The I
Pe

ITEM NO.

30109 0 13721132

The Indispensable Pentium Book

Hans-Peter Messmer

ADDISON-WESLEY
PUBLISHING
COMPANY

Wokingham, England • Reading, Massachusetts • Menlo Park, California • New York
Don Mills, Ontario • Amsterdam • Bonn • Sydney • Singapore
Tokyo • Madrid • San Juan • Milan • Paris • Mexico City • Seoul • Taipei

The programs in this book have been included for their instructional value. They have been tested with care but are not guaranteed for any particular purpose. The publisher does not offer any warranties or representations, nor does it accept any liabilities with respect to the programs.

Many of the designations used by manufacturers and sellers to distinguish their products are claimed as trademarks. Addison-Wesley has made every attempt to supply trademark information about manufacturers and their products mentioned in this book. A list of the trademark designations and their owners appears on page XIV.

Cover designed by Chris Eley
and printed by The Riverside Printing Co. (Reading) Ltd.
Typeset by someTimes GmbH, Munich.
Printed in the United States of America.

First printed 1995

ISBN 0-201-87727-9

British Library Cataloguing in Publication Data
A catalogue record for this book is available from the British Library.

Library of Congress Cataloging in Publication Data applied for.

Contents

Introduction

Dear Reader,

This *Indispensable Pentium Book* will provide you with in-depth information about Intel's high-end chip. But that's not all – in a broader sense, I will also discuss the concepts that led to the 'classic' CISC processors and detail the innovative strategies that make use of the modern RISCs.

Who should read this book

This book aims to address those who are interested in knowing more about the inner workings of modern microprocessors. For beginners who are less well acquainted with modern processors, I have included Part 1 as an introduction to the world of microprocessors.

This book is for:

everybody who wants to or who has to understand the ideas and functioning of modern microprocessors, either as a professional or as a private user;

hardware designers who want to take as much advantage of the new Pentium features as possible;

users who want to upgrade their PCs with a Pentium and who would like to understand the possible gain;

dealers who wish to advise their customers well;

and last but not least,

curious people who want to look beyond the horizon and learn about the ideas behind such magic words as, for example, 'superscalar architecture', 'dynamic branch prediction' or 'speculative execution and dynamic register renaming'.

The indispensable contents of this book

The book is divided into five major parts which are self-contained and can be used independently.

Part 1, including Chapters 1 to 5, introduces the subject of microprocessors and explains the basics of classical CISCs.

Part 2, which includes Chapters 6 and 7, focuses on the technology and the ideas behind the term RISC.

Part 3, including Chapters 8 to 13, presents a detailed view of the Pentium, especially discussing its advanced features.

Part 4, encompassing Chapters 14 and 15, provides extensive information about the external support and bus systems required to make full use of the Pentium's performance.

Part 5, including Chapters 16 and 17, is dedicated to various competing RISC implementations and some seemingly mysterious ideas of the next millennium – fuzzy logic and neural nets.

The extensive Appendices summarize the Pentium instruction set and possible instruction pairings.

Finally, the Glossary is a small but nevertheless comprehensive computer encylopedia which explains most terms and concepts related to microprocessors and personal computer hardware in general.

Acknowledgements

This book is the result of a lot of work – not only by the author but also by many other people who I would like to thank very warmly. In particular, thanks to Nicky Jaeger who looked after me and the manuscript at all times. I also have to thank Jane Kerr and Alison Woodhouse for carefully copy-editing and proofreading the manuscript. Moreover, I would like to thank all the companies and individuals who assisted me in writing the book by providing written or verbal information.

Hans-Peter Messmer
Quito, Ecuador, June 1995

Part 1
Microprocessor basics and classic CISC concepts

If you look at the mass market for powerful general-purpose microprocessors, you will find that there are two different processor families that lead in the central processing unit (CPU) industry. These are the 80x86 family from Intel and the 68000 series from Motorola. Both of these, including the i386 and 68040, are pure complex instruction set computer (CISC) processors. It's a pity that the two families are not compatible: the way in which instructions are handled internally, the language in which the instructions are given, and how the addresses are allocated in the memory (RAM) or the I/O address areas are completely different. The 68000 series are used mainly in Apple Macintosh machines (recently also equipped with a pure reduced instruction set computer (RISC) processor, the PowerPC), which are the biggest competitors to IBM compatible PCs. Even though the Pentium is the fifth in the 80x86 series, I would like to use the i386 in this first part as far as examples are required. The fact that the i386 is the last pure CISC model of the 80x86 family (the i486 uses partial RISC principles) makes this chip a good example of classical CISC technology in the microprocessor field. I should also add that there are other companies that produce 80x86 compatible CPUs, sometimes even better than Intel itself, the largest of which are AMD and Cyrix. Now, a short list of the key features of the i386:

- ▶ 32-bit general-purpose and offset register
- ▶ 16-byte prefetch queue
- ▶ Memory management unit (MMU) with a segmentation unit (SU) and a paging unit (PU)
- ▶ 32-bit data and address bus
- ▶ 4-Gbyte physical address space
- ▶ 64-Tbyte virtual address space
- ▶ i387 numerical coprocessor with IEEE standard 754-1985 for floating-point arithmetic
- ▶ 64 k 8-, 16- or 32-bit ports
- ▶ implementation of real, protected and virtual 8086 mode

Now let us give our undivided attention to the general basics of microprocessors and CISC concepts. The following is a list of the most important characteristics of CISC microprocessors:

- ▶ extensive (complex) instructions
- ▶ complex and efficient machine instructions
- ▶ micro-encoding of the machine instructions
- ▶ extensive addressing capabilities for memory operations
- ▶ relatively few, but very useful, registers

1 The function and general structure of the CPU

The CPU is the central part of the computer. It performs all of the logical and arithmetic operations. The CPU reads the data from memory, processes it accordingly, then loads it back to memory. In addition, the CPU controls other parts of the computer such as the disk drives, video adaptors, and so on. Figure 1.1 shows the general set-up of our example, the i386, the classic CISC microprocessor.

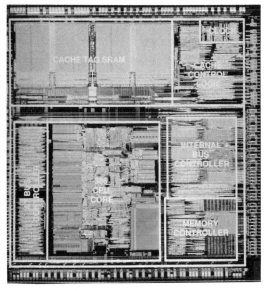

Figure 1.1: The i386 CPU as part of the i386SL. The i386 is the most powerful CISC member of Intel's 8086 family. It forms the CPU core in the i386SL. Source: Intel GmbH (Germany).

1.1 The CPU: The heart of every computer

For the completion of every logical and arithmetic operation (or process), the CPU uses the *bus unit (BU)*, the *instruction unit (IU)*, the *execution unit (EU)* and the *addressing unit (AU)*. In the bus interface, there is a so-called *prefetch queue*, which reads instructions from the memory and prepares them for the CPU. The EU performs the data processing (addition, comparing, and so on), and includes a *control unit (CU)*, an *arithmetic and logic unit (ALU)* and a number of registers. In the i386, for example, the prefetch queue is 16 bytes. The AU has a *memory management unit (MMU)* with an integrated *segmentation unit (SU)* and a *paging unit (PU)* (see Figure 1.2).

General-purpose registers are used as a fast internal data memory for the CPU. The EU reads data from one or more registers, sends it to the ALU for manipulation, then reads it back to one or more of the registers. This is a typical example of a register-to-register operation, because the source of the data and the result remain in the same register(s). A typical CISC microprocessor can also use source data and product data directly from memory and send it back to memory. This is a memory-to-memory, register-to-memory or memory-to-register operation. Besides the general-purpose registers, there are also segment registers for memory management, control registers, and many others.

The bus interface is the link to the other components. It includes the data, address and control buses. The buses carry instructions from the memory in the prefetch queue to the IU. The IU controls the EU, allowing the ALU to carry out the instruction.

The CPU reads data from, or writes data to, the memory via the data bus. This part of the memory is given an address that is calculated by the processor with the aid of the AU and sent to the memory subsystem via the address bus. In the i386, for example, the address calculation depends on the operational mode – real mode, protected mode or virtual 8086 mode. The read or write sequence is sent through the bus interface; the BU supplies the bus address and, if necessary, the data to be written or the data from the memory in the applicable address. The processor communicates with the memory in the same way when reading instructions. This *instruction fetching* however, does not occur with a specific read instruction, but is carried out automatically by the BU. The data that is read – that is, the instructions – is not written to a register in the EU, but is transferred to the prefetch queue. Later, the IU reads the instruction or data from the prefetch queue, decodes it and sends the decoded instruction to the EU.

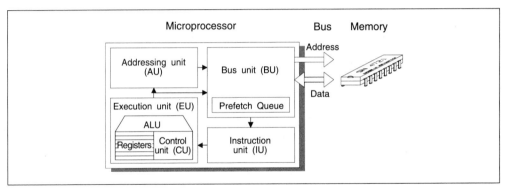

Figure 1.2: The structure of a typical CISC microprocessor, the i386.
The i386 includes a bus interface for reading and providing data and instructions, with a prefetch queue, an IU for controlling the EU with its registers, as well as an AU with an MMU and a PU for generating memory and I/O addresses.

Instructions and data find themselves in the same physical memory. However, the physical memory is often divided into different logical parts (often called *segments*) containing the instructions or data (this is the case for the i386). In modern computers, there is basically no division between instruction and data memory. In the early days of computer technology, there was a strict division between memory for instructions and memory for data.

1.2 CPU, main memory and segmentation in real mode

The 8086, as the first 80x86 CPU, divided the available memory into segments. The later CPUs, from the 80286 to the Pentium, do exactly the same. As the 8086 has only 20 address lines compared to the 32 of the i386, it can address a maximum of only 2^{20} bytes (1 Mbyte) of memory. This is why the physical address space is a maximum of 1 Mbyte. Each of the general-purpose registers in the 16-bit 8086 processor (then, almost revolutionary in comparison to its 8-bit 8080 predecessor) is still only 16-bit, and therefore can only address a maximum of 2^{16} bytes (64 kbytes). The 8086 divides the physical address area into 64k segments with a capacity of 64 kbytes. In a segment, the position of a byte is given by an *offset*. Offsets are stored in the general-purpose registers. The segments are controlled by the segment registers CS to ES (two additional segment registers FS and GS are installed from the i386 on). The CPU uses a segment:offset pair to access the memory. The segment of a specific memory object (byte, word, double word, and so on) is indicated by the segment register, the offset in the applicable segment by the general-purpose register.

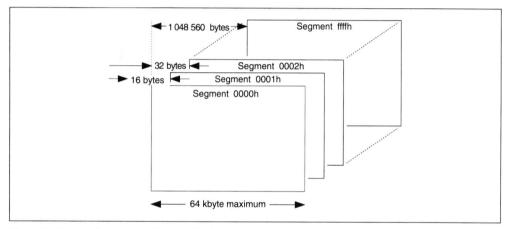

Figure 1.3: Segment interleaving. The 8086 divides the address space of 1 Mbyte into 64k segments of 64 kbytes each. By doing this, successive segments are shifted by 16 bytes and overlap by regular distances of 16 bytes – they are interleaved.

The 16-bit segment register can address segments like the 16-bit offset register of the 8086, each of which is 64 kbytes in size (64k = 65 536). The theoretically possible address space is therefore 64k * 64 kbytes = 4 Gbytes. This is not possible with the 20-bit address bus of the 8086, which is only capable of addressing 1 Mbyte. The segments are spaced 16 bytes apart (see Figure 1.3). When the value of a segment register is increased by 1, the segment simply moves 16 bytes and not a complete segment of 64 kbytes. In comparison, when the offset register is increased by 1, the memory object only moves one position (1 byte). A change in the segment register value causes a significantly larger (16 times) result than a change in the offset register value. This is a characteristic of *real mode*. The 8086 can only work in real mode. The i386 (or Pentium) only operates in real mode after it is switched on or after a processor reset. It can, however, be switched into real mode with a specific instruction during protected or virtual 8086 mode. The addresses are then calculated completely differently. More details are given later.

The address of an object in real mode is calculated with a simple formula:

`16 * Segment + Offset`

or similarly:

`10h * Segment + Offset`

Simply stated, this means that the segment register is shifted four bits to the left and the offset is added. The four bits that were not affected by the shifting of the segment register are set to zero. The AU carries out this movement and performs the addition process: after the segment address has been moved four bits to the left, an adder in the AU adds the new segment address and the offset to calculate the *linear address* (see Figure 1.4).

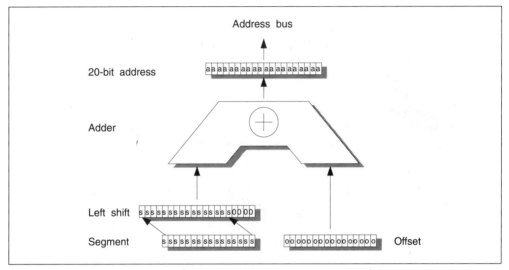

Figure 1.4: Combination of segment address and offset in 80x86 real mode.
In real mode the AU shifts the segment register value left by four bits, thus multiplying the segment value by 16, and adds the offset. The result is a 20-bit address.

The segment and offset are normally given in the hexadecimal segment:offset format.

```
Example: 1F36:0A5D means segment 1F36, offset 0A5D;
         according to the above formula the linear address is:
         1F36h * 16 + 0A5Dh = 7990 * 16 + 2653 = 130 493.

         Alternatively we can use the segment shift by four bits:
         1F360h + 0A5Dh = 1FDBDh = 130 493.
```

Note that two different segment:offset pairs in real mode can give the same memory address (this is not possible in protected mode, for several reasons).

```
Example: 1FB1:02AD means segment 1FB1, offset 02AD; thus we get for the address:
         1FB1h * 16 + 02ADh = 8113 * 16 + 685 = 130 493.
```

As already explained, this method of address calculation is a characteristic of real mode or even of the 8086. In 80x86 protected mode, the segment and the offset are completely separate. The segment register has a different use and there is no simple formula like that mentioned previously. Therefore, the 80286 has a maximum *logical address space* of 1 Gbyte, and the i386 can have up to 64 Tbytes for each task (program). This logical address space is, however, restricted by the segmentation logic of the 80286 to a maximum *physical address space* of 16 Mbytes because of its 24 address lines (2^{24} = 16M). In the i386, 4 Gbytes are available. Note, however, that the actual memory capability of a computer is often considerably less than this maximum value.

The *virtual 8086 mode*, implemented for the first time in the i386, is a substantial innovation for the running of real-mode programs in the multitasking environment of the protected mode. In this mode, the i386 calculates the addresses using the formula described previously for real mode, but access to the memory and the peripherals is monitored and protected from unauthorized and incorrect instructions by the mechanism characteristic of protected mode, which is discussed later.

1.3 Information representation in the computer

The CPUs mentioned in the previous section and other components, including the processor, consist mainly of transistors that digitally switch between the on and off conditions. This immediately leads to a binary or two-value representation of the information. The computer has to be able to use this on/off (often called 1/0) information. This appears abstract at first. However, a look at our daily lives shows us that the implementation of this abstract representation is constantly with us. Since childhood, we have become so used to it that we do not notice it any more. Even the information medium that you are using at present (this book) is filled with symbolic representation: 26 letters (from a to z) and six special characters (.,:;?!) of the English language. The 10 digits (0 to 9), our conventional numbers, are a further form of information representation. The difference in the information representation used in a computer is that there are only two symbols (0 and 1). From this you can see that the information representations that we use in our daily lives have to be converted into a 1/0 format before they can be of use to a computer. For the conversion, a *code* is necessary, and so we come to the following line:

S C

Firstly, I will state that S and C are different; secondly, I will state that they are the same. Don't put the book down on the grounds that the author is talking rubbish: it is just a matter of perspective. Both statements are correct. With this, we come immediately to an important distinction, namely the *meaning* or the *use* of information and its *representation*. If you refer to the Latin alphabet, the first statement is correct; S and C are two different letters, they also have different meanings. It it completely different, however, if you take the S from the Latin alphabet and the C from the Cyrillic alphabet: the C in the Cyrillic alphabet has the same meaning as the S in the Latin alphabet that we normally use (ice hockey fans will already know this, as the previous world champions had CCCP instead of USSR, for Union of Soviet Socialist Republics, on their shirts). The meaning of an object is abstract, basic and independent of its specific representation (learned mathematicians know something about the properties and definitions of an object in high level mathematics). After all, Shakespeare can be understood in many languages even though he wrote his works in English. The meaning of information (for example, the content of *Hamlet*) is the same even after translation, even though the words themselves, when translated into other languages, are different.

An further example of the subtle distinction between meaning and representation is the use of roman and arabic numbers. The numbers XIV and 14 have the same value (the same meaning) but are represented differently. In the roman numbering system, only the seven characters M, D, C, L, X, V and I are available; on the other hand, our decimal system uses the 10 characters 0 to 9. In the same way that the Cyrillic and Latin alphabets or the roman and arabic numerals have to be converted, we must change our way of thinking in order to understand the way in which a computer represents information. Today the *ASCII code* dominates for the use of text in letters, digits and punctuation marks. There are several different codes for numbers, which come from a mathematical background (for example, the two's complement or IEEE format). Now, a short trip into the on/off world of the computer – the binary system.

1.3.1 Decimal and binary systems

A further important distinction applies to the terms 'digit' and 'number'. A digit is one of the characters between 0 and 9; a number, on the other hand, has a value. The usual *decimal numbers* are represented by the 10 (and therefore decimal) digits 0 to 9. With this method, there are a total of 10 possibilities (0 to 9). The computer can only understand two possibilities, namely 0 and 1.

Now I would briefly like to examine the interpretation of a decimal number. This numbering system is also known as a *position system* because every position in a decimal number has a specific value: the position at the far right has the value of 1, the second position from the right has a value of 10, the next position to the left has a value of 100, and so on. The current position value is then multiplied by the applicable digit. These parts of the decimal number are then added together to give the complete number.

```
Example: The interpretation of the number 429 is as follows: 4*100+2*10+9*1, or expressed with
         powers: 4*10²+2*10¹+9*10⁰.
```

This method continues for larger numbers and has no boundary (the Romans, however, used the letter M to indicate a thousand). The 10 is known as the *base* of this numbering system; the base is usually the same as the quantity of different digits. In the computer there are only two, instead of the usual ten, digits. Here, the ten is replaced with two and we then have a *binary* (or *dual*) *system*. Numbers in a binary system are indicated by a 'b' at the end of the number.

```
Example: The (binary) number 110101101b means 1*2⁸+1*2⁷+0*2⁶+1*2⁵+0*2⁴+1*2³+1*2²+0*2¹+1*2⁰ or,
         equally, 1*256+1*128+0*64+1*32+0*16+1*8+1*4+0*2+1*1 = 429.
```

With this, we have two different representations of the number 429 – 429 in the decimal system and 110101101b in the binary or dual system. The binary method can be used for larger numbers in exactly the same way as the decimal system. It is quite easy to see the main disadvantage of the binary system: much more room is needed to write down a binary number than a decimal number.

Altogether, there are eight binary positions, or *bits* (from *binary digit*), in a byte. Two connected bytes are known as a *word*, four bytes as a *double word* and half a byte (four bits) as a *nibble*. With a single byte, it is possible to represent $2^8 = 256$ different numbers from 0 to 255, or 256 different symbols, which are in some way numbered from 0 to 255 (comparable to the ASCII code mentioned earlier).

This, of course, is not yet the end for the binary system. Many more bytes can be grouped together into units in order to represent very large numbers. This is done in the same way that the comma or space is used in very large decimal numbers: in the number 7,396,124, the commas break the number up into three groups of decimal digits (or single, kilo, mega and other powers of 10 groupings), so that it can be read easily.

In the binary system, the grouping of two bytes into a word can give an area from 0 to 65 535 (2^{16}–1). This is known as an *unsigned integer* (or *unsigned*). A double word of four bytes can give an area of 4 294 967 295 (2^{32}–1) and is known as an *unsigned long integer* (or *unsigned long*).

1.3.2 ASCII and EBCDIC code

Originally, the ASCII code was a 7-bit code, whereby 2^7 different characters could be represented; it has since evolved into *extended ASCII code* with 8 bits (1 byte), but is still known as ASCII code. It allocates a character to each of the 256 different values of a byte. The given value is, therefore, the ASCII code of the applicable character. For the Latin and Cyrillic alphabets, this is perfectly adequate, even when you take into consideration punctuation marks, digits and special characters. For Japanese characters, of which there are more than 2000, this is naturally not the case. Anyway, a high resolution graphics adaptor is necessary just to show these characters on the screen.

The first 32 ASCII characters are defined as *control codes* and are used to send messages about the transmitted data. ASCII (an abbreviation of *American Standard Code for Information Interchange*) was first developed for data transmittal – thus, for example, the control character ^D (EOT or End Of Transmission) is used for the end of data flow. In Appendix A you will find a table containing the symbols, characters and codes of the expanded ASCII code from IBM. There is no hidden or deeper meaning to the order of ASCII codes and characters. Someone, at some time, used this choice because he or she thought that this list was useful. Anyway, letters, characters, punctuation marks and perhaps a few graphical symbols are all that are necessary to write Christmas greetings, for example, on a computer.

```
Example: ASCII code 90:        upper case Z
         ASCII code 206:       block graphics character ╬
         ASCII code 13 (CR):   control code for Carriage Return
```

The main purpose of the ASCII code is to represent text. Thus, text data is often referred to as ASCII data. A sequence of a number of ASCII codes, or more precisely a sequence of characters represented by their ASCII codes, is called a *string*. The length of a string can vary considerably in comparison to the size of an unsigned integer: from a ' ' (empty string) to a sentence, a paragraph or even a complete book. In addition, the length of the string must be given. BASIC accomplishes this through a string descriptor, which includes the length (and the address) of a string. DOS and a number of other programming languages, such as C, end the string with the ASCII code 0. This is known as an *ASCIIZ string* (Z = zero).

As I explained previously, the order in which the characters and code are given is purely a matter of choice, as long as it does not become too impractical. It is no wonder that other codes exist. The *EBCDIC code* is one of them. It is, however, only used in large IBM computers and other compatible mainframes. If it was not for IBM's domination of the market for mainframes, it would have disappeared long ago.

You can of course create your own personal code, and use the letter A or the letter group Ab as number 1, for example. Data compression programs do this by changing the codes. It is possible to reduce a large amount of data into fewer bits. The ASCII code actually contains 64 letters and digits, which are adequate for normal text, and 196 control, graphic and other characters that are not normally needed. If these characters were removed, the new code could be reduced to 6 bits, reducing the amount of data by 25%, without loss of information.

1.3.3 Hexadecimal representation and hexadecimal numbers

The representation of numbers and ASCII codes in the form of 0s and 1s is no small thing when dealing with large amounts of data. If you combine four bits (a nibble) in a group, you can create a new numbering system ($2^4 = 16$), called the *hexadecimal system*. With four bits, it is possible to represent 16 different digits; in addition to the normal digits 0 to 9, we need an additional six hexadecimal digits '10' to '15'. The letters A ('10') to F ('15') are generally used.

In order to differentiate between a hexadecimal number and a decimal number, an h or an H (for *h*exadecimal) is positioned after the number (for example, 2Fh) or 0x is added before the number (for example, 0x2F in C). The conversion between the hexadecimal and the decimal system is analogue, as it is between the binary and decimal systems; the only difference is that base 16 is used in place of base 2.

```
Example: Unsigned decimal integer 60 000
         Binary number              1110 1010 0110 0000b
                                     =
```
$$1*2^{15}+1*2^{14}+1*2^{13}+0*2^{12}+1*2^{11}+0*2^{10}+$$
$$1*2^9+0*2^8+0*2^7+1*2^6+1*2^5+0*2^4+0*2^3+0*2^2+0*2^1+0*2^0$$
```
         Hexadecimal number   ea60h=
```
$14*16^3+10*16^2+6*16^1+0*16^0$

```
Example: ASCII code 97, corresponding character 'a'
         Decimal:      0110 0001b  97
         Binary:       0110 0001b
         Hexadecimal:  61h
```

The hexadecimal system allows a more compact way of writing, which, through the use of base 16, still communicates with the hardware and its 0/1 method of operation.

1.3.4 Integers and two's complement

We have already met positive binary integers in the description of the binary system. Here I would like to quickly discuss the system again. Every binary digit (every bit) of a positive integer is given a value, as in the decimal system. The complete value is obtained by adding these individual values. Normally positive integers are included in a word (2 bytes or 16 bits).

```
Example: The positive integer 10110000 10101101b means in decimal notation a value of:
```
$1*2^{15}+0*2^{14}+1*2^{13}+1*2^{12}+0*2^{11}+0*2^{10}+0*2^9+0*2^8+1*2^7+0*2^6+1*2^5+0*2^4+1*2^3+1*2^2+0*2^1+1*2^0$
$=1*32768+0*16384+1*8192+1*4096+0*2048+0*1024+0*512+0*256+1*128+0*64+1*32+0*16+1*8+1*4+0*2+1*1$
$=45\ 229$

As you can see from the example, the digit sequence of the binary number has no influence on the digit sequence of the decimal number. This makes understanding of the binary system difficult at first, but after a while you will get the feel of it.

Long positive integers of four bytes (32 bits) function in exactly the same way. It is probably better not to give a page long example.

Naturally, besides the positive integers, the negative integers are also important, even if only to describe a cold and frosty winter. The representation of a negative integer in the computer is only possible in a roundabout way, because the normally used minus sign is not used. The simplest plausible solution would be to add an additional bit in front, to indicate if the integer is positive (0 in front) or negative (1 in front). This is not possible for practical reasons. The reason for this is that the subtraction of an integer is the same as the addition of the two's complement of the integer, even though it is more complicated than the additional bit method. This results in a considerably simpler ALU in the CPU. A negative integer is represented in its two's complement: all of the 0s in the equivalent positive integer are replaced with a 1 and all of the 1s are replaced with a 0. The value 1 is then added to the result. In this way, a possible amount carried over is ignored.

```
Example: Positive integer 20307:  0100 1111 0101 0011b
         Negative integer -20307:
         Complement             1011 0000 1010 1100b
         Add one              +                   1b
         Result                 1011 0000 1010 1101b
```

These signed integers (or integers for short) generally contain two bytes (16 bits); their values range from −32 768 (−2^{15}) to 32 767 (2^{15}). The number 111 111 111 111b in two's complement representation is no longer the decimal 65 535, but −1. You can see that for negative integers in two's complement representation, the most significant bit (the bit at the far left) is always 1. This bit does in fact take on the function of a front sign bit. It is only the interpretation of the subsequent positions that is different to the simple method mentioned previously. With a simple sign bit, the negative integer −20 307 would become 1100 1111 0101 0011b (in comparison to the two's complement representation 1011 0000 1010 1101b).

In order to convert a negative number in two's complement representation into a decimal number, it is necessary to reverse the procedure given in the previous example.

```
Example:  Binary number 1100 1011 0001 1111b in two's complement representation, interpretation
          as signed integer:
          Binary               1100 1011 0001 1111b
          Subtract one         1100 1011 0001 1110b
          Complement           0011 0100 1110 0001b
          Result                         -13537
          (minus sign as 1100 1011 0001 1111b is a negative number)
```

Two's complement representation is possible in the same way for large negative numbers, with a value range from −2 147 483 648 (−2^{31}) to +2 147 483 647 (2^{31}−1).

As I explained previously, the reason for using two's complement representation for negative numbers is that the subtraction of a number (the subtrahend) from another number (the minuend) is mathematically the same as adding the two's complements of the subtrahend and the minuend. The formation of two's complements is very simple for an electronic circuit. Complementing can be carried out by a series of NOT gates, and the subsequent addition of 1 can be performed by the same adder, as can the addition of the minuend and the two's complement of the subtrahend. In this instance, the subtraction rule is as follows:

Minuend − Subtrahend = Minuend + Two's Complement (Subtrahend)

```
Example: Calculate 197 - 43
                197d = 0000 0000 1100 0101b
                 43d = 0000 0000 0010 1011b
Two's complement(43d)  = 1111 1111 1101 0101b
thus      197 - 43     = 0000 0000 1100 0101b
                        +1111 1111 1101 0101b
                        1 0000 0000 1001 1010b
The leading 1 is ignored as a carry, the result is 0000 0000 1001 1010b or 154 decimal.
```

An integer in two's complement representation can be extended easily to a larger format without changing its value. To do this, only the sign bit; that is, the highest order bit of the number, needs to be written to all newly arising bits. This is called *sign extension*.

```
Example: Extend 16-bit integer 1101 1001b (decimal -39) to 32 bits.
```

The leading bit is 1, thus all newly arising 16 bits have to be filled with 1s: 1111 1111 1101 1001b; this long integer also represents a value of −39.

Generally, the method of extending signed integers to signed long integers can be written as follows:

```
16-bit integer:
Snnn nnnn nnnn nnnn (S: sign; n: binary number 0 or 1)
Extension to long 32-bit integer:
SSSS SSSS SSSS SSSS Snnn nnnn nnnn nnnn
```

This method is also applied to the extension of numbers with length other than 16 bits accordingly. Please note that both the initial and the new, extended number need to be given in two's complement representation. Unsigned integers, on the other hand, are extended to the new format by filling all newly arising bits with 0s. The contraction of a format into a less extensive format can be carried out, of course, only if the initial number does not exceed the range of values for the new format.

1.3.5 BCD numbers

A further format for integers is the *binary coded (BCD) decimal number*. In this case, each of the decimal digits (0 to 9) is given by the value of a byte. Note that the bytes of the *binary value* represent the digit, and not the ASCII code.

```
Example: Decimal number 63
         BCD 0000 0110  0000 0011b

         The first byte 0000 0110 means digit 6, the second one 0000 0011 digit 3.
```

You already know that normal BCD numbers use a lot of space. A byte can represent 256 different digits, whereas BCD numbers use only 10, corresponding to the decimal base. They do, however, have a distinct advantage as a conversion between decimal and binary numbers is not necessary.

Each byte gives the digit of the corresponding decimal place, and the decoding is very simple, especially for the human user. The so-called *packed BCD* numbers take up a little less space. Each nibble of a byte gives a decimal digit.

```
Example: Decimal number 63 (see above)
        Packed BCD    0110 0011

        The first nibble 0110 of the byte means digit 6, the second nibble 0011 digit 3.
```

The density is double the size. For all that, practically a hundred decimal numbers (from 0 to 99) can be represented with one byte.

Slowly, another problem arises: all of the formats mentioned so far, whether they are ASCII code, unsigned integers, two's complement, BCD or packed BCD, appear similar at the hardware level – namely, as a series of 0s and 1s contained in bytes or numbers of bytes. The reason for this is, that with only these two symbols (0 and 1) available, there is no possibility of introducing an additional symbol for the minus sign. Even the 1 at the front of a two's complement representation to indicate a negative integer is no different from the binary digit 1. The same naturally applies to the marking of hexadecimal numbers with an h, or to BCD numbers. It all depends on the interpretation of a given series of binary numbers.

```
Example: Binary sequence 1001 0111b (hexadecimal 97h)
Interpretation as unsigned integer:     151 decimal
Interpretation as two's complement:    −105 decimal
Interpretation as packed BCD:           97 decimal
Interpretation as ASCII code:          character 'a'
```

In addition, there are even more possibilities for interpreting binary sequences, for example, floating-point numbers of different formats, or *processor instruction codes*, made up of one or more bytes, which instruct the processor to perform a particular action (to shift a value, to compare it to another, to add a value, and so on). A quick look into the memory would show all of these formats as a series of 0s and 1s. The computer can read these different formats because the format of the applicable binary sequence that the processor can expect is encoded into the instruction for the CPU. The CPU then decodes the applicable binary sequence. An example of this is in the two i386 multiplication instructions, MUL and IMUL. MUL multiplies two unsigned integers and interprets its operand accordingly; IMUL, on the other hand multiplies two signed integers. If the stored operands for MUL and IMUL have the wrong format, a failure is produced. This, however, is the responsibility of the programmer. It can be seen that 'naked' bytes have different meanings, depending on their interpretation.

1.3.6 Little-endian format and Intel notation

80x86 processors must read or write operands and other values from the memory in a specific format. The i386 and the other members of the 80x86 family store a word, double word or other value in such a way that the lowest value byte is located at the lowest memory address, and the highest value byte is located at the highest memory address. This is known as the *little-endian* format. You are already used to writing the highest value of number at the far left and the lowest value at the far right – a million is written as 1 000 000, not 000 000 1. Addresses, however, increase from left to right. In little-endian format, the data appears to be switched in comparison to the normal way of writing. This can lead to considerable confusion. As the 80x86 CPUs are the most well known that use the little-endian format, it is also known as Intel notation. The *big-endian* format stores the lowest value byte in the highest address, and the highest value byte in the lowest address, exactly opposite to the little-endian format. The 68000 series from Motorola, for example, uses the big-endian format.

1.3.7 Scientific notation and biased exponent

Number formats appear to have no end – here, I would like to explain floating-point numbers and their different formats. Arithmetic calculations use part and mixed numbers (for example, 1/8 and 146.108). The basis for the internal computer representation of these numbers is called *scientific notation* or *floating-point representation*. In the following decimal notation, the value of the number is given by the *mantissa* ±M (a number between 1 and 9 with a + or – sign) and the power of the *base* B (with a value of 10) with an *exponent* ±E. It looks like this:

```
Number value = ±M * B±E
```

An example would perhaps make this clearer:

```
Example: Scientific notation with decimal base.
1/8 = 0.125 = 1.25*0.1 = 1.25*10⁻¹       thus: mantissa 1.25, base 10, exponent −1
−146.108 = −1.46108*100 = −1.46108*10²   thus: mantissa −1.46108, base 10, exponent 2
```

Thus, the term floating-point representation becomes clear: the decimal point is moved until one digit of the mantissa is positioned before the decimal point and all the other digits are positioned after. With the addition of the exponent, the value of the number is the same. In fixed-point numbers, the decimal point does not move and so the possible value range is considerably reduced. Today, nearly all computers use floating-point numbers.

Scientific notation has a considerable disadvantage in exact calculation with decimal fractions. Unfortunately, some fractions, such as 1/7 or pi for example, produce repeating and non-repeating recurring numbers. To cope with this, unending positions are required for the mantissa – but this is not possible. Only fractions with a denominator as a product of 2 and 5 can be represented as a finite decimal number. All other numbers are stopped when a specific number of mantissa decimal places has been reached. The number 3.141 592 653 6 is not *exactly* pi, but an approximation to 11 decimal places. The number of mantissa decimal places is known as the *accuracy*.

Floating-point numbers in the decimal system are not quite so easy to convert into the decimal system as integers. Let us look at the decimal floating-point number 4.907. In the same way that we interpret 729 as $7*100+2*10+9*1$, we can interpret 4.907 as follows:

```
4.907 = 4*1+9*0.1+0*0.01+7*0.001
      = 4*10⁰+9*10⁻¹+0*10⁻²+7*10⁻³
```

This interpretation of 4.907 is very similar to that of 729, exept that the negative power of base 10 is used for the values after the decimal point. It is possible to use this method for both positive and negative exponents:

```
146.108 = 1*100+4*10+6*1+1*0.1+0*0.01+8*0.001
        = 1*10²+4*10¹+6*10⁰+1*10⁻¹+0*10⁻²+8*10⁻³
```

The computer represents floating-point numbers internally in an analogue form, using the binary system instead of the decimal system.

```
Example:  1.11001011 * 2^1101 in the binary system means
[1*2^0+1*2^-1+1*2^-2+0*2^-3+0*2^-4+1*2^-5+0*2^-6+1*2^-7+1*2^-8]*2^13
=[1*1+1*1/2+1*1/4+0*1/8+0*1/16+1*1/32+0*1/64+1*1/128+1*1/256]*8192
=[1*1+1*0.5+1*0.25+0*0.125+0*0.0625+1*0.03125+0*0.015625+1*0.0078125+1*0.0039063]*8192
= [459/256] * 8192 = 14 688
= [1.7929688] * 8192 = 14 688
As an integer in conventional binary representation, this would mean a value of 14 688 = 0011
1001 0110 0000b.
```

Negative numbers can also be written in scientific notation, both in the mantissa and in the exponent: number = "mantissa*base$^{\pm exponent}$. The two's complement representation that works so well for negative integers is not used here. The implementation of floating-point arithmetic using electronic circuits is a lot more complicated than with integers. For example, two floating-point numbers can not easily be added together because their exponents will most likely be different. Firstly, the CPU must internally check and convert the exponents before it can add the mantissas. For this reason, the electrical circuits used for floating-point arithmetic are often found on a separate coprocessor. The i386 only contains an ALU for integer arithmetic, and not for floating-point calculations. These are performed separately by the i387 coprocessor. In floating-point numbers, an additional sign bit is used for the mantissa and the exponent is represented with a bias. With this representation, the bias is automatically subtracted during the interpretation of the floating-point number. This corresponds to the shifting of the exponent zero value. With this method, negative exponents can be represented by a positive exponent value. Thus:

```
Number = ±Mantissa*2^Exponent-Bias
```

It seems surprising that the two floating-point numbers $1.110\ 010\ 11 * 2^{100\ 011\ 00}$ and $1.110\ 010\ 11 * 2^{1101}$ represent the same value. As I explained earlier, it all depends on the interpretation of the number. After many years of confusion in the area of floating-point numbers, there is now a widely accepted standard for floating-point numbers – the IEEE format. This is explained in the following subsection.

1.3.8 The IEEE standard format

Figure 1.5 shows the IEEE format for the short real, long real and temporary real floating-point types, which are 32, 64 and 80 bits long, respectively, and all use biased exponent.

The values of floating-point numbers in IEEE format are interpreted as follows.

```
Value = (-1)^S * (1+M_1*2^-1+M_2*2^-2+...+M_23*2^-23) * 2^E7...E1E0-127 (short real)
Value = (-1)^S * (1+M_1*2^-1+M_2*2^-2+...+M_52*2^-52) * 2^E10...E1E0-1023 (long real)
Value = (-1)^S * (M_0+M_1*2^-1+M_2*2^-2+...+M_63*2^-63) * 2^E14...E1E0-16383 (temporary real)
```

In the mantissas of the short real and long real formats shown in Figure 1.5, the mantissa position M_0 is missing. In addition, the interpretation of these formats always begins with a '1'. Behind this apparent inconsistency lies a considerable amount of ingenuity. These IEEE formats concern a *normalized representation* of floating-point numbers. A decimal number in scientific notation with normalized representation is indicated by a digit from 1 to 9 in front of the decimal point. The exponent is adjusted so that the value of the number is not changed. For example, you write $7.183 * 10^3$ in normalized representation, and not $71.83 * 10^2$ or $0.7183 * 10^4$. The value of the three numbers is the same. The same applies to the IEEE format of floating-point numbers, which are also written in normalized representation. A digit other than zero must be located before the decimal point.

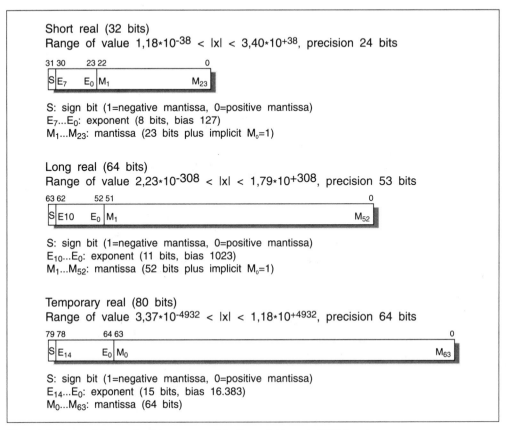

Short real (32 bits)
Range of value $1{,}18*10^{-38} < |x| < 3{,}40*10^{+38}$, precision 24 bits

S: sign bit (1=negative mantissa, 0=positive mantissa)
$E_7...E_0$: exponent (8 bits, bias 127)
$M_1...M_{23}$: mantissa (23 bits plus implicit $M_o=1$)

Long real (64 bits)
Range of value $2{,}23*10^{-308} < |x| < 1{,}79*10^{+308}$, precision 53 bits

S: sign bit (1=negative mantissa, 0=positive mantissa)
$E_{10}...E_0$: exponent (11 bits, bias 1023)
$M_1...M_{52}$: mantissa (52 bits plus implicit $M_o=1$)

Temporary real (80 bits)
Range of value $3{,}37*10^{-4932} < |x| < 1{,}18*10^{+4932}$, precision 64 bits

S: sign bit (1=negative mantissa, 0=positive mantissa)
$E_{14}...E_0$: exponent (15 bits, bias 16.383)
$M_0...M_{63}$: mantissa (64 bits)

Figure 1.5: Short real, long real and temporary real floating-point types in IEEE format.

In the binary system, there is such a digit – the 1. This shows that the first mantissa position (M_0) in normalized representation is always 1. When it is known that floating-point numbers in IEEE format are always given in normalized representation, therefore, M_0 will always be 1 and so it is not necessary to store it. The stored mantissa value only gives the digits after the decimal point in a binary floating-point number. With this method it is possible to gain, almost free of cost, an extra digit to increase the accuracy of the mantissa. If necessary, the decimal point can be shifted and the exponent adjusted accordingly until the number '1' is located before the decimal point.

Example: $0.0011011 * 2^{01011}$ is not normalized, thus shift the point and adjust the exponent
$0.0011011 * 2^{01011} \to 0.011011 * 2^{01010} \to 0.11011 * 2^{01001} \to 1.1011 * 2^{01000}$ (normalized representation)

The 23 to 30 (short real) and the 52 to 60 (long real) give the biased exponent. In order to determine the true exponent, you have to subtract the bias value from the stored exponent. With the short real format you subtract 127; with the long real format 1023. Values smaller than 127 or

1023, respectively, in the stored exponent indicate a negative exponent and represent numbers smaller than 1. The choice of the bias values of 127 and 1023 is more or less random, but they do produce logarithmic symmetry due to their middle position between the maximum and minimum possible values.

Finally, the S bit gives the sign of the mantissa, and thus the whole number.

```
Example: 365.827 99 = 3.658 279 9 * 10² in short real format is as follows:
c3b6e9fc = 1100 0011 1011 0110 1110 1001 1111 1100b
```

mantissa: $2^{-2}+2^{-3}+2^{-5}+2^{-6}+2^{-8}+2^{-9}+2^{-10}+2^{-12}+2^{-15}$
$+2^{-16}+2^{-17}+2^{-18}+2^{-19}+2^{-20}+2^{-21}$=0.429 015 64
add implied '1': 1.429 015 64
exponent: 135–bias(127) = 8
sign: 1 = negative number

```
Thus the number is −1.429 015 64 * 2⁸ = −1.42901564 * 256 = 365.827 99
```

The values 255 and 2048 for the biased exponent in short real and long real format, respectively, are defined in the IEEE format as *not a number (NAN)*, and so are not considered as numbers, accordingly.

A problem that often occurs, especially in scientific and technical calculations such as weather forecasting and the aerodynamic forces acting on an aircraft wing, is that many successive calculations with very large differences in the sizes of numbers are possible. If the multiplication and addition of many such numbers occur with many interim results, the result can quickly become inaccurate. An extreme example would be $[(1+10^{-100})-1]*10^{200}$. If the number $1+10^{-100}$ is stored as 1 because not enough decimal places are available and afterwards 1 is subtracted, the interim result is 0. When this is multiplied by the large number 10^{200}, the result remains small, also 0. If, on the other hand, the number $1+10^{-100}$ had been correctly stored and then 1 had been subtracted, the interim result would have been 10^{-100}. Multiplied afterwards by 10^{200}, the result is now 10^{100}. If you consider this number as a quantity of atoms, a lot of universes are represented, as opposed to the 0 atoms of the first case – a considerable difference.

In order to increase the accuracy of interim results in expansive calculations, it is necessary to use mathematic coprocessors such as the Intel 80x87 family or even software emulation that uses the internal temporary real format of 80 bits. This format need not necessarily be normalized as the short and long real formats are, because the M_0 bit of the mantissa is contained in the format. It is not, as previously explained, always 1 through implication.

Something totally non-mathematical appears in the signed bit, an apparently positive and negative zero. Mathematically speaking, this is impossible. There is exactly one, and only one, zero. The reason for the sudden appearance of two different zeros is that the floating-point format, and therefore also the coprocessor, defines the number by representation, whereas mathematics are based on attributes. Even if all of the bits in the short and long real formats are zero, it does not mean that the actual value of the number is zero. Ultimately, the M_0=1 bit remains by definition. Should the simple floating-point number 00000000h really represent the value zero, or perhaps because M_0=1 is implied, the value $1*2^{-127}$?

Even this has been considered and a clear definition is given: (1) If the mantissa is 0 in a floating-point number in the normalized format with the smallest possible exponent, the value 0 is represented; (2) If the exponent has the smallest possible value and the mantissa has a value other than 0, the mantissa is not normalized and the stored mantissa bit gives the mantissa value without the implied $M_0=1$. This number can only be represented with a gradual under-flow. The number, despite being too small for normalized representation, can be represented if normalization is not applied and leading zeros are used instead.

```
Example: 00000011h in short real format
sign 0b:          positive number
biased exponent 0000 0000b:   exponent -127, thus no normalized mantissa
mantissa 000 0000 0000 0000 0000 0011 = 2⁻²¹ + 2⁻²² = 3*2⁻²²
value of this number: mantissa * 2exponent = 3*2⁻²² * 2⁻¹²⁷ = 3*2⁻¹⁴⁹ = 4.203 895 5 * 10⁻⁴⁵
The smallest possible normalized number, according to the short real format, however, is:
00800000h=1*2⁻¹²⁶=1.175 494 4 * 10⁻³⁸.
```

1.3.9 The MSBIN format

To give the complete picture, I would like to describe the MSBIN format for floating-point numbers. It is used by the GWBASIC and BASICA interpreters from Microsoft and IBM, respectively.

The bias value is 129 for both of the MSBIN formats, as opposed to 127 with the short real format of the IEEE standard. Values in MSBIN format must be interpreted as follows:

```
Value = (-1)ˢ * (1+M₁*2⁻¹+M₂*2⁻²+...+M₂₃*2⁻²³) * 2E7...E0-129 (short real)
Value = (-1)ˢ * (1+M₁*2⁻¹+M₂*2⁻²+...+M₅₅*2⁻⁵⁵) * 2E7...E0-129 (long real)
```

The accuracy of the long real format is almost twice as great as that of the short real format. The value range is, however, not larger. The MSBIN long real format can always be converted into the IEEE long real format, but conversion in the other direction is only possible if the value of the IEEE number is less than $1.7*10^{38}$ and more than $3.0*10^{-39}$.

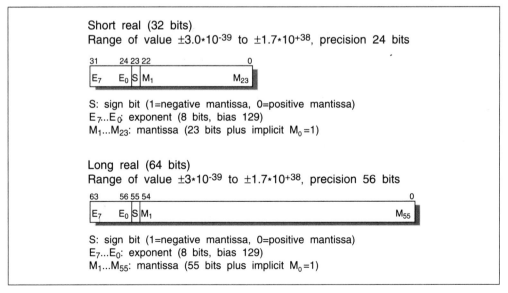

Figure 1.6: MSBIN formats for short real and long real.

```
Example: 5.294 * 10⁷ = 1.577 734 9 * 2²⁵
in IEEE short real: 0cc9f337h
00001100110010011111001100110111
```

$$\text{Example: } 5.294 * 10^7 = 1.577\ 734\ 9 * 2^{25}$$

in IEEE short real: 0cc9f337h

00001100110010011111001100110111

mantissa: $M_0(=1)+2^{-1}+2^{-4}+2^{-7}+2^{-9}+2^{-10}+2^{-11}+2^{-14}$
$+2^{-15}+2^{-18}+2^{-19}+2^{-21}+2^{-22}+2^{-23}=1.577\ 734\ 9$

exponent: $2^4+2^3+2^0=25$

sign: +

in MSBIN short real: 1949f337h

0001 1001 0100 1001 1111 0011 0011 0111

mantissa: $M_0(=1)+2^{-1}+2^{-4}+2^{-7}+2^{-9}+2^{-10}+2^{-11}+2^{-14}$
$+2^{-15}+2^{-18}+2^{-19}+2^{-21}+2^{-22}+2^{-23}=1.577\ 734\ 9$

sign: +

exponent: $2^4+2^3+2^0=25$

as long integer (52 940 000): 0327cce0h

The example clearly indicates that the IEEE and MSBIN formats are completely incompatible.

2 Basic 80x86 register architecture and logical memory access

This chapter introduces the basic register architecture of the 80x86 family as well as the logical memory access (also known as logical memory addressing). You will find only the most important topics that are necessary to understand the following discussions about CISC concepts and RISC innovations.

2.1 General-purpose and segment registers

The general-purpose registers in the i386 are 32-bit, but because of the need for compatibility with their 16-bit 8086/186/286 predecessors they can also be used as 16-bit or 8-bit registers. Figure 2.1 shows all of the registers in the i386. The registers for memory management are used in protected mode. As an introduction, I would like to discuss the most important registers in the i386 that are already used in real mode. These are the general-purpose and segment registers, the flag register and the CR0 control register. The lower value word of the CR0 control register was implemented in the 80286 as the machine status word (MSW), which regulates the switching into protected mode and contains the status information necessary for protected mode operation. The processor has a lot more internal registers – for example, if storage is needed for interim results of an ALU calculation. These temporary registers are not accessible and I do not wish to go into detail at this point. Only the segment descriptor cache register will be described in connection with protected mode.

The i386 has seven general-purpose registers (EAX to EBP), six segment registers (CS to GS), an instruction pointer (EIP), a stack pointer (ESP) and a flag register (EFLAG). The general-purpose registers, instruction pointer, stack pointer and flag register are all 32-bit, whereas the segment registers are only 16-bit. Because of the 32-bit maximum size of the general-purpose register, the i386 can have offsets of 32 bits, such as 0 to 4G-1. Segments can also be considerably larger with an i386 than is possible with an 8086, but that is not surprising for a fourth generation. With all 32-bit registers, it is also possible to communicate only with the two lower byte values. They are marked as AX to DI (general-purpose registers), IP (instruction pointer), SP (stack pointer) and FLAG (flag register). The lower value word of the four general-purpose registers (AX to DX) can be subdivided even further into two register bytes, namely AH and AL for the AX register. Therefore, the i386 can also process single data bytes. The EAX register, with the subdivisions AX, AH and AL is used as a special accumulator. The majority of, and fastest executing, instructions are available to EAX (and the subdivisions AX and AH, AL). The ECX (or CX) register is mainly used as a count register during programming and the execution of loops. Every loop pass reduces the value in CX by 1, until CX reaches a value of zero. Table 2.1 shows the conventional designations of the registers and a summary of their main uses. The i386 32-bit processor is the successor to the 16-bit 80286 CPU and is fully compatible with it. It is necessary for the 32-bit registers of the i386 to communicate with the 16-bit, so the 32-bit registers are designated with an E (for extended) at the beginning. In comparison, the 80286 possesses only the usual AX register and so on. The use of the i386 register with 32-bit or 16-bit depends on the operating mode, which can be selected. This will be explained later. A further quality of the i386 is its backwards compatibility to all previous 80x86 microprocessors, including the 8086 and the

80286. Therefore, the i386 can do everything that its predecessors, the 8086 and 80286, are capable of. In the following section, I describe some of the general-purpose registers and segment registers in more detail.

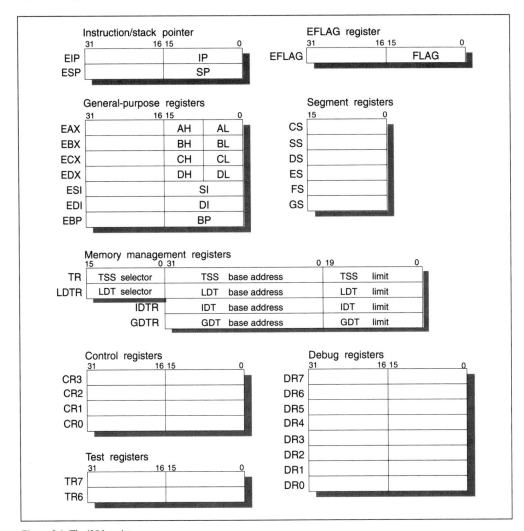

Figure 2.1: The i386 registers.

Register

32-Bit	16-Bit	8-Bit	Name	Task
EAX	AX	AH, AL	Accumulator	Multiplication/division, I/O, fast shifts
EBX	BX	BH, BL	Base register	Pointer to base address in data segment

Register				
32-Bit	**16-Bit**	**8-Bit**	**Name**	**Task**
ECX	CX	CH, CL	Count register	Count value for repetitions, shifts, rotates
EDX	DX	DH, DL	Data register	Multiplication, division, I/O
EBP	BP		Base pointer	Pointer to base address in stack segment
ESI	SI		Source index	Source string and index pointer
EDI	DI		Destination index	Destination string and index pointer
ESP	SP		Stack pointer	Stack pointer
	CS		Code segment	Segment of instructions
	DS		Data segment	Standard segment of data
	SS		Stack segment	Segment of stack
	ES		Extra segment	Freely usable segment
	FS		Extra segment	Freely usable segment
	GS		Extra segment	Freely usable segment
EIP	IP		Instruction pointer	Offset of instructions
EFLAG	FLAG		Flags	Indicators for processor status and operation results

Table 2.1: The i386 registers and their uses.

2.2 Code segment, instruction pointer and program execution

As I explained previously, the processor fetches instructions from memory and then executes them, in order to run a program. The code segment and the instruction pointer form the basis for this automatic reading. The code segment sets the segment for the next instruction. The instruction pointer gives the offset for the next instruction to be read. The value or register pair, code segment:instruction pointer, thus defines the next instruction in memory to be executed. The processor can then read and carry out the instruction. The code of the instruction tells the processor how many bytes it must read, so that the whole instruction is contained in the processor. Instructions for the 80x86 are between 1 and 15 bytes long.

When the instruction is executed, the instruction counter is incremented by the number of bytes contained in the executed instruction. With a short 2-byte instruction, the instruction counter is increased by two, the code segment:instruction counter pair then refers to the next instruction to be executed. The next instruction is read and executed in the same way. Subsequently, the processor increments the instruction counter again. The read and the incrementation are both carried out by the processor completely independently. No action from the control program or from the user is necessary. Once activated, the CPU will continuously read in and execute instructions.

The prefetch queue and the bus interface play an important role in instruction fetching. As I stated earlier, the instruction is first read into the prefetch queue, which then passes it to the instruction unit (IU). If, after the instruction bytes have been passed to the control unit (CU), there are as many bytes free in the prefetch queue as the processor data bus is wide, the bus interface will read the applicable number of bytes from the memory into the prefetch queue. For example, the i386 has a four byte (32-bit) data bus. It will, therefore, independently read in four bytes when four bytes are free in the prefetch queue. In this way the processor uses the data bus optimally; when the i386 carries out an instruction that does not cause an immediate memory access (for example, the addition of two registers), the bus interface can load the prefetch queue without hindering the currently active instruction. Immediately after an instruction has been executed, the next instruction is available and so need not be read from memory. Obviously, a memory access as a result of an active instruction (for example, after the use of MOV, register, memory) has priority over the reloading of the prefetch queue. Parallel to the execution of the currently active instruction and the reloading of the prefetch queue, the IU decodes the next instruction and prepares it for the execution unit (EU) and for execution. The EU carries out the instruction in a specific number of clock cycles. Simple instructions such as CLC (clear carry) need two clock cycles, whereas complicated instructions such as a task switch via a gate in protected mode need more than 300.

From this description you can immediately see that there is a uniform instruction flow from the memory to the processor. In other words, a program is executed sequentially. Today, the intention is to perform as many independent steps as possible, in parallel, in order to increase the capabilities of the computer. The Pentium can use three independent pipelines for parallel processing.

The uniform flow of instructions can be interrupted and redirected by conditional and unconditional jumps and branchings. This is very important for the logical structure of a program, because a computer should frequently perform different things, depending on the specific instructions. In order to carry out a jump or a branching (which is nothing more than a jump under specific conditions), only the value of the instruction pointer and, if necessary, the code segment need to be changed. With a so-called near call or near jump, the code segment remains unchanged; only the new value of the EIP is loaded. The instruction flow is also located in the same segment. With a far call or jump, in comparison, the code segment is also changed and an *intersegment call* or *intersegment jump* is executed. The processor writes to a different segment for the program execution. In addition, with this sort of jump, the prefetch queue is completely emptied so that the bytes that have been read in are not included with the new instruction.

Example: The value in the code segment register CS is equal to 3d4f, the value of the instruction pointer is equal to 10de. Thus the next instruction is located at address 3d4f:10de. The code at this address is 8ce0. The CU decodes this 2–byte code and determines the instruction:

MOV EAX, FS

It should carry over the value of the extra segment FS in the 32-bit accumulator register EAX. After the execution of this instruction, the value of the instruction pointer is increased by two because MOV EAX, FS is a 2-byte instruction. The value of EIP is then 10e0; the value of the code segment CS remains unchanged.

Example: The value of the code segment is equal to 4fe0, the value of the instruction pointer is equal to 2a34. Thus the next instruction is located at address 4fe0:2a34. The code at this address is 751b. The CU decodes this code and determines the instruction:

JNZ 2a51

This occurs with a specific branching (JNZ; jump if not zero) to the instruction with the address 2a51. Here, the code segment is not changed, even when the jump condition is fulfilled and the processor executes a jump. Usually, a comparison of two values occurs before such a specific branching occurs. The processor sets or resets specific flags depending on the result of the comparison. The flags are also necessary for the logical flow of a program.

If the result of the previous example is not equal to zero, the program will branch: the instruction pointer IP is loaded with the value 2a51 and the i386 continues with the address 4fe0:2a51. If, on the other hand, the result of the comparison is equal to zero, no jump occurs and the instruction continues uniformly. With this, the instruction pointer EIP simply increases by two to 2a36, because JNZ 2a51 is a 2-byte instruction. Note that the 1-byte jump address 1b in the opcode 751b is relative to the instruction pointer EIP after the loading of the 2-byte opcode. From this, the target address for the example is calculated as 2a34 (old EIP value) +2 (2-byte instruction) + 1b (jump width), which gives 2a51.

The 32-bit instruction pointer EIP makes possible programs up to a maximum of 4Gbytes, whereas its 16-bit 80286 predecessor only allowed programs of up to 64 kbytes, with the use of the 16-bit offset register. With a change in the code segment possible through the use of a specialized instruction (the loading of CS with a specific value), larger programs are possible. It is important to note that the code segment can be changed, but not the instruction pointer. There is no direct loading instruction for the EIP. The value in the instruction pointer can only be changed with a conditional or unconditional jump (or call) to another program. Far calls and far jumps automatically influence the value in the code segment CS.

The i386 instruction set, with 206 instructions and additional instruction variations, is very extensive in relation to the register width and its addressing methods – a true CISC device. In Appendix C, all of the i386 instructions are listed as part of the Pentium instruction set.

2.3 Stack segment and stack pointer

The stack segment and its stack pointer have a further special use. Every program is normally assigned a stack segment, where it can store the value of a register or a memory operand with the use of the PUSH instruction. The PUSHF instruction copies all of the flags, and the PUSHA instruction all of the general-purpose registers, to the stack. In the other direction, it is possible to use the instructions POP, POPF and POPA to remove the applicable data from the stack and to write the memory operand or the flag to a register.

Note that the stack reduces to smaller values of the stack pointer ESP (Figure 2.2). If data is stored on the stack, the value of ESP is reduced by four, because a complete double word (4 bytes) is always written to the stack. When the i386 operates in 16-bit mode, naturally only 2 bytes are written to the stack and the value of ESP is only reduced by two with every PUSH. This also applies to the 16-bit 8086 and 20286 predecessors. If the stack is empty, the stack pointer takes on its largest value. After the word has been stored, the stack pointer indicates the last stored word in the stack. Firstly, a PUSH instruction increases the value of the stack pointer ESP, then the register or memory value is stored in the stack.

The main causes of program crashes, especially in the development phase, are called *stack over-flows*. This occurs when the capacity of the stack is exceeded and the processor wishes to write additional data to it using a further PUSH instruction. This is, of course, not possible. A stack overflow is easy to identify in real mode: when ESP has a value of 0, the stack is full and every further PUSH instruction will lead to a stack overflow.

The disadvantage is that, in real mode, the application must test before every PUSH instruction, to confirm that the stack has enough free capacity. In protected mode, the i386 can identify such a failure automatically: the protected mode is not so named for nothing.

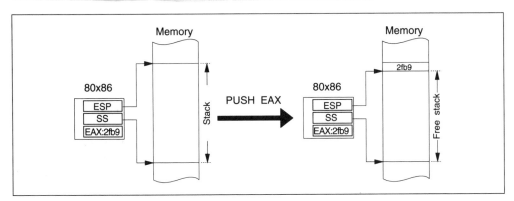

Figure 2.2: Stack and stack pointer.
The 80x86 uses the stack mainly as a temporary storage for return addresses or register values. By means of PUSH EAX you are saving the accumulator value EAX on the stack. Simultaneously the stack pointer is decremented by four. Thus the stack grows downwardly, that is towards lower addresses.

A further important use of the stack is as an intermediate storage medium for the use of data that can not easily be accessed without PUSH and POP. The trap flag is such an example. The stack is, however, mainly used for storing parameters and procedures of subroutines. Parameters for procedures containing one or more PUSH instructions of the current program are also stored there. The applicable procedure can then use these parameters with one or more POP instructions, as applicable, or through the use of an addressing via the base pointer BP.

In the i386, a specific instruction pair is used to produce these procedure stacks: ENTER (stack frame creation) and LEAVE (stack frame deletion). In addition, the applicable procedure uses the stack to store local variables. Depending on the user's programming language, the applicable procedure must reset the stack to its previous condition before the current program is reactivated with a RETURN, or the current program wipes the stack after completion with a RETURN. In this way, the stored parameters and the temporary local variables are deleted.

The PUSH SP instruction has a special characteristic, that is the writing of the stack register itself to the stack. The i386 (and all other 80x86 processors with the exception of the 8086/8088) first writes ESP to the stack, then ESP is reduced (by two or four). The 8086/8088, on the other hand, first reduces SP (by two), then copies SP to the stack.

2.4 Data segment and memory addressing

Next to the code and stack segment registers, the data segment (DS) register also has a special use. It is important when an instruction reads data from, or writes data to, the memory – this means when memory operands are necessary. The offset of the memory operand is usually contained in a general-purpose register, and the DS:offset pair refers to the applicable value. The DS data segment register is normally used as an offset associated segment register. When it is necessary to read or write a value into another segment, the segment register DS must be loaded with the value of the new segment, or a segment prefix must be used so that the data register DS is replaced with an extra segment register ES to GS. More on this subject follows.

Through the use of different segments for code, stack and data, the logically different steps of a program are separated. The protected mode uses this fact to prevent program failures. Obviously, all of the segment registers can contain the same value. In this case, there is no longer any separation between code, stack and data.

2.5 Addressing types and instruction encoding

In Section 2.2, instructions such as JNZ and MOV were discussed. However, when a program requires a specialized editor or the DOS instruction TYPE, such codes are not used. JNZ and MOV are called *mnemonic codes*, or *mnemonics* for short. These short names only serve as support for the programmer, repeating the operation of the applicable instruction in a shorter form.

2.5.1 Mnemonics and the assembler

An *assembler* interprets the mnemonics and carries out the applicable encoding in a *machine code* instruction for the processor. Machine code instructions are (naturally) a series of zeros and ones contained in one or more bytes. The instruction TYPE, as a 'text indicator' interprets all of the codes as ASCII characters, which produces apparently confused nonsense. For example, if TYPE is used in conjunction with the previously used mnemonic code JNZ 2a51, the screen will show: *Q.

As well as converting mnemonics and machine code, an assembler can also make other things easier. For example, many assemblers can handle macros (for this reason, called *macro assemblers*), carry out various addressing schemes and process variables, and jump positions (JNZ) as well as procedures (CALL subroutines) symbolically. The assembler then converts these instructions into the applicable machine code instructions. An assembler is the closest thing to an artificial programmer.

In the explanations of the machine code instructions that follow, I have used mnemonic codes and elements of assembler programming (for example, symbolic jump positions or the designations of procedures). In Appendix C you will find a complete list of instructions for the i386 and the Pentium. If you are not familiar with these instructions, you should take a quick look at the list, to get a feel for the vocabulary of your computer.

2.5.2 Addressing

If a register such as the accumulator EAX is loaded with a value through the use of MOV EAX, the following three possibilities can be used.

Immediate operand: MOV EAX, 6a02h

The accumulator register EAX is loaded with the value 6a02h. This value was included at the time of programming and is part of the program code; this means it is read by the code segment CS, and not by the data segment DS or an extra segment. The value 6a02h is a part of the instruction that is loaded from the bus interface into the prefetch queue. The control unit, however, passes it on to the EAX register and not to the execution unit, as it would for an instruction.

Register operand: MOV EAX, EBX

The register EAX is loaded with the value in the register EBX. As in the above example, EAX is a register operand (or destination operand). Here, the source operand is also a register (EBX).

Memory operand: MOV EAX, mem32

In place of mem32, the assembler must insert the *effective address* of the symbolic operand mem32. If the effective address is already known by the assembler, representing static size, it inserts the unchanged value during the assembling procedure. In this case, mem32 is called a *direct memory operand*. Usually, such direct memory operands in a macro assembler are indicated with a symbol (such as *array*). If the effective address is dynamic (if the address can change during runtime, for example, a register with a previously unknown value), then the CPU calculates the effective address during runtime. In this case, mem32 is an *indirect memory operand*.

The effective address is understood to mean the offset of an operand contained in the chosen segment (usually DS). The effective address can be constructed of up to four elements.

Displacement: MOV EAX, array [0]

The first element of the array is loaded into the accumulator. *Array[0]* is a symbolic designation of how a macro assembler can operate in order to make the work of a programmer easier. In an assembled program, there is a number in place of *array[0]*, which indicates the address of the symbolic *array[0]*. If, for example, the address of array [0] is 0f2h, the instruction would be MOV EAX, [0f2h]. Don't confuse this with an immediate operand: with a displacement, the value gives the applicable address and not the value itself. In our example, the value in the DS segment with an offset of 0f2h is loaded, not the value 0f2h itself.

Base register: MOV EAX, [EBX]

The instruction loads the operand in the DS segment with the offset given by the value in the register BX into the accumulator. If, for example, EBX contains the value 0f2h, this instruction is equivalent to the previous example MOV EAX array[0]. The main logical difference between [EBX] and array[0] is that the value of BX can be changed dynamically during the program execution, while array[0] is a fixed and constant value for the runtime of the program. With the dynamic changing of EBX, it is possible to use multiple loops for the complete array, similar to the BASIC instruction FOR I=1 TO 9 ... NEXT I. The base registers are EBX and EBP.

Index register: MOV EAX, [ESI]

In this base form, the use of the index register has the same rules as the use of the base registers. Additionally, the index register has another possibility, the assignment of a scaling factor. The index registers are ESI and EDI.

Scaling factor: MOV EAX, [ESI*4]

To calculate the effective address for this example, the value of the ESI index register is multiplied by four. With this example, it is possible to index array elements by four. The i386 carries out the scaling (or multiplication) with a factor greater than 1, without support. The values 1, 2, 4 and 8 can be used as scaling factors. The scaling factor was introduced into the addressing capabilities beginning with the i386: the 8086 and 80286 have to operate without scaling factors.

Displacement, base registers, index registers and scaling factors can be used in any combination. In this way, very complicated and multidimensional addresses can be defined, such as those necessary for array elements. These complex possibilities for the definition of effective addresses clearly differentiate a CISC processor from a pure RISC CPU; one major demand of the RISC concept is that only two instructions, with simpler definition of the effective address (usually with a type of base register), can access the memory: LOAD and STORE. Nested addressings, as in the following example, were not foreseen in the original RISC concept.

Example: A 10-element array is given, which defines various bodies; each element has a structure of height:width:depth:cross-section. The partial elements, height and so on, each comprise 1 byte. The array starts at 0c224h. The following program fragment loads the depths into the accumulator EAX:

```
MOV EBX, 0c224h      ; load base address into EBX
MOV ESI, nr          ; load element number into ESI
MOV EAX, [EBX+ESI*4+2] ; load depth (displacement of 2 bytes compared to the beginning
                     ; of the element)
                     ; of element number (element size = 4 bytes, thus scaling 4)
                     ; of array (starting at base address in EBX) into accumulator EAX
```

The i386 normally uses the DS segment register (or SS where EBP is the base register). The i386 also has the three extra segment registers ES to GS and the code segment register CS. In order to activate DS or SS for a data access, it is necessary to use a *segment override*. The assembler recognizes such an override, where the identification of the applicable segment in the memory operand is separated by a colon. If, in the above example, it is necessary to address a field in a segment that will be defined by the value in the ES segment register, the instruction MOV EAX, ES:[EBX+ESI*4+2] must be used. Such a segment override is useful, if a segment need only be addressed infrequently. If, on the other hand, a series of instructions accesses the ES segment, it is better to load the value from ES into DS. The value of ES can then be accessed frequently from DS and the processor does not need to perform an ES override.

2.5.3 Instruction encoding

In the subsection on displacement, I quickly explained that in the given example, the assembler converts the instruction MOV EAX, array[0] to MOV EAX, 0f2h. But how does the i386 know that 0f2h represents a displacement (an address) and not a value, where the value in the address DS:0f2h and not the value 0f2h itself should be loaded into the AX register? The key to this is contained in the encoding of the instruction.

The processor does not understand symbolic instructions such as MOV AX, ES:[BX+SI*4+2] (with this, ASCII encoding would also be inadequate), only bytes or series of bytes. An assembler or compiler converts symbolic instructions into a long series of bytes. For this, every instruction is divided into four main parts:

Prefix(es)	Opcode	Operand(s)	Displacement/Data

The most important part is the *opcode* (operation code). It consists of one or two bytes and describes the instruction in simple terms. If the first byte is 00001111b, the opcode consists of two bytes. If the first byte starts with the bit sequence 11011 (27 in decimal, corresponding to ESC), the instruction is for the mathematics coprocessor (the i387). Simple instructions without operands such as CLC (clear carry flag = reset carry flag) consist of only 1byte opcodes. Complex instructions with prefixes and many operands/displacements/data can, however, in the i386, consist of up to 15 bytes. The opcode contains information pertaining to the prefix, operand and displacement/data of the instruction, as necessary. The two least significant bits of the opcode frequently indicate the direction of data transfer (register to register/memory or memory to register) as with the use of 8-/16- or 8-/32-bit operands (for example, AL, AX or EAX).

The *operand(s)* field defines which register uses which direct or indirect memory operands. The *displacement/data* field indicates a displacement or an immediate operand that is already known at assemble time.

The IU knows if a MOV instruction with displacement or an immediate operand is necessary with the different opcodes. The IU then controls the EU accordingly, so that the MOV instruction with displacement or the immediate operand is executed. With a displacement, the EU tells the AU to load the value in the address DS:0f2h from the memory into the accumulator through the bus interface. If 0f2h is an immediate operand, the i386 loads the value 0f2h from the prefetch queue into EAX as part of an instruction. In the first case, an additional memory access is necessary while the EU processes the immediate operand at once.

If, with the displacement of an operand, it is necessary to use the offset address 0f2h in the extra segment ES, FS or GS in place of the normal data segment DS, a *prefix* is attached to the instruction code instead of using an additional opcode. This segment override prefix causes an extra segment (also CS and SS) to override the standard data segment DS. Table 2.2 shows all of the valid segment override prefixes for the i386.

Segment	Prefix
CS	00101110 (2eh)
DS	00111110 (3eh)
SS	00110110 (36h)
ES	00100110 (26h)
FS	01100100 (64h)
GS	01100101 (65h)

Table 2.2: Segment override prefixes.

There are other prefixes in addition to these segment override prefixes. They are used for repeating string operations (with REP), the control of the bus (with LOCK) and the changing of operands (16- or 32-bit) and address sizes (16- or 32-bit). The advantage of a prefix over an additional opcode lies in the fact that prefixes are only added when an instruction requires it. In comparison, the encoding contained in an opcode would increase the size of the code for each instruction, if it were to include the information that is only used as necessary with the prefix. With this method, either the length of the opcode or its complexity is increased. The as-required encoding with prefixes uses less memory space and the programs are compacted. Disregarding extensive memory accesses, instructions using the segment override prefix in instruction fetching, where the standard data segment DS is replaced by another segment (ES, FS, GS, SS or CS), are carried out in the same time. With the constant and automatic reloading of the prefetch queue in the background, the additional memory access, due to the prefix, only rarely slows down the operating speed, for example, when the prefetch queue is reset after a jump or a function call.

Assemblers recognize automatically from designations such as EAX or ES: the operand size with respect to which segment should be used and the corresponding opcode, operand(s) and displacement/data. In addition, they insert the necessary prefix independently.

3 Micro-encoding of machine code instructions

We have already come across the mnemonics and encoding of instructions and addressing in Section 2.5. Now we need to answer the question, how does the i386 (or other CISC processor) use this coded bit flow in order to execute the required instructions with the necessary data? In this chapter, we will learn about the fundamental characteristics of CISC processors – in fact, the *micro-encoding* of machine code instructions. CISC and RISC processors do not just differ from each other by the extent of instructions (today, there is very little numerical difference), but mainly in the 'internal workings'. Let us move now to the microprogramming concept.

Figure 1.2 showed that the instructions are read into a prefetch queue. An attached decoding unit then decodes them. With microprogrammed processors, an instruction is not executed directly, but is available, in a microcode ROM within the processor, as a microprogram. Figure 3.1 shows the basic concept schematically.

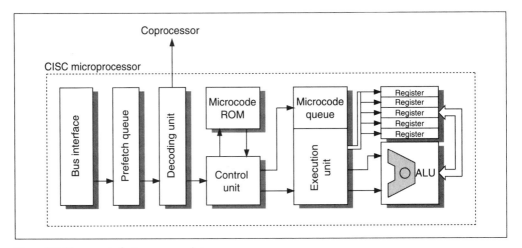

Figure 3.1: The concept of microprogramming.
With microprogramming the processor fetches the instructions via the bus interface into a prefetch queue, which in turn transfers them to a decoding unit. The decoding unit separates a machine instruction into many elemetary micro-instructions and applies them to a microcode queue. The micro-instructions are transferred from the microcode queue to the control and execution unit so that the ALU and the registers are driven accordingly.

The processor decoding unit must, therefore, decode the read instruction first; that is, split it into the actual instruction, the type of address, extent and type of relevant register, and so on. All of this information is contained in the opcode, prefix operand and displacement/data. The control unit calls the necessary microprograms in relation to the applicable values, in order to execute the instructions with the help of the ALU, register, and so on. It becomes apparent that the decoding process and the preparation for executing the necessary microprograms require a specific amount of time. The decoding time can, therefore, be equal in length to or even longer than the execution time of the instruction itself. Thus, the execution time of an instruction consists of the decoding time and the duration of execution. In addition to the relief of the bus interface, the prefetch queue plays a further important role. Since it already contains the next available instructions, prior to executing the current instructions, the decoding unit can stock up work in advance, by decoding the next instruction and preparing it for execution in the control unit, while the execution unit is still busy processing the current instruction.

In the following text, I would like to briefly present the steps for the MOVS/MOVSB/MOVSW/ MOVSD (move data from string to string) instruction. This instruction is one of the most powerful i386 machine code instructions, and is typical for a CISC processor. Intel specifies the following i386 operations for the instruction:

```
IF (instruction = MOVSD) OR (double word operand available)
  THEN Operand size <- 32;
  ELSE Operand size <- 16;
FI;

IF address size = 16
  THEN SI=SourceIndex and DI=DestinationIndex;
  ELSE ESI=SourceIndex and EDI=DestinationIndex;
FI;

IF Operation of byte-type
  THEN
    [DestinationIndex] <- [SourceIndex];
    IF DF=0
      THEN IncDec <- 1
      ELSE IncDec <- -1
    FI;
  ELSE
    IF Operand size = 16
      THEN
        [DestinationIndex] <- [SourceIndex];
        IF DF=0
          THEN IncDec <- 2
          ELSE IncDec <- -2
        FI;
      ELSE
        [DestinationIndex] <- [SourceIndex];
        IF DF=0
          THEN IncDec <- 4
          ELSE IncDec <- -4
        FI;
    FI;
FI;

SourceIndex <- SourceIndex + IncDec
DestinationIndex <- DestinationIndex + IncDec
```

The individual operations are represented by matching microcodes in the microcode ROM and are executed by the execution unit (EU) with the assistance of logic gates, the ALU and the bus interface. You can see that a considerable number of internal micro-instructions are executed for the instruction MOVSx. Intel specifies that the execution time of the instruction is eight processor clock cycles (PCLK). If the instruction is repeatedly executed with a prefix of REPxx, then the first execution of MOVSx requires eight clock cycles, but each subsequent execution requires only four. The complete IF-THEN-ELSE-FI block only has to run through at the start, in order to determine the operands, addresses and IncDec quantities. Each following run only defers the data from source to the destination operation. For this, four processor clock cycles are required (including the test for the completion of all repetitions).

A very complex circuit would be necessary in order to implement this operation as a hardwired logic. On the other hand, however, the microcodes repeatedly access the same hardware logic elements. The EU has a microcontrol pointer analogue to the EIP instruction pointer of the 'entire processor', which addresses the micro-instructions in the microprogram memory. The complexity of the MOVSx instruction is due to the binary encoding in the microcode ROM and not to a circuit layout. Similar aspects also led to the general development of microprocessors or free programmable computers. Also in this case, the one-off, fixed and relatively simple circuit structure is repeatedly used by a program, which is stored in memory. It would be possible, for example, to implement a program such as AmiPro, in principle, by hardwired logic purely in hardware. The technical difficulties, would, however, be enormous. I am sure that you can imagine that considerably more components would be required, more even than the Pentium has. Instead, it is better to transfer the complexity of AmiPro into a program memory, where the individual instructions can be stored in coded form. A further advantage is that the content of the memory can be altered much more quickly and more easily than a circuit.

One disadvantage of micro-encoding can be seen immediately: the execution speed is much slower than that of direct hardware implementation. The reason behind this is that many individual steps and individual decisions are necessary (thus, many clock cycles), whereas a pure hardware implementation disposes of the whole instruction in one go.

Microprogramming has developed over a period of time, having many advantages. For instance, for a very compact instruction code, the size of the instructions, and, thus, the memory requirement, is small. You can get 256 different instruction codes in one byte, if each modification of the type of address, register concerned and so on is regarded as an individual instruction. In the early 1960s the core storage (made of ferromagnetic rings), which in those days was the write and read memory, was the most expensive and, unfortunately, also the slowest component of a computer, having a typical average access time of $1\,\mu s$. Today, a good DRAM will achieve $0.060\,\mu s$ and a fast SRAM approximately $0.012\,\mu s$. However, in those days, ROMs could be realized with an access time of 100–200 ns, which, moreover, were considerably cheaper than core memories. For a single access of the write or read memory, the processor could execute between 5 and 10 ROM accesses. In other words, while the prefetcher is reading an instruction code from the write/read memory, the processor is capable of internally extracting and executing between 5 and 10 micro-instructions from the microcode ROM. Even in those days, micro-encoding had a minimal effect on reducing the speed of instruction execution.

Because of the high cost and sluggishness of the core memories, it was necessary to reduce the load of program code on the write/read memory. The alternative was to load the complex program code into the cheaper and faster (microcode) ROM in the processor. This resulted in microprogramming. Of course, in the 1960s, there were no microprocessors, but more or less just enormous processor cards. Even since the introduction of microprocessors themselves, the concept of microprogramming has not changed. Today, the majority of microprocessors (with the exception of pure RISC implementation) are still micro-encoded. The Pentium is no exception. The fact is that the majority of commonly used and relatively simple instructions are available in hardwired form; however, complex instructions such as MOVSx, as mentioned previously, are still micro-encoded.

An additional advantage of microprogramming is that, in simple terms, compatibility can be achieved with earlier processors. All that is required is to maintain the old code and implement it with additional instructions for the newer, more efficient, processors. To that end, the micro-code ROM is simply enlarged in the processor and the microcodes of the new instructions are also stored. Thus, in theory, a new generation of processors is created. It is, therefore, hardly surprising that the higher family members of the different processor families have an ever increasing number of powerful instructions, thus leading to the evolution of CISCs.

At the end of the 1970s, the relationship between the access time of the internal microcode ROM and the external main memory slowly but surely reversed. The slower core storages were completely replaced by semiconductor memories, as the result of great advances in memory technology. Today, because of high integration, mainly in memory chips, and the resulting reduction in price, processors are much more costly than memory, and it no longer has any bearing whether or not the instruction code is compact.

The concept of microprogramming can be casually linked, in a certain way, to that of a simple BASIC interpreter. In this case also, the instruction is split into its component parts – that is, interpreted, then executed in accordance with the decoded component parts. Micro-programming does not know powerful instructions such as GWBASIC, nor can instructions be nested like, for example, PRINT(STRLEN("ww"+A$+STRING(20, "q"))+9).

The equivalent for the hardwired instructions in RISC processors would be a compiled program. Here, instructions would be executed immediately without the influence of higher level (interpreter and microcode) programs. I am sure that you are aware of the difference in speed between an interpreted and a compiled BASIC program. It is no great surprise that RISC processors work instructions on a much quicker basis than CISC processors. A realistic factor of three or even four can be applied to comparable processors. In order to achieve this, though, other criteria are also necessary, for example pipelined working-off of machine code instruction, ideally in several independent pipelines, and of course, not forgetting the software side of things. You will learn more about these crucial RISC processor characteristics later. In the meantime, let us deal with the general basic components of an electronic chip.

4 In-depth for the technically minded: MOS transistors and logic gates – the foundations of a processor

Today, microprocessors and memory chips are the most complex of integrated circuits (IC). They are constructed from the smallest possible electronic components. The most important of these is the metal oxide semiconductor field effect transistor (MOSFET). In general, the logic gates and complex logic circuits, such as AND gates and full adders, consist of these components.

4.1 The MOSFET

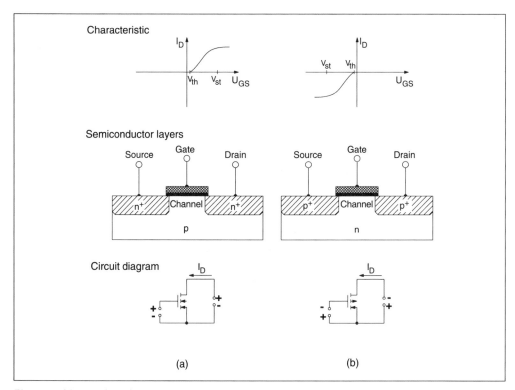

Figure 4.1: (a) An n-channel MOSFET and (b) a p-channel MOSFET.

The MOSFET is known for its simple structure and low power consumption. This is very important, when you consider that for one million transistors each having a power consumption of one hundred thousandth of a watt, the total power requirement is already 10 W. In reality, the overheating of these highly integrated chips is becoming more and more of a problem. Figure 4.1 shows n-channel and p-channel MOSFETs. The n-channel MOSFET consists of a p-type semiconductor substrate (mostly silicon), located between two n^+-type regions (the gap between them in ICs is approximately 0.5–5 μm). These two outer regions are known as *source* and *drain*. The p-type semiconductor does not contain the quantity of negative electrons necessary for the flow of current. This is due to the deposition of atoms (impurities) that have fewer electrons (p-type material such as boron) or more electrons (n-type material such as phosphorus or arsenic) in comparison to silicon. The '+' indicates an area with a high number of such impurities. A *channel* is formed between the two regions. The conductivity of the channel, and consequently the resistance of the MOSFET, can be controlled by a *gate* made from metal or polycrystalline silicon. This is isolated from the substrate by a layer of oxide. From top to bottom, the layers are metal, oxide and semiconductor, giving rise to the acronym MOS transistor. By applying a voltage to the gate, the number of charge carriers in the channel increases. A positive gate voltage produces negative charge carriers (electrons), which are drawn into the channel. A positive voltage repels the charge carriers from the channel. The number of charge carriers that are available increases as the voltage increases, and with this there is a reduction in the channel resistance. Note that the word 'transistor' is actually an abbreviation derived from *'transfer resistor'*. The current I_D (and also the current delivered by the MOSFET), between source and drain is dependent upon the gate voltage (U_{GS}) (between gate and source). Current flow only commences once the predetermined voltage threshold V_{th} is exceeded. A further increase in current flow is linearly proportional to an increase in gate voltage U_{GS}. On reaching the saturation value V_{st}, any further increase in the voltage (U_{GS}) has no further effect on the current. The MOSFET is said to be in a state of saturation. The proper definition for the MOSFET described here is an *n-channel MOSFET with isolated gate*.

A p-channel MOSFET can be constructed on a similar basis. All that is required is to replace the n-regions with p-regions (see Figure 4.1(b)). A significant difference between the two types is the opposing relationship of the channel current with respect to the gate voltage (U_{GS}). In this case, the conductivity decreases from a maximum value to zero with an increase in U_{GS}. The increasingly positive gate voltage repels the positive charge carriers from the channel, thus increasing its resistance.

The characteristics between the threshold voltage V_{th} and the saturation voltage V_{st} shows an almost linear relationship between the applied voltage and the current (or the current produced by the MOSFET resistance). In *analogue circuits*, the MOSFET is operated in this proportional area, in order to amplify the signals, so that their relative intensity remains equal. This is, for example, the case in a radio receiver, where as little distortion as possible should be apparent. In principle, in analogue technology, there is an infinite quantity of intermediate levels available between minimum and maximum values (for example, the minimum and maximum volume of a piece of music).

However, in a *digital circuit*, the operation of the MOSFET is totally different. Here, the voltage (U_{GS}) between gate and source lies either below (or in the range of) the threshold voltage V_{th} or above (or in the range of) the saturation voltage V_{st}. Therefore, digital technology uses these characteristic areas, which on the grounds of distortion are not available using analogue techno-logy. This results in two stable and positive transistor conditions, which are the OFF and the ON conditions. In the OFF condition, the MOSFET is totally closed, possessing an infinite value of resistance, and between source and drain the maximum voltage drops. In comparison, the MOSFET in the ON condition possesses the ideal resistance of zero, allowing the maximum current to flow; thus, the voltage drop between source and drain is minimal (equivalent to threshold voltage V_{th}). In other words, the transistor operates in the same manner as a switch with the two positions of ON and OFF. Digital circuits make use of the existence of these exactingly defined and stable conditions. Classic logic will not tolerate imprecise ideas, such as possible, almost and so on. Fuzzy logic attempts to integrate these natural ideas using exact mathematics, doing so with great success (more about this later). As a result of the two clearly defined and distinguished switching conditions, digital circuits lead directly to dual or binary (two-valued) logic.

From corresponding bias voltages, resistance combinations and so on, the MOSFET ON/OFF logic conditions are represented by fixed voltage values. A list of the corresponding voltages for various families of logic circuits is given in Table 4.1.

Family	U_0 (V)	U_1 (V)
NMOS	−1...+1	5...10
CMOS	1...2	4...15
TTL	0...0.5	2.5...5
ECL	ca. 3	4...5
IIL	ca. 1	2...5

NMOS: logic with n-channel MOS transistors
CMOS: logic with complementary MOS transistors
TTL: (bipolar) transistor–transistor logic
ECL: (bipolar) emitter coupled logic
IIL: (bipolar) integrated injection logic

Table 4.1: The logic levels of various families.

4.2 The CMOS inverter as a low power element

The MOS transistor discussed above has, when compared to a bipolar transistor (the conductivity of which is not controlled by a gate *voltage*, but instead by a base *current*), a very small power consumption. Currently, however, with the integration of many millions of transistors on one chip (a 4 Mbit DRAM memory chip contains more than four million transistors and four million capacitors), the power consumption is quite considerable. Therefore, there is a further requirement to reduce the power consumption. To fulfil this requirement the CMOS technique is employed, its basic element being a *CMOS inverter*. A CMOS inverter is simply achieved from the parallel switching of a p-channel and a n-channel MOSFET, as shown in Figure 4.2. Both MOSFETs are connected in series between ground (GND; earth) and the supply voltage (Vcc). As I have already mentioned, the MOSFET gate is isolated from the substrate, and thus from the source and drain, by a thin layer of oxide, thus preventing a current flow through the gate. It is necessary, in order for the current to flow from Vcc to GND, that both transistors are simultaneously conductive. Only then will a current path between ground and supply voltage exist. As the characteristics in Figure 4.1 show, there is no overlapping of the conductivity from p-channel and n-channel MOSFETs. Therefore, one of the two MOSFETs is always OFF, and there will never be a current flow. If the voltage U_E is adequately positive (greater than the threshold voltage V_{thn} of the n-channel MOSFET Tr_n) at the input E, then the n-channel MOSFET conducts and the p-channel MOSFET Tr_p is closed. With adequate negative voltage U_E (less than the voltage threshold V_{thn} of the p-channel MOSFET Tr_p), the p-channel MOSFET is conductive and the n-channel MOSFET is closed. Both transistors are off between V_{thn} and V_{thp}.

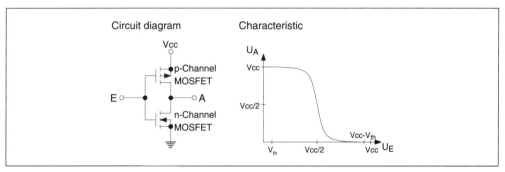

Figure 4.2: The CMOS inverter.
A CMOS inverter consists of two MOSFETs with opposite conductivity which are connected between ground and Vcc. By means of this a characteristic with sharp transition can be obtained.

From this, it is apparent that MOSFETs are not controlled by a gate current, but instead by the gate voltage. The voltage U_A delivered to output A can be used to control MOSFETs in succeeding stages and thus process signals (or data). The voltage U_A at output A changes as a result of a deviation in the input voltage U_E:

▶ If U_E is sufficiently negative, then Tr_p conducts and Tr_n is closed, output A is connected to Vcc, and the CMOS inverter produces a logic 1 (or logic 0 with negative logic).

▶ If U_E is sufficiently positive, then in this case Tr_n conducts and Tr_p is closed, output A is connected to ground, and the CMOS inverter produces a logic 0 (or logic 1 with negative logic).

As the characteristic in Figure 4.2 shows, due to the extremely sharp transition between Vcc and ground, the CMOS inverter accomplishes the requirements almost perfectly with two clearly defined and separate logic conditions. Also, as CMOS elements require very little power consumption when compared to normal MOS chips, then we are hypothetically killing two birds with one stone. A current will only flow by switching over the output voltage between Vcc and ground, in order to charge or discharge the respective layers of the CMOS transistor to their respective capacities. CMOS elements have a small *static power consumption*, which is caused mainly by current leakage, which in turn is caused by the gate oxidation layer (which is never absolute). Additionally, there is a *dynamic power consumption* caused by a toggle in the voltage U_A at output A as a result of a change in the input voltage U_E. Since, with every toggle, the semiconductor layers are charged and discharged, the dynamic power input is proportional to the toggle frequency (P~v). CMOS elements (for example, the i387) with a fast clock speed therefore require more current than those with a slow clock speed. This is useful in the application for a Notebook, because when in power-down mode, the clock frequency is reduced to zero. This only leaves the very small static power consumption. Energy saving can amount to as much as 99.99% (this is not a printing error).

As Goethe once said, where there is light, there is also shadow. Of course CMOS technology does have a disadvantage; a CMOS inverter always has to have two MOSFETs, whereas a MOS transistor only requires one (that is, itself). In comparison, the integration density of CMOS inverters is smaller than that of MOS transistors. By clever arrangement of the different layers on the substrate, almost the same quantity can be obtained. It is only the extent of the technology required that is greater.

4.3 AND and OR gates as logical basic elements

In this section I would like to introduce you to the two most basic elements of logic circuits, the AND and the OR gates. They implement the abstract AND and OR combination of two quantities E1 and E2 by means of an electronic circuit and two signals. Table 4.2 shows the truth tables for the AND and OR combinations.

E1	E2	AND value A	OR value A
0	0	0	0
0	1	0	1
1	0	0	1
1	1	1	1

Table 4.2: Truth table for AND and OR combinations.

The OR operation is in fact a representation of the mathematical OR and is not to be confused with the colloquial either/or. This is implemented by the XOR operation. Many logic operations are constructed from the AND and OR operations. AND and OR take over the role of 0 and 1 from the natural numbers.

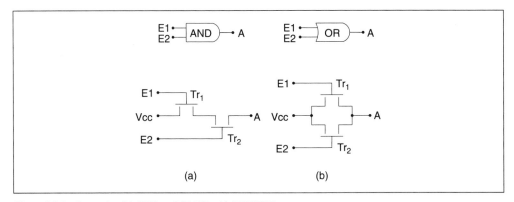

Figure 4.3: Implementing (a) AND and (b) OR with MOSFETs.

In the following text I have assumed that logic 1 is represented by a high level signal and logic 0 by a low level signal. A circuit must be constructed for the AND operation, whereby only two high level signals at both E1 and E2 inputs produce a high level signal at output A, whereas the OR operation, which already has a high level signal at one of the E1 or E2 inputs, produces a high level signal at output A. In Figure 4.3 you can see a simplified implementation of this requirement using MOSFETs. The two n-channel MOSFETs Tr_1 and Tr_2 in Figure 4.3(a) only switch the supply current Vcc through to output A if both E1 and E2 input signals are at a high level; that is, logic 1. If either one of the E1 or E2 input signals is equivalent to 0, then one of the transistors Tr_1 or Tr_2 closes, and the output A produces a low level signal representing logic 0. Thus, the circuit shown in Figure 4.3(a) implements an AND operation for input signals E1 and E2. The symbol shown above the circuit diagram in the illustration is a standard symbol, used to represent an AND gate as a functional unit in logic circuit diagrams.

Figure 4.3(b) shows the implementation of an OR gate from the two n-channel MOSFETs Tr_1 and Tr_2. In this case, it is enough for one of the two MOSFETs to be switched on in order to provide output A with a high level signal. Therefore it is sufficient that E1 or E2 is at a high level. The symbol given is the standard symbol used for an OR gate in logic circuit diagrams. The logic gates represented are 2-input AND and 2-input OR gates respectively. Without any problems, the circuits can be extended to n-input AND and n-input OR gates. This is done simply by inserting and connecting n MOSFETs in series (AND) or in parallel (OR) between Vcc and output A.

4.4 An advanced example: The full adder

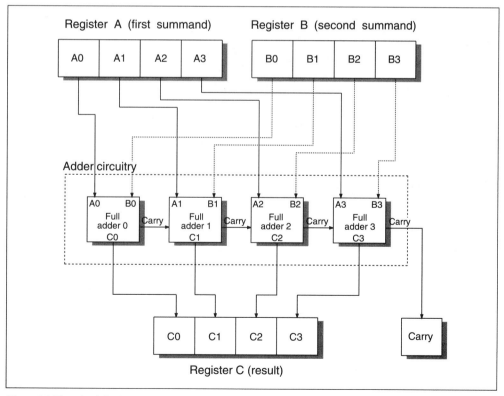

Figure 4.4: The 4-bit full adder.

In the following text I would like to introduce you to an application of the AND, OR and XOR gates, namely that of a full adder. This has the function of adding pairs of binary numbers. As an example, Figure 4.4 shows a 4-bit full adder, which adds the contents of a pair of 4-bit registers and delivers a total value and a carry (so far as is available).

The single bits A0 to A3 of register A with the first summand, together with the single bits B0 to B3 of register B with the second summand, are passed to the full adders 0 to 3 contained in the adder circuitry. Each of the full adders delivers a result bit C0 to C3 as well as a carry. The result bits are received by register C and the carry bit from the third full adder is received by a carry register. Register A of the i386, for example, can equal the accumulator EAX, register B can equal register EBX, register C can also equal accumulator EAX and the carry register can equal the carry flag in the flag register EFLAG.

Thus, the full adders 1 to 3 produce three inputs for the two summands and the carry from the previous level as well as two outputs for the result and the carry of the next level. The carry has to spread from the first to the last of the full adders, from where it has to reach the carry register. The correct result is only available once the carry has reached the last of the full adders.

The full adders 0 to 3 are all identical (apart from the first full adder in the example given in Figure 4.4, which does not receive a carry). Table 4.3 shows the combinations of the three bits A_x, B_x and $Carry_x$, which have to run through the full adders in order to produce a correct result.

A_x First summand	B_x Second summand	$Carry_x$ from previous stage	C_x result	Carry
0	0	0	0	0
0	0	1	1	0
0	1	0	1	0
0	1	1	0	1
1	0	0	1	0
1	0	1	0	1
1	1	0	0	1
1	1	1	1	1

Table 4.3: Combining summand and carry bits in the full adder.

You can see a possible implementation of the truth table using AND, OR and XOR gates in Figure 4.5. The two summand bits are fed to an XOR gate to create a total in one of the four full adders. The output signal of the first XOR gate together with the carry bit of the previous level is then passed to a second XOR gate. The resulting output signal produces the corresponding total bit. Using the three AND gates, the carry bit can ascertain whether or not at least two of the fed bits A_x, B_x and $Carry_x$ are equal to 1, and whether the combination in an OR gate can be approved. If you analyse the circuit logic, you end up with the combinations in Table 4.3.

Full adders such as this have very fast working speeds, their working speed being dependent upon the transistor circuit speed in the logic gates. The i386 has full adders such as these in its ALU, which are capable of an addition within two processor clock cycles; that is, for 40 MHz only 50 ns is required. On the other hand, the carry, dependent upon the size of the i386

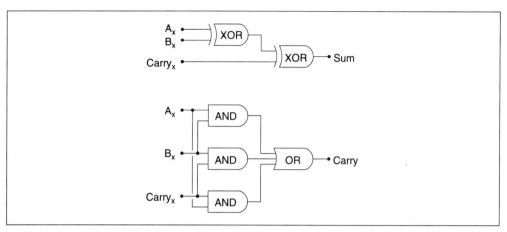

Figure 4.5: Implementing the full adder truth table.

register, has to spread over 32 levels. The circuits can often be simplified at element level for total implementation with MOS transistors (for example, some gates can share transistors). This saves components and increases integration.

5 First steps to performance increases

In this chapter I would like to introduce you to a couple of strategies that lead to significant increases in the performance of computers using CISC processors.

5.1 Reading instructions and prefetching

As I have mentioned before, the prefetch queue has the purpose of relieving the bus system, because the prefetcher is constantly reading new instruction bytes as soon as enough space becomes available in the prefetch queue. A double word is always read if four bytes are free in the i386 queue. This automatic instruction fetching is linear, which means that the prefetcher commences with a start address and always reads the following word or double word. By this action, it ignores any jumps and branches.

Normally, as a result of a double word, which has no multiples of four, with address being accessed, the bus interface reads a complete double word at a double word address. The only exception applies when a CALL or jump instruction, which does not represent a double word address, is transferred to a memory address. In this case, the prefetcher only reads one to three bytes via the bus unit until a double word is reached. Subsequently, a complete 32-bit double word with double word address is always read (as long as four bytes are free in the prefetch queue).

Memory accesses obtained as the result of machine code instructions, for example MOV reg, mem, have, of course, priority over instruction fetching. When the i386 executes such an instruction, the prefetch queue has to wait. When executing instructions without memory access, for example ADD reg, reg and the internal execution of an instruction in a phase, which does not require memory accesses, then the prefetcher can read a double word into the prefetch queue, without interruption and the need to disturb the performance of instructions in the i386.

The i386 stops prefetching if the instruction unit (IU) records a CALL or jump instruction and actually assigns the call or jump (that is, the call or jump condition is achieved). In this instance, the i386 empties its prefetch queue, invalidates the microcodes of the already decoded instructions in the microcode queue and commences the jump address by reading the new instructions. Prefetching is then executed linearly until a further CALL or jump instruction is executed.

This all works well, as long as the prefetch queue is constantly topped up at the same speed at which the processor executes the instructions. With a jump or procedure call that exceeds the boundaries of the prefetch queue (this is very often the case), the i386 empties its prefetch queue and commences with the target address by reading the new instruction byte. This is, of course, also applicable to RET or IRET instructions. The problem is that the next instruction not only has to be read, but also decoded. Note that i386 instructions can contain 15 bytes, so up to four bus cycles can be necessary, each with two processor clock (PCLK) cycles, in order to read an instruction. These eight PCLK cycles also require time for decoding and execution. The execution times given in manuals always refer only to the execution time itself. Therefore they are only valid if the instruction has been fully read and decoded. In most cases, prefetching makes sure that instructions are ready for execution. If you imagine what it would be like without prefetching, where for every instruction the instruction reading and decoding time would be apparent, then you will quickly realize the performance advantage that prefetching achieves.

The control unit must wait for a long period for the next decoded instruction after a jump or procedure call to an address, which is outside the previously read code area. If the jump target is still within the queue and the instruction contains very few bytes, resulting in it being fully read, then all that remains is for it to be decoded. The instruction reading cycle is dropped. Where no jump is to be executed (because the jump conditions, for example, JNE, are not fulfilled), then the i386 continues without delay.

If you examine a complicated program using a debugger, you will realize that it is teeming with JUMPs and CALLs. For example, the compiler converts many of the language C's CASE statements into a quantity of conditional JUMPs. If the target address is outside the area covered by the prefetch queue, then the i386 has to start with instruction fetching and decoding from the beginning. The converting of the source code into an unfavourable sequence of JUMP instructions can badly effect the execution time of a program. Assembler programmers should take note of this. Unfortunately, optimizing compilers from well-known manufacturers are also known to skip outside the prefetch boundaries, sometimes without good reason.

5.2 Coprocessors

Coprocessors produce an increase in performance aimed at certain types of applications. Generally speaking, a coprocessor is a mathematical coprocessor that supports the CPU in calculating complicated mathematical expressions using floating-point arithmetic at the hardware level. The i387 is the mathematical coprocessor for the i386. It supports the i386, aimed directly at the calculation of mathematical expressions with floating-point arithmetic. This includes addition, subtraction, multiplication and division of floating-point arithmetic, and the calculation of square roots, logarithms and so on. All i386 address types are available to the i387 for memory operands.

5.2.1 Functional expansion and performance gain

The four basic types of arithmetic using integers are already integrated with the i386. The entire mathematical structure is based upon the use of integers, for the smallest of operations such as 1 times 1, to transcendental logarithms. In principle, the i386 can execute all mathematical calculations on its own. The programs necessary for this are identified as being *software emulations* of the i387. By the implementation of these functions at a hardware level instead of a software level, the i387 floating-point calculations are executed at a much higher speed. Table 5.1 shows the gain in performance. As you can see, the increase in speed lies somewhere between 50 and 500 times faster. Application programs, such as CAD or numerical control of machinery and robots, which require the intensive use of mathematical calculations using floating-point numbers, would be executed at a much faster rate when using a coprocessor. The factors of 50 to 500 only refer to the mathematical calculations themselves. To a large extent, application programs must also be able to perform other functions, such as the input and output of data, user guidance and so on. When considering all factors, it is realistic to say that speed will be increased by a factor of between two and ten times. On the one hand, for the representation of a circle using a CAD program, a coprocessor will help with the necessary calculation of the points of the circle. On the other hand, the points of the circle must also be shown on the monitor. The i387 does not assist the CPU in the necessary accessing of the video memory.

Floating-point operation	i387	Emulation on the i386
Addition/subtraction	0.7	125
Multiplication (single precision)	0.9	125
Division	2.6	250
Square root	3.5	1500
Tangent	9.8	1000
Exponentiation	9.6	1350
Load (double precision)	0.9	100
Store (double precision)	1.6	130

For the emulation typical average values are given; more or less effective programming using i386 instructions may increase or decrease the values.

Table 5.1: Floating-point calculations on the i387 and i386 (execution times in µs at 33 MHz clock rate).

The concept of coprocessors is not just limited to the expansion of the CPU to handle decimal values. For example, there are also I/O coprocessors, like that of the 82389, which supports the exchange of data between the i386 and the system bus. Generally speaking, every coprocessor, which has a specific task in supporting the CPU, is designated as a coprocessor. Examples of these are used for mathematics, I/O graphics and other applications. Coprocessors are often referred to as processor extensions, which is a more appropriate definition because the coprocessors extend the function of the CPU.

5.2.2 Number formats and floating-point instructions

In addition to logic operations, the i386 can also perform arithmetical operations. For this it also uses numbers. The i386 supports the following number formats:

▶ signed and unsigned integers (16-bit)
▶ signed and unsigned long integers (32-bit)
▶ packed and non-packed binary coded decimal numbers (8-, 16-bit)

The i386 is only able to emulate floating-point arithmetic, treating it internally as if it were a chain of characters. The coprocessor emulation program then separates the 32-, 64- or 80-bit floating-point number into its constituent parts – sign, mantissa and exponent – then processes them separately using the installed four basic types of arithmetic. The emulation program subsequently formulates the result back to that of a chain of characters, in the floating-point arithmetic format.

As a mathematical coprocessor, the i387 processes the floating-point arithmetic directly, without the requirement of separating the sign, mantissa and exponent. The i387 also goes a step further, by internally interpreting all numbers, from integers with a length of 16 bits to temporary real floating-point numbers, as 80-bit floating-point numbers in temporary real format in accordance with the IEEE standard representation. The i387 supports the following number formats:

▶ signed and unsigned integers (16-bit)
▶ signed and unsigned long integers (32-bit)
▶ packed and non-packed binary coded decimal numbers (8-, 16-bit)
▶ short real (32-bit)
▶ long real (64-bit)
▶ temporary real (80-bit)

From the list of i387 instructions, there are two instructions, *load* and *store*, that have special importance for the management of number formats. Using the load instruction, a number is loaded from memory into one of the i387 registers and, at the same time, converted into the 80-bit temporary real format. Using this number format, the i387 executes all of the necessary calculations, from simple comparisons to complicated logarithms or tangent calculations. The store instruction is the counterpart to load: it stores a number located in the i387 in the temporary real format, into memory. For this, the i387 again carries out the conversion automatically.

You are probably aware that the conversion of number formats is complicated and time consuming. For example, it takes up to 53 clock cycles to load a 16-bit integer from memory into the i387, and for the associated format conversion. In the case of a binary coded decimal (BCD) number, this process can take up to 97 clock cycles. The unloading takes even longer. For simple calculations, such as addition, subtraction and multiplication using floating-point numbers, the additional workload necessary to convert the format is greater than the advantage gained from processing floating-point numbers in the i387. For this reason, many applications use i386 software emulation for floating-point arithmetic, and only access the coprocessor when dealing with long and complicated calculations, such as logarithms, because the coprocessor can execute these tasks much more quickly. Simple spreadsheet calculations, such as the creation of totals and average values for a column or a row, are often executed at the same speed, with or without a coprocessor. On the other hand, three-dimensional CAD applications often require trigonometrical functions such as sine and tangent, in order to calculate projections onto a particular plane. You can calculate the sine of a (floating-point) value of x using the following equation:

$$\sin x = x - x^3/3! + x^5/5! - x^7/7! +- \ldots \quad (3!=1*2*3=6, \; 5!=1*2*3*4*5=120 \text{ and so on})$$

Depending upon the value of x, more or less $x^n/n!$ places are required in order to determine the value of $\sin x$ with sufficient accuracy. As you can see from the formula, a considerable number of extensive arithmetic floating-point multiplications and floating-point divisions are necessary to calculate the potential x^n. Considerable time is required by the i386 using software emulation, whereas the i387 can use its calculating ability to the full.

When looking at the i387 instructions a little more closely, it becomes apparent that the i387 does not recognize machine code instructions in order to transfer data from its register into a register of the i386. For example, you cannot shift a 32-bit integer from the i387 into the accumulator EAX of the i386. The data transfer takes place via the main storage area, thus making it slow. This is due to the need to always have two memory accesses and a format conversion.

This is also the reason why simple calculations with floating-point arithmetic can be executed at the same speed using an i386 with an optimized emulator as with an i387. This changes significantly with the i486 and the Pentium which include the coprocessor on-chip (i486), or where the 'coprocessor' is already part of the internal instruction pipeline (Pentium). Here, no time-consuming writing and re-reading of data to and from memory (with the associated format conversions) is necessary to establish the communication between the integer core and the floating-point unit.

5.3 Multiprocessor systems

If, by the use of a coprocessor, the performance of a computer system is improved, then it should also be possible to bring together many processors, in order to produce a super-computer. In reality, there are already a number of high performance computers in operation that use many processors, for example, the Cray YMP (maximum of 64) or the connection machine (maximum of 65 536 processors). There are also a number of smaller systems, for example, the UNIX server and PC-based workstations and servers of the future, which, at times, use two to four CPUs. Using prudent foresight, Intel has already introduced the concept of a multiprocessor system with the introduction of the 8086 MULTIBUS, which implements a base for many processors working together. In this section I would like to address the ideas behind a multiprocessor system, and of course the associated problems. Note that the combination of an i386 and its i387 coprocessor is not regarded as a two-processor system. In this sense, the pairing of the i386/i387 represents more of a single processor made up of two chips. This does not apply to the new Pentium (or i486DX, for that matter), because the coprocessor is already integrated into the CPU chip. Put more simply, in addition to an arithmetic and an integer unit, the Pentium and i486 also have a floating-point unit.

Multiprocessor systems create the hardware base for powerful multitasking operating systems, which must execute many tasks at the same time (in parallel). Therefore, one possibility for the implementation of a multiprocessor system is for each processor to execute a separate task. Thus, it is not necessary for a disrupted task to run on the same processor once the system has been reactivated: physically, the main memory is the same. In principle, such a multiprocessor system can be replaced by many single processor systems, because each task is run through only one processor. It becomes more interesting (but also more complicated) if a task is divided between many processors, as each processor calculates a portion of the program task. This, unfortunately, leads immediately to communication and synchronization problems. For example, if part of a task, which is on one processor, is waiting for a result that is being calculated on another processor, then it has to know which processor is able to deliver the result, and, furthermore, it has to arrange for the transfer of the result from the processor. Of course, all of this will only work if the processor in question has actually finished the calculation.

There is also the possibility of integrating many processors into one chip, or at least the logic sections. This is actually the case, within limits, for the class of superscalar processors, to which the Pentium belongs. In this instance, the communication problems are transferred from one or more processor boards to a single silicon chip. However, the problems themselves remain the same.

Extensive multiprocessor systems with many processors are ideally suited for applications that contain many isolated program sections. An example of this would be the spell checker for a long document. In this case, each processor is able to dedicate itself to checking one word. A more serious example is that of weather forecasting: under no circumstances is the current weather affecting North America going to affect the weather in central Europe in the next five minutes (the speed of sound at approximately 300 m/s as an upper limit for pressure and particle circulation within the atmosphere is nowhere near enough). On the other hand, over a time period greater than a couple of days, we see things in a different light. Many central European autumn/winter storms actually start in the Caribbean or further north. The storms are drawn across the Atlantic in the direction of Europe. At first, a multiprocessor system used for weather forecasting has to calculate the short-term weather in small cells, each cell having its own processor. Subsequently, the processors must communicate with one another, in order to swap and transfer the weather data from the small cells so that the long-term forecast for a continent can be predicted. Multiprocessor systems such as these greatly accelerate the rate at which a weather forecast can be produced. The greatest advantage is that many simple and readily available processors can be linked together, in order to achieve the performance of a highly complicated and expensive supercomputer chip.

As I have already mentioned, communication between individual processors produces considerable problems. Switching nodes are needed, which have the capacity to connect two processors, and software (existing in the form of a permanent type or microprogram), which controls the connection. Using the first of the connection machines with their 64k (=65 536) 6502 processors (simple 8-bit CPUs, which are well known from the C64), the connection was achieved over a maximum of 10 switching paths. It can be said that the connection machine implements a type of hypercube, whereby the lines of communication pass over the edges of the cube. From their inception, the transputers from INMOS were designed for multiprocessor operation. For every chip there is a CPU and a connecting unit. Thus, they can be joined together without difficulty to form a multiprocessor system.

Unfavourable configurations of multiprocessor systems or unmatched software can lead to the application of communication being greater than that of the calculation. The result of this is that the performance reduces once the optimum quantity of processors has been exceeded. There is no linear increase in performance for multiprocessor systems: communication paths become longer and the communication between the processors themselves becomes more complicated. Here, the relationship between the performance curve and the quantity of processors is directly related. The greater the harmony between the computer and its application (and vice versa) the better the performance. For example, the connection machine performs better when generating weather forecasts or calculating aerodynamic factors for aircraft wings than when calculating a satellite flight path that is under the influence of disturbances. This is because each subsequent satellite position is dependent upon its previous position and the disturbance.

Multiprocessor systems with similar processors, which generally execute the same tasks (that is, program operation), can be identified as being *symmetrical multiprocessor systems*. In comparison, systems using a combination of specialized processors (for example, standard CPUs, graphic processors, network processors and so on) are termed *asymmetrical multiprocessor systems*. The individual processors of a multiprocessor system can access either their own local memory or the main memory. I think it is quite obvious that coordinating access is no simple matter, especially when you consider that a slower running processor must not overwrite an already updated entry.

After this somewhat general statement, it is time to go back to the i386. Even this processor implements a few things in the support of simple multiprocessor systems. The key to this is formed by the two signals HOLD and HLDA. In the first instance, the applicable signals use accesses to the i386 to control the bus slot. This bus can be, for example, the memory bus for the main storage, the X-bus for the I/O address space or an extensive system bus for other components, such as the internal bus slots or adaptors in a PC. Additionally, there are several types of controller and buffer (data memory), which can be inserted between the local bus, which is connected directly to the i386, and the other previously mentioned buses. More or less, these are responsible for access coordination. Figure 5.1 shows a simple schematic diagram for the implementation of a multiprocessor system using three i386 CPUs.

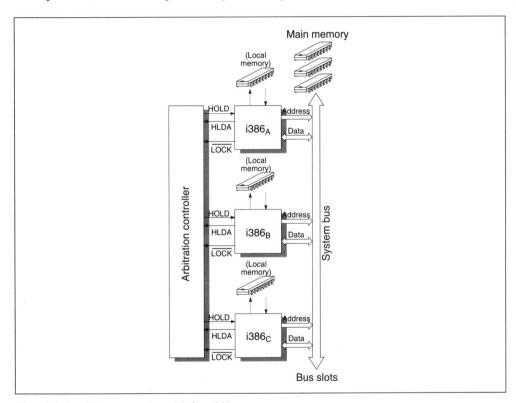

Figure 5.1: A multiprocessor system with three i386 processors.

Bus access authorization is controlled by an arbitration controller. If, for example, i386$_A$ accesses the main storage, then the arbitration controller feeds a high level HOLD signal to each of the other processors i386$_B$ and i386$_C$. These, in turn, normally react by activating the AHOLD signal, which indicates that they will not execute a bus cycle and that i386$_A$ has sole access between the bus and main storage. i386$_A$ will not release control if it is executing a so-called *locked bus cycle*. This is the case if an access to a data unit exceeds the double word limit (thereby making two bus cycles necessary), or if an instruction is called using a LOCK prefix to execute a locked cycle. In both cases $i386_X$ activates the $\overline{LOCK}$ signal to indicate to the arbitration controller that such a cycle is taking place. When $i386_A$ has executed the required access, the arbitration controller once again deactivates the HOLD signal. $i386_B$ and $i386_C$ react in turn by deactivating the HLDA signal, thus giving them renewed access to the bus under control from the arbitration controller. It is possible, by the implementation of further control logic (for example, from each respective bus controller to each $i386_X$), for the respective $i386_X$ to continue using its local memory, while another is accessing the system bus and with it, for example, main memory execution.

Figure 5.1 shows a typical example of a simple multiprocessor system with many bus controllers. These have to share a single bus, and in doing so can only access individually and within a clearly defined hierarchical structure. EISA (Extended Industry Standard Architecture) and MCA (Micro Channel Architecture; IBM) systems implement such an arbitration scheme, in order to permit the CPU (for example, 386 with possibly an i387 coprocessor installed) and the external bus controller (for example, the DMA controller, network processors and so on), to access the main memory and expansion channel. As bus control is obtained by another processor, the i386/i387 can proceed to execute the pre-loaded instructions, as long as no further memory access is necessary. Especially calculation-intensive floating-point instructions, which only refer to internal registers, can then be executed in parallel with the work being performed by the other chips. Thus, a simple multiprocessor system is achieved, but for a high-performance parallel computer, this is not adequate. Firstly, the memory would have to be sub-divided between local and global RAM, and secondly, the implementation of equal and parallel communication using many parallel buses between the processors (and additional pro-gramming) would be required. It is, however, perfectly adequate for the personal computer. When connected into a LAN, the concept of multiprocessing is achieved. This is because each workstation has its own local powers of calculation, and communication between the individual processors is made possible by the server.

Part 2
The basic elements of RISCs

In this part, I would like to introduce you to the general basic elements of RISC processors. In addition to the hardware level, the software level plays an equally important role. The implementation of RISC elements in classic CISC processors in order to improve their performance, is described in Chapter 7.

6 Basic RISC elements at the hardware and software levels

In addition to CISC (complex instruction set computer), there is the more recent and more powerful RISC (reduced instruction set computer). CISC refers to microprocessors such as those belonging to the Intel 80x86 family, or the Motorola 68000 series used in Apple computers. The processor is known for its large instruction set, consisting of more than 300 machine instructions, its complex addressing schemes and the micro-encoding of the processor instructions, which were explained in Chapter 3. In comparison, RISC processors such as the Intel i860/i960, the MIPS R2000 and R3000, or Sparc processors have a much smaller – that is reduced – set of instructions. The reduction of the extensive instruction set to fewer, and therefore more highly optimized, machine code instructions is not the only well-known characteristic of RISCs: there are many other innovative principles involved. RISC is, in fact, the result of an amazing realization.

6.1 Surprising result: Less is more

Through advances in the integration of electronic components, it became possible to store more and more microcodes in the microcode ROM of the processor. Thus, very complex instructions, such as repeated string operations, or extensive task switch algorithms, could be implemented. When you think about it, how many programmers have knowledge of 300 sets of instructions, and in particular, those that are very seldom used, or used only under special circumstances? An example of this is REPE SCAS (repeat scan string). This instruction is powerful, because it can repeatedly scan a complete string for a bit pattern. But when is it actually required? Instead, in preference, many programmers use a combination of, for example, MOV and TEST, two regularly occurring and well used instructions. A significant disadvantage of such highly complex and rarely used instructions is that, due to their complexity, they require vast amounts of microcode, and therefore occupy a considerable amount of space available in the on-chip microcode ROM. The necessary capacity increase of the microcode ROM reduces the space for the processor logic units and therefore reduces performance. In the mid-1970s, IBM performed a detailed statistical investigation, the unexpected but impressive results of which led to the development of RISCs:

▶ In a typical CISC processor program, approximately 20% of the instructions are responsible for taking up 80% of program time.

▶ In some cases, the execution of a sequence of simple instructions runs quicker than a single complex machine code instruction that has the same effect.

In the first instance, the result is due to the different, but, in principle, simple tasks executed by the computer. The complex instructions are aimed mainly at very few, highly complex, tasks that seldom occur. In addition to this, the programmer's familiarity with simple instructions must be considered. Furthermore, programs have significant number of branches (some statistics relate to figures of up to 30% of program code for jumps, calls and so on). Thus, the very simple MOV, TEST and branch instructions make up the majority of the machine code instructions that are used.

The decoding time is mainly responsible for the second result. The instruction execution time issued by processor manufacturers is only valid for instructions that have been decoded and are already available for execution – the decoding time is not taken into consideration. The decoding of very complex instructions can take a long time, whereas many simple instructions can be decoded much more quickly, and,in many circumstances, can be used to perform the same task.

When looking at the first result a little closer, what is more obvious than reducing the quantity of instructions to the necessary 20%, and optimizing them such that they can be executed in the shortest possible time? Considerations such as this led to the concept of RISC processors, which are no longer micro-encoded, but instead execute each instruction by hardwired logic without the need to access a microprogram. Therefore, most instructions can be completed within a single clock cycle. Using an i386, the instruction MOV reg, reg requires two clock cycles, whereas with the i486 it requires only one.

The RISC concepts of the individual manufacturers are, naturally, slightly different. However, many of the essential points are similar, such as:

▶ Reduction of the instruction set.

▶ Instruction pipelining: the interleaved execution of many instructions.

▶ Load/store architecture: only the load and store instructions have access to memory, all others work with the internal processor registers.

▶ Unity of RISC processors and compilers: the compiler is no longer developed for a specific chip, but instead, at the outset, the compiler is developed in conjunction with the chip to produce one unit.

▶ A modified register concept: in some RISC processors, for a fast subroutine call, the registers are no longer managed as ax, bx and so on but exist in the form of a variable window which allows a 'look' at certain register files.

The investigation into and the later development of RISC systems took place mainly at two American universities: Stanford and Berkeley. The working groups each developed concepts, similarly based upon the essential points, but having characteristics that differ from each other (mainly applicable to the treatment of pipeline stalls and the register concept). Therefore, RISC CPUs are often differentiated by the implementation of the *Stanford* or *Berkeley concept*.

6.2 RISC characteristics at the hardware level

In this section, I would like to introduce briefly the most important characteristics of RISC implementation at the hardware level. However, most RISC processors deviate greatly from the individual points of these puritanical requirements.

6.2.1 Reduction in the instruction set

Although there are currently quite a number of interpretations of the RISC abbreviation (such as regular instruction set computer, because of the unified instruction format), RISC was originally derived from the reduction of the highly complex CISC instruction set. This is reflected in the number of available instructions. It is referred to in the following two examples. The first prototype that implemented the Berkeley RISC concept had 31 instructions and was called the *RISC I*, whereas, its successor, the *RISC II*, had 39. The simplicity of the processor structure is shown by the reduced number of integrated transistors: in the RISC II there were only 41 000 (in comparison to more than three million in the Pentium). For the implementation of the MIPS concept, the Stanford University prototype processors, *MIPS* and *MIPS-X*, each required 32 machine code instructions. In addition to this, 25 000 and 50 000 transistors, respectively, were required in order to integrate the processor functions. What is also interesting is that the MIPS-X had an additional 100 000 transistors for an on-chip instruction cache – double the number of transistors required for its own processor functions. Today, it is normally the case that the supporting units, for example, data and instruction cache, or branch target buffer, take up more space on the processor chips than the highly efficient CPU itself.

As a result of the simple structure, due to the reduced instruction set and, therefore, the minimized amount of electronics of a typical RISC processor, the development time is much reduced when compared to that of CISC CPUs. Generally speaking, a factor of three is applied to the development period for a RISC processor, compared to that of a comparable CISC processor. In the case of the SPARC processor MB86900, only three engineers and half a year were needed between its conception at the end of 1984 and the fully functioning chip in April 1985. To justify this, though, it has to be realized that it was only possible because the Sun engineers tackled the development of gate arrays and, therefore, only the logic was involved, and not the manufacturing technology of highly integrated circuits. Despite this, it is still a remarkably short time scale. Intel required three years for the development of the Pentium. This alone is an indication that the Pentium is not just a large RISC processor.

6.2.2 Hardwired instructions

The most important characteristic of the RISC processor is hardwired instructions (or, put somewhat better, the hardwired control unit (CU)). This means that in a RISC processor, the execution unit (EU) in the CU is no longer controlled with the assistance of extensive microcodes. Instead, the whole operation is achieved in the form of hardwired logic. This greatly accelerates the execution of an instruction. As fewer instructions need to be implemented for RISC, the CU and EU can be larger and more efficient than those of CISC processors, without the need to take up more space on the chip. For example, the extensively coded functions of a CISC processor, such as the multiplication of two integers, is achieved in a RISC processor by complex circuitry (multiplier). Figure 6.1 emphasizes this point.

A possible implementation of the multiplication function in a CISC processor would be to successively move the multiplicand one position to the left and to add up the subtotals, if the corresponding position in the multiplicator is a 1. With a 0, the multiplicand is simply moved a further position to the left. For this, the CISC CPU only requires a full adder (see Section 4.4), whereby in each case, the CU, under the control of the microcodes for the multiplication function in the adder, only repeats the movement of the multiplicand one position further and adds the subtotals of the previous addition.

Thus, the required microcode would look something like this (a language similar to C is used):

```
multiplicand[32]
multiplicator[32]
result[64]
result=0
for (i=0;i<32;i++){
  if multiplicator(i)==1{
    result=result+multiplicand
  }
  multiplicand<<
}
```

With a 32-bit multiplication instruction, the operation is completed after a maximum of 32 runs. The complexity of a multiplication instruction lies in the microcode. Because a 0 as the corresponding digit of the multiplicator does not need to run through the addition step, the multiplication time varies depending on the actual multiplication value.

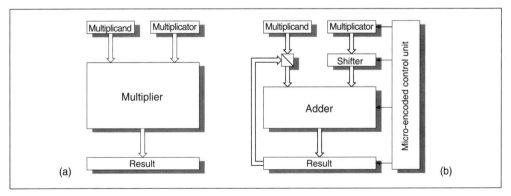

Figure 6.1: The multiplication of two numbers in (a) a RISC and (b) a CISC CPU.
The RISC CPU has a complex hardware multiplier which multiplies the two numbers in the multiplicand and multiplier registers and stores the product in the result register.
In a CISC CPU, on the other hand, a simple adder circuitry is driven by the micro-encoded CU so that the multiplicand is successively shifted to the left by a shifter and the value increased thus is repeatedly added to the multiplicand or partial result, until the result register contains the final result.

You will regularly see specifications of from...to... in the information relating to the execution speed of complex CISC instructions. In other words, the same CISC instruction can have varying execution times; this would seriously interfere with the flow of instructions in a RISC CPU.

Such a multiplication would be executed completely differently in a powerful RISC CPU. In place of an adder, which is often required for the execution of single multiplication instructions, the RISC CPU has a hardwired multiplication unit. A characteristic of the multiplication unit is that, independent of the multiplicand and multiplicator values, it executes a multiplication in the same number of clock cycles, thus executing them more quickly because of its increased performance. The CU already knows, at the time of release of the multiplication instruction, when the EU is going to deliver the result. As a result of this, the components of the RISC CPU can be dynamically synchronized more efficiently with one another. This is essential for the efficiency of the instruction pipeline – another characteristic element of RISC processors.

6.2.3 Non-destructive operation

Unlike the majority of CISC processors, which have a reduced register set, RISC processors are generally non-destructive. This means that after the execution of an instruction, the operands remain unchanged and available; the instruction result is stored in another register. As you have already seen in Part 1, the i386 adopts a destructive method for all two-operand instructions if both operands are not readily available as operands in the instruction flow, but instead are represented as register and/or memory operands.

Example: ADD eax, mem32
The i386 adds the 32-bit memory operand mem32 to the content of the accumulator EAX and writes the result into the accumulator EAX again. Thus the initial accumulator value – that is, the register operand – is overwritten and destroyed.

The above example can be expanded to include register-register, register-memory or memory-memory instructions. In addition, the i386 32-bit processor can multiply two 32-bit numbers, the result extending to 64-bits. The most significant double word is stored in the EDX register, so that this register value can also be destroyed.

Contrary to this, RISC processors operate in a non-destructive manner in accordance with the requirement (not always maintained) – that is, the source operands remain after execution of the instruction. Therefore, RISC is sometimes referred to, and interpreted as, a *reusable information storage computer*. Subsequently, the operand values can be used for further calculations, without the need to download them from memory. Under normal circumstances, RISC processors work with three operands – two source operands, src1 and src2, and a destination operand dest.

Example: ADD dest, src1, src2
The RISC processor adds the two register operands src1 and src2 and writes the result into the destination register dest. Therefore the initial register values scr1 and src2 remain unchanged and are not destroyed.

The reason for this non-destructive requirement is that a faster RISC processor should be less likely to access a slower memory. In addition to this, as a result of the load/store architecture, it is not possible to give a memory operand in the instruction. If the same operand is required quickly – for example, twice consecutively – then a LOAD instruction and its corresponding memory access is saved. Remember that the i386 instruction given above, ADD eax, mem32, implicitly executes a LOAD. In comparison, RISC CPUs implement rather more, equivalent general-purpose registers in the form of a register file, so that enough registers are available for non-destructive operation. This was not the case in the earlier CISC processors. They had very few general-purpose registers (sometimes only two), which functioned asymmetrically. For example, only the accumulator could be specified as the target operand.

6.2.4 Instruction pipelining

The execution structure of an instruction is, as a result of the basic microprocessor working principles, the same for the majority of machine code instructions. The following steps must be carried out:

- read the instruction from memory (instruction fetching)
- decode the instruction (decoding phase)
- where necessary, fetch operand(s) (operand fetching phase)
- execute the instruction (execution phase)
- write back the result (write-back phase)

The instruction is decoded during the decoding phase and, in most cases, the operand addresses are determined. In a CISC processor this instruction step is performed by the bus interface and the prefetcher, as soon as there is enough space in the prefetch queue. Even the second step, the decoding of the instruction, is executed in the decoding unit prior to the instruction execution itself; thus, the decoded microcode is available in the microcode queue. The remaining three steps are executed by microcode in the EU under the control of the CU. In normal circumstances, a single clock cycle is not sufficient, or the clock cycle must be very long – in other words, the clock frequency is very low.

The implementation of instruction pipelining has one aim: single-cycle machine instructions. This means that, ideally, each machine code instruction is executed within one processor clock cycle, or, put another way, only one clock cycle per instruction is necessary; thus, clocks per instruction (CPI) =1. However, it is important to note that an instruction is not *executed* within a cycle, but, instead, that an instruction is *completed* for every cycle. What at first appears as linguistically subtle has enormous consequences and forms the basis of instruction pipelining. Here, each executable instruction is divided into a set quantity of substeps, and the processor executes every substep in a single stage of a pipeline. This is shown graphically in Figure 6.2.

As you can see from the figure, the processor commences with the execution of the nth instruction, as soon as the $(n-1)^{th}$ instruction has left the first pipeline stage. In other words, the CU starts the instruction fetching phase for the nth instruction, as soon as the $(n-1)^{th}$ instruction enters the decoding phase. In the given example of a five-stage pipeline, under ideal circumstances, five instructions can be found in different execution phases. It can be optimistically assumed that a processor clock cycle (PCLK) is necessary per instruction phase and, therefore, an instruction is always executed within five clock cycles. As there are five instructions in the pipeline simultaneously, which are each displaced by one clock cycle, an instruction result is available from the pipeline for each clock cycle (that is, each step contains an instruction in differing stages). Normally, a register is situated between the individual pipeline steps: it serves as the output register for the preceding pipeline step and, at the same time, as the input register for the following pipeline step.

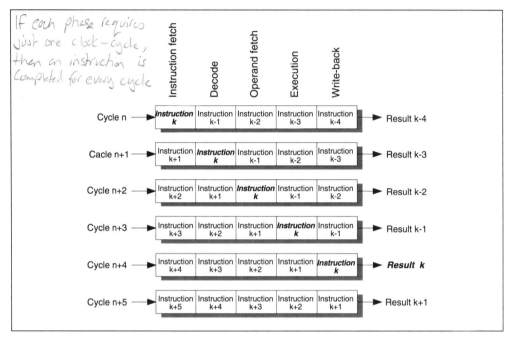

If each phase requires just one clock-cycle, then an instruction is completed for every cycle

Figure 6.2: Instruction pipelining.
Every instruction is broken down into partial steps for execution in the five-stage pipeline. The partial steps are executed within one single clock cycle. Thus, for example, the instruction k needs five cycles for completion. At the pipeline output an instruction result is available with each clock cycle.

In comparison, without pipelining (as is normally the case with CISC processors), only the nth instruction is started; thus, the instruction fetching phase of the nth instruction only starts after the (n-1)th instruction is completed. If in such a CISC processor the internal circuitry operates as fast as the RISC processor, and the individual instruction phases last one clock cycle, then the overlapping of the instructions alone leads to an increase in speed by a factor of five.

You are probably asking yourself why manufacturers did not consider using instruction pipelining right from the start. This is mainly due to two reasons. Often, during the individual subphases, similar, if not identical, joins appear. An example (known in the i386) is the instruction ADD eax, [ebx + ecx]. Both the determination of the operand address [ebx + ecx] and the instruction execution (ADD) itself require an adder. If the CU of a CISC CPU needs to determine the operand address and the instruction result, it can access the same adder twice; in this case, only one adder is required. In a RISC CPU the situation is totally different due to instruction pipelining. Both the decoding step and the execution step must have an adder; therefore, two adders are required. Even a common adder would not solve the problem. If, for example, the two instructions ADD eax, [ebx + ecx] and MOV edx, [eax + ecx] follow one another with an additional instruction in between, then instructions in the same clock cycle require the adder: the instruction ADD eax, [ebx + ecx] for the determination of the addition result (ADD) in the execution phase, and the instruction MOV edx, [eax + ecx] for the determination of the operand address [eax + ecx] in the decoding phase. Thus two adders are necessary, or the instruction MOV edx, [eax + ecx] has to be delayed, until the addition of the first instruction is complete. This causes a reduction in performance. The creation of instruction pipelines leads to redundant components on the chip. This results in a higher degree of integration being necessary, which was not available until a few years ago. But the simplified structure of RISC CPUs almost cancels out the increased complexity of the pipeline stages.

A further problem associated with the implementation of instruction pipelining can be seen in both of the previously mentioned instructions, ADD eax, [ebx + ecx] and MOV edx, [eax + ecx]. The value of the eax register for the address calculation of the second operand in the MOV instruction, is only known after the execution phase of the ADD instruction. On the other hand, the MOV instruction can already be found in the decoding phase, where the operand addresses [eax + ecx] are generated, while the MOV instruction is still in the execution phase. At this time, the decoding phase cannot determine the operand address. The RISC CPU control unit must recognize such *pipeline interlocks*, and react accordingly. The simplest solution is to delay the operand calculation in the decoding phase by one clock cycle. Another possibility is offered by optimized compilers. They can simply insert NOPs (no-operation opcodes) or restructure the program code so that obstacles never occur. In this example, it is apparent from the start that RISC hardware and software form a unit. In the next section you will learn more about pipeline interlocks. The coordination of the individual pipeline steps is not a trivial matter; this is one of the reasons why instruction pipelining was introduced relatively late into microprocessors.

I would like to further emphasize that the five-stage pipeline represented in Figure 6.2 is just an example. With some processors, the phases are combined into one single phase; for example, the decoding phase and the operand fetching phase (which is closely linked to the decoding phase), may be executed in a single pipeline stage. The result would be a four-stage pipeline. On the other hand, in an effort to increase the clock speed still further, the individual instruction phases can be subdivided even further, until each element has its own subphase. Thus, through simplicity, very quick pipeline stages can be implemented. Such a strategy leads to *superpipelined architecture* with many pipeline stages (10 or more).

Another possibility for increasing the performance of a RISC microprocessor is the integration of many pipelines. With this method, the result is a *superscalar* with pipelines operating in parallel to one another. As I am sure you can imagine, the complexity of coordinating the components with each another is increased still further. Here, not only the individual pipeline stages have to cooperate, but also the different pipelines themselves. This is not that simple and so the Pentium (the first x86 superscalar) does not always run both of its pipelines in parallel, except when using 'paired' instructions. With pure RISC implementation, the superscalar architecture is simpler to realize, because one of the main reasons for the coordination difficulties is the complex addressing methods of CISC CPUs. A superscalar could, perhaps, also be identified as a multiprocessor system on a single chip. Examples of superscalar architecture include Intel's i860 and i960 RISCs, the Pentium (with restrictions), and the IBM/ 6000 POWER. The parallel execution of many machine code instructions in parallel pipelines is either instructed explicitly by the opcode (as in the i860), or the CPU automatically recognizes when instructions can be executed in parallel (the pairing rule in the Pentium). Well-coordinated hardware and optimized program code with respect to parallel operation enable

CPI values of less than one – in other words, on average, the processor executes more than one machine instruction for each clock cycle. While CISC CPUs normally attain MIPS (million instructions per second) values that are notably below the clock rate (for example, approximately 15 MIPS for the 33 MHz i386), in ideal circumstances, superscalar RISCs attain MIPS values that are currently double the clock rate (for example, about 160 MIPS with the 100 MHz Pentium). These are, of course, theoretical values, which are influenced by many other factors in practice.

A comparison can be made between the pipelined processing of instructions in a microprocessor and the assembly of a car on a production line: Imagine the situation where a complete car has to be assembled in one single 'clock cycle' (on the production line, in two to five minutes depending upon the work requirement). Apart from the fact that it would not be possible to gain access to the necessary number of workers at the same time, it would end up more like a Monty Python sketch, and the result would be a vehicle lacking quality and, therefore, unsellable.

6.2.5 Pipeline interlocks

An important requirement for the best possible use of the pipeline is for each instruction phase to be completed at the same time. In the example shown in Figure 6.2, this means that all machine instructions will be executed within exactly five processor clock cycles. In this instance, reference is also made to a unified time characteristic of the instruction. This requirement cannot be fulfilled in the case of a delayed load and delayed branch. In addition, data dependencies or interlocks between the individual pipeline levels also lead to undesired delays in the flow of instructions.

Delayed load

If a memory operand occurs in the instruction, the CPU has to fetch the operand from the cache, or worse, from main memory. Even an access of the extremely fast on-chip cache of the 100 MHz Pentium requires a clock cycle equivalent to 10 ns. However, if the operand has to be fetched from the slower DRAM main memory, even with an optimistic 60 ns access time, six additional clock cycles are necessary. The continued transfer of the instruction from the operand fetch stage to the execution stage then has to be delayed accordingly. Alternatively, the processor can execute NOPs. Program execution is slowed down by both processes – this is known as a *delayed load*. In order to execute loading as quickly as possible, and to make the pipeline operands available immediately after transfer from memory, many RISC CPUs perform a *load forwarding*. For this, the operand from memory is not sent to the register and then transferred to the pipeline or ALU; instead, the control unit sends the operand immediately to the ALU after it has been read. Furthermore, it holds it ready in an intermediate register, in order to finally store the value in the referenced register.

Pure RISC implementation has a load/store architecture, in which only the two Load and Store instructions have access to memory. In comparison, all other instructions (such as ADD or MOV) refer to internal processor registers (instructions such as ADD reg, mem are, therefore, not possible). Even the load/store architecture leads to delayed loads, not just instructions with extensive addressing, like the instruction ADD eax, [ebx + ecx] mentioned earlier. In this case considerably more difficulties can arise; the Pentium, as an 80x86 compatible chip, has much to deal with.

Now, back to pure RISC architecture and the occurrence of delayed loads when using load. As an example, we will use the following instruction:

```
LOAD reg1, mem
ADD dest, reg1, reg2
```

This leads immediately to a delayed load because the ADD instruction is already in the operand fetching phase, while the LOAD instruction is awaiting execution; it must wait a long time until mem is available in register reg1. The Berkeley concept uses *scoreboarding* to deal with this pipeline obstruction. For this, a bit is attached to each processor register. For machine instructions that refer to a processor register, the bit is initially set by the control unit to show that the register value is not yet defined. The bit is cleared if the register is written to during the execution phase and receives valid content. If a subsequent instruction wishes to use the register as an operand source, it checks whether the scoreboarding bit is set; that is, the content is undefined. If this is the case, then the control unit holds back the execution of the new instruction until the storage stage writes to the register and resets the associated scoreboarding bit. If, in the given example, memory requires two clock cycles in order to make the operand available, the ADD instruction is delayed by two clock cycles via the set scoreboarding bit.

The Stanford concept also handles these delays with scoreboarding, in that the compiler simply inserts many NOPs to attain a delay. The Stanford concept does not require hardware support for pipeline obstructions during operation. For the example given, a MIPS compiler (MIPS RISC CPUs implement the Stanford concept) produces the following code:

```
LOAD reg1, mem
NOP
NOP
ADD dest, reg1, reg2
```

Straight away, you should be able to see the major disadvantage: the number of NOPs inserted is determined by the access time of memory. This can lead to big problems. The quantity of NOPs that have to be inserted depends on whether the operand is already available in the fast on-chip cache, the slightly slower L2 cache or the slow main storage area. The position of an operand in memory at the time of operation is, naturally, unknown at the time of compiling. In addition to this, the access time in processor cycles depends on the clock speed, the quality of memory chips used, and the current operating mode (normal, page mode or refresh). This means that for the conversion of the source code, the compiler must always adopt the worst case; thus, it must insert many NOPs. The code produced must always be specific to the machine and model, otherwise the result is a deterioration in performance. Compared with the CISC or a personal computer, the requirements of the whole system increase significantly. Luckily, some problems (including the subsequent jump delay) can be cured with the aid of an optimized compiler. You will learn more about this in Section 6.3.

At this stage I would like to point out that for RISC CPUs, wherever possible, a *data and instruction alignment* is performed. Data and instruction sizes always start at a limit set by the data bus width (for example, double word limit for a 32-bit data bus). Thus, the need for two consecutive memory accesses to load a data object into the processor, for example, an i386 memory access crossing a double word boundary, is eliminated. This would only further obstruct the RISC pipeline. As a result of the current reduction in the price of memory chips, it is no great waste to store 8 bits in a 32-bit double word and to leave the remaining 24 bits empty.

Delayed jump and delayed branch

Jump and branch instructions constitute a large number of the machine code instructions (according to investigations, approximately 30%). They have an undesirable effect on instruction pipelining. The instruction fetching phase takes place in the first pipeline stage, and the current instruction pointer value determines the address of the instruction to be fetched. If a jump or branch occurs – that is, if a branch instruction leads to a new instruction address – then the new value for the instruction pointer is only known after the execution phase. This is identified as a *delayed jump* or *delayed branch*, because the jump or branch is executed with a delay. While the jump or branch instruction was passing through the pipeline, many more new instructions were being loaded into the pipeline. This does not cause a problem if the processor does not execute the jump, because the program execution is continued sequentially. This, of course, is not the case if the jump or branch is actually executed. Depending on the length of the pipeline, the processor has already partially executed a number of instructions, which, due to the branch, should not actually have been executed. This can lead to further problems. For example, if the instruction that follows the jump instruction is already in the execution phase, possible changes could occur to processor flags or other things, because during the write-back phase of the jump instruction the value of the instruction pointer is changed. Therefore, the CU must ensure that such effects do not occur, and that once the jump instruction is executed, the pipeline is flushed. Alternatively, the compiler can also insert one or more NOP instructions directly behind the jump instruction. These have no effect. This process is shown schematically in Figure 6.3.

Note that the NOPs are in the sequential control flow and not in the jump target. This means that the NOPs are almost always executed completely, independently of whether or not the jump is actually executed.

A better method is to rearrange the code generated, so that the processor can execute useful instructions instead of NOPs, without producing nonsense. The positions where previously the NOPs were located are identified as being *branch delay slots*, in which the compiler can insert other instructions. This also applies to the structure of the optimized compiler (see Section 6.3).

Data and register dependency

I briefly mentioned data and register dependency during the discussion on instruction pipelining. The problem always occurs if a later instruction n+1 (or n+2) requires the result of the instruction n from an earlier pipeline stage. This can occur, for example, if the value of an operand read during the operand fetching phase is not known, because the corresponding instruction is still in the execution phase. An example would be:

```
ADD reg1, reg2, reg7
AND reg6, reg1, reg3
```

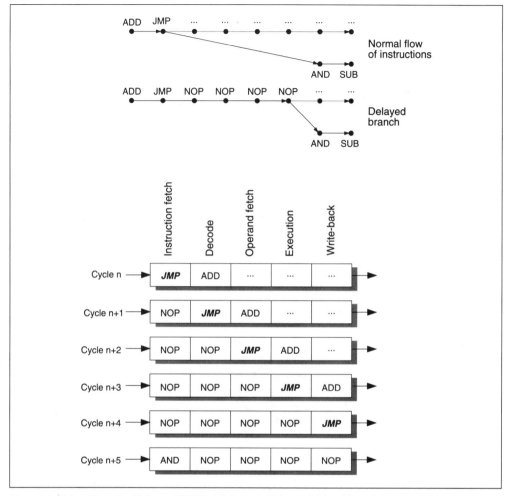

Figure 6.3: Delayed branch with inserted NOPs. Without pipelining and delayed branch the processor would continue execution with the first instruction at the jump target (here AND) immediately after the branch instruction. Because of instruction pipelining more or fewer NOPs have to be inserted after the JMP instruction (four NOPs with the five-stage pipeline) so that the processor does not provide any wrong result. Not before cycle n+4 the processor carries out the write-back of the operation result; that is, it writes the instruction pointer with the jump target address. Therefore, instruction AND at the target address can not occur before cycle n+5.

To begin with, both of the registers reg2 and reg7 are added and the result passed to reg1. The instruction that follows directly, uses the new content of reg1 in order to create an AND value in conjunction with reg3, and to pass this result to reg6. For this, it is necessary that the result of the addition exists in reg1. The writing back of the result only occurs in the final pipeline stage. At this moment in time, the given example of the AND instruction would find itself in the execution phase – in other words, the operand fetching phase delivers a false register value. This problem can be solved either by scoreboarding (Berkeley concept) or by inserting NOPs (Stanford concept). Both lead to pipeline delays and, therefore, a reduced calculating efficiency. With NOPs, for example, the following code is produced:

```
ADD reg1, reg2, reg7
NOP
NOP
AND reg6, reg1, reg3
```

Note that the inserted NOPs do not reduce the processor MIPS because a NOP is also an instruction. The effective calculating efficiency, in the sense of performing a certain task (such as three-dimensional calculations), is reduced drastically. Calculating efficiency is more than just MIPS or FLOPS (floating-point operations per second).

Also, in the case of a register dependency the number of NOPs, and thus delays caused by them, can be decreased, similarly to load forwarding, by so-called *register bypassing*. This, for example, causes the ALU to supply the result of the ADD instruction at the same time as the last pipeline stage (write-back of the instruction result) and the input to the ALU. The value of reg3 for the operand fetching phase is located at another ALU input, so that subtraction can be performed immediately. In this way, the writing back of the addition result into the register reg1, and the operand fetching phase for reg1, are no longer applicable. Such coordination of the pipeline stages is, of course, very complicated, and there is an additional increase in the hardware workload. The technology of bypassing and forwarding generally saves register read and write access, which do not contain logical operations.

There is a direct escalation of the problems with pipeline interlocks in superscalar processors: in this case, data dependencies do not just occur between individual stages of one pipeline, they also occur between the stages of differing pipelines. On these grounds, the Pentium only uses its pipelines for so-called 'simple' instructions, which reduces the probability of data dependencies right from the start. It is of no use if the instructions are active, in parallel, in both pipelines, but cannot be completed because one is waiting for a result from the other. An intelligent rearranging of the machine code instruction, as well as the thrifty insertion of NOPs via the compiler, can lead to drastic increases, without the need for any additional transistors. More on this subject follows in Section 6.3.

6.2.6 The horizontal machine code format

Few and simple instructions and, in particular, the customary RISC load/store architecture, enable a horizontal machine code format and a unified length of machine instruction. This means that the individual positions in the opcode always have the same meaning. In addition, each position of the operand field in the opcode is often attached to a register. Naturally, this causes an increase in redundancy because, for the coding of eight registers, only three bits are necessary ($2^3=8$), whereas with pure horizontal code, eight bits are required, where each bit represents one of the registers. This greatly reduces the amount of decoding; therefore, the decoding phase can be reduced and the pipeline decoding stages can be simplified. For example, the i860 normally uses a 32-bit instruction format with predetermined segregation in the individual fields (see Figure 6.4).

The figure shows that the i860 operates in a non-destructive fashion, because there are always two source registers *src1* and *src2* as well as a target register *dest* available. The 5-bit fields src1, src2 and dest code each of the 32 registers – that is, the i860 codes the registers vertically. Also, as with a two-register instruction, for example, MOV dest, src1, or even a 0 register instruction, such as NOP, the three register fields in the opcode are not removed and, therefore, the opcode is not shortened. Instead, the processor simply ignores the register fields. This leads to the opcode having a unified length of 32 bits.

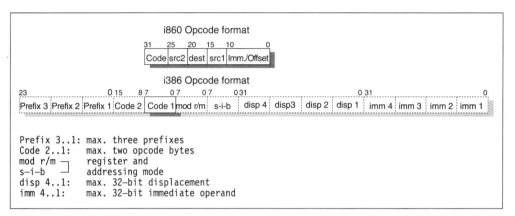

Figure 6.4: The horizontal 32-bit opcode format of the i860 and, as a comparison, the highly encoded vertical opcode format of the i386. The i386 format varies between one byte (for example, NOP or INT 2) and 15 bytes.

In comparison, CISCs generally use a vertical machine code format, which is characterized by its compactness and powerful coding. The result is that the opcodes have differing lengths (with an i386, between 1 byte for NOP and a maximum of 15 bytes). This is especially true of the x86 processors, with their prefixes and their various addressing formats, such as that in Figure 6.4, showing the general opcode format of the i386. The decoding of such highly coded instruction formats can only be performed with the help of microcode, because the necessary decoding circuitry would be too complicated. This decoding disadvantage is somewhat reduced by the prefetch queue, because the decoding unit of the CPU can already decode the instructions in the prefetch queue, at the same time as a previous instruction is in the execution phase. The decoding becomes really critical as the result of a jump or branch from the prefetch queue, because here the amount of decoding, in addition to the instruction execution, is extreme.

6.2.7 Support from on-chip caches

The main storage in a RISC system is regarded as a brake for two reasons. In the first instance, even with a modern 60 ns DRAM memory, the access time has a braking effect on a 50 MHz RISC processor with its 20 ns cycle time, making a large number of wait states necessary. In addition to this, delays are caused during instruction execution in the RISC CPU by delayed loads. This causes fast clocked RISC processors to wait desperately for an on-chip cache because, as is often the case, even fast L2 caches are regarded as being too slow. On-chip caches are notably faster than L2 caches, because above all, fewer clock cycles are necessary for the backup and reproduction of registers during a task switch, or the call and subsequent return of a subroutine. Normally, a RISC CPU has two separate caches: one for the program code and one for data. The bus width can thus be doubled in order to simultaneously reload or restore the data and code caches. The two caches cause a *cache consistency* problem, because data with the same address may be present in both caches, and an overwrite, for example, will change data in the data cache, but leave code in the code cache unchanged. The processor must constantly monitor and react to all read and write processes in, or from, the on-chip cache, so that no cache inconsistencies occur. With the Pentium, this is achieved with the assistance of MESI (modified, exclusive, shared, invalid) protocols and snooping (see Part 3).

At this stage, I would also like to point out that the CPU is not just supported by on-chip caches. For example, some RISC processors even integrate a quicker interrupt controller. The management of hardware interrupts by an external controller is extremely long-winded and is responsible for reducing the processor efficiency, especially if complicated INTA (interrupt acknowledge) sequences have to be executed. On-chip interrupt controllers can effect this more quickly. The Pentium does not integrate such an interrupt controller. Instead, Intel has developed an improved external interrupt controller, the 82489DX, so that hardware interrupt requests are run appreciably quicker than with the previous 8259A.

6.2.8 Coprocessor architecture

The few instructions of a RISC CPU are entirely sufficient for the running of 'common' programs. In comparison, floating-point instructions like those in CISCs must be implemented with the assistance of complicated integer routines. RISC processors also demand a mathematical coprocessor. This, though, has nothing to do with the reduced instruction set (only the unnecessary integer and string instructions are eliminated). There are coprocessors for the majority of RISC CPUs: they support the CPU in respect of floating-point operations, for example, MB86910 for the SPARC (scalable processor architecture) processor MB86900. They are implemented either as separate chips, or together with the CPU on a single chip.

The second solution offers a considerable speed advantage, because there is no data transfer between the CPU and the coprocessor. In addition, the synchronization of CPU core and coprocessor can be managed more simply if both units are located on the same chip. This happens either by scoreboarding (Stanford) or by inserting the necessary number of NOPs (Berkeley). A new synchronization between the CPU and the processor is necessary, because the execution of complex floating-point instructions takes much longer than the addition of two integers in the CPU, for example SIN dest, src for the calculation of the sine of src, (the sine of a value is determined with the help of many multiplications and additions). The Transputer T800 and the Pentium are examples of RISC processors that integrate the mathematical coprocessor in the processor chip.

Deviating from the pure RISC concept, with its hardwired instructions, are the coprocessors that frequently use microcode, at least for complex transcendental instructions. This is necessary because even a hardwired control unit for a multitude of transcendental floating point instructions (SIN, COS, ARCTAN, LOG and so on), with an accuracy of 80 bits, would be considered too large and too slow for current very large-scale integrated (VLSI) technology.

The new generation of RISC processors, and the Pentium, no longer have an on-chip coprocessor. Instead, the floating-point unit is implemented as part of the pipeline. The first three pipeline phases (instruction fetching phase, decoding phase and operand fetching phase) are identical for integer and floating-point instructions. Only at the execution stage do the paths of the instructions split: integer instructions are processed in the conventional CPU pipeline, whereas floating-point instructions are transferred to the floating-point pipeline for execution. The Pentium also does this. The separation of the CPU and coprocessor no longer exists. Integer and floating-point instructions are processed in the same manner; no explicit instruction and operand transfer from the CPU to the coprocessor takes place.

In comparison, not so long ago (for example, with the i486) a coprocessor was integrated with the CPU interface on the chip. It is simple to see the reasoning behind this: a complete coprocessor was available in the form of the i387, thus, the reduced development cost and the time saved meant that the available coprocessor logic with its smaller structure size could be implemented on the i486 chip. The development of a combined integer/floating-point unit or pipeline would have been much more complicated. Only now, with the Pentium, has Intel caught up. However, the integration of CPU core and coprocessor on the same i486 chip has led to inproved floating-point performance, because the long route via the I/O ports and buffer is no longer required for the execution of an instruction, and the exchange of data between the CPU and coprocessor.

6.2.9 Register files

To avoid unduly braking a RISC processor, as few memory accesses as possible should be executed. In other words, many operands must be stored in the processor itself. This requires a large number of processor registers, the structure of which is generally very simple: it is sufficient to use simple flip-flops, similar to the memory cells of static RAM (SRAM). It is better to turn disadvantages into advantages and, thus, throw out the old concept of general-purpose registers used in CISCs (originally just a continuation of the limited integration possibilities from 20 years ago).

At this point, I would like to introduce you to the final characteristic, the register files of modern RISC CPUs. Typically, they comprise between 32 and 2048 (or even more) registers with uniform qualities. There is no special register available (like, for example, ECX in the i386 for counting loops). A simple general-purpose register file is the simplest register structure for a RISC processor (see Figure 6.5(a)). It consists of 32 registers in a stack, similar to the eight floating point registers FP(0) to FP(7) that we learned about previously in the i387. RISC processors using the Stanford concept (for example, MIPS, MIPS-X, R2000, R3000) generally work with such a register file. The advantage of this extensive collection of registers – the i386 only has the seven registers EAX, EBX, ECX, EDX, ESI, EDI and EBP available for use as general-purpose registers – is that they vastly reduce load/store memory accesses. If the processor carries out a subroutine call (via a CALL), then a larger quantity of register values have to be stored than is the case with a CISC containing fewer registers, because the subroutines also wish to use all of the 32 registers, in order to reduce memory accesses to a minimum.

In order to overcome this problem of saving complete register files when a subroutine is called, some RISC CPUs implement so-called *multiple register files*. Each subsection of these multiple register files contains its own complete logical register file. They are managed by a *register file pointer* (see Figure 6.5(b)). When a CALL occurs, the register file pointer is simply switched one file further (upwards), and then points to a register file that is currently not in use. This is then assigned to the called subroutine. In this way, the storing of register values in memory for a CALL becomes unnecessary. If a RETURN from the subroutine causes a return to the called program, then the CPU simply switches the register file pointer back by one. The program can then, once again, see the old register values.

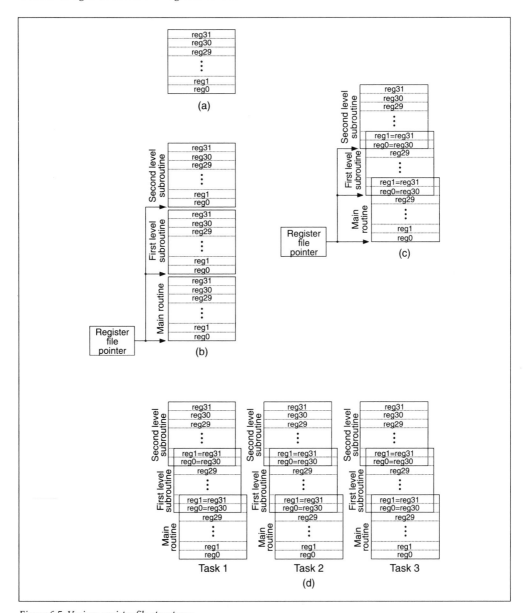

Figure 6.5: Various register file structures.
(a) Simple register file (MIPS, R2000, R3000), (b) several logical register files for each nesting level; one physical register file, (c) partially overlapping register files for each nesting level; one physical register file (RISC I/II, SPARC) and (d) several physical register files for fast task switches; several physical register files.

Because programs with more than 10 subroutine levels are very rare at present, it is sufficient to have approximately 320 registers in ten register files, without causing too much of a problem. However, should more subroutines occur, a register file overflow is produced, and the operating system has to unload one or more register files from memory, or store virtual registers in memory (memory addresses). This strategy of having different nesting levels does not just prevent memory accesses within the routine; in addition, a subroutine is executed at very high speed. More than 10 subroutine levels occur, above all, in recursive procedures which repeatedly call themselves, such as sorting algorithms.

In order to transfer parameters between the calling program and the subroutine, a corresponding amount of data has to be copied from the register file of the calling program to that of the subroutine. This problem can be cleverly overcome by partially overlapping the register files in the different sublevels (see Figure 6.5(c)), for example, each register file should be sectioned into input parameters, local variables, output parameters and perhaps also global variable sectors. If the output parameter sector of the calling program overlaps with the input parameter sector of the called subroutine, there is no need for a parameter transfer. The subroutine already receives its input parameters during a CALL when the register file pointer is switched. In the same way, the calling program receives the result when the register file pointer is switched back with a RETURN. This procedure is known as the *procedure window method* because, as a result of the CALLs and RETURNs, a *register window* is moved across the whole multiple register file (which contains all of the register files).

Overlapping simultaneously offers two advantages. Firstly, explicit parameter transfers can be saved by copying register values, and secondly overlapping reduces the quantity of registers required in order to maintain a large number of logical registers.

The degree of overlapping and the size of the register window can be implemented statically or dynamically, depending on the conditions at the time of compiling (thus, the quantity of the local variables of a procedure, as well as the quantity of parameters to be transferred/returned). In the latter case, this is referred to as *register windows with variable size*. A typical implementation of this concept would be the execution of the multiple register files as a ring memory, which solves the problem of register data file overflow at the same time.

Like the keyboard buffer in a PC, the ring memory is managed, for example, by a start and an end pointer. If the pointer values indicate a register file overflow, then the register file, as indicated by the start pointer, is saved in memory so that there is enough space for a register file of a lower subsection level. As a RETURN returns to the level directly above, it is most advantageous to remove the highest level register files from memory.

One problem encountered with the register window method as described here has not been solved; instead, it has been worsened. With a task switch or task change, all register values of the current task in all of the physical register files have to be stored in memory, then the register values of the register files for the new task have to be reloaded. Therefore, depending on the current nesting level of the procedures, and the quantity of procedure variables, a more or less extensive memory access is necessary. The problem can be solved by the hardware, by implementing many independent physical register files (see Figure 6.5(d)). Then, a corresponding pointer selects the currently valid physical register file. SPARC processors with 2048 registers in many physical register files can more or less immediately execute not only a procedure call, but also a task change, because all that is necessary is the switching of a pointer. Compare this to the complicated memory access when the i386 (or, of course, the Pentium) executes a task switch. For this, the i386 saves all register values in the task state segment of the current task, and loads its registers with the values from the task state segment (TSS) of the newly activated tasks.

6.2.10 Dynamic register renaming and speculative execution

Dynamic register renaming is closely related to multiple register files. Here, a reference to a certain register with a certain logical name (r08, for example) can be switched through to any register, implemented in the processor. For example, if the processor has a single register file comprising eight registers but physically implements 32 registers, any of these eight logical registers can be mapped by the register renaming logic to any of the 32 physical registers. Unlike a register window (where these eight registers are mapped onto a contiguous subset of eight physical registers), here, the corresponding eight physical registers need not be contiguous (logical register r00 can be mapped to physical register R23, and logical register r01 can be mapped to physical register R07, for example).

Dynamic register renaming is used for out-of-order execution of instructions in superscalar processors or for speculative execution. In scalar RISC processors with only one execution pipeline, all instructions are terminated in the order in which they are loaded into the pipeline, that is, instructions cannot pass an earlier instruction. This may change in a superscalar because perhaps the instruction in the second pipeline can be executed quicker than in the first pipeline (simpler instructions requiring fewer clock cycles, no interlocks, no load/store delay etc.). In this case, the quicker instruction writes in its last stage into the respective logical register, but this register is assigned the corresponding physical register only after the scheduler has confirmed the correctness and has resolved the initial instruction order again. The key point is that the pipeline can continue execution of the next instruction at once (and write back another result to the same logical register, that is, address the same logical but another physical register at once), whereas without dynamic register renaming the write-back stage has to wait until the addressed logical (equal physical) register is free for the write-access.

Dynamic register renaming is also used for so-called speculative execution. Speculative execution means that after a branch prediction, the processor continues program execution without waiting for the branch to be verified. In the course of instruction execution it is likely that the CPU overwrites registers which have been used earlier and whose contents should have been preserved if the prediction is verified as false later. With dynamic register renaming, the speculative branch predicted by the branch prediction logic addresses the usual logical registers which are, however, mapped onto different physical registers. If the prediction is verified to be correct later, the renaming logic simply makes the register mapping of the predicted branch the 'real' mapping. If the branch is verified to be incorrect, then the renaming logic switches back to the 'old' mapping before the branch. Nesting of these branches can occur if another branch instruction occurs before the earlier branch can be verified in a pipeline stage. Today's high-end microprocessors allow four and more branch nesting levels. Register renaming and speculative execution are often used for 80x86-compatible processors which use RISC technologies to enhance performance. The eight general-purpose registers of the 80x86 make them a natural target for register renaming. Note that the previously mentioned register windows are usually employed for subroutine calls and task switches whereas dynamic register renaming is used for ordinary program execution. Of course, dynamic register renaming is also valuable for sub-routine calls and task switches. A further advantage is that dynamic register renaming uses the physically available register set more economically than register windows, because frequently a program branch doesn't use all the registers available in the processor.

6.3 RISC characteristics at the software level

RISC machines, for the implementation of high level language architecture, require the support of an optimized compiler in order to achieve high efficiency of any sort. Firstly, RISC systems also use high level language compilers (mainly C) for system software (for example, UNIX, the very widespread operating system, is written almost entirely in C). In this case, the assembler plays almost no part at all, because the compiler manufacturer has packed all of his know-how into the compiler with respect to the optimization of the RISC code for the respective processor. The programming 'by (assembler) hand' would, in only a few cases, produce the same perfor-mance as when using compilers – the dogma applicable to CISC machines, that time-critical applications have to be programmed in assembler, is turned around by RISC machines and their associated compilers. Without high level languages, an application programmer has to concentrate on the technical details such as the pipelines and their interlocks, a very extensive and therefore error-prone task.

6.3.1 RISC processor and compiler as an indivisible unit

An important characteristic of the RISC concept is the processor and compiler unit. Until recently, it was normal for one development team to develop the processor, and another to be responsible for the compiler and system software. The dialogue between processor and software took place via a defined interface, that of the processor instruction set. Toady's RISC concepts create a single unit right from the start.

The early synchronization of hardware development and the machine code instruction set is absolutely necessary because of the hardwiring of the control unit. A change to the instruction set, or even to a single machine code instruction, requires a total redesign of the control unit – a rather extensive enterprise. In comparison, the microcode in the micro-encoded units of the CISC processor can, even after development of the hardware, be changed within certain limits so that the content of the microcode ROM is suitably matched. For example, a few new instructions can be inserted, or already implemented instructions can be modified, without the need for extensive changes to the control unit of the CPU.

The RISC chip only contains instructions that reduce the work of the compiler and accelerate program execution. The distribution frequency of the instructions from a runtime analysis of currently available programs has determined the reduced instruction set. The homogeneity of the compiler and the processor enables considerably more effective program optimization, using the compiler, than is possible with commercial CISC processors and a thrown-in compiler.

Statistical analyses into the frequency of machine code instructions actually executed have shown that, to a large extent, they depend on the language used and, thus, the compiler. One result showed that, for example, the 10 most frequently used Fortran machine code instructions have a runtime portion of up to 60%. For the generation of code using a COBOL compiler, the same machine code instructions take up a mere 8% of the executed code quantity. This led to the development of RISC processors for certain program languages. Examples of these are *SOAR (Smalltalk On A RISC)* for Smalltalk, and *SPUR (Symbolic Processing Using RISC)* and *COLIBRI (Coprocessor for LISP on the Basis of RISC)* for LISP. This clearly shows the changing rolls of hardware and software, in order to achieve the best possible efficiency (some scientists even refer to the brain as being a form of hardware, which produces its own software). However, with a CISC, it is normal to have to develop a program language and the compiler (or assembler of the lowest level) for a given processor.

The restricted number of instructions in a RISC processor limits the instruction selection for the compiler. In this respect, compiler construction is simplified. The less powerful instructions (for example, there are no string instructions, as is the case with the i386) lead to extensive machine programs because complex calculations, which can be executed in a CISC processor with a single instruction, require many instructions in a RISC CPU. Typically, a compiler produces 50% more object code for a RISC processor than is necessary for the same task in a CISC CPU. Compilers for RISC processors must be highly optimized in order to make use of the performance advantage using fast instruction execution, and not lose performance due to the need to process more instructions. The optimization includes not only the elimination of dead or invalid code, the optimization of multiple repeated loops or of register coordination, but also the prevention of pipeline interlocks by specifically rearranging the code segments. This further complicates compiler development.

The high level language programmer does not notice any difference between a RISC and a CISC CPU; in both cases, the syntax and semantics of the high level language are the same. However, with RISC, the use of a high level language improves the portability of the program right from the start. Until now, this has not been the case with the PC. As these programs usually address the BIOS or even the hardware functions directly, the PC programs, even at source code level, are almost not portable, or only portable after modification. This is currently changing with the introduction of hardware independent operating systems such as OS/2 and Windows NT.

6.3.2 Jumps and delay slots

An important task of the compiler is to optimize the code so that no, or as few as possible, pipeline interlocks occur. The most aggravating pipeline obstructions emerge during subroutine calls and, above all, during branching. This is because the target address is known only in the final pipeline stage, but is required in the first pipeline stage for the reading of the instruction to the target address. For a five-stage pipeline, the execution of the subsequent instructions must be halted for four clock cycles, until the target address is available in the final stage. In this respect, the load instructions are also critical, because their execution is dependent upon the slower memory, leading to many idle cycles of the CPU. Load forwarding reduces the number of idle cycles by one clock cycle. Pipeline interlocks through register dependency can be smoothed with the help of the bypass or forwarding principle, if the result of the execution is supplied to the operand fetch stage while bypassing the write-back stage.

I would like to illustrate, in the following 'worst case example' of a conditional branch (jump if true), the solution of a pipeline interlock problem with the aid of a compiler. It is assumed that the compiler produces the following code sequence during the initial pass, prior to optimization:

```
ADD r3, r2, r1
AND r0, r5, r6
JMPT r0, label
NOP             <- Delay slot
...
label:SUB r1, 5, r6
...
```

Depending on the result of the AND instruction, the JMPT instruction causes a jump to *label*, or a continuation of the sequential instruction execution. If you consider the code produced, you can see that the ADD instruction does not refer to a register, which is relevant for the execution of the branch (the instruction effects neither the AND conditions nor the evaluation in JMPT). On the other hand, depending on the number of pipeline stages after the JMPT instruction, the compiler has inserted NOPs in order to give the pipeline time to make available the target address after JMPT in the instruction fetch stage. The insertion of NOPs is similar, in terms of performance, to a hold on the pipeline as soon as the JMPF appears in the decoding stage. In this case, only the JMPF instructions would run through the pipeline; all other instructions are barred. This, of course, decreases the efficiency of the computer. The insertion of NOPs acts as a form of occupational therapy for the pipeline stages, because the first effective instruction is loaded only after the complete execution of the JMPF instructions and the write-back of the target address in the instruction fetching stage of the pipeline.

Therefore, code optimization is necessary. The subsequent operation of the code optimizer in the compiler replaces the NOP instruction in the delay slot, with the ADD instruction from the first line of the example. In this way, after optimization, we get the following code with a delayed branch:

```
AND r0, r5, r6
JMPT r0, label
ADD r3, r2, r1 <- Delay slot
...
label: SUB r1, 5, r6
...
```

The effects of both instruction sequences are identical; they have the same semantics. The only difference is that one NOP instruction is saved during code reorganization. Correspondingly, one less clock cycle is required to execute the code sequence. Depending on the number of pipeline stages and, therefore, the delay slots and the number of previous instructions that do not affect branching, two NOPs can, of course, be replaced by two effective instructions. This, incidentally, also reduces the quantity of the code: the programs produced are more compact.

Such a code change is always possible for an unconditional jump (with JMP), a procedure call (with CALL) or a procedure return (with RETURN) because in these instances, conditions are not tested. Therefore, the jump or call of preceding instructions has no effect on the jump or call target. The rearranging of code is only successful for conditional jumps if the instruction that follows the jump or call instruction does not influence the conditional value and, therefore, the jump target. In practice, the delayed branch process reduces the number of NOPs necessary to about 10% of the NOPs before the optimization phase (the longer the pipeline, the more NOPs are necessary; superpipelined architecture increases this problem). The same applies to the delayed load. In 90% of cases (taken from statistical analyses), a value from an independent instruction can be inserted into the delay slot and executed while the bus interface loads the value from memory. Therefore, you can see that improvements, not just on the hardware side – such as register bypassing or load forwarding for reducing the number of register accesses – but also in the compiler – that is, the software – can contribute to an increase in speed.

A further problem occurs with a jump or call to a distant target address. Such an instruction is not normally found in the processor prefetch queue; instead, it is found in memory. In addition to the delay caused by a jump or subroutine call, there is the delay caused by a memory access. This is only relevant for a conditional jump if the jump is actually executed and the instruction pointer is changed accordingly. Otherwise, either the pipeline is stopped or the inserted NOPs are executed until it is clear that the instruction pointer will not be altered.

In order to make the delay caused by the executed jump or the subroutine call as short as possible, some RISC processors implement a *branch target cache* or *jump target cache*. This is a memory cache for a target address, namely that of the target address of the jump or subroutine call, which delivers the first few instruction codes to the target address (for example, the first instructions of the subroutine). In this way, the instruction codes can be fetched immediately from the pipeline instruction fetching stage and decoded in the decoding stage, while the bus interface reads the subsequent instructions from memory. The Pentium goes a stage further than this branch target cache, by implementing a *branch prediction buffer*. It not only stores the target address and a few instructions at this address, but also attempts to predict, through statistical analysis of the previous branches and a predetermined algorithm, whether or not the jump will actually be executed.

6.4 Development trends in the RISC world

Currently, the so-called *Beyond RISC Architecture* , which has a combination of RISC and CISC characteristics is being discussed and even implemented in applications. Associated with this, for example, is the micro-encoding of the floating-point units on the chip, which until now were only implemented on a separate coprocessor. This, of course, leads to nothing other than a new abbreviation, *CRISP*, which stands for *Complexity Reduced Instruction Set Processor*. Here, as a result of the increasing complexity of the problems associated with RISC workstations and RISC processors, the puritanical RISC rules are broken. Examples include extensive scientific and graphical applications, and also the area of artificial intelligence. All of them require a maximum rate of (parallel) performance which, in the future, could not be solved by a single, though extraordinary, processor. On this basis, during the architecture development, modern RISC CPUs are designed for multiprocessor operation. Superfast circuits based on gallium arsenide (GaAs) and the use of superconducting effects are currently undergoing research.

7 RISC elements in classical CISC processors

At present, just as CISC principles find acceptance in many modern RISC processors (for example, the micro-encoding of the on-chip floating-point units), certain RISC concepts can also be found in high performance CISCs. In the first instance, this affects the partial hardwiring of the units, in order to execute frequently used instructions in the shortest time, as well as extensions to the pipelined processing of the instructions and the integration of on-chip caches. An example of this is the i486 from Intel. In the next section I would like to briefly introduce the i486 and the implementation of RISC technology on this chip.

7.1 The i486 in brief

In some respects, the i486 represents a hybrid between CISC and RISC processors. The frequently used instructions (for example, MOV) are hardwired in RISC fashion and are therefore executed extremely quickly. In comparison, complex and less commonly, used instructions are available in micro-encoded form. A sequence of simple instructions can, therefore, be quicker than a complex instruction with the same effect. The instructions are executed in a five-stage pipeline. The hardwiring of some instructions, and also the partial use of RISC technology, is not always visible.

The i486 integrates, on one chip, an improved i386 CPU, an improved coprocesser when compared to that of the i387, and a cache controller including 8 kbytes of cache memory. The i486 can be obtained as versions with 25 to 50 MHz clock frequencies, or even 100 MHz with internal clock tripling (the i486DX4). Using the 32-bit data bus, it is possible to transfer data at a rate of up to 160 Mbytes/s in burst mode. Mainly as a result of hardwiring and instruction pipelining, the i486 is approximately three times faster than an i386, clocked at the same frequency. To achieve this, more than a million transistors are incorporated in the thumb-sized i486 chip. In comparison, at the beginning of the PC/XT age of the personal computer, the 8086 had only a fiftieth of this quantity.

Closely in line with the requirements of the PC market, the i486 is fully compatible with the i386/i387 combination. It uses the same instructions and types of data; it uses the same real, protected and virtual 8086 modes, and performs memory segmentation and demand paging in the same way. As the coprocessor is on the same chip as the CPU, data transfer between them is quicker. The i486 shows its main strengths in calculation-intensive applications such as CAD or computer graphics.

7.2 The internal structure of the i486

Through the integration of three previously separate functional units into one chip – the CPU, coprocessor and cache controller – the internal structure of the i486, in comparison to the i386, has also become considerably more complicated. For the i386 processor family, three separate microprocessors were necessary – the i386 CPU, the i387 coprocessor and, for example, the 82395 cache controller. Figure 7.1 shows schematically the internal structure of the i486.

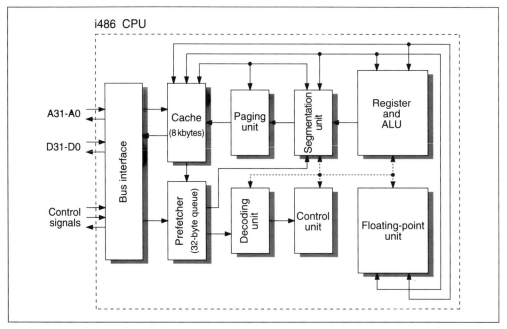

Figure 7.1: The internal structure of the i486.
The i486 integrates on a single chip not only an improved CPU core, but also a more powerful i387 as well as a cache controller and an 8 kbyte cache. The prefetch queue has been enlarged to 32 bytes.

As with all microprocessors, the connection to the surrounding environment is through the bus interface. The bus interface receives or sends data through the data bus D31-D0, and, with the help of the address bus A31-A2 and the byte enable signals $\overline{BE3}$-$\overline{BE0}$, addresses memory and I/O address space. Through the control bus, it sends information about the condition of the i486 and receives instructions from external devices. The on-chip cache is directly connected to the bus interface. This integrated 8-kbyte cache memory is used as both a data and code cache. In contrast, powerful RISC CPUs, and also the Pentium, use separate data and code caches for the independent buffering of instructions and program data. Thus, the i486 cache buffers the data and instructions then passes them on to the registers, ALU, floating-point unit or prefetcher, as applicable. During a bus cycle that requires an access to external cache memory – a so-called *second level cache* or *L2 cache* – two clock cycles are necessary, whereas only one clock cycle is necessary when using internal cache. Even though 8 kbytes is very small, it produces an enormous increase in the speed of operation.

If data or instructions that are not buffered in the cache must be read from memory, the register or prefetcher accesses the bus interface directly. This can occur when the required data is dispersed, or when a jump instruction to an address in a different part of memory is required.

After the cache, the paths of the data and instruction codes separate. The data bytes are passed on to the registers or floating-point unit; the instruction bytes are sent to the prefetch queue, which, in the i486, consists of 32 bytes. The decoder unit decodes all instructions in the prefetch queue, then passes them on to the control unit (CU) that controls the registers, the ALU, the segmentation unit and the floating-point unit. The decoder and the execution unit (EU) are parts of the five-stage i486 pipeline, which I will explain later. Many instructions pass through the partially hardwired control unit of the i486 and are carried out immediately – that is, they are not processed by a microprogram. The prefetcher separates immediate operands or displacements in the instruction flow and passes them on to the ALU or addressing unit (AU), which consists of the paging unit and the segmentation unit, as applicable.

The data bytes that have been read are transferred to the segmentation unit, the registers, the ALU or the floating-point unit and are processed. The two 32-bit data buses together form the internal 64-bit data bus for the transfer of data between the CPU core, corresponding to the i386, and the floating-point unit, corresponding to the i387. Unlike the i386/i387 combination, no I/O bus cycles are necessary for the transfer of opcodes and data between the CPU and the coprocessor. In addition, the data transfer occurs internally with a width of 64-bits compared to the 32-bit data bus of the i386/i387. This, of course, makes a noticeable difference to the execution speed of floating-point instructions, and enables the i486 to process ESC instructions considerably quicker than the i386/i387 combination.

For the generation of addresses, the i486 uses a segment and an offset register, as do all of the 80x86 family of processors. In the segmentation unit, the contents of both registers are combined to form the linear address. When in protected mode, the segmentation unit executes an access check at the same time, in order to ensure the protection of the separate tasks and the system. When paging is active, the linear address determined in the segmentation unit is then converted to a physical address in the paging unit. Without paging, the linear address is also the physical address. The bus interface sends out the physical address and, if necessary, the data to be written, or reads in the addressed data.

The bus interface of the i486 contains four write buffers for the acceleration of write accesses to external memory. If the i486 bus is not immediately available, for example, because the processor is currently executing a cache line fill, then the data is first written to the write buffer. The internal buffers can be filled at a rate of one write operation for each processor clock cycle; the data is written to the four buffers in the sequence in which the data should be supplied from the i486 to the data bus. If, after the cache line fill, the processor becomes available again, the bus interface independently loads the data in the write buffers onto the bus. If, on the other hand, the i486 bus is free during a write operation, the write buffers are bypassed and the data to be written is transferred immediately to the bus. If the write operation represents a cache hit, in both cases the data is also stored in the on-chip cache.

In order to increase the processor efficiency still further, the i486 can transpose the sequence of read and write operations on the bus. This is the case if all write accesses that are waiting in the write buffers represent cache hits and the read access is a cache miss. The i486 will first carry out the read access and then the write access. This is possible because the read access does not affect a memory position that must first be updated by the write access.

7.3 The i486 pipeline

The different CPU units of the i486 can, in a sense, operate in parallel, in that during the execution of an instruction, the next instruction can be decoded and the instruction following that can be fetched. The i486 pipeline is, therefore, more of a relatively loose connection between the separate functional units than the closely joined model shown in Figure 6.2. A reason for this is the very different complexity and execution time of the separate instructions (which is reflected in the large difference in workload required for decoding). Through the parallel operation of the prefetcher, decoder and EU, as well as a register write stage, instruction pipelining is performed. A 'true' RISC pipeline – that is, a pipeline with closely joined stages – is first realized in the Pentium. Figure 7.2 shows the functional structure of the i486 pipeline.

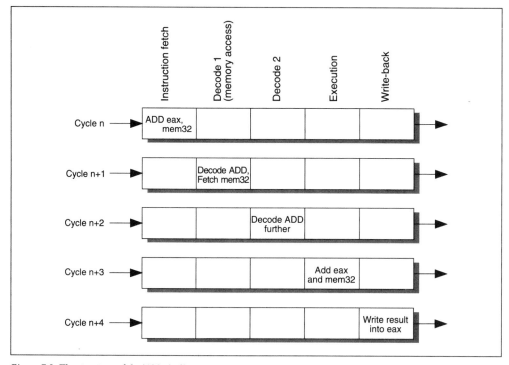

Figure 7.2: The structure of the i486 pipeline.
The i486 ppeline comprises one prefetch stage, two decoding stages, one execution stage and one write-back stage. The figure shows, as an example, the execution of an ADD eax, mem32 instruction.

The first stage in the pipeline – the prefetch stage – reads 16-byte instruction blocks from memory into the prefetch queue and, simultaneously, into the on-chip cache. For this, the i486 can use the burst mode. In total, the prefetch queue has enough room for two such 16-byte units; it contains 32 bytes and so is twice the size as that in the i386.

The decoding unit forms the second and third stages in the i486 pipeline. It converts simple machine instructions directly into control instructions for the CU, and more complex machine instructions into microcode jump addresses. In the latter case, the microcode is transferred to the CU, where it controls the execution of the instruction. The fact that the first decoding stage can instigate a memory access has a considerable effect on the performance of the pipeline. Decoding stages one and two correspond to the decode and operand fetch stages in the true RISC pipeline model shown in Figure 6.2.

The two-stage decoding is necessary due to the complex CISC instructions of the i486; it does however, also produce considerable improvements in performance when memory operands need to be loaded. In this case, the first decoding stage sends out memory access. If the operand is located in the on-chip cache, it can be read from the on-chip cache in one clock cycle, during which the instruction is processed in the second decoding stage. Memory operand is, therefore, available during the execution phase of the instruction without hindering the pipeline. This is true for the combination of a load instruction (for example, MOV eax, mem32) and a subsequent instruction that uses or affects the loaded operand (such as ADD eax, ebx). The ADD instruction is immediately available for the operand mem32 loaded into the accumulator EAX. This is also true if the ADD instruction contains a memory operand similar to the example shown in Figure 7.2. In this way, the i486 pipeline supports effective program code that already exists, but which is not optimized for the pipelining of instructions, for example, through the rearranging of code and delayed load. In addition to the register-register instruction MOV eax, ebx, memory-register instruction MOV eax, mem32 is also executed in only one clock cycle.

During the execution step, the CU interprets the control signals or the microcode jump addresses and controls the ALU, floating-point unit or other logic element of the i486 in order to carry out the instruction. This can take one or more clock cycles, depending on the instruction. This characteristic differs greatly from RISC methodology, in which every pipeline step should be executed in one single processor clock cycle. The execution of the subsequent already decoded instruction is obstructed, until the current instruction has been fully executed.

The last pipeline stage writes the result of the instruction into the target register (if the instruction specified a register as the target) or a temporary register for the output back to memory (if the instruction specified a memory operand as the target).

Part 3
The one-chip supercomputer: The 166 MIPS superscalar Pentium

People have had to wait a long time for the secrets surrounding the i486 successor to be made public. The name itself was unclear – speculation ranged from the i586 to the P5. The Pentium, as it was finally christened, was presented to the general public in March 1993. It should represent a major step forward by implementing the most modern RISC technology, and also have a great advantage over its competitors by being completely binary compatible with its predecessors from the 8086 to the i486DX/2. According to Intel, the Pentium at 100 MHz with optimized code, should reach a command throughput rate of 166 MIPS, compared to 54 MIPS for the i486DX2-66. Note that the Pentium can also carry out very complicated commands, which must be emulated in true RISC CPUs by multiple element commands. In this section, I explain which RISC principles are realized in which areas (the i486 compatible command set alone, with more than 400 machine code commands, puts at least the 'R' into question), and which requirements must be fulfilled in order to use the full capabilities of the Pentium.

8 The Pentium superscalar implementation

Firstly, I would like to present the characteristic features of the Pentium in the following list:

- ▶ two (almost) independent integer pipelines and a floating point pipeline – thus, the Pentium implements a superscalar architecture.
- ▶ dynamic branch prediction.
- ▶ short command execution times through many hardwired commands.
- ▶ binary compatibility, also for complex i386 functions through a microprogrammed CISC unit.
- ▶ separate data and code caches each with 8 kbytes, write-back strategy and supporting of the MESI (modified, exclusive, shared, invalid) cache consistency protocol.
- ▶ wider 64-bit data bus with pipelined burst mode for quicker cache line fills and write-backs.
- ▶ memory management unit (MMU) for demand paging.
- ▶ additional error detection functions such as internal parity check, self test and JTAG boundary scan test.
- ▶ execution tracing for external monitoring of internal command execution.
- ▶ operates in real, protected and virtual 8086 modes.
- ▶ hardware debug support through probe mode.
- ▶ system management mode for implementing power saving functions.
- ▶ performance monitoring for the optimization of code sequences.
- ▶ full binary compatibility with all x86 and x87 predecessors – the greatest advantage.

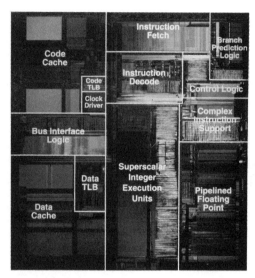

Figure 8.1: The Pentium. Source: Intel GmbH (Germany).

In Figure 8.1, you can see a photograph of an unbonded Pentium chip. The separate elements can be seen clearly. Regular structures represent memory, such as the two caches, the translation lookaside buffers (TLBs) and the branch trace buffer. The very complicated control and execution units show more chaotic wiring. The chip shown has more than three million transistors.

8.1 The internal structure of the Pentium

The Pentium, like its i386 and i486 predecessors, is a 32-bit processor but has a 64-bit data bus. This is not a contradiction, because the data bus serves the on-chip caches and not the 32-bit processor directly. The external and the internal buses are connected through the caches. The internal data paths of the Pentium are between 128 and 256 bits wide, so that the transfer of data and codes can be carried out very quickly. Figure 8.2 is a block diagram of the Pentium.

As usual, the bus interface represents the connection to the outside world – in the Pentium, through the 64-bit data bus and the 32-bit address bus. Both on-chip caches are directly connected to the bus interface. Unlike the i486, two separate and independent 8-kbyte caches for code and data are provided; the cache line size is 32 bytes. The i486 contains only a single, unified cache of 8-kbyte capacity with a cache line size of 16 bytes. Each cache is connected to its own TLB, so that the paging unit (PU) of the MMU can quickly convert linear code or data addresses into physical addresses. In addition to the standard 4-kbyte pages, 4-Mbyte pages are provided for the support of larger systems with a linear memory model. The caches use physical addresses; the data cache can work with both write-through and write-back strategies as necessary.

The control unit (CU), which controls the five-step integer pipelines, u and v, and the eight-step floating-point pipeline, forms the heart of the Pentium. In this case, the term integer refers to all commands that do not contain floating-point operations, such as addition, comparison, move and jump commands. In this way, the Pentium can carry out any sort of command in the u pipeline, and a command indicated as simple in the v pipeline, simultaneously. Under the right conditions, the Pentium can thus execute two integer commands in one single clock cycle. The first four steps of the floating-point pipeline overlap with those of the u pipeline, so that the integer and the floating-point pipeline can only work in parallel under certain conditions. In comparison to an i486DX of similar clock speed, the Pentium floating-point unit executes floating-point commands up to 10 times faster. This is achieved through the integration of a hardware multiplier and divider, and also through the implementation of quicker algorithms for the microcoded floating-point commands. The two pipelines are supplied with codes by two independent 32-byte prefetch buffers. Only in this way is it possible to have overlapping command execution in the two pipelines.

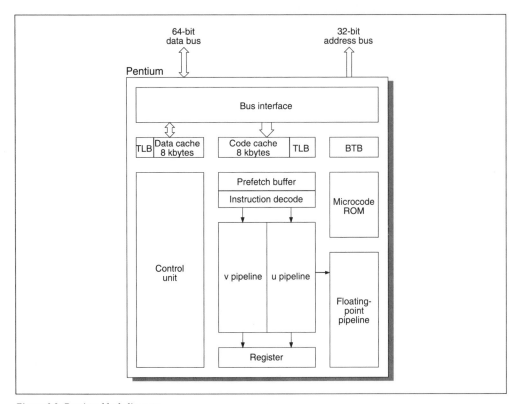

Figure 8.2: Pentium block diagram.

The branch prediction logic gives the Pentium an essential advantage over the i486 for the handling of branches, which can cause considerable delays, especially for processors with command pipelining. It consists of a CU and a branch trace buffer (BTB). It stores the target address of the branches and also statistical information concerning the frequency of the current branch, that is, how often the branch has been executed (also known as *taken branch*), or not executed. In this way, the branch prediction logic can reliably predict branches, and cause the Pentium to use the most likely target address for command fetching. Pipeline stalls, caused by emptying the pipeline (through a pipeline invalidate or flush), and also the subsequent command fetching, are considerably reduced and so the program execution is accelerated.

As an x86 and x87 compatible microprocessor, the Pentium must, of course, support all commands of the microcoded i386 and i387 processors. This is not possible using the hardwired CU, especially when considering the very complex commands and functions of protected mode and of task switches and the transcendental functions of the floating-point unit. For this reason, the Pentium contains microcode in a support unit ready for these complex functions. The support unit controls the pipelines with the help of the microcode, in order to carry out complex functions. The microcode is constructed in such a way that it can use both pipelines of the Pentium at the same time. Thus, even microcoded commands in the Pentium run much quicker than in the i486. Simpler functions, on the other hand, such as all ALU functions, are performed by the hardwired logic in accordance with the RISC principle.

8.2 The Pentium registers

In this section, I would like to briefly present the registers of the Pentium. They include the general-purpose, segment, status and control registers, as well as the registers of the floating-point unit. With the exception of the control register CR4 and the test register TR12, all registers are already implemented in the i386 and i486. Exclusively in the Pentium, a new pair of bits has been added to the registers implemented previously in the Pentium's predecessors.

8.2.1 The general-purpose, segment and memory management registers

The general-purpose registers in the Pentium, as in the i386 and i486, are each 32 bits wide, but can be addressed as 16- or 8-bit registers, due to the need for compatibility with the 8086/186/286. Figure 8.3 shows all of the registers of the Pentium integer unit. The memory management register and parts of the control registers CR0 to CR4 are used only in protected mode.

The Pentium has seven general-purpose registers EAX to EBP (as expected on compatibility grounds), six segment registers CS to GS, an instruction pointer, a stack pointer ESP and a flag register EFlag. The general-purpose registers, instruction pointer, stack pointer and flag register are each 32 bits wide; the segment registers, on the other hand, are only 16-bit. The 32-bit maximum size of the general-purpose registers in the Pentium gives offsets with a length of 32 bits, thus from 0 to 4G-1. With all 32-bit registers, it is also possible to address only the two least significant bytes. They are identified as AX to DI (general-purpose registers), IP (instruction pointer), SP (stack pointer) and flag (flag register). The least significant word of the four general-purpose registers AX to DX can be divided still further into two register bytes, for example AH and AL for the AX register. In this way, the Pentium can also work with single data bytes. The division of, for example, the 32-bit accumulator EAX into AX and then further into AH and AL is the result of compatibility with the 16-bit 8086 and 80286 CPUs. The full 32-

bit registers are identified by the prefix E (for *extended*), as in the i386 and i486. In the following subsections, I discuss the various general-purpose and segment registers in brief.

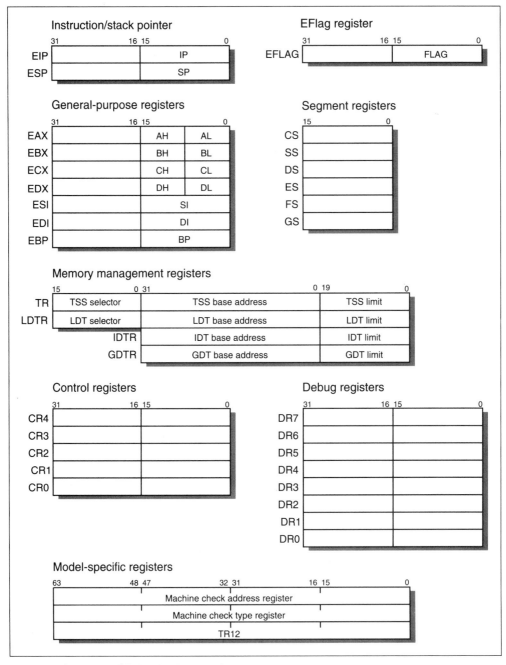

Figure 8.3: The registers of the Pentium integer unit.

Accumulator EAX

The accumulator is used mainly as a temporary storage area for data and for holding operands. This special use of the accumulator is historically so because microprocessors originally had only one register (the accumulator), so only one operation could be executed. An example would be the addition (accumulation) of values. It is only in the past 10 years that micro-processors have had many registers – SPARC RISC CPUs can have up to 2048 registers. The Pentium accumulator still has its uses, because many instructions are optimized for it with respect to the execution speed. The instructions are executed by a reference of the accumulator at a higher speed than if, for example, the EBX register was used. In addition, some register reference instructions are only valid for the accumulator. An example of this would be input/output data to and from ports.

The 32-bit accumulator (EAX) can be reduced to a 16-bit (AX) accumulator. In addition, it can be divided into two 8-bit sub-accumulators, the higher value accumulator byte AH from AX and the lower value accumulator byte AL from AX.

```
EXAMPLE:
MOV ah, al   ; the value in the low-order accumulator byte al is moved
             ; into the high-order accumulator byte ah
```

Base register EBX

The base register is used to store a value temporarily, or as a pointer to the start of a data object (for example, the start of an array) by indirect addressing. The 32-bit register can also be reduced to a 16-bit register (BX) and further reduced to 8-bit BL and BH registers.

```
Example:
MOV eax, [ebx]   ; load 32-bit accumulator EAX with the value
                 ; which is stored at the base address EBX
```

Count register ECX

The conventional use of the count register is to determine the number of loop, string instruction (REP) or shifting and rotation (SHL, ROL and so on) repetitions. After completion of the loop (for example, after the loop instruction), the value in ECX is reduced by one. You can also use ECX or CX as a standard general-purpose register to store data temporarily. Furthermore the 32-bit ECX register can be reduced to a 16-bit CX register and further subdivided into two 8-bit CL and CH registers.

```
Example:
MOV ecx, 08h    ; load ecx with 08h
start:          ; define begin of loop
  IN al, 70h    ; read al via port 70h
  MOV [ebx], al ; write content of al to memory location [ebx]
  INC ebx       ; increment address ebx by one
LOOP start      ; 8 repetitions (until ecx is equal 0)
```

Data register EDX

The EDX data register is normally used for the temporary storing of data. The EDX and DX have an important task during data input and output to and from ports: EDX contains the I/O addresses (from 0 to 65 535) of the respective ports. Only with the help of the EDX data register is it possible to communicate with I/O addresses greater than 255. The 32-bit EDX register can also be divided into a 16-bit DX register and further subdivided into two 8-bit DL and DH registers.

```
Example:
MUL EDX, ESP ; load stack pointer into register EDX
```

Base pointer EBP

The EBP base pointer can be used like the EAX, EBX, ECX or EDX registers to store data temporarily. Its main function, however, is that of a pointer to the base of stack frame. The EBP is then used for accessing procedural arguments. Unlike other registers, this is not assigned to the standard data segment in the applicable DS register but to the SS segment register. A memory access normally uses the SS:EBP registers. A segment override also replaces the SS stack segment with another segment, for example the ES extra segment.

```
Example: Procedure call with BP as stack frame base (MASM 5.0)
              PUSH sum1            ; push first summand onto stack
              PUSH sum2            ; push second summand onto stack
              PUSH sum3            ; push third summand onto stack
              CALL addition        ; add up all three

addition   PROC NEAR              ; near-call with four bytes for old eip as return address
           PUSH ebp               ; save base pointer
           MOV  ebp, esp          ; move stack pointer into base pointer; esp points to old
                                  ; base pointer bp on the stack; sum1, sum2, sum3 are
                                  ; local variables
           MOV  eax, [ebp+8]      ; load sum1 into eax
           ADD  eax, [ebp+12]     ; add sum2 to sum1 in eax
           ADD  eax, [ebp+16]     ; add sum3 to sum1+sum2 in eax
           POP  ebp               ; restore old base pointer
           RET                    ; return
addition   ENDP
```

Source index ESI

Like a 32-bit general-purpose register, the source index can also be used for temporary data storage. Its strength, however, is as a pointer during string operations – that is, as an index for an object within an array. The array base is often set by the EBX base register. In string instructions, the ESI mostly indicates single bytes, words or double words contained in the output (source) string. In addition, the ESI is automatically incremented or reduced (depending on the value of the direction flag) when a string instruction is repeated using the REP prefix. For example, you can transfer data quickly between two points in the memory using the MOVS instruction and the REP prefix.

```
Example: Display string "message:" underlined on a monochrome monitor with MOVSD
string    DB    16 DUP ('moeⓐs◎s◎a◎g◎e◎:◎')
                                  ; provide string to move with MOVSD in buffer called string
                                  ; (◎ = ASCII code 1 is the attribute for underlining)
          MOV  ax, @data          ; load 16-bit data segment of buffer string into ax
          MOV  ds, ax             ; adjust ds to data segment of string
          MOV  ax, b800h          ; move segment of monochrome video RAM to ax
          MOV  es, ax             ; load video segment into extra segment es
          CLD                     ; ascending order
          MOV  ecx, 4             ; transfer 4 words with 4 bytes each (2 characters + 2
                                  ; attributes)
          MOV  esi, OFFSET string ; load address of string into source index
          MOV  edi, 00h           ; display string in upper left corner of monitor
                                  ; (corresponding offset 0 in video RAM)
          REP  MOVSD              ; transfer a double word four times
```

With REP MOVSD edi and esi are incremented by four after each double word transfer and then point to the next double word in string.

Destination index EDI

The destination index is the partner of the ESI source index. The EDI can be used for temporary data storage or, like the ESI, as a pointer, but at the end of an operation. In string instructions, the EDI indicates bytes, words or double words in the string. The EDI is automatically incremented or decreased (depending on the value of the direction flag) when instructions using the REP prefix are used.

Example: See source index.

A further group of registers are the so-called segment registers. The Pentium has six of them: CS, DS, SS, ES, FS and GS. The extra registers FS and GS are not included in the 16-bit predecessors, the 8086 and the 80286. In contrast to the general-purpose registers, the segment registers were not increased to 32-bit when converted from the 16-bit 80286 to the 32-bit i386.

Code segment CS

The code segment builds a data block for holding the instruction and the addressed data. The instructions contained in the segment are addressed via the extended instruction pointer (EIP). This does not change the content of the CS. Only a far-call (or far-jump) and an INT can automatically change the CS content. In protected mode, the Pentium automatically checks the contents of the segment register during a change to make sure that the applicable task can access the new segment.

Data segment DS

The data segment usually contains the data for the active task. To be exact, the DS is the standard data segment – many instructions (such as MOV) use this data segment only to address data in the memory with an offset. The Pentium can only change this setting with a so-called segment override using another (extra) segment. By using DS as a standard data segment, the program code is more compact, because not every applicable data segment is given for each instruction.

Stack segment SS

The stack segment contains data that can be addressed with stack instructions such as PUSH, POP, PUSHALL and so on. The stack forms a special section in the memory, normally used for a CPU return address. In addition, the so-called local variable or local data of procedures is normally stored on the stack. When a procedure is finished, the segment will be overwritten by a new procedure.

The stack instructions use the value of SS to store data on, or read data from, the stack. Note that the storing of data on the stack (for example, with the instruction PUSH EAX) automatically results in the reduction of the ESP stack pointer, corresponding to the size of the stored data. In this way, the PUSH EAX instruction reduces the value of ESP by four. Consequently, the stack 'grows' from higher to lower memory addresses.

Extra segments ES, FS and GS

The extra segments and their registers are used mainly for string instructions. ES, FS and GS can also be used to address data not contained in the standard data segment (DS) because of the method of segment override. Using DOS and the IBM BIOS of the personal computer, ES is frequently used as a segment indication of a buffer at the start of a function.

Thus, there are four data segments available to the Pentium: the DS as a standard data segment and the three extra segments ES, FS and GS. The six segment registers play a considerable part in all three operating modes for organizing and addressing the memory.

8.2.2 The EFlags

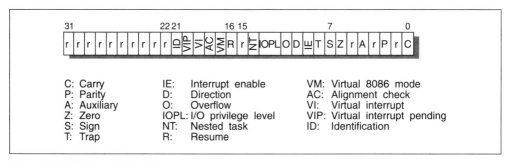

Figure 8.4: The EFlags of the Pentium.
The Pentium comprises several flags that indicate the result of the previous operation or the current processor status.

In advance of conditional jumps or branches that are necessary for the logical structure of a program, a logical comparison of two quantities (the checking of a condition) is usually processed, as the word 'condition' implies. The flag register is of greater importance in this context; the specific flags are set (flag equal to 1) or reset (flag equal to 0) depending on the result of the comparison. In addition, some instructions, such as ADC (addition and carry), set and reset specific flags. They also indicate the current processor status and control the identification of maskable interrupts and other reactions of the Pentium. They are known as EFlags because only the lower value 16-bit flags were available to the 8086. They are shown in Figure 8.4.

Next, I would briefly like to introduce each of the Pentium flags. The list also indicates in which processor each flag was originally implemented.

C, carry (8086)

Carry is set if the execution of an i386 instruction produces a carry or a borrow for the destination operand. This is the case during a 32-bit addition if the sum of two 32-bit numbers produces a result greater than 4G-1. Carry is set by the STC (set carry) instruction, reset by the CLC (clear carry) instruction and complemented with the CMC (complement carry) instruction.

P, parity (8086)

Parity is set if the result of an operation has an even number of set bits. Parity is set exclusively by the processor – an explicit set or reset through software is not possible.

A, auxiliary carry (8086)

The auxiliary carry flag is used and set by arithmetic operation of binary coded decimal (BCD) values, if an operation produces a carry or borrow for the four least significant bits of an operand (the BCD values use only the lower four bits of a byte, see Section 1.3.5).

Z, zero (8086)

Zero is set by the processor in case the result of an operation is zero. An example of this would be the subtraction of two numbers with the same value, or the bit logic AND with a value of zero.

S, sign (8086)

Sign equals the most significant bit of the result of an operation (0 = positive, 1 = negative result) and so is only of significance for signed numbers. Sign is important for comparison operations because, in general, the result is the difference between the two numbers. Sign is then set or reset by the Pentium, depending on the result of the subtraction.

T, trap (8086)

When trap is set, the processor issues an interrupt 1 by itself after every step. Trap belongs to the exceptions class. Real-mode debuggers use trap mainly in order to run a program step by step: they use the interrupt to check the individual steps of a program. Trap can not be set or reset by a specific instruction. This is only possible, in a roundabout way, with the use of the

PUSHF (put the flags onto the stack) and POPF (write the flags on the stack back to the flag register) instructions. PUSHF puts the flags onto the stack, where they are manipulated. These altered flags – that is, after setting trap – are then written back to the flag register by the POPF instruction.

IE, interrupt enable (8086)

If the IE flag is set, the Pentium recognizes hardware interrupt requests; in other words, it reacts to an active signal at the INTR (interrupt request) input. This leads to an INTA (interrupt acknowledge) sequence with the interrupt controller. Unlike trap, this flag can be explicitly reset with the CLI instruction and set with the STI instruction. Interrupts must be blocked for applications that do not allow interrupts. An excessively long interruption can cause problems for realtime applications (it is possible for received bytes to be lost at the serial port interface). Normally, the operating system should change this flag. This applies mainly to the multitasking environment.

D, direction (8086)

The direction flag sets the direction of string operations with the REP prefix (such as REP MOVS). If the direction flag is set, character strings are worked from higher to lower addresses; otherwise, from lower to higher addresses. You can explicitly set the direction flag with STD and explicitly reset with CLD.

O, overflow (8086)

The Pentium sets the overflow flag, if the result of an operation is too large or too small for the format of the target operand.

IOPL, I/O protection level (80286)

This 2-bit flag defines the minimum necessary protection level that a task needs to access the I/O address space during protected mode operation. Typically, this is controlled by the operating system, and so the IOPL flag is controlled in most cases by the operating system (OS/2, UNIX and so on). The flag has no use in real mode. More information on the protection of I/O address spaces is given in Section 11.3.10.

NT, nested task (80286)

A multitasking operating system uses nested task in protected mode in order to know whether several tasks are loaded and, at the same time, whether a task has been interrupted. Explained in another way, a set NT flag means that at least one task switch has been performed and that there is an inactive task state segment (TSS) in the memory. The back link entry in the active TSS then points to the TSS of the previously interrupted task.

R, resume (i386)

The resume flag controls the restarting of a task after a breakpoint interrupt through the debug register of the Pentium. When resume is set, the Pentium debug tasks are temporarily disabled. This means that the task can be resumed at the breakpoint, without a new debug exception error occurring (the Pentium would otherwise go into a breakpoint exception/resume loop when it encountered a breakpoint).

VM, virtual 8086 mode (i386)

You can switch the Pentium into the virtual 8086 mode by setting the VM flag. This is only possible in protected mode, and then only through a gate. If the VM flag is later reset, the Pentium returns to normal protected mode. VM has no significance and no effect in real mode. For the acceleration of interrupt handling in virtual 8086 mode, the two additional VIF and VIP flags have been implemented in the Pentium (see below). In real mode, the VM flag has no use (and therefore no effect).

AC, alignment check (i486)

If the AC flag is set, the Pentium issues an exception and the corresponding interrupt 17 (11h) if an alignment error occurs. The alignment check only affects programs with a privilege level of 3, misalignments are ignored in programs with the privilege levels 0 to 2. Alignment errors occur with word accesses to an odd address, double word accesses to addresses that are not multiples of four, or 8-byte accesses to addresses that are not multiples of eight. The alignment check has been implemented for multiprocessing with processors that require an alignment of data and code, examples of which are the i860 and other RISC processors that use a uniform instruction or data format (for example, the 32-bit principle).

VI, virtual interrupt (Pentium)

The VI flag is a virtual version of IE for the sending of interrupts in virtual 8086 mode.

VIP, virtual interrupt pending (Pentium)

The VIP flag works together with the VI flag, so that each task in virtual 8086 mode can have its own virtual version of the IE flag. In this way, interrupts are considerably accelerated and the CLI and STI instructions no longer lead to an exception.

ID, identification (Pentium)

The ID flag indicates whether the processor supports the CPUID instruction for its identification. If you can set and reset the ID flag, then CPUID will be carried out correctly and will deliver information concerning the type and functional capabilities of the processor.

The special significance of the flag register comes from the fact that all instructions for specific branches, more or less check the extensive combinations of the flags, which are set or reset by the processor as a result of the normal predetermined comparison instructions.

Example: If the value in register AX is equal to 5, the program shall branch to HOLDRIUM:

```
CMP ax, 5      ; compare register AX with value 5
JZ HOLDRIUM    ; jump to HOLDRIUM
```

Firstly, the processor carries out the comparison CMP ax, 5 in which the value 5 is subtracted from AX and the applicable flags are set. In the previous example, 5 is subtracted from the value of the AX register and the zero flag set, if the result is equal to zero (AX contains the value 5). If, however, AX is greater than 5 (the result of the subtraction is greater than zero), the Pentium resets the sign and zero flags (sign = 0, zero = 0). If AX is smaller than 5 (the result of the subtraction is less than zero), zero is set to 0 and sign is set to 1 (negative result). Complicated branch instructions, such as JBE (jump if below or equal), test several flags simultaneously (in this example, sign and zero) to determine if the jump conditions have been met.

8.2.3 The control registers CR0 to CR4

The Pentium contains five separate control registers and four memory management registers for the protected mode, and eight debug registers. The control and debug registers are all 32-bit. In Figure 8.5 you can see the structure of the control registers CR0 to CR4.

Control register CR0

The control register CR0 contains eleven entries that are, in part, already implemented in the 80286 to i486. The list shows in which processor the field is already implemented.

The *machine status word (MSW)*, known from the 80286 for supporting the 16-bit protected mode of the 80286, is located in the lower value word of the CR0 control register. The TS, EM, MP and PE bits are the same as in the 80286. On compatibility grounds, the lower value MSW of the CR0 register continues to use the 80286 instructions LMSW (load MSW) and SMSW (store MSW). These are, more or less, a form of sub-instruction of the MOV CR0, value instruction, or MOV value, CR0, respectively.

```
Example: The i386 shall be switched into protected mode by setting the PE bit in CR0.
1st possibility:   MOV CR0, 0001h ; set PE bit by MOV instruction with 32-bit operand;
2nd possibility:   LMSW 01h       ; set PE bit by LMSW instruction with 16-bit operand.
```

PE, protection enable (80286)

If you set this bit, the Pentium switches into protected mode. Resetting with the MOV CR0, value instruction with CPL=0 will switch the Pentium back to real mode.

MP, monitor coprocessor (80286)

If the MP bit is set, then a WAIT instruction can issue the 'no coprocessor available' exception, which leads to an interrupt 7. MP is used for synchronization between the CPU and the floating-point unit before the Pentium. In the Pentium, MP should be set.

EM, emulate coprocessor (80286)

If the MP bit is set, then an ESC instruction generates the 'no coprocessor available' exception leading to an interrupt 7. The handler can then emulate floating-point instructions. This only applies to the i386 or the i486SX, neither of which has a floating-point unit. In the Pentium (and also the i486DX), the EM bit should be reset, because a floating-point unit is integrated.

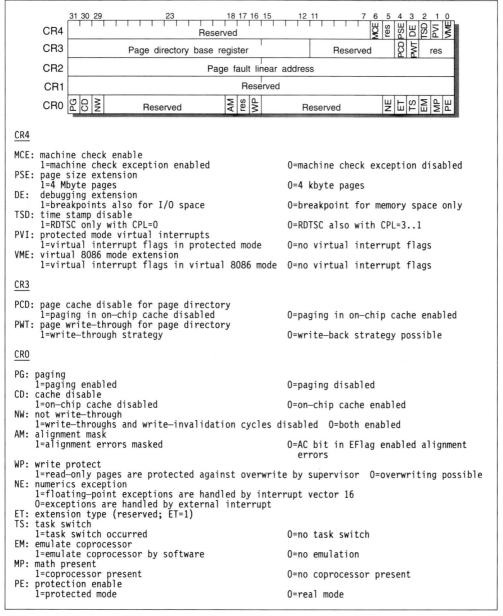

CR4

MCE: machine check enable
    1=machine check exception enabled   0=machine check exception disabled
PSE: page size extension
    1=4 Mbyte pages   0=4 kbyte pages
DE: debugging extension
    1=breakpoints also for I/O space   0=breakpoint for memory space only
TSD: time stamp disable
    1=RDTSC only with CPL=0   0=RDTSC also with CPL=3..1
PVI: protected mode virtual interrupts
    1=virtual interrupt flags in protected mode   0=no virtual interrupt flags
VME: virtual 8086 mode extension
    1=virtual interrupt flags in virtual 8086 mode   0=no virtual interrupt flags

CR3

PCD: page cache disable for page directory
    1=paging in on–chip cache disabled   0=paging in on–chip cache enabled
PWT: page write–through for page directory
    1=write–through strategy   0=write–back strategy possible

CR0

PG: paging
    1=paging enabled   0=paging disabled
CD: cache disable
    1=on–chip cache disabled   0=on–chip cache enabled
NW: not write–through
    1=write–throughs and write–invalidation cycles disabled   0=both enabled
AM: alignment mask
    1=alignment errors masked   0=AC bit in EFlag enabled alignment
                                                 errors
WP: write protect
    1=read–only pages are protected against overwrite by supervisor   0=overwriting possible
NE: numerics exception
    1=floating–point exceptions are handled by interrupt vector 16
    0=exceptions are handled by external interrupt
ET: extension type (reserved; ET=1)
TS: task switch
    1=task switch occurred   0=no task switch
EM: emulate coprocessor
    1=emulate coprocessor by software   0=no emulation
MP: math present
    1=coprocessor present   0=no coprocessor present
PE: protection enable
    1=protected mode   0=real mode

Figure 8.5: The structure of the control registers CR0 to CR4.

TS, task switch (80286)

If this bit is set, a task switch has occurred; in protected mode, the Pentium has run into a task gate at least once. The TS bit is important for determining whether the coprocessor is working on an additional instruction for the old task, or has already started with the newly activated task. The CLTS instruction directly resets the TS bit – in other words, it is not necessary to use the indirect MOV CR0, value method.

ET, extension type (Pentium)

In the i486, the ET bit always equals 1. It indicates that i387 coprocessor instructions are supported. In the Pentium, this bit is also reserved (=1).

NE, numeric error (i486)

The NE bit controls the behaviour of the Pentium when a non-masked numerical exception occurs. If the NE bit is set, the exception is handled through interrupt 16; the Pentium issues an interrupt 16. This is the standard procedure for the Pentium. If, on the other hand, NE is reset (equals 0), the exception is dealt with by an external hardware interrupt handler, because of the need for compatibility with other PC systems. The signals $\overline{\text{IGNNE}}$ and $\overline{\text{FERR}}$ are used for this purpose. If the $\overline{\text{IGNNE}}$ input receives an inactive signal with a high level, and a floating-point error occurs, the processor stops the program execution and activates the $\overline{\text{FERR}}$ signal. An external interrupt controller can use this signal and can send out a hardware interrupt request through the INTR pin of the Pentium. The controller gives the vector of the applicable handler to the Pentium. In PCs, $\overline{\text{FERR}}$ is identical to IRQ13, and so an interrupt 75h is generated.

WP, write protect (i486)

With the WP bit, you can protect pages that are designated as read-only (write protected) from being overwritten by a supervisor; that is, a program with a privilege level of 0 to 2. In the i386 on the other hand, such read-only pages can, in principle, be overwritten. With the WP bit, it is possible to protect data sections, in units of a page, from being overwritten. The protection mechanism of protected mode only protects complete segments and not parts of segments. Operating systems with flat memory models such as UNIX, for example, make use of this in order to emulate segment protection in the segmented memory model, for protection at page level.

AM, alignment mask (i486)

Through the AM bit, you can determine whether the AC bit in the EFlag register can generate an alignment exception and the corresponding interrupt 17. A set AM bit permits exceptions; a reset AM bit masks the AC flag. The AM bit has higher priority than the AC flag. Note that an alignment exception is only issued if CPL=3; misalignments are ignored for CPL=0 to CPL=2, despite the AM and AC bits being set.

NW, not write-through (i486)

With the help of the NW bit, you can control the write operations for the activated on-chip data cache. If the NW bit is reset, all write data is also sent out through the pins – that is, written to the main memory or an L2 cache – thus, a write-through is carried out independently of whether a cache hit or miss occurs. In addition, invalidation cycles are permitted, in which an entry is deleted from the cache if the invalidation address causes a cache hit. If NW is set (equals 1), all write-throughs and write invalidation cycles are disabled. If this is the case, the data is not 'written through' to the memory – the value is only located in the internal cache and not transferred to the main memory; no signal appears at the pins. This enables a write-back strategy. Invalidation cycles are ignored if the NW bit is set.

CD, cache disable (i486)

The CD bit controls the operating mode of the two on-chip caches. In principle, if the CD bit is set, the code and data caches are not refilled after a cache miss, thus, cache line fills are disabled. Note that despite this, cache hits can occur. In order to completely disable the on-chip caches, you must set the CD bit and, additionally, carry out a cache invalidation. Whether the addressed value is actually transferred to the cache, following a cache miss with active caches (CD=0), does not depend on CD alone, it also depends on the signal at the $\overline{\text{KEN}}$ pin and the PCD bit in the page table entry for the applicable page in which the data lies. Only when all three values equal 0 is code or data transferred to the applicable cache, when a cache miss occurs.

PG, paging enable (i386)

With the PG bit, you can enable (PG=1), or disable (PG=0) the PU in the MMU of the Pentium. With the PU disabled, the Pentium will not perform any address translations; the linear address, after addition of offset and segment base, automatically represents the physical address of the memory object.

On the other hand, with an active PU the Pentium carries out a further address translation in addition to the segmentation, in order to produce the physical address from the linear address. Paging can only be used in protected mode. The control registers CR2 and CR3 only have an effect if the PG bit is set.

Control register CR1

The control register CR1 is reserved and currently has no use.

Control register CR2

After a page fault (for example, the page stored externally and marked as not present in the page table entry), the control register stores the linear address of the instruction that caused the page fault. In this way, the program execution can be restarted with this instruction, after the externally stored page has been transferred to memory.

Control register CR3

With an active paging unit, the Pentium stores the 20 most significant bits of the page directory address – that is, the first level page table, in the control register CR3. Additionally, two further entries (PWT and PCD) are included.

PWT, page write-through (i486)

If paging is active, the PWT bit is sent from the PWT output of the Pentium for all cycles that do not require paging (for example, INTA sequences or TLB updates). For cycles that do require paging, the PWT pin sends out the value of the PWT bit in the page table entry. Through PWT, the strategy of an L2 cache can also be controlled on a cycle basis, if non-paged cycles are performed.

PCD, page cache disable (i486)

The PCD bit is similar to the PWT bit described above. If paging is enabled, the PCD bit is sent from the PWT output of the Pentium for all cycles that do not require paging. As above, for cycles that do require paging, the PCD pin sends out the value of the PCD bit in the page table entry.

Control register CR4

The control register CR4, newly implemented in the Pentium, supports the extensions for the virtual 8086 mode and other different properties. For this, six control bits have been included, which I would like to explain in the following text.

VME, virtual 8086 mode extension (Pentium)

A set VME bit enables the support of virtual interrupt flags in virtual 8086 mode. In this way, interrupts are executed quicker, and the performance in virtual 8086 mode increases. The virtual 8086 monitor is then no longer required. The associated task switches are unnecessary.

PVI, protected mode virtual interrupts (Pentium)

In protected mode, the PVI bit has a similar purpose to the VME bit in virtual 8086 mode. A set PVI bit enables the supporting of virtual interrupt flags in protected mode. In this way, programs that were originally designed for execution with CPL=0 can, under certain circumstances, be executed with CPL=3. In particular, CLI and STI do not send out the exception 0dh, they only change the VIF flag in the EFlag register and no longer the IE flag, which now determines the response of the Pentium to external hardware interrupt requests.

TSD, time stamp disable (Pentium)

By setting the TSD bit, the RDTSC instruction that reads the value of the time stamp counter becomes a so-called privileged instruction. It can then only be executed with CPL=0, without generating a protection exception.

DE, debugging extension (Pentium)

If you also want to cover the I/O address space with breakpoints, you must set the DE bit to the value 1. The Pentium then interprets the 10b combination of the R/W_x bits (invalid in the i386/i486) as a breakpoint for I/O write and I/O read accesses.

PSE, page size extension (Pentium)

With the help of PSE, you can set the size of a page to be managed by the PU. A set PSE bit sets the page size at 4 Mbytes; with a reset PSE bit, the PU will use the standard page size of 4 kbytes.

MCE, machine check enable (Pentium)

By setting the MCE bit, you enable the machine check exception. You will find more on this subject in Section 13.6.

8.2.4 The debug registers DR0 to DR7

Debugging in a multitasking environment is a very difficult matter because a program has to be checked while breakpoints, changes in registers and other influences on the debugger are being executed. Real-mode debuggers frequently write bytes to specific breakpoints with the code 11001100 for the INT 3 instruction. When the program reaches such a breakpoint, the processor produces an interrupt 3, which the debugger intercepts. In order to continue the program execution, the debugger overwrites the code 11001100 with the byte previously located at the applicable breakpoint.

In the protected mode of the Pentium, this is no longer possible, because it is, in principle, impossible to write to the code segments. The debugger can neither replace the old byte with the opcode 11001100 of INT 3, nor can it undo the replacement in order to continue with the program execution, without producing a protection error. A further serious disadvantage of the real mode strategy is that it is not possible to access a specific data area. For determining wild pointers in a program (a frequently occurring bug, especially in C programs) this would be a great advantage. A Pentium in protected mode usually operates in a multitasking environment, in which other tasks are also active besides the debugger. This is why the debugger must be considerably more aware of what possible direct influence it can have on the computer (including the consequences of overwriting specific program code). Therefore, hardware support for the debugger is necessary.

In the Pentium, this is achieved with eight debug registers (DR0 to DR7), each of 32 bits. They support debuggers at the hardware level in both protected and virtual 8086 modes. Their structure, as shown in Figure 8.6, is identical to the debug registers in the i386/i486. Only the R/W_x bits are extended by the 10b combination. The 10b combination is enabled by setting the DE bit in the CR4 control register. In the i386 and i486, this combination was reserved; that is, invalid.

if 1, then the cause of the debug exception was a result of an instruction access in a debug register

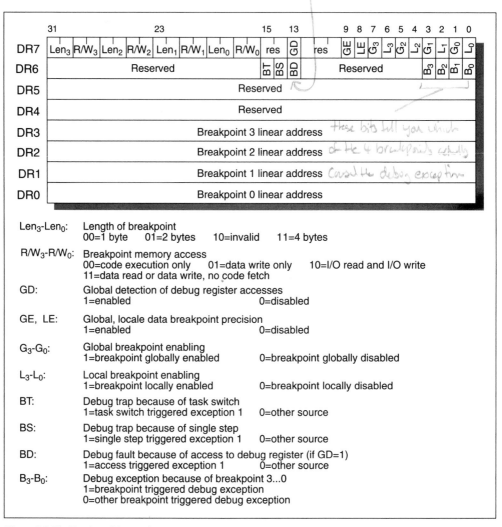

these bits tell you which of the 4 breakpoints actually caused the debug exception

Len$_3$-Len$_0$:   Length of breakpoint
00=1 byte   01=2 bytes   10=invalid   11=4 bytes

R/W$_3$-R/W$_0$:   Breakpoint memory access
00=code execution only   01=data write only   10=I/O read and I/O write
11=data read or data write, no code fetch

GD: Global detection of debug register accesses
1=enabled   0=disabled

GE, LE: Global, locale data breakpoint precision
1=enabled   0=disabled

G$_3$-G$_0$:   Global breakpoint enabling
1=breakpoint globally enabled   0=breakpoint globally disabled

L$_3$-L$_0$:   Local breakpoint enabling
1=breakpoint locally enabled   0=breakpoint locally disabled

BT: Debug trap because of task switch
1=task switch triggered exception 1   0=other source

BS: Debug trap because of single step
1=single step triggered exception 1   0=other source

BD: Debug fault because of access to debug register (if GD=1)
1=access triggered exception 1   0=other source

B$_3$-B$_0$:   Debug exception because of breakpoint 3...0
1=breakpoint triggered debug exception
0=other breakpoint triggered debug exception

Figure 8.6: The Pentium debug registers.

In the following paragraphs I would like to briefly explain the register entries. If you require more information about this specialized hardware aspect of the Pentium, please refer to a more specific programming handbook for the Pentium.

You can define four breakpoints. Their linear addresses (that is, the address after the addition of offset and segment base, but without paging) is stored in the debug address registers DR0 to DR3. The two debug registers DR4 and DR5 are reserved in the Pentium for future use. The entries in the debug control and status registers DR6 and DR7 control the behaviour of the Pentium if the instruction execution meets a breakpoint. The entries R/W$_0$ to R/W$_3$ define, for each breakpoint independently, when the Pentium issues a debug exception, leading to an interrupt 1. With a set DE bit, you can choose between instruction execution, data reading and writing and also I/O accesses. For the R/W_x bits, the following interpretations can occur, if the DE bit in the CR4 control register equals 1:

▶ 00b: Stop only for instruction execution (instruction fetching)

▶ 01b: Stop only for data write accesses to memory

▶ 10b: Stop for I/O read and I/O write accesses

▶ 11b: Stop for data read and write accesses, but not instruction fetching

If the DE bit is reset, the 10b value is invalid; for R/W_x, you can only use 00b, 01b or 11b. The entries LEN_0 to LEN_3 define, for each breakpoint separately, the extent of the breakpoint area. You can globally enable the breakpoints with the bits G_0 to G_3; the Pentium then sends out a debug exception if any task refers to the specified memory position. This is useful if you want to check the interaction of a number of tasks in a multitasking environment. On the other hand, the bits L_0 to L_3 enable the breakpoints locally; the Pentium then sends out a debug exception, only when a specific task (usually the one loaded into the debugger) refers to the specified memory position.

The bits GD, BT, BS, BD and B_3 to B_0 indicate the source of a debug exception. A set GD bit leads to a debug exception if an instruction attempts to access a debug register. The GD bit is always reset when the exception handler is called, so the handler has access to all of the debug registers. The three bits BT, BS and BD indicate the source of a debug exception. If a task switch to a task occurs, in which the T bit in the TSS is set, then the Pentium sets the BT bit (breakpoint task switch) to 1. If the T flag is set, then the Pentium generates a debug exception after every instruction and sets BS (breakpoint single step) in order to indicate the cause. A set BD bit indicates that the accesses to the debug register are blocked by the GD bit, and that an instruction has attempted to access the debug register. Finally, the four breakpoint assigned bits B3 to B0 indicate the actual breakpoint that caused the debug exception.

8.2.5 The memory management registers

Besides the control and debug registers, the Pentium has four memory management registers (Figure 8.7). They operate as memory managers and divide the memory into segments during protected mode.

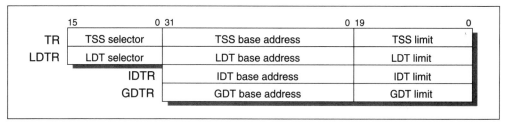

	15 0	31 0	19 0
TR	TSS selector	TSS base address	TSS limit
LDTR	LDT selector	LDT base address	LDT limit
IDTR		IDT base address	IDT limit
GDTR		GDT base address	GDT limit

Figure 8.7: The Pentium memory management registers.

8.2.6 The test register

The test registers TR6 and TR7 for checking the TLB are implemented in the Pentium as part of the model specific register. The test registers are described in Chapter 13 in conjunction with the applicable test functions.

8.2.7 The model-specific registers

The model-specific registers of the Pentium consist of the machine check address register, the machine check type register, the test registers TR1 to TR12, the time stamp counter, the control/event select register, and the two counters 0 and 1. For accesses to these registers, the two new instructions RDMSR (read model-specific register) and WRMSR (write model-specific register) have been implemented. The RDMSR instruction has the format shown in Table 8.1.

Register	Call value	Return value
RDMSR:		
EAX		MSR content (low-order double word)
ECX	MSR number	
EDX		MSR content (high-order double word)
WRMSR:		
EAX		MSR content (low-order double word)
ECX	MSR number	
EDX		MSR content (high-order double word)

MSR, model-specific register.

Table 8.1: Format of instructions RDMSR and WRMSR.

The three model specific registers have the MSR numbers shown in Table 8.2.

Model-specific register	MSR number	Used for
Machine check address register	00h	Physical address of erroneous bus cycle
Machine check type register	01h	Type of erroneous bus cycle
TR12	0eh	Control register for branch trace message special cycle
Time stamp counter	10h	Read/write of internal 64-bit counter

The other MSR numbers are reserved by Intel for test registers TR1 to TR11 as well as the control and status registers of the performance monitoring feature.

Table 8.2: Numbers of the model-specific registers.

The Intel model-specific registers are used in this way only in the Pentium. Possibly, in future processors of the 80x86 family and in Pentium derivatives such as the Pentium overdrive and so on they will no longer be implemented, or at least not in the same way. All model-specific registers are 64 bits wide. Figure 13.2 shows the structure of the machine check type register.

The test register TR12 is explained in Section 13.4; its structure is shown in Figure 13.3. The test registers TR6 and TR7 support the testing of the TLBs. The other test registers are used to check the other internal components.

Note that the RDMSR instruction, together with the target time counter, has the same effect as the RDTSC instruction (read time stamp counter). RDTSC, however, is a self-standing instruction, which is independent of the actual implementation of the time stamp counter; as the model-specific register 10h, it is also available for future processor generations. As the RDMSR signal requires a longer execution time than the RDTSC instruction, you should use RDTC wherever possible. In addition, RDMSR is only executable in protected mode with CPL=0; RDTSC, on the other hand, can be used by applications with CPL=3..1, providing that the TSD bit in the CR4 control register is reset.

8.2.8 The registers of the floating-point unit

There are many individual general-purpose registers (EAX, EBX and so on) as well as segment registers (CS, DS and SS) that are available for access in the Pentium's integer core. The floating-point unit, though, has a register stack containing eight 80-bit registers (R1 to R8) as well as various control and status registers (Figure 8.8).

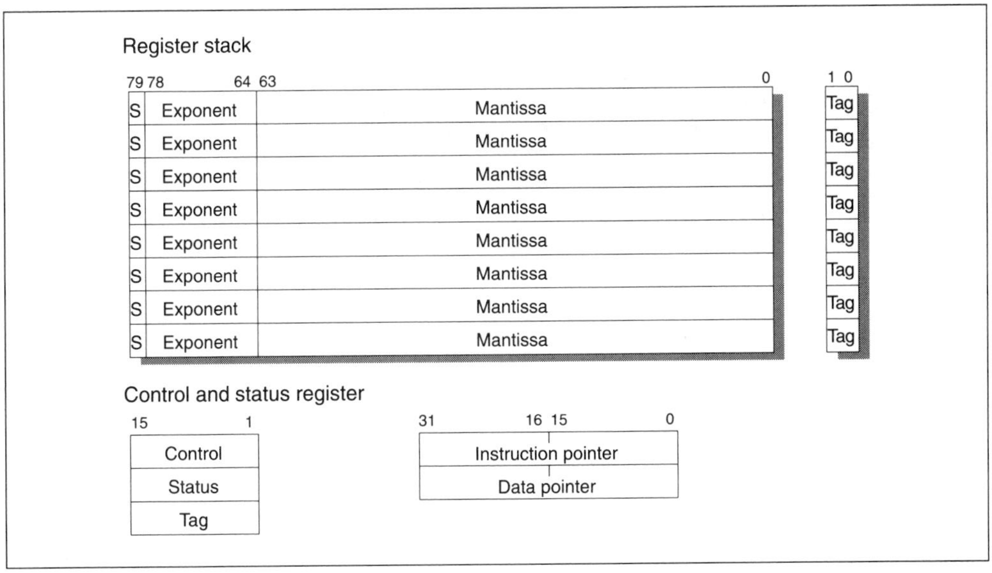

Figure 8.8: Internal Pentium floating-point registers.

The eight data registers correspond to the temporary real format and each is divided into three sections: sign S, 15-bit exponent and 64-bit mantissa. They are organized as a stack and not as individual registers. The 3-bit field (TOP) in the status word (Figure 8.9) shows the current 'Top' register. TOP has similar qualities and tasks to those of the stack pointer ESP. These can, via floating-point instructions such as FLD (floating load and push) and FSTP (floating store and pop), which are similar to the integer instructions PUSH and POP, reduce TOP by 1 and place a value in its respective register or increase TOP by 1 and take off the applicable stack register.

The stack increases downwards to register smaller numbers. Most instructions implicitly address the top register in the stack; that is, the register with the stored number in the TOP field of the status register. You can also explicitly specify a register with many floating-point instructions. Note that the explicitly specified register is not absolute but relative to TOP.

Example: FLD st(3) addresses the third register, but which of registers R0 to R7 is actually accessed depends on TOP. If, for example, TOP is equal to 5 then register 2 is accessed. If TOP is equal to 1, then FLD st(3) means an invalid operation because the register R(-2) does not exist. The i387 reports an error.

Information relating to the current floating-point condition is held in the status word. The Pentium can write the status word to memory using the instructions FSTSW/FNSTSW (store status word) or into the AX register with FSTSW AX (implemented from the i486 onwards). The Pentium can then examine the status word in order to determine, for example, the cause of an exception.

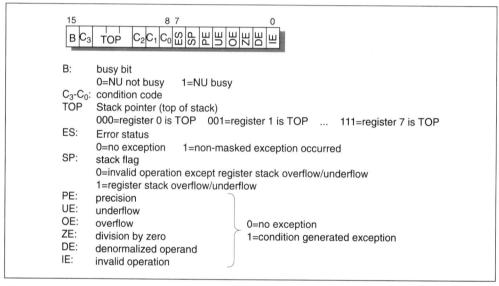

Figure 8.9: Format of the floating-point status word.

The B bit is only partly available due to compatibility with the 8087 and is always equal to the ES bit. On no account does B produce any data with regard to the condition of the numeric unit and therefore the pin $\overline{\text{BUSY}}$. The Pentium error status is indicated by the ES bit. If ES is set, then an unmasked exception occurred, the cause of which is given by bits SP to IE. Bit SP is used to differentiate between invalid operations caused by register stack underflow or overflow and invalid operations with other causes. If *SP* is set and an underflow or overflow of the stack register has occurred, then, with the help of bit C_1, it is possible to differentiate between an overflow ($C_1=1$) and an underflow ($C_1=0$). For an interpretation of the condition code C_3-C_0 of a comparison or similar operations, see Table 8.3. These are similar to the EFlags. Note that, in this relationship, the Pentium operates with two floating-point zeros. The three TOP bits form the stack pointer for the registers R7 to R0 located at the top.

Instruction type	C_3	C_2	C_1	C_0	Meaning
	0	0	x	0	TOP > operand (instruction FTST)
Compare	0	0	x	1	TOP < operand (instruction FTST)
Test	1	0	x	0	TOP = operand (instruction FTST)
	1	1	x	1	TOP cannot be compared
Investigate	0	0	0	0	Valid, positive, denormalized
	0	0	0	1	Invalid, positive, exponent=0 (+NAN)
	0	0	1	0	Valid, negative, denormalized
	0	0	1	1	Invalid, negative, exponent=0 (−NAN)
	0	1	0	0	Valid, positive, normalized
	0	1	0	1	Infinite, positive (+∞)
	0	1	1	0	Valid, negative, normalized
	0	1	1	1	Infinite, negative (−∞)
	1	0	0	0	Zero, positive (+0)
	1	0	0	1	Not used
	1	0	1	0	Zero, negative (−0)
	1	0	1	1	Not used
	1	1	0	0	Invalid, positive, exponent=0 (+ denormalized)
	1	1	0	1	Not used
	1	1	1	0	Invalid, negative, exponent=0 (− denormalized)
	1	1	1	1	Not used

Table 8.3: Pentium floating-point condition codes.

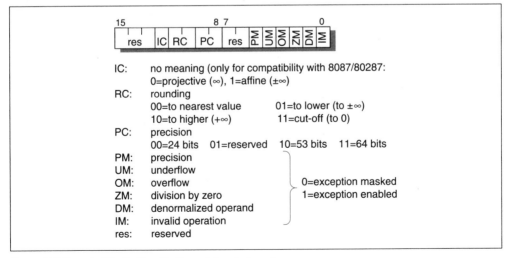

IC: no meaning (only for compatibility with 8087/80287:
       0=projective (∞), 1=affine (±∞)
RC: rounding
       00=to nearest value   01=to lower (to ±∞)
       10=to higher (+∞)   11=cut-off (to 0)
PC: precision
       00=24 bits   01=reserved   10=53 bits   11=64 bits
PM: precision
UM: underflow
OM: overflow   0=exception masked
ZM: division by zero   1=exception enabled
DM: denormalized operand
IM: invalid operation
res: reserved

Figure 8.10: Format of the Pentium floating-point control word.

Under certain circumstances, the Pentium produces a coprocessor exception. These exceptions can be individually masked. What is more, you can determine different modes for rounding and precision. The control word is used for this purpose, the structure of which is shown in Figure 8.10.

In the Pentium, the IC bit has no purpose when handling infinite dimensions, because the Pentium complies strictly to the IEEE standard when handling floating-point numbers. On the grounds of compatibility with the 8087 and the 80287 the IC bit is available but has no effect. The Pentium always handles infinite quantities in the affine sense of ±∞, even if you set IC to 0. The two RC bits control the rounding in the defined way. The accuracy of the calculations is set by the PC bits, in order to achieve compatibility with the older coprocessors from the 8-bit era. PC only has an effect on the result of the ADD, SUB, MUL, DIV and SQRT instructions.

The remaining control word bits PM, UM, OM, ZM, DM and IM control the generation of an exception and the resulting interrupt. Altogether, the Pentium uses six different floating-point exceptions. You can mask the exceptions individually using bits PM, UM, OM, ZM, DM and IM. The Pentium then executes a standard routine to deal with the respective errors using a so-called standard on-chip exception handler. This is an integral part of the chip.

There is a further available status register, the *tag word*. Its construction is shown in Figure 8.11. Tag_7–Tag_0 contain information, that identifies the contents of the eight data registers R7–R0. The coprocessor uses this information to perform certain operations at an increased speed. Using this process, the Pentium can very quickly determine empty and non-empty stack registers or determine certain values such as NAN, infinity and so on without the need to decode the value from the respective register. Using the FSTENV/FNSTENV (store environment state) instructions, you can store the tag word in memory and examine it.

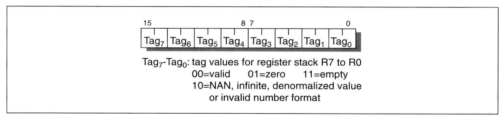

Figure 8.11: Format of the tag word.

8.3 The integer pipelines u and v

The Pentium, like the i486, uses RISC concepts to improve calculation performance. One of these is the implementation of instruction pipelining. While the i486 only contained a single instruction pipeline, the Pentium can call on two integer pipelines, they are known as the u pipeline and the v pipeline. Under certain conditions, they can operate in parallel and execute so-called paired instructions.

8.3.1 Pipeline structure

The two Pentium pipelines each contain five stages for instruction execution, namely instruction fetch (IF), decoding 1 (D1), decoding 2 (D2), execution (EX) with ALU and cache accesses, and register write-back (WB). The main pipeline u can carry out all instructions of the x86 architecture. This includes existing complex instructions in microcode format. The v pipeline, on the other hand, is used only for so-called simple integer instructions and the floating-point unit instruction FXCH. The grouping of instructions into instruction pairs and their parallel execution in both of the pipelines must conform to certain rules. These are explained in Section 8.4.1. In this Section, I would like to discuss the basic structure and the functioning of the two integer pipelines. Figure 8.12 shows the five-stage structure of the two integer pipelines. For the figure, it is optimistically supposed that instruction pairing is possible for every paired group of instructions and every clock cycle. Thus, for each cycle, two results leave the pipelines.

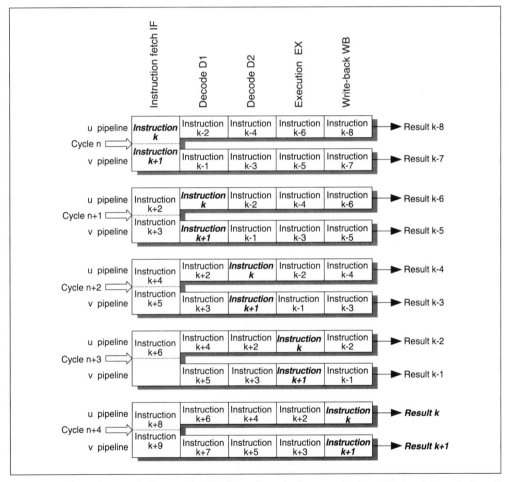

Figure 8.12: The two integer pipelines u and v. The figure shows the five-stage structure of the two integer pipelines. It is assumed that instruction pairing is possible for every two instructions and, therefore, in each clock cycle. Thus, with every clock cycle two results leave the pipelines.

The *instruction prefetch stage* IF, collects two instructions (one for each pipeline) from the on-chip code cache (cache hit) or from an external storage device (cache miss). The first stage contains two independent 32-byte prefetch buffers, only one of which is actually active, and fetches code, at any given time. The prefetch buffers work together with the BTB, in order to implement the dynamic branch prediction. More information on dynamic branch prediction is given in Section 8.7. The currently active prefetch buffer reads the instructions in a predefined sequence, and then passes then on to the decoders, until it reaches a branch (JMP, Jcc) or a call (CALL) instruction. At this point, the branch prediction logic becomes active, and, with the help of the stored entry in the branch target buffer, predicts whether the branch will actually be carried out (*taken branch*), or the instruction flow will be sequentially continued (*not taken branch*).

In the first case (*taken branch*), the currently active prefetch buffer is disabled, and the other prefetch buffer commences with the instruction fetching at the position that the BTB predicted. Thus, instruction fetching is continued as if the branch will actually be executed. At this point in time, other instructions – such as the instruction that calculated the branch condition for Jcc – find themselves in the pipeline at various stages of completion. However, it is not yet known whether the branch will actually be carried out; the Pentium will first determine this in the EX or WB stage (this is why it is a prediction). If the prediction is later found to be false, the Pentium pipeline is emptied, the incorrectly carried out instruction is deleted, and the other prefetch buffer continues the prefetching at the correct address.

The second stage of the Pentium pipeline, the *first decoding stage D1*, consists of two parallel working decoders, which both perform first stage decoding of the instructions passed on from the instruction prefetch stage. In this first D1 stage, the Pentium also determines whether the two *k* and *k+1* instructions are paired and, thus, whether the instructions can be executed in parallel in the u and v pipelines. The rules for this are explained in Section 8.4.1. If parallel execution is possible, then the first instruction *k* is loaded into the u pipeline, the sequentially following *k+1* instruction is then loaded into the v pipeline. The two instructions then run through this pipeline in parallel.

If the two instructions cannot be executed at the same time because one of the pairing rules has not been complied with, then only the first instruction *k* is loaded into the u pipeline. In the next cycle, the instruction prefetch stage only supplies the subsequent instruction *k+2*. The instruction decoding stage D1 then checks whether the pairing rules are fulfilled for the two instructions *k+1* and *k+2*.

Instruction prefixes are decoded in the instruction decoding stage D1 and passed on to the u pipeline. The pairing rules prevent prefixes – that is, apart from the 2-byte opcode prefix 0fh for the Jcc instruction – from being passed through the v pipeline. For each prefix, a processor clock cycle is necessary, so every prefix delays the execution of the proper instruction in the u pipeline by one cycle. After all prefixes have been loaded into the u pipeline, the proper instruction code is transferred, which then enables it to be paired with another instruction. All paired instructions must enter the D1 stage at the same time and must also exit the D1 stage at the same time. If necessary, the instruction in the u pipeline or the v pipeline is delayed until the instruction in the other pipeline can be transferred to the following D2 stage.

The *second instruction decoding stage D2* forms the third stage of the Pentium pipeline. Its purpose is to determine operand addresses. In the Pentium, unlike the i486 pipeline, instructions with an immediate operand and a displacement (such as ADD [array], 08h), and also instructions with base and simultaneous index addressing (such as MOV dword ptr

[ebp][edi], value), can be executed in the D2 stage in a single clock cycle. The i486 requires two clock cycles for this. As in the D1 stage, all paired instructions must both enter and exit the D2 stage together. Correspondingly, all 'quicker' instructions in the u pipeline, or the v pipeline must be suitably delayed when necessary. The D2 stage also performs the segment access checks in protected mode.

The *execution stage EX*, the fourth pipeline stage, deals with all occurring ALU and cache accesses, in order to perform all ALU operations, and to load memory operands from the cache. Instructions with an ALU and a cache access, such as ADD eax, mem32 (ALU access: ADD, cache access: mem32), require more than one clock cycle in this stage. The execution stage also checks branch predictions for all instructions in the u pipeline, and all instructions in the v pipeline with the exception of conditional jumps. Conditional jumps in the v pipeline are first verified in the WB stage. Here also, as in the D1 and D2 stages, paired instructions must enter the execution stage at the same time, but it is not absolutely necessary that they leave it together. Instructions in the u pipeline can overtake those in the v pipeline, but not the other way round. Thus, u pipeline instructions in the EX stage are never delayed; a v pipeline instruction is only delayed when it will be executed quicker than the instruction in the u pipeline. If the instruction in the u pipeline has already left the EX stage and has entered the next WB stage, the EX stage cannot be refilled with the next instruction from the D2 stage. This is only possible when the paired instruction in the v pipeline has also entered the next WB stage.

The *write-back stage* WB writes back the result of the instruction to the register. It also writes back to the processor status and EFlag registers. In this way, the instruction execution is completed. In addition, branch predictions for conditional jumps of the v pipeline are checked for correctness; that is, the result of the branch instruction is simply compared to the prediction. Unlike the pipeline stages D1, D2 and EX, it is not necessary for paired instructions to enter the WB stage at the same time; the instruction in the u pipeline can enter the WB stage one or more clock cycles earlier. This does not affect the sequence of instructions: the instruction in the v pipeline immediately follows the u pipeline instruction in the sequential instruction flow.

8.3.2 Pipeline stalls

In the Pentium, pipeline stalls can be caused by a cache miss, if a memory operand should be loaded or written to. Above all, this affects the D2 and EX stages. It also applies to the loading of instructions, if the instruction itself is not found in the on-chip code cache. This occurs mostly with branches that are not stored in the BTB. This affects the IF stage. Additionally, it is possible that specific instructions – above all, complex micro-encoded instructions – require more than one clock cycle in a pipeline stage. This immediately leads to a pipeline stall for the subsequent instructions in the previous pipeline stage. Thus, the Pentium is far from the RISC concept of accomplishing a uniform instruction execution time. It must, however, also fulfil binary compatibility with the CISC instruction set of the i386. The microcode for complex instructions is laid out such that it can simultaneously use the two Pentium pipelines, thus executing a form of internal instruction pairing of elementary instructions. In this way, for example, string instructions with REP prefixes can be executed much more quickly than in the i486, firstly because both of the parallel pipelines can be used, and secondly because the 64-bit data bus is twice the width. A REP MOVSD can be emulated by repeating the following instruction:

```
MOV eax, [esi]
ADD esi, 04h
MOV [edi], eax
ADD edi, 04h
```

Here, the source and target addresses esi and edi, respectively, are ideally located in the on-chip data cache. The instructions MOV eax, [esi] and ADD esi, 04h, and also MOV [edi], eax and ADD edi, 04h can each be paired. Further optimization through the microcode, which can immediately address processor elements, leads to the fact that after the first transfer of a double word in the string, the transfer time is reduced to one cycle per double word.

8.3.3 Instruction pipelining and interrupts

Exceptions and software interrupts are recognized by the Pentium when the corresponding instruction is executed in the execution stage of the pipeline. All instructions already located in the following pipeline stages are completed. Instructions in the prefetch and decoding stages, on the other hand, are deleted. In the i386, which has no pipeline, the processor need not invalidate an instruction. The Pentium then jumps to the handling routine, either through the interrupt vector tables or through an interrupt gate.

On the other hand, external hardware interrupt requests are asynchronous and are triggered by a signal with the corresponding level at an interrupt input. For this, it is necessary for the Pentium to continually check the actual interrupt input. This always occurs when a new instruction is loaded into the execution stage EX. As with a software interrupt or an exception, the Pentium completes all instructions that are located in subsequent pipeline stages, and the instructions in the prefetch and decoding stages are deleted. Through the superscalar architecture of the Pentium, it is possible for two instructions to be located in parallel in the u and v pipelines when an interrupt occurs.

The interrupt is handled when the instructions in both pipelines have been completed. You can stop the sampling of the INTR input by resetting the IE interrupt flag; the Pentium then only recognizes the non maskable interrupt (NMI). In addition to the hardware interrupts known from the i386, the signals R/$\overline{\text{S}}$, $\overline{\text{FLUSH}}$, $\overline{\text{SMI}}$ and INIT are also implemented as interrupts. This means that the activation of these signals will possibly not lead to the immediate interruption of the program execution; this will occur only when the next instruction is loaded into the EX stage of the pipeline.

Instructions that remain in the EX stage for more than one cycle, and also pipeline stalls, cause a delay in the recognition of the interrupt. This is similar to the i386 without instruction pipelining. The i386 checks the interrupt inputs when it has executed an instruction. Due to the large variation in execution times of the various micro-encoded instructions, the average interrupt delay time is clearly more than one processor clock cycle. The difference between the i386 without a pipeline and the superscalar Pentium is that in the Pentium, an interrupt is recognized even though the previous instruction has not yet been completed. The i386, on the other hand, completely finishes every instruction before it checks whether there is an interrupt request. During the interrupt checking, no instructions are active.

If a number of interrupt requests occur simultaneously, the Pentium handles them in accordance with the following priorities:

R/S̄	Highest priority
FLUSH	
SMI	
INIT	
NMI	
INTR	Lowest priority

In Table 8.4, all of the exceptions are shown, along with the matching interrupt vectors. Some exceptions can occur as traps or faults; the saved instruction address then refers either to the instruction immediately following the error (trap) or to the instruction itself (fault). The abort 08h (double fault), switches the Pentium into shutdown mode, which it can only leave after an NMI or a reset.

Vector (hex)	Vector (decimal)	Meaning	Type	Real mode	Implemented from
0h	0	Division by zero	Fault	Yes	8086
1h	1	Debug (via trap flag or Breakpoint register)	Trap/ Fault	Yes	8086/i386
3h	3	Breakpoint via INT 3	Trap	Yes	8086
4h	4	Overflow detection with INTO	Trap	Yes	8086
5h	5	BOUND	Fault	Yes	80186
6h	6	Invalid opcode	Fault	Yes	8086
7h	7	No coprocessor present	Fault	Yes	8086
8h	8	Double error	Abort	Yes	80286
9h	9	Segment overflow coprocessor	Fault	Yes	80286
Ah	10	Invalid task state segment	Fault	No	80286
Bh	11	Segment not present	Fault	No	80286
Ch	12	Stack exception	Fault	Yes	80286
Dh	13	General protection fault	Trap/ Fault	Yes	80286
Eh	14	Page fault	Fault	No	i386
Fh	15	Reserved by Intel	—	—	—
10h	16	Coprocessor error	Fault	Yes	80286
11h	17	Alignment error	Fault	No	i486
12h	18	Machine check error	*	Yes	Pentium
13h–19h	19–31	Reserved by Intel	—	—	—
1ah–ffh	32–255	Maskable interrupts	—	Yes	8086
00h–ffh	0–255	Software interrupts via INTn	—	Yes	8086

* Model-specific.
Note: interrupt 02h handles an NMI.

Table 8.4: Pentium exceptions and interrupts.

In real mode, as previously in the i386 and i486, the first 1024 (1 k) bytes are reserved for the interrupt vector tables. Like its two 32-bit predecessors, the Pentium manages these tables, also in real mode, through the interrupt descriptor table register (IDTR), which is one of the memory management registers. It stores the base address and the limit of the real mode descriptor table. After a processor rest, the IDTR is loaded with the value 00000000h for the base and 03ffh for the limit. This corresponds exactly to a 1 kbyte table in segment 0000h at offset 0000h. With the help of the two LIDT (load IDTR) and SIDT (store IDTR) instructions, you can change this value and store the table with a different size, at a different position in the real mode address space. Note that the table can also store all of the vectors for the interrupts that can possibly occur. Otherwise, an exception 8 (double error) is the result.

8.4 Instruction pairing in the integer pipelines

For the simultaneous execution of two integer instructions, two instructions must be paired. The paired instructions are mostly executed within one clock cycle, so that through the superscalar architecture of the Pentium, two integer instructions can be completed in one clock cycle. In the instruction flow, the instruction of an instruction pair that is loaded into the v pipeline immediately follows the instruction loaded into the u pipeline; it is in fact a pair, and not just two instructions that are executed. A very important feature of the Pentium compared to other superscalar implementations is that the Pentium carries out this instruction pairing automatically and independently. With most other superscalars (such as the i960 and the i860, for example), the compiler must specifically call parallel processing in the pipelines. Pentium, in comparison, requires neither software control instructions nor specific dual instructions in order to use the superscalar architecture. This is also necessary with respect to compatibility with the Pentium's x86 predecessors, because they only contained a micro-encoded CU (8086 to i386), or only one pipeline (i486), so that instructions could not be executed in parallel. Instruction pairing and the parallel execution of two instructions in the superscalar architecture of the Pentium is, thus, completly transparent to the programmer. Naturally, this in no way means that the correspondingly adapted encoding, and the sequence of the instructions, does not play an important part in improving the performance. Even slight changes in the code sequence to avoid register dependency can produce substantial improvements in performance. You will find more details concerning optimization strategies for the Pentium in Section 11.7.

8.4.1 Pairing rules

In the following subsections, I would like to introduce the list of rules and limitations for instruction pairing.

Rule 1

Both instructions of a pair must be simple. The simple instructions of the Pentium are completely hardwired – inputs of microcode from the microcode ROM are not necessary. In this way, they can normally be executed in a single clock cycle. The simple instructions include (ALU indicates any arithmetic or logical instruction, such as ADD or AND, for example):

▶ MOV reg, reg/mem/imm
▶ MOV mem, reg/imm
▶ ALU reg, reg/mem/imm
▶ ALU mem, reg/imm
▶ INC reg/mem

▶ DEC reg/mem
▶ PUSH reg/mem
▶ POP reg/mem
▶ LEA reg, mem
▶ JMP/Jcc NEAR/CALL
▶ NOP

Rule 2

Unconditional jumps JMP, conditional jumps Jcc near, and function calls can only be paired if they occur as the second instruction in a pair – that is, loaded into the v pipeline. This is necessary in order to give the branch prediction logic and the prefetch buffers the opportunity to predict the jump, or for the instruction prefetching to switch from one prefetch buffer to another, as necessary. If such a jump or call were the first instruction of a pair, then the instruction sequentially following the branch instruction would be automatically loaded into the v pipeline and executed. This results in nothing more than the non-execution of a branch; in this case, branch prediction is irrelevant.

Rule 3

The shifting by one position (SAL/SAR/SHL/SHR reg/mem, 1), or an immediate operand (SAL/SAR/SHL/SHR reg/mem,imm) and rotations by one position (RCL/RCR/ROL/ROR reg/mem,1) must occur as the first instruction in an instruction pair – that is, they must only be loaded into the u pipeline.

Rule 4

No register dependencies must occur between the instructions in an instruction pair, such as the following, for example:

```
MOV eax, 0001h
ADD ecx, eax
```

In this example, the ADD instruction in the v pipeline must be held until the MOV instruction in the u pipeline has written the result (here, 0001h in eax). On one hand, this cancels out the advantages of instruction pairing, because the two instructions can no longer be executed in parallel. On the other hand, this is not possible due to the structure of the two integer pipelines, because both of the instructions should enter the D1, D2 and EX stages of the pipeline simultaneously. However, the operand fetch stage D2 can only deliver the operand for the instruction in the v pipeline after the execution stage EX has determined the value for the instruction in the u pipeline.

Register dependencies that make instruction pairing impossible are not restricted to the explicit register dependency given in the example using the two instructions MOV and ADD. Indirect or implicit dependencies can also occur, if registers or flags are concerned that are not explicitly given in the instruction. For example, the multiplication instruction IMUL mem32 stores the 64-bit product of the multiplication eax∗mem32 in the register pair edx:eax. Thus, two registers are implicitly concerned. ALU instructions in the u pipeline, which modify the flags in the EFlag register, such as CMP (the flags carry, overflow, parity, sign, zero and auxiliary carry are set according to the result), cannot be paired with an ADC instruction (add with carry) or SBB instruction (subtract with borrow) in the v pipeline due to the implied dependency on the EFlag register. In addition to the minuend and subtrahend, the ADC and SBB instructions also use the carry flag as an input.

Rule 5

Instructions with a prefix (for example, the segment override, the LOCK or the repeat prefix), can only occur in the u pipeline. The decoding stage sends the prefixes through the u pipeline at a rate of one prefix per clock cycle. The only exception is the 0fh prefix, which indicates the 2-byte opcode. 0fh forms the first byte of the opcode; the actual opcode itself follows. 0fh can occur in connection with a conditional branch Jcc and is the only prefix that can be loaded into the v pipeline, but only if the instruction is actually a Jcc. Only in this way is it possible for conditional jumps to obey rule 2. Note that the 0fh prefix in connection with an instruction other than Jcc can only be executed in the u pipeline. After all prefixes have been loaded into the u pipeline, the actual instruction code is transferred and, subject to rules 1 to 4 and 6, paired with another instruction.

Rule 6

As the last limitation, the two instructions executed in parallel must not simultaneously refer to a displacement and an immediate operand. This occurs, for example, in the following instruction ADD array[02h],08h. In this case, array[02h] represents the displacement and 08h the immediate operand.

8.4.2 Deviations

Rules seldom exist without exceptions (as these examples confirm). Above all, this applies to data processing. For instruction pairing in the Pentium, the following deviations apply.

Deviation from rule 1

The simple instructions ALU reg, mem and ALU mem,reg, require two and three clock cycles, respectively. For this reason, suitable provisions on the hardware side ensure the delay of other paired instructions in the pipeline stages D1, D2 and also EX (in the case where ALU reg,mem or ALU mem,reg is executed in the v pipeline), to stop the slower simple instructions from overtaking and, thus, inverting the instruction sequence in the WB stage.

A further delay occurs with a so-called read–modify–write instruction, for example ALU mem,reg, because, firstly, the memory operand is fetched from the memory (read), secondly, it is added to the value in the reg register (modify), and, finally, it is sent back to memory (write) as the target operand. When two such read–modify–write instructions are paired, which is quite possible as they both represent simple hardwired instructions, then the write accesses must be completed one after the other. This causes two additional cycles, which must be added to the three cycles for ALU mem, reg.

Deviation from rule 4

Comparison and branch instructions can be paired. This occurs very often because, in general, a conditional branch precedes a comparison. Above all, especially in programs that are not optimized for the pipelined processing of instructions (known as delayed branch), these two instructions immediately follow each other. On the one hand, it is important that the two instructions can be paired, in order to increase the performance of the Pentium. On the other hand, this is also possible without causing problems, because conditional branches are controlled by the branch prediction, which takes place in the instruction fetch stage and is, thus, prior to the production of the jump condition, and the jump is executed (taken branch) or not executed (not taken branch) independently of the jump condition. The actual jump execution is only executed after the verification in the EX or WB stages, as applicable, if the jump condition has already been evaluated.

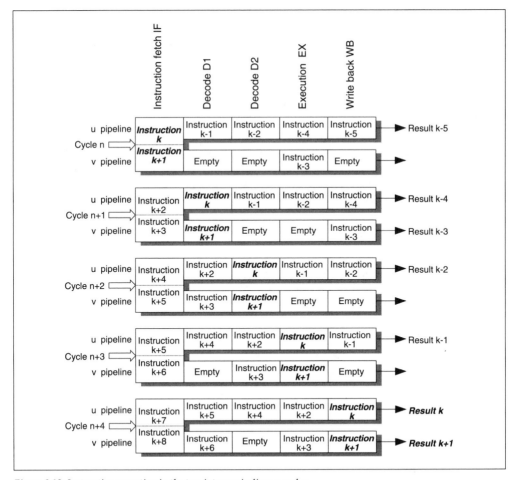

Figure 8.13: Instruction execution in the two integer pipelines u and v.
In the example shown, instruction pairing is not always possible. The instructions k-4 and k-3, k and k+1, k+2 and k+3 as well as k+5 and k+6 can be paired. The instructions k-5, k-2, k-1 and k+4 can only be executed individually. The result flow 'splutters'.

The PUSH and POP instructions are a further, frequently occurring, instruction combination that indicates an implicit register dependency. Usually, immediately after calling a subroutine using CALL, all registers used by the subroutine are saved on the stack using a number of PUSH instructions. Thus, the implicit register dependency occurs through the stack pointer ESP. Similarly, this occurs immediately before a RETURN, if the registers of the called routine are restored by the corresponding number of POPs. Here also, the implicit register dependency occurs through the stack pointer ESP. In this way, even the instruction sequences frequently occurring in older programs can make use of the superscalar architecture of the Pentium. A special hardware assembly handles ESP dependencies caused by PUSH and POP in an appropriate way. This is also very simple because every PUSH instruction reduces ESP by a value of two or four depending on whether the Pentium is in 16- or 32-bit mode, and every POP instruction increases ESP by a value of two or four, also depending on the mode. An additional note – the instructions PUSHA (PUSH All) and POPA (POP All) were implemented in the 80186/88. They save all of the registers on the stack or restore all of them, respectively. Due to the demands of DOS and most Windows programs for compatibility with the 8086, it was not possible for these instructions to be used in existing programs. PUSHA and POPA cannot be paired with other instructions, because they are implemented as microcode. However, the microcode controls the u and v pipelines simultaneously, so that in this case also the superscalar architecture of the Pentium can be used to the full. This is done in an optimal way, as the microcode is fully tuned to both of the pipelines. Figure 8.13 shows the instruction execution in the two integer pipelines, when instruction pairing is sometimes possible and sometimes not possible.

8.5 The floating-point pipeline

In addition to the two integer pipelines, the Pentium also contains a floating-point unit, which executes floating-point instructions in a pipelined way.

8.5.1 Structure of the floating-point pipeline

Unlike the u and v pipelines, the floating-point pipeline contains eight stages. The first five stages IF to WB are shared with the u pipeline. The pairing rules prevent the parallel execution of integer and floating-point instructions.

Only the FXCHG instruction, which exchanges the two elements of the register stack in the floating point unit, can be executed simultaneously with another floating-point instruction in the v pipeline. Figure 8.14 shows a schematic representation of the structure of the floating-point unit.

As the pairing of integer and floating-point instructions is not possible because of the pairing rules, the u and the floating-point pipelines can share the first five pipeline stages. In this way, the floating-point pipeline uses the WB stage of the u pipeline as the first execution stage, which likewise, performs write operations, namely to the register stacks FP(0) to FP(7) of the floating-point unit. In addition to an adder, a multiplier and a divider are also included in the hardware, in order to accelerate floating-point multiplications and divisions. The register stack, as in the x87 coprocessors and the i486DX, contains eight 80-bit registers, which all store floating-point numbers in the temporary real format.

The floating-point unit of the Pentium is completely compatible with the x87 coprocessors and the on-chip coprocessor of the i486DX. However, there are a number of internal differences. The floating-point unit of the i486DX was implemented as a an on-chip coprocessor, while the floating-point unit of the Pentium is an integral part of the CPU (as the joint use of the first five pipeline stages by the u pipeline and the floating-point unit shows). Together with improved algorithms, and the hardware multiplier and divider, the calculation performance is increased; the Pentium typically executes floating-point instructions between two and five times faster than the i486DX2. In the ideal situation, the floating-point pipeline can load and execute a floating-point instruction and, additionally, the FXCHG instruction in the v pipeline, with every clock cycle.

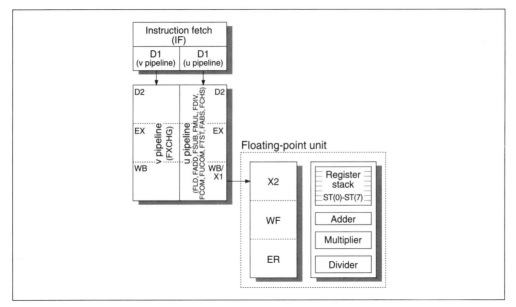

Figure 8.14: The structure of the Pentium floating-point unit.
The floating-point unit implements a pipeline with eight stages. It shares the first five stages with the u pipeline. An adder, multiplier and divider are implemented in hardware. The register stack comprises eight 80-bit registers, which all hold floating-point numbers in temporary real format.

The floating-point pipeline of the Pentium carries out all floating-point instructions (with the exception of FXCHG in the v pipeline), in accordance with the eight-stage pipeline model shown in Figure 8.15.

The first stage IF, as previously explained, reads in the instruction and then passes it to the first decoding stage D1. The second decoding stage D2 produces the operand addresses, for example the instruction FLD mem_real for the loading of the memory operand mem_real after TOP, and the simultaneous conversion of mem_real into the temporary real format. In the EX stage, the data cache and the register operand are read, as is the case with the FSTORE instruction, which converts data from internal 80-bit representation into the representation of the memory target.

Depending on the instruction, like all other stages, this stage need not necessarily execute any-thing (this is the case with the NOP integer instruction, which in pipeline stages only leads to a wait procedure).

The last stage shared with the u pipeline, X1, handles floating-point instructions in a similar, but not identical, way to integer instructions. For the u pipeline, X1 represents the register write stage WB, which updates the register content and the status register. X1, as the first floating-point execution stage, has a similar function in the floating-point pipeline; an operand read from the data cache or memory is converted into the temporary real format and is written to one of the registers in the register stack FP(0) to FP(7).

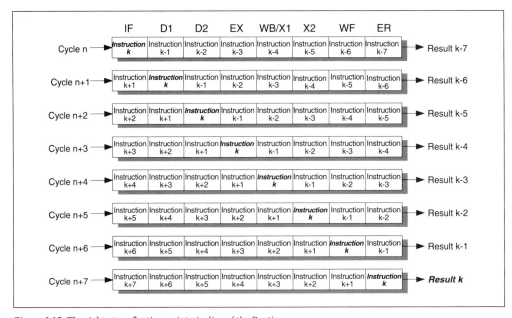

Figure 8.15: The eight-stage floating-point pipeline of the Pentium.

In addition to this, the X1 stage has the task of identifying so-called *safe instructions*. This is also known as *safe instruction recognition (SIR)*. Safe instructions do not cause an overflow, underflow or exception through an inaccuracy. In addition, they require no Pentium micro-codes in order to handle internal masked exceptions and to deliver the corresponding results (for example, 0 in the case of an underflow). For this reason, the X1 stage examines the operand values and the opcode of the instruction. If it finds the current instruction to be safe, then the subsequent floating-point instruction – providing that there is one at hand – leaves the EX stage and enters the X1 stage, as soon as the previous instruction has proceeded to the second exe-cution stage X2. If it is not certain that the current instruction is safe, then the subsequent instruction in the EX stage is held up – and thus the complete pipeline – until the current instruction has left the last ER stage without producing an error. In this way, unsafe instructions are prevented from interfering with subsequent instructions and, thus, from producing uncontrollable exception conditions in the floating-point unit – this could occur, above all, because of the floating-point unit's heavy reliance on pipelining. The holding back of the pipeline always causes a delay of four processor clock cycles in the subsequent instruction – even if the current instruction does not produce an exception. This also applies where an integer instruction follows a pair of floating-point instructions; the integer instruction has to pass through the EX and X1 stages anyway. If the X1 stage estimates the two floating point instructions to be unsafe, then the integer instruction in the ER stage is delayed by four cycles.

The X1 stage examines the opcode and the operands on a simple basis: they must fulfil the four following conditions:

▸ the opcode must define the FADD, FSUB, FMUL or FDIV instructions
▸ both operands (in the internal temporary real format) must have an exponent without bias; that is, smaller than 1fffh
▸ both operands must have an exponent without bias; that is larger than -1fffh
▸ the exception for an imprecise result must be masked

The required exponent values guarantee that, for the given instruction, no exponent greater than 3ffdh, or less than -3ffdh will be produced; the result produces neither an overflow nor an underflow for the temporary real format.

The three stages that follow are only implemented in the floating-point pipeline and are totally independent of the u pipeline. The sixth stage of the floating-point pipeline, the second FP execution stage X2, performs the actual execution of the floating-point instructions, such as the calculation of the sine or logarithm of an operand. Above all, this second execution stage X2 requires more clock cycles for calculating complicated transcendental functions (sometimes up to 100). In the meantime, the u and v pipelines can execute further integer instructions. Thus, it is not strictly parallel processing; more accurately, it should be called *concurrent processing*. The *FP register write stage WP*, which follows, performs all rounding tasks and writes the result to an 80-bit register of the FP register stack. Finally, the ninth and last *ER stage* of the floating-point pipeline deals with errors that may occur and updates the status word accordingly.

8.5.2 Register bypass

The floating-point pipeline also contains two *register bypasses* for the acceleration of instructions that require the results of previously executed instructions as operands. The first bypass connects the output of the X1 stage with the input of the EX stage. In this way, the operand loaded from memory and converted into the temporary real format can perform an FLOAD instruction as soon as the operand read stage EX for the subsequent instruction has been executed. Thus, in the next clock cycle, the operand is available for the instruction that follows and need not, firstly, be stored in the register stack by X1 and, secondly, reread from the register stack by EX during the subsequent cycle. The second bypass connects the output of the WF stage directly to the input of the EX stage. With this, the result of an instruction is available for the next instruction, without the delay of the write operation. The bypasses do not stop the operation of the X1 and WF stages: it is obvious that these stages still carry out the write operation to the register stack. They supply results to the instructions that follow, in parallel to executing the write operation to the applicable register, whereby a clock cycle is gained.

8.5.3 Instruction pairing

There are also pairing rules for floating-point instructions, in order to execute two instructions at the same time. They are, however, considerably more restrictive, because 'full' floating-point instructions require stages IF to X1 of the u pipeline and X2 to ER of the floating-point pipeline, of which only one of each is available. Only the instruction FXCHG for exchanging two register values on the register stack ST(0) to ST(7) can, in certain circumstances, be executed in the v pipeline, in parallel to another floating-point instruction. Many floating-point instructions address the TOP register (top of stack) at the top of the register stack, explicitly or implicitly, as the source or target operand.

With only eight floating-point registers ST(0) to ST(7), stack overflows can quickly occur. In order to prevent this, and also to be able to use lower lying register values, for example as source operands, the value in TOP must be exchanged frequently with other register values. The FXCHG instruction serves this purpose; it is often used in this way and thus slows down the instruction execution – especially where it cannot be executed in parallel to another floating-point instruction. The following rules apply to the pairing of floating-point instructions.

Rule 1

A floating-point instruction can only be paired with an FXCHG instruction; other pairings of floating-point instructions with each other are not possible.

Rule 2

Only the following floating-point instructions can be paired with the FXCHG instruction:

▶ FLD memreal32/memreal64/ST(i)
▶ all types (normal, integer, with or without POP) of the instructions FADD, FSUB, FMUL, FDIV, FCOM, FUCOM, FTST, FABS and FCHS.

Rule 3

All instructions that neither represent an FXCHG instruction nor belong to the instruction group defined in rule 2 are processed as single instructions in the u pipeline.

Rule 4

The FXCHG instruction must be the second of the pair – that is, it must be loaded into the v pipeline. If the subsequent instruction is other than FXCHG, then it is executed as a separate instruction in the u pipeline – that is, not paired.

It is no great problem if an FXCHG instruction cannot be paired; it requires only one clock cycle for execution. However, you should ensure that floating-point instructions are paired with subsequent FXCHG instructions as much as possible during programming. Above all, this has an effect with quick floating-point instructions, such as FADD or FMUL, for example, which under favourable conditions require only one clock cycle.

On the other hand, it is unimportant whether or not the FXCHG instruction is paired with an FDIV instruction. FDIV requires a minimum of 39 clock cycles, so an acceleration of only approximately 2% occurs if FXCHG can be paired with FDIV (39 clock cycles compared to 40 without pairing). With the one-cycle instructions FADD and FMUL, this can lead to a doubling of the execution speed (one clock cycle, as compared to two without pairing).

8.5.4 Malfunction of the floating-point divider

Since June 1994, a serious malfunction of the floating-point divider in the Pentium's floating-point unit has been known at Intel. The public was not informed before the end of 1994 (as is, unfortunately, usual in this field of business). It appears in one in nine thousand million floating-point divisions and mainly affects the accuracy of the result. Intel indicates a maximum of 10^{-9} for the accuracy error, but errors of 10^{-5} are also known. Unfortunately, there is no roundabout way to avoid these inaccuracies by hardware. Only an emulation of the floating-point division by software avoids such problems (but this is, of course, not a recommended method in view of the floating-point performance). Intel states that for the typical end user, this malfunction should occur only once in 27 000 years. This seems to be absolutely too low because a 100 MHz Pentium needs only about one hour to execute nine thousand million floating-point divisions (39 CLK cycles per FP division). Taking into account the larger load of the processor for ordinary integer instructions, you can expect a calculation error, when using programs that deal with floating-point arithmetic, nearly every day. Pure mathematical applications for determining eigenvalues or solving differential equations, for example, suffer much more often from the malfunction. The most serious problem is that you cannot trust the results of a very complex calculation. You can only state that the result is (still very) likely to be true or sufficiently exact.

The malfunction appears for the three instructions FDIV, FIDIV and FPREM, if divisions with certain numbers are executed. The dividend–divisor pairs most widely discussed on the Internet are:

▶ dividend=4 195 835, divisor=31 457 27, quotient=1.333 739 07, inaccuracy=6 101 661$*10^{-5}$

▶ dividend=5 505 001, divisor=294 911, quotient=1.866 660 00, inaccuracy=3.487 859$*10^{-5}$

▶ dividend=1, divisor=1 824 633 702 441, quotient=1.212 659 62$*10^{-12}$, inaccuracy=3.725 290$*10^{-9}$

There are, of course, a lot of other dividend–divisor pairs that lead to serious inacuricies. It is, however, impossible to determine (or store) all dividend–divisor pairs; for the 80-bit temporary real format, we have 2^{80} possibilities for the dividend and 2^{80} possibilities for the divisor, thus, in total $2^{160}=1.46*10^{48}$ possibilities. A 100 MHz Pentium would need $5.8*10^{41}$ s=$1.8*10^{34}$ years to calculate all results (in comparison, the age of the universe is only about $2*10^{10}$ years).

The mask revision of the Pentium chip now provides error-free floating-point dividers (or, probably better, floating-point dividers without known malfunctions). If you buy a Pentium, you should ask whether it was produced with the new mask or not. If you are not doing profound mathematics on your Pentium PC, the erroneous chips could be sufficient, so ask for a cheap and old Pentium (the error rate of about 10^{-10} will hardly affect desktop publishing or word processing, for example).

8.6 Serializing the instruction execution

For many situations and instructions, it is essential that an instruction is completed before the next instruction is transferred for execution into the Pentium pipeline. An example of this is an OUT instruction, which switches an external gate for the address line A20, in order to emulate the 'stone-age-like' address wraparound of the 8086. This switching informs the Pentium through the A20M signal that it also masks the address line A20 for internal accesses to the on-chip cache. If the instruction following the OUT instruction does not switch into, or switches back from the wraparound condition, then pipelined instruction execution can lead to problems. The OUT instruction is first executed in the EX stage and, in this way, an I/O bus cycle to the A20 gate is executed. The subsequent instruction finds itself in the second decoding stage D2, and so has already been read in and partly decoded. For this reason, the instruction fetching for the instruction is not influenced by the switching of the gate and so, possibly, an incorrect instruction has been collected.

The switching of the A20 gate, and also other hardware elements that immediately influence the execution of instructions in the Pentium, is the responsibility of the BIOS and, for this reason, hardware-like even though it is accomplished with software. Thus, the software must be able to influence the instruction pipelining realized by fixed hardware within set limits, in order to prevent such fatal situations. This is accomplished through *serializing* the instruction execution. This means that the next instruction is only loaded into the first pipeline stage when the current instruction has been fully completed and has left the last stage. Additionally, serializing causes emptying of the prefetch queue. Thus, all register, memory and flag updates are finished before the next instruction is read into the pipeline from the instruction fetching stage. All write accesses that are awaiting execution in the internal write buffers are performed; the Pentium then waits for the activation of the $\overline{\text{EWBE}}$ signal, in order to be sure that additional subsystems (such as an L2 cache) have also completed all write operations. Note, however, that modified cache lines in the on-chip data cache are not written back; if this is necessary, a WBINVD must be executed, whereby the WBINVD instruction automatically issues a serialization.

The Pentium controls its internal pipeline as described for a serializing of the instruction execution, if one of the following (serialization) instructions is executed:

▶ MOV control register/debug register (except for CR0)
▶ INVD, INVLPG, WBINVD
▶ IRET, IRETD
▶ LGDT, LLDT, LIDT, LTR
▶ CPUID
▶ RSM, WRMSR

Above all, the instruction CPUID is useful for serialization, because it can be carried out at every protection level without causing a protection exception and, in addition, does not influence control registers and EFlags in any way; only the four general-purpose registers EAX, EBX, ECX and EDX are overwritten with an identification code. The i486 and, particularly, the earlier micro-encoded 80x86 CPUs without an instruction pipeline implicitly perform a serialization as soon as a jump or a branch instruction occurs. Every jump or branch instruction empties the prefetch queue (and also, in the i486, the instruction pipeline), so that after every JMP or Jcc the instruction fetching starts with an empty prefetch queue and pipeline; thus, a serialization is performed. In the Pentium, this is generally not the case, because emptying of the prefetch buffers and pipeline should be prevented by the branch prediction. Here, an explicit serialization instruction must be executed in order to achieve serialization, for example, CPUID. Incidentally, the implicit serialization in the 8086 to i486 via a jump or branch instruction reduces the performance considerably, because these instructions occur frequently, and after each instruction the prefetch queue must be loaded. The instruction also has to be decoded before it can be executed.

8.7 Dynamic branch prediction

The branch prediction logic represents substantial advantage for the handling of branches compared to the i486, especially for processors with instruction pipelining, which can be slowed considerably by prefetch delays.

8.7.1 Construction and functionality of branch prediction logic

The branch prediction logic consists of a control unit and the branch trace buffer or branch target buffer (BTB). The BTB represents a type of cache with a total of 256 entries, which, as a tag, contain the addresses of instructions that immediately precede the branch instruction. Furthermore, as an actual cache entry, it contains the target address of the jump and also history bits that deliver statistical information about the frequency of the current branch. In this respect an executed branch is known as a *taken branch* and a non-executed branch is known as a *not taken branch*. The dynamic branch prediction predicts the branches according to the instructions that the Pentium has executed previously.

Every branch is assigned one of four 'taken' conditions by the history bits: strongly taken, weakly taken, weakly not taken and strongly not taken. If a branch is taken, the history bits are updated according to the chain strongly not taken → weakly not taken → weakly taken → strongly taken. For example, if the initial history bits indicated a weakly not taken state, then, after the branch is taken, the history bits are updated to the weakly taken state. The same applies for not taken branches; the history bits are updated in the opposite direction: strongly taken → weakly taken → weakly not taken → strongly not taken. For example, if the initial state was the weakly not taken state, then after the (not taken) branch, the history bits indicate strongly not taken. If the history bits already refer to strongly taken, and the branch is taken, no further update is carried out The same applies if the history bits indicate a strongly not taken state, and the branch is not taken. When a new entry is made in the BTB (usually after a BTB miss; that is, no entry exists in the BTB for the current branch), the history bits for this branch or entry are initialized to the strongly taken condition. This is justified because most of the branches run through at execution time refer to jumps back to the beginning of a loop.

The prefetch buffer and the BTB work together, in order to fetch the most likely instruction after a jump. Note that the Pentium supplies the address of the instruction in the D1 decoding stage to the BTB – that is, the EIP address of the instruction that precedes a jump instruction, and not the EIP address of the jump instruction itself. This is true for all instructions; a BTB hit can only occur for one branch instruction. With a BTB hit, the branch prediction logic delivers the address of the jump target instruction, as the instruction fetch address, to the IF stage of the pipeline. If many branch instructions occur in a program, the BTB, like all caches, will at some point become full, then BTB misses also occur for branch instructions. A BTB miss is handled as a not taken branch. The dynamic BTB algorithms of the Pentium independently take care of the reloading of new branch instructions, and the 'noting' of the most likely branch target. In this way, the branch prediction logic can reliably predict the branches. In the Pentium, it causes either the sequentially next instruction (for a prediction of 'branch not taken') or the instruction at the jump target address (if the prediction is 'branch taken') to be loaded into the prefetch stage IF of the pipeline. Pipeline stalls caused by emptying the pipeline (pipeline invalidations or flushes) and also the subsequent explicit instruction fetching are clearly reduced, and the program execution is accelerated.

Usually, preceding a conditional branch, a comparison of two numbers occurs, for example, either explicitly through CMP or implicitly through SUB. The execution of this comparison takes place in the fourth EX stage, and the writing of the EFlag register takes place in the fifth WB stage. At this point, the subsequent CMP instruction is already in the second decoding stage D2 or the execution stage; in the case of an instruction pairing, this can even be in the same stage as the comparison instruction. The prediction for unconditional jumps (using JMP) and conditional jumps (using Jcc) of the u pipeline, and calls (using CALL) can first be checked in the execution stage EX. For conditional jumps of the v pipeline, the prediction can first be checked in the register write stage WB.

If the prediction is shown to be correct, as is nearly always the case with unconditional jumps and procedure calls (only incorrect or old BTB entries from a different task can change this), then all instructions loaded into the pipeline after the jump instruction are correct, and the pipeline operation is continued without interruption. Thus, if the prediction is correct, branches and calls are executed within a single clock cycle, and in accordance with the pairing rules, in parallel to other instructions. If, in the EX or WB stages, the prediction is found to be incorrect, then the Pentium empties the pipeline and tells the instruction fetching stage to fetch the instruction at the correct address. Finally, the pipeline restarts operation in the normal way. Unconditional jumps, conditional jumps and procedure calls already in the EX stage are verified. This takes three clock cycles longer. Conditional jumps in the v pipeline, in which the verification takes place during the WB stage, require four clock cycles. The dynamic algorithms can, however, generally avoid such situations with the history bit.

Note that these types of execution only affect near CALL/JMP/Jcc. Far calls in protected mode with a change to the CS segment register, which occur with a call, interrupt or task gate, require considerably longer time. The large 32-bit segments with 4 Gbyte storage capacity make such intersegment calls unnecessary – especially if the code is specific to the 32-bit architecture of the Pentium or its i386 and i486 predecessors. This is not currently the case with Windows and, of course, the old real-mode applications that run in DOS boxes under Windows, OS/2 or Windows NT. Anyone expecting to win at Indianapolis in a Ford Model T would also be a little bit disappointed.

This, and the very high performance concept of delayed branches, cannot be used in the Pentium for two reasons. Firstly, all already existing programs for the x86 processors, from the 8086 to the i486, do not fill the delay slots after a branch instruction with one or more significant instructions, or simply the required number of NOPs. Until the i386, this was not at all possible, because every instruction following a branch or a procedural call would only be executed in the case of a branch not taken, due to the strict sequential execution of instructions. With a branch not taken, inserted NOPs would only slow down the program execution, and with a taken branch no performance advantage at all would result. In addition, the corresponding hardware precautions for a delayed branch come into play, whereby the instruction in the delay slot sequentially following the actual branch instruction would also be executed. This would only be a possibility with very complex hardware that, for example, must know independently when instructions can and must be rearranged, so that a correct delayed branch is performed – a task for which, not without reason, an optimized compiler was included during project planning of RISC processors. However, branch prediction is almost as successful as the delayed branch concept, in that already existing programs can also benefit from the quicker execution of branch instructions.

8.7.2 Effects of branch prediction: an example

Even in the i486, which already includes many RISC concepts such as instruction pipelining, the effects of executed branches (taken branches) is very fateful. They delay the instruction execution quite considerably. As a short explanation, I would like to discuss the following example from the point of view of the Pentium and the i486. The init_loop is important in the example, as it is run a hundred times for field initialization.

```
Example: Initialize array with 100 double words ffffffffh.

mov edx, ffffffffh  ; load initialize value into edx
lea eax, array      ; store start address of array in eax
mov ecx, eax+396    ; load address of last field element into ecx

init_loop:          ; begin of initializing loop
  mov [eax], edx    ; set field element to ffffffffh
  add eax, 04h      ; next field element
  cmp eax, ecx      ; determine whether last address has been reached; that is, whether eax–
                    ; exc>0
  jbe init_loop     ; loop again, if last address has not yet been reached
```

In the i486, the four instructions MOV, ADD, CMP and JBE are executed sequentially, because only one pipeline is available. The first three instructions each require only one clock cycle. The problem occurs with the conditional jump JBE, which is executed 99 times – in other words, a jump back to the MOV instruction is initiated. For such a taken branch, the i486 requires three clock cycles. So in the i486, six cycles are required for each loop operation (for comparison the i386 requires 13 cycles).

This is completely different in the Pentium. The four loop instructions can be paired, so the execution sequence is as follows:

```
u Pipeline        v pipeline

mov [eax], edx    add eax, 04h
cmp eax, ecx      jbe init_loop
```

The first instruction line is executed in one cycle. If it establishes the branch prediction for jbe as correct, then the second line is also executed in only one cycle. Thus, in total, only two clock cycles are required to complete the operation of the loop. This is three times quicker than the i486. A false prediction by the BTB logic would cause a delay in the execution of four clock cycles, because the JBE instruction is located in the v pipeline. Due to the operation of the initialization loop a hundred times, it is very likely that the BTB logic will produce an erroneous branch prediction, at least with the first loop operation, because as yet, the BTB has no 'experience' with the outcome of the CMP and JBE instructions. Also, it is quite likely that the BTB will predict an erroneous branch for the last loop operation, because of the history bits and the previous 99 taken branches. Thus, branch prediction gives a great advantage when frequently repeated loops are required, as is often the case with the implementation of algorithms employed in the calculation of mathematical expressions, or with visualization of processor results.

Note that the BTB is not a branch target cache (BTC). A branch target cache only stores the first instruction at a branch target address, and not whether the branch will actually be executed. Thus, the BTC is a type of code cache but, unlike a true code cache, only stores a specific number of instruction bytes at the branch target addresses, and not a large quantity of sequential codes. As an example, the branch target cache of the Am29000 (see Section 16.6.1) contains 512 bytes and stores the first four 32-bit instructions of 32 branch targets. The BTB should only prevent delays caused by slow main memory; pipeline stalls caused by branches are not rectified in this way.

8.7.3 Side effects

In some cases, branch prediction can cause a few specific side effects, which I would briefly like to bring together here. Through the use of the instruction address in the D1 stage, sometimes when a BTB hit occurs, instructions are read in from the IF stage that have nothing to do with the current instruction flow. The cause can be a context change through a task switch, a false branch prediction, or simply a BTB that has not been updated. The Pentium then loads codes into the pipelines, the execution of which will never be completed, because the EX or WB stage will evaluate the branch as incorrect and the pipelines will then be emptied. This is not so bad with respect to loss of performance through false prediction. Further, through inadequate BTB entries (mainly due to incorrect branch target entries), it is possible that the IF stage fetches code, in protected mode, which already lies outside the CS segment limit – and for this reason, may not even represent code at all. Usually, such instructions are deleted from the pipeline before completion due to the lack of branch prediction validation. If this is not the case, the protection logic of the Pentium intercepts such accesses in protected mode and issues a protection exception. Code accesses to externally stored pages are not possible through such BTB false predictions, because they are deleted from the pipeline before they generate a paging exception and request the operating system to reload the required page.

8.8 BiCMOS technology: Quick and economical

Unlike any of its predecessors, the Pentium must perform a trade-off between a higher speed of operation and lower energy usage per semiconductor component. The speed requirement comes from the need to achieve the highest possible execution speed for the individual instructions. For this, the electronic signals must be propagated very quickly through many components (mainly transistors). High performance CPUs for supercomputers or very efficient workstations are therefore constructed using bipolar technology. An example is the MIPS R6000 using emitter-coupled logic (ECL) technology. The disadvantage of bipolar transistors is their higher energy needs; the advantage is a much shorter switching time between the on and off conditions. CMOS components, on the other hand, use less power. However, they normally operate more slowly than bipolar transistors. Because of its more than three million transistors, the Pentium cannot be constructed as a single bipolar chip – the power losses would immediately lead to overheating.

Using BiCMOS technology, the Pentium unites the advantages of the two technologies. Bipolar transistors are used where speed is of the utmost importance. This occurs particularly in the last stage of complex circuits, for example in the ALU. These circuits are characterized by many stages, through which the logic signals must propagate. The quick and greatly amplifying bipolar transistors ensure that the signals are output at the correct time. The lower output resistance of the bipolar transistors causes a much stronger signal to be sent from the circuit. The CMOS transistors, on the other hand, with their relatively high input resistance, are inserted at the beginning of the circuit. They are also inserted where the transfer speed would not be affected, for example, in the registers and buffers that store data only temporarily, or in circuits with only a few stages, such as the prefetch logic.

If the Pentium only implemented ECL technology, the power consumption would be two to three times greater – approximately 30 W. Without contact cooling or a large heat sink, the heat produced could not be shed. In normal situations, such a chip would be unusable, or would require very expensive cooling equipment. On the other hand, a Pentium using only CMOS technology would end up with a clock frequency of less than 50 MHz. You are probably asking yourself how the i486DX can handle internally 66 MHz without problems, while the Pentium can not. The reason for this is simply that the Pentium is much more complicated and that the signals must pass through considerably more circuit elements. Every CMOS element has a time cost of between 0.2 and 1 ns; in a cycle time of 15 ns at 66 MHz, between 15 and 75 elements can be used. Thus, complicated circuits with more switching elements (including the input and output wiring gates for each component) brake the signal flow.

If you look at Figure 4.4, you can see that even a simple 4-bit adder contains a great number of stages through which the signal must flow. However, the Pentium does not contain a 4-bit adder in the floating-point unit; in its place, it has a 64-bit adder for adding the mantissas of temporary real numbers. Thus, the signal must flow through 64 stages, each with a number of elements. In multipliers, the signal takes even longer to flow through, because of an even more complicated circuit structure. Thus, normal but extremely fast CMOS transistors are too slow (consider that, in 1 ns, a commercial aircraft will move only 0.000 02 mm; this corresponds to the wavelength of ultraviolet light – light itself will move only 30 cm), and must be replaced by faster bipolar transistors.

Future technical developments will almost certainly reduce the switching time of CMOS elements (which depends on the size of the element; that is, the degree of integration and the potential difference between the layers of the element), so that, before long, more energy efficient Pentiums will be produced.

8.9 Pentium-comparable chips

The word 'comparable' in the heading indicates a revolution in the field of 80x86-compatible microprocessors; Intel is no longer the one and only supplier of genuine 80x86 technology. Instead, its main competitors have freed themselves more and more from slave-like compatibility down to the microarchitecture and microprogram level. This was and is necessary to close the gap between the leading Intel processors and the successive compatible chips of one to two generations. Money is made mainly with new chips where no or little competition exists. In the previous two generations (i386 and i486) the basic architecture and operating modes did not change significantly. Even Intel is concentrating on the microarchitecture to enhance performance (some advances have been added to the Pentium, however, with the support of virtual interrupts, for example). On the other hand, the changes mainly refer to registers and functions at a very low level as, for example, performance monitoring or probe mode. These are, however, only important for developing quick compilers or operating system kernels. They are not absolutely decisive for the ordinary user, even at the level of an advanced operating system like Windows NT or OS/2. So these subjects can be left over to board and system or compiler designers who, with the help of the respective company, make use of the new functions in the development stage of their products. Once finished, the end user will not notice any difference between a Pentium and, for example, an M1-based machine (despite some performance differences that may occur, depending on the applications).

The three companies NexGen, Cyrix and AMD were forced to free themselves from Intel microcode (which was used, for example, by AMD in the 386 and some 486-compatible chips, and led to the typical court battles where, as usual, both lost and the attorneys won). If they had wanted to construct a real Pentium-'compatible' chip, they could not have started development before the Pentium was available in the market. So it would not have been possible to close the gap to less than two years (the usual development cycle for processor architectures and – more importantly – the necessary process technologies for production). So all three decided to already start development when still nothing was known about the Pentium. Of course, the basic RISC and other principles for enhancing the performance were known to all, and all three tried to implement them (to a far greater extent than Intel in its Pentium) in their products. You will therefore find some technologies that are very hot topics today (nearly one and a half years after Intel presented the Pentium to the public), and that can also be expected to be incorporated in the Pentium's successor (the P6, as it is frequently named). All companies claim that their chips outperform the Pentium with real-world applications, but at the time of writing, this could not be confirmed. Nethertheless, I quote the companies' values (it can be assumed that Intel also tries to put its processors in the best light, so all performance indices should be comparable).

8.9.1 NexGen Nx586 and Nx587

This Pentium-comparable chip, the first available in the market, was designed by Next (the supplier of the NextStep operating system) and is produced by IBM. It supports all 80x86 instructions and the registers visible to the programmer and user (or to system and application programs). Of course, it has a lot of internal registers and functions that are not accessible on the level of 80x86 instructions. This processor is a two-chip set consisting of the 'main' processor Nx586 and the separately available floating-point unit Nx587. The Nx586 has three exeution units (two integer and one addressing unit), which can operate in parallel. Further, it incorporates separate instruction and data caches, each with 16 kbytes of memory on-chip. Both caches are four-way set-associative, which leads to more cache hits the the Pentium's two-way set-associative caches. The L1 data cache is write-through. Because the floating-point unit is missing, there was enough space to integrate an L2 cache controller on-chip, which manages an external, unified L2 cache for data and code. This L2 cache is write-back, and is accessed through a separate dedicated L2 cache bus. Therefore, the Nx586 (463 pins) can not be pin-compatible with the Pentium. Moreover, ordinary memory is addressed through the Nx586 bus, incompatible with the Pentium's bus.

The main kernel concept of the Nx586 is that all 80x86 CISC instructions are translated to a special RISC instruction set, the so-called NexGen *RISC86* instructions. In the worst case, a 3:1 ratio of CISC to RISC instructions appears. Most of the simpler 80x86 instructions (such as, for example, ADD reg, reg) are translated to one single RISC86 instruction. The decoder translates one CISC instruction per CLK cycle and dispatches up to three RISC86 instructions per clock to the three Nx586 pipelines (two integer and one addressing pipeline). These are a minimum of seven stages long, with maximum length depending on the CISC–RISC86 translation. The RISC pipelines within the Nx586 implement advanced concepts like branch prediction, speculative execution and register renaming, with 14 registers (onto which the eight 80x86 general-purpose registers are mapped). The Nx586 core also allows out-of-order execution and termination of instructions, but they must retire (written back to the 80x86 registers) in the order the instructions are dispatched to the pipelines. The floating-point unit is available separately as the Nx587 'coprocessor'. This should minimize the system price for users who hardly ever use floating-point arithmetic. All features together add up to performance that is more or less the same as that of the Pentium.

A special concept is that all RISC86 instructions can also be used stand-alone – that is, a RISC86 assembler or compiler can directly generate RISC86 code, which is fed directly into the three Nx586 pipelines. Therefore, very powerful operating systems or programs can be generated while compatibility with older 80x86 programs is maintained – an interesting approach to combine powerful, modern software and compatibility.

8.9.2 Cyrix M1

Few facts were known about this interesting chip at the time of writing. According to Cyrix, it has 32 general-purpose registers with dynamic register renaming. Its superscalar pipelines with seven stages support speculative execution with four nesting levels (because 32 registers are implemented, but the 80x86 architecture has only eight) and branch prediction. Cyrix claims a 30% performance advantage over the equally clocked Pentium.

8.9.3 AMD K5

For AMD, the K5 marks an important step towards being a 'grown-up' supplier of high-end microprocessors. After years of dependency on Intel microcode or architectural concepts and licences, the K5 implements a purely AMD design and microcode, and integrates 4.1 million transistors.

It has five parallel execution units: two integer, one floating-point, one branch and one load/store unit (the Pentium has only two integer pipelines, u and v, and a floating-point unit). They can operate in parallel on five RISC-like instructions (in the Pentium, a maximum of two pipelines can be active), the so-called *R-ops*. The majority of R-ops execute in a single processor clock cycle. The pipelines are five-stage. The 'brain' of the K5 is a very powerful decoder; it converts the 80x86 CISC instructions into one or more R-ops. Four of these R-ops are dispatched at one time to the RISC core, thus, the K5 is a so-called four-way issue superscalar. The conversion of the CISC instructions into the R-ops begins with the inloading into the instruction cache (I cache), where they are tagged with additional information. This predecoding resolves the instruction boundaries between the 80x86 instructions (which can encompass anything between 1 and 15 bytes) as well as branch prediction. The decoder then decodes the CISC instructions further with the help of the tags; an 80x86 instruction which decodes into three or fewer R-ops is called a fast instruction; more complex CISCs address microcode in an on-chip ROM, which consists of a more or less long series of R-ops that are dispatched four at a time to the pipelines.

It is not necessary for the four R-ops that are dispatched simultaneously to come from the same 80x86 instruction. Instead, they can be decoded from different CISC instructions and, moreover, from different branches when speculative execution is active, for example. The R-ops that are dispatched to the five units four at a time can execute and terminate out of order, but must retire in order. Therefore, the K5 supports out-of-order execution, branch prediction and speculative execution. Also dynamic register renaming with 16 general-purpose registers that map onto the eight 80x86 GP registers is possible.

Another interesting solution refers to the branch prediction implemented in the K5. Unlike the Pentium and other processors, the K5 does not use a separate BTB, but appends the predicted branch address to every branch instruction stored in the I cache; one prediction is possible per 16-byte cache block. Therefore, a maximum of 1024 branch predictions is possible (the Pentium has 256 BTB entries and possible predictions). Once a branch instruction is loaded into the I cache, it is initialized as not taken. Afterwards, the prediction is reversed every time it is wrong. The Pentium handles the prediction more intelligently. The execution units are supported by a 16-kbyte I cache and an 8-kbyte data cache, both of which are four-way set-associative (the Pentium is two-way associative) to improve the hit rate. On the other hand, the K5's floating-point unit is not as fast as that in the Pentium, but floating-point instructions are hardly ever used by the 'typical' user. Altogether, AMD claims a 30% performance advantage of the K5 compared to an equally clocked Pentium, and that the design leaves enough space to enhance the performance even more, so that the K5 design could also compete with the Pentium successor P6.

9 Caches and the MESI protocol

In this chapter, I would first like to discuss the general basics of cache memory and then examine their use in the Pentium. Fast-clocked processors naturally require fast memory with short access times. What is the use of a 100 MHz Pentium if it has to insert five or more wait states for every memory access? Today's DRAM chips have standard access times of at least 60 ns. The page and static column modes, and also memory organization, can reduce this to 35 ns. Even in the 33 MHz i386, this was too slow; it is even worse for the Pentium, especially when you look at the considerably longer cycle time of the DRAMs. SRAM components offer a way out, using CMOS or BiCMOS technology with a typical access time of between 15 and 20 ns – one wait state for a 100 MHz Pentium. Only ECL or bipolar SRAMs achieve access times of 10 ns, which would serve the Pentium without wait states. For comparison, in 10 ns, a commercial aircraft flying at 850 km per hour would move only 0.002 mm, or less than a tenth of the diameter of a hair. SRAM chips are unfortunately very expensive and are larger than DRAMs; for these reasons, they are not compatible with an 8-Mbyte main memory.

9.1 The cache principle and cache strategies

A cache attempts to combine the advantages of fast SRAMs with the cheapness of DRAMs, in order to achieve the most effective memory system. You can see the cache principle in Figure 9.1.

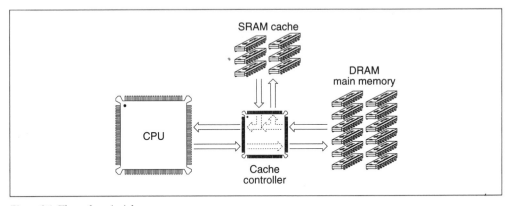

Figure 9.1: The cache principle.
Between the CPU and the main memory DRAM a fast cache SRAM is provided. It holds the frequently accessed data and delivers it very quickly. The process is controlled by a cache controller, which may implement various write strategies as, for example, write-through or write-back.

A cache unit is inserted between the CPU and the main memory. It consists of a cache controller and a cache SRAM. They may be included on the same chip as the CPU (on-chip cache) or may exist as a separate component. There are also mixes (such as the MIPS R3000), where the cache controller is included on the CPU chip and the actual cache memory is formed by external SRAM chips. On-chip caches are, today, typically between 4 and 16 kbytes in size;

external caches in personal computers are between 256 and 512 kbytes. Thus, the cache memory is typically between 10 and 1000 times smaller than the main memory.

As most successive memory accesses affect only a small address area, the most frequently addressed data is held in a small high-speed memory – the cache. The advantage with this is a very much reduced access time, which, added up over many closely packed memory accesses, produces a considerable increase in speed. The data and code that is not currently required can be stored in the slower main memory, without a great slowing down effect on the program execution. The cache principle of using a small SRAM cache memory and a large but slower DRAM main memory combines the speed advantages of SRAM chips with the lower cost of DRAMs.

When the CPU reads data, as usual, it sends out the corresponding memory address. However, here the cache controller is located between the processor and the main memory address. It determines whether the requested data is available in the SRAM cache. If this is the case, it is known as a *cache hit*. On the other hand, if the data is only available in the main memory, it is known as a *cache miss*. In the first case, the cache controller reads the data from the quicker cache memory and passes it on to the CPU. This usually takes place without wait states – that is, with the maximum bus speed. The read access is completely intercepted by the cache and the main memory knows nothing about it. (This design is also known as *look-through cache* because the CPU has to 'look through' the cache system; for a *look-aside cache*, the cache system resides 'aside' the CPU–memory path and 'snoops' all memory accesses to provide the read more quickly if they are stored in its fast SRAMs.)

On the other hand, if a cache miss occurs, the cache controller must first read the data from the main memory, thus the read access is switched through to the main memory. As this usually takes longer, an appropriate number of wait states are required; the cache controller disables the ready (or an equivalent) signal, so that the CPU inserts wait states. The cache controller addresses the main memory simultaneously. The internal organization of most caches requires that when a cache miss occurs, not only the requested data bytes but a complete *cache line* is read from the main memory into the SRAM cache. This operation is known as a *cache line fill*. For this, it is possible that changed data must first be stored in the main memory, before the new data in the cache line can be read into the SRAM cache. The cache controller is intelligent enough to perform bus cycles independently for the writing and reading of data to or from the main memory, respectively. The data bytes addressed by the CPU are immediately passed on by the cache controller – that is, before the transfer of the whole cache line is completed.

Cache lines are typically 16 or 32 bytes large. The reason for this is that the data and program codes, as already explained, are formed into blocks and, therefore, it is quite likely that the next access will require a value contained in the same cache line. This increases the hit rate. In addition, most cache controllers implement a so-called *burst mode*, through which a complete data block, which contains more bytes than the data bus is wide, is read (whereby multiple bus cycles are required, in order to read in the complete block). The burst mode almost doubles the bus transfer rate, so a complete cache line can be read much more quickly than a single value. Thus, the organization of the caches into cache lines increases the system performance.

If, on the other hand, the CPU writes data, the cache controller determines whether the data is also located in the SRAM cache. If this is the case, the data from the CPU is written to the SRAM cache. There are three different strategies for the further operation of the cache controller: write-through, write-back (also known as copy-back) and write-allocate. The first two strategies affect a cache hit, the last a cache miss.

The simplest case is the *write-through strategy*, which is implemented in most caches. A write operation from the CPU always leads to the transfer of data to the main memory, even with a cache hit; all write operations are switched through to the main memory. Naturally, this also involves the writing to and updating of the applicable entry in the cache. Write-through has the disadvantage that all write operations must also be switched through to the much slower main memory. Without further measures this would, in principle, switch off the cache for write operations, and an unjustifiably long write access time would be the result. For this reason, write through caches use fast write buffers, which buffer the write accesses. However, depending on its size, this is only possible until the buffer is full. Thus, multiple write accesses invariably lead to wait states. On the other hand, the write-through strategy in a multiprocessor system automatically ensures main memory consistency, because all updates are switched through to the main memory. The cache consistency, however, is not so safe in a multiprocessor system. It is possible that a different CPU has overwritten the main memory; the cache of a different CPU would know nothing of this. Only an inquiry cycle can re-establish the consistency.

A *write-back cache* collects all write operations and only updates the cache entry, not the content of the main memory. Only after the corresponding instruction is the changed cache line copied to the main memory, in order to update the information therein. In the Pentium, this instruction can be initiated by software, for example through the WBINVD instruction (write-back and invalidate data cache), or through a hardware signal such as $\overline{\text{FLUSH}}$, for example, implicitly as the result of a cache miss, where one cache line is exchanged with another (see below), or through an internal or external inquiry cycle. The disadvantage of the write-back cache is that the exchanging of cache lines takes longer, because the data must first be written to memory before the new data can be read into the cache. However, this disadvantage is usually more than compensated by the fact that the previous write accesses need not be switched through to the slower main memory.

The two cache strategies described do not, however, make clear the behaviour when a cache miss occurs during a write operation – that is, the required address is not located in the cache. If the cache implements a *write-allocate strategy*, then the cache controller fills the cache space for a cache line with the content for the address to be written. Usually, the data is firstly written through to the main memory; the cache controller then reads into the cache the applicable cache line with the entry to be updated. Because the data is initially written through, the CPU can immediately restart the program execution. The cache controller performs the write allocate independently in parallel with the CPU operation. In the worst case, it must first write a changed cache line to the main memory before it can use the cache line for the new data. For this reason, and because of the clearly complicated cache implementation, most caches do not use a write-allocate strategy. Write accesses that lead to a cache miss are simply switched through to the main memory and ignored by the cache.

If other processors or system components have access to the main memory, as is the case, for example, with the DMA controller, and the main memory can be overwritten, the cache controller must inform the applicable SRAM content that the data is invalid, if the data in the main memory changes. This is also the case if a number of caches are available in a system, and are connected to different CPUs. Such an operation is known as a *cache invalidation*. If the cache controller implements a write-back strategy, and with a cache hit only writes data from the CPU to its SRAM cache, the cache content must be transferred to the main memory under specific conditions. This applies, for example, when the DMA chip should transfer data from the main memory to a peripheral unit, in which current values are only stored in SRAM cache. This type of operation is known as a *cache flush*.

The strategies described are not restricted to those hardware caches with SRAM and a cache controller. Software caches must also satisfy these requirements. As an example, most operating systems make use of any number of disk buffers, in order to accelerate floppy and hard disk accesses. Our much-loved DOS uses the CONFIG.SYS instruction BUFFERS for this purpose. With this, it ensures that the operating system can make use of a specific number of buffers, which operate as a cache between the CPU, the main memory and the floppy or hard disk controllers. Similarly to the way in which you can write-back the on-chip data cache of the Pentium to the main memory with a WBINVD instruction and then invalidate it, you can force DOS to perform a buffer flush with the 0dh, 5d01h and 68h functions of INT 21h. Older versions of the hard disk cache SMARTDRV.SYS only use the write-through strategy, and so caches are only effective during read accesses.

9.2 Cache organization and cache hit determination

In this section, I would like to explain the different types of cache organization and also the associated concepts such as direct mapped, two-way, tag and associative memory. The best way to describe such things is to use an example; for this purpose, in the following description, I would like to assume that the cache has been constructed for a 32-bit processor. Its size is 8 kbytes, a cache line contains 32 bytes, and it is laid out as a two-way set-associative cache. This corresponds to the on-chip code or data cache of the Pentium.

The cache controller internally splits the 32-bit address from the CPU kernel of the Pentium into a 20-bit tag address A31–A12, a 7-bit set address, and a 3-bit double word address (corresponding to a 5-bit byte address) (Figure 9.2, top). A cache entry consists of a cache directory entry and the corresponding cache memory entry. The cache directory contains information such as which data is stored in the cache; the actual data itself is stored in the cache memory entry. The cache directory can be stored internally in the cache controller, or in an external SRAM. For this reason, most cache systems require more SRAM chips than is actually necessary according to their memory capacity. This is because one or more SRAM chips must store the cache directory, while the others store the actual data. For a two-way cache, the cache directory entry contains a 20-bit tag address for each way and also, typically, a write protection bit, a valid bit and two LRU-bits (last recently used), which are used together for both ways. The cache memory entry – that is, the corresponding cache line – is 32 bytes in size, as per the above assumptions, and so contains four quad words, each of 64-bits (the width of the Pentium data bus). These four quad words correspond to the four transfer cycles of burst mode for a cash line fill of the Pentium. However, the Pentium, as a 32-bit processor, works with double words, and so a cache line contains eight double words. This is represented graphically in Figure 9.2 (middle).

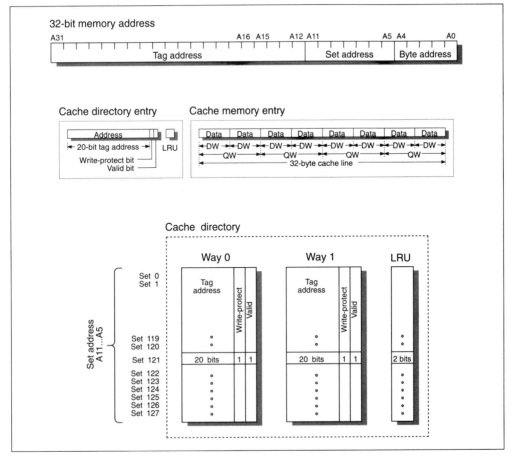

Figure 9.2: Memory address, cache entry and two-way cache directory.

9.2.1 Concepts

In the following subsections, I would briefly like to explain the important concepts that often occur in connection with caches.

Tag

The tag is the largest part of a cache directory entry. With its help, the cache controller determines whether a cache hit or a cache miss has occurred. The tag stores the tag address – that is, the address bits A31–A12 of the corresponding cache line (cache memory entry). The tag address is only valid with a set valid bit, otherwise it or the cache line contains incorrect values. For example, after a cache flush, the valid bits of all cache lines are reset and, in this way, all entries are identified as invalid. If the write protection bit is set, then the corresponding cache line cannot be overwritten. This is necessary, for example, so that a cache line fill can be completed without interruption, and so that a cache line fill cycle does not overwrite data that has already been changed by the CPU, before the cache line is completely contained within the SRAM cache.

Set

Every tag and the corresponding cache line are elements of the set. The 7-bit set address A11–A5 define the required set from 128 possibilities. Thus, in principle, a set is composed of a cache directory entry and the corresponding cache memory entry together, for each way.

Way

The way concept indicates the associativity of the cache system. For a given set address, the tag addresses of all ways are simultaneously compared with the tag part of the address given out by the CPU, in order to ascertain whether it is a cache hit or a cache miss. The example is of a two-way set-associative cache: it has two ways. Thus, a data group that corresponds to a cache line can be stored in the cache at two different positions. Each way in the example cache contains 128 sets with a cache line size of 32 bytes each. This, according to the capacity formula equals ways times sets times cache line size, giving the stated 8 kbyte cache memory. A set entry for the two ways together is a 2-bit LRU entry assigned; the cache controller uses them to determine which of the two cache lines should be replaced after a cache miss. There are a number of different algorithms for this.

Note that in this context the memory address at the top of Figure 9.2 contains no entry for the way. With the way, the associativity comes into play. A direct mapped cache only has one way, thus it is not associative; a data group can – if stored in the cache at all – only be stored at one position in the cache, subject to the 12 least significant bits. As an example, the data corresponding to the binary address xxxx xxxx xxxx xxxx xxxx ssss sssx xxxxb would always be stored in the set sssssss. The entry previously stored here must be replaced by the new one. In a two-way set-associative cache, the data corresponding to the binary address xxxx xxxx xxxx xxxx xxxx ssss sssx xxxxb would also always be stored in the set sssssss. Here, however, two ways are available for every set and so it is not absolutely necessary to overwrite the previous entry. If a cache line in the other way is free, then the cache controller can store the data in the second way. This increases the hit rate of the cache, as here, two entries are available for the same set address. Four-way set-associative caches have a correspondingly higher hit rate; however, the technical complexity is also increased.

Cache line

The cache line forms the complete data portion that is exchanged between the cache and the main memory. In a cache line, the double word for the 32-bit data bus is given by the address bits A4–A2. A cache line is either completely valid or completely invalid; it cannot be partially valid. Even when the CPU only wishes to read one byte, all 32 bytes of the applicable cache line must be stored in the SRAM cache, otherwise a cache miss will occur. The cache line forms the actual cache memory; the cache directory is used only for its management. Cache lines usually contain more data than is possible to transfer in a single bus cycle. For this reason, most cache controllers implement a block or burst mode, in which preset address sequences enable data to be transferred more quickly through the bus. This is very simple for cache line fills or the writing back of cache lines, because they always represent a continuous and aligned address area.

Content addressable memory

The associative memory concept often appears in connection with caches. It is also known as *content addressable memory* or *(CAM)*. This identifies its principle of operation. Usually, data in a memory is explicitly communicated with through its address. In an associative memory, however, this is achieved through a part of the data itself stored in memory – hence the name CAM. In order to read information from the CAM, a section of the information in question is input into the CAM. This should agree with a section of information already stored. If this is the case, the CAM sends out all of the information associated with that section; in this way, it 'completes' the section. As the section of information input to the CAM is only part of the information content, it is possible that sections of other information also agree, and, as such, are sent out. The result can be ambiguous, but this should not be surprising with associations – you yourself may associate 'Sea' with many things, such as holidays, beaches, swimming, sunburn and so on. If there is no resulting agreement at all with the data stored, then the CAM will not send out any data. This is as it is in real life: a sensible association with avfjnweflkad is, at least, difficult.

9.2.2 Cache hit determination

A cache performs associative addressing set by set. Thus, the association takes place in both ways. The addressing of the set, however, is explicitly given by the set address A5–A11. The information section for the associative addressing is given by the tag address in the set. This tag address is compared to the tag addresses A12–A31 from the CPU. If they agree, the cache controller associates the whole applicable cache entry – that is, the complete cache line that belongs to the corresponding way of the set with the correct tag address. In Figure 9.3, you can see the determination of a cache hit or cache miss schematically for the case of a two-way set-associative cache with 8-kbyte memory capacity.

The CPU kernel puts the 32-bit address of the data to be read onto the address bus. This is taken by the cache controller and split, as shown in Figure 9.2, into the tag, set and byte addresses. The tag address is immediately passed on to the tag address comparator. The controller uses the set address A5–A11 in order to choose a set in the cache directory for both way 0 and 1, and to send out the tag address for the set to the tag address comparator. The cache controller transfers the cache line from the SRAM data memory, corresponding to the set given in the 128-bit data buffer. The data buffer selects a double word from the cache line through the double word address A2–A4. Now it only requires the go ahead from the tag address comparator (an active enable signal) in order to actually put the data on the data bus. The tag address comparator compares the tag address from the CPU with the tag address from the cache directory. If the two agree, it activates the enable signal to the data buffer; the data is then available. If the two tag addresses are different, the output is blocked and a cache miss is indicated by the hit/miss signal. The cache controller must then address the main memory in order to transfer the data to the CPU and to begin the cache line fill. The selection and comparison operations described are performed in the same manner for both ways. Thus, among other things, two comparators, two data buffers and so on are required. The quantity increases as the associativity increases; that is, it grows in line with the number of ways. Therefore, the direct mapped caches are the simplest; the occasionally used eight-way set-associative caches are the most complicated. If the tag address from the CPU agrees with a tag address in any one of the different ways, a cache hit results; otherwise, a cache miss.

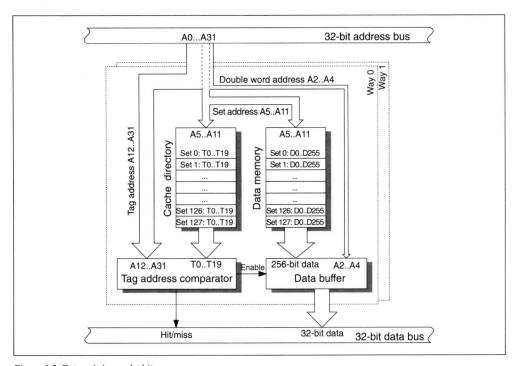

Figure 9.3: Determining cache hits.

The 20-bit tag address divides the 4-Gbyte address space of the Pentium into 2^{20} cache pages, each of 4 kbytes. Through the 128 sets, a page is further divided into 32-byte cache lines. Each of the two ways uses 256 of these cache lines.

Naturally, there are types other than the two-way set-associative cache described. In a four-way set-associative cache, for example, there are four ways in total (0 to 3). A direct mapped cache, on the other hand, contains only a single way. Of course, quantities of sets other than 128 can also be formed. For example, a typical L2 cache with 256-kbyte memory capacity, organized as a four-way set-associative cache with a cache line size of 32 bytes will have a total of 2048 sets. With this structure, the address partitioning is different to that shown in Figure 9.2: the byte address A4–A0 remains unchanged, the set address contains the 11 address bits A15–A5, and the tag address, the 16 most significant address bits A31–A16.

9.2.3 Replacement strategies

The cache controller uses the two corresponding LRU bits of a set of cache lines (see Figure 9.2) to identify the way of the set most recently addressed. This enables an *LRU strategy*: if the last access was accomplished through the use of way 0, the controller sets the LRU0 bit and resets the LRU1 bit. If, on the other hand, the last access was accomplished through way 1, LRU0 is reset and LRU1 is set. The controller updates the LRU bits with every memory access to the applicable set. A cache reset or a cache flush resets both LRU bits. If a cache miss occurs during a cache read, the cache controller replaces a cache line by the addressed data; it executes a cache line fill. The LRU strategy ensures that the cache line of a set in the way that was not the last to be addressed is overwritten with a new cache line; that is, the one with a reset LRU bit. It is also possible to use only one LRU bit. This binary value indicates which cache line was last used: a value of 0 indicates way 0, a value of 1 indicates way 1. Caches with more than two ways must correspondingly extend the LRU algorithm with additional LRU bits. In a direct mapped cache the LRU strategy serves no purpose, because only one way exists, so the cache controller does not require any assistance in selecting the cache line to be overwritten.

In addition to the LRU strategy, the cache controller can also exchange the cache lines randomly. This is also known as *random replacement*. The frequency of accesses to the individual cache lines then has no influence on their 'permanence' in the cache. Comprehensive statistical analyses have shown that there is very little difference between the efficiency of an LRU and a random replacement algorithm. Because it is less complex, the random replacement algorithm is easier to implement and it also works more quickly, because it does not require conditional operations.

The definition and implementation of the replacement strategy relies solely on the judgement of the cache system designer. Which cache construction and replacement strategy is chosen depends on the application, the cache size and the available (financial) resources.

9.3 Cache consistency and the MESI protocol

A major problem occurs as soon as two caches are available in a system. They can be, for example, a combination of an on-chip cache and an external L2 cache, or two separate caches for two CPUs in a multiprocessor system. The basic difficulty lies in the fact that the consistency of the data in the two different caches must be assured – this is no simple task. It is, for example, essential that every CPU always reads the most up-to-date data; on the other hand, very old data can also be overwritten. Similar problems can occur in single caches. A write-through cache updates all of the data including the main memory; a write-back cache requires an explicit instruction to ensure that data modified in a cache line fill is also stored in the main memory.

Right from the start, the Pentium was designed as a CPU for use in a multiprocessor system. In addition, it already includes two independent caches on its chip. Thus, cache inconsistencies cannot be avoided without taking further precautions. For this purpose, Intel has developed the MESI protocol for cache lines, which is briefly presented in the following section. Its application in the on-chip code and data caches, and also where an L2 cache is included, is discussed in Sections 9.4 and 14.2.

9.3.1 The four MESI states

The MESI protocol gives every cache line one of four states, which are managed by the two MESI bits. MESI is an abbreviation of modified exclusive, shared, invalid. The four terms also identify the four possible states of a cache line. The state of a cache line can be changed by the processor itself (through read and write operations, and also through internal snooping), or by external logic units, such as other processors or an L2 cache controller (through external snooping). But first of all, the four MESI states; at any given time, a cache line will have any one of the following four states.

Modified M

The data of a cache line that is marked as modified is available only in a single cache of the complete system. The line can be read and written to, without the need for a write access through an external bus. Note that the actual value need not necessarily be located in the main memory as well.

Exclusive E

An exclusive cache line, like the M cache line, is stored in only one of the caches in a system. However, it is not changed by a write access; that is, modified. Thus, the values are identical to those in the main memory. As an exclusive cache line is only stored in a single cache, it can be read and overwritten without the need for an external bus cycle. After an overwrite, the cache line is identified as modified.

Shared S

A shared cache line can also be stored in other caches in the system, it is – as the name suggests – shared with a number of other caches. A shared cache line always contains the most up-to-date value; in this way, read accesses are always served by the cache. Write accesses to a shared cache line are always switched through to the external data bus independently of the cache strategy (write-through, write-back), so that the shared cache lines in the other caches are invalidated. The address given out during the bus cycle is used as an external inquiry cycle for invalidating the cache lines in the other caches. At the same time, the content of the main memory is also updated. The write operation in the local cache itself only updates the content of the cache; it is not invalidated. Shared indicates the state with the least 'privileges' for a valid cache line.

Invalid I

A cache line marked as invalid is logically not available in the cache. The cause could be that the cache line itself is empty or contains an invalid entry; that is, not updated. Invalid or empty tag entries also cause cache lines to be marked as invalid. Every access to an invalid cache line leads to a cache miss. In the case of a read access, the cache controller normally initiates a cache line fill (if the line can be cached and its transfer into the cache is not blocked). A write access, however, is switched through to the external bus as a write-through. The MESI protocol will not provide a write allocate.

Table 9.1 lists the MESI states and also their causes and effects.

MESI state	Cache line valid?	Values in memory are	Copy exists in another cache?	Write access refers to*
M	Yes	Invalid	No	Cache
E	Yes	Valid	No	Cache
S	Yes	Valid	Possibly	Cache/memory subsystem
I	No	Unknown	Possibly	Memory subsystem

* Memory subsystem means main memory or L2 cache.

Table 9.1: The four MESI states.

The definitions of the four MESI states clearly show that the MESI protocol has been developed for a write-back cache without a write-allocate strategy for write misses. In order to be able to use the MESI protocol for a write-through cache, all valid cache lines must be held in the shared state; the modified and exclusive states cannot occur. In accordance with the MESI protocol, all write accesses must then be switched through to the external bus. This can, for example, be accomplished easily in the Pentium, in that the WB/$\overline{\text{WT}}$ signal is always held at a low level. As an additional note, this WB/$\overline{\text{WT}}$ signal enables the setting of individual cache lines as either write-through or write-back. Note that the MESI protocol is only employed in memory cycles and not in I/O or special cycles. These cycles are directly switched through to the external bus, so the cache is not affected. The write-through strategy is, above all, necessary for accesses to the video RAM of graphic adaptors; after all, changes should also be shown immediately on the monitor and not just stored (invisibly) in the cache.

9.3.2 Transitions of the MESI states

The state of a cache line can change in a read access, a write access or an inquiry cycle (snooping). The following rules apply to the transition of the various states into another. They are given separately for the three types of access. Figure 9.4 shows the corresponding transition diagram.

Read accesses

▶ M to M (R_1): the read access has led to a hit; the data is available in the cache and is transferred to the CPU.

▶ E to E (R_2): as above, the read access has led to a hit; the data is available in the cache and is transferred to the CPU.

▶ S to S (R_3): the read access has led to a hit; the data is available in the cache and is transferred to the CPU. Summed up, it is clear that according to the cache principle, a cache hit has no influence on the state of the cache, or the stored data during a read access.

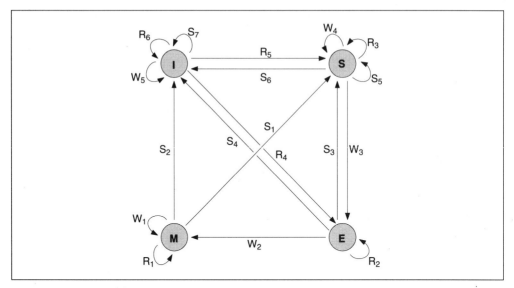

Figure 9.4: Transitions of the MESI states.

▶ I to E (R_4): the read access has led to a miss; the data is not stored in the cache. The cache controller sends out an external read cycle in order to read the data. As the cache line is in the exclusive state at the end, the addressed data must be cacheable, so that the cache controller can execute a line fill, and a write-back strategy must be implemented for it.

▶ I to S (R_5): as above, the read access has led to a miss; the data is not stored in the cache. Here also, the cache controller sends out a cache line fill in order to read the data. As the cache line is in the shared state at the end, the addressed data must be cacheable, so that the cache controller can execute a cache fill, and a write-through strategy must be implemented for it.

▶ I to I (R_6): the read access has led to a miss; the data is not stored in the cache. However, the cache controller cannot execute a line fill in order to load the cache line. Thus, it remains invalid.

Write accesses

▶ M to M (W_1): the write access has led to a hit; the data is available in the cache and so is updated. According to the MESI protocol, this relates to a write-back cache, so that no write-back cycle is sent through the external bus.

▶ E to M (W_2): as above, the write access has led to a hit; whereby the cache line was not previously overwritten. The cache controller then overwrites the cache line and annotates it as modified. According to the MESI protocol, this case also relates to a write-back cache, so no write-back cycle is sent through the external bus.

▶ S to E (W_3): the write access has produced a cache hit. As the original line is marked as shared, it could also be stored in other caches. According to the MESI protocol, this entry must be invalidated, so the cache controller sends a write cycle through the external bus.

Thus, the line is now only stored in the local cache; due to the write-through cycle, the entry in the main memory is also updated. The cache line can then be identified as exclusive.

▶ S to S (W_4): here also, the write access has produced a cache hit. However, W4 relates to a write-through cache. For this reason, all subsequent write accesses are switched through to the bus – that is, the write-through strategy is also actually implemented; the cache line remains identified as shared.

▶ I to I (W_5): the write access has led to a miss; the data is not stored in memory. The MESI protocol does not include a write-allocate strategy. For this reason, the missing entry is not loaded into the cache from the main memory. The cache line remains invalid.

Snooping

▶ M to S (S_1): the inquiry cycle has hit a modified cache line; it should not be invalidated. Despite this, the applicable cache line is written back to the main memory.

▶ M to I (S_2): as above, the inquiry cycle has reached a modified cache line that, here, should be invalidated. The applicable cache line is written back to the main memory.

▶ E to S (S_3): the inquiry cycle has hit a cache line marked as exclusive. It has not been modified and so need not to be written back to the main memory. This transition serves to transfer a line previously located in only one cache into another cache in addition. The cache line is then no longer exclusive; it must be marked as shared.

▶ E to I (S_4): as in S_3, the inquiry cycle has reached a cache line marked as exclusive. It also has not been modified and so need not to be written back to the main memory. S_4 also serves to transfer a line previously located in only one cache into another cache in addition. Unlike S_3, the cache line is invalidated, so it is available in a different cache as an exclusive cache line.

▶ S to S (S_5): the inquiry cycle has reached a cache line that is marked as shared. This interaction only informs the system that the applicable cache line is available in the cache. No bus activity results.

▶ S to I (S_6): the inquiry cycle has reached a cache line marked as shared. It has not been modified and so need not be written back to the main memory during the subsequent invalidation. The external controller that is performing the inquiry then knows that its copy has been updated.

▶ I to I (S_7): the inquiry cycle has found a cache line that is marked as invalid; that is, it does not contain valid data. No bus activity results; the controller performing the inquiry can ignore the content of the local cache for the applicable cache line.

Inquiry cycles are initiated by external bus controllers in order to determine whether the Pentium on-chip cache contains a specific cache line, and which MESI state it currently has. Such external inquiry cycles affect the code and data caches. Details concerning their operation are contained in Section 12.6. For locked accesses, the Pentium invalidates the addressed cache lines independently of their output state; it marks them as invalid.

9.4 The Pentium on-chip caches

In the Pentium, two separate and independent 8-kbyte caches for code and data are provided. In this way, no collisions are possible between instruction prefetching and data accesses occurring in one of the pipeline stages; the data and code caches work in parallel and can be addressed simultaneously. Each cache is laid out as two-way set-associative; each cache line is 32 bytes long, giving a total of 128 sets. The burst mode with its four transfer cycles, one after the other, and the 64-bit data bus can be used to their full extent for cache line fills or write-backs. Together with bus pipelining, the 100 Mhz Pentium achieves a line fill rate of 528 million bytes per second (equal to 508 Mbyte per second).

9.4.1 On-chip code and data caches

The data cache fully supports the MESI protocol. In this way, the write-through or write-back strategy of the data cache, according to the MESI protocol, can be individually set for each 32-byte cache line using the shared state. The code cache – except, of course, through an automatic reloading during instruction fetching – cannot be written to, and so only supports the shared and invalid states. Together with the setting of individual pages as cacheable or not cacheable through the PCD and PWT bits in the page directory or page table entry, this makes the cacheing of code and data in the Pentium very flexible to configure – it can be adjusted to requirements. By resetting and setting the CD bit in the CR0 control register, the two caches can be enabled or disabled. The exchange strategy and the MESI protocol are implemented as fixed parts of the hardware, so the Pentium can independently execute the cache line fills and the consistency algorithms without the influence of software, such as the operating system.

The tags of the data cache have three ports, so that two data accesses through the u and v pipelines, and also snooping can be executed in the same clock cycle. Note that the tags only ascertain whether the required address is stored in the cache. The data cache memory itself – and thus the cache lines – only have one port, whereby the entries at double word limits are interleaved, so that data from two data accesses to the same cache line can be handled through one port. Each tag entry is parity protected by a bit; each data byte of the data itself has a parity bit. In this way, minimum protection against data errors is included.

The tags of the code cache also have three ports, so that a split line access to the upper 16-byte half of a cache line, the lower 16-byte half of the subsequent cache line (this corresponds to a 32-byte window, shifted by 16 bytes, for the transfer of code to the 32-byte prefetch buffers) and an inquiry cycle can all be accomplished in one clock cycle. This allows simultaneous code fetch and inquiry if the instruction to be fetched crosses a line boundary in the code cache (the code fetch uses the split line access capability – that is, two simultaneous accesses to the code cache through two ports – and the inquiry cycle uses the third port). The code cache is connected to the 32-byte prefetch buffers through a 256-bit bus. For this reason, the complete cache line can be loaded into the buffer in only one cycle. The tag entry of the code cache is parity protected, as are those of the data cache; every tag has a parity bit, as does every 8 bytes of the code area.

The replacement of cache lines in the two on-chip caches is accomplished through an LRU algorithm, which replaces the least used entry in the two ways by the new data. For the implementation of the LRU algorithm, every set contains an LRU bit, which points to the least frequently used entry. In addition, every tag also requires information about the current MESI state of the applicable line. In the data cache, this is achieved by two MESI bits, which binary codify the four possible MESI states, modified, exclusive, shared and invalid. As the code cache only supports the shared and invalid states, one MESI bit is sufficient. Figure 9.5 shows the somewhat different structure of the tag and memory entry for the on-chip caches of the Pentium, as compared to that shown in Figure 9.2.

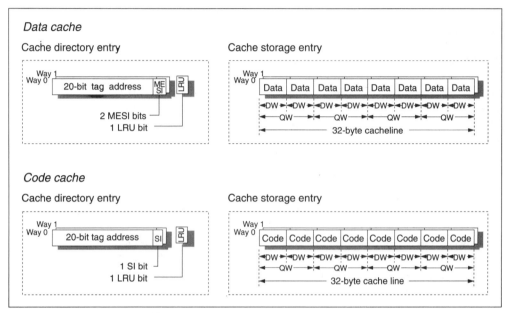

Figure 9.5: Structure of the tag and storage entries.

Through the separate caches for code and data, and also through instruction pipelining, a disadvantageous side effect occurs if a program changes its own code during its execution. This is the case in real mode programs, for example when a debugger overwrites instructions with the 1-byte opcode for INT 3, in order to insert breaks. In this case, where the Pentium will overwrite code that has already been read into the code cache and transferred to the prefetcher – the change is ignored because the write operation only affects the data path of the Pentium and not the code path. In the i486, it was necessary to execute a jump instruction after every code change in order to empty the prefetch queue and the instruction pipeline. In the Pentium, this is not possible because the branch prediction prevents such pipeline flushes. It is also not necessary because, due to the linear address, the Pentium automatically knows whether a write access also affects the address, which is already located in the prefetch stage of the pipeline or the pipeline itself. Thus, it is not necessary to insert a jump instruction after a code modification. Overwrites affecting code that is not yet loaded into the prefetch queue or the instruction pipeline, but which does lie in the code cache, are intercepted by internal snooping cycles that invalidate the corresponding entry in the code cache. In this way, the changed instruction is reloaded from the main memory at the next cache line fill, if it is required for execution in the Pentium.

9.4.2 The translation lookaside buffers

Every cache has its own translation lookaside buffer (TLB) assigned to it, so that the PU of the MMU can quickly convert code or data addresses into physical addresses. The caches use physical addresses; that is, the conversion of the linear address into the corresponding physical address must be accomplished before the access to the cache. Accesses to page tables in memory are only executed if the applicable TLB (for code or data) does not contain an entry for the addressed page. Two TLBs are assigned to the data cache: the first is for managing the standard 4-kbyte pages, the second is for the newly implemented 4-Mbyte pages. The first TLB has capacity for 64 entries. It is laid out as a four-way set-associative cache with 16 sets. The second TLB is also a four-way set-associative cache, but it has only eight entries (and so only two sets). Both of the data caches have two ports, through which two separate linear addresses from the two pipelines can be translated into two physical addresses. The replacement of TLB entries is accomplished by a pseudo-LRU algorithm, which is included as part of the hardware. In many RISC processors (such as the i860 and R3000), this is left to software, so that the operating system can react flexibly to a TLB miss. Like the data cache itself, the TLB of the data cache is protected by a parity bit; each tag and each data entry has its own associated parity bit.

The code cache has only one TLB, which is used for both the standard 4-kbyte pages and the new 4-Mbyte pages. It has a capacity of 32 entries and is configured as a four-way set-associative cache with eight sets. Thus, the code cache TLB is much smaller than the data cache TLB, which you can see clearly in the photograph (Figure 8.1). Code accesses are executed in the linear instruction flow in a very similar way to data accesses. Thus, the code cache TLB does not require as many entries in order to achieve just as good a hit rate (typically 99% or more). The code cache TLB contains only one port because only one bus to the prefetch buffers is required. The code cache TLB is protected by one parity bit per tag and one parity bit for each data entry.

Applications with CPL=3 to CPL=1 cannot address the TLBs; this is only possible with system programs with CPL=0. The management of pages and their external storing and reading in is, after all, the responsibility of the operating system kernel. If the system entry in the page table changes, the TLBs, or the applicable entry at least, must be invalidated because the change will be written to memory or to the cache. The Pentium, however, does not automatically know that an access to a page table entry has been executed, and that it must change the corresponding TLB entry. All of the TLBs are invalidated by loading the CR3 register, for example through the instruction MOV cr3, eax or through a task switch (the TSS contains an entry for CR3). This is necessary if the complete address conversion has changed (for example, as the result of a task switch). If, however, you only overwrite the individual entries, for example, through shifting a page in the physical memory, then it is sufficient to invalidate the corresponding entry in the TLB. This is accomplished with the help of the INVLPG mem32 instruction (invalidate TLB entry mem32). If the address from mem32 agrees with an entry in the TLB, this entry is invalidated.

9.4.3 Operating modes and registers for controlling the on-chip caches

The activation of the on-chip cache and the cache strategy therein is mainly set by the CR0 control register. Its structure is shown in Figure 9.6. The two bits CD (cache disable) and NW (not write-through) influence the on-chip caches. The effects of the four possible combinations of the two control bits are given in the following subsections.

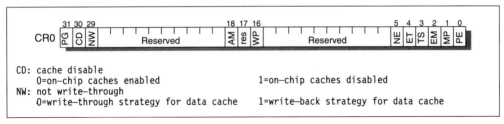

CD: cache disable
  0=on-chip caches enabled   1=on-chip caches disabled
NW: not write-through
  0=write-through strategy for data cache   1=write-back strategy for data cache

Figure 9.6: The structure of the control register CR0.

CD=0, NW=0

Read accesses are dealt with by the applicable cache when a hit occurs in a code or data cache. Misses initiate a cache line fill, if the values are cacheable ($\overline{\text{KEN}}$ at a low level); the loaded cache line is then stored in the exclusive or shared state, depending on the external signal WB/$\overline{\text{WT}}$. Thus, the on-chip caches are fully enabled. Write accesses only update the data cache during a hit to an exclusive cache line. Only during a hit to a shared cache line or a miss is an external write bus cycle initiated. Thus, the cache operates using a write-back strategy according to the MESI protocol. In addition to this, cache lines marked as shared can be changed to the exclusive state providing that a cache hit occurs during a write operation, the PWT pin is at a low level (corresponding to a write-back strategy for the applicable page), and the memory subsystem sends a high level signal to the WB/$\overline{\text{WT}}$ pin. Finally, with CD=0, NW=0, the on-chip caches support inquiry cycles and the corresponding invalidations.

CD=0, NW=1

The Pentium intercepts this invalid bit combination and issues a general protection error corresponding to the interrupt 0dh.

CD=1, NW=0

Read accesses are dealt with by the applicable cache when a hit occurs in a code or data cache. Misses do not initiate a cache line fill, because the cache is disabled by CD=1. Write accesses update the data cache when a hit occurs. The data to be written only appears on the external bus as well if a hit to a shared cache line or a miss occurs. The write-back strategy is set by NW=0, even if the cache (or, more accurately, the cache line fill) is officially disabled. In addition to this, cache lines identified as shared, as described above, can be changed to the exclusive state. Even though the caches are in fact disabled, they still support inquiry cycles and the corresponding invalidations.

CD=1, NW=1

Read accesses are dealt with by the cache when a hit occurs in a code or data cache. Misses do not initiate a cache line fill, because the cache, as above, is disabled by CD=1. Write accesses update the data cache when a hit occurs, but because of NW=1, are never switched through to the external bus. When a hit occurs to an exclusive cache line, its MESI state is changed to modified; the state of shared lines is not changed. Thus, the data cache further supports the MESI protocol. In other words, the MESI protocol logic is connected to the activation logic. For a write miss, the write access is switched through to the external bus. Only if all available cache lines are marked as invalid are all write cycles actually switched through to the main memory. The caches support neither inquiry cycles, nor invalidations.

In order to achieve high performance levels, you must set the CD and NW bits to 0 – that is, enable both caches and set the write-through strategy for the data cache. However, after a Pentium reset, these two bits are set – that is, equal to 1. Thus, after a reset, the on-chip caches are disabled and the standard strategy is write-back. If you wish to disable the on-chip caches after a prior activation, it is not sufficient simply to set the CD bit, In addition, the NW bit must be set, and, finally, a cache flush must be performed with INVD, or better still WBINV. The last step is necessary because cache hits can also occur when the cache is disabled, if the cache contains cache lines that are still marked as valid. Thus, the CD bit only disables cache line fills. If there are no valid cache lines, this is, however, equivalent to a full cache deactivation.

The MESI transitions and the results of inquiry cycles in Pentium are controlled and given, respectively, by a number of different signals. Table 9.2 lists the input or output signals. Figure 9.4 shows the transition diagram.

Transition	Signal
Read access	
M→M (R_1)	None
E→E (R_2)	None
S→S (R_3)	None
I→E (R_4)	$\overline{\text{CACHE}}$=0, $\overline{\text{KEN}}$=0, WB/$\overline{\text{WT}}$=1, PWT=0
I→S (R_5)	$\overline{\text{CACHE}}$=0, $\overline{\text{KEN}}$=0, WB/$\overline{\text{WT}}$=0 or $\overline{\text{CACHE}}$=0, $\overline{\text{KEN}}$=0, PWT=1
I→I (R_6)	$\overline{\text{CACHE}}$=1 or $\overline{\text{KEN}}$=1
Write access	
M→M (W_1)	None
E→M (W_2)	None
S→E (W_3)	PWT=0, WB/$\overline{\text{WT}}$=1
S→S (W_4)	PWT=0, WB/$\overline{\text{WT}}$=0 or PWT=1
I→I (W_5)	None
Inquiry cycle	
M→S (S_1)	INV=0, $\overline{\text{HIT}}$=0, $\overline{\text{HITM}}$=0
M→I (S_2)	INV=1, $\overline{\text{HIT}}$=0, $\overline{\text{HITM}}$=0
E→S (S_3)	INV=0, $\overline{\text{HIT}}$=0
E→I (S_4)	INV=1, $\overline{\text{HIT}}$=0
S→S (S_5)	INV=0, $\overline{\text{HIT}}$=0
S→I (S_6)	INV=1, $\overline{\text{HIT}}$=0
I→I (S_7)	INV=0, $\overline{\text{HIT}}$=1 or INV=1, $\overline{\text{HIT}}$=1

Table 9.2: Signals for MESI transitions and inquiry cycles.

R_4 to R_6 (see Figure 9.4) are controlled in the Pentium by the $\overline{KEN}$ signal (for cacheable data) and the WT/$\overline{WB}$ signal (for the write-through or write-back cache strategies).

9.4.4 Cache flush

The on-chip caches can be flushed both by external hardware and by software instructions. The Pentium then carries out a cache flush. The hardware-initiated cache flush is achieved by a low level signal at the $\overline{FLUSH}$ pin of the Pentium. This can be done, for example, through a gate that is controlled by external hardware (for example, the reset button on the computer housing). The Pentium then writes all modified lines in the data cache back to memory and marks all entries in the code and data caches as invalid. Finally, it executes a special cycle, the flush acknowledge cycle, to indicate the end of the cache flush. Special cycles are handled in Section 12.5.

For cache emptying through software, the two instructions INVD (invalidate data cache) and WBINVD (write-back and invalidate data cache) are available. The INVD instruction invalidates all entries in the code and data caches, but does not write back the modified cache lines to the main memory. Finally, it sends the special flush cycle through the bus, to indicate that invalidation has been executed. The WBINVD instruction, on the other hand, writes back all of the modified lines of the data cache before the invalidation. Only then are the entries in the code and data caches invalidated. To indicate the completion of the write-back and the invalidation to the external system (for example, an L2 cache), first the write-back cycle is executed, then a special flush cycle is sent through the bus.

9.4.5 Cacheing at page level

In addition to the individual definitions of the cache strategy and the activation of the cache at a cache line level, with an active PU, it is also possible to influence cacheing at page level. The two bits PCD (page cache disable) and PWT (page write-through) are used for this. They are included in the page directory and the page table entry, and control the activation of cacheing (PCD) and the cache strategy (PWT), respectively. In Figure 9.7, you can see the structure of the entries. The PCD and PWT bits are shown. You will find a more detailed explanation of the other fields in Section 11.5.4.

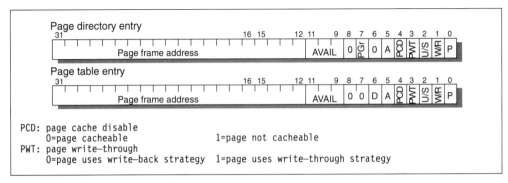

Figure 9.7: Page directory and page table entries.

The PCD bit controls the cacheing of the corresponding page. If it is reset, the page data can be transferred to the on-chip cache; that is, a cache line fill is executed, if $\overline{\text{KEN}}$ is also at a low level. If, on the other hand, the PCD bit is set (equals 1), then no data of the written page can be loaded into the cache, even if there is nothing to stop it on the hardware side (low level $\overline{\text{KEN}}$ signal). If the PWT bit equals 0 – that is, reset – then the cache should use a write-back strategy for the data of the page. If PWT is set (equals 1), then the page requires a write-through strategy. Naturally, the value of PWT has no effect if no cacheing is necessary for the page.

During a memory access, the effective values of PCD and PWT are given respectively by the PCD and PWT pins of the Pentium. You will find more information concerning the applicable pins in Chapter 10. If an L2 cache is available, the signals can be used to individually match an applicable cache strategy to the current memory access.

10 The pins and signals of the Pentium

In the Pentium, all components must be supplied with a stable operating voltage and a very sizeable current of more than 3 A at 100 MHz. This occurs through the 50 Vcc and 49 GND pins. Together with the 168 signal pins, the Pentium requires the large total of 267 pins. Six additional pins are not used; in connection with the 82496 cache controller, two of these pins are used as an interface between the Pentium and the cache controller. The Pentium comes in a monstrous pin grid array housing with 273 pins. The pins are not only used for the input and output of the supply voltage and signals; they are also used as a heat sink. Finally, the Pentium can 'burn' up to 13 W, almost all of which is converted into heat. Heat production per unit area is thus considerably higher than that of the heating system radiator in your room. Figure 10.1 shows the pins of the Pentium schematically.

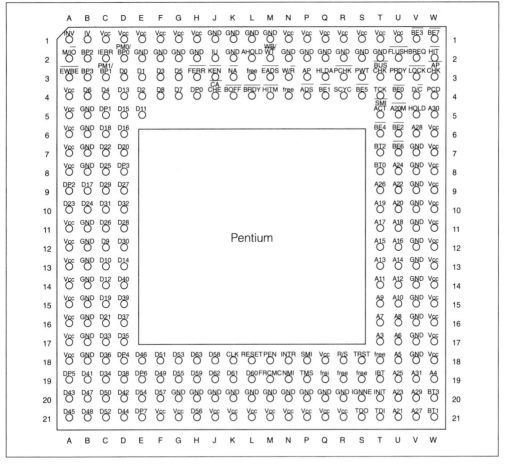

Figure 10.1: The Pentium pin layout.

In this chapter, I would like to present this large number of pins and explain the input and output signals. The sequence is alphabetical.

$\overline{\text{A20M}}$ (I)

Pin U5

If this address 20 mask pin is at a low level, then before every memory access, the Pentium internally masks the address bit A20. This also affects all accesses (look-ups) to the two internal cache memories. In this way, the Pentium emulates the wrap-around of the 8086 at the address 1M. $\overline{\text{A20M}}$ must only be activated in real mode.

A31–A3 (I/O)

Pins T9–T17, U8–U21, V6, V19–V21, W5, W19

These 29 pins provide the 29 most significant bits of the 32-bit address for write and read operations and, in this way, represent the 29 most significant address lines of the Pentium.

The three least significant address bits A0 to A2 are coded by the eight byte enable signals $\overline{\text{BE0}}$–$\overline{\text{BE7}}$. In an inquiry cycle, the external logic uses the 27 signals A31–A5 to transfer the inquiry address to the Pentium.

$\overline{\text{ADS}}$ (O)

Pin P4

A low level address status signal at this pin indicates that the Pentium has started a new bus cycle, and that the pins W/$\overline{\text{R}}$, D/$\overline{\text{C}}$ and M/$\overline{\text{IO}}$ give valid signals for the definition of the bus cycle, and that the pins $\overline{\text{BE0}}$–$\overline{\text{BE7}}$ and also A31–A3 give valid address signals. With a high level signal at the ADS pin, the pins detailed deliver non-defined signals.

AHOLD (I)

Pin L2

If this address hold pin receives a high level signal, a different bus controller can access the address bus of the Pentium, in order to perform an inquiry cycle for the Pentium. If AHOLD is active, the Pentium does not use its address bus A31–A3, BT3–BT0 and AP; all other signals remain active, so data for previously sent bus cycles can still be transferred.

AP (I/O)

Pin P3

In addition to parity formation for the data bus, the Pentium also supports parity formation for the address bus. Unlike DP7–DP0, AP is given out for the complete 29-bit address bus part A31–A3. For every write cycle, the Pentium sends out the AP parity bit, so that parity is achieved. When reading data, the system must send a signal to the AP pin that causes even parity (for A31–A3 and AP). Systems that do not support this parity function usually fix AP at Vcc or GND. In a read operation, the AP associated signal does not influence the program execution; the Pentium reacts to an address parity error only by activating $\overline{\text{APCHK}}$ two CLK cycles after the activation of $\overline{\text{EADS}}$ by the interrogating subsystem.

$\overline{APCHK}$ (O)

Pin W3

After the reading in of an external address during an inquiry cycle, the Pentium sends out a signal through the address parity check pin that indicates whether the transferred address bits A31–A3 and the address parity bit AP are consistent (thus, together give an even parity). If $\overline{APCHK}$ is at a low level, then an address parity error has occurred. $\overline{APCHK}$ is sent out by the interrogating subsystem two CLK cycles after the activation of $\overline{EADS}$ and remains active for one CLK cycle. The system need not necessarily serve or use $\overline{APCHK}$, or the other parity checking signals.

$\overline{BE7}$–$\overline{BE0}$ (O)

Pins U4, U6, U7, Q4, S4, T6, V1, W1

These (byte enable) signals indicate which byte group of the 64-bit data bus will actually transfer data in the current bus cycle. $\overline{BE0}$ corresponds to the least significant data byte D7–D0, $\overline{BE7}$ corresponds to the most significant data byte D63–D56. During a cacheable read cycle, all data lines must be used with a valid data signal independently of $\overline{BEx}$ values because, in principle, the Pentium carries out a cache line fill for such read accesses.

$\overline{BOFF}$ (I)

Pin K4

If the backoff pin receives a $\overline{BOFF}$ signal with a low level, the Pentium disables its bus at the next clock cycle. It disconnects all pins that are also disabled by a HOLD/HLDA cycle and interrupts all currently running bus cycles. After the deactivation of $\overline{BOFF}$, the Pentium restarts the interrupted bus cycle anew, in that all necessary address, data and control signals for the interrupted cycle are given out again; in other words, it starts the interrupted bus cycle again from the beginning.

BP3–BP2, PM1/BP1–PM0/BP0 (O)

Pins B2, B3, C3, D2

The breakpoint pins BP3–BP0 correspond to the debug registers DR3–DR0. An active signal indicates the occurrence of a breakpoint for the corresponding register (if the breakpoint is active). Through the two bits BP1 and BP0 in the debug mode control register DR4, you can set whether PM1/BP1 or PM0/BP0 should be used as a breakpoint pin (BPx=1) or for performance monitoring. BP3–BP0 enables breakpoint hits to be instantaneously seized by external hardware. Otherwise, an internal breakpoint interception only runs after a delay, because the Pentium must, first of all, internally produce the corresponding exception and jump to the handler using a relatively long-winded interrupt call.

$\overline{\text{BRDY}}$ (I)

Pin L4

The burst ready signal at this pin indicates whether the addressed peripheral system, for example the main memory, or an I/O device has already completed the requested access ($\overline{\text{BRDY}}$=low), or requires more time ($\overline{\text{BRDY}}$=high). Memory components or peripheral devices that react too slowly for the Pentium's higher cycle rate cause the Pentium, with the help of the $\overline{\text{BRDY}}$ signal, to insert one or more wait states. Above all, this is the case if neither the on-chip cache of the Pentium nor the second level cache (when available) contains or can load the required data, thus making a lengthy main memory access necessary. In this way, the Pentium waits until the addressed subsystem has completed the access. A wait state is a processor clock cycle; that is, a CLK cycle long.

BREQ (O)

Pin V2

Through the bus request signal BREQ, the Pentium indicates that it has requested the internal bus. It is possible that the Pentium cannot use the bus at this moment (due to an active AHOLD, HOLD or $\overline{\text{BOFF}}$ signal). Despite this, BREQ is still sent out and can be used by the bus operation logic in order to give the Pentium priority after the deactivation of AHOLD, HOLD or $\overline{\text{BOFF}}$.

BT3–BT0 (O)

Pins T7, T8, W20, W21

The three branch trace signals BT2–BT0 give the bits A2–A0 the linear branch address (the other address bits through A31–A3) during a branch trace message cycle; BT3 defines the standard operand size. If BT3 is active (high level), then the standard operand size is 32-bit, otherwise it is 16-bit. A set ET bit in the test register TR12 instructs the Pentium to execute such a branch trace message cycle and to send out the signals BT3–BT0 for every activation of IBT.

$\overline{\text{BUSCHK}}$ (I)

Pin T3

The subsystem addressed during a bus cycle can use the bus check pin to inform the Pentium of an incomplete bus cycle; that is, the cycle was finished, but the subsystem could not correctly execute the cycle (data read, data write or other access and so on) as instructed by the Pentium. If $\overline{\text{BUSCHK}}$ is active (at a low level), then the Pentium stores the addresses and values according to the control signals, in the machine check register. A set MCE bit in the CR4 control register then leads to a machine check exception corresponding to interrupt 18 (12h).

$\overline{\text{CACHE}}$ (O)

Pin J4

An active $\overline{\text{CACHE}}$ signal indicates that the current memory cycle sent by the Pentium is internally cacheable. If the Pentium initiates a memory read cycle or an instruction fetching cycle and $\overline{\text{CACHE}}$ is active (at a low level), then the Pentium extends the memory read cycle to a cache line fill in burst mode, providing the addressed memory subsystem activates $\overline{KEN}$ and, in this way, informs the subsystem that the required data or codes are cacheable. If $\overline{KEN}$ remains inactive, then despite an active $\overline{CACHE}$, the Pentium will not perform a cache line fill. The cause may be, for example, that with a memory mapped I/O, a control register is located at the addressed memory position. An inactive $\overline{CACHE}$ signal, independently of the $\overline{KEN}$ signal level, always leads to a single transfer without internal cacheing of the transferred data or code bytes. If $\overline{CACHE}$ is activated by the Pentium for a write cycle, then it executes a write-back of a cache line in burst mode. Write-throughs to the external memory are executed with an inactive $\overline{CACHE}$. These are write operations that lead to a cache miss in the on-chip data cache. The Pentium does not execute a cache line fill for such write cache misses. The $\overline{CACHE}$ signal could also be described as a burst instruction signal, because an active $\overline{CACHE}$ signal with a low level always results in a burst mode and the transfer of 32 bytes of code or data. In principle, I/O cycles are not cacheable, because usually a control or status register is lurking behind the addressed port.

CLK (I)

Pin K18
The clock signal is sent to this pin. The Pentium uses this signal as the internal processor clock signal PLCK.

D63–D0 (I/O)

Pins A10, A20, A21, B4, B9, B10, B19–B21, C4, C6–C21, D3–D7, D9–D17, D19–D21, E3–E5, E18, E20, F3, F4, F18–F20, G3, G4, G18, G19, H18, H19, H21, J18, J19, K19, L19
These 64 pins form the bi-directional 64-bit data bus of the Pentium for the input and output of data. Thus, the Pentium data bus is double the width of that in the i386. This, above all, increases the speed with which the two internal caches are filled or emptied. During a data read operation, the data at these pins is taken as soon as $\overline{BRDY}$ signal is active (i.e. reaches a low level).

D/$\overline{C}$, M/$\overline{IO}$, W/$\overline{R}$, (O, O, O)

Pins V4, A2, N3
The data/control (1=data cycle, 0=instruction/special cycle), memory/IO (1=memory cycle, 0=I/O cycle) and write/read (1=write cycle, 0=read cycle) signals at these pins set the current bus cycle type. The possible signal combinations have the following meanings:

▶ (000) interrupt acknowledge sequence
▶ (001) special cycle
▶ (010) reading from an I/O port
▶ (011) writing to an I/O port
▶ (100) instruction fetching
▶ (101) invalid
▶ (110) reading of data from memory
▶ (111) writing of data to memory

The special cycles are:

▶ $\overline{BE7}=\overline{BE6}=\overline{BE5}=\overline{BE4}=\overline{BE3}=\overline{BE2}=\overline{BE1}=1, \overline{BE0}=0$: shutdown
▶ $\overline{BE7}=\overline{BE6}=\overline{BE5}=\overline{BE4}=\overline{BE3}=\overline{BE2}=\overline{BE0}=1, \overline{BE1}=0$: internal cache flush (INVD, WBINVD)
▶ $\overline{BE7}=\overline{BE6}=\overline{BE5}=\overline{BE4}=\overline{BE3}=\overline{BE1}=\overline{BE0}=1, \overline{BE2}=0$: stop
▶ $\overline{BE7}=\overline{BE6}=\overline{BE5}=\overline{BE4}=\overline{BE2}=\overline{BE1}=\overline{BE0}=1, \overline{BE3}=0$: write-back cycle (WBINVD)
▶ $\overline{BE7}=\overline{BE6}=\overline{BE5}=\overline{BE3}=\overline{BE2}=\overline{BE1}=\overline{BE0}=1, \overline{BE4}=0$: flush acknowledge
▶ $\overline{BE7}=\overline{BE6}=\overline{BE4}=\overline{BE3}=\overline{BE2}=\overline{BE1}=\overline{BE0}=1, \overline{BE5}=0$: branch trace message cycle

DP7–DP0 (I/O)

Pins A9, A19, C5, D8, D18, E19, E21, H4

The Pentium supports the formation of parity for the data bus; that is, it sends out the parity bit DP7–DP0 for every byte of the data bus D63–D0 during every write cycle, so that even parity is achieved. When reading data, the system must send signals to the pins DP7–DP0 that will give an even parity. Systems that do not support this parity function, usually fix DP7–DP0 at Vcc or GND. The signals sent to the pins during a read operation do not influence the program execution, if $\overline{PEN}$ is not simultaneously active; that is, at a low level. With an active $\overline{PEN}$, the addresses in the applicable read cycle and the type of cycle are stored in the MCA and MCT registers, respectively. Through a set MCE bit in CR4, the Pentium sends out a machine check exception corresponding to interrupt 18 (12h). If $\overline{PEN}$ is not active, the only reaction of the Pentium to a data parity error is the activation of the $\overline{PCHK}$ signal two CLK cycles after the activation of $\overline{BRDY}$ by the addressed subsystem.

$\overline{EADS}$ (I)

Pin M3

An active low level signal at this external address pin indicates to the Pentium that an external bus controller has sent a valid address to its address pins. The Pentium uses these addresses during inquiry cycles.

$\overline{EWBE}$ (I)

Pin A3

An active low level signal at this external write buffer empty pin informs the Pentium that the external system (for example, a second level cache) is ready to take write data from the Pentium. If, on the other hand, $\overline{EWBE}$ is inactive (at a high level), the system must first execute an additional write cycle before the Pentium can proceed with transferring data. Only when $\overline{EWBE}$ is again active can the Pentium continue with the write operation.

$\overline{FERR}$ (O)

Pin H3

This pin sends out an active signal with a low level, if a non-masked exception occurs in the floating-point unit of the Pentium. In this way, the Pentium can be built into a system (mostly personal computers) that can, for reasons of compatibility with the i386/i387 combination, issue a coprocessor interrupt in order to indicate such a coprocessor fault.

$\overline{\text{FLUSH}}$ (I)

Pin U2
If the cache flush pin receives a $\overline{\text{FLUSH}}$ signal with a low level, then the Pentium writes back to memory all changed cache lines of the on-chip data cache and invalidates both on chip caches (data and code cache). An active $\overline{\text{FLUSH}}$ forces the Pentium to execute a cache flush. After the completion of the cache flush, the Pentium initiates a flush acknowledge cycle (see D/$\overline{\text{C}}$, M/$\overline{\text{IO}}$ and W/$\overline{\text{R}}$).

$\overline{\text{FRCMC}}$ (I)

Pin M19
The signal at this functional redundancy checking master/checker input indicates to the Pentium during a reset and its subsequent initialization whether it should operate as a master or a checker. As a master (high level $\overline{\text{FRCMC}}$), the Pentium controls the bus according to the usual bus protocol (for example, it activates the address and control signals). In checker mode, on the other hand, the Pentium determines the signal level at all output (O) pins (with the exception of $\overline{\text{IERR}}$ and TDO) and compares them with internal values. $\overline{\text{IERR}}$ is activated if the signal levels are not the same as the internal values.

$\overline{\text{HIT}}$ (O)

Pin W2
The $\overline{\text{HIT}}$ signal indicates the result of an inquiry cycle. If a hit occurs in the on-chip data or instruction cache, the Pentium drives the $\overline{\text{HIT}}$ signal to a low level. If a miss occurs, the pin sends out a low level signal.

$\overline{\text{HITM}}$ (O)

Pin M4
The hit modified line signal, similarly to $\overline{\text{HIT}}$, indicates the result of an inquiry cycle. If a changed line in the on-chip data cache is referenced, the Pentium activates the $\overline{\text{HITM}}$ signal at a low level. If a miss, or a hit to an unchanged line occurs, the pin sends out a signal with a high level. An external system can then use $\overline{\text{HITM}}$ during bus arbitration, to prevent a different bus controller from using the applicable data before the Pentium has written back the content of the changed line to memory.

HOLD, HLDA (I, O)

Pins V5, Q3
The two bus hold request and bus hold acknowledge pins are used for bus arbitration – that is, for controlling the transfer of the control of the local bus between the different local bus controllers. If a different bus controller (for example, a DMA controller or an external CPU)

wishes to have control, it sends a high level signal to the HOLD input of the Pentium. If the control transfer is not internally blocked by an active $\overline{\text{LOCK}}$ signal, or the current operation of an instruction, then the Pentium reacts with an active HLDA signal. This is a sign to the requesting bus controller that it can take over the control of the local bus, and must now generate the necessary bus control signal. The new bus controller keeps the HOLD signal active until it wishes to hand back control of the local bus (or until it must). It will then deactivate the HOLD signal, and the Pentium then retakes control. HOLD and HLDA play an important bus arbitration role in EISA (Extended Industry Standard Architecture) and microchannel systems.

IBT (O)

Pin T19

The instruction branch taken pin gives out a signal with a high level if the Pentium executes a branch internally. With a set ET bit in the control register TR12, the Pentium will also execute a branch taken message cycle.

$\overline{\text{IERR}}$ (O)

Pin C2

An active internal error signal with a low level at this pin indicates an internal error in the Pentium. This could be a parity error when reading internal data fields; the Pentium, working as a controller, then activates IERR and goes into a shutdown condition. In checker mode, $\overline{\text{IERR}}$ is activated if the received value at the output pins does not agree with the internally calculated values.

$\overline{\text{IGNNE}}$ (I)

Pin S20

If this ignore numeric error pin receives a low level signal and the NE bit in the control register CR0 is reset (thus, equals 0), then the Pentium will ignore numerical errors (exceptions) and continue to execute floating-point instructions. Despite this, $\overline{\text{FERR}}$ is activated. If $\overline{\text{IGNNE}}$ is at a high level (thus, inactive), and the next floating point instruction is a FINIT, FCLEX, FSTENV, FSAVE, FSTSW, FSRCW, FENI, FDIDI or FSETPM, then the Pentium executes the new instruction instead of the exception. If $\overline{\text{IGNNE}}$ is at a high level, and the subsequent instruction is other than those listed above, then the Pentium stops the instruction execution and waits for an external interrupt. If the NE bit in the control register CR0 is set, $\overline{\text{IGNNE}}$ has no effect.

INIT (I)

Pin T20

A signal with a high level at this initialization pin for a minimum of two CLK clock cycles sets the Pentium into a defined initial start condition in a similar way to a reset. However, unlike a reset, the internal caches, write buffers, model registers and floating-point registers are not reset, but retain their values. In addition to a reset and changing the value of the PE bit in the control register CR0, INIT also enables another possibility: switching the Pentium back into real mode. In this way, driver programs that were developed for the 80286 and only switch back into real mode when reset operate in the Pentium at a much higher speed. With a reset instruction from a keyboard controller, a corresponding external logic uses the INIT input in place of the reset input. In this way, a complicated and lengthy reset is avoided and the Pentium again runs in 80286 compatible real mode after only two clock cycles.

INTR (I)

Pin N18
With every clock signal CLK, the Pentium checks the status of the INTR signal. A high level indicates that an interrupt request from a hardware unit exists. If the interrupt flag IE in the EFlag register is set, then the processor completes the active instruction and, afterwards, immediately executes an INTA cycle in order to read the applicable interrupt number from the interrupt controller. The Pentium then calls the corresponding handler via the interrupt vector table (real mode) or the interrupt descriptor table (protected mode). By resetting the IE flag, the checking of INTR can be suppressed and, in this way, hardware interrupt requests can be masked.

INV (I)

Pin A1
During an inquiry cycle, a high level invalidation request signal at this pin leads to the invalidation of the applicable cache line, if a hit occurs. A low level marks the cache line as shared if a hit occurs. If no hit occurs, INV has no effect. Upon an active $\overline{\text{EADS}}$ signal, the addresses are transferred to A31–A5.

IU (O)

Pin J2
If the Pentium has completed an instruction in the u pipeline, for a CLK cycle, it sends out a signal with a high level from this instruction/u pipeline pin.

IV (O)

Pin B1
If the Pentium has completed an instruction in the v pipeline, for a CLK cycle it sends out a signal with a high level from this instruction/v pipeline pin. IU and IV are used for externally monitoring the pipeline activity.

$\overline{\text{KEN}}$ (I)

Pin J3
Through $\overline{\text{KEN}}$ (cache enable), the Pentium determines whether the current cycle is 'cacheable' – that is, whether the addressed address area can be transferred to the cache. If that is the case, and if the Pentium has sent out a cacheable cycle (thus, $\overline{\text{CACHE}}$ is active), then the current read access is expanded to a cache line fill cycle. The Pentium will then read a complete cache line into one of its two on-chip caches. As $\overline{\text{KEN}}$ information originates in a memory subsystem,

specific address areas of hardware devices can be protected from cacheing by $\overline{KEN}$. This is useful, for example, for accesses to memory mapped I/O areas because at the applicable memory address, control and status registers are to be found instead of storage cells.

$\overline{LOCK}$ (O)

Pin V3

With an active $\overline{LOCK}$, – that is, a low level signal at this pin – the Pentium will not pass control of the local bus to another bus controller which requests control using HOLD. Thus, it executes a locked bus cycle and does not respond to a HOLD request with an acknowledge (HLDA).

$\overline{NA}$ (I)

Pin K3

The next address signal is used for the implementation and control of address pipelining. The address decoder system of the computer indicates with, a low level signal at this pin, that the new values for $\overline{BE0}$–$\overline{BE7}$, A3–A31, W/$\overline{R}$, D/$\overline{C}$ and M/$\overline{IO}$ can be transferred to the decoder before the current cycle is completed. In this way, the next bus cycle has already begun before the current bus cycle ends with a $\overline{BRDY}$ signal. The Pentium carries out address pipelining, in that it begins the applicable bus cycle two CLK cycles after the activation of $\overline{NA}$. $\overline{NA}$ is latched in the processor and is activated with the next clock cycle, the Pentium 'notes' it as a type of pipeline request.

NMI (I)

Pin N19

If this pin receives a signal with a high level, then the Pentium issues an interrupt 2 which, unlike INTR, cannot be masked by the interrupt flag IE. Thus, it is a non-maskable interrupt. After the completion of the current instruction, the Pentium, in all conditions, stops the program execution and attends to the interrupt. Note that, unlike INTR, no INTA sequence is executed.

PCD, PWT (O, O)

Pins W4, S3

The page cache disable signal at this pin indicates the value of the PCD bit in the CR3 control register, the page table entry or the page directory entry for the current page. Thus, at this pin, the Pentium delivers external cacheing information on a page basis. The page write-through signal at this pin indicates the value of the page write-through bit PWT in the CR3 control register, the page table entry or the page directory entry for the current page. Thus, at this pin, the Pentium delivers external write-back or write-through information on a page basis. Individually, the pins deliver the following signals in specific circumstances.

If the on-chip caches are disabled by CD=1 in the CR0 control register, the PCD pin logically, always gives out a high level signal (for disabled). With disabled paging through PG=0 in the CR0 control register, the Pentium gives out a signal at PCD with a level corresponding to the value of the CD bit in the CR0 control register. The PWT pin gives out a signal with a low level (corresponding to write-back). The PCD and PWT bits are assumed to be 0. If both the on-chip caches and the paging unit are active (CD=0 and PG=1 in the control register CR0), then the values of the PCD and PWT bits in the page directory entry (for 4-Mbyte pages), or page table entry (for 4- kbyte pages) are given out at the PCD and PWT pins. Such entries are found in the TLB.

Furthermore, there are bus cycles that do not support paging even though paging is active, namely TLB refreshes. These cycles read the page directory or page table entries in order to store them temporarily for new pages in the TLB. The signals at the PCD and PWT pins and, thus, the effective internal values of the PCD and PWT bits, are defined according to the following sources:

▷   Access to page directory entry: PCD and PWT from the control register CR3
▷   Access to page table entry: PCD and PWT from the corresponding page directory entry

$\overline{\text{PCHK}}$ (O)

Pin R3
After the reading of data, the Pentium gives out a signal through the parity check pin, which indicates whether the transferred data bits D63–D0 and the parity bits DP7–DP0 are consistent. Only the data bytes explicitly identified as active with $\overline{\text{BEx}}$ are checked. If $\overline{\text{PCHK}}$ is low, then a parity error has occurred. $\overline{\text{PCHK}}$ is given out by the addressed subsystem two CLK cycles after the activation of $\overline{\text{BRDY}}$; it remains active for one CLK cycle. The system need not necessarily supply or use $\overline{\text{PCHK}}$ or any of the other parity checking signals.

$\overline{\text{PEN}}$ (I)

Pin M18
Together with the MCE bit in the CR4 control register, the signal at this parity enable pin defines whether the Pentium should send out a machine check exception corresponding to interrupt 18 (12h) if a data parity error occurs (for D63–D0, DP7–DP0) during a read cycle. With an active $\overline{\text{PEN}}$, the Pentium stores the address bits and the values of the bus control signals in the machine check registers. If the MCE bit is also set, then the Pentium sends out a machine check exception.

PRDY (O)

Pin U3
A signal with a high level at this probe ready pin indicates that the Pentium has stopped normal operation and has gone into probe mode as a reaction to a low level R/$\overline{\text{S}}$ signal. PRDY is used for the implementation of the new Intel debug ports, through which a debugger can be supported by external hardware.

PWT (O)

Pin S3

In a bus cycle that does not support paging, even though paging is active, PWT indicates the value of the PWT bit in the CR3 control register. With disabled paging, the Pentium always gives out a low level signal at PWT.

RESET (I)

Pin L18

If this pin receives a high level signal for a minimum of 15 CLK cycles, then the Pentium completely stops what it is doing and carries out an internal processor reset. In addition, all caches are invalidated (changed cache lines are not written back). The Pentium checks the signals at $\overline{\text{FLUSH}}$, $\overline{\text{FRCMC}}$ and INIT, in order to determine the operating condition after such a reset.

R/$\overline{S}$ (I)

Pin R18

A signal with a low level at this resume/stop pin interrupts the currently running program execution. The Pentium restarts the instruction execution when the signal changes to high level.

SCYC (O)

Pin R4

With a 16- or 32-bit access over a double word limit, or a 64-bit access over a quad word limit (a so-called misaligned access), the Pentium must carry out two memory accesses in order to read in, or to write, words, double words or quad words, respectively. With two sequential locked cycles ($\overline{\text{LOCK}}$ at a low level), for example a locked read–modify–write cycle, four accesses are required. The Pentium then gives out an active split cycle signal at the SCYC pin, in order to indicate that more than two locked bus cycles will follow. In the example given, four locked cycles are necessary, two for reading and two for writing. Such locked read–modify–write cycles are performed in order to ensure data integrity in a multi-bus controller system – that is, the Pentium reads, modifies and writes a data unit (for example, a variable) without another bus controller having permission to access the data using HOLD and the subsequent bus arbitration.

$\overline{\text{SMI}}$ (I)

Pin P18

An active low level signal at this input for a minimum of two CLK cycles causes the Pentium to activate the $\overline{\text{SMIACT}}$ signal, if it reaches an instruction boundary. In addition, it waits initially for the completion of all write cycles and the activation of $\overline{\text{EWBE}}$. The Pentium then stores the register values in the SMRAM (system management RAM), and branches to the SMM (system management mode) handler, in order to carry out the necessary functions. An RSM (resume from system management mode) instruction reloads the register values from the SMRAM back into the Pentium and enables the processor to resume the interrupted program.

$\overline{\text{SMIACT}}$ (O)

Pin T5
An active low level signal at this system management interrupt active pin indicates to the system that the Pentium is currently running in system management mode and only accesses the SMRAM.

TCK (I)

Pin T4
This test clock pin is sent a test clock signal for the boundary scan test. Synchronous with this clock signal, test data and status information is input and output.

TDI (I)

Pin T21
This test data input pin is sent TAP (test access port) instructions and data serially synchronized with TCK. The instructions and data are necessary for the boundary scan test.

TDO (I)

Pin S21
From this test data output pin, instructions and result data from the boundary scan test are sent out. It is serially synchronized with TCK.

TMS (I)

Pin P19
If this test mode select pin receives a high level signal, the test access port sends out the JTAG test logic for the boundary test scan. If TMS remains at a high level for five TCK cycles or more, then it restarts the test logic independent of the currently active condition.

$\overline{\text{TRST}}$ (I)

Pin S18
An active signal with a low level at this test reset pin initializes the boundary scan test logic.

WB/$\overline{\text{WT}}$ (I)

Pin M2
A signal with a high level at this write-back/write-through pin defines the corresponding cache line as write-back, or otherwise write-through, during a memory access. In this way, the cache

lines can be configured individually as write-back or write-through. WB/WT, together with PWT, is necessary for the implementation of the MESI protocol.

Free

Pins L3, N4, Q19, R19, S19, T18
These pins should always be held in a free (floating) condition. If a second level cache is available with an 82496 cache controller, the two pins L3 ($\overline{\text{BRDYC}}$) and N4 ($\overline{\text{ADSC}}$) serve as pins between the Pentium and the cache controller. You will find more information concerning the cache subsystem in Section 14.2.

Vcc (I)

Pins A4–A8, A11–A18, C1, D1, E1, F1, F21, G1, G21, H1, J21, K21, L21, M21, N1, N21, P1, P21, Q1, Q18, Q21, R1, R21, S1, T1, U1, W6–W18
These pins receive the supply voltage ((+5 V for the 60 and 66 MHz Pentium, +3.3 V for the 90 and 100 MHz P54C), in order to supply the Pentium with current. Up to 3.2 A flows through Vcc (thus, 64 mA maximum for each pin).

GND (I)

Pins B5–B8, B11–B18, E2, F2, G2, G20, H2, H20, J1, J20, K1, K2, K20, L1, L20, M1, M20, N2, N20, P2, P20, Q2, Q20, R2, R20, S2, T2, V7–V18
These pins are connected to ground (earth; usually 0 V).

11 Pentium operating modes

The Pentium can be operated in a number of different modes. When switched on, or after a reset, it starts in real mode as do all other 80x86 processors. It can also be switched to protected and virtual 8086 mode. In order to improve the performance in continually developing virtual 8086 mode, a few new improvements have been introduced compared to the i386 and i486, which, above all, increase the speed of interrupt handling. Completely new are the system management mode for reducing energy consumption, and the probe mode for supporting debuggers with the Pentium hardware. The paging functions in the Pentium have also been expanded. For supporting larger systems with a linear memory model, 4-Mbyte pages have been included in addition to the standard 4-kbyte pages.

11.1 Pentium real mode

On compatibility grounds, the Pentium can operate in real mode in addition to the more modern protected and virtual 8086 modes. In this mode, it forms linear addresses in the same way as the 8086, with the multiplication of the segment register value by 16 and the addition of the offset. With the 8086, the addresses are strictly limited to 1M because the 20-bit adder in the addressing unit only has a 20-bit bus. The combination of the highest segment and offset register values of ffffh in each case produces a linear address of ffff0h + ffffh=10ffefh, which lies above the highest address fffffh that the 8086 can allocate (all 20 address lines equal 1). The 8086, therefore, carries out a so-called *wraparound*, as the leading '1' is simply ignored. The 8086 allocates the address 0ffefh, which is located lower in the memory.

With the Pentium, the limit to 20 bits does not apply, of course, because it has a 32-bit adder with a 32-bit address bus located in the addressing unit and can therefore produce 32-bit addresses. The Pentium, therefore, does not produce the address 0ffefh, but the full address 10ffefh in order to break the 1M barrier by ffefh, or almost 64 kbytes. The corresponding data is stored in extended memory. For strict (and completely stupid) compatibility with the real mode of the 8086, personal computers have an additional gate installed that, in specific circumstances, blocks the A20 signal (which applies to the leading '1'). In this way, the wraparound of the 8086 is emulated. The gate is mainly controlled by the keyboard controller under the supervision of the HIMEM.SYS driver, which delivers a defined program interface for the A20 gate.

The address generation in the real mode of the Pentium is different to the 8086 and 80286 in another way. With its 32-bit offset register and help from address prefixes, the Pentium can actually produce 32-bit addresses. If the content of a 32-bit offset register is used as an address and the value of the effective address is over ffffh, the Pentium produces a so-called pseudo-protection exception without an error code, which leads to an interrupt 12 or 13 (see Section 11.2). In this way, a halt is called to the production of linear addresses beyond 10ffefh (which is a pity, because otherwise the complete Pentium address space of 4 Gbytes would be available in place of a meagre 1 Mbyte).

In real mode, all of the instructions specific to protected mode such as LLDT (load local descriptor table – a data structure that is available only in protected mode) are as useless as the unnecessary opcodes.

11.2 Interrupts and exceptions

From the combined efforts of the bus interface, prefetch queue, execution unit and so on. of the processor, it is easy to see that the processor can carry out instructions endlessly. As soon as an instruction has been executed, the next is loaded and executed. Even if it appears that the computer is inactive, ready for you to type in an instruction (such as DIR, for example), it does not mean that it has stopped working, only to start again when instructed to. Many more routines run in the background, such as a keyboard check, to determine whether a character has been typed in. Thus, a program loop is carried out. Only notebooks with power management actually stop the processor from functioning after a specific time without an instruction. The first key press reactivates the CPU immediately.

For the intentional stoppage of the processor during continual operation, interrupts are used. For example, a periodic interrupt called the timer interrupt is used in the PC to update the internal system clock regularly. The Pentium (and 80x86s in general) has a total of 256 different interrupts (0 to 255). Intel has reserved the first 32 interrupts for use by the processor.

There are three categories of interrupts, which depend on the source:

- software interrupts
- hardware interrupts
- exceptions

11.2.1 Software interrupts

Software interrupts are initiated with an INT instruction. For example, the instruction INT 10h issues the interrupt with the hex number 10h. Figure 11.1 shows the procedure for carrying out an interrupt in real mode.

In the real mode address space of the Pentium, 1024 (1k) bytes are reserved for the interrupt vector table. This table contains an *interrupt vector* for each of the 256 possible interrupts. In the 8086, the position of this table was preset by the hardware. The Pentium, in real mode, manages this itself and is a little more flexible. From all memory management registers (see Figure 8.7) the interrupt descriptor table register (IDTR) is already valid in real mode. It stores the base address and the limit of the real mode descriptor table. After a processor reset, the IDTR is normally loaded with the value 00000000h for the base and 03ffh for the limit. This corresponds exactly to a 1-kbyte table of segment 0000h and offset 0000h. Through the two Pentium instructions LIDT (load IDTR) and SIDT (store IDTR), it is possible to change the base and limit values, and thus to change the table size and to move it to a different position in the real mode address space.

Note, however, that the table must be able to record all of the vectors for all possible interrupts, otherwise an exception 8 would result (see below).

Every interrupt vector in real mode consists of four bytes and gives the jump address of the *interrupt handler* for the particular interrupt in the segment:offset format. Since the interrupts usually only have one cause (such as the request of an operating system function or receipt of data at the serial interface), the interrupt handler handles the interrupt in the applicable way.

For example, it carries out the operating system function or receives the character. Through the replacement of the handler, the interrupt can simply take on another function.

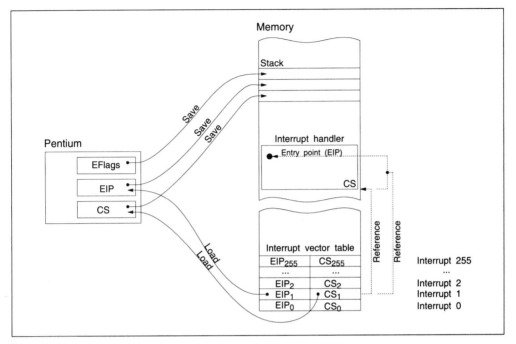

Figure 11.1: Interrupts in real mode.
When an interrupt is issued to the Pentium the processor automatically transfers the current flags, the instruction pointer EIP and the code segment CS onto the stack. The interrupt number is internally multiplied by four and then provides the offset in segment 00h where the interrupt vector for handling the interrupt is located. An interrupt vector is an address in the segment:offset format which represents the entry point of the applicable handler. The Pentium loads EIP and CS with the values in the table.

The coordination of interrupts and interrupt vectors is accomplished on a one-to-one basis. This means that the interrupt 0 is assigned the interrupt vector 0 (at the address 0000:0000) and the interrupt 1 is assigned the interrupt vector 1 (at the address 0000:0004) and so on. The Pentium only has to multiply the number of the interrupt by four to establish the offset of the interrupt vector in segment 0000h. The overwriting of the interrupt vector table with incorrect values has a catastrophic effect on the Pentium. The next interrupt will not be able to find the applicable jump address, causing the computer to crash.

When an interrupt occurs, the Pentium automatically carries out the following procedure (see Figure 11.1), without any further input from the program:

▶ The Pentium puts the EFlags CS and EIP – in this sequence – onto the stack (flags CS and IP in 16-bit mode)
▶ the interrupt and the trap flag are reset
▶ the Pentium addresses the interrupt vector in the interrupt vector table corresponding to the number of the interrupt and loads EIP (or IP in 16-bit mode) and CS from the table

CS:EIP of the interrupt vector gives the entry point of the interrupt handler. In this way, the processor continues its work with the interrupt handler. The return to the current program occurs with an IRET.

Example: INT 10h

The processor saves the current flags, CS and EIP, on the stack, clears the interrupt and trap flags and reads the interrupt vector at location 0000:0040. The two bytes at 0000:0040 are loaded into EIP, the two bytes at 0000:0042 into CS (note the Intel format low–high).

 Note that the Pentium, in 32-bit mode, loads the offset value of the handler into EIP, but the offset in the interrupt vector table is only 16-bit because of the need for compatibility with the 16-bit 8086 and 80286 predecessors. The two most significant bytes in EIP are simply filled with the value 0000h.

The encoding of an INT instruction is also interesting:

INT 3   for all others:

| 11001100 | | 11001101 | vvvvvvvv |

11001100 and 11001101 represent the opcode, and *vvvvvvvv* indicates the number of the interrupt. Thus, the INT 3 instruction consists of only one byte. You will find out more about this interrupt in Section 11.2.3. For all other interrupt instructions, only one immediate addressing is possible; this means that the number of the interrupt vector is part of the instruction. In this way, the number of the interrupt cannot be held in a register or memory operand.

Software interrupts are synchronized with program execution, which means that every time the program gets to the point where there is an INT instruction, an interrupt is issued. This is considerably different to hardware interrupts and exceptions.

11.2.2 Hardware interrupts

As the name suggests, these interrupts are set by hardware components (with timer interrupts, for example, by the timer component) or by peripheral devices such as a hard disk. There are two basic types of hardware interrupts: *non-maskable interrupts (NMI)* and *(maskable) interrupt requests (IRQ)*. Normally an interrupt controller is used for these IRQs, which can control a number of such interrupts and pass them on to the processor depending on their priority.

When the computer sets an NMI, the NMI terminal of the processor (pin N19 in the Pentium) receives an active signal. The Pentium finishes the current instruction and immediately afterwards, carries out an interrupt 2 in exactly the same way as before. An NMI is usually the result of a serious hardware problem, such as a memory parity error or a bus error.

An NMI is different in that it cannot be suppressed (or masked, as its name suggests). An NMI always pushes its way to the forefront. Because it normally indicates a serious failure, this, however, is understandable and also correct: a computer with incorrectly functioning hardware must be prevented from destroying data.

Interrupt requests, on the other hand, can be masked with a reset interrupt flag IE. In real mode, this can be accomplished with the CLI instruction. All interrupt requests at the INTR connection (pin N18) are ignored. The opposite STI instruction reactivates these interrupts. Note that the software instruction INT xx specifically carries out a CLI. This means that it blocks all interrupt requests. It is therefore necessary to carry out an STI to reactivate the interrupt requests after an INT instruction, otherwise the computer would be 'deaf'.

Interrupt requests are usually issued by a peripheral device. An example would be where the serial interface informs the Pentium that it has just received a character. This and other hardware interrupt requests are controlled by the interrupt controller. When it receives a signal from a unit to indicate that the unit has requested an interrupt, the interrupt controller sends the interrupt request signal (IRQ) to the INTR input (pin N18) of the Pentium. If the processor can handle the interrupt (IE is set), the Pentium sends the confirmation signal INTA (interrupt acknowledge) by setting each of the control signals M/$\overline{\text{IO}}$ D/$\overline{\text{C}}$ and W/$\overline{\text{R}}$ to a low level (see Section 12.5). During the INTA cycle, the interrupt controller delivers the number of the active interrupt. The processor continues in the same way as explained previously and addresses the applicable interrupt handler.

Hardware interrupts (NMI and IRQ), unlike software interrupts, are asynchronous to the program execution. This is understandable because, for example, the serial interface does not always receive a character at the same point in a program. This depends on whether or not the serial interface is connected to a device and if the device is actually switched on. This makes the detection of program errors very difficult if they occur only in connection with hardware interrupts.

11.2.3 Exceptions

We have already learned about two sources of interrupts; a third originates in the processor itself. Interrupts produced by the Pentium are known as *exceptions*. The production of an exception corresponds to that of a software interrupt. This means that an interrupt is issued, the number of which is set by the Pentium itself. The cause of an exception is usually an internal processor error caused by system software, which can no longer be handled by the processor alone.

Exceptions are distinguished according to three classes: faults, traps and aborts. The characteristics of these three classes are as follows:

▶ Fault: a fault issues an exception prior to completing the instruction. The saves the EIP value then points to the instruction that led to the exception. By loading the saved EIP value (for example, with IRET) the Pentium is able to re-execute the instruction, hopefully without issuing an exception again. One example of a fault is the exception segment not present. The Pentium has the ability to reload the segment and attempt another access.

▶ Trap: a trap issues an exception after completing instruction execution. Thus, the saved EIP value points to the instruction immediately following the instruction that gave rise to the exception. The instruction is therfore not re-executed. Traps are favourable if the instruction has been executed correctly but the program should netherthemore be interrupted. This holds, for example, in the case of debugger breakpoints. Here the instructions should be executed, and the debugger only checks the register contents and so on. Re-executing the corresponding instruction would lead to a faulty instruction flow.

▶ Abort: unlike faults and traps, an abort does not always indicate the address of the error. Therefore, after an abort the recovery of program execution is not always possible. Aborts are only used to indicate very serious failures such as, for example, hardware failures or invalid system tables.

Many exceptions are used when the Pentium operates in protected mode. In real mode, only the following exceptions are used (the processor with which each exception was implemented is given in parentheses):

▶ Division by 0 (exception 0; 8086): if, with the instruction DIV or IDIV, the devisor equals zero, then the result of the operation is not mathematically defined and the Pentium cannot reply.

▶ Single step (exception 1; 8086): if the trap flag is set, the Pentium issues an interrupt 1 after each separate step. The trap flag is automatically reset by the Pentium when an interrupt is issued, so that the processor can continue with the interrupt routine. Debuggers use the trap flag and intercept the interrupt so that the program can be carried out step by step.

▶ Breakpoint (exception 3; 8086): in the Pentium, a breakpoint exception can occur in two different ways. The Pentium contains an internal debug register which assists it in issuing an interrupt 3 under specific circumstances. In addition, a debugger can set a breakpoint in place of an instruction, in which the instruction (or its first byte) is overwritten with the op-code 11001100 for the INT 3 instruction. When the program reaches this point, the Pentium issues an interrupt 3 and the program is interrupted. For continuation of the program, the debugger overwrites the opcode 11001100 with the byte existing previously at this location and carries out an IRET. Of course, the Pentium can also use the INT 3 instruction to issue a software interrupt 3. This also applies to all of the other exceptions, except that there is no reason for the subsequent interrupt as the source of the interrupt lies in a processor error and not in an explicit software interrupt.

▶ Overflow with INTO (exception 4; 8086): if the overflow flag is set and the INTO instruction is sent, the processor produces an interrupt 4.

▶ BOUND (exception 5; 80186): the Pentium will issue an interrupt 5 if an index in a field is checked with the BOUND instruction and is found to lie outside the boundaries of the field.

▶ Invalid OPCODE (exception 6; 8086): if the instruction unit comes across an opcode without an associated instruction, the processor will send out an interrupt 6. The causes of invalid opcodes are usually incorrect assemblers or compilers, or a program error that causes a jump to a position that does not contain an opcode, but a data word that the instruction unit interprets as an opcode.

▶ No coprocessor available (exception 7; 8086): if the instruction unit receives an opcode for a coprocessor instruction (an ESC instruction) and there is no coprocessor installed, the Pentium issues an interrupt 7.

▷ IDT limit too small (exception 8; 80286): if the limit of the IDT is too small for the vector of the interrupt, the Pentium issues an interrupt 8. This is often the case when a program has read and incorrectly changed the IDT.

▷ Stack exception (exception 12; 80286): the stack pointer ESP delivers a value higher than ffffh for the stack access. This can occur because ESP represents a 32-bit register and its value is not restricted to 1M. The Pentium then sends out an interrupt 12 to stop the allocation of linear addresses above 10ffefh in real mode.

▷ General protection error (exception 13; 80286): a 32-bit offset register delivers an effective address higher than ffffh for a memory access. As for the stack pointer ESP, the allocation of linear addresses above 10ffefh in real mode is stopped; in this case the Pentium issues an interrupt 13.

▷ Coprocessor error (exception 16; 80286): an error occurs in the floating-point unit and the Pentium activates the $\overline{FERR}$ signal.

11.2.4 The floating-point exceptions

The following list shows the cause of each exception as well as the respective standard handler. For an unmasked exception, the applicable bits are set in the status word of the floating-point unit (see Figure 8.9); the Pentium issues an exception 16 – coprocessor error.

▷ Precision (PE, PM): the result of an operation cannot be represented exactly in the determined format. The coprocessor continues its tasking without further action if the bit is PM.

▷ Underflow (UE, UM): the result is different to zero, but too small to represent in a determined format. If UM is equal to 1, the Pentium cancels the normalization of the result and displaces the mantissa leading 1 to the right until the exponent conforms to the chosen format. Each displacement to the right results in a division of the mantissa by 2, therefore the value of the exponent must be increased by 1. This process is known as a *gradual underflow*.

▷ Overflow (OE, EM): the result is too large for the determined format. If the exception is masked, the Pentium produces a code internally for the value $\pm\infty$ and uses this for further operation.

▷ Division by zero (ZE, ZM): the divisor is equal to zero, the dividend different to zero. On mathematical grounds, the result is not definable (thus not equal to $\pm\infty$). Undefined things are difficult to work with. The Pentium produces internally an encoding for $\pm\infty$ for masked exceptions.

▷ Denormalized operand (DE, DM): at least one operand or the result of the operation cannot be represented in normalized form (having the smallest possible exponent with a mantissa different to zero). If DM=1, then the Pentium continues to operate with the denormalized number without any further action.

▷ Invalid operation (IE, IM): either an overflow or an underflow of the register stack has taken place (PUSH on a full register stack or POP on an empty register stack). Either an undefined mathematical operation, for example $0 \div 0$, $\infty \div \infty$ or $\infty - \infty$, should be executed, or a NAN value used as an operand. The Pentium produces either a predetermined NAN value or outputs a NAN value as a result for a masked exception.

11.3 Pentium protected mode

Protected mode was originally implemented in the 80286 to protect (as its name suggests) the different tasks in a multitasking operating system against invalid or incorrect accesses. Two essential differences compared to the real mode are the completely different way in which linear addresses for a memory object are calculated, and the size and implementation of access checks of programs for code and data with respect to hardware. The following section details the special characteristics of the protected mode.

11.3.1 Segment selectors, segment descriptors and privilege levels

As previously described, in real mode the addressing unit of the Pentium simply multiplies the value of the segment register by 16 in order to determine the base address of the applicable segment. The address contained in such a 64-kbyte segment is then given by the offset. In protected mode, the values in the segment registers are interpreted completely differently; they represent so-called *selectors* and not base addresses. Figure 11.2 shows the organization of such a segment selector.

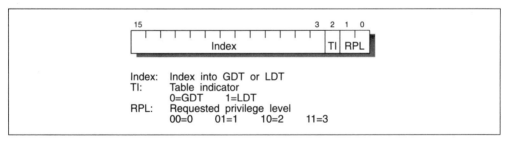

Figure 11.2: Structure of a segment selector.

The selector is 16 bits long and completely fills the 16-bit segment register. The two least significant bits 0 and 1 specify the *requested privilege level (RPL)* from which a program can access the segment – here, we are first confronted with an access check of the protected mode. The value of the RPL field in the segment selector of the code segment CS is known as the *current privilege level (CPL)*; this refers to the privilege level of the currently active program. The active program can access data segments that have a privilege level the same as or higher than the CPL. The value of RPL can also be larger than the value of CPL, which means that the segment set by the selector is accessed with a lower privilege level. The larger of the CPL and RPL values defines the *effective privilege level (EPL)* of the task. The Pentium has in total four privilege levels (PL) 0 to 3. Note that 0 is the highest and 3 is the lowest privilege level – a higher value indicates a lower privilege level and vice versa. An RPL of 0 does not restrict the privilege level of a task at all, whereas a selector with RPL 3 can only access segments that have a privilege level of 3, independently of the CPL.

Programs with lower privilege levels (a higher CPL) can only access a segment with a higher privilege level (lower CPL) in strictly defined circumstances. For this, the Pentium uses so-called *gates* to 'open the door' to segments with higher privileges. In this way, the Pentium hardware implements a method of protection included in the task through the use of the different privilege levels. Figure 11.3 graphically shows the four privilege level concept. Access to the highest level – the operating system core with PL=0 – is only possible through the gates.

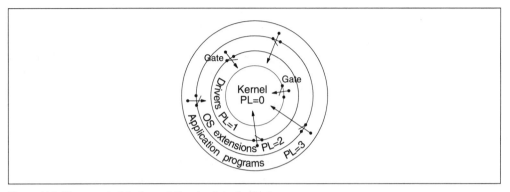

Figure 11.3: The concept of the four privilege levels in the Pentium.

Usually the most critical part (the kernel) of the operating system uses the highest privilege level 0. The kernel consists of the routines for memory control, for task switches and for the handling of critical errors, and so on – the most basic processes for maintaining the operation of the computer. Many instructions that directly affect the status of the processor or computer, such as LGDT (load global descriptor table), for example, or LMSW (load MSW), are only carried out by the Pentium in protected mode when the applicable program has privilege level 0. This should prevent applications from corrupting the operating system due to program errors or hackers gaining uncontrolled access to data.

Operating systems should not only manage and control the computer, but should also perform the data management function, signal outputs and so on for applications. In DOS, the PC accomplishes this with the interrupt 21h, the *DOS function distributor*. Such *operating system functions* run mostly with PL=1. Also, unit and device drivers (for example, for controlling interfaces and disk drives) usually operate with this level. Less critical operating system functions such as support for a graphical user interface (GUI), in comparison, use PL=2.

The lowest privilege level of all tasks is used by *applications*. They should only use the computer, not control it. Through the use of a lower level (higher PL value), data and codes of other programs, and the operating system, are well protected from bugs in applications. One of the main causes of a total system failure under DOS is, for example, the unwanted overwrite of the interrupt vector table. A subsequent interrupt finds a corrupt jump table and so crashes. In protected mode, on the other hand, the operating system reacts with an error message, which immediately interrupts the program containing the error, if an application attempts to change the interrupt table. All other tasks continue to run, unaffected and uninfluenced. As a side effect, this also helps programmers to locate bugs. This naturally assumes that the operating system (such as OS/2 or Windows NT) is error free – a requirement that is, due to the complexity of multitasking operating systems, unfortunately not realistic, especially for the short period after the release of a new version.

In the following explanation, the task concept often occurs. First, a few words to explain this concept: a task includes the applicable program (for example, AmiPro) and data (or text), as well as the necessary system functions (for example, the data management at the hard disk level). Under Windows, for example, it is possible to start AmiPro and load text ready for processing. In order to edit an additional text file in parallel, it is possible to load the additional file into AmiPro and to switch between the two AmiPro windows. In this way, two texts are loaded into one program. AmiPro and the two texts together form a *single* task. Another possibility for editing the second text is to start AmiPro again. Windows accomplishes this with an additional window. The second text file is then loaded into the more recently started AmiPro. In this case also, it is possible to switch between the two windows. The main difference to the first example is that now two programs have been started, that is two AmiPros with a text file loaded into each. Each program, together with its corresponding text, is a task. Even though the program is the same in both cases, the PC is running *two* tasks.

The Pentium provides a separate stack for every privilege level (PL=0 to PL=3) of a task. For the previous example, there would be a stack available for the application AmiPro (PL=3), the functions of the user interface (PL=2), the operating system functions for data management (PL=1) and the kernel (PL=0) (see also Figure 11.3).

The 2-bit segment register (Figure 11.2) specifies the so-called *table indicator (TI)* – that is, whether the global (TI=0) or the local (TI=1) descriptor table for the location of the segment in the memory should be used. These two tables are used mainly for the segmenting of the memory in protected mode. In protected mode, the Pentium uses the segment selector in the segment register as an index for the global or local descriptor tables.

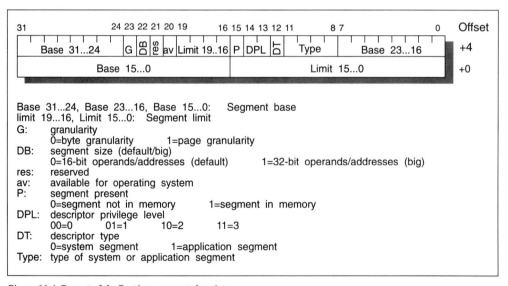

Figure 11.4: Format of the Pentium segment descriptor.

The *global descriptor table* is a list in the memory that describes the segment sizes and addresses in memory in the form of *segment descriptors*. The construction of such a segment descriptor is shown in Figure 11.4.

Every descriptor contains eight bytes. This descriptor table is known as global, because it describes the segments that are usually available for all tasks (when they have access to the privilege levels and applicable gates). The *local descriptor table* is also a list of similarly constructed segment descriptors. In contrast to the global descriptor table, the local descriptor table is only available to the currently active task – in other words, when the task changes, the local descriptor table also changes.

The 32 *base* bits of the segment descriptor specify the start address of the described segment in the memory (see Figure 11.5). These 32 bits of the base addresses correspond to the 32 address lines of the Pentium. In protected mode, addressing can be performed using these 2^{32} bytes or 4 Gbytes. The base entry of the segment descriptor specifies the start address of the applicable segment in this very large address space. Figure 11.5 shows how the segment descriptor sets the start of the segment.

In real mode, each segment is defined as being 64 kbytes in size, even if only a small amount of data is actually stored in a segment. The setting of the distance between the segments to 16-byte makes certain that a maximum of 15 bytes are lost (or empty). The uncoupling of the segment in protected mode changes this completely, because, depending upon the selector value in the segment register, sequential segments should, on no account, be physically stored in the memory sequentially. Every segment descriptor, therefore, refers to an entry limit in the least significant byte of the descriptor, in order to actually define the size of the segment (see Figure 11.5).

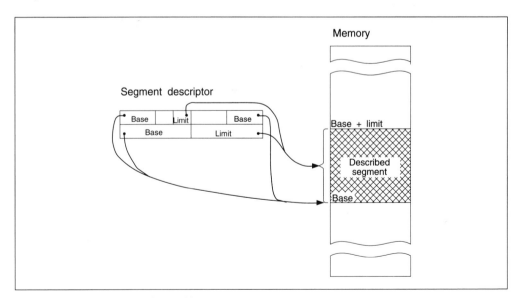

Figure 11.5: Segment descriptor base and limit.
In protected mode a segment descriptor defines a segment. The base address indicates the physical start of the segment in memory, the limit its size.

Through the 20 bits of the entry limit, segments in protected mode are possible up to a maximum of 1 Mbyte with byte granularity, and 4 Gbytes with page granularity. The actual segment limit (or size) of the segment described by the descriptor depends on the granularity bit G as well as the 20-bit entry limit. Note that in the Pentium, a page is 4 kbytes (=4096 bytes) in size.

```
Example: limit=1000, G=0:  segment limit 1000 bytes
         limit=1000, G=1:  segment limit 1000*4kbyte=4 096 000 bytes
```

The full address area of the 32-bit offset register comes only from the page granularity. In this case, the smallest assignment unit for a segment is 4 kbytes in size; this means that the memory is sectioned into portions of 4 kbytes. This is only suitable for larger systems; for PC users, segments of 1 Mbyte are most suitable so that the memory can be used more beneficially. OS/2 and Windows NT use a so-called *flat memory model*, in which a single 4-Gbyte segment contains all tasks. This means that segmentation is almost irrelevant. In its place, memory sections in pages are used as a further protection mechanism.

You will remember that the 32-bit offset registers EAX and so on. can be reduced to 16-bit and also further to 8-bit registers. In addition, every program code that was developed for the 8086 and 80286 16-bit processors requires 16-bit addresses. On compatibility grounds, the Pentium must also be able to use such addresses in addition to new 32-bit program code. For this reason, the DB bit is important. It indicates whether the Pentium should use 16- or 32-bit operands for the descriptor described segment in the case of data segments, and whether 16- or 32-bit addresses should be used for a code segment. If DB=0, the Pentium uses 16-bit operands or 16-bit addresses. Note that the DB bit equals 0 for standard values given for an 80286 segment descriptor. The 80286 code can, therefore, be carried over to the 32-bit architecture of the Pentium without a problem, because all operands and addresses are normally handled as 16-bit. Also, the other 80286 standard values use the 16-bit architecture with 24-bit address bus calculation.

With a reset DB bit, operands and addresses can be expanded to 32-bit for specific instructions with the so-called *operand size prefix 66h* and the *address size prefix 67h*. The operand size prefix sets the size with the DB bit of the applicable *data* segment; the address size prefix sets the size with the DB bit of the applicable code segment. With a reset DB bit (DB=0), the applicable segment uses 16-bit operands and 16-bit addresses. The prefix then instructs the Pentium to use 32-bit operands or 32-bit addresses in place of the standard 16-bit. If, on the other hand, the DB bit is set, the segment uses the standard 32-bit. An operand or address prefix forces the Pentium to use a 16-bit operand or a 16-bit address, respectively, in place of 32-bit. The great advantage of using the DB bit and prefixes is that the Pentium does not need different opcodes for similar instructions, such as MOV ax, mem16 and MOV eax and mem32, that are sometimes 16-bit and sometimes 32-bit. This reduces the number of opcodes necessary for the implementation of an extensive instruction set, and so also the average encoding complexity. These prefixes lead to a more compact program in exactly the same way as segment override prefixes.

```
Example: The opcode for the two instructions MOV eax, [01h] and MOV ax, [01h] is equal to
10111000 in both cases. The Pentium distinguishes them according to the DB bit and operand size
prefix. It is assumed that the DB bit in the code segment descriptor is cleared – that is, the
Pentium uses 16-bit displacements as standard. With a cleared DB bit in the data segment des-
criptor an assembler has to insert the operand size prefix 66h in front of the opcode in the
first case. We get the following instruction encoding:
```

```
MOV eax, 01h: 66 b8 00 01 (the instruction transfers the 32-bit value at offset 01h into the
32-bit accumulator eax)
MOV ax, 01h:     b8 00 01 (the instruction transfers the 16-bit value at offset 01h into the
16-bit accumulator eax)
```

If DB is set in the corresponding data segment descriptor then, in the second case, the assembler inserts the operand size prefix 66h in front of the opcode because the Pentium now uses 32-bit quantities as standard. The encodings are:

```
MOV eax, 01h:     b8 00 01 (the instruction transfers the 32-bit value at offset 01h into the
32-bit accumulator eax)
```

```
MOV ax, 01h:  66 b8 00 01 (the instruction transfers the 16-bit value at offset 01h into the
16-bit accumulator eax)
```

The *DT* bit in the segment descriptor defines the type of descriptor. If DT equals 0, the descriptor describes a system segment, otherwise an application segment. The *type* field indicates the type, and *DPL* the privilege level (from 1 to 3) of the applicable segment. DPL is also known as the descriptor privilege level. Finally, the *P* bit indicates whether or not the segment is actually located in the memory. The *vf* bit in the segment descriptor is for the use of the operating system or the user. The Pentium does not use it and Intel has not reserved it for any future use.

11.3.2 The global and local descriptor tables

The index or higher value 13 bits of the segment selector (see Figure 11.2) specify the number of the segment descriptor in the descriptor table that the applicable segment describes. With these 13 bits, a maximum of 8192 different indices are possible, so the global and local descriptor tables can each contain a maximum of 8192 entries of 8 bytes, or a total of 64 kbytes. In this way, each table describes up to 8192 different segments. The construction and size of the segment descriptors for the local descriptor table (LDT) and the Global descriptor table (GDT) are identical. The table indicator (TI) in the selector indicates whether the segment selector is contained in a segment register of the GDT or the LDT. If the Pentium wishes to access an entry in the GDT or the LDT, it multiplies the index value of the selector by eight (the number of bytes in each descriptor) and adds the result to the base address of the corresponding descriptor table. The Pentium uses five registers (see Figure 11.6) for the management of the local and global descriptor tables and also the interrupt descriptor tables and tasks described later in this section. They are the control register CRO, and the four memory management registers: the task register (TR), and the registers for the local descriptor table (LDTR), the interrupt descriptor table (IDTR) and the global descriptor table (GDTR).

The least significant word of the control register is known as the machine status word (MSW) in the 80286, and can also be addressed in the Pentium in this way on compatibility grounds. The most significant PG bit activates or deactivates the paging unit. The use of the bits in the control register CRO was discussed previously in connection with the control registers.

The PE bit (protection enable) is of special importance for the protected mode. When set to 1, the Pentium immediately switches into protected mode. It can be reset with the MOV CRO, xxxxxxxx xxxxxxxx xxxxxxxx xxxxxxx0b instruction, a processor reset or a Pentium triple fault. The base addresses of the global and local descriptor tables are stored in the GDT and LDT registers respectively. These registers are loaded with the applicable values by the load routine of the operating system (GDTR) or by the operating system itself (LDTR). In contrast to the LDT, the zero entry (beginning with the base address of the GDT) of the GDT cannot be used. Any write to the zero entry leads directly to the exception 'general protection error'. In this way, a non-initialized GDTR is prevented from being used.

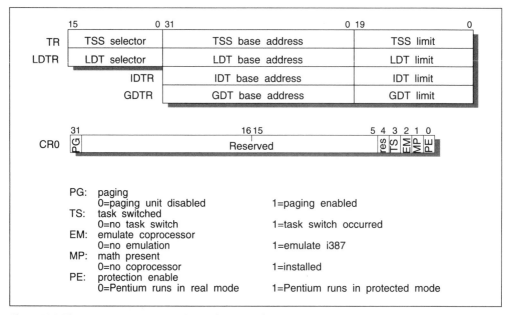

Figure 11.6: The memory management and control registers for the Pentium protected mode.

A special feature of GDT is that the Pentium uses it for building up the complete segment and, therefore, the whole memory management. In the GDTR (see Figure 11.6), the processor stores both the base address and the limit (the size of the GDT in bytes) of the global descriptor table – the GDTR thus refers to the GDT in the memory. In contrast, the Pentium manages the local descriptor table dynamically because many LDTs are possible (compared to only one possible GDT). For every local descriptor table, there is an entry in the GDT. In this way, the LDTs are managed similarly to segments (see Figure 11.7). The GDTR therefore contains a *segment descriptor*, but the LDTR contains a *segment selector*.

The GDTR can be loaded with the segment *descriptor* mem64 by the LGDT mem64 instruction. The operating system loader must carry out this step before the Pentium can be switched into protected mode. If not performed, the memory management will not function correctly. In contrast, the LDTR is loaded with a segment *selector* by the LLDT reg16 or the LLDT mem16 instructions. The segment selector sets the applicable entry in the global descriptor table, which contains the descriptor for the required local descriptor table. The consistent management of the descriptor tables is controlled only by the operating system (OS/2, Windows NT and so on); the application programmer cannot influence this process. In protected mode, the instruction to load the descriptor table registers LDTR and GDTR must be initiated by a task with a privilege level of 0, usually the kernel of the operating system. This is not surprising, since memory management is also the responsibility of the operating system. All attempts to change the descriptor table registers by an application with PL=3 cause the exception 'general protection error' and the interrupt 0dh.

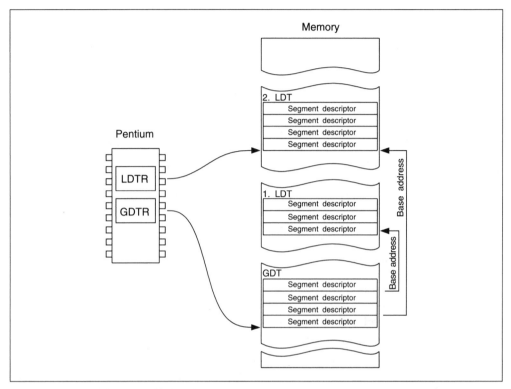

Figure 11.7: The local descriptor table (LDT).
The Pentium GDTR points to the GDT in memory, which may hold segment descriptors for various LDTs. The LDTR then indicates (similar to a segment selector) the number of the segment descriptor in the GDT, which in turn defines the corresponding LDT.

For each task, the operating system delivers the global and also a local descriptor table. This is advantageous in that segments that are used by a number of tasks (for example, a segment with an operating system function), are stored in the GDT and the segments that are used by the current task (such as program code or program data), are stored in the LDT. In this way, different tasks can be isolated from one another. Each task can use a maximum of two complete descriptor tables, containing up to 8192 entries, where the zero entry in the GDT is not used. This leads to a maximum of 16 383 segments. Every segment in the Pentium can contain up to 1 Mbyte (granularity bit equals zero) or 4 Gbytes (G bit set). This produces a maximum *logical* or *virtual address space* of 16 Gbytes or 64 Tbytes, respectively, for each task. In the latter case, this is an immense size. If a bit is represented in terms of approximately 10 mg of wheat grain, 64 Tbytes with eight bits each would equate to more than 5 billion (US: trillion) tonnes (5 000 000 000 000 t) of wheat. This would solve the world food shortage for at least 2000 years.

This theoretical logical address space, is of course considerably larger than the *physical address space* of the Pentium (4 Gbytes maximum). It is, therefore, either not possible to have all of the segments in the memory at the same time, or the segments are very small. A remedy for this is the storing of some segments in an external device (such as the hard disk) by the operating system. The *P* bit in the segment descriptor is used for this purpose (see Figure 11.4). A set P bit indicates that the described segment is actually located in the memory, whereas a reset P bit indicates that the applicable segment has been stored externally by the operating system. The Pentium issues an exception (segment not available) and the applicable interrupt 0bh if there is an attempted access to the externally stored segment. The corresponding interrupt handler can then reload the applicable segment into the memory, usually after it has removed a different segment from the memory and stored it externally so that there is enough room in the memory. The Pentium hardware supports this *swapping* process in that exceptions are produced. The actual loading and external storing of segments must be performed by the operating system. The Pentium only sends out the trigger (the exception) for the process. The Pentium can use more virtual address space than there is actual physical address space available.

11.3.3 The segment descriptor cache register

If, in protected mode, the Pentium loads a segment selector into a segment register, the Pentium hardware automatically and independently checks whether or not the active task should be allowed to access the newly loaded segment. For a positive result of this check, it is essential that the value of the effective privilege level EPL of the task is lower, or equal to the descriptor privilege level DPL of the loaded segment. If this is not the case, the Pentium issues the exception 'general protection error' in order to stop the illegal access. If the access is valid, the processor loads the base address and the limit of the selector designated segment into the applicable *segment descriptor cache register* (see Figure 11.8).

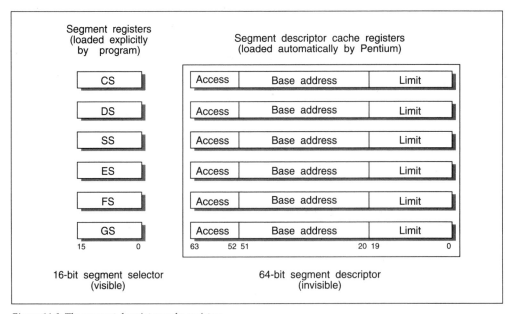

Figure 11.8: The segment descriptor cache registers.

In protected mode, every segment register is assigned such a segment descriptor cache register. The cache register is only used internally in the Pentium; programmers have no access to it. For every instruction that changes a segment register entry, the processor automatically reads (that is, without further software instructions) the limit, base address and the access privilege bit for the segment, from the GDT or LDT into the relevant cache register. This multiple memory access automatically activates the $\overline{\text{LOCK}}$ signal of the Pentium. The purpose of the cache register is that, following the address calculation of an operand and the verification of the access privilege, the Pentium does not need to access an entry in the descriptor table in the memory, as it can access the data in an internal processor register with much greater speed. In the following description of the Pentium and its operating modes, I refer to 'segment descriptor in the GDT or LDT', but remember that the Pentium only addresses the GDT and LDT during the first descriptor access. Subsequently, the internal cache register is always used in their place.

11.3.4 Switching into protected mode

Should a switch into protected mode occur, the operating system or the ROM BIOS must assemble the required tables in the memory and, at least, initialize the GDTR and IDTR registers with the appropriate values. When this has taken place, the system, or the ROM BIOS, sets the PE bit in the CRO control register with the MOV CRO, value instruction. The Pentium then switches into protected mode. With the PC, it is also possible to switch the Pentium into protected mode using the 89h function of the INT 15h interrupt. Because of the need for compatibility with the 80286, the Pentium can also be switched into protected mode with the 80286 LMSW (load machine status word) instruction. Note that LMSW only addresses the least significant word of the CRO control register. In contrast to MOV CRO, value, for example, it cannot activate the paging.

The Pentium can leave protected mode by a simple method, in that a task with PL=0 (the highest privilege level) can reset the PE bit with a MOV CRO, value instruction. The Pentium then immediately switches back into real mode. In the 80286 this is, unfortunately, not possible. Once switched into protected mode, the PE bit of the 80286 can no longer be reset in order to switch the 80286 back into real mode. The reason for this is probably that Intel could not imagine how anyone (or rather, DOS) could ignore the innovative protected mode. In the 80286, the real mode should only perform the necessary preparation to enable switching into protected mode. A return from protected mode to real mode seems absurd (it is, if you compare the physical real mode address space of 1 Mbyte to the 4 Gbytes of protected mode). First the compatibility principle and then the market significance of DOS forced Intel to include a way of returning from protected mode into real mode (and here all DOS users sweat, despite memory expansion and so on, even today!).

The 80286 can only be switched back into real mode by a processor reset. In this way, the initialization routine is called up, and the processor again works in real mode. Naturally, this is not simple. The ROM BIOS of the AT knows, from a shutdown status entry in the CMOS RAM, whether the PC should be rebooted or switched back into real mode. Strictly speaking, the return from protected mode to real mode is contrary to the protection principles of the protected mode. A virus or other type of troublemaker, already at work in the susceptible and unprotected real mode, can also have unlimited access to system elements in protected mode.

11.3.5 The addressing of memory in protected mode

In real mode, the determination of the linear address of an object is quite simple: the addressing unit multiplies the value of the corresponding segment register by a factor of 16, then adds the offset. Protected mode, in comparison, requires considerably more steps (Figure 11.9):

▶ With the aid of the segment selector in the applicable segment register, the Pentium determines whether the global or the local descriptor table should be used for the access.

▶ The base address of the global or local descriptor table is determined with the help of the GDTR or LDTR memory management registers, respectively.

▶ The Pentium multiplies the index entry in the segment selector by eight, and adds the result to the base address of the descriptor table; in addition, the Pentium checks whether the determined value does not exceed the segment limit; if this is the case, than the processor issues a general protection fault according to interrupt 0dh.

▶ With the help of the segment descriptor (8 bytes) in the addressed descriptor table, the base address and the limit of the segment are now determined.

▶ The address adder in the addressing unit of the Pentium adds this base address and the offset; furthermore, the Pentium checks that the obtained value is less than the limit of the applicable segment; if that is not the case, the processor issues a 'general protection fault' exception and the corresponding 0dh interrupt.

▶ Thus, the determined address represents the linear (and, without paging, also the physical) address of the object.

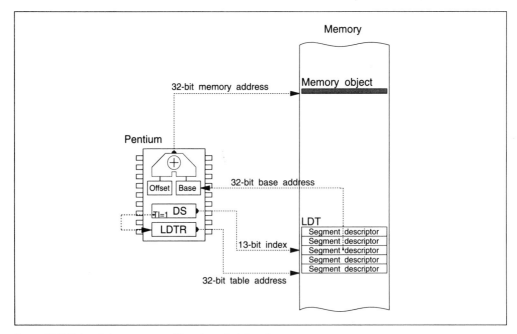

Figure 11.9: Determining a memory address in protected mode.

Here, the advantages of the segment descriptor cache register are again clear: with the help of the cache registers, in most cases the descriptor need not actually be read in, as mentioned previously. Often, after the first access to the segment, the required values are already stored in the cache registers. All later accesses can use this on-chip value.

The method described, indicates the logical way in which the Pentium determines linear addresses. All checks run parallel to the calculation; in addition, after the first access, all important data is already contained in the cache registers. Perhaps somewhat surprisingly, this complicated calculation and check procedure does not result in a loss of performance (in protected mode, the Pentium uses a large quantity of additional transistors for this purpose), in comparison to the simple address calculation in real mode. Apart from the instructions that explicitly or implicitly load a new segment descriptor, and so invalidate the applicable entry in the segment descriptor cache register, all memory accesses in protected and real mode are executed at the same speed.

11.3.6 Segment and access types

After this short trip into addressing, we must once again return to the segment descriptor. An additional pair of bit fields have not yet been discussed (see Figure 11.4).

The DT bit (*descriptor type*), like the four type bits in the segment descriptor, gives the type and rights of an access to the described segment. If DT is set (DT=1), then the described segment is an *application segment* – that is, the segment contains program code or program data. In addition to applications, system routines, which are used for managing the computer down to the kernel level of the operating system, also belong to such programs. In comparison, the *system segments* and *gates* (DT=0) describe reserved data structures, which are used to control and monitor a number of tasks running parallel in the computer, or for the call of procedures and jumps to segments with a different privilege level.

Application segments

If DT=1, the segment is handled like an application segment, so the *type* field in the segment descriptor has the following composition:

Bit	11	10	9	8
Meaning	EXE	E/C	W/R	A

Table 11.1 contains all of the possible combinations of the EXE, E/C, W/R and A bits and their applicable meaning.

In a more exact sense, there is a difference between data and programs: data is the information that should be processed or worked on; the program, in comparison, represents the tool that helps to accomplish the processing or work on the data. The main difference is that the program is not usually changed during the execution, whereas the data should be worked on and, therefore, changed. This computer-related differentiation of the general term 'data' is again found in the segment descriptors: there are executable (that is, program) and non-executable (that is, data) segments. In the descriptor, the difference is indicated by the EXE bit: if EXE equals 1 (set), then it is handled as a program segment, otherwise as a data segment.

Type	EXE	Content	E	W	A	Meaning
0	0	Data	0	0	0	Read only
1	0	Data	0	0	1	Read only, accessed
2	0	Data	0	1	0	Read/write
3	0	Data	0	1	1	Read/write, accessed
4	0	Data	1	0	0	Read only, expand down
5	0	Data	1	0	1	Read only, expand down, accessed
6	0	Data	1	1	0	Read/write, expand down
7	0	Data	1	1	1	Read/write, expand down, accessed
			C	R	A	
8	1	Code	0	0	0	Execute only
9	1	Code	0	0	1	Execute only, accessed
10	1	Code	0	1	0	Execute/read
11	1	Code	0	1	1	Execute/read, accessed
12	1	Code	1	0	0	Execute only, conforming
13	1	Code	1	0	1	Execute only, conforming, accessed
14	1	Code	1	1	0	Execute/read, conforming
15	1	Code	1	1	1	Execute/read, conforming, accessed

Table 11.1: Application segment types (DT=1).

Data segments are always implicitly identified as readable – that is, the program may usually read, but not overwrite, the data. This is only possible if the W *(write)* bit is set. Every segment overwrite attempt that has a reset write bit (W=0) causes a 'general protection error' exception and the 0dh interrupt. Thus, stack segments must always be identified as writable (W=1), because the stack is a local temporary storage and is continuously overwritten (PUSH) and read (POP). Provision for the data segment to extend downwards and upwards is included in the Pentium. The direction is defined by the E *(expand down)* bit. It changes the significance of the limit: in a segment that extends upwards (E=0), the offset of an object must be smaller or equal to the limit. On the other hand, with a segment that extends downwards (E=1), the offset must always have a larger value than the limit exhibits. If this is not the case, the Pentium again sends out a 'general protection error' exception and the 0dh interrupt. In general, the stack segment always expands downwards, because a push instruction decrements the stack pointer ESP and so the stack expands downwards. Normally, data and code segments extend upwards.

If the Pentium accesses data or code in a segment, it automatically sets the A *(accessed)* bit in the applicable descriptor. The operating system can then ascertain which segments are accessed frequently. This is important, in order to implement swapping of segments. The swap routine of the operating system resets the accessed bits of the loaded segments at regular intervals. Every later access to a segment then sets the A bit again. Through a periodic evaluation of the set and reset A bits, the system can determine which segments are frequently, and which infrequently, addressed. The swap routine gives preference to the least used segments, and stores them externally, in order to keep the number of required swaps to a minimum. A similar strategy occurs in the *demand paging* which is supported by the paging unit of the Pentium: more on this later.

In contrast to data segments, program segments are always implicitly identified as not writable (read only). The Pentium should never attempt a write access to such a code segment; a 'general protection error' exception would be the result. This is part of the protection philosophy of the protected mode, and is used for protection against program errors. A frequent cause of system crashes in DOS programs, for example, are bugs that overwrite program code. The chances of this occurring are reduced by the write protection of code segments.

However, sometimes it is necessary to overwrite code or immediate operands (which are part of the instruction flow and, for this reason, are code segments) during the execution of a program. For this purpose, the implementation of the protected mode allows a data and a code segment to overlap. For example, a segment can be identified as a code segment, when a second segment with the same base and the same limit is defined as a data segment. In this roundabout way, with the help of a so-called *alias* and the data segment, the Pentium can overwrite code. Naturally, this is not without danger because, in principle, the same source of errors mentioned previously can occur.

Through the setting of the R *(read)* bit in the segment descriptor of a code segment (R=1), the segment is not only carried out (that is, read from the bus interface exclusively into the prefetch queue), but a task can, with the help of a MOV instruction, also transfer data from this code segment into a general-purpose register. This is necessary when data (such as immediate operands or tables) is embedded in program segments. Above all, the ROM BIOS of a PC frequently contains embedded tables for the hard disk type, and base addresses of the monitor memory, and so on, which must be read by the start program of the BIOS when the PC is switched on. If a table should only be read, it is possible to save a difficult and error-prone alias, through the use of the R bit. The value in the code segment is then only read and not written. In this way, a program crash due to the overwriting of code is prevented.

The segment descriptor produces an accessed bit for a code segment, in the same way as for a data segment. Thus, code segments can also be stored in an external memory object, through the use of the swap routine. In place of the expand down bit (E bit) of data segment descriptors, the code segment descriptor provides the C *(conforming)* bit. Program segments identified as conforming can also be addressed directly by code segments with lower privileges, without the need for a difficult roundabout way through a gate. Typically, all functions of the operating system (such as library and coding functions) that do not use a protected part of the system elements are prepared in conforming segments. Thus, applications can access a few critical functions, without needing to pass through a call gate.

System segments

The Pentium has three basic types of system segments (see Table 11.2), namely *task state segment (TSS)*, *local descriptor table (LDT)* and *gate*. They are used for memory management (LDT) and the calling of tasks and procedures. If DT is reset (DT=0), a system descriptor describes a system segment. The Pentium then interprets the value in the *type* field of the descriptor, as shown in Table 11.2. For example, if a local descriptor table is described by a system segment descriptor, the type field refers to entry 2 (0010b). In addition to the system segments, gates also exist.

Type	Meaning	
0	Reserved	
1	Available 16-bit TSS	System segment
2	LDT	System segment
3	Active 16-bit TSS	System segment
4	16-bit call gate	Gate
5	Task gate (16+32-bit)	Gate
6	16-bit interrupt gate	Gate
7	16-bit trap gate	Gate
8	Reserved	
9	Available 32-bit TSS	System segment
10	Reserved	
11	Active 32-bit TSS	System segment
12	32-bit call gate	Gate
13	Reserved	
14	32-bit interrupt gate	Gate
15	32-bit trap gate	Gate

Table 11.2: System segment and gate types (DT=0).

Table 11.2 clearly shows that most of the gates and the task state segments for the 80286 and the Pentium are different. The cause is the 32-bit architecture of the Pentium, which, in comparison to the 80286, has 32-bit offsets and permits 32-bit stack values. Due to the need for compatibility, the Pentium can use the 80286 system segments without problems. Of course, this is not the case in reverse. The TSS defines the condition of an active (busy) or interrupted (available) task; in the Pentium, this is mainly for the hardware support of multitasking operating systems. Note that TSS and LDT descriptors are only permissible in the GDT as entries, and are not allowed into the LDT. Further TSS and gate details are included below.

The base address entry of a system segment descriptor for an LDT defines the start of the table in the memory, as is the case for a 'normal' segment. As the LDT consists of entries, each containing eight bytes, the entry limit in the system segment descriptor is the corresponding factor of eight.

In protected mode, the Pentium uses so-called *gates* to control task access to data and code in segments with a higher privilege level. The gates implement substantial protection against un-authorized or incorrect accesses to foreign data and programs. If an application requires opera-ting system functions, (for example, to open or close files), then the gates guarantee that the access is error-free, otherwise an exception would be produced. The application cannot bypass the protection mechanism without alerting the operating system. DOS, in comparison, is com-pletely blind. An incorrect access does not necessarily cause an immediately obvious problem in the computer. Mostly, it is only apparent after the system has already crashed. This sometimes makes the debugging of real-mode applications quite complicated. If an application attempts to call a function with an incorrect jump address, it is retained by the computer as unforeseeable. In protected mode, the gates define the access to foreign routines for applications. You will learn more about gates in the next section.

11.3.7 Control transfer and call gates

A near call or a near jump transfers the control to a procedure or an instruction that is located in the same segment as the CALL or JMP instruction. Such a transfer only changes the value of the instruction pointer EIP, and the Pentium simply checks whether EIP exceeds the limit of the segment. If the offset lies within the correct area, the call or jump is carried out, otherwise, the Pentium sends out the usual 'general protection error' exception.

Extensive tasks are mostly made up of more than one code segment. Many code segments are available. An access to a code segment other than the active one causes, for example, a far call, a far jump or an interrupt. In all three cases, the current segment selector in the code segment register is replaced by a new one. In real mode, such an *intersegment call* simply loads the instruction pointer EIP and the code segment CS with the appropriate new values that give the entry point of the routine. Naturally, this is not so easy in protected mode; the loading of a code segment requires an extensive check procedure.

The way in which a far call or a far jump is carried out depends on the privilege level of the active task and the target segment:

▶ If the target segment of the call or jump has the same privilege level (PL) as the segment from which the call originates, then the Pentium carries out the far call by directly loading the target segment selector into the code segment CS. In this case, the Pentium simply checks whether the new value in the instruction pointer EIP exceeds the set area of the limit entry in the target segment, and whether the type of the target segment (EXE=0 or 1) is consistent with the call.

▶ If the target segment is indicated as conforming, and its privilege level is higher than that of the initial segment, then the far call is carried out in the same way as described for the previous example. The Pentium then carries out the code in the conforming segment with a privilege level (CPL) that corresponds to the lower privilege level of the called segment, and not to the higher privilege level of the conforming segment. This prevents programs with lower privilege levels from obtaining higher privilege levels, through the back door use of a conforming segment, and so from achieving accesses to protected system areas.

▶ If the target segment has a different privilege level to the initial segment, and it is not identi- fied as conforming, the far call can only be accomplished through the use of a call gate.

In the first two cases, the Pentium simply loads the target segment selector into the CS register, loads the instruction pointer value into EIP, and then executes the program. This is similar (with the exception of checking), to a far call or far jump in real mode. In the third case, on the other hand, the segment selector of the target segment for the far call or far jump does not point to the target segment itself, but first to a so-called *call gate*.

The handling of interrupts is generally an inherent, and also critical, function of the operating system kernel, because interrupts affect the computer immediately. Therefore, an interrupt call usually results in a change of the privilege level (for example, when an application with PL=3 is stopped with an interrupt, and an interrupt handler in the kernel with PL=0 is called). The interrupt must use an interrupt or trap gate, in order to activate the interrupt handler (see below). I will explain the use of task gates in Section 11.3.9.

The call, interrupt and trap gates permit jumping to a routine in another segment with a different privilege level. Gates are defined by the DT=0 bit in the segment descriptor, and a value of the type field from 4 to 7 and from 12 to 15. They are also part of the system segments. Table 11.2 shows all of the gate descriptors that are valid for the Pentium.

The organization of Pentium *gate descriptors* is shown in Figure 11.10. Call gates are used not only to call procedures using a far call, but also for all unconditional and conditional jump instructions using a far jump. Call gates can be used in local and global descriptor tables, but not in the interrupt descriptor table. Here, only trap and task gates are allowed.

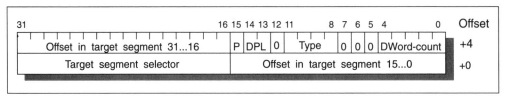

Figure 11.10: Format of a Pentium gate descriptor.

As Figure 11.10 clearly shows, the organization of a gate descriptor is considerably different to that of a 'normal' segment descriptor: For example, the base address of the segment is missing. In its place, a 5-bit field *D Word-count* is provided, and the bits from 5 to 7 in the second descriptor double word are set to 0. In addition, the second word is reserved for a segment selector. It defines the target segment for the far call or far jump and, together with the offset in the least significant and most significant word, gives the jump address. To actually allocate the jump address in the Pentium, a further descriptor access is necessary. The gate finally contains only the target segment selector, not its linear address. In this way, the Pentium grabs two segment descriptors (see Figure 11.11) for a far call or a far jump through a call gate. The first access loads the gate descriptor; the second then loads the base address of the applicable segment. The addressing unit of the Pentium adds this base address of the target segment, set by the segment selector in the gate descriptor, to the offset given by the gate descriptor. The resulting value represents the jump address.

With an entry in the type field, the Pentium knows whether the target segment selector for the CS register of a far call or a far jump directly represents a code segment or a gate descriptor. In the first case, the processor checks whether the direct call is permitted (for example, whether or not the target segment is identified as conforming), and, depending on this, whether it should be carried out, or an exception produced. In the last case, in comparison, it first loads the segment descriptor given by the call gate. The meaning and purpose of this strategy lies in the fact that a gate defines an exact and correct jump point, so that the applicable code cannot give an incorrect call or jump target. This is particularly important if the code calls operating system functions. An incorrect jump point in these routines normally leads to a total system crash; an incorrect gate, on the other hand, only causes the loss of the task and the production of an error message.

I have already mentioned previously that each task of the four different privilege levels has its own stack. Naturally, data must be transferred frequently between these tasks, so the code of a different level has access to the data of the called code. For this access, the system or the compiler/assembler carries the number of double words (each of four bytes) to be copied, in the field

Dword-count. With a call to the call gate, the Pentium automatically transfers these words from the stack of the calling, to the stack of the called procedure. With these five bits, a maximum of 31 double words (that is, 124 bytes) can be transferred. This should be sufficient for the transfer of parameters; if not, it is possible to construct a far pointer to transfer a data structure containing the required parameters.

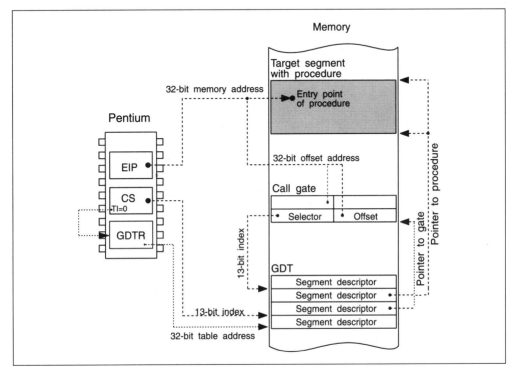

Figure 11.11: Far call via a gate and a segment descriptor.

For reasons of compatibility, the Pentium can also use 80286 gates. The 80286 gates are different only in that bits 31 to 16 are reserved (that is, equal 0) for the target offset of the call or jump, and that the Dword-count field does not indicate double words but normal 16-bit words. The reason for this restriction is the 16-bit architecture of the 80286. If the Pentium comes across an 80286 gate, it interprets the Dword-count field as word-count, and only copies the corresponding number of words (each of 16 bits). Obviously, the Pentium also checks the access privileges for a call through a gate. The following privilege levels are used in this checking:

▶ CPL
▶ RPL of the segment selector for the call gate
▶ DPL of the gate descriptor
▶ DPL of the segment descriptor for the target segment of the call or jump

The DPL entry of the gate descriptor sets which privilege level should be used for the gate. Gates are used, for example, to transfer control at the highest privileged levels (for example, the operating system) or code of the same privilege level. In the latter case, this is not absolutely necessary (it is also possible directly, as explained previously), but always possible. Note that only call instructions, and not jump instructions, can use gates to call routines with a lower privilege level (higher PL). Jump instructions can only use call gates for a control transfer to a code segment with the same privilege level, or to a conforming segment with the same or higher privilege level.

For a jump instruction to a segment that is not identified as conforming, the different privilege levels must fulfil the following conditions:

▶ The value of the effective privilege level (EPL), which is the maximum of CPL and RPL, must be smaller or the same as the DPL value of the gate descriptor.

▶ The DPL of the target segment descriptor must be the same as the CPL of the applicable program.

In comparison, for the execution of a CALL or a jump instruction to a conforming segment, the following two conditions must be met:

▶ The value of the EPL, which is the maximum of CPL and RPL, must be smaller or the same as the DPL value of the gate descriptor.

▶ The DPL value of the target segment descriptor must be less than or equal to the CPL value of the applicable program.

For a call through a call gate of a procedure with a higher privilege level, the Pentium does the following:

▶ The CPL value is changed so that it reflects the new privilege level.
▶ The Pentium transfers control to the called procedure or the addressed data.
▶ In place of the previously used stack, the stack of the new privilege level is used.

In this way, the stacks of all privilege levels are defined in the task state segment (TSS) of the relevant tasks (see Section 11.3.9).

Perhaps I should stress here that all of these extensive checks are carried out by the Pentium *automatically* and *independently*, without the corresponding presence of a software instruction in the instruction flow. In place of these software instructions, extensive microprograms are stored in the microcode ROM of the Pentium, which monitor, on-line, all accesses in protected mode.

11.3.8 The interrupt descriptor table

In addition to the registers for the global and local descriptor tables, and the task register, the Pentium has a further register for the *interrupt descriptor table* (*IDT*; see Figure 8.7). In real mode, the 1024 (1k) least significant bytes of the address space are reserved for the 256 entries of the interrupt vector table, corresponding to the 256 interrupts of the Pentium. Every table entry contains the jump address (target) of the applicable interrupt handler in the segment:offset format.

The 256 Pentium interrupts from 0 to 255 are also available in protected mode. Unlike the real mode, the interrupt handlers are no longer addressed with a double word in the segment:offset format, but through a gate, because every interrupt call causes considerable disruption to the running of the program. Only task, interrupt and trap gates are permitted as entries in the IDT, and every entry contains eight, instead of four, bytes. To even things up, through the entry limit in the IDTR (see Figure 11.12), the actual size requirements of the interrupt descriptor table can be adapted. If, for example, a system only requires the 64 interrupts from 0 to 63, an IDT with 64 entries of eight bytes is sufficient (that is, 512 bytes). If an interrupt is issued for which there is no longer an entry in the IDT (in this case, for example, an INT 64), the Pentium switches into shutdown mode and signals this through the corresponding level of the signals $D/\overline{C}$, $M/\overline{IO}$, $W/\overline{R}$ and $\overline{BE7}-\overline{BE0}$ (see Section 12.5). In real mode, the linear address of the interrupt descriptor table is preset by the hardware; it uses the first 1024 bytes of the address space. In protected mode, in comparison, the table can be located anywhere in the memory, because the base address of the IDT, as well as the table limit, is stored in the IDTR (see Figure 11.12).

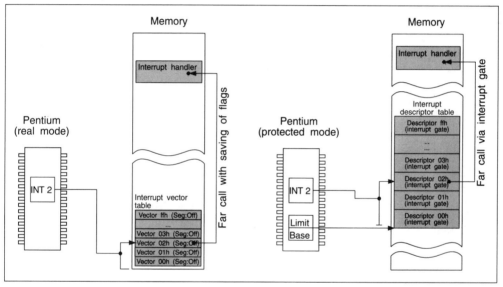

Figure 11.12: Interrupt tables in real and protected mode.
In real mode the interrupt number is simply multiplied by four to evaluate the offset in the segment 00h where the applicable interrupt vector is stored. In protected mode the IDTR points to a descriptor table, which holds the gates to the corresponding interrupt handlers.

Before the Pentium can be switched into protected mode, the initialization program that runs in real mode must compose the IDT as well as the GDT, and load the base address and limit into the IDTR. If this does not occur, the system will crash with an almost 100% certainty, before the IDT can be made available in protected mode. The initialization table refers somewhere (exactly *where* is not possible to say) for each exception and interrupt, or sends out a further exception error, which cannot be handled. When switched on, or when the processor is reset, the Pentium loads a value of 000000h for the base address, and 03ffh for the limit, from the IDTR. These values correspond to the reserved area for the interrupt vector table in real mode.

The interrupt, trap and task gates have the same composition as a call gate (see Figure 11.10). Only the Dword-count entry has no use. Interrupt and trap gates define entry points in a handler, through the offset and segment selector entries, in the same way as the call gate. The segment selector, like the call gate, refers to the applicable segment descriptor in the LDT or GDT, which contains the base address of the corresponding segment. In this way, the entry point of the interrupt handler is clear and correctly defined. Interrupt and trap gates differ in that an interrupt call through an interrupt gate resets the IE and T flags; the trap gate, on the other hand, does not.

The task gates are of special significance for the completion of tasks. In the following section, I explain what the Pentium does if it meets a task gate during the execution of an interrupt, CALL or jump instruction.

11.3.9 Multitasking, TSS and task gates

The complete protection functions of the Pentium, above all, have a purpose – the support of a multitasking operating system through the Pentium hardware. With an efficient PC system, a number of tasks should, more or less, run in parallel. Actually, a processor only *appears* to execute tasks in parallel: the separate tasks are only carried out for a short time, interrupted, then, after another short period, they are restarted again at the same point. In order to achieve this, the condition of the task at the point of interruption must be completely protected, otherwise the task will not be restarted at the same position or under the same conditions as at the time of the interruption.

A similar, although clearer and simpler, operation already occurs under MS DOS. If a hardware interrupt occurs, such as a timer interrupt, for example, the processor saves all registers on the stack, the interrupt is executed, and all of the registers are again loaded with the old values from the stack. With this, it is very important that the CS:EIP register pair is saved, because it gives the position in the program where it has been interrupted.

It is no doubt sensible, due to the extensive protection functions of the Pentium and the requirements of a number of tasks running in parallel, not just to save only the two CS and EIP registers. In the following paragraph, a certain system segment, known as the task state segment (TSS), is discussed. This represents a complete segment that is used exclusively for storing the condition of a task. Figure 11.13 shows the composition of the TSS.

As you can see, in addition to the complete offset and segment registers in the TSS, there is also the ESP pointer and segment SS for the stacks of the different privilege levels, the selector for the local descriptor table (LDT) used by the task, and the saved CR3 register, which gives the base address of the page directory for the described task. The *I/O map base* entry gives the address of an I/O map, which is used together with the IOPL flag for the protection of the I/O address space in protected mode. You will find more on this subject later. The *back link* field contains a segment descriptor that refers to the TSS of the previous interrupted task. The entry is only valid if the *NT* bit (nested task) in the EFlag register is set. If the T bit (debug trap bit) is set and there is a task switch (for example, when the TSS is loaded), the Pentium produces a debug exception and the corresponding interrupt 1.

If the corresponding TSS descriptor in the LDT or GDT refers to the value 1 in the type field (80286 compatible TSS) or the value 9 (Pentium TSS), the descriptor described TSS is available. The task described by the TSS can be started. If an entry 3 (80286 compatible TSS) or 11 (Pentium TSS) is located in the type field, the TSS is identified as active (busy). Such a TSS described task is active and need not be expressly activated. That aside, it must not be activated, because the stored TSS still contains the old values. In principle, contrary to procedures, tasks are not re-entrant. First, when the current (active) task is interrupted (for example, in order to activate another task), the Pentium saves all of the current values of the active task in the corresponding TSS, and then loads the values of the task to be started into the segment, offset and control registers. This occurs completely *automatically*, without the further influence of software.

31 16 15 0	Offset
I/O map base	0 0 0 0 0 0 0 0 0 0 0 0 0 0 0 0 T	+100 (64h)
0 0 0 0 0 0 0 0 0 0 0 0 0 0 0 0	Task LDT selector	+96 (60h)
0 0 0 0 0 0 0 0 0 0 0 0 0 0 0 0	GS selector	+92 (5ch)
0 0 0 0 0 0 0 0 0 0 0 0 0 0 0 0	FS selector	+88 (58h)
0 0 0 0 0 0 0 0 0 0 0 0 0 0 0 0	DS selector	+84 (54h)
0 0 0 0 0 0 0 0 0 0 0 0 0 0 0 0	SS selector	+80 (50h)
0 0 0 0 0 0 0 0 0 0 0 0 0 0 0 0	CS selector	+76 (4ch)
0 0 0 0 0 0 0 0 0 0 0 0 0 0 0 0	ES selector	+72 (48h)
EDI	+68 (44h)
ESI	+64 (40h)
EBP	+60 (3ch)
ESP	+56 (38h)
EBX	+52 (34h)
EDX	+48 (30h)
ECX	+44 (2ch)
EAX	+40 (28h)
EFLAG	+36 (24h)
EIP	+32 (20h)
CR3 (PDBR)	+28 (1ch)
0 0 0 0 0 0 0 0 0 0 0 0 0 0 0 0	SS for CPL2	+24 (18h)
ESP for CPL2	+20 (14h)
0 0 0 0 0 0 0 0 0 0 0 0 0 0 0 0	SS for CPL1	+16 (10h)
ESP for CPL1	+12 (0ch)
0 0 0 0 0 0 0 0 0 0 0 0 0 0 0 0	SS for CPL0	+8 (08h)
ESP for CPL0	+4 (04h)
0 0 0 0 0 0 0 0 0 0 0 0 0 0 0 0	Back link to previous TSS	+0 (00h)

Figure 11.13: The Pentium task state segment (TSS).

How, then, does the Pentium know when to interrupt a task, and which new task it should reactivate – in other words, what forms the trigger for a task switch? The key lies in the task gates (after studying Table 11.2, what else can be expected?). Figure 11.14 shows the construction of such a task gate. Note that there is no difference between the structure of the task gates for the 80286 and the Pentium, unlike the other gates and system segments.

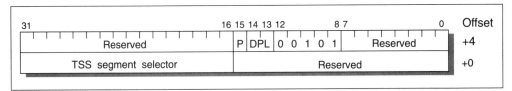

Figure 11.14: The task gate descriptor.

The TSS segment selector in the task gate refers to the segment descriptor that is described by the TSS of the activated task. If the Pentium encounters a task gate during the execution of a CALL instruction, a jump instruction or an interrupt, it carries out a so-called task switch.

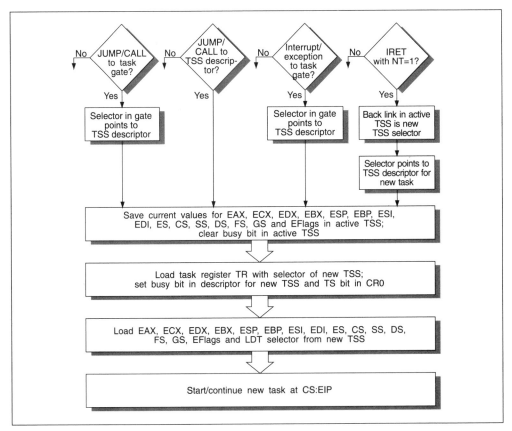

Figure 11.15: Issuing and executing a task switch.
The Pentium executes a task switch if a JUMP or CALL instruction encounters a task gate or a TSS descriptor, an interrupt or an exception hits a task gate, or if an IRET instruction occurs with a set NT bit.

The Pentium stores the condition of the currently active task into the TSS set by the TR task register (see Figure 11.6), and writes the value 1 (80286 compatible TSS) or 9 (Pentium TSS) into the type field of the applicable TSS descriptor. In this way, the TSS is identified as an available TSS. Finally, the Pentium loads the new TSS segment selector from the task gate descriptor into the task register and reads in the base address, limit and access privileges of the task gate descriptor, from the LDT or GDT (depending on which table of the segment selector is referred to in the task gate). In order to conclude the task switch, the processor identifies the applicable TSS descriptor in the type field as busy – that is, it writes the value 3 (80286 compatible TSS) or 11 (Pentium TSS) into this field. Finally, the Pentium loads the values for the segments and offsets stored in the new TSS into the corresponding register. The CS:EIP register pair now points to the instruction of the newly activated task that was interrupted previously; its execution is then re-continued from the point of interruption. Figure 11.15 shows the four ways in which task switches can be initiated, and the processes by which the Pentium accomplishes them.

Tasks called for the first time – that is tasks that are newly loaded – are activated by the Pentium in the same way. Here, the CS:EIP register pair refers to the start instruction of the program, and not to the instruction at the point of interruption.

Example: The active task is the word processor AmiPro which is currently performing page formatting. Now a timer interrupt occurs. During the processing of the corresponding interrupt handler the Pentium encounters a task gate that points to a C compiler, which processes a routine for string output. The Pentium suspends executing AmiPro and activates the C compiler. For this purpose it saves all registers in the TSS of AmiPro and loads its registers with the values that are stored in the C compiler's TSS. The C compiler is restarted and continues compiling the string output routine. After a short time another timer interrupt occurs. But now the C compiler is suspended and instead CorelDRAW! is activated to set up the invitation for my anniversary party. The next interrupt activates the word processor again via the AmiPro task gate ... This permanent suspending and restarting of tasks is carried out very quickly, therefore the user gets the impression that the computer is executing all programs in parallel.

It is the operating system's responsibility to allocate an applicable amount of processor time to each of the separate tasks. The control of task switches can only be achieved by the operating system; the programs themselves have no way of influencing the process in a true multitasking operating system such as OS/2 or Windows NT. When a new task is started, the operating system produces a new TSS for this task. A multitasking operating system is quite complicated and must be able to carry out very complex operations quickly. Above all, this applies if a considerable number of additional interrupts occur (for example, because signals continually come in from the serial interface or the network adaptor), which will usually lead to a task switch. In real mode under DOS, in comparison, only an interrupt handler is called, and the CS and EIP registers together with the flags are saved (10 bytes). However, during a task switch, the Pentium must save 104 bytes of the active TSS and then load 104 bytes for the new task. This may not seem to be the most effective implementation of task switches, but it is no problem for many of the extremely fast RISC processors (Sparc, for example).

OS/2, UNIX and Windows NT are examples of multitasking operating systems (or operating system extensions), and also, to a lesser extent, normal Windows (in which the tasks themselves decide when to pass control to another task; that is, when to permit a task switch). Multitasking operating systems are supported very effectively by the Pentium: the operating system only has to provide a task gate, a TSS descriptor and a TSS for the task switch. The Pentium saves the old contents of the registers and loads the new values independently and automatically. No software instruction to the operating system is necessary; in other words, during a task switch, the Pentium saves the 104 bytes of the old TSS and loads the 104 bytes of the new TSS completely independently.

Unfortunately, in my opinion (and also many other people's), the above-mentioned functions are not available in the most widely used DOS operating system. Also, drivers such as SMARTDRV.SYS and RAMDRIVE.SYS, which at least partly operate in protected mode, only produce a GDT and an IDT, more or less, in order to swap extensive byte groups between the 1-Mbyte base memory and extended memory. OS/2 and Windows NT are the first systems to make extensive use (as intended by the Intel development engineers) of the task switches and the considerable and also very useful access checks.

11.3.10 Protection of the I/O address space with the IOPL flag

In general, the Pentium communicates with the registers in external hardware components (such as the hard disk controller or the control register of the DMA chip) through the I/O ports. However, the control and monitoring of the hardware is the responsibility of the operating system alone. For this, it mainly uses drivers with the privilege level PL=1. Thereby, the I/O address range is also included in the access protection area in protected mode. Ports, however, are not addressed with the help of a segment register, so this form of access protection is not available here.

The Pentium accomplishes the protection of the I/O address space with two completely different strategies: the IOPL flag in the flag register and the I/O permission bitmap in the task state segment (TSS). Firstly, the IOPL flag.

The value of the IOPL flag is set by the minimum privilege level that a code segment must refer to in order to access the address space; that is, CPL ≤ IOPL. If the CPL value of the active task is greater (has a lower privilege level), the IN, OUT, INS and OUTS I/O instructions lead to the already well-known 'general protection error' exception. Rational applications running under a rational operating system carry out such accesses exclusively through the operating system. A few rational applications under an irrational operating system (such as DOS) do this directly, in some cases, to increase the performance and, in other cases, to enable communication with specific components. In addition to the above-mentioned immediate I/O instructions, the CLI and STI instructions also depend on the IOPL flag. The six instructions together are known as *IOPL sensitive* instructions, in that the value of the IOPL flag has an influence on their execution.

The grounds for this restriction are immediately clear, if we consider the following situation: a system function reads, for example, a data set from the hard disk, and is interrupted by a task switch; the newly activated task then communicates immediately with the control register in the controller using an I/O instruction. If, in protected mode, the second immediate access to the control register was not strictly forestalled by the protection of the I/O space using an exception, the system routine interrupted by the task switch would be in a completely different condition after its reactivation. The PC ignores or, worse, deletes such data. There is no explicit instruction available for changing the IOPL flag (such as CLI or STI for the interrupt flag). This is only possible in the Pentium with the POPF (POP flags) and the PUSHF (PUSH flags) instructions. These two instructions are, however, privileged – they can only be executed in a code segment with the highest privilege level of CPL=0. This is usually reserved for the operating system kernel – applications can not, therefore, change the IOPL flag. When this is attempted, the processor sends out (once again) the 'general protection error' exception. The flags are part of the TSS and so can be different from task to task. It is possible that one task has access to part of the I/O address space, but another task has not.

This global securing strategy for the I/O address space using the IOPL flag is already implemented in the 80286. In addition, the Pentium can individually protect the ports. This protection strategy for the ports is implemented especially with regard to the virtual 8086 mode.

11.3.11 Protection of the I/O address space with the I/O permission bitmap

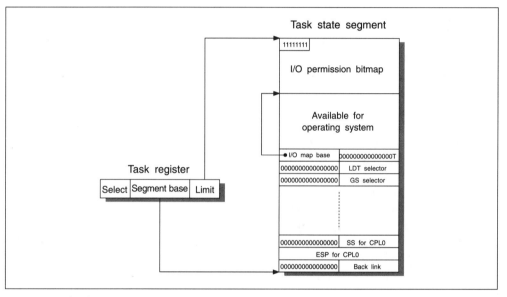

Figure 11.16: The I/O permission bitmap in the Pentium TSS.
The Pentium protects the I/O address space not only by means of the IOPL flag in a global manner, but also via the I/O permission bitmap, which is stored in the Pentium TSS. A set bit protects the corresponding port and gives rise to an exception if an unauthorized access attempt occurs.

In addition to the global protection through the IOPL flag, the Pentium has a further protection mechanism for accesses to the I/O address space, the so-called *I/O permission bitmap*. It is part of the TSS of the respective tasks, so different tasks can refer to different I/O permission bitmaps. The *I/O map base* entry in the TSS descriptor gives the offset within the TSS where the corresponding I/O permission bitmap begins. It stretches to the end of the TSS, as it defines the limit entry of the Pentium TSS descriptor. The I/O permission bitmap need not, therefore, begin immediately after the entries for the register in the TSS. Moreover, an almost arbitrarily sized area can lie between the I/O map base entry and the start of the I/O permission bitmap; this space can be used by the operating system for storing information. Figure 11.16 schematically shows the I/O permission bitmap in the Pentium TSS. Note that the most significant byte of the map (the byte immediately before the end of the TSS) must have the value 11111111b (ffh). Only a Pentium TSS can be used for the I/O permission bitmap; an 80286 TSS cannot be used because it has no I/O map base entry.

A TSS indicates to the Pentium that a valid I/O permission bitmap is present, in that the I/O map base is contained in the TSS. If the value indicates a base outside the TSS, the Pentium ignores all of the checks that are associated with the I/O permission bitmap, then the access protection for the I/O address space is only accomplished with the IOPL flag.

The I/O permission bitmap is an access protection of the second level: if the value of the CPL and IOPL for the active task permits an access to the I/O address space, the Pentium also examines the I/O permission bitmap, in order to determine whether or not the required port can actually be addressed. The basis for this is the one-to-one association between the I/O address and the corresponding bit in the map. This means that the port with the address 0 is associated with the bit contained in the map that has an offset of 0, and the port with address 1 is associated with the bit that has an offset of 1, and so on. When the bit in the map corresponding to the port is set (equals 1), and there is an access to the applicable port, the Pentium sends out the 'general protection error' exception. If this bit is reset, the processor continues with the I/O operation.

The length of the map sets the additional number of protected ports. It is, therefore, not necessary for the I/O permission bitmap to cover all of the available I/O addresses. All of the ports that are not included in the bit are automatically assigned a set bit. An access to a map that is not included in the map automatically produces an exception. In an ISA PC, it is sufficient, for example, to protect the 3ffh least significant ports using a map. Access to ports with a higher address can only mean a program error, because beyond these I/O addresses, no more physical ports are available. The Pentium, then, automatically sends out an exception. You can again see that the protection mechanism of the protected mode not only protects programs and the system, but also offers a substantially simpler method for localizing bugs. In order to protect the complete I/O address space with its 64k 8-bit ports, a total of (64k ports)/(8 bits for every byte) + (8-bit 11111111) – that is, 8193 bytes – is necessary.

A 16-bit port has two, and a 32-bit port four, sequential bits assigned to it. Only if both, or all four, respectively, assigned bits are simultaneously reset can the Pentium perform an I/O operation. If only one of the bits equals 1, the processor issues an exception.

```
Example: The bitmap is  11111111 11101100 00001100 10111100
                        L___T___J L_____T_____J
                        End of the map           Map

First case: 8-bit ports
Locked ports      2, 3, 4, 5, 7, 10, 11, 18, 19, 21, 22, 23
Unlocked ports    0, 1, 6, 8, 9, 12, 13, 14, 15, 16, 17, 20
Second case: 16-bit ports
Locked ports      2, 4, 6, 10, 18, 20, 22
Unlocked ports    0, 8, 12, 14, 16
Third case:
Locked ports      0, 4, 8, 16, 20
Unlocked port     12
The 8-bit, 16-bit and 32-bit ports can, of course, also be mixed depending on the register
width of the I/O device at the corresponding address.
```

I would like to mention at this point that the Pentium does not use the IOPL flag in virtual 8086 mode; it achieves the protection of the I/O address space exclusively through the I/O permission bitmap. In this way, the Pentium can emulate the characteristics of the 8086, for an 8086 program that runs in virtual 8086 mode, under a protected mode operating system. The I/O permission bitmap is implemented especially with regard to the virtual 8086 mode.

11.3.12 Protected mode exceptions

In protected mode, in comparison to real mode, more exceptions are implemented, the main purpose of which is to indicate error conditions. The reason for these new exceptions lies in the additional checks required for protected mode. The following list contains the new exceptions.

▶ Double fault (exception 8): if two exceptions occur one after the other (for example, an exception occurring when the handler is called after a previous exception), before the first can be handled, and it is not possible for the Pentium to carry out both of the exceptions, then the Pentium sends out an interrupt 8. In this case, the Pentium cannot always handle both exceptions sequentially, if both in each case represent an exception 0 (division by 0), 9 (coprocessor segment overflow), 10 (invalid task state segment), 11 (segment not available), 12 (stack exception) or 13 (general protection error). Thus, if exceptions 11 and 13 occur, an exception 8 is produced.

▶ Coprocessor segment overflow (exception 9): if part of a coprocessor operand is protected or not available, the Pentium issues an interrupt 9.

▶ Invalid task state segment (exception 10): every task switch with an invalid TSS produces an interrupt 10 (0ah). The reason for this is an inconsistency in the TSS (for example, the segment indicated by CS can not be carried out, or a selector exceeds the applicable table limit).

▶ Segment not available (exception 11): if the Pentium attempts to access a segment that is not available in the memory – that is, the present bit is reset in the corresponding descriptor – then the Pentium issues an interrupt 11 (0bh).

▶ Stack exception (exception 12): if an instruction attempts to exceed the stack segment limit, or the segment indicated by SS is not available in the memory (for example, after a task switch), the Pentium issues an interrupt 12 (0ch).

▶ General protection error (exception 13): if the protection rules in the protected mode of the Pentium are violated, and the cause can not be associated with one of the exceptions 8–12, interrupt 13 (0dh) is the result.

▶ Coprocessor error (exception 16): if the coprocessor functions are not emulated by a software library in the Pentium (the EM bit in the CRO control register equals 0), and the Pentium has an active signal from the coprocessor at the $\overline{\text{ERROR}}$ pin (a low level signal), then the Pentium sends out an interrupt 16 (10h). The active $\overline{\text{ERROR}}$ signal indicates an error condition in the coprocessor (for example, an underflow or an overflow).

11.3.13 Summary of the protection mechanism in protected mode

The protection mechanism in the protected mode of the Pentium applies mainly to instructions that read and control the condition of the CPU, or that access code and data segments. In this way, incorrect or inadequate instructions that crash the system or block the CPU should be prevented (such as an erroneously placed HLT instruction). In addition, protected mode should prevent data and code segments from being used incorrectly and thereby affecting the system integrity. For this purpose, the Pentium implements three groups of protection mechanisms:

▶ Restricted usage of segments. For example, code segments, in principle, cannot be written to, and data segments can only be written to if the write bit (W) is set. Accessible segments are written to through the GDT or LDT; all other segments cannot be reached by the task.

▶ Restricted access to segments. The different privilege levels, and the use of CPL, DPL, EPL and RPL, restrict the access of programs with a specific privilege level (CPL, RPL and EPL) to data and code of other segments (DPL). Permitted call-up mechanisms (call gate, and so on) are the only possible exceptions.

▶ Privileged instructions. Instructions that immediately influence the condition of the CPU (such as LGDT and LLDT) or that change the descriptor tables can only be executed by tasks with CPL or IOPL values of a higher privilege level.

In protected mode, if one of these protection mechanisms is violated, the Pentium immediately issues an error exception.

11.3.14 The protected mode and memory duplication of instruction and data pointers in the floating-point unit

If the floating-point unit executes a numerical instruction, the Pentium notes the control, status and tag word. In addition, there are two registers available, which contain the instruction and a possible operand address. If a floating-point exception occurs, and if the Pentium generates an interrupt as a result of this, then by using the instruction FSTENV/FNSTENV, the handler can store the environment in the memory and subsequently determine the cause of the exception. With this, the handling of a floating-point error is greatly eased.

The memory representation is differentiated depending upon whether or not protected or real mode is active, and whether the Pentium is currently operating using 16- or 32-bit operands and offsets. The different formats are shown in Figure 11.17

The floating-point instruction FSETPM is implemented only on the grounds of compatibility with the 80287. In the 80287, the registers for operands and instruction addresses are available in the coprocessor, which means, in reality, that the 80287 must know whether an address is to be executed in protected or in real mode. Otherwise, in the case of an exception, the pointer is stored in an incorrect format. Thus, the Pentium continues to support the instruction FSETPM, by ignoring it, but at the same time does not produce an 'invalid opcode' error message.

11.4 Pentium virtual 8086 mode

The virtual 8086 mode of the Pentium has been expanded because of its importance for DOS compatibility with the OS/2 and Windows NT operating systems, and also because of the operating system extension Windows. In this way, the performance should be improved. The main problem was that, up to the i486, DOS programs very often issued interrupts in order to call operating system functions. The handling of such interrupts in a real-mode manner, but under the protected mode monitor in virtual 8086 mode, takes a very long time. The main reason for this is the lengthy switching between the virtual 8086 program, the virtual 8086 monitor and the emulation routines for the required operating system functions.

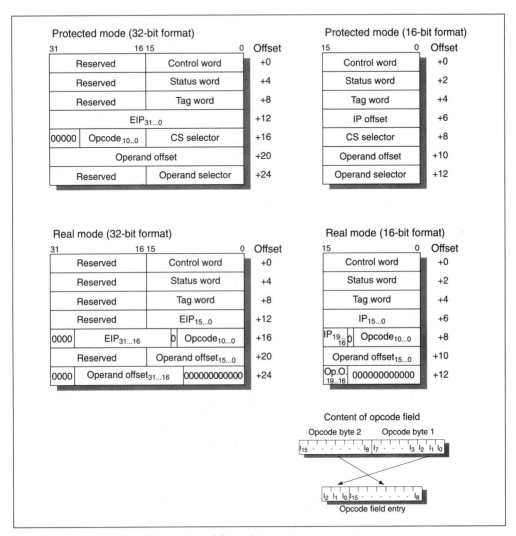

Figure 11.17: Memory images of instruction and data pointer.

11.4.1 The control and status flags for the Pentium's virtual 8086 mode

The EFlag register and the new CR4 control register are important for the activation and control of the Pentium's virtual 8086 mode. Figure 11.18 shows the structure of the two registers. The important bits for virtual 8086 mode are indicated.

The transformation of addresses according to virtual 8086 mode is activated by setting the VM flag in the EFlag register. However, the Pentium must already be running in protected mode. Note that virtual 8086 is not actually an operating mode; the Pentium continues to operate in protected mode with its corresponding protection functions. Only the formation of linear addresses from the segment and offset register values are carried out as in the 8086 or the Pentium real mode. With a reset VME bit in CR4, the Pentium's virtual 8086 mode is completely compatible with that of the i386/i486. This mode is detailed in Section 11.4.2. By setting the VME bit you can, however, enable the new virtual 8086 mode functions of the Pentium. Then, the two bits VIP and VI in the EFlag register also come into play. VI is a virtual copy of the normal interrupt flag; a set VIP flag permits individual virtual interrupt flags for the 8086 program in virtual 8086 mode. More on this subject is given in Section 11.4.3.

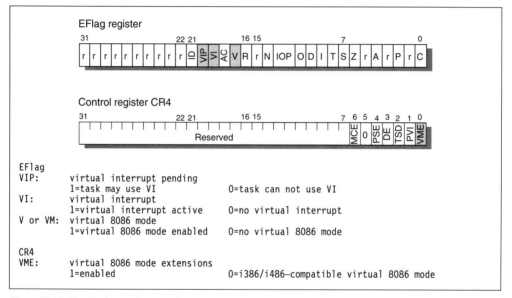

Figure 11.18: Flags and control register for Pentium virtual 8086 mode.
The bits significant for the Pentium virtual 8086 mode are indicated.

11.4.2 The i386/i486 compatible Pentium virtual 8086 mode

In addition to the 32-bit architecture and paging, the virtual 8086 mode was a fundamental innovation of the i386 in comparison to its predecessor, the 16-bit 80286. Together with the functions of the paging unit, it generates enormous possibilities for the protected multitasking operation of real-mode programs that are not truly multitasking-compatible (what a contradiction!).

The motive for implementing the virtual 8086 mode lies in the number of real-mode programs available for the PC that run under DOS, and the fact that the market did not react to the protected mode of the 80286. Almost all i386 CPUs are brought onto the market for use in real mode under MS DOS, which, incredibly, can still only address the first of 4096 Mbytes in the 32-bit address space. In real mode, neither the extensive protection mechanisms of protected mode nor the paging mechanism of the i386 could be used.

The virtual 8086 mode should provide some redress, in that it enables operation of unchanged real-mode programs developed for the 8086, even if it does not make the most of the protection mechanisms of protected mode. The advantage with this is that so-called *virtual 8086 tasks* can run in parallel with other virtual 8086 tasks or Pentium tasks. In this way, it is possible to utilize multitasking with real-mode programs that are not multitasking-compatible. With the assistance of the paging unit, in principle it is possible to run any number of real-mode programs in parallel. This makes the most of all of the DOS windows under Windows or OS/2. Alternatively, it is possible to use a proper protected mode operating system with the corresponding protected mode applications.

Virtual machines and virtual 8086 monitors

In virtual 8086 mode, the hardware of the Pentium and the *virtual 8086 monitor* form a so-called *virtual machine*. The virtual machine gives a program or user the impression that the complete computer is available to him alone. He is, however, only part of a multi-user system. The virtual machine can apparently refer to a single hard disk, a single disk drive and a single set of data and programs. In reality, these components are only part of a considerably greater complete system, which can generate and control many such virtual machines. The system can, for example, divide the physically available size of the hard disk into many smaller portions, each of which can be made exclusively available to a virtual machine. Not without reason, is it frequently possible to gauge the importance of a user by the virtual platform made available by the system manager.

Mainframes make extensive use of this strategy, and in this way, can support more than 1000 users, each with a virtual machine. With a single-user system under a multitasking operating system such as OS/2, for example, virtual machines for different users are not formed. In their place, the system produces a separate virtual machine for every task. Windows in enhanced mode and OS/2 make use of virtual 8086 mode to form such virtual machines, in order to permit the running of real-mode programs, in a DOS window, in parallel with protected mode applications.

Just a few more words on the virtual 8086 monitor: this monitor, of course, has nothing to do with the screen, but represents a system program (typically part of the operating system kernel), which is used to produce and manage (thus monitor) the virtual 8086 tasks. The Pentium hardware uses a TSS to produce a set of virtual Pentium registers. Further to this, a virtual memory is formed corresponding to the first Mbyte of the linear address space. A real-mode program then has the impression that a normal 8086 is available. The processor then carries out physical instructions that affect these virtual registers and the virtual address space of the task. The purpose of the virtual 8086 monitor is essentially to supervise the external interfaces of the virtual machine – that is, of the virtual 8086 task. The interfaces are formed from interrupts, exceptions and I/O instructions, through which the virtual 8086 task can logically communicate with the other parts of the system. The exceptions and interrupts take on the role of physical interfaces (for example, the control registers) in a normal 8086 PC. The monitor makes sure that the virtual 8086 machine fits into the extensive Pentium system in protected mode, as a separate task without the possibility of interfering with other tasks, or the Pentium operating system itself.

Addresses in virtual 8086 mode

At first sight, the main difference between real mode and protected mode is the way in which the addresses are calculated. In real mode, the Pentium simply multiplies the value of the segment register by 16 in order to determine the base address. In protected mode, on the other hand, the segment register is used as an index in a table in which the base addresses of the segment are stored. In this way it is, for example, not possible to lock onto the linear address of an object immediately from the segment and offset register values. Many real-mode programs, however, do exactly this. Proper execution in protected mode is, therefore, impossible.

If the Pentium is in virtual 8086 mode and has to run 8086 programs, it must calculate the linear address of an object in the same way as the 8086 in real mode for the reasons stated above. Thus, in virtual 8086 mode, the Pentium produces the linear address of an object by multiplying the value of the applicable segment register by 16 and then adding the offset, as in real mode. There is, however, a difference between the 8086 and the Pentium, in that the Pentium makes use of 32-bit offset registers and the 8086 does not. Virtual 8086 tasks can produce linear 32-bit addresses through the use of an address size prefix. If the value in a Pentium offset register in virtual 8086 mode exceeds 65 535 or ffffh, the Pentium issues a pseudo protection exception, in that it generates the exception 0ch or 0dh but not the error code. As in the normal real mode, the combination of a segment ffffh with an offset of ffffh in virtual 8086 mode leads to an address 10ffefh, which is beyond the first Mbyte in the real mode address space. The Pentium can then break through the 1 Mbyte barrier of real mode by almost 64 kbytes in virtual 8086 mode.

Entry into and exit from virtual 8086 mode

The Pentium can easily be switched into virtual 8086 mode – the VM (*virtual mode*) flag in the EFlag register is simply set. Note that, in addition, the Pentium must already be working in protected mode. A direct jump from real into virtual 8086 mode is not possible. The VM flag can only be set by code with the privilege level 0 (the operating system kernel), a task switch through a Pentium TSS, or an IRET instruction that collects the EFlags with a set VM bit from the stack. A task switch automatically loads the EFlags from the TSS of the newly started task. In this way, it is not necessary for the operating system itself to decide at each task switch whether the newly started task should be carried out in protected or virtual 8086 mode. Moreover, the TSS of the operating system makes this decision only when the TSS for the task is created; it is necessary to set the Eflag entry, ensuring that the task will always be carried out in virtual 8086 mode. A 16-bit 80286 TSS, on the other hand, cannot change the most significant word in the EFlag register containing the VM flag, because of the reduction of the flag entry to 16-bit.

The Pentium quits virtual 8086 mode when the VM flag is reset. This is possible through the use of a Pentium TSS or an interrupt – that is, an exception that refers to a trap or an interrupt gate. The Pentium then returns to the normal protected mode, in order to carry out other protected mode tasks. This is more clearly illustrated in Figure 11.19.

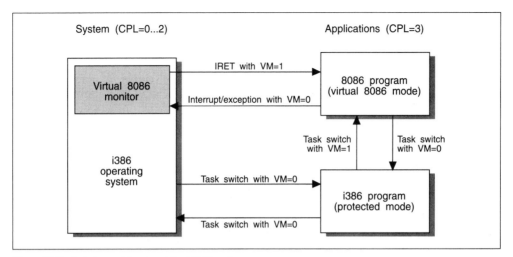

Figure 11.19: Entering and leaving virtual 8086 mode.

In virtual 8086 mode, all 8086 registers are available and are expanded to 32-bit (through the use of a preceding E). The new Pentium registers, FS, GS, debug register and so on, are also available. Further to this, a virtual 8086 task can use the new instructions that were implemented in the 80186/286/386 such as BOUND, LSS and so on. Although the mode is called virtual 8086 mode, it would be more accurate to call it virtual Pentium real mode.

Tasks in virtual 8086 mode

In addition to the hardware platform of the Pentium, it is necessary to use a number of software components in order to assemble a virtual machine that can execute an 8086 program in virtual 8086 mode. These are:

▶ the 8086 program itself (real mode)
▶ the virtual 8086 monitor (protected mode)
▶ operating system functions for the 8086 program (real or protected mode)

You can see that the Pentium hardware only supports the virtual tasks; on its own, it is not sufficient. The same applies to the normal protected mode. The Pentium hardware supports a multitasking operating system through the use of automatic access checks and so on. in protected mode. That on its own is not sufficient, but enables a lot more work to be done by the system programmer in order to set up a stable system. Without protected mode, a multitasking operating system would still be possible in principle, but without the hardware support, it would be much more difficult to program and keep stable (and it is better to say nothing at all about the performance).

As an example in the following explanations, consider an editor that normally runs under MS-DOS. It represents the 8086 program for the real mode. The virtual 8086 monitor is usually part of the operating system kernel in the protected mode of the Pentium, because the monitor has an immediate effect on the system (for example, memory management). In addition, the editor requires the normal operating system functions, such as the opening and closing of data files (also a function of INT 21h).

The three parts together form a *virtual 8086 task*. It is managed by a Pentium TSS. In this way, it is possible to call the virtual 8086 task like any other, and specifically for the protected mode formulated task, through a task switch and the Pentium TSS. The 8086 program can be embedded in a multitasking environment.

The virtual 8086 monitor runs in protected mode with the privilege level PL=0 and contains routines for loading the 8086 programs and for handling interrupts and exceptions. In comparison, an actual 8086 program has a privilege level of CPL=3 (after all, it is only an application). In virtual 8086 mode, the first 10fff0h bytes of the Pentium linear address space (from 4 Gbytes equals 100 000 000h) are used by the 8086 program, as in real mode. Addresses outside this area cannot be used by the 8086 program. The addresses beyond 10ffefh are available to the virtual 8086 monitor, the Pentium operating system and other software.

The virtual 8086 task is now only missing the normal operating system functions of the 8086 operating system (in our case, above all, those of INT 21h). For the implementation of this, there are two strategies:

▶   The 8086 operating system runs as part of the 8086 program – that is, the 8086 program and MS-DOS form a unit. In this way, all of the necessary operating system functions are available.
▶   The Pentium operating system emulates the 8086 operating system.

In the first case, the previously used real-mode operating system can be used almost unchanged. Every virtual 8086 task has its own exclusively reserved copy of MS-DOS (or any other real mode operating system). In this way, many different operating systems can run simultaneously in a Pentium system: the high level Pentium operating system watches over the protected mode programs and the virtual 8086 monitor, just as it does for the different 8086 operating systems for the 8086 programs in virtual 8086 mode. This produces a serious problem: the operating system functions of MS-DOS, and also other systems, are called by interrupts; the interrupt handlers are the most critical areas of the Pentium top level operating system itself. A very complicated procedure is required in order to eliminate this problem (see below).

If a number of virtual 8086 tasks should run in parallel, as is the case with, for example, DOS boxes in Windows or OS/2, it is easier to make use of the second possibility. In this case, the real-mode operating system of the 8086 tasks is emulated by calling the Pentium operating system.

In protected mode, the execution of I/O instructions depends on the value of the IOPL flag. If the CPL value is too high in comparison to the IOPL (that is, a privilege level that is too low), an exception is produced. In virtual 8086 mode, the I/O instructions are, therefore, no longer dependent on the IOPL flag – the I/O space is protected solely by the I/O permission bitmap. The instructions PUSHF, POPF, INTn, IRET, CLI and STI still react to the value of IOPL, because instructions such as PUSHF, POPF, CLI and STI affect flags and, therefore, can influence the condition of the processor. The changing of flags in the extensive and protected environment of the Pentium system, with possibly many parallel running virtual 8086 and protected mode tasks, can only be the responsibility of the virtual 8086 monitor or the Pentium operating system, and not the responsibility of antiquated and inferior MS-DOS programs.

The dependence of the instructions INTn and IRET on the IOPL allows the possibility of intercepting operating system calls of 8086 programs through interrupts. If the value of IOPL is less than 3 (the CPL value of the 8086 program), the virtual 8086 monitor intercepts every software interrupt with an INT instruction. If the 8086 operating system is part of the 8086 program, then the monitor passes on the interrupt to the 8086 operating system embedded in the 8086 program. In this way, the call and result are adapted to the Pentium environment. In the other case, the monitor, as part of the Pentium operating system, emulates the required functions of the 8086 operating system. Note, however, that the handling of interrupts in real mode and protected mode appear very different.

The 8086 program is usually written for an 8086 processor (or a Pentium in real mode). The virtual 8086 task uses an interrupt vector table in real mode form with the interrupt vectors in the CS:IP format. The table begins at the linear address 0000h and contains 1 kbyte. Also in virtual 8086 mode, the Pentium does not use these real mode tables directly, first of all it uses an INT instruction of the 8086 program to call the corresponding handler of the Pentium operating system through the IDT. It then quits the virtual 8086 mode. The flow of an interrupt in virtual 8086 mode can be seen in Figure 11.20.

As usual with an interrupt, the Pentium stores the EFlags on the stack. Thus, the called handler knows by means of the stored flag whether or not the VM flag was set at the time of the interrupt – that is, whether or not the interrupt stopped a virtual 8086 task. If VM is set, the interrupt handler passes control to the virtual 8086 monitor. The monitor itself can handle the interrupt or, again, pass control to the interrupt handler of the 8086 program. For this purpose, the monitor checks the interrupt vector table of the interrupted 8086 task, in order to determine the entry point of the real mode interrupt handler. Through an IRET instruction (with the privilege level PL=0 of the monitor), the Pentium switches back into virtual 8086 mode and calls the handler. After the real mode interrupt handler has finished, the completed IRET instruction of the real mode handler is sent again to the virtual 8086 monitor. After it has prepared the stacks for the return, a further IRET is sent. In this way, the Pentium restarts the virtual 8086 program that was stopped by the interrupt. The interrupt is served in this roundabout way through the IDT monitor handler from the real-mode handler of the 8086 task. As you can clearly see, it forces an interrupt to use a very extensive and, therefore, protracted procedure. In the Pentium, the process is more optimized.

A distinguishing feature of MS-DOS programs is the repeated setting and resetting of the IE interrupt flag, in order to control the operation of hardware interrupts in critical code sections. The Pentium operating system, which is responsible for the whole machine, cannot tolerate such interference. It is the responsibility of the operating system alone to decide whether a hardware interrupt request should be served immediately, after a short time or not at all. In virtual 8086 mode, there are also the PUSHF, POPF, CLI and STI instructions that depend on the IOPL, because they can directly (CLI and STI) or indirectly (PUSHF and POPF) change the IE flag. The monitor intercepts these instructions and processes them in such a way that they are compatible with the whole Pentium system. The reason for the interference of the monitor when an IOPL-dependent instruction is issued by an 8086 program is clear: the 8086 program is under the impression that these instructions should be executed as in real mode.

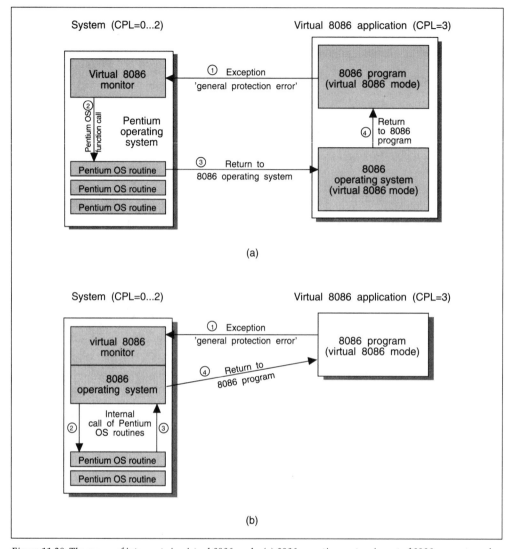

Figure 11.20: The course of interrupts in virtual 8086 mode. (a) 8086 operating system is part of 8086 program, and (b) 8086 operating system is emulated by virtual 8086 monitor.

A further critical area for multitasking systems is the I/O ports, because with their help the processor can access the registers of hardware components. Here also, the Pentium operating system cannot tolerate interference from an 8086 program in virtual 8086 mode. Many real-mode programs, unfortunately, access the I/O ports directly; under MS-DOS, this is no great problem – the PC crashes regularly anyway. Under a multitasking system, on the other hand, most programs can only do this by a roundabout way through the operating system so that accesses to the I/O ports are coordinated. After all, a task containing errors should not affect other tasks or other users in a multi-user system. In virtual mode, the I/O port access problem does not exist, as the system protects the critical ports through the use of the I/O permission bitmap and not the IOPL flag. The I/O instructions are no longer IOPL sensitive even though the Pentium is running in protected mode. In this way, the virtual 8086 monitor can, in one respect, permit an 8086 program to access critical I/O ports directly. If, for example, an 8086 program targets a plug-in board programmed for controlling a robot, the registers would not be used by another program and so for this port, a conflict would never occur – the roundabout way through the Pentium operating system would only cause delays and would not provide any additional protection. With the help of the permission bitmap, however, critical ports such as the registers of a monitor screen control chip or a hard disk controller are protected against unauthorized and possibly erroneous accesses. The virtual 8086 monitor intercepts such accesses and handles them accordingly.

11.4.3 The extensions to the Pentium virtual 8086 mode

Most information concerning the Pentium's extensions to virtual 8086 mode is, unfortunately, a closely guarded Intel secret. For this reason, I can give only a brief overview of the new functions (as far as they are not too speculative). They mostly affect the lengthy switching between the 8086 program, virtual 8086 monitor and protected mode operating system for interrupts in virtual 8086 mode. In order to bypass this and to increase the speed of program execution, you must set the VME bit (virtual mode extensions) in the CR4 control register to 1.

The extensions of the Pentium for the virtual 8086 mode mainly affect the management of virtual interrupts through the virtual interrupt flag VIF and the virtual interrupt pending flag VIP in the EFlag register. It is also possible to redirect interrupts in virtual 8086 mode (thus, 8086-type interrupts) with the help of a so-called *redirection bitmap*. You can also use the concept of virtual interrupts in normal protected mode. For this purpose, the EFlag register contains the protected mode virtual interrupt flag PVI.

Redirection bitmap

As I have already explained in Section 11.4, software interrupts, above all, represent a considerable problem in virtual 8086 mode. On one hand, 8086 DOS programs can only communicate with DOS functions if INT 21h is called. On the other hand, the handling of interrupts – whether software interrupts, hardware interrupts or exceptions – was originally the responsibility of the operating system, or in this case the virtual 8086 monitor. As you can see in Figure 11.20, a considerable software overhead is associated with every interrupt call of an 8086 program in virtual 8086 mode. We already know three possible ways of handling, for example, an INTn instruction in virtual 8086 mode; I would like to briefly repeat them here:

▶ The virtual 8086 monitor intercepts the interrupt (more accurately put, it generates the exception 0dh) and handles it accordingly (for example, it emulates the DOS functions). The 8086 program is restarted with an IRET.

▶ The virtual 8086 monitor intercepts the interrupt, but transfers control to a handler, which is part of the virtual 8086 task. Typically here, the 8086 program, the virtual 8086 monitor and the 8086 operating system (thus, mostly DOS), are combined into a virtual 8086 task. As usual, the monitor intercepts the interrupt, but, for its handling, calls an 8086 procedure through the 8086 interrupt vector table. After completion, IRET restarts the 8086 program.

▶   As above, the virtual 8086 monitor intercepts the interrupt, but leaves the handling of the
    interrupt to a procedure of the higher level protected mode operating system. After its acti-
    vation by the exception, the monitor calls an operating system function. Here also, IRET
    restarts the 8086 program.

The extension of the Pentium's 8086 mode enables the possibility of using the redirection
bitmap to redirect a software interrupt of the virtual 8086 task directly to an interrupt handler.
The interrupt handler is given at segment 0:offset 0 in the interrupt vector table of the virtual
8086 task. Thus, software interrupts call a real-mode interrupt handler through an INTn
instruction in exactly the same way as in real mode, whereby the address is given in real mode
format in the real-mode interrupt vector table.

Virtual interrupts

As I have already explained in Section 11.3.10, the execution of certain instructions depends on
the value of the IOPL flag. These so-called IOPL-sensitive instructions include CLI, STI, PUSHF,
POPF, INTn and IRET – instructions that influence the condition of the processor and, therefore,
the behaviour of the system. An IOPL value of less than 3 causes an 0dh exception, if one of
these instructions occurs and no virtual 8086 mode extensions have been enabled by VME=1.
INTn and IRET are handled by the redirection bitmap where CPL is less than 3. Only the four
instructions CLI, STI, PUSHF and POPF remain, of which CLI and STI are of especially great
importance, because the interrupt flag is initially reset after an INTn in real mode and so external interrupt requests are masked. For this reason, many 8086 interrupt handlers use STI, in
order to allow hardware interrupts. In the same way, 8086 programs mainly use CLI in order to
protect time critical code areas from an interruption, and, for this purpose, to forestall external
hardware interrupts.

For this reason, the virtual 8086 monitor implements software interrupt flags that, after an
exception caused by a CLI or STI instruction of the 8086 program, are compared by the monitor
accordingly. The virtual 8086 extensions of the Pentium now include a hardware interrupt flag
VIF and also a virtual interrupt pending flag VIP for the virtual 8086 mode, so that instructions
which change the value of the interrupt flag IF (thus, CLI, STI, PUSHF and POPF) do not necessarily cause an exception that the virtual 8086 monitor will intercept. Instead, these
instructions affect the virtual interrupt flag VIF instead of the interrupt flag IE.

The handling of hardware interrupts when the virtual 8086 extensions are active is a two-step
operation. The interrupt initiated by the activation of the INTR input calls a protected mode
interrupt handler through a gate; the handler deals with the interrupt accordingly and sets the
VIP flag on the stack. The interrupt handler is left and the interrupted 8086 program is resumed
with an IRET. We again find ourselves in virtual 8086 mode. Here, the Pentium reacts to a VIP
flag in a similar way to a hardware signal at the INTR input. CLI, STI, PUSHF and POPF only
influence the masking of interrupts locally for the virtual 8086 task and not globally for the
whole system.

11.5 Paging on the Pentium

A further essential component of the Pentium is the paging unit located in the memory management unit. Its connection with paging and the new possibilities it introduces, also with respect to the virtual 8086 mode, are detailed in the next section. The paging function of the Pentium, compared to the i386 and i486, contains a new feature. In addition to the standard 4 kbyte pages, pages of 4 Mbytes are also possible in the Pentium. In this way, larger systems that use a linear memory model are supported. The cache strategy of the on-chip caches can be set separately for each page.

11.5.1 Logical, linear and physical addressing and paging

The Pentium has a logical address space of 64 Tbytes per task due to the 32-bit offset register and the 16-bit segment register, which includes a 13-bit segment selector. As the base address in the segment descriptor is 32-bit, these virtual 64 Tbytes are mapped onto a maximum physical address space of 4 Gbytes. The combination of the base address of a segment and the offset within a segment gives the so-called *linear address* by means of an address adder. This means that these addresses indicate the position of a memory object in a linear fashion. You will find with a larger address that the memory object is higher (further) in the memory. The segment number – that is, the segment selector – is no different. A larger selector can point to a segment deep in the memory – after all, it is only a table index that contains the addresses. Representation of 64 Tbytes with the 4 Gbytes is possible, because not all of the 64-Tbyte segments need to be available (P bit of the segment descriptors) and not all of the segments reach the maximum capacity of 4 Gbytes.

If all Pentium address lines are used, the 32-bit addresses can be transformed into a *physical address*, which is also 32-bit. Each address in the 4 Gbyte logical address space is represented by a memory object in one of the many memory chips. Until now, the physical address space of 4 Gbytes has not been realized by any PC (this is not likely to change for some time). Only using supercomputers or massively parallel operating machines is it possible to work with these quantities today.

We have already come across one way of making the virtual address space larger than the actual physically available memory, in Section 11.3. When a P bit is present in the segment descriptors, it indicates whether or not the applicable segment is in memory. If the processor attempts to address a segment whose P bit has been cleared – that is, it is no longer in memory – then the exception 'Segment not present' is sent. Once this has happened, the operating system can load the segment in question into memory, and give the instruction a new opportunity to access the segment. It is possible that a program, or a number of tasks, will refer to more segments than are able to fit into memory at any one time. As required, the unloaded segments are simply read to memory. If no more space is available in memory, the system will unload one or more of the other segments to make space available for the new segment.

The constant swapping of whole segments is a little ridiculous, since in most cases only locally grouped data or code is referred to. For example, in order to read a single program statement from an unloaded 1-Mbyte segment, the complete Mbyte must be loaded from disk to memory.

It is quite possible that the following memory access will require that this segment be rewritten to disk to make way for another unloaded segment. This is, of course, much too complicated.

Luckily, it is for our benefit that consecutively referenced codes and data tend toward forming a block – in other words, it is improbable that a subsequent access will refer to a position in the memory that is far away from the previous access. Therefore, it is better to swap smaller blocks, known as *pages*, than to swap complete segments. This process is simply known as *paging*. To this end, each segment is subdivided into an equal number of much smaller pages. It is only these smaller pages that are unloaded and loaded. An ordinary Pentium page is 4 kbytes or 4096 bytes long.

As all of the segments must be located in the available physical memory, which, as previously mentioned, is considerably smaller than 4 Gbytes, all segment base addresses and, of course, all memory object linear addresses are found within the address area of the physical memory. With a main memory storage area (RAM) of 4 Mbytes, for example, all of the linear addresses are smaller than 4M. Put another way, the total linear address space from 4M to 4G is unused; this is approximately 99.9% of the address space. Many pages could be stored in this space.

It is paging strategy to map a very large virtual address space onto a much smaller physical main storage address space, as well as the large address space of a mass store (generally a hard disk). Today, only rarely do hard disks have a memory capacity that matches the Pentium physical address space of 4 Gbytes. Paging is achieved in fixed portions, namely that of pages, mentioned above. The ordinary Pentium page size is set at 4 kbytes; this is determined at hardware level and cannot be altered. Thus, the total Pentium virtual address space contains one million pages. In most cases, not all pages are actually loaded with data. Pages containing data can be found either in the memory or stored on the hard disk.

Whether or not the Pentium actually uses this paging mechanism is dependent upon the PG bit in the CRO register. If PG is set (PG=1), the Pentium will activate its paging unit and perform paging. Otherwise, the PU will be deactivated. Since the operating system is required to administer and, if necessary, unload or read the pages, this cannot be achieved by the PG bit alone. The Pentium hardware supports paging in a similar manner to the protected mode or 8086 virtual mode. The operating system is responsible for capturing and performing the requirements of the paging exceptions, and for searching and reading the unloaded pages and so on.

Thus, the Pentium performs a double address mapping. Initially, memory object segments and offsets are combined, giving a linear address in the linear address space of 4 Gbytes, equivalent to one million pages. Subsequently, the applicable pages from the one million pages, equivalent to the linear addresses in a physical address, or an exception 'page not present', are converted for reading.

11.5.2 Page directory, page tables, page frames and the CR3 register

For the determination of a linear address from a segment and offset, it must be known where the respective segment starts. This information is contained in the descriptor tables. There are two levels of such tables. The global descriptor table (GDT) creates a type of 'main directory', in which the local descriptor tables (LDT) are stored as 'root directories'. The descriptor table addresses are stored in the GDTR and LDTR, respectively. Using the information stored in this space, the segment and offset can be combined to form a 32-bit address, which can be used as a physical address in an unchanged manner when paging is deactivated.

For example, in a PC with a Pentium processor and 16 Mbytes of main storage space, the segment starts at 160000h, the offset is a3d20h. Thus, the linear address is 203d20h. The byte with the number 2 112 800, or 0000 0000 0010 0000 0011 1101 0010 0000b, is addressed. Since the main storage area is limited to 16 Mbytes, the eight most significant bits are always equal to 0; that is, the address will always read 0000 0000 xxxx xxxx xxxx xxxx xxxx xxxx, where x is equal to the binary number 1 or 0. In a similar manner to the representation of segment and offset in the form of a linear address, the implementation of mapping a linear address onto a physical address is carried out. This is achieved using a two-step directory and a register, which in turn defines a sort of 'main directory'. A table defines the mapping between linear and physical addresses. For this, a special interpretation of the linear address is required (see Figure. 11.21).

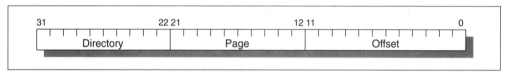

Figure 11.21: Interpreting the linear address with active paging.

In the activated paging unit, the 10 most significant bits of the linear address indicate the number of the applicable page table in the page directory. This corresponds to the current linear address. The 10 bits that follow define the page number of the established page table. Subsequently, the 12 least significant bits indicate, in the usual manner, the offset within the defined page. The 12 bits are sufficient for this task, because a page only consists of $2^{12} = 4096$ bytes. However, a segment requires a 32-bit offset. A linear address is represented by a physical address, which is specified by *DIR* for a page table, by *page* for a page within the page table and finally by *offset* to indicate an offset in the given page (see Figure 11.22) This can be interpreted in another way: Paging remaps the 20 most significant address bits onto new values, whereas the 12 least significant address bits are taken over, unchanged, as an offset.

It is easy to understand the reasoning behind having two page table levels. Each page table entry comprises four bytes (see Figure 11.23). If every page (of 4 kbytes) of the linear address space of 4 Gbytes (equivalent to one million pages) was represented by a single page table in the memory, this would on its own require 4 Mbytes just for the page tables. In some cases, this would fill the main storage area. The creation of a second level makes it possible to administer page tables of a lower level as if they were themselves pages. They are similar to a normal page in that they are only 4 kbytes. With the assistance of the operating system, the Pentium loads and unloads second level page tables like normal pages. It is only the 4-kbyte page directory that must be constantly maintained in the memory. Its base address is saved by the CR3 register.

Both the page directory and the second level page tables each have 1024 (1k) page table entries, each with a length of 4 bytes. Figure 11.23 shows the structure of such a page table entry.

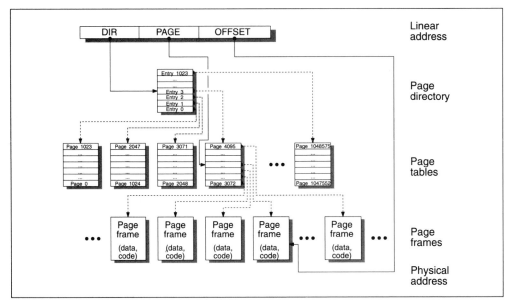

Figure 11.22: Mapping of a linear address onto a physical address with active paging.
After combining segment and offset into a linear address the resulting linear address is split into a 10-bit page directory address, a 10-bit page address and a 12-bit offset, if paging is enabled. Every page comprises 4 kbytes, thus the full address space is divided into 4-kbyte blocks.

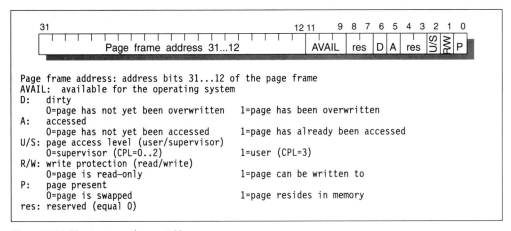

Figure 11.23: The structure of a page table entry.

The *P* bit (page present) indicates whether the respective page is in memory (P=1) or stored outside (P=0). In the latter case, the remaining 31 bits of the page table entry contain information, with regard to where the page is located on the hard disk or other memory medium. Therefore, the entries that follow it have no meaning.

If the page is present in the memory (P=1), the 20 most significant bits specify the address of the *page frame* for the page. A page frame is a memory area the size of a page (4 kbytes), which stores the page data. The addresses of page frames are always integer multiples of 4k (4096d or 1000h): 0, 4096, 8192 and so on, and 0000h, 1000h, 2000h and so on. To some extent, the page frames create a frame in which the page data is stored.

In the linear 32-bit address, the Pentium paging mechanism replaces the 20 most significant address bits with the 20 page frame address bits, in order to create the physical addresses. The 12 least significant bits of the linear address specify the memory object offset within the page (or the page frame). The 12 least significant bits in the page table entry have the purpose of administering the respective page via the bits AVAIL to P. During active paging and in the page contained in the memory, the Pentium joins the 20 bits of the page frame address, together with the 12 offset bits of the linear address, to form a physical 32-bit address. If, on the other hand, the page is not loaded (P=0), the Pentium releases a 'page fault' and the corresponding interrupt 0eh. The operating system paging routine intercepts the interrupt and loads the necessary page into an available page frame in the main storage area.

This loading and unloading of pages triggered by the page fault exception also occurs if a memory object such as a double word no longer fits on one page and is split over two pages.

In general, the Pentium processor constantly addresses the physical double word addresses 0, 4, 8 and so on for single bus cycles and the physical quad word addresses 0, 8, 16 and so on for burst cycles.

If a double word does not commence at the boundary of such a double word, or if a quad word does not commence at the boundary of such a quad word, the Pentium has to execute two memory accesses, each of which starts with a double or quad word, respectively. In the example given, the last four bytes of the first page are addressed, in which the two least significant bytes of the double word are found. Subsequently, the processor accesses the first four bytes of the next page. This is loaded if it is not currently in memory. Thus, the processor can address the two most significant values of the double word. The 4-kbyte size of the page does not cause any problems. In the worst case, two page fault exceptions are issued and two pages are loaded into memory.

There are obvious advantages, when compared to the unloading of complete segments. The mostly smaller pages of 4 kbytes can be loaded and saved quickly. In addition to this, programs prefer a localization of memory access – that is, they mostly address data in close proximity. Thus, despite the relatively small 4-kbyte page size in comparison to the 4-Gbyte linear address area (a factor of 1 million), there is a very high probability that the data will be found in the memory and therefore will not require writing to memory. In the case of large segments, only the necessary fragments to be worked on are loaded. The computer runs much faster when using paging than if it were to work with complete segments.

Several bits are provided for in the page table entries to administer the second level pages and page tables (see Figure 11.22). If the Pentium has accessed a page – that is, data has been read or written – then the A Bit (accessed) is set in the respective page table entry. If the operating system regularly erases the A Bit, it can tell which pages are used frequently. As a result, it stores the least frequently used pages outside memory, in order to reduce the amount of read and write accessing of the hard disk. Thus, paging runs almost without delay.

The *D* bit (dirty bit) identifies pages the content of which has been altered (overwritten). When the bit is erased, the page does not require writing to disk, because the disk still contains an unchanged copy of it. If, however, the D bit is set, the operating system can see that a change to the data has taken place. It writes additional information, in order to find the page at a later date, and also writes the page data to disk. Read-only code segments are hardly ever written; they are nearly always only read.

In addition to segment protection in protected mode, the Pentium includes further protection at page level, through paging itself. Unlike segments, for which there are four privilege levels (0 to 3) available, the paging protection mechanism only recognizes two, *user* and *supervisor*. The supervisor level is attached to programs with privilege levels CPL=0 to CPL=2 – operating system, unit drivers, operating system expansion – whereas user is attached to the application programs. The page privilege level is determined by the *U/S* bit (user/supervisor). U/S=0 is valid for the operating system, system software, and so on. (CPL=0, 1, 2); U/S=1 is valid for application program codes and data (CPL=3). Using the *R/W* bit, individual pages are identified as being read-only (R/W=0) or read and write (R/W=1). On the other hand, however, the segmenting mechanism protects the data on a segment basis when in protected mode.

A violation of the paging protection mechanism, for example, an attempt to write to a read-only page (R/W=0) or using user access on a supervisor page, leads to 'page fault', and the associated interrupt 0eh.

The three *AVAIL* bits are available to the operating system for page management. All other bits are reserved.

In the Pentium, segmenting and paging produce duplicate address conversions. Segmenting produces the base address of the segment from the virtual address in the segment:offset format with the help of the descriptor tables and the segment descriptors, and, with the addition of the offset, forms the linear address in the large linear address space. Paging converts this linear address into a physical address of the usually much smaller physical address space or to a 'page fault' exception. This procedure is shown in Figure 11.24. In most cases, the Pentium can execute this conversion without a time delay, due to the segment descriptor cache register and the translation lookaside buffer.

The conversion of linear to physical addresses in paging, in addition to producing the linear address from the segment and offset, does of course increase the workload. Luckily, this seldom leads to an actual time loss. The reason behind this is that the Pentium cache memory refers to where the most recently used page table entries are stored. This cache memory is known as a *translation lookaside buffer (TLB)*. Only if a page table entry is to be used which is not yet in the TLB and which, therefore, must be read first from memory, will the address translation be somewhat delayed by the additional memory access. However, the whole situation becomes more complicated if the page table with the entry is stored on disk. Firstly, the page table has to be read to memory, then the entry has to be read by the processor. Luckily, this case is rare and so produces very few time delays, as a result of intelligent algorithms for page table administration and their operating system entries. The gain, when comparing a very large virtual address space to a small physical address space by paging, is extremely large.

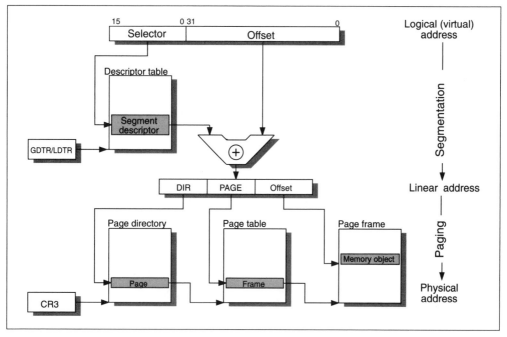

Figure 11.24: The double address translation with segmentation and paging.

The TLB is usually implemented as an n-way set-associative memory. It is an integrated part of the processor chip, and does not require any external SRAM memory. Like other cache memories, each entry consists of the tag and the actual cache data. The data entry contains the most significant value bits of the associated physical address, which must be translated from linear to physical address.

If the physical address of the page format is already stored in the TLB when a page table access occurs, the Pentium uses it internally, in order to produce physical 32-bit addresses. Otherwise, the processor first has to read the page table entry. Intel specifies a 98% TLB hit rate – in other words, 98% of all memory accesses for code and data refer to a page whose frame address is already contained in the TLB.

The Pentium has test registers for the testing of the TLBs these being the test instruction register TR6 and the test data register TR7. They are discussed in Section 13.3.3.

11.5.3 4-kbyte and 4-Mbyte pages

The single and, at the same time, considerable difference between the paging function in the Pentium and that in i386/i486 is represented by the new 'large' 4-Mbyte pages. A new bit is provided in the page directory entry for its management, the page size bit SIZ. Figure 11.25 shows the structure of the page directory and page table entries.

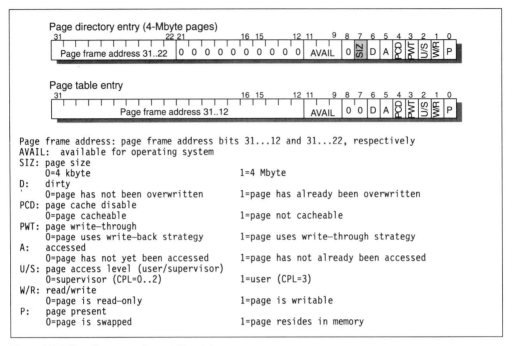

Page frame address: page frame address bits 31...12 and 31...22, respectively
AVAIL: available for operating system
SIZ: page size
    0=4 kbyte   1=4 Mbyte
D: dirty
    0=page has not been overwritten   1=page has already been overwritten
PCD: page cache disable
    0=page cacheable   1=page not cacheable
PWT: page write–through
    0=page uses write–back strategy   1=page uses write–through strategy
A: accessed
    0=page has not yet been accessed   1=page has not already been accessed
U/S: page access level (user/supervisor)
    0=supervisor (CPL=0..2)   1=user (CPL=3)
W/R: read/write
    0=page is read–only   1=page is writable
P: page present
    0=page is swapped   1=page resides in memory

Figure 11.25: Page directory and page table entries.
The new SIZ bit is marked.

The *SIZ* bit is the only new bit, it indicates the actual size of the applicable page. Pages of 4 Mbytes can only occur in the page directory and are only managed by the page directory entry; page table entries are, thus, only relevant to 4-kbyte pages. A set SIZ bit defines a page size as 4-Mbyte memory capacity. The page directory entry then contains the 10 most significant bits of the corresponding page frame address in the bits 31 to 22; the bits 21 to 12 equal 0 (for a 4-kbyte page, these positions contain an additional 10 bits for the *page frame address*). In addition, the dirty bit *D* must be defined here, because the page directory entry points directly to a page and the page content could have changed. Note that in the TLB of the on-chip data cache, eight separate entries are provided exclusively for the 4-Mbyte pages (a total of 64 for 4-kbyte pages). The TLB of the on-chip code cache does not differentiate between 4-kbyte and 4-Mbyte pages.

For the 4-Mbyte pages, the interpretation of the linear address, as compared to that described in Section 11.5.2 and shown in Figure 11.21, must also be modified somewhat. This is because the pages now begin at a 4-Mbyte limit, but within a page an object is still addressed with an offset. For a page address space of 4 Mbytes, all 22 address bits are necessary (2^{22}=4M), so that according to the normal partitioning, the 22 least significant address bits of the linear address for this offset contained in the page are used. This corresponds exactly to the previously used 10-bit page table and 12-bit offset address. The page table address is, however, no longer necessary if the pages are already managed by the page directory (thus, the first level page table). Therefore, the 10-bit page frame entry is superfluous. Figure 11.26 shows a comparative representation of both the 4-kbyte and 4-Mbyte page interpretations.

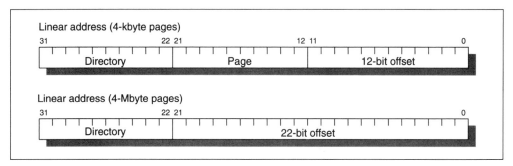

Figure 11.26: *The interpretation of a linear address when paging is enabled for 4-kbyte and 4-Mbyte pages.*

If SIZ is reset, as is normally the case with the i386 and i486 entries, the page can only store 4-kbytes. The other fields are already explained, and so I will not repeat them.

11.5.4 Paging control register

The control registers CR0 and CR2 to CR4, which are shown in Figure 11.27, are important for the paging function. All fields required for paging are marked in the figure. A more comprehensive explanation, including the other control bits, was given in Section 8.2.3.

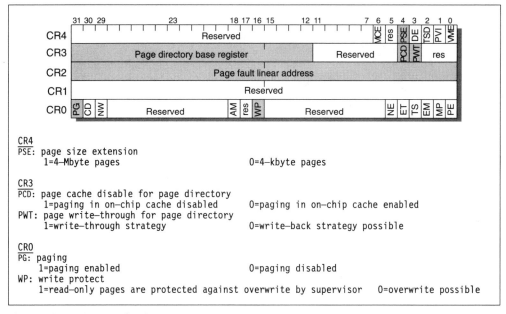

Figure 11.27: *Paging control registers.*
The fields significant for paging are marked.

The *PG* bit in the CR0 control register enables (PG=1) or disables (PG=0) the paging unit of the Pentium. With a disabled PU, the Pentium does not perform any address translations; after the addition of the offset and segment base, the linear address automatically represents the physical address of the memory object. Paging can only be used in protected mode. With the *WP* bit, you can protect pages in the page table entry that are identified as read-only (write protected) from being overwritten by a supervisor – that is, a program with a privilege level of 0 to 2.

After a page fault, the control register CR2 stores the linear address of the instruction that caused the page fault.

With an active PU, the Pentium stores the 20 most significant bits of the page directory address in bits 31...12 of the control register CR3 – that is, the first level page table. When paging is active, the *PWT* bit is sent out from the PWT output of the Pentium for all cycles that are not subject to paging (for example, INTA sequences or TLB updates). For cycles that are subject to paging, on the other hand, the PWT pin gives out the value of the PWT bit in the page table entry. The PCD bit is similar to that described above for the PWT bit. When paging is active, the *PCD* bit is given out at the PWT output of the Pentium for all cycles that are not subject to paging. Cycles that are subject to paging are similar to that above in that the value of the PCD bit in the page table entry is given out at the PCD pin.

The CR4 control register, newly implemented in the Pentium, is used for enabling the 4-Mbyte page size. With the help of the *PSE* bit, you can enable the possibility for pages to store 4 Mbytes of data. Whether a specific page is actually 4 Mbytes long, or must content itself with the standard size of 4 kbytes, is set in the applicable page table entry (see Figure 11.25). A set PSE bit permits 4-Mbyte pages; with a reset PSE bit, the PU will only use standard pages with a size of 4 kbytes.

11.5.5 Paging and virtual 8086 mode

As long as only one virtual 8086 task is running, no difficulties will be experienced when using the main storage area. The first 10fff0h bytes of the linear address space are reserved for the virtual 8086 task; the operating system and all other tasks occupy the addresses above. What happens to video memory? Many 8086 programs write directly to the video memory, in order to release text or graphics more quickly. This is because neither DOS nor the BIOS has efficient routines for text and graphic output. To complicate matters further, DOS programs write to the entire screen from top left to bottom right. Many tasks running in parallel that output data to the screen can lead to disarray, especially if one part of the task data is output in text mode and another part in graphic mode (for differing graphic modes). In turn, these difficulties have led to the development of the Presentation Manager for OS/2 or the API for Windows, which should create a uniform interface with the screen for all programs. Of course, older 8086 programs will not know anything about this.

The answer to the problem is paging: using paging, the address space, which is reserved for the video RAM, can be copied to a video buffer in the main storage area. The video buffer creates a 'virtual' screen. The virtual 8086 monitor is capable of deciding which data in the video buffer is addressed and in what form and to which part of the actual video RAM the data is sent. In addition, the virtual 8086 monitor captures all I/O instructions, that address the graphic adaptor register and, for example, change the video mode. Using this, it is possible to assign an 8086 program to a window on the screen for data output, and to process differing video modes of the 8086 program. For example, the virtual 8086 monitor converts 8086 program data from text output mode to a graphical representation, which then appears in the form of a window in Windows or OS/2.

As I have already mentioned, the 8086 program of a virtual 8086 task occupies the lower 10fff0h byte of the *linear address space*. Using paging, you can hold in, and run from memory, many virtual 8086 tasks in parallel. To achieve this, the paging unit must copy the lower 10fff0h byte of the linear address space for the differing virtual 8086 tasks to varied physical address spaces. This can be done by differing page table entries for the first 10fff0h byte, equivalent to 272 pages, each having 4 kbytes for the individual virtual 8086 tasks. The page directory page register CR3 is stored in the Pentium TSS and, thus, the page sequence will also be changed by a task switch. Therefore, each virtual 8086 task can use another address area for the same linear addresses between 000000h and 10ffefh; for example, the first virtual 8086 task can occupy the physical address from 000000h to 10ffefh, the second from 10fff0h to 11ffdf and so on.

Thus, the individual virtual 8086 tasks and consequently, the 8086 programs are isolated from one another. In addition, the other advantages of paging can be used; for example, a very large address space. If the 8086 programs do not change the 8086 operating system – that is, they do not overwrite its code – many such 8086 programs can share one copy of the 8086 operating system and also the ROM code. The program code always remains the same; the differences in the 8086 operating system for the individual virtual 8086 tasks lies only in the value of the CS, EIP, SS, ESP, DS and so on registers. It is these that are stored in the Pentium TSS of the individual virtual 8086 task, and thus define the code condition for the individual tasks, without the need for different operating system codes. It is therefore possible to have economical use of the available memory.

When there is a bug in an 8086 program, it is possible that the 8086 operating system will be inadvertently overwritten. Thus, one program error has an effect on the operation of others, this being an obvious violation of the protection mechanism of the protected mode. This can be prevented by identifying the pages for the 8086 operating system in the page tables as read-only (R/W=0), because every write attempt leads to an exception. If, in the case of a legal update of an 8086 operating system table (for example, the interrupt vector table in the real mode format), the monitor can take over the responsibility for the operation. If there is an illegal attempt to write, the virtual 8086 monitor interrupts the 8086 program. A secondary effect is that you can recognize program errors much more quickly.

A destruction, caused by an overwrite of the 8086 program or the 8086 operating system, that is exclusively available for the respective task is no worse. It only crashes the erroneous 8086 program. In order to protect the virtual 8086 monitor against every attack, it is enough that one of the following precautionary measures is fulfilled:

▶ The first 10fff0h bytes of the linear address space are exclusively reserved by the Pentium operating system for the 8086 program and the 8086 operating system. Pentium protected mode applications and system programs are loaded such that they always lie beyond the 10fff0h address. Virtual 8086 tasks cannot produce addresses beyond 10ffefh without causing an exception.

▶ The pages of the virtual 8086 monitor are identified in the respective page table as being supervisor pages (U/S=0). As the 8086 program of the virtual 8086 tasks always runs with CPL=3 commensurate to the user level, it cannot, therefore, overwrite the virtual 8086 monitor. Such an attempt will lead to an exception, which stops the monitor, in order to interrupt the erroneous 8086 program.

Do not expect too much from the 8086 compatibility of OS/2 or Windows. The problem with real-mode applications under DOS is quite simply that many programmers apply their skills and knowledge to 'out-trick' DOS, to obtain the maximum possible performance from a PC. Thus, such programs, for example, read the interrupt vector table and sometimes jump directly to the entry point of the handler, or they overwrite an interrupt vector directly using a MOV instruction instead of using a much slower DOS functional call. Such contrived strategies do improve performance under DOS, but at the same time the Pentium operating system or the virtual 8086 monitor is being regularly 'out-smarted'. The PC itself is unwilling to execute such 'expert programs' for compatibility. Despite of this, the virtual 8086 mode is a powerful instrument, particularly when used together with the paging mechanism of the Pentium, for embedding older real-mode programs in a multitasking environment.

11.5.6 Paging exceptions

In addition to the previously mentioned exceptions, paging can lead to a further exception, namely:

Page fault (exception 14): If, during the conversion of a linear to a physical address, the paging unit determines that the required page table or the page itself is stored externally, or if the task that wishes to read the data in a page is only running at the user level but is, however, identified as being supervisor level, then the Pentium issues an interrupt 14 (0eh). The operating system can load the respective page or page table into memory, or can register an access error.

11.6 The system management mode of the Pentium

The 100 MHz Pentium, with its typical power consumption of between 13 and 16 W, is not exactly predestined for use in notebooks (unless you have a mid-sized solar panel or a portable car battery handy). But this is not necessarily the reason for the system management mode in the Pentium: extensive desktop systems can also make good use of system management mode, in order to implement a second address space that is completely separate from the normal memory. Here, for example, recovery routines can be stored in case a complete system shut-down occurs due to defective hardware components, or a total power loss (if the system management RAM is buffered by a battery). Additionally, the system management mode (SMM) enables a power-down mode, so that when it is not being used, such as at night or during the weekend, the computer switches off. If no activity occurs for a specific (and often adjustable) time, an external monitoring unit generates a system management mode interrupt (SMI), and the Pentium goes into system management mode. Depending on the configuration and the programming of the computer, it can then, more or less, shut down units one after the other, for example the power-eating monitor or the disk drives, or first save the content of the memory to the hard disk, and then adjust the memory refreshing (with a 32-bit main memory, this saves a lot of power). Finally, it is possible to stop the Pentium, in that the monitoring unit simply switches off the clock signal. The only power now required is for the monitoring unit, the battery-buffered SMM RAM, and the Pentium for its static power consumption (a few mW) – a power saving of more than 99% compared to full operation.

The main advantage compared to switching off the computer is that, for example, after a key or mouse movement, the system is again fully available after a short time (namely, after activation of the CPU, memory refresh, disk drives and the monitor, and also the refilling of the main memory from disk), so that on Monday morning, it is in the same condition as when you went home for the weekend on Friday afternoon. The whole operation takes only a few seconds, as compared to a never-ending boot operation (especially if a number of disk drives and device drivers are loaded), the starting of Windows or OS/2, the logging into a network, and the calling of all programs that you require for work. You can also confidently leave such a computer permanently connected to telecommunications, for example, a fax machine with its corresponding fax adaptor installed, in receive mode. When nothing is happening on the telephone line, it will fall into a deep and energy saving sleep, but is immediately awake as soon as an external fax machine wishes to send a fax. After a few tone signals, the computer is ready to receive, stores the fax data on disk, then goes into 'sleep' mode again. Now, the more serious SMM implementation in the Pentium.

11.6.1 Entry into the SMM through the system management mode interrupt SMI

The Pentium includes two interfaces for system management mode, namely $\overline{SMI}$ (input) and $\overline{SMIACT}$ (output). The Pentium goes into SMM as soon as it receives an active $\overline{SMI}$ signal with a low level at its $\overline{SMI}$ input (pin p18). It is controlled by the changing of the $\overline{SMI}$ signal from a high to a low level – thus, the $\overline{SMI}$ signal can then return to a high level without causing the Pentium to leave SMM. This is only possible with an explicit RSM (resume from system management mode) instruction. The SMI is an interrupt newly implemented in the Pentium; unlike reset, for example, it only occurs at instruction boundaries, thus only if the Pentium wishes to load a new instruction into the execution stage of its pipelines. Only R/$\overline{S}$ and $\overline{FLUSH}$, which are conceptualized as interrupts, have a higher priority than $\overline{SMI}$. The interrupt hierarchy is, thus, as follows:

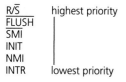

R/$\overline{S}$ highest priority
$\overline{FLUSH}$
$\overline{SMI}$
INIT
NMI
INTR   lowest priority

After capturing an active $\overline{SMI}$ signal, the Pentium first waits for the execution of all memory operations and the activation of $\overline{EWBE}$. This means that no more data located in the Pentium, or in the write buffers of a memory subsystem, needs to be saved. Then, the Pentium sends out an active signal with a low level from the $\overline{SMIACT}$ output, for as long as it remains in SMM. Finally, the Pentium stores its actual processor condition – that is, its current register values – in memory, starting at the physical address 3ffa8h, and initializes its registers for system management mode according to Table 11.3. The handler for the $\overline{SMI}$ is executed starting at the address 38000h.

Register	Value
EAX, EBX, ECX, EDX,	Undefined
EBP, ESI, EDI	Undefined
EFlag	00000002h
EIP	00008000h
CS	3000h (base address=30000h)
DS, ES, FS, GS, SS	0000h (base address=00000000h, limit=ffffffffh, standard size=16 bits)
CR0	PE=EM=TS=PG=0, others unchanged
CR4	00000000h
DR6	Undefined
DR7	00000400h
GDTR, LDTR, IDTR, TR	Undefined

Table 11.3: Pentium initialization in SMM.

As you can see from the table, the protection enable PE bit and the paging bit PG are reset, so that the Pentium performs address calculations in SMM in accordance with real mode without paging. Thus, it moves all segment values four bits to the left and adds the corresponding offset. This address is given out as the physical address without further alteration. The only difference to 'real' real mode is that the limit is not restricted to 1M; instead, all 32 bits, corresponding to an address space of 4 Gbytes, can be used. In real and virtual 8086 mode, on the other hand, the Pentium produces an exception if an offset exceeds the value of 0000ffffh.

During the time that SMM is active, all further SMIs are ignored. However, a flush is identified and executed. If the Pentium receives an NMI and an INIT, it notes them but does nothing. Only when the Pentium has left SMM are NMI and INIT handled accordingly. In addition, the IE flag is reset when SMM is entered, so that all interrupt requests through the INTR input are blocked.

Thus, neither an NMI nor an interrupt request is attended to. This is necessary, because the memory addressing in SMM resembles real mode. However, SMM can also be activated when the Pentium is running in protected mode. The differing interrupt formats (vector, descriptor) would then, without fail, lead to a crash. SMM should also be completely separate from the rest of the system, so that the previously valid handler cannot possibly handle the interrupts in SMM adequately. Thus, the SMM program must first initialize the interrupt vector table in SMM. Note that although all interrupts are blocked, exceptions, as internal processor interrupt sources (in addition to an explicit INT instruction), can, however, still occur. This can only be prevented by an absolutely error-free program code.

11.6.2 The structure of SMM RAM

For SMM, an address space between 30000h and 3ffffh using battery-buffered SRAM chips has been included. The SRAM chips use the memory addresses of the DRAM that is usually located there. For this purpose, the external hardware can use the $\overline{\text{SMIACT}}$ signal, for example, as a chip select signal, and thus address the SRAM chips ($\overline{\text{SMIACT}}$ at a low level), or the normal main memory ($\overline{\text{SMIACT}}$ at a high level). In this way, it is possible for SMM to use memory that is completely separate from normal memory, due to fixed hardware circuitry. The system condition in all other modes is not then influenced by SMM. This, or a similar use of $\overline{\text{SMIACT}}$, is completely optional: if the external hardware simply ignores the $\overline{\text{SMIACT}}$ signal, then the Pentium addresses the normal main memory between 30000h and 3ffffh, also in SMM. Naturally, this is not a job for the developer. It is solely the responsibility of the system designer to use the $\overline{\text{SMIACT}}$ signal in the most suitable way to give an effective SMM. Through the physical separation of normal and SMM RAM achieved in this way, SMM is completely clear for both application programs and the operating system. Generally, the SMM RAM is mapped onto the physical 4-Gbyte Pentium address space as shown in Figure 11.28, if $\overline{\text{SMIACT}}$ is active.

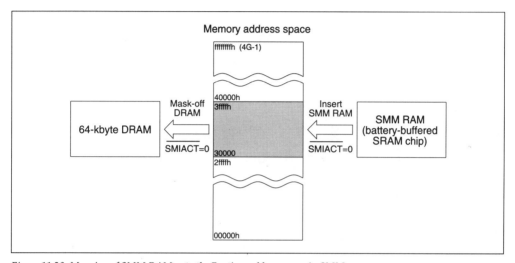

Figure 11.28: Mapping of SMM RAM onto the Pentium address space in SMM.

The SMM RAM is either 32 kbytes or 64 kbytes in size. The SMM RAM is logically divided as shown in Figure 11.29, independently of the choice of SMM RAM size and the use of the SMIACT signal.

The lower 32 kbytes between the addresses 30000h and 37ffffh are optional. The address 3800h, or 3000:8000h according to the real-mode notation segment:offset, is the entry point – that is, the first instruction of the SMM handler. The 32 256 bytes between 3000:8000h and 3000:fdffh are available for the code and data of the SMI handler. Located here are, for example, the complete routines for saving the contents of memory to disk or for deactivating individual components.

Note that the Pentium can also produce addresses outside the 64-kbyte SMM RAM; then, in SMM, it can also access data outside the area reserved for SMM. Usually, however, the SMI handler should be restricted to the 64 kbytes of the SMM RAM.

The CPU register dump is also attached to the handler area in SMM RAM. It consists of 512 bytes. When the SMI signal is activated and SMM is entered, the Pentium automatically – that is, without further influence from software (with the exception of the Pentium's microcode) – stores all register values that are necessary for the restoration of its original condition in this area. In this way, after an RSM instruction, the Pentium can continue from the point where it was interrupted by the system management interrupt. Table 11.4 shows the organization of the register dump in SMM RAM.

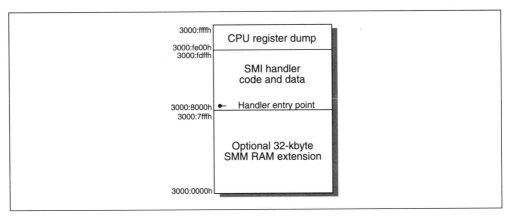

Figure 11.29: The logical structure of SMM RAM.

Offset	Register content	Offset	Register content
fffch	CR0	ffc4h	TR
fff8h	CR3	ffc0h	LDTR
fff4h	EFlag	ffbch	GS
fff0h	EIP	ffb8h	FS
ffech	EDI	ffb4h	DS
ffe8h	ESI	ffb0h	SS
ffe4h	EBP	ffach	CS
ffe0h	ESP	ffa8h	ES
ffdch	EBX	ff04h-ffa7h	Reserved
ffd8h	EDX	ff02h	Halt auto restart
ffd4h	ECX	ff00h	I/O trap restart
ffd0h	EAX	fefch	SMM identification
ffcch	DR6	fef8h	Register dump base
ffc8h	DR7	fe00h-fef7h	Reserved

Table 11.4: Pentium register dump in SMM RAM.

Note that in the case where the size is 16 bytes, the most significant word of the corresponding 32-byte entry is reserved. Reserved areas must not be used, because Intel has included them for possible future changes to the implementation of SMM.

The registers indicated in Table 11.4 are automatically saved upon an SMI and restored with an RSM instruction. All indicated register values can be read by the SMM handler. This does not apply for overwriting. If the Pentium leaves SMM, only the general-purpose registers, the flags and the instruction pointer can be overwritten, the changed values are then loaded back into the applicable registers. Obviously, the complete register dump area in SMM RAM can be over-written (as long as part of it is not write protected by hardware). This overwriting does not, however, have any affect on the restarting of the interrupted mode. Table 11.5 shows, for each register, whether it can be saved and restored, read and overwritten.

Register	Save/ restore	Read	Write
EAX, EBX, ECX, EDX, EBP, EDI, ESI	Yes	Yes	Yes
EFlags, EIP	Yes	Yes	Yes
CS, DS, ES, FS, GS, SS	Yes	Yes	No
CR0, CR3, DR6, DR7, TR, LDTR	Yes	Yes	No
CR1, CR2, CR4	Yes	No	No
Base, limit and so on in segment descriptor cache registers for CS, DS, ES, FS, GS, GDT LDT, IDT	Yes	No	No
DR0–DR7, STn, control/data word tag word, memory images (FPU)	No	No	No

Table 11.5: Save, read and write conditions of the registers.

All registers that, according to Table 11.5, are saved and restored but do not explicitly occur in the register dump (Table 11.4) are stored in, and restored from, the section of the register dump indicated as reserved. However, Intel has not specified a fixed definition for their format and addresses, so they can occur at other positions in other processors or models. Note that you, yourself, must take responsibility and ensure that the content of each register is restored after a change performed in the last block. Their values will not be saved. This only occurs with the floating-point and debug registers. You can assume from this that they are seldom used in the SMM handler.

Of all the registers, only the offset register and the flags can be changed. An error in an offset after the return to an interrupted mode, for example, would be discovered quickly by the protection mechanism of protected mode and would lead to an exception. Thus, the overwriting of the offset register and flags is not especially critical for the whole system. In addition, the SMM handler, more or less, belongs to the kernel of the system, so you can assume that it is error-free.

In addition to the saved registers in the register dump, you will also find the four control fields, halt auto restart, I/O trap restart, SMM identification and register dump base.

The *halt auto restart* entry (offset ff02f) controls the behaviour of the Pentium if it was in a halt condition when it entered SMM. For this purpose, the Pentium sets halt auto restart to 1 if it receives an $\overline{\text{SMI}}$ and goes into SMM when in a halt condition. Otherwise, the value of halt auto restart equals 0. The $\overline{\text{SMI}}$ handler can change halt auto restart, in order to re-enter the halt condition or not, after the return to the interrupted mode. If halt auto restart was equal to 1 and the handler does not change this value, then after the RSM instruction, the Pentium will return to the HLT instruction that initiated the halt condition. Thus, the Pentium will be brought to a standstill again. If, on the other hand, the handler resets the halt auto restart entry, then the Pentium restarts the program execution after the HLT instruction and, in this way, leaves the halt condition. If halt auto restart was reset when entry into SMM occurred, then the $\overline{\text{SMI}}$ has occurred during normal program execution; the Pentium is not in a halt condition. In this case, the $\overline{SMI}$ handler must not change the value of halt auto restart.

Due to the asynchronicity of $\overline{SMI}$, it is possible for I/O instruction to be interrupted. If the *I/O trap restart* entry (offset ff00h) has a value of ffffh, the Pentium carries out the interrupted I/O instruction again after a return to the interrupted program through an RSM. If the value is 0000h, on the other hand, the Pentium restarts the program execution with the following instruction and does not repeat the I/O instruction. When the register dump is saved, the Pentium automatically sets the trap restart entry to 0. Note that I/O trap restart can then only be set to ffffh by the $\overline{SMI}$ handler if the interrupted instruction was actually an I/O instruction. Otherwise, the Pentium would do something unexpected.

The *SMM identification* (offset fefch) indicates the revision level and the functional capabilities of the implemented system management mode, it contains 32 bits. The 16 least significant bits 0 to 15 define the revision level. Bit 16 is the I/O trap restart bit; if it is set (thus, equal to 1), then the processor supports an I/O trap restart. Bit 17 represents the SMM RAM relocation bit. If it is set, an SMM RAM relocation is supported. The 14 most significant bits are reserved.

The Pentium contains an internal register in which the base address for the register dump is stored. When switched on, the Pentium sets the value to 30000h. The current value is stored in the *register dump base* entry (offset fef8h) when system management mode is entered and, from there, reloaded into the register after an RSM. If the $\overline{SMI}$ handler changes the value of this entry in the SMM RAM, the old value in this register is overwritten when the new value is written back. In this way, you can change the base for the register dump and, in the same way, also change the base of the SMM RAM in the 4-Gbyte address space. Thus, the SMM RAM is relocated. The SMM RAM relocation bit in the SMM identification entry indicates whether the applicable CPU supports such an SMM RAM relocation, and thus contains a register for the register dump, whose content will be overwritten with a return from SMM. Note that the register dump base must lie at a 32-k limit. The new value is only changed back to its original value when the Pentium is switched on or reset, and not by an INIT.

11.6.3 Program execution in system management mode

The Pentium starts operation in system management mode at 3000:8000h – that is, its instruction pointer EIP is automatically loaded with the value 8000h and the CS register is loaded with 3000h. The EIP, and also the base value of the CS register, can be changed during the program execution. When the SMM handler is called, the Pentium automatically resets the PE bit and the PG bit in the CR0 control register, so that the Pentium now operates in an extended real mode: extended because, unlike normal real mode, the offset registers can use their full 32-bit width, in order to address the 4-Gbyte memory. If the Pentium activates SMM, the segment limits of all segment registers are internally set to ffffffffh and their bases (with the exception of CS, of course) are set to 00000000h. Even the loading of a new value into the segment register does not change the limit stored in the segment descriptor cache register. As in real mode, the segment register values are simply multiplied by 16 (moved four bits to the left), in order to determine the base address of the segment. Generally, SMM uses 16-bit operands and 16-bit addresses. However, you can also use prefixes, in order to produce 32-bit operands and 32-bit addresses. With the segment registers alone, as in real mode, you can only produce addresses within the first Mbyte of memory due to the formation of the address. This also applies to all far jumps, far calls and interrupts. In addition, note that when the Pentium is in SMM, it also manages the interrupts in real mode format – that is, it requires an interrupt vector table at 0000:0000h. Only if the SMM handler moves the base of the interrupt vector table in the SMM RAM using an LIDT instruction, and constructs an interrupt vector table there can the Pentium correctly attend to the interrupt, isolated from the normal main memory.

Through the deactivation of $\overline{KEN}$ for the address area between 3000:0000h and 3000:ffffh, the system designer must ensure that the Pentium transfers neither code nor data from the SMM RAM into the on-chip caches, or invalidates the cache before the execution of RSM. Otherwise, because the SMM RAM is enclosed and mapped onto the memory address space of the Pentium, the cache would contain code and data of the $\overline{SMI}$ handler after the original mode has been restored.

11.6.4 Returning from system management mode

The Pentium only leaves SMM after an explicit RSM (resume from system management mode) instruction. The deactivation of the $\overline{SMI}$ input signal, however, does not set the Pentium back into the condition it was in before interruption. Note that the RSM instruction is only valid in SMM. In all other modes, it leads to an invalid opcode exception. To execute an RSM instruction, the Pentium restores all registers from the register dump. You also have the possibility of specifically influencing the restoration, by changing specific values in the register dump of the SMM RAM. Inconsistent values, however, lead to a shutdown of the Pentium. Note that during the execution of the RSM instruction, the Pentium does not restore every register; it only replaces those detailed in Table 11.4. If the SMM handler has also changed other registers, then you must ensure that these registers are restored to their original condition, before RSM is initiated.

11.7 Code optimization

The use of superscalar architecture and instruction pipelining to the full is only possible if the program code is tuned to the Pentium's set-up. As I have already explained, branch prediction, for example, is used to increase the execution speed in the Pentium as much as possible for already existing 80x86 code. Code already available in binary form cannot, or not without difficulty, be retrospectively optimized. This, of course, is simpler for source program that has been produced in a high level language. An optimizing compiler that has been optimized for the Pentium can produce better code that, for example, makes better use of the pipelines and leads to fewer stalls, if the code is then recompiled. The development of compilers and system software written in assembler is supported in the Pentium by performance monitoring. In this way, for example, the hit rate for the on-chip caches and the instruction flow through the pipelines can be monitored and, thus, the code can be optimized. However, even simple rules for the use, or not, of specific instructions, registers and addresses can accelerate the program considerably.

11.7.1 Simple straightforward optimization

In this section, I would like to explain a few simple but nonetheless effective ways of optimizing code. The reasons behind the advantage, in most cases, are the superscalar architecture of the Pentium and instruction pipelining.

Address generation interlock AGI

As far as possible, prevent register dependencies, especially when using registers to generate addresses, for example:

```
SUB ebx, 0008h
MOV eax, [ebx]
```

This leads to so-called address generation interlocks (AGIs). Even though, in principle, both instructions can be executed in one clock cycle, the MOV instruction must wait a clock cycle in the decoding stage D2, because the address [ebx] can only be calculated when the SUB instruction has reached the WB stage. Also, because of the register dependency through ebx, the two instructions SUB and MOV can not be paired. This produces the first delay; the clock cycle delay described occurs additionally. Compare the following instruction sequence:

```
SUB edx, 0008h
MOV eax, [ebx]
```

The two instructions mentioned above (SUB ebx, 0008h and MOV eax, [ebx]) require two additional clock cycles: one because of the register dependency through ebx, and one additional clock cycle due to the delayed address calculation for [ebx]. Note that instructions that can lead to such an additional delay need not necessarily follow one another. Because of the parallel pipelines u and v, the distance between them can be up to three instructions, if all instructions can be paired; for example:

```
(u pipeline)      (v pipeline)

SUB ebx, 0008h    INC ecx
DEC edi  MOV eax, [ebx]
```

With this instruction sequence (admittedly, this is fictitious), the MOV instruction in the second line requires the result of SUB in the first line for the address calculation. In the instruction flow, the four instructions occur in this sequence:

```
SUB ebx, 0008h
INC ecx
DEC edi
MOV eax, [ebx]
```

This means that the first SUB instruction produces a delay of the address calculation three instructions later (namely for MOV eax, [ebx]). Note that implicit register accesses also occur frequently; these are already coded into the instruction and, thus, do not occur explicitly in mnemonic code, for example, PUSH, POP and MUL. The delays described for the address calculation can mostly be eliminated by changing the sequence of the code; optimizing compilers and assemblers for the Pentium do this automatically, of course.

Data alignment

Because of the possibility of split line accesses to the on-chip code cache of the Pentium, the codes need no longer be aligned with the cache line limit, so that they do not cause access delays. Alignment errors of data in the on-chip data cache, on the other hand, are penalized by three additional clock cycles. This is especially bad, because a data access required by an instruction that is already located in one of the pipelines thus causes an access delay, which produces a stall in the pipeline. Delayed code accesses, however, are cushioned by the large prefetch buffer. For the alignment of the data, the following rules apply:

▶ 16-bit words must be completely contained in an aligned 32-bit double word, the two least significant address bits A1/A0 thus can only contain the combinations 00b, 01b or 10b; 11b leads to a misalignment.
▶ 32-bit double words must be aligned at a 4-byte limit.
▶ 64-bit quad words must be aligned at an 8-byte limit.

Prefixes

As I already explained in Section 8.3.1, the instruction prefixes are decoded in the instruction decoding stage D1 and then passed on to the u pipeline. The pairing rules prevent prefixes from being transferred to the v pipeline, with the exception of the 2-byte opcode prefix 0fh for the Jcc instruction. A processor clock cycle is required for each prefix, so that every prefix delays the actual instruction execution in the u pipeline by one cycle. Only when all prefixes have been loaded into the u pipeline is the actual instruction code transferred. Thus, prefixes should be reduced to a minimum. Above all, address sizes, operand sizes and segment overwriting prefixes occur frequently. Thus, as far as possible, use 32-bit operands and 32-bit addresses in 32-bit segments, and 16-bit operands and 16-bit addresses in 16-bit segments. The 8-bit registers al, ah and so on are not affected, because they are self-standing, and, in principle, 8-bit wide registers are coded into the opcode. Only the use of EAX or AX, for example, depends on the standard size of the segment and the prefix.

Registers

Some registers in the Pentium – contrary to the symmetrical strategy of true RISC processors – as previously in its 80x86 predecessors, are more advantageous than others for the execution speed, and, above all, for encoding. This applies to the EAX register and the DS register. Because of its position as an accumulator, instructions using EAX are frequently coded with fewer bytes. This applies similarly to the use of the standard data segment DS in place of ES, FS and GS. The additional data segments must be enabled by the corresponding segment override prefix; DS, on the other hand, is implicitly always active for data accesses. Thus, the use of DS saves an instruction byte and, therefore, a decoding cycle.

One-cycle instructions

As far as possible, use one-cycle instructions – that is, instructions that can usually be executed in a single clock cycle. Such instructions are mostly simple and can therefore be paired with other simple instructions. Complex instructions such as ENTER or LOOP, for example, require many clock cycles and cannot be paired with other instructions. On the other hand, complex string instructions with a REP prefix for long character strings are often quicker than their 'manual' execution using many MOV instructions. The reason for this is that the microcode for complex string instructions, with respect to the superscalar architecture, is already optimized to a level (namely the individual elements of the u and v pipeline) that cannot be achieved by an optimizing compiler.

11.7.2 High optimization with performance monitoring

Next to the virtual 8086 mode extensions in the Pentium, performance monitoring is the second most complex innovation, which, to a large degree, Intel has kept under lock and key. Here also, for this reason, I can give only a brief and somewhat speculative overview of the corresponding functions.

Performance monitoring enables a number of parameters, which provide a vital contribution to the overall performance of a Pentium system to be determined exactly. These include, for example, the hit rate of the on-chip cache, the number and length of pipeline stalls, and the hit rates in the TLB and BTB. They depend greatly on the quality of the program code produced, and so performance monitoring represents a useful tool for compiler developers and system programers, for producing the most effective code for the Pentium. This clearly points to the fact that the superscalar architecture of the Pentium, despite compatibility targeted branch prediction, can only be used to the full if the code has been optimally tuned to the Pentium's hardware elements. This is nothing more than an unerring indication of the use of RISC concepts.

Hardware elements for performance monitoring

For the implementation of performance monitoring, the Pentium contains a time stamp counter (TSC), two programmable event counters CTR0 and CTR1, two pins PM0/BP0 and PM1/BP1 that are associated with the two event counters, and a control/event select register (CESR). All performance monitoring elements are not influenced by an SMI or an INIT; in particular, they are not restored.

As a single element, TSC can be addressed by an executable instruction at user level, namely RDTSC (read time stamp counter) if the TSD bit in the CR4 control register is reset (CPL=0 is required for TSD=1). All other registers are accessible only through the RDMSR and WRMSR instructions. You can also access TSC with RDMSR and WRMSR. All performance monitoring registers are also accessible through the test access port (TAP); for this purpose, the probe register is provided in the TAP controller; more on this later.

The TSC is, as previously explained, a 64-bit wide counter, which is triggered by processor clock signals and is incremented at every cycle (for comparison, at 100 MHz, it will take $2^{64} * 10\text{ns} = 1.9 * 10^{11}\text{s}$ or almost 6000 years for TSC to overflow; a 32-bit counter, on the other hand, would be exhausted after less than one minute). By reading the time counter before and after the execution of a procedure, for example, you can very precisely determine the time required for the procedure based on the processor cycle time. In this way, TSC forms the basis for all time evaluations in connection with optimization. As an example, it can be determined very accurately whether a complex micro-encoded instruction (such as REP MOVS) from Intel uses the two pipelines in an optimal way, or whether it can be executed more quickly with a sequence of simple hardwired instructions (such as MOV). Above all, this is most interesting for compiler developers because it allows them to test algorithms for code optimization.

In addition to the 64-bit TSC, two programmable 40-bit event counters CTR0 and CTR1 are available. They can be individually assigned to different events in order to count their occurrences. These two counters are directly connected to the two pins PM0/BP0 and PM1/BP1 which, when configured as performance monitoring interfaces, send out signals through the debug mode control register. They then indicate the current activity of the counter. This is the standard setting after a reset; they are then configured as performance monitoring interfaces.

The event counter can count the occurrences of a specific event and its duration, and can also be made available to inquiry programs. This includes, for example, data read and data write operations, TLB hits and TLB misses, hits and misses to lines in the on-chip data cache, snoop cycles, BTB hits or erroneous predictions, pipeline stalls and so on. All in all, you could say that with performance monitoring, almost all operations can be evaluated in respect of duration and frequency. This gives useful information about the efficiency of code produced by a compiler or programmed (assembled) by hand.

Access through the test access port

I have already explained above that the performance monitoring registers can also be accessed through the TAP. The test access logic operates in parallel to the Pentium's CPU and therefore does not disturb the program execution. Accesses to the performance monitoring register with the help of the RDMSR, WRMSR and RDTSC instructions, on the other hand, are part of the instruction flow and must be performed by the interrogating Pentium CPU itself. The actual method chosen, in order to make use of performance monitoring, is purely a matter of personal preference. The main advantage in using the RDMSR and WRMSR instructions is that performance monitoring can be carried out purely on a software basis and thus without additional hardware. Implementing an access through TAP, on the other hand, is not quite so simple because external hardware is required. For compensation, other TAP functions are also available (see Section 13.2).

A probe register is included in the TAP controller for supporting performance monitoring. You can address it in exactly the same way as the other TAP registers (such as the runbist register). The data for the probe data register is synchronized with TCK, and is serially input through TDI and output through TDO. Intel has extended the TAP instruction set by a number of instructions for performance monitoring.

12 The Pentium bus and its bus cycles

The memory addressing described previously is of a purely logical nature. In reality, in order to read and write data, the Pentium must be able to transmit and receive various control signals, and, of course, it also needs power for its circuitry. Right from the first day of delivery, the Pentium could run at 66 MHz (and now 100 MHz). The three pipelines of the Pentium achieve a throughput that, in the case of instructions with intensive memory accesses, would completely overload the bus of, for example, the i386. Thus, a characteristic of the Pentium's bus is its uncompromised alignment with a quick second level cache. Frequently required instructions and data are held ready in the two on-chip caches, which can be read or written to in a single clock cycle. For the connection to the second level cache (L2 cache), the Pentium's data bus has been widened to 64-bit, so that the on-chip caches can be reloaded and written back with suffi-cient speed: 32 bits would be insufficient if all three pipelines execute an instruction for every CLK cycle (without blockages) and, additionally, carry out a memory access where possible. The Pentium attempts to execute memory accesses, as far as possible, as cache line fills or write-backs.

A direct connection with the DRAM main memory without an L2 cache is not possible due to the 100 MHz clock frequency. With a CLK cycle time of only 10 ns, the SRAM cache itself, must also act very quickly. Thus, only the most modern DRAM chips with page or static column mode and internal refreshing, and high quality SRAM chips with a corresponding cache con-troller, can be used for the Pentium. Cacheing and the necessary memory subsystems are more accurately described in Chapter 9 and Section 14.2. But, first, the characteristic properties of the Pentium's bus.

12.1 Characteristics of the Pentium memory and I/O subsystems

The Pentium contains an external 64-bit bus. Note that these 64 bits only refer to the external bus width. Internally, the Pentium is a 32-bit processor, just like the i386 or i486 – in other words, its registers and the processing track of the pipelines are 32 bits wide. Both the L2 cache and the main memory are usually organized as 64-bit memory. Despite this, the Pentium can also address individual bytes, words, or double words through the byte enable signals $\overline{BE7}$–$\overline{BE0}$. Every bus cycle addresses memory through A31–A3 at quad word limits – thus, in multiples of 8 (0, 8, 16 and so on).

Accesses to memory objects that stretch over such a boundary, for example, quad word accesses that are not a multiple of eight – also known as misaligned accesses – are split into two conse-cutive accesses by the Pentium. The physical address space of the Pentium comprises 4 Gbytes and is thus the same size as that in the i386 (and i486). Of course, the memory can also be formed as a 32-, 16- or 8-bit memory. The address bits A2, A2 and A1, and A2–A0, respectively, must then be decoded from the $\overline{BEx}$ signals (I am quite sure that no one would have the need to connect the Pentium to an 8-bit memory). The video RAM of ISA and EISA graphic adaptors are examples of 16- and 32-bit memories, respectively.

The Pentium includes a burst mode for quickly filling and saving the cache lines. The burst read mode, already known from the i486, has been extended to include a burst write mode, which can read and write twice as many bytes, due to the doubling of the data bus width. Compared to the i386 and the i486, the address pipelining has also been further improved, so that in pipelined burst mode a maximum data transfer rate of 528 million bytes (at 66 MHz) is possible. The Pentium attempts to execute all read and write accesses as burst cycles. Only accesses to the I/O address space and non-cacheable address areas in memory (such as register addresses for memory mapped I/O, for example) are executed as single transfer cycles.

Unlike memory accesses, accesses to the I/O address area have not been widened to 64-bit. The maximum width here is only 32-bit. The reason for this is that I/O accesses, in principle, do not pass through the on-chip data cache; instead, they are directly 'switched through' to the bus. Thus, cacheing only affects memory and not the I/O ports. The Pentium can also address 8- or 16-bit ports. The I/O subsystem must decode the port address bits A2–A0 from the byte enable signals $\overline{BE7}$–$\overline{BE0}$.

12.2 The signal path between CPU and memory

Up until now, we have only encountered how the Pentium, with the assistance of its segment and offset registers, logically organizes and addresses data. In reality, to read data from, or write data to, the memory, the Pentium has to physically address the memory (using the address bus) and transfer the data (via its data bus). Such a bus cycle, in which data is read or written, follows a definite and strictly defined sequence of address, data and control signals. In addition, the Pentium provides its address pins A31–A3 and $\overline{BE7}$–$\overline{BE0}$ with the physical address of the memory object on completion of segmentation and paging, via the addressing unit and the bus interface.

The Pentium signals are not normally used directly for the control of the memory or the system bus. On the contrary, an additional bus controller is usually available, which makes all bus signals available to the memory device with sufficient strength. Today, the bus controller is, together with the address and data buffers and additional control circuitry, the main part of a highly integrated system controller (for example the Plato chipset for the Pentium, including L2 cache controller, bus controller and memory controller). It frequently embraces the functions of earlier support chips, for example, DMA chip 8237, programmable interval timer 8253/8254 and the programmable interrupt controller 8259. However, at this point, I do not wish to go into any further depth regarding support chips. Figure 12.1 shows the principal signal paths between the processor and the memory.

If the Pentium wishes to read data from memory, it transmits an address to the *address buffer*, via its address bus. If the $\overline{ADS}$ signal is active, the address buffer accepts the address bits and locks them. At this point, $\overline{BE0}$–$\overline{BE7}$ define which data bus line should actually transfer the data. In order to address the correct word in the main storage area, an *address multiplexer* is available. It selects the chosen word from the main memory with the assistance of the *memory controller*. The data that has been read is then transferred from the main memory to the memory buffer. Subsequently, the *memory buffer* transfers the data to the *data buffer*, from which the Pentium can read the data. Figure 12.1 represents a memory system without a cache. The memory and data buffers can also be identical, to prevent an extra transfer from the memory to the data buffer from occurring. Such matters are entirely dependent upon the individual design of the mother board. The developer has almost total freedom, because the layout is transparent for software. Data transfer is only achieved by electrical signals, and not by software instructions.

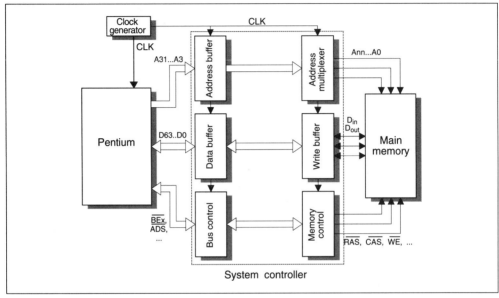

Figure 12.1: The path between processor and main memory.
Usually the processor does not access the memory directly. Instead a bus controller, for generating the necessary control signals for the bus, and various buffers, for temporary storing and amplifying of the data and address signals, are provided between the Pentium and the RAM. The memory controller drives the main memory, so that it outputs correct data or writes it to the appropriate location. The buffer and control elements shown as individual components in the figure are usually parts of one single highly integrated system controller.

12.3 Accesses to memory and the Pentium bus cycle

In this section, I would like to present accesses to memory, and also the essential bus cycles. The Pentium carries out the same cycles, independently of whether the external memory system represents a quick second level cache or a slower DRAM main memory. The only difference is that in the latter case the $\overline{\text{BRDY}}$ signal is returned later, thus the Pentium inserts more wait states. Note that the Pentium is running at a maximum of 66 MHz externally.

The Pentium bus can have one of six possible conditions, which I would briefly like to detail at this point, along with their usual abbreviations (according to Intel notation). Each condition has a duration of one CLK cycle. Naturally, many such cycles can follow consecutively.

▶   Ti (idle condition): the Pentium does not execute a bus cycle: it waits. Ti is the wait or ready condition.

▶ T1: the bus condition corresponding to the first clock cycle of a bus transfer cycle. Burst cycles, in particular, can take many clock cycles.

▶ T2: the bus condition corresponding to the second, or later, clock cycle of a bus transfer cycle. During T2, write data is typically given out by the Pentium, or read data is transferred.

▶ T12: in this bus condition, two clock cycles are pending. The first cycle is not yet complete (and is in condition T2), the second has just been sent (and is in condition T1). T12 only occurs with pipelined addressing if the Pentium has already given out the address for the subsequent transfer before the current bus cycle has been completed.

▶ T2P: in this bus condition also, two clock cycles are pending. The first cycle has not yet been completed (and is in condition T2), but the second is already in the second or later clock cycle (and is also in condition T2). T2P follows T12 if, during pipelined addressing, T12 has already been completed, but the first cycle has still not been terminated.

▶ TD (dead condition): the dead condition indicates a pending cycle, whereby the Pentium must first allow a clock cycle to elapse, in order to execute a write operation after a read operation, and vice versa. The Pentium uses TD during pipelined addressing.

12.3.1 Single transfer cycles

The single transfer read and single transfer write cycles are the two simplest memory access cycles of the Pentium. During their execution, data 8, 16, 32 or 64 bits in size is transferred from memory to the Pentium, or from the Pentium to memory. Figure 12.2 shows a read cycle without pipelining and wait states. Only the most important control signals are represented in the figure.

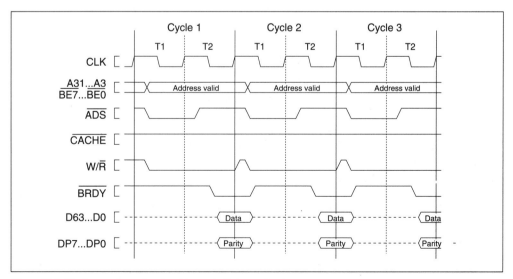

Figure 12.2: Single transfer read cycle without pipelining and wait states.

During the first clock cycle T1, the Pentium first sends out the addresses A31–A3, the $\overline{\text{BEx}}$ signals corresponding to the data width of the access, and also the control signals W/$\overline{\text{R}}$ and $\overline{\text{CACHE}}$. Finally, it activates the $\overline{\text{ADS}}$ signal in order to indicate the validity of the address and bus control signals. The Pentium uses the $\overline{\text{CACHE}}$ signal, which is, however, inactive for this cycle – that is, held at a high level. In this way, it indicates that the current cycle is a single transfer cycle.

After a period of time, depending on the speed of the memory subsystem, the subsystem delivers the addressed data and activates the $\overline{\text{BRDY}}$ ready signal. The subsystem can, more or less, optionally deliver the parity bits corresponding to the active $\overline{\text{BEx}}$ signals. For the memory read cycle described, the data and parity bits are immediately available, so no wait states are required. (Wait states and wait cycles are discussed in Section 12.3.2.) Thus, $\overline{\text{BRDY}}$ is activated by the memory subsystem before the end of the T2 cycle.

Single transfer write cycles in the Pentium are (apart from the opposite direction of the data signal flow) not very different. Figure 12.3 shows a typical write cycle without wait states, after which two read cycles follow.

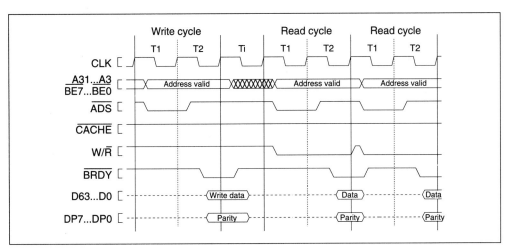

Figure 12.3: Single transfer write cycle without pipelining and wait states.

Here also, the Pentium first sends out the addresses A31–A3, the $\overline{\text{BEx}}$ signals corresponding to the data width of the access, and also the control signals W/$\overline{\text{R}}$ and $\overline{\text{CACHE}}$. In this case, W/$\overline{\text{R}}$ is at a high level because a write access is required. Finally, the Pentium activates the $\overline{\text{ADS}}$ signal, in order to indicate the validity of the address and bus control signals. The $\overline{\text{CACHE}}$ signal is also inactive here, indicating a single transfer cycle. During T2, the Pentium also delivers the write data and the necessary parity bits. The subsystem takes the data and then sends back an active $\overline{\text{BRDY}}$ signal. Now the Pentium is ready for the next cycle. The write cycle described is accomplished without wait states.

In Figure 12.3, a Ti clock cycle (i=idle; that is, empty) follows the write cycle first, then a read cycle and finally a further read cycle.

In single transfer mode (read and write), a data transfer without wait states requires at least two CLK cycles. With a data bus width of 64 bits, this leads to a maximum data transfer rate of 264 million bytes/s (equal to 254 Mbytes/s). This can be doubled in pipelined burst mode to 528 million bytes/s (equal to 508 Mbytes/s).

12.3.2 Wait states or wait cycles

If the memory or peripheral device cannot conclude a read or write request within the two T1 and T2 cycles, then the memory controller holds the $\overline{\text{BRDY}}$ signal at a high level. This indicates to the Pentium that it should implement another T2 instruction cycle, in order to give the memory or peripheral device more time to conform to the request. This is known as a *wait cycle* or a *wait state*. If, on completion of the additional T2, the $\overline{\text{BRDY}}$ signal is still at a high level, then the processor inserts another wait cycle (and another, and another and so on). Figure 12.4 shows a write bus cycle with one wait state (or wait cycle).

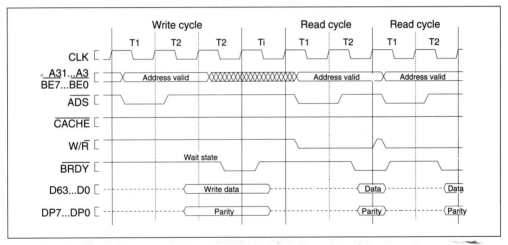

Figure 12.4: Single transfer write cycle with one wait state.
The Pentium inserts one or more wait states if the accessed device is not able to follow the fast clocked Pentium and does not activate the $\overline{\text{BRDY}}$ signal (with a low level) in time.

In Figure 12.4, the nth bus cycle leads to a wait cycle; the (n+1)th, however, does not. The Pentium maintains the write data active until the end of the first system clock CLK2 after the last T2 of the current bus cycle. If two bus cycles follow immediately after each other, this means that the write data is active until, at least, the end of the first system clock CLK2 of the *next* bus cycle.

Of course, the number of wait cycles for writing data can differ to that for reading data. DRAM main memories can, in fact, write data quicker than read it. The reason for this is that when writing it is sufficient to transfer the memory controller address and the value of the data byte. The memory controller executes the write process independently using the stored data from the data or the memory buffer, while the Pentium can devote itself to another process, and not have to wait for the conclusion of the write process resulting from a slow memory device. In contrast, when reading, the CPU has no other choice but to wait for the completion of the internal reading process in the main storage area. Prior to this, no other data will be available.

The number of wait cycles can also depend on the location of the memory. The main storage area on the mother board operates with far fewer wait states than, for example, the video RAM on a graphics adaptor, which in a PC is also part of the Pentium address space. Anything up to 50 wait states can occur in this case. The cause of this is not an incorrectly chosen memory chip, but the low clock rate of 8 MHz for the connection between the plug-in board and the adaptor (the Pentium can run at up to 66 MHz externally). Furthermore, the video RAM is not always accessible in many graphic adaptors, thus further delays occur.

The number of wait states was previously determined by the board design, or could be ascertained by a jumper, depending on how fast the installed memory chips were. In those days, the memory controller reacted in a standard manner with a predetermined delay of the $\overline{\text{BRDY}}$ signal. Today this process is out of date. Modern and efficient concepts, such as cache memory, or page interleaved memory touch on statistical considerations, therefore a flexible output of the $\overline{\text{BRDY}}$ signal is required, because the exact number of wait cycles for the individual memory access cannot be predicted. This requires a number quantity of wait cycles in relation to the actual installation.

12.3.3 Quad word boundary

The Pentium represents a 32-bit processor with a 64-bit data bus. Thus, the main memory is normally organized as a physical 32-bit memory. This means that the Pentium always physically addresses the byte addresses 0, 8, 16, ..., with 4G-8. In fact, logically, quad words (32-bit) can start at an address that is not a multiple of eight. However, the quad word can not be physically read or written to such an address in one attempt. If a quad word is to be stored or read to an address that does not represent such a quad word address, the Pentium bus interface splits the quad word access into two accesses. The first access reads or writes the least significant part of the quad word, the second accesses the most significant part. Such a quad word part is between one and seven bytes long (eight bytes would, of course, be a quad word access at a quad word address).

This process is totally transparent to the software – in other words, the hardware is responsible for the division and double memory access without the influence of software. Thus, the programmer can sort data into a preferential form, without having to worry about quad word boundaries.

During the two-part access, the memory is physically addressed by the quad word addresses 0, 8, and so on, but is only read or written by the predetermined bytes $\overline{\text{BE0}}$–$\overline{\text{BE7}}$. Furthermore, the Pentium can also read and write individual bytes, 16-bit words or 32-bit double words. A single access is all that is required, providing that a 16-bit data word does not exceed the quad word boundary.

Figure 12.5 represents a read access. The bus interface executes an access twice when accessing the quad word with the address 2f05h. Initially, the three bytes with the addresses 2f05h, 2f06h and 2f07h are read. This occurs as a result of the processor producing the 2f00h address and simultaneously setting the byte enable signals as shown: $\overline{\text{BE0}}$=1, $\overline{\text{BE1}}$=1, $\overline{\text{BE2}}$=1, $\overline{\text{BE3}}$=1, $\overline{\text{BE4}}$=1,

$\overline{BE5}$=0, $\overline{BE6}$=0, $\overline{BE7}$=0. Thus, the three least significant bytes of the quad word are read to the address 2f05h. Immediately after this, the CPU provides the 2f08h address and simultaneously sets $\overline{BE0}$=0, $\overline{BE1}$=0, $\overline{BE2}$=0, $\overline{BE3}$=0, $\overline{BE4}$=0, $\overline{BE5}$=1, $\overline{BE6}$=1, $\overline{BE7}$=1. Thus, the byte is read to the address 2f08h. The bus interface combines the first three bytes and the last five bytes that were read into a quad word at the address 2f05h. Thus, from the double access, the Pentium has addressed a quad word that does not start at a quad word address. In order to write a word to such an address, the same process is run in reverse.

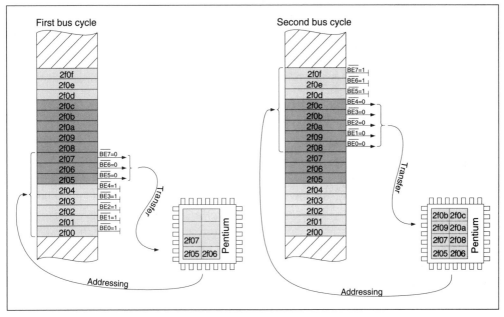

Figure 12.5: Access to a quad word that does not begin at a quad word boundary.
As the memory of the Pentium is organized in 64-bit portions, the Pentium is not able to access quad words directly that do not start at quad word boundaries. Instead the Pentium has to split such an access into two successive accesses. In both accesses a whole quad word is addressed, but only the required one to seven bytes are actually fetched and combined into one single 64-bit quad word. The Pentium bus interface carries out the double access automatically.

Bytes with the address $8n$ (n=0 to n=G/2) are always carried over the data bus lines D7 to D0, and bytes with the address $8n+1$ via D15 to D8. The same applies for bytes with the address $8n+2$, which always use the lines D23 to D16, and bytes with the address $8n+3$, which use lines D31 to D24, and so on. Finally, bytes with the address $8n+7$ use lines D63 to D56. Something similar applies to ports. Generally, during both part accesses, the memory controller executes a complete 64-bit access and can, in each case, also output all 64-bits to the data bus. However, either the system controller or the Pentium will accept the byte, for which $\overline{BEx}$ (x=0–7) is at a low level.

It is clear that reading or writing of a quad word to an address that is not a multiple of eight always requires two bus cycles, whereas the access of a quad word to a quad word address only requires one bus cycle. Therefore, it is advantageous, even when unnecessary, to always sort the data in memory, so that quad words start with a quad word address and 16-bit words and 32-bit double words do not stretch such quad word addresses. This procedure only applies to data because code fetching is carried out through the code cache, which is always filled with a burst cycle addressing 64-bit double words at double word boundaries. But the transfer of the opcodes from the code cache to the prefetcher can start at any address (for example, if a jump to an odd address occured). In order to reach a quad word address, the processor, if required, reads one to seven bytes first, before continuing at quad word boundaries.

12.3.4 Burst cycles

For the transfer of larger quantities of data, the Pentium implements a bus mode known as burst mode. In normal single transfer mode, a bus cycle without wait states requires two clock cycles. Thus, every two processor cycles, the Pentium can read or write a value. In burst mode, the time for the transfer of a value is reduced to a single clock cycle; the transfer rate is doubled. The Pentium uses burst mode for cacheable read cycles, and also for write-back cycles when writing back a complete cache line. In a burst cycle, four bus cycles are used to transfer 32 bytes, which must be connected and must each lie at a 32-byte limit (this is usually a cache line of the two on-chip caches). Thus, burst mode is directly targeted at cache line fills and write-backs.

For the $\overline{BRDY}$, $\overline{CACHE}$ and $\overline{KEN}$ signals, the Pentium independently decides whether a burst cycle should be executed, or if a single transfer is sufficient. A burst cycle is started by a normal memory access that requires two clock cycles. In Figure 12.6, you can see the flow of the important signals for a burst read cycle.

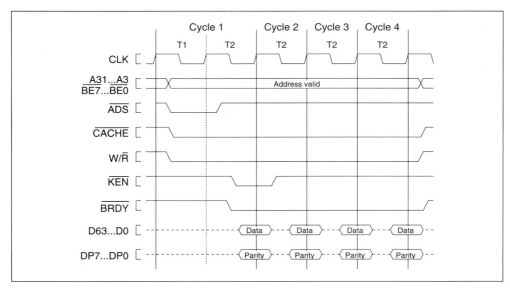

Figure 12.6: Burst read cycle without wait states and pipelining.
In burst mode, the bus cycle for a 32-byte address area is reduced from two processor clock cycles to one cycle. Only the first access lasts two clock cycles. Thus, a cache line of the internal caches can be filled very quickly.

If the Pentium initiates a read cycle, it first sends out the address of the object to be read through its address bus, and activates the $\overline{ADS}$ signal in order to indicate that the address and control signals are valid. For a burst cycle, the $\overline{CACHE}$ signal from the Pentium and the $\overline{KEN}$

signal from the memory subsystem also play an important role. The Pentium indicates to the subsystem, through an active $\overline{\text{CACHE}}$ signal with low level, that the addressed object can be transferred to the on-chip cache, and thus the read access is cacheable. If the $\overline{\text{KEN}}$ signal delivered by the memory subsystem is active, then the Pentium independently and automatically extends the single transfer to a cache line fill, in order to store the addressed object in the on-chip cache. The cache line fill is necessary for this, because no individual bytes, words, double or quad words are stored in the cache; instead, complete cache lines of 32 bytes are always used. The memory subsystem then only activates $\overline{\text{KEN}}$ if the addressed object does not lie in an area that blocks cacheing. An example of such a blocked area is the memory mapped register, which is addressed through the normal memory address space, but which takes on control responsibilities. The 'cacheing' of such registers would simply bring the control to a standstill. A further example is the video RAM of graphic adaptors in personal computers. Changes to the screen (such as the insertion of a text line) should also be indicated and not just temporarily stored in the on-chip cache.

Because burst cycles are limited to an address area that begins at a 32-byte limit, after receiving the start address, the memory subsystem can independently calculate the other three burst addresses, without the need to decode further address signals from the Pentium. The Pentium only sends the address and $\overline{\text{BEx}}$ signals during the first cycle; they are not changed during the subsequent three bus cycles. In order to satisfy the limitations and adjust the 32-byte partitions to such 32-byte limits, a specific fixed sequence of addresses in burst mode has been defined. You can see this sequence in Table 12.1.

First address output by the Pentium	Second address	Third address	Last address
0h	8h	10h	18h
8h	0h	18h	10h
10h	18h	0h	8h
18h	10h	8h	0h

Table 12.1: Address sequence for burst read cycles.

The definition of the sequence is necessary, because the first address given out by the Pentium need not necessarily define a 32-byte boundary; it can lie anywhere in the address space. After the decoding of the start address, the external memory subsystem must calculate the sequence of the addresses given, and then follow the sequence when memory is addressed. The Pentium receives the data without sending out any more addresses, and then divides the data delivered by the subsystem according to the quad word entries in the applicable cache line. The address sequence is not cyclic; it is given in the indicated form, in order to support two-way interleaving of the DRAM main memory. This reduces the access time. Independently of whether the byte enable signals are active or inactive for the first cycle, 64 bits plus eight data parity bits are always returned. In the case of a burst cycle, the memory subsystem must ignore the $\overline{\text{BEx}}$ signals and use the full 64-bit address bus.

The burst mode in the Pentium is considerably different to that in the i486 (for which the 80x86 burst mode was first implemented). In the i486, a burst cycle is explicitly initiated by a $\overline{\text{BLAST}}$

signal (which is not available in the Pentium) during T2 of the first cycle. In addition, a burst transfer in the i486, in principle, begins with an address at a 16-byte limit (because of the 32-bit data bus of the i486, its burst mode is proportionally limited to 16 bytes). Burst mode in the i486 can only be used for a read transfer and not for the writing of data. Because the i486 on-chip cache is implemented as a write through cache, this is, however, not absolutely necessary, since every write access to bytes, words or double words is switched through to the memory sub-system. The write-back cache of the Pentium, on the other hand, requires that burst mode also be used for write transfers. In Figure 12.7, you can see the signal flow for such a write burst transfer.

The signal flow is not very different to that of the burst read cycle. Only the W/$\overline{\text{R}}$ signal is different, in that it is at a high level to indicate the write transfer.

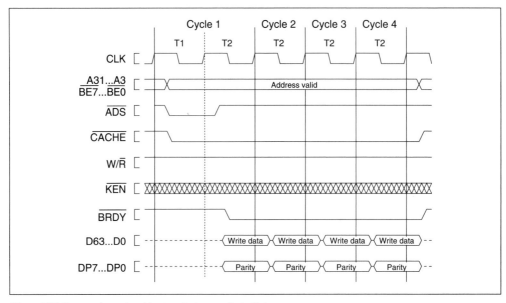

Figure 12.7: Burst write cycle without wait states and pipelining.
The Pentium uses the burst write ccyle to carry out a cache line write-back.

In addition, $\overline{\text{KEN}}$ is ignored, because all data available in the on-chip cache is obviously cacheable and an entry in the on-chip cache will be emptied and not refilled. A burst write cycle is always a write-back cycle for a modified line in the data cache. The Pentium indicates this with an active $\overline{\text{CACHE}}$ signal with a low level. For the on-chip code cache, no write-backs can occur, because the data stored there should never be overwritten. Thus, burst write cycles always affect the data cache; burst read cycles, on the other hand, affect both the data and code caches. Write-back cycles occur in the following cases:

▶ The replacement of a modified cache line with a line from memory (L2 cache or main memory); this is the result of a cache miss in the data cache.
▶ In an inquiry cycle, in accordance with the MESI protocol, a hit occurs for a modified line in the data cache.
▶ A Pentium internal snoop has reached a modified line in the data cache.

▶ An external activation of the $\overline{\text{FLUSH}}$ signal has initiated a cache flush.
▶ The Pentium carries out an internal WBINV (write-back and invalidate) instruction.

A further considerable difference, compared to the burst write cycle, is the address sequencing necessary for burst write operations. As they are exclusively the consequence of cache line write-backs, the first address sent out always defines a 32-byte boundary; for this reason, differing address sequences as in Table 12.1 do not occur. Instead, the memory subsystem can simply increase the target address by eight for every subsequent bus cycle. Thus, the address sequence is set to 0h → 8h → 10h → 18h. 0h is given by the Pentium; 8h, 10h and 18h by the memory subsystem.

Thus, a burst cycle can read in or write a maximum of 32 bytes. With a data bus width of 64 bits, therefore, four read cycles are necessary; for the Pentium in burst mode 2+3=5 clock cycles are required. The transfer rate of 32 bytes every five clock cycles in the 100 MHz Pentium corresponds to a burst transfer rate of approximately 610 Mbyte/s (or 640 million byte/s). Address pipelining (see below) can also reduce the first burst bus cycle to a single CLK cycle; then only four clock cycles are necessary to transfer 32 bytes, so the transfer rate is increased to 763 Mbyte/s or 800 million byte/s. Note, however, that for these impressive figures, the rate only applies for an access time of 40 ns or 0.040 μs. Even high performance hard disks with numerous heads driven in parallel, or an array of coupled disk drives, seldom achieve more than 5–10 Mbyte/s. Thus, the processor bus does not represent the hold-up; the whole system is usually slowed down at other points.

Wait states can also be inserted in burst mode, if the memory subsystem cannot follow quickly enough. Such an access is known as a slow burst cycle. Figure 12.8 shows the signal flow.

The Pentium inserts wait states in burst mode if the addressed memory subsystem is late in activating the $\overline{\text{BRDY}}$ signal. The bus cycle is then simply extended by a T2 clock cycle. Note that the example shown in Figure 12.8 is still handled as a burst cycle – that is, the Pentium only sends out the first address. All subsequent addresses must be produced independently by the memory subsystem in accordance with Table 12.1. Thus, burst mode does not only increase the speed of data transfers, it also accelerates the production of addresses.

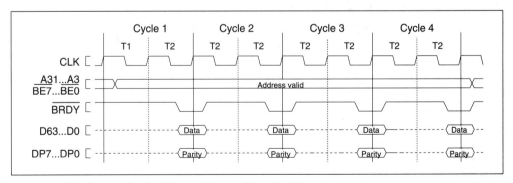

Figure 12.8: Slow burst read cycle with one wait state without pipelining.
The Pentium can also insert wait states in burst mode. For this purpose, the addressed memory subsystem returns the active $\overline{\text{BRDY}}$ signal later.

12.4 Address pipelining or pipelined addressing

The Pentium can transfer the next address to the decoder at the same time that the data transfer logic is still busy with data reading or writing. Thus, the decoder logic and address buffer can work in advance. Subsequent accesses are interleaved: the addressing logic receives the new address prior to the end of the current bus cycle. This principle is shown in Figure 12.9.

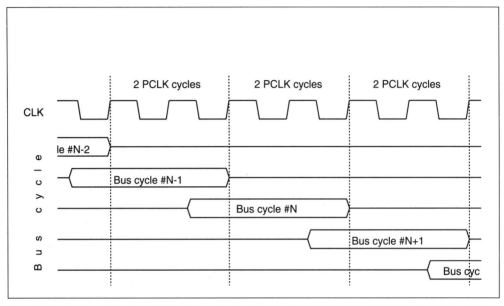

Figure 12.9: Pipelined addressing. With active pipelined addressing the processor outputs the following address before the current bus cycle has terminated. By means of this the addressed device is able to decode the new address, while the previous data is still being transferred.

In this way (according to the example), consecutive bus cycles require three clock cycles, but the effective time is reduced to two CLK cycles as a result of overlapping the bus cycles. This inter-linking, or overlapping, of input and output data and addresses of consecutive bus cycles, is known as *pipelined addressing* or *address pipelining*. The signals flow continuously as if in a pipeline.

Pipelined addressing is only an advantage if several memory accesses are to be executed one after the other. During the first access, the processor has to start the pipelining, by producing the address of the first access. This is similar to the production line at a car factory: several hours pass before the first car can be assembled and eventually leave the production line. Once the production line (or the 'vehicle pipeline') is full, a new car will leave the assembly area every couple of minutes. Pipelined addressing is especially advantageous for extensive memory accessing, as occurs, for example, with a task switch or when loading the processor cache register in protected mode. The aim and principle of pipelined addressing are similar to those for instruction pipelining (for example, in the u and v pipes of the Pentium).

The Pentium implements address pipelining, in addition to the increased bus band width, to further increase the data throughput. A special feature of the Pentium address pipelining is that it is 'aware' of two different types of bus cycle, and, with the help of address pipelining, can execute them consecutively, if the CPU pipelines are already working on other tasks. In this way, on one hand, the time between the address output and the data input or output is increased further to that caused by the use of slower memory components. On the other hand, the first bus cycle in burst mode can also be reduced to a single clock cycle, whereby the data transfer rate of 406 Mbyte/s (or 426 million byte/s) can be increased by 25% to 508 Mbyte/s or 528 million byte/s. Figure 12.10 shows two consecutive cache line fills in burst mode with active address pipelining.

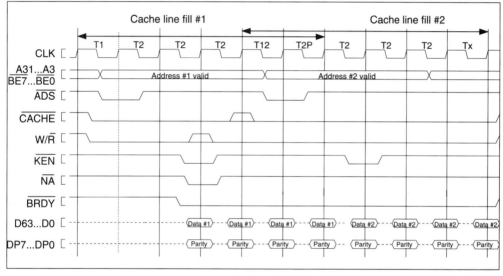

Figure 12.10: Pipelined cache line fills in burst mode without wait states.
The figure shows two successive cache line fills, which are carried out in burst mode. By means of address pipelining the second cache line fill overlaps the first one, and the data transfer can be carried out within four CLK ccyles.

Address pipelining is controlled by the $\overline{\text{NA}}$ (next address) signal. In Figure 12.10, the Pentium first sends out an initial burst for a cache line fill, in the way described above. It prepares the start address and activates $\overline{\text{ADS}}$ and $\overline{\text{CACHE}}$. If the addressed subsystem has decoded this address, and is ready to take the next cache line fill address for decoding, then it sends an active $\overline{\text{NA}}$ signal to the Pentium. For this, it is not necessary for memory to have already transferred all data packets of the burst to the Pentium. The subsystem can then decode the address given out in T12, while the third data transfer of the previous burst is still in operation. Immediately after the transfer of the last eight bytes from cache line fill 1, the memory subsystem delivers the data (and the parity) for cache line fill 2, so a CLK cycle is saved. Two or more such bursts can then be executed consecutively, for example, if a task switch is executed where a complete TSS must be saved and a new one loaded. Address pipelining is not limited to burst read cycles. Burst write cycles and single transfers can also use address pipelining. Locked and write-back cycles, of course, must not overlap other types of cycle.

The Pentium monitors how many $\overline{\text{BRDY}}$ signals have been returned, and therefore knows which burst is currently being executed. A maximum of two burst cycles (single burst transfers) can be active at any one time. Thus, as long as the last data packet of cache line fill 1 in Figure 12.10 has not been transferred to the Pentium, and the corresponding $\overline{\text{BRDY}}$ has not been activated, no new $\overline{\text{ADS}}$, nor the corresponding addresses, will be sent out.

12.5 Special cycles

The Pentium's special cycles have the task of informing the other devices of specific internal processor operations. This is achieved through the normal bus of the Pentium – in other words, the Pentium sends the necessary control signals, and also $\overline{\text{ADS}}$, in order to indicate that, as usual, it has sent out a bus cycle with valid signals. A special cycle takes place if the Pentium sends out the D/$\overline{\text{C}}$ and M/$\overline{\text{IO}}$ signals at a low level, and the W/$\overline{\text{R}}$ signal at a high level. Six special cycles have been provided; the Pentium identifies them through the byte enable signal $\overline{\text{BEx}}$, as you can see in Table 12.2.

$\overline{\text{BE7}}$	$\overline{\text{BE6}}$	$\overline{\text{BE5}}$	$\overline{\text{BE4}}$	$\overline{\text{BE3}}$	$\overline{\text{BE2}}$	$\overline{\text{BE1}}$	$\overline{\text{BE0}}$	Special cycle	Reason
1	1	1	1	1	1	1	0	Shutdown	Triple fault, parity error
1	1	1	1	1	1	0	1	Flush	INVD, WBINVD
1	1	1	1	1	0	1	1	Halt	HLT instruction
1	1	1	1	0	1	1	1	Write-back	WBINVD instruction
1	1	1	0	1	1	1	1	Flush acknowledge	$\overline{\text{FLUSH}}$ signal
1	1	0	1	1	1	1	1	Branch trace message	Taken branch

1=high signal level; 0=low signal level.

Table 12.2: Pentium special cycles (D/$\overline{C}$=M/$\overline{IO}$=0, W/$\overline{R}$=1).

The external system (such as the system controller) must also confirm such a special cycle by activating $\overline{\text{BRDY}}$. In this section, I would like to discuss briefly the meaning and cause of the different special cycles.

A Pentium *shutdown*, which is indicated by a shutdown cycle (11111110), usually has a serious background: either a further exception has occurred during the call-up of the double fault exception handler (thus, a triple fault), or an internal parity fault in a logic field or microcode ROM has occurred. The processor interrupts the current operation, goes into shutdown mode and waits for an NMI, INIT or RESET signal. Here, the data cache content is not written back to the main memory. This is a possible task for the restart routine, in order to wake the Pentium from its shutdown sleep and to set the computer working again.

The *halt* cycle (11111011) is closely related to shutdown. It is sent out if the Pentium executes an explicit HLT instruction and thus enters the halt condition. Here also, the Pentium stops all operations and waits to be reactivated. As for a shutdown, this can be through an NMI, an INIT or a RESET; it can also be achieved through the activation of the INTR signal (if the IE flag is set and thus interrupt requests are permitted). Here, as with a shutdown cycle, the content of the data cache is not written-back to the main memory.

The Pentium sends out a *flush* special cycle (11111101) if it has executed an INVD (invalidate cache) or WBINVD (write-back and invalidate cache). Note that in the case of WBINVD, the Pentium firstly executes a write-back cycle and then sends out a flush cycle. The flush special cycle only shows that the internal cache has been invalidated; it does not indicate whether the changed data cache content has also been written back. The external system can use the flush special cycle, for example, in order to send out a cache flush for the L2 cache, if one is available. Without this special cycle, the external system could otherwise not differentiate between a cache flush with a write-back of the modified cache lines through WBINVD, and a normal write-back. With this, and the subsequently described write-back special cycle, when the computer must be switched off, the system can successfully save all data, and then finally give the system manager the OK to physically switch off the system.

The Pentium sends out a *write-back* special cycle (11110111) only after a WBINVD instruction has been executed. In this way, it indicates that all modified cache lines in the on-chip data cache have been written back to the main memory (or to an intermediate second level cache). The system can use the write-back special cycle, for example, to finally write-back all modified cache lines in the L2 cache to the main memory. Immediately after a special write-back cycle, the Pentium sends out an addition flush cycle.

A further special cycle that affects the writing back and invalidation of the on-chip data cache is the *flush acknowledge* special cycle (11101111). The Pentium sends this special cycle through the bus if an external unit (such as the system controller) has applied an active signal with a low level to the $\overline{\text{FLUSH}}$ input, in order to initiate a write-back and a cache invalidation, and the Pentium has executed these operations. In this way, the system controller can differentiate between a cache flush through software (an INVD or WBINVD), and a cache flush through hardware (an active $\overline{\text{FLUSH}}$ signal). The flush acknowledge cycle, like the write-back special cycle, indicates a write-back and invalidation of the cache lines. The flush special cycle, on the other hand, only indicates an invalidation.

The *branch trace message* special cycle (11011111) is implemented as the sixth special cycle. The Pentium sends it out if the ETE bit (execution tracing enable) is set in the TR12 test register, and the Pentium has executed a branch immediately beforehand. Note that during the branch, it activates the IBT (instruction branch taken) signal. Furthermore, during the branch trace message special cycle, the Pentium sends out the linear address (thus, the address without regard to the translation caused by paging, which may be active), to its address pins A31–A3 and the branch target pins BT2–BT0; thus, A31–A3 and BT2–BT0 form the linear 32-bit address of the branch target. Additionally, through the BT3 signal, it indicates whether the standard operand size is 32 bits (BT3=high level) or 16 bits (BT3=low level). Thus, BT3 corresponds to the DB bit (bit 30) in the corresponding segment descriptor. The branch trace message special cycle is part of execution tracing, which has been implemented in the Pentium in order to establish externally the internal activity of the CPU. This also includes the two IU and IV signals, which indicate the completion of an instruction execution in the u and v pipelines, respectively.

12.6 Inquiry cycles and internal snooping

Inquiry cycles are used for the implementation of the MESI protocol for multiprocessor systems. In this way, it is possible for an external unit to determine whether the data at a specific address is stored in the on-chip cache of the Pentium. In addition, the external unit can invalidate the stored data and, thus, the whole corresponding cache line. This is necessary so that the data in a multiprocessor system is always consistent. If a processor changes a value in its on-chip cache so that this value is also stored in the on-chip cache of a different CPU, and this other CPU also modifies the value, then it is no longer absolutely clear which of the two changed values is current – that is, valid.

For an inquiry cycle, the external unit must transfer the physical address of the data to the Pentium. Thus, the transfer direction in the usually unidirectional address bus must be turned around. This is achieved with the help of the AHOLD signal. After the external system has sent an active AHOLD signal with a high level to the Pentium and has then waited for two CLK cycles, it transfers the inquiry address to the Pentium through A31–A5. A4 and A3 are ignored, because a complete cache line is always addressed in an inquiry cycle (only units of cache lines can be read and written back to the on-chip caches). The final activation of $\overline{\text{EADS}}$ instructs the Pentium to fetch the address given and to use it as an inquiry address. Thus, for inquiry cycles, $\overline{\text{EADS}}$ has the same purpose as $\overline{\text{ADS}}$ has for normal bus cycles. The INV signal must also be sent with the addresses A31–A5. In the case of an interrogation or inquiry hit, it indicates whether the applicable cache line should be marked as invalidated or shared. INV has no effect for inquiry misses.

In an externally initiated inquiry cycle, as in normal memory accesses, the tag logic of the on-chip cache checks whether the address is located in the tag memory, and thus whether the corresponding value is available in the on-chip cache. In an inquiry cycle, the address originates in the external logic; in a normal memory cycle, on the other hand, from the CPU kernel. In both cases, the address comparator compares the cache control, tag and transferred addresses, in order to determine a hit or a miss. If a hit has occurred in the code or data cache, the address comparator, and therefore the Pentium, sends out an active signal with a low level from the $\overline{\text{HIT}}$ pin. If a miss occurs, the $\overline{\text{HIT}}$ output sends out a signal with a high level. The Pentium requires two CLK cycles in order to determine a hit or a miss and to send out the $\overline{\text{HIT}}$ signal; thus, it occurs two CLK cycles after the activation of $\overline{\text{EADS}}$. If a hit for a modified cache line is at hand (which is only possible for the data cache), then the Pentium sends out an active $\overline{\text{HITM}}$ signal (hit modified) with a low level. An active $\overline{\text{HITM}}$ also means that the Pentium contains the latest version of the data. Thus, it is important for harmonization in multiprocessor systems, for example, in which the individual CPUs communicate through the main memory and also access it.

If, during an inquiry cycle, a hit to a modified line in the data cache occurs (there are no modified lines in the code cache), then the Pentium writes back the applicable line to memory. Thus, it sends out a burst write-back cycle. In this way, it is ensured that the inquiring system contains the latest data. Figure 12.11 shows the signal flow for the case where an inquiry cycle finds a modified line.

As the INV signal is at a high level, the written back line is then invalidated. $\overline{\text{HIT}}$ and $\overline{\text{HITM}}$ are active two CLK cycles after $\overline{\text{EADS}}$. After the actual inquiry cycle and during the first four CLK cycles, the Pentium carries out the burst write-back cycle beginning with the activation of $\overline{\text{ADS}}$ two clock cycles after $\overline{\text{HIT}}$ has been sent out. In principle, $\overline{\text{HIT}}$ does not change its value between the two inquiry cycles; thus, it remains at a low level. $\overline{\text{HITM}}$ remains at a low level until two CLK cycles after the last $\overline{\text{BRDY}}$ of the burst write-back cycle. If AHOLD is still active at the start of the write-back, and thus the Pentium is prevented from using its address bus, then the memory subsystem uses the addresses A31–A5 delivered by the inquiring unit for the write-back cycle. In this way, A31–A5 always give the start address of a cache line. The external system can also deactivate AHOLD before the Pentium begins with the cache line write-back. If this is the case, the Pentium sends out the write-back address. An inquiry cycle can occur a maximum of every two CLK cycles. If a modified cache line is reached, the Pentium first writes back all 32 bytes, and only then accepts the next inquiry cycle.

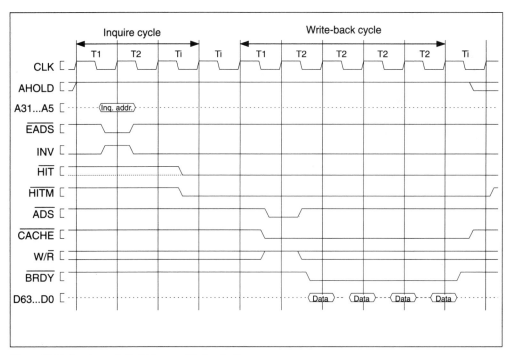

Figure 12.11: Inquiry cycle that hits a modified cache line.

In addition to this externally (through $\overline{\text{EADS}}$) initiated inquiry cycle, there is also internal snooping. It is used mainly for checking the consistency of the two independent on-chip caches, the code and data caches of the Pentium. Above all, in real mode the same data can be available in both the code and data caches, as an indirect result of prefetching. Internal snooping is neither initiated by an $\overline{\text{EADS}}$ nor by the activation of $\overline{\text{HIT}}$ or $\overline{\text{HITM}}$, even though it is similar to the effects of inquiry cycles. Internal snooping can occur in the following three cases:

▶ The CPU kernel of the Pentium accesses the code cache, and this access results in a miss. If the cache line with the addressed value is actually located in the data cache, but the code cache is loaded with the same line from memory, it is possible that the two lines have differing content even though they represent the same memory address. This is the case if the entry in the data cache is modified, but has not yet been written back. In this case, snooping causes the data cache line to be written back before the code cache is loaded. If the line is in fact located in the data cache, but is marked as shared or exclusive, then the snooping cycle only invalidates the cache line.

▶ The CPU kernel accesses the data cache, and this access leads to a cache miss (read access), or a write-through (write access) to the L2 cache or the main memory. If the corresponding cache line is also stored in the code cache, it is invalidated there by snooping. The reason for this is that in the first case (read access), an external unit could have changed the entry in the external memory, without the knowledge of the Pentium. The cache line fill following the miss loads the correct version of the value into the data cache; the corresponding entry in the code cache is then invalidated. In the second case (write access), the Pentium will change the value in the external memory with an almost 100% certainty due to the write-through. In this way, the entries in the corresponding cache line of the on-chip code cache are, of course, no longer correct.

▶ If the A or the D bit (accessed and dirty bit, respectively) of a page table or page directory entry is overwritten as the result of an access or a change to the corresponding page, the Pentium carries out internal snooping. If the corresponding cache line is available in one of the on-chip caches and is marked as valid, then the Pentium invalidates the entry. If the line is available and has also been modified, it is first written back, and only then invalidated. This is necessary, in order to permit central management of pages that affect the shared main memory and are also used by the processors in the system. The external storage of a page, possibly with an explicit saving to an external mass storage, is decided by the frequency and type of access to this page. One could also regard the main memory as a 'cache' between the CPU and the mass storage device.

12.7 I/O address space of the Pentium and peripherals

Until now we have only learned about addressing of the memory using offset and segment, and the physical addressing with the assistance of the 32-bit address bus. For example, the memory is addressed with the instructions MOV reg, mem or MOV mem, reg. In addition to the memory area, the Pentium has a so-called *I/O address space*, which can be accessed with the machine instructions IN, OUT and so on via ports. This address space, as in its predecessors, includes 64k 8-bit ports, 32k 16-bit ports and 16k 32-bit ports, or an equivalent mix of them. Thus, the Pentium has two totally separate address spaces – the memory and the I/O space – both of which are addressed via the data and address bus.

Accesses to the I/O address space are accomplished with a maximum width of 32 bits; the remaining 32 bits of the 64-bit Pentium data bus are then unused. The Pentium identifies an I/O bus cycle through a low level M/$\overline{\text{IO}}$ signal. As in other 80x86 processors, the port addresses 0f8h to 0ffh are reserved. They are used in the i386 for communication between the CPU and the coprocessor. In principle, I/O accesses bypass the cache and are sent directly through the bus, as they normally only address control or status registers. If an I/O write access was intercepted by a cache control register, and only later written back to the corresponding cache line through the bus, it would produce unexpected consequences at unexpected and unknown times. I/O write accesses are also not temporarily stored in the write buffers. The I/O address space can only be addressed logically with the help of the accumulator; the memory, on the other hand, can be addressed by all registers. In addition, the segment registers for the I/O address space have no significance. It can be said that the 64k port represents its own segment, which is addressed by IN and OUT. The Pentium ports and the I/O address space are mostly used for addressing *registers* in peripheral devices. The IN or OUT instruction (and variations) makes direct contact between the processor accumulator and the peripheral device register, and transfers data between them. This means that when the Pentium executes an *I/O mapped I/O* (or *I/O mapped input/output*), the registers are located in the I/O address space, in contrast to the so-called *memory mapped I/O*, where the peripheral device registers are located in the conventional memory address space. They are addressed with the normal memory instructions, for example, MOV mem, reg. A suitable decoder and controller logic then accesses a register instead of a memory cell.

12.7.1 I/O addressing

If the Pentium wishes to address a port, then it produces the low level $M/\overline{IO}$ output signal. The system controller recognizes that an access to the I/O address space should be executed. In addition, via $W/\overline{R}$, the transfer direction is determined as Pentium → port ($W/\overline{R}$=1) or port → Pentium ($W/\overline{R}$=0). The writing of data to a port or the reading of data from a port is performed in the same manner as reading and writing data to and from the memory.

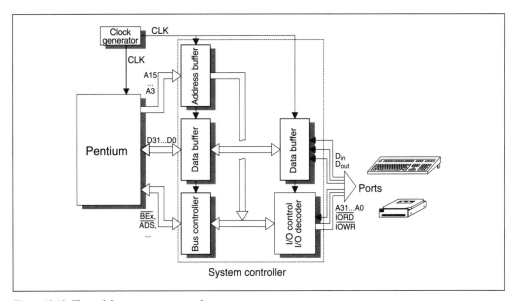

Figure 12.12: The path between processor and ports.
Usually the processor does not access the I/O address space directly, but instead via a bus controller, as is also the case for main memory. The bus controller generates the necessary control signals for the bus and various buffers for temporary storing and amplifying of the data and address signals. These intermediate circuits are today integrated into one single system controller.

Figure 12.12 shows the path for the data transfer between processor and ports. Like the reading and writing of data to and from the main memory, the CPU gives an address to the address buffer and controls the bus controller using the status signals M/$\overline{\text{IO}}$, D/$\overline{\text{C}}$, and W/$\overline{\text{R}}$. If data need to be transferred to a port (with OUT), the Pentium provides additional information. The bus controller logic recognizes from the M/$\overline{\text{IO}}$ control signal that an access of the I/O address space and not the memory should take place. Thus, instead of the memory controller, the I/O controller is activated, which decodes the address signal from the address buffer and addresses the appropriate port. This applies in most cases to a register in a peripheral device (for example, keyboard or hard disk) or in a hardware component (for example, the mode controller register in a DMA chip). Thus, data can be transferred between the processor and a register in the I/O address space of the PC. The Pentium can address a maximum of 64k 8-bit ports, such that the 16 most significant lines A31–A16 are always at a low level for access to a port.

12.7.2 I/O cycles

Figure 12.13 shows the bus cycle for a write access of the I/O address space. A comparison with Figure 12.3 shows that the bus cycle and the associated signals agree, with the exception of M/$\overline{\text{IO}}$, with which a write access to the memory is made.

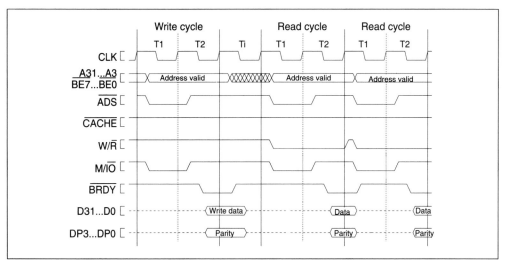

Figure 12.13: Pentium bus cycle for a write access to the I/O address space.

12.8 The internal bus buffers of the Pentium

To ease the burden of the external bus and to preventing unnecessary wait states if the bus is currently occupied, the Pentium includes a number of internal buffers. Above all, they should cushion write accesses to the external memory system (L2 cache or main memory) and, in this way, improve the performance. For this, the Pentium contains three groups of bus buffers.

12.8.1 Write buffers

The bus interface of the Pentium contains two 64-bit write buffers; each buffer is assigned to one of the two pipelines u or v. They should prevent the braking of the Pentium pipelines if the external bus is not immediately available because, for example, a cache line fill is currently being executed, or the previous memory access has not yet been completed and the Pentium has not received a valid $\overline{BRDY}$ for the previous bus cycle. Without write buffers, the pipeline would have to be held for a minimum of five clock cycles (the minimum length of a cache line fill in burst mode), if a cache line fill is currently active and the external bus is occupied. The CPU kernel of the Pentium can write to both write buffers simultaneously, for example, if two paired instructions in the u and v pipelines must each execute a memory write access that leads to a cache miss. If they are both written during the same clock cycle, the write buffer of the u pipeline has priority over that of the v pipeline, because the instruction in the u pipeline is sequentially the first in the instruction flow. If the two write buffers are not filled in the same cycle, then the one written first has priority, independently of whether it is assigned to the u or v pipeline. The Pentium adheres strictly to the sequence of write operations. This also applies to cache hits. All write accesses that are awaiting execution in the write buffers must be completed before subsequent read accesses can be executed, In the i486 on the other hand, read and write accesses can be rearranged to a certain degree, providing this does not cause a disturbance, and the rearrangement increases the speed of program execution (see Chapter 7). Note that only write memory accesses are temporarily stored in the two write buffers. Write accesses to the I/O address space bypass the write buffers and are directly switched through to the external bus, but only after the write accesses waiting in the write buffers have been completed. The same applies to IN instructions. They are only executed – that is, forwarded to the external bus for an I/O read cycle – after the memory waiting write accesses have been executed and, thus, the write buffers have been emptied.

12.8.2 Write-back buffers

In addition to the 64-bit write buffers, the Pentium contains three 32-byte write-back buffers. Each of these buffers encompasses a complete cache line and supports the Pentium during write-backs of cache lines in the on-chip data cache. A 32-byte buffer is available for each of the possible causes of a cache line write-back. The first write-back buffer stores the cache line to be written back, if during the replacement of a cache line after a cache miss or a cache flush, a modified line must be written back to the external memory. The second buffer has been provided for external snooping, and stores the cache line to be written back, if the inquiry cycle has reached a modified entry in the on-chip data cache. Finally, the third write-back buffer supports the writing back of a cache line, if an internal snooping process reaches a modified entry in the on-chip data cache. The internal and external snoops are used for the implementation of the MESI protocol and to ensure cache consistency in a multiprocessor system with multiple caches. If a number of buffers store write data, then the following priority sequence applies:

▶ write-back buffer for external snoops
▶ write-back buffer for internal snoops
▶ write-back buffer for cache line exchanges
▶ write buffer from Section 12.8.1

12.8.3 Line fill buffers

In addition to the previously described write buffers, the Pentium contains two additional line fill buffers, which support cache line fills. They are each 32 bytes wide (one cache line). The first line fill buffer is assigned to the on-chip data cache, the second to the on-chip code cache. If the Pentium reads a complete cache line, during a burst cycle, into the on-chip data or code cache, then the bus interface does not successively fill the on-chip cache with the transferred 8-byte groups. Instead, it first transfers them to the corresponding line fill buffer. Only when all 32 bytes of the applicable cache line have been stored in the line fill buffer is the complete cache line transferred to the code or data cache. Cache line fills are usually the result of a cache miss in the on-chip code or data cache. Thus, the Pentium requires the data as quickly as possible. In accordance with the address sequence for burst read cycles shown in Table 12.1, the requested bytes are transferred from the memory subsystem during the first cycle of the burst and are immediately passed on to the CPU kernel of the Pentium. Thus, the CPU kernel uses them for instruction execution, before the burst read cycle has been completed and the line fill buffer has been filled. This also applies where, due to a cache miss, a modified cache line is exchanged with another and stored externally. Only after the line fill buffer has been completely filled is the modified line to be saved transferred to the write-back buffer for the cache line replaced, and the new cache line loaded from the line fill buffer. This is necessary, because the cache line fill for the new cache line, and also the writing back of the modified cache line, should be executed by burst cycles, which must not be interrupted.

13 New performance-related Pentium features

In addition to the superscalar architecture, a number of other performance enhancing elements have been implemented in the Pentium, which support the user or system developer. These include, for example, a somewhat changed reset, and different test functions for the checking of the chip or the monitoring of bus activity during operation. Above all, in multitasking environments the Pentium can make usually somewhat difficult debugging easier, through its hardware debug functions. Finally, the complete system, from hardware to software (for example, the operating system and compilers), can be optimally tuned through execution tracing and performance monitoring, in order to improve the performance of the computer.

13.1 Pentium reset, Pentium initialization and self-test

In addition to the reset through an active signal at the L18 RESET pin, the Pentium can also execute a true initialization. The processor initialization is sent out if a signal with a high level is received at the T20 INIT pin for a minimum of two CLK cycles. Thus, an INIT is very quickly identified. The resulting initialization sets the Pentium back into real mode and initializes the segment and offset registers. The internal caches, write buffers, model registers and floating-point registers, however, are not written back; instead, they maintain their values. The two translation lookaside buffers (TLBs) and the branch target buffer (BTB) are the exceptions; even though they represent a form of cache, they are invalidated by an INIT. INIT serves as a quick way of resetting the Pentium into real mode by means of external hardware (for example, the keyboard controller of the AT) in place of a privileged MOV CR0, value instruction, for resetting the PE bits. Thus, Intel appears to be convinced that someone will have the idea of using the Pentium in real mode with 80286 memory expansion.

An extensive reset of the Pentium is sent out when the system control receives a high level signal at the RESET pin for a minimum of 15 CLK cycles. If the signal then returns to a low level, the Pentium checks the signal levels at the $\overline{\text{FLUSH}}$, $\overline{\text{FRCMC}}$ and INIT pins, in order to determine the operating condition and the necessary checks, and also to carry out an internal initialization. The Pentium can execute a check through the internal self-test BIST (built-in self-test), the functional redundancy checking (FRC) or the tristate test mode.

The internal self-test is enabled if a high level signal is received at the INIT input, while the reset signal sinks back to a low level. The self test takes approximately 2^{19} CLK cycles; at 100 MHz, this corresponds to approximately 5 ms. Without BIST, the Pentium is ready for operation after 150–200 CLK cycles, thus, after approximately $2\,\mu$s. BIST's first responsibility is to check the microcode ROM and the internal logic fields (PLAs). This section of BIST is hardwired. The subsequent BIST part is implemented as microcode and checks all caches, and also the TLBs and the BTB. These checks are executed under the control of the microcoded section of BIST because of their complexity. The Pentium stores the result of the BIST check in the EAX register. A value of 00000000h indicates an error-free BIST conclusion; a value other than zero indicates an error, and the chip is then unusable. Even in this operating condition, the Pentium activates the $\overline{\text{IERR}}$ signal if it discovers an internal parity error; it then goes into a shutdown condition.

The FRC is used for checking the external systems (for example, a second Pentium) using a Pentium processor. The Pentium enters FRC if the $\overline{\text{FRCMC}}$ signal is at a low level one clock cycle before the completion of reset. Then, with the exception of $\overline{\text{IERR}}$ and TDO, the Pentium stops sending signals through its output pins. Instead, it checks the level of the signals received. If the levels determined in this way do not agree with those internally calculated, then the Pentium activates the $\overline{\text{IERR}}$ signal, in order to indicate the fault externally. If FRCMC is at a high level one clock cycle before the completion of reset, then the Pentium operates as a master; that is, it sets all output pins and signals in accordance with the applicable bus cycle. The signal levels at the output pins are not checked. Through FRC the individual processors in a multiprocessor system can be mutually checked on a Pentium basis, for example.

The tristate test mode is used for the implementation of hardware checks for a complete board. For this, the Pentium stops all external outputs and bidirectional connections so that the board cannot receive any signals at all from the Pentium. The high level test logic can then execute a hardware check more easily and locate any possible errors more simply. The Pentium only leaves the tristate test mode with an additional reset.

A reset, and also an initialization through INIT, changes the value of certain registers. Table 13.1 indicates the corresponding values for the individual registers.

Register	Value	
	Reset	Initialization
(ALU/integer)		
EAX	00000000h	00000000h
EBX, ECX	00000000h	00000000h
EDX	identific.*	identific.*
EBP, ESP	00000000h	00000000h
ESI, EDI	00000000h	00000000h
EIP	0000fff0h	0000fff0h
CS	f000h+	f000h+
DS, ES, FS, GS	0000h#	0000h#
SS	0000h#	0000h#
EFLAG	00000002h	00000002h§
CR0	00000000h	
CR2, CR3, CR4	00000000h	00000000h
LDTR, TR	00000000h§	00000000h**
GDTR, IDTR	00000000h**	00000000h++
DR0–DR3	00000000h	00000000h
DR6	ffff0ff0h	ffff0ff0h
DR7	00000400h	00000400h
TR12	00000000h	00000000h
all others	nnnnnnnnh	nnnnnnnnh
(FPU)		
Control word	0040h	uuuuh

Register	Value Reset	Initialization
Status word	0000h	uuuuh
Tag word	5555h	uuuuh
FIP, FEA, FOP	00000000h	uuuuuuuuh
FCS, FDS	0000h	uuuuh
FSTACK	0000000000h	uuuuuuuuuuh
Caches	nnnnnnnnnnn	uuuuuuuuuuu
Cache TLBs	nnnnnnnnnnn	nnnnnnnnnnn
BTB, SDC	nnnnnnnnnnn	nnnnnnnnnnn

n, not defined.
u, unchanged.
* Processor identification number 00000500h + model
+ Base address = ffff0000h, limit = ffffh (segment descriptor cache register)
# Base address = 00000000h, limit = ffffh (segment descriptor cache register)
§ CD, CW unchanged, bit 4=1, all others=0
** Selector = 0000h, base address = 00000000h, limit = ffffh
++ Base address = 00000000h, limit = ffffh

Table 13.1: Pentium register contents after a reset or initialization.

The Pentium restarts operation in real mode after a reset, unless FRC or tristate test mode is active. After internal initialization, the CS:EIP pair is located at the memory address f000:0000fff0. As the 12 most significant address lines A31–A20 of the address bus are held at a high level, the Pentium sends out the physical address ffffff0h.

After the first JMP or CALL instruction over a segment limit that leads to the reloading of the CS register and, thus, the base and limit entry, the address lines A31–A20 return to a low level. All further code and data addressings interpret the segment values strictly in accordance with the rules of real mode – that is, the segment values are simply multiplied by 16, and the Pentium only addresses objects within 1M.

Also in the Pentium, IDTR is loaded with the values 00000000h for the base and 03ffh for the limit after a processor reset. These values correspond to the reserved area for the interrupt vector table in real mode. It is possible for the two LIDT (load IDTR) and SIDT (store IDTR) instructions to change these values, and, in this way, the interrupt vector table used by the Pentium in real-mode can be shifted to any other position in the real mode address space. Note that the table also stores the vectors for every possible interrupt that can occur. Otherwise, an exception 8 is the result.

13.2 The JTAG boundary scan test

In addition to the test modes of the Pentium described previously, which are executed during a reset depending on the FLUSH, FRCMC and INIT signals, the Pentium also contains a so-called boundary scan test, in accordance with the standard IEEE 1149.1. This permits the external checking of the Pentium's logic units and their circuits by means of software, even after the completion of manufacture and their inclusion in the computer. In addition, the Pentium can be explicitly instructed to perform the internal BIST self-test.

The JTAG test is supported by the five TCK (test clock), TDI (test data input), TDO (test data output), TMS (test mode select) and $\overline{\text{TRST}}$ (test reset) pins. As Figure 13.1 shows, a boundary scan register and a JTAG logic, or a TAP controller which is accessed through the test access port (TAP), are available on the Pentium chip. The test must be performed by an external logic, which uses the JTAG test bus with the five TCK, TDI, TDO, TMS and $\overline{\text{TRST}}$ pins. Note that the chip integrates the actual Pentium processor and, additionally, the JTAG logic. All references to the Pentium in this book refer to the Pentium part of the chip.

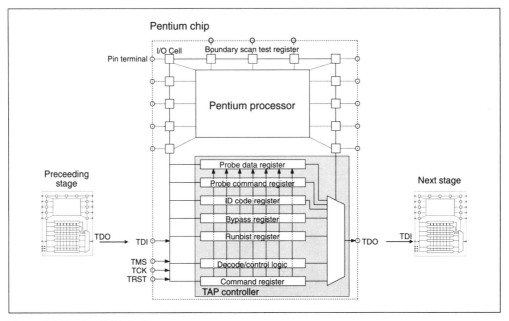

Figure 13.1: Pentium TAP structure.
The input TDI and the output TDO can be connected to the output of a circuit in a preceding stage and the input of a circuit in a successive stage, respectively.

The scanning path is located between the input pin TDI and the output pin TDO. A 1-bit write register is provided for each pin, through which all applicable inputs and outputs from the Pentium flow. If TAP control is not active, these registers pass on the supplied data to the corresponding pin, or to the Pentium, without change. If JTAG mode is active, the 1-bit write registers are configured as input or output cells. The input cells intercept the value at the corresponding input pin and store it. No further influence on the Pentium takes place, because the Pentium does not support the INTEST instruction of JTAG. Active output cells, on the other hand, store the value which then appears at the corresponding pin.

The write registers are not only connected to the input/output pins of the Pentium; they are also connected to each other. In this way, they form a pathway between TDI and TDO. In addition, there are a total of five control cells at many positions. Data in the 1-bit write registers is moved from TDI to TDO every TCK cycle, without being changed during the process. The name boundary scan should now also be clear: through the write registers located at the 'boundary', the 'boundary values' of the Pentium are scanned and sent out through TDO. All of the 1-bit write registers, or input/output and control cells joined together, form the so-called boundary scan register. The control cells determine the transfer direction for bidirectional pins (such as D63–D0, for example), or cut off the output pin (such as $\overline{\text{ADS}}$, for example) – that is, they go into a tristate condition. A 1 in the corresponding control cell defines the applicable bidirectional pin as an input and so cuts off the output pin. A 0 selects the bidirectional pin as an output and so activates the output pin. The control signals always work in conjunction with a group of pins. Table 13.2 lists the control cells and their corresponding groups.

Control cell	Pin group
DISABUS	A31–A3, AP, BT3–BT0
DISBUS	$\overline{\text{ADS}}$, $\overline{\text{BE7}}$–$\overline{\text{BE0}}$, $\overline{\text{CACHE}}$, SCYC, M/$\overline{\text{IO}}$, D/$\overline{\text{C}}$, W/$\overline{\text{R}}$, PWT, PCD, $\overline{\text{LOCK}}$
DISMISC	BREQ, $\overline{\text{APCHK}}$, $\overline{\text{SMIACT}}$, PRDY, IU, IV, IBT, BP3, BP2, PM1/BP1, PM0, BP0, FERR, $\overline{\text{HITM}}$, $\overline{\text{HIT}}$, $\overline{\text{PCHK}}$, HLDA
DISFRC	$\overline{\text{IERR}}$
DISWR	D63–D0, DP7–DP0

Note: DIS stands for disable, because a 1 disables the corresponding output.

Table 13.2: JTAG control cells and assigned pin groups.

The boundary scan path is gone through in the following way (note the control cell DISxxx):

TDI→free→free→free→RESET→$\overline{\text{FRCMC}}$→$\overline{\text{PEN}}$→R/$\overline{\text{S}}$→NMI→INTR→$\overline{\text{IGNNE}}$→$\overline{\text{SMI}}$→INIT→free→CLK→free→A3→A4→A5→A6→
A7→A8→A9→A10→A11→A12→A13→A14→A15→A16→A17→A18→A19→A20→A21→A22→A23→A24→A25→A26→A27→
A28→A29→A30→A31→BT0→DISABUS→BT1→BT2→BT3→$\overline{\text{BE7}}$→$\overline{\text{BE6}}$→$\overline{\text{BE5}}$→$\overline{\text{BE4}}$→$\overline{\text{BE3}}$→$\overline{\text{BE2}}$→$\overline{\text{BE1}}$→$\overline{\text{BE0}}$→SCYC→D/$\overline{\text{C}}$→PWT→
PCD→W/$\overline{\text{R}}$→$\overline{\text{ADS}}$→$\overline{\text{ADSC}}$→PRDY→AP→$\overline{\text{LOCK}}$→HLDA→$\overline{\text{APCHK}}$→$\overline{\text{PCHK}}$→$\overline{\text{HIT}}$→$\overline{\text{HITM}}$→DISBUS→BREQ→$\overline{\text{SMIACT}}$→A20M→
$\overline{\text{FLUSH}}$→HOLD→WB/WT→EWBE→EADS→BUSCHK→AHOLD→BRDYC→BRDY→KEN→NA→INV→BOFF→IU→IV→$\overline{\text{CACHE}}$→
M/$\overline{\text{IO}}$→BP3→BP2→PM1/BP1→PM0/BP0→DISMISC→$\overline{\text{FERR}}$→$\overline{\text{IERR}}$ DISFRC→DP0→D0→D1→D2→D3→D4→D5→D6→D7→DP1→
D8→D9→D10→D11→D12→D13→D14→D15→DP2→D16→D17→D18→D19→D20→D21→D22→D23→DP3→D24→D25→
D26→D27→D28→D29→D30→D31→DP4→D32→D33→D34→D35→D36→DISWR→D37→D38→D39→DP5→D40→D41→
D42→D43→D44→D45→D46→D47→DP6→D48→D49→D50→D51→D52→D53→D54→D55→DP7→D56→D57→D58→D59→
D60→D61→D62→D63→IBT→TDO

Other important JTAG registers include the bypass, the ID code, the runbist and the instruction registers. The most significant bits of all registers are connected with TDI and the least significant bits with TDO. The bypass register, like the other cells, is a 1-bit write register and is used to 'short circuit' TDI and TDO. After the corresponding BYPASS instruction to the TAP controller, only a single TCK cycle is necessary in order to send a given value from TDI to TDO, instead of the usual 180 CLK cycles. The bypass register is initialized with a '0' (which then represents the first value given to TDO).

The ID code register stores 32-bit identification information for examining the chip. In the case of the Pentium, the following contents apply: bit 0=1, bits 1 to 11=manufacturer (Intel =09h), bits 12 to 27=part number (bits 12 to 16=model 01h, that is, DX; bits 17 to 20=generation 05h, that is, Pentium; bits 21 to 27=type 01h, that is, CPU), bits 28 to 31=version (not defined in the Pentium). The 32-bit Pentium ID code is thus x02a1013h (x=undefined). The runbist register stores the 1-bit test result after an internal self-test. A successful test stores the value 0. Any other value indicates that the Pentium is, more or less, damaged. The boundary scan test is executed with the help of a defined test instruction set, which currently contains five instructions. The nine most significant bits of the 13-bit instruction register are reserved. The four least significant bits store the corresponding instruction bit for the five EXTEST, IDCODE, RUNBIST, SAMPLE/PRELOAD and BYPASS instructions. They are listed below, together with their 4-bit opcodes.

▶ EXTEST (opcode xx0h): this instruction tests the external circuits of the Pentium (or the chip generally, using the JTAG test). For this, the Pentium sends out from output pins the values stored in the individual cells of the boundary scan register, and reads the values sent to the Pentium's input pins into the corresponding cells. Bidirectional pins are handled as input or output pins depending on the value in the control cell. Note that the data sent to the input pins, and which is read into the cells, is not transferred to the Pentium. Thus, it has no influence whatsoever on the behaviour of the Pentium. The Pentium must be reset after an EXTEST instruction.

▶ SAMPLE/PRELOAD (opcode xx1h): depending on the condition of the TAP controller, this instruction scans the condition of the input/output pins of the Pentium, or establishes data for the output pins. In capture DR condition (see below), the values that are sent out by the Pentium to the output pins, and the values received by the Pentium at the input pins, are transferred to the cells of the boundary scan register, and can then be read from TDO. In update DR condition, this instruction establishes the data that the Pentium chip sends out from its output pins to the board on which it is mounted, using an EXTEXT instruction.

▶ IDCODE (opcode xx2h): this instruction connects the ID code register with TDI and TDO. Through the switching (toggling) of TCK, the ID code is then given out through TDO, and can be used by the external test logic. After an initialization or a Pentium reset, the instruction register contains the opcode for IDCODE.

▶ RUNBIST (opcode xx7h): this instruction connects the runbist register to TDO and loads the value '1'. The BIST is then activated. If the test is successful, it overwrites the '1' in the runbist register with a '0'. When BIST has been completed, after approximately 2^{19} processor clock cycles (not TCK cycles), the test value can be read through TDO. Note that BIST can also be initiated if a high level signal is received at the INIT input during a processor reset. In this case, however, the test result is available in EAX.

▶ BYPASS (opcode xxfh): this instruction connects the bypass register with TDI and TDO, and breaks the connection between TDI/TDO and the boundary scan register. In this way, the data input to TDI is sent out to TDO, unchanged, after only one TCK cycle. BYPASS is used for implementing checks for complex circuits, if individual components need to be tested without being removed from the circuit. This naturally assumes that all components to be tested support the JTAG test. Thus, the TDI input of the Pentium can, for example, be connected to the TDO output of a different component, and the TDO output, to the TDI input of another chip. In this way, it is possible to form very long scan paths over a complete board.

▶ PRIVATE: all other opcodes are reserved and can be used by the chip manufacturer for its own purposes. Generally, they have no effect; they are more or less NOPs.

In addition to the test data, the instructions are also serially sent to the Pentium through the input pin TDI. The clock signal at the TCK pin is used for this purpose. Therefore, the TAP controller must be aware of which register (boundary scan register, instruction register and so on) the input data bits have been defined for. For this purpose, a clearly defined condition sequence for the TAP controller has been implemented. Starting with the reset condition, which the TAP controller receives after the activation of $\overline{TRST}$ or of TMS for a minimum of five TCK cycles, the different controller conditions are executed in a set sequence, depending on the different combinations of TMS and TCK. For this, TCK is used as the driving clock cycle and TMS as the branch signal, which selects the different branches of the condition diagram. These conditions also include the capture DR and update DR conditions described above. They affect the data transfer from TDI to TDO through the boundary scan register. The instruction register is loaded when the TAP controller is located in the instruction branch of the condition diagram. Thus, the tester (an external logic for performing the JTAG test) must define the transfer sequence of the serial test data exactly, and must also include the activation of the TMS and TCK signals: a far from trivial task.

I would also like to point out that this JTAG test is not limited to microprocessors. Manufacturers also perform similar tests for DRAM and SRAM chips, in order to check whether the chips operate correctly, or contain faults after their manufacture. For this purpose, different data is serially sent to the on-chip test control, and is written to the memory cells as a test sample. Finally, the data is read back by the on-chip test control, in order to determine whether or not it has been changed. Many chip faults can only be discovered by specific data patterns.

The external addressing of individual memory cells and an external data comparison would take far too long. For this reason, most modern chips perform this check internally. Similarly to that in the JTAG test, the extensive test data is very quickly input serially through a specific pin, and only the result data – chip ok or not – is then output through a pin. A noteworthy point is that the very complex on-chip test logic is only used when the chip is checked by the manufacturer. After delivery, it lies dormant. The integration of such a test logic into the chip is, however, considerably cheaper than the time necessary to check the memory chip externally – another clear indication of the advances made in the integration of electronic components.

13.3 Fault detection functions of the Pentium

The Pentium includes a number of different functions for the identification of data and address faults. They only affect the internal functional units, such as the microcode ROM, and the bus interfaces with the address and data buses. FRC is also a part of the fault detection function. This is described in Section 13.1.

13.3.1 Detecting internal errors

The Pentium carries out a parity check of the following memory fields:

- data/code cache memory entry
- data/code cache tag entry
- data/code TLB memory entry

▶ data/code TLB tag entry
▶ microcode ROM

Intel states that 53% of all functional units in the Pentium are checked. This parity check takes place continually (on-line) in the background; in other words, it is completely transparent for the machine code; the user usually knows nothing of it – except when the error detection logic discovers a parity fault during the reading of a memory field entry. If this is the case, the Pentium sends out an active low level signal from its $\overline{\text{IERR}}$ output and goes into shutdown mode (apart from where the fault makes this impossible). This internal fault checking is also executed for all memory fields during a BIST, in order to check their internal consistency.

13.3.2 Detection of faults at the bus interface

In addition to the internal parity check, the Pentium can also check the parity of the external data and address buses. For this purpose, in addition to the actual data and address bus interfaces D63–D0 and A31–A3, respectively, it also contains eight data bus parity interfaces DP7–DP0 and an address parity pin AP. In addition, with the help of the $\overline{\text{BUSCHK}}$ signal, it can also identify general bus faults.

Data parity fault

During a write cycle (single or burst), in addition to the data at pins D63–D0, the Pentium also gives out the eight parity bits DP7–DP0, so that for every data byte (according to the byte enable signals $\overline{\text{BE7}}$–$\overline{\text{BE0}}$), even parity is achieved. The external system can use the parity information to check the inner consistency of the data.

In a read cycle, the external system can transfer the parity information together with the data bytes. The Pentium checks whether the resulting parity is even and sends out the corresponding signal from the $\overline{\text{PCHK}}$ pin. If the signal is at a low level, the Pentium has detected a parity fault. No further action results, as long as the external system does not send an active signal with a low level to $\overline{\text{PEN}}$ during the transfer of the data and parity bits. If this is the case, the Pentium stores the physical address (corresponding to the signal on the address bus) in the machine check address (MCA) register and stores the type of cycle that caused the parity fault in the machine check type (MCT) register. You can see the structure of the MCT register in Figure 13.2.

If the CHK bit is set, then the four bits LOCK, M/$\overline{\text{IO}}$, D/$\overline{\text{C}}$ and W/$\overline{\text{R}}$ indicate the type of cycle and the MCA register contains the physical fault address. Note that a set LOCK bit indicates an active – that is, low level – $\overline{\text{LOCK}}$ signal. If the MCE bit in the new CR4 control register is also set, then the processor also issues the machine check exception corresponding to interrupt 18 (12h). Both the MCA register and the MCT register are 64 bits wide. They are read-only and can be addressed by using an RDMSR (read model specific register) instruction. The reading of the MCT register resets the CHK bit. Thus, you should always read the MCA register first, before you access the MCT register.

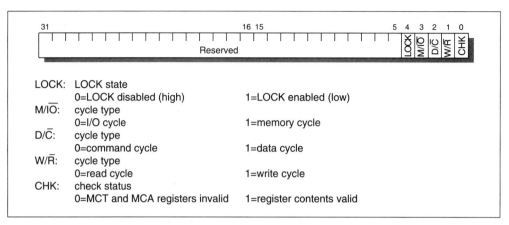

Figure 13.2: The structure of the machine check type register.

Address parity error

For most bus cycles, the address bus is unidirectional and always gives out an address. Thus, the Pentium does not perform an address parity check, but it does produce an address parity bit at AP so that even parity occurs. Note that only the address bits A31–A5 are used in the calculation of parity; A4 and A3 are ignored. A31–A5 and AP together include an even number of 1s, and thus have even parity.

The parity of an address is only checked by the Pentium for an inquiry cycle, because here, the transfer direction of the address bus is reversed. The external system delivers the inquiry address at A31–A5 (corresponding to a cache line) and also a high or low level signal at AP. If the Pentium detects an address parity fault, it activates its $\overline{\text{APCHK}}$ (address parity check) output and, from there, sends out an active signal with a low level. Unlike a data parity fault, an address parity fault has no continuing effect on the behaviour of the Pentium. The external system can use $\overline{\text{APCHK}}$ or simply ignore it, if no address parity check is implemented.

General bus fault

The immediate identification of a bus fault is the responsibility of the external subsystem. The cause can be, for example, a time overrun fault of the memory or an I/O device, or an incorrect functioning of the hardware in general. The subsystem indicates this to the Pentium, in that it sends an active signal with a low level to the $\overline{\text{BUSCHK}}$ pin. The subsystem must also send an active $\overline{\text{BRDY}}$, so that the Pentium can identify the $\overline{\text{BUSCHK}}$. In a similar way to a data parity fault, the Pentium then stores the physical address (corresponding to the signal on the address bus) in the MCA register, and stores the type of cycle that caused the general bus fault in the MCT register. If the MCE bit in the CR4 register is also set, the Pentium also sends out the machine check exception corresponding to interrupt 18 (12h).

13.3.3 Other check functions

The Pentium also contains many other functions for checking the internal hardware components, especially the TLBs of the BTB, the parity test function and the two pipelines. What use is
the best possible built-in parity test function if it is unreliable? The possibility exists to send out
a parity error intentionally, for example, in order to check the parity protected cache lines and
BTB, and also the TLB entries. The correct functioning of the parity check logic activates $\overline{\text{IERR}}$.
Finally, as can be predicted, the Pentium goes into a shutdown condition.

The on-chip caches of the Pentium can also be checked with the help of test registers (in total,
the Pentium contains 12 of them). The TLB is a small cache, which, as a cache line, contains the
physical address of a linear address (representing the tag). Naturally, for cache checking, it is
generally necessary to write, read and change cache lines, and also the corresponding tag, MESI
status and LRU entries.

The two test registers TR6 and TR7 are used in the Pentium for checking the function of the
TLBs in the paging unit. Note that for the code and data caches, two separate TLBs are
provided, and that the data cache TLB is further subdivided into a 64-entry TLB for 4-kbyte
pages, and also an 8-entry TLB for 8-Mbyte pages. Because the TLBs also represent caches, they
are checked in a similar way to the on-chip code and data caches. The TLBs convert a linear
address into a physical address.

In addition to the TLBs in the paging unit and the on-chip caches, you can also check the BTB
with the help of the test registers. The BTB also represents a cache and is thus checked in a
similar way to the on-chip code and data caches.

Unfortunately, these topics have not been disclosed to the public by Intel. I can only say that the
check procedure is similar to that for the i386's TLB, but any further speculation is not justified.

13.4 Execution tracing

The program execution sequence or program execution tracing is used for the external
monitoring of internal program execution in the Pentium. Execution tracing has been newly
implemented in the Pentium. The processor indicates if a pipeline has completed an instruction,
or whether a branch has occurred, through the signals at the three output pins IU, IV and IBT,
and also the branch trace special cycle. The signals IU, IV and IBT are given out by the Pentium
without further programming. Because it also initiates a branch trace message special cycle, you
must also set the tracing bit TR in the test register TR12 (see Figure 13.3).

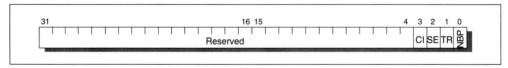

Figure 13.3: The control register TR12 for enabling the branch message special cycle.

The IU and IV signals indicate the sequential termination of a program; IBT (instruction branch
taken) indicates a branch. If the u pipeline has completed an instruction – that is, the instruction

has left the last stage of the pipeline – then the Pentium sends out an active signal with a high level from its IU pin. Note that IU can only be disabled if the completed instruction has not led to a branch. However, this does not mean, for example, that the instruction can be a JNZ. Only if the zero flag equals 0 (thus, the previous comparison has delivered a 'dissimilar zero'), is the branch also executed and IBT activated. This is known as a 'taken branch' in Intel's new method of identification. This is similar for the v pipeline. Note, however, that the v pipeline can only complete an instruction at the same time as the u pipeline. If one of the two is a taken branch, then the v pipeline always executes the branch. Table 13.3 lists the possible combinations of the IU, IV and IBT signals and indicates the cause of their activation. In addition to conditional and unconditional jumps, taken branches also include procedure calls (CALLs), interrupts, RETs and IRETs, and also specific segment descriptor load operations, serialization instructions and most exceptions.

IU	IV	IBT	
0	0	0	No instruction completed (at least the u pipeline contains a not-completed instruction)
0	0	1	Invalid
0	1	0	Invalid
0	1	1	Invalid
1	0	0	u pipeline has completed an instruction other than a branch
1	0	1	An instruction completed in the u pipeline led to a branch
1	1	0	u pipeline and v pipeline each completed an instruction other than a branch
1	1	1	u pipeline and v pipeline each completed an instruction; the instruction in the v pipeline led to a branch

Table 13.3: Activation of IU, IV and IBT during execution tracing.

The IU, IV and IBT signals are sent out at the same time as the completion of the instruction in the last pipeline stage. However, the (optional) branch trace message cycle can be delayed in comparison to the instruction completion. This is caused by fluctuating bus activity. If the Pentium bus is in an idle condition Ti, then the message cycle can be sent immediately through the bus. If, on the other hand, a cache line fill, a write-back or a locked cycle is active, then the message cycle is delayed accordingly. The delay does not just depend on the currently active cycle of a burst transfer, it also depends on the number of wait states required. The internal instruction execution in the pipelines and the bus activity can, however, be executed in parallel. In order not to completely eliminate the external system from the concept, between the activation of the first IBT signal and the execution of the corresponding branch trace message cycle, the Pentium also sends out a maximum of two further IBT signals. Otherwise, the instruction execution in the pipelines would be held up until the bus activity has died down and the Pentium can perform the first message cycle.

For the complete picture at this point, I would briefly like to repeat the signals and data given out by the Pentium during a branch trace message cycle:

$\overline{BE7}=\overline{BE6}=\overline{BE4}=\overline{BE3}=\overline{BE2}=\overline{BE1}=\overline{BE0}=1;\overline{BE5}=0$
$D/\overline{C}=M/\overline{IO}=0,W/\overline{R}=1$

A31-A3: bits 31..3 of branch target linear address
BT2-BT0: bits 2..0 of branch target linear address
BT3:   1=standard operand size 32 bits; 0=standard operand size 16 bits

The external system must quit the cycle by sending back $\overline{\text{BRDY}}$. The Pentium inserts wait states until it receives an active $\overline{\text{BRDY}}$. Execution tracing can be used to write information concerning the flow of a completed program to an external memory. This supports debugging at the hardware level, because a completed program containing faults can be examined later, step by step. Above all, this is important where faults only occur in conjunction with a specific asynchronous hardware condition (for example, where hardware interrupts occur). Such conditions are only randomly produced, so if the program is started again, it may run without faults.

13.5 Hardware debug support and probe mode

Section 8.2.4 detailed part of the way in which the Pentium supports hardware debugging. However, this only concerns the supporting of a debugging program, and thus of software, through the debug registers of the Pentium. In this way, for example, breakpoints for different access types can be set, so that the Pentium itself sends out an exception corresponding to interrupt 01h if the breakpoint condition is fulfilled. These functions have been provided to support hardware that directly accesses the Pentium's registers and directly monitors the program execution. For this purpose, the new probe mode has been implemented together with the debug port. Intel suggests a 20-pole connection to the external hardware debugger. You can see the suggested contact layout in Figure 13.4.

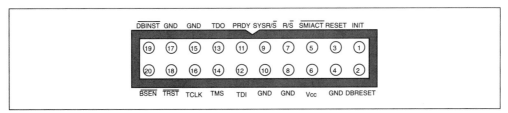

Figure 13.4: Contact scheme of the debug port.

An external debug hardware has only to be connected in order to perform the debugging. The pins of the debug port shown in the figure are connected to the Pentium and also to other components on the mother board. Table 13.4 shows the signals used and to what they are connected. Different configurations are possible depending on the complexity of the system and the performance capability of the external debugger. Thus, Table 13.4 shows those signals as MIN (for minimum configuration) which, in principle, must be used in order to enable the debug functions and probe mode. All MAX signals, on the other hand, are only necessary for the maximum spread of functions, for example if the examined Pentium is part of a multiprocessor system with an extensive boundary scan path. I and O indicate the signal direction – that is, whether the applicable signal must be output (O), or input (I) to the system through the corresponding debug port pin.

Signal	Pin	Name	Connected to	I/O	Configuration
INIT	1	Initialization	System reset logic	O	MIN
DBRESET	2	Debugger reset	System reset logic	I	MIN
RESET	3	Reset	System reset logic	O	MIN
$\overline{\text{SMIACT}}$	5	SMI active	Pentium	O	MIN
R/$\overline{\text{S}}$	7	Run/stop	Pentium	I	MIN
SYSR/$\overline{\text{S}}$	9	System run/stop	System R/$\overline{\text{S}}$ logic	O	MAX
PRDY	11	Probe mode ready	Pentium	O	MIN
TDI	12	Data input	Pentium	I	MIN
TDO	13	Data output	Pentium	O	MIN
TMS	14	Mode select	Pentium	I	MIN
TCLK	16	Clock signal	Pentium	I	MIN
$\overline{\text{TRST}}$	18	Boundary scan reset	Pentium	I	MIN
$\overline{\text{DBINST}}$	19	Debugger installed	Pentium (R/$\overline{\text{S}}$)	I	MAX
$\overline{\text{BSEN}}$	20	Boundary scan enab.	System scan logic	I	MAX
Vcc	6	Power supply			
GND	4, 8, 10	Ground			
	15, 17				

Table 13.4: Debug port signals and connections.

I would now like to introduce only the signals vital to the minimal configuration. The data and control signals TDI, TD0, TMS, TCLK and $\overline{\text{TRST}}$ for the boundary scan are described in Chapter 10 and Section 13.2. The INT, RESET and $\overline{\text{SMIACT}}$ have also been discussed (see Chapter 10). The external debugger sends the DBRESET signal through the debug port of the on-board system reset logic, in order to instruct it to reset the Pentium and, if necessary, the other system components. The Pentium is then supplied with a RESET or INIT signal, as necessary, by this system reset logic. The two signals R/$\overline{\text{S}}$ and PRDY are essential for the debug port and its associated probe mode. They were also described in Chapter 10, but because of their importance, I would briefly like to describe them again.

R/$\overline{\text{S}}$

A low level signal at this resume/stop pin interrupts the currently running program. R/$\overline{\text{S}}$ is implemented as an interrupt – that is, the Pentium identifies the signal at instruction limits. The Pentium immediately enters probe mode. When the signal switches back to a high level, the Pentium restarts the program execution.

PRDY

A high level signal at this probe ready pin indicates that the Pentium has reacted to a low level R/$\overline{\text{S}}$ signal by interrupting normal operation and has gone into probe mode.

The maximum configuration signals SYSR/$\overline{\text{S}}$, DBINST and $\overline{\text{BSEN}}$ form the basis for the embedding of the debug port into an extensive boundary scan system for examining not only the Pentium, but also the connections to the memory controllers of other buffer components, for example. Typically, SYSR/$\overline{\text{S}}$ indicates that an R/$\overline{\text{S}}$ signal from the system should be passed on to the Pentium as an $R/\overline{S}$ signal – that is, the external debugger activates $R/\overline{S}$ as the result of an active SYSR/$\overline{S}$. The $\overline{\text{DBINST}}$ signal indicates to the system that the external debugger is connected to the debug port, thus, it is installed. Gates, buffers and latch switches in the system are typically activated by $\overline{\text{DBINST}}$, so that the debug port can supply the corresponding signals, or receive signals from the system. An active $\overline{\text{BSEN}}$ signal indicates that the external debugger is currently performing a boundary scan in place of another scan logic. Otherwise, the other scan logic can send the corresponding control and data signals TDI, TDO, TMS, TCLK and $\overline{\text{TRST}}$.

In probe mode, only the normal CPU activity is shut down; inquiry cycles are still supported. The probe register of the TAP controller can be addressed and the different internal Pentium registers can be read and changed through the boundary scan path. Thus, the TAP control is not influenced by an $R/\overline{S}$ signal. After the corresponding configuration, probe mode can also be enabled by a debug exception in place of the applicable interrupt. In this way, extensive examinations are possible into the behaviour of the Pentium and programs. As I explained in Section 13.4, execution tracing is used to support debugging at a hardware level.

13.6 The machine check exception

When compared to the i486, the Pentium includes a new exception – the machine check exception. It leads to an interrupt 18 (12h). Note that this exception is only active if you set the MCE bit (machine check enable) in the CR4 control register. Otherwise, the Pentium ignores any exception conditions that occur. The reason for this is that an interrupt 18, like all interrupts from 0 to 31, is reserved by Intel. However, many system suppliers (such as IBM), have not, for example, prevented the calling of BIOS functions through an interrupt that falls within this area. In the PC, for example, INT 18h addresses a function that determines the actual memory size.

After a reset, the MCE bit in the CR4 control register is reset, thus the Pentium does not generally send out a machine check exception. Unlike the other exceptions, such as page fault or general protection fault, if a machine check exception occurs you can determine neither the instruction for which the exception has occurred nor the exact cause of the fault. The reason for this is that a machine check exception is synchronized with bus activity, and not with the execution of instructions. As an example, a memory access using MOV mem,reg can be sent through the bus a number of clock cycles after MOV mem,reg has already been completed. This results in the fact that the restarting of program execution after a machine check exception is practically impossible. However, this is not required in every case, because the exception occurs either as the result of a data parity fault in the Pentium, or from an active $\overline{\text{BUSCHK}}$ signal from the bus system. Both represent a very serious hardware function fault, making the memory content and the computer functions completely unreliable. The 64-bit machine check address register stores the actual physical address given out on the address bus when an MCE exception occurs; the 64-bit machine check type register stores the type of active bus cycle. The structure of the machine check type registers is described in Section 13.3.2.

13.7 CPU identification with CPUID

Usually, programs run on all 80x86 CPUs identically – the processors are compatible. Nevertheless, it is sometimes advantageous (in the case of system software, such as the BIOS) to know on which type of processor the code will be executed. As an example, it is not possible to switch an 8086 into protected mode, or to use virtual 8086 mode, which is so useful under Windows, in an 80286. Using the built-in self-test included in all post-i386 processors, the determination of the processor type when switched on is not difficult for the BIOS. It would, of course, be a little more complex if a driver or another program wished to know the processor type later. Only an intelligent – and thus extensive and slow – routine can determine the type of CPU installed. Programmers will therefore be pleased to know that a new instruction included in the Pentium – CPUID – easily identifies the type of processor installed using a single instruction.

Before you can execute the CPUID instruction on an unknown installed processor, you must first determine whether or not the CPU actually supports this instruction. This is done simply by sending out CPUID. If the instruction is not supported, the processor produces an invalid opcode exception. You must intercept this exception and the resulting interrupt and handle them in a suitable way. In protected mode, this is very difficult, because it is not possible for an application program to change the interrupt handler without initiating a further protection fault exception. That is exactly what would be necessary in order to intercept the first exception. For this reason, Intel has inserted a new flag in the EFlag register: the ID flag. If the application program can set and reset the ID flag, then the installed processor supports the CPUID instruction. This procedure with a new flag is much simpler and quicker than the interception of an invalid opcode exception.

The new CPUID instruction, in addition to identifying the Pentium, also delivers information concerning which special features are supported. A number of identification levels are provided for CPUID; the Pentium supports levels 0 and 1; higher levels are reserved for future models and processors. In order to execute the CPU identification, you must first load the value 0, corresponding to the lowest identification level, into the EAX register, and then issue the CPUID instruction. The Pentium then returns in EAX the highest identification level that it supports (currently 1). The three EBX, ECX and EDX registers, in this sequence, contain a 12-byte identification in clear text, namely 'GenuineIntel'. Expressed more accurately, the registers contain the following values: EBX=756e6547h (='Genu'), ECX=49656e69h (='ineI') and EDX=6c65746eh (=ntel'). Note that in little-endian format, the 'G' in EBX is stored in the least significant nibble of BL. Future Pentiums, and possibly clones from other manufactures, will almost certainly return a different character string. The issuing of the CPUID instruction with an EAX value of 01h delivers an identification value to the EAX register similar to the identification data in the ID code register of the TAP controller. In addition, the EDX register indicates which special functions the installed processor supports. In this case, EBX and ECX are reserved and deliver the values 00h. You must first make sure that the CPU also supports the CPUID instruction with an EAX value equal to 01h by issuing the CPUID instruction with an EAX value of 00h. You will find the call and return values of CPUID in Table 13.5.

Register	Call value	Return value
EAX	00h	01h (maximum identification level)
EBX		'Genu'
ECX		'inel'
EDX		'ntel'
EAX	01h	Identification value*
EBX		Reserved (=0)
ECX		Reserved (=0)
EDX		Feature flags+

* bits 31..12	reserved (=00h)
bits 11..8	processor family (05h for Pentium)
bits 7...4	model (01h for ordinary Pentium)
bits 3...0	revision

+ bits 31..9:	reserved (=00h)
bit 8:	CMPXCHG8B (1=implemented, 0=not implemented)
bit 7:	machine check exception (1=implemented, 0=not implemented)
bit 6:	reserved
bit 5..1:	implemented special functions
bit 0:	on-chip FPU (1=yes, 0=no)

Table 13.5: Call and return values of CPUID.

Note that the identification value of the CPUID instruction deviates from the identification information contained in the TAP controller. For the first Pentiums delivered, the CPU identification is xxxxx510h, as compared to x02a1013h (x=undefined). In addition to the identification of the installed CPU, CPUID in the Pentium can also be used for the serialization of the instruction execution, if it is necessary for all previous instructions (with the exception of the write operation that is actually required) to be completed before the Pentium can execute the next instruction.

13.8 Multiprocessing

At the end of this Pentium section, I would briefly like to discuss the clearly identifiable target for the reasoning behind the Pentium's architecture: multiprocessing. Through multiprocessing, a number of processors in a computer system should be able to operate simultaneously and execute one or more tasks in parallel. Modern operating systems, such as Windows NT, support multiprocessing right from the start, and independently divide the responsibilities among the processors contained in the system. Thus, multiprocessing is essentially the responsibility of the software; the hardware can only deliver support. The Pentium accomplishes this mainly through the MESI protocol and locked bus cycles.

A multiprocessor system based on Pentiums automatically contains multiple caches: namely, the two on-chip caches of the Pentium as a minimum. In addition, a larger L2 cache would also be available in such a system, so that the memory accesses of the individual CPUs are not braked too severely. This leads straight to the problem of cache consistency, because a value can be available in one or more of the on-chip caches, and also in the L2 cache. The MESI protocol eliminates this problem, even if more memory accesses are then required than would be necessary in the case of a single on-chip cache. The external cache and bus control for the L2 cache and the main memory must also support the MESI protocol, and provide suitable control signals. Otherwise, it is possible that a Pentium has changed data without the knowledge of the other Pentiums. Figure 13.5 shows schematically a multiprocessor system based on Pentiums with a shared memory bus, through which the individual processors and the L2 cache controller access the main memory.

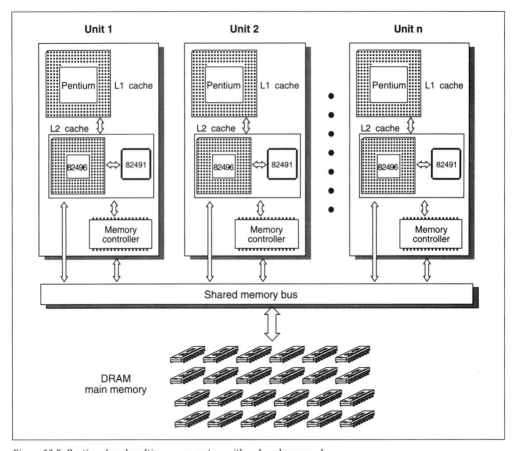

Figure 13.5: Pentium-based multiprocessor system with a shared memory bus.

Further difficulties include the communication between the individual processors and memory, and the sequence of write accesses if multiple processors execute a program together. The basis for the elimination of these problems is that specific accesses to memory – through which the individual CPUs swap data with the help of *semaphores* and, thus, communicate with each other – are not disrupted or interrupted by other processors. The $\overline{\text{LOCK}}$ signal already implemented in the 8086 is used for this purpose (MULTIBUS, an Intel bus for multiprocessor systems was even provided in the 8086). Through the activation of $\overline{\text{LOCK}}$ – that is, an output $\overline{\text{LOCK}}$ signal with a low level – the Pentium can *atomically* perform memory accesses that require multiple successive bus cycles. Other processors or components cannot then interrupt the bus cycle sequence for the duration of the complete access; the access is inseparable. The Pentium activates the $\overline{\text{LOCK}}$ signal if the LOCK prefix is used for the BTS, BTR, BTC, XCHG, XADD, CMPXCHG, CMPXCHG8B, INC, DEC, NOT, NEG, ADD, ADC, SUB, SBB, AND, OR and XOR instructions. Naturally, LOCK is then only reliable and effective if the named instruction actually changes the memory content; AND, for example, must have a memory operand as a target. Many operations, such as INTA sequences, segment descriptor, page directory and page table changes, and also the XCHG instruction, automatically activate $\overline{\text{LOCK}}$. The system designer of a multiprocessor system is responsible for the correct usage of the $\overline{\text{LOCK}}$ signal: with many processors, this is, a far from trivial task, especially if the performance is not to suffer.

Part 4
External Pentium support

This part introduces the external systems that are necessary so that the Pentium's efficiency can be used to the maximum. Without such support, the Pentium would either be hampered by simple but time consuming commands that could be better executed on a more specialized and simpler chip, or would have to insert vast numbers of wait cycles. In either case, performance would be drastically reduced.

14 General supporting systems

Included in these general subsystems are the interrupt, cache, memory and DMA subsystems. They are necessary to reduce the response time of the whole system to a minimum. At 100 MHz, you could even regard a time scale of 10 clock cycles as being ultra-fast. This, alone, clearly shows the requirements placed on the subsystems.

14.1 The interrupt subsystem and the high performance interrupt controller 82489DX

Right from the beginning, the Pentium was set out for scalable multiprocessor systems – in other words, by the simple addition of a Pentium/system unit, a system can be modified, becoming more efficient, without the need for a complete restructuring of the whole system and software. In order to achieve this, the interrupt subsystem has to be matched accordingly. Therefore, after more than 10 years, Intel has developed a replacement for the widely used PIC 8259A: the *Advanced Programmable Interrupt Controller APIC 82498DX*. It is available at a maximum of 50 Mhz; typically, it is available at 33 MHz – a vast improvement in contrast to the lazy 8 MHz of the 8259A. All internal registers are a minimum of 32 bits wide (as compared to 8 bits with the 8259A), so that during a register access, considerably more data can be transferred or read. Intel recommends the implementation of the 82489DX in the memory address space – that is, memory mapped I/O – in order to maximize performance. The APIC can, of course, be situated in the I/O address space: the data is transferred over the same data bus. Intel specifies that for a typical file server (which has to execute a considerable number of interrupts, the result of a continuous flow of requests from the workplace), a performance gain of 8% is achieved purely by using the 82489DX instead of the 8259A. In the following sections I would briefly like to introduce its special characteristics. First, though, a short, general summary of the external interrupts and their handling.

14.1.1 External hardware interrupts and their handling

There are many components in a computer that are only required for use by the processor from time to time. This includes, for example, the serial port that can asynchronously receive data from a modem (thus, the chip is also known as UART). Here, a relatively long period of time can elapse between two characters or two character blocks, during which time the processor executes one or more other programs. If, for example, a PC is waiting for characters to enter via the serial interface or network adaptor, there are two methods of collecting them:

▶ the interface is periodically checked to see if a data has entered *(polling)*
▶ the interface itself indicates that it has received data *(interrupt driven data exchange)*.

The disadvantage of polling is clear: to a large extent, the processor is busy with the query and so the performance of the foreground program becomes slower. The other possibility is mainly realized with the aid of a hardware interrupt, so that the interface activates an IRQ in order to indicate to the processor that it has received data and is ready to transfer it to the processor.

A hard disk is a typical example of another peripheral device that operates using interrupt driven data exchange (better still, the hard disk controller). By computer standards, a hard disk is occupied for a relatively long period with moving and positioning the read/write head and reading specific data. During this time, the computer is not required to wait (this should not happen in multitasking operating systems either); instead, it can accept other tasks. Only when the drive has read the data does the controller activate the controller signal in order to arrange for the processor to serve the hard disk. You can see that a powerful interrupt subsystem is all the more important, depending on the number of components available in the system (CPUs, peripheral devices and so on).

Since usually more than one such interrupt source is available in a system, but the processor only has a limited number of interrupt terminals (in addition to NMI, the Pentium only includes the INTR pin), the signal has to be directed via a programmable interrupt controller. This is a peripheral chip, which collects external interrupt requests, manages them and sends them on to the processor, as an interrupt request in a certain sequence. As the CPU (or better still, the interrupt handler) in this case knows the cause of the interrupt exactly, the execution speed is quicker. As an example, a character is available (serial or network interface), or a sector can be transferred (hard disk). The periodic checking of peripheral devices is dropped, and the extent of the program for the operation of peripherals is reduced. Potential candidates for interrupt driven communication are all components that exchange data with the main memory and the CPU.

For more than 10 years, the Intel (or clones produced by other manufacturers) PIC 8259A has been very successful in the PC sector. Three registers are available in the 8259A for the recognition and management of interrupt requests from peripheral elements: the interrupt request register (IRR), the in-service register (ISR) and the interrupt mask register (IMR). It has eight interrupt lines, IR0–IR7, which accept the interrupt requests and redirects them to the IRR. In order to issue an interrupt request, the relevant peripheral device drives the signal level accordingly at pins IR0–IR7. With this, the 8259A sets the associated bit in IRR, which is retained by all devices that have currently issued an interrupt request. Since it is possible for several peripheral devices to issue a hardware interrupt and, therefore, that several bits can be set in the IRR, a priority encoder in the 8259A only transmits the bit with the highest priority.

The following steps are carried out for a hardware interrupt from a peripheral device in the PC, with an interrupt subsystem based on the 8259A:

▶ One of the interrupt request lines IR0–IR7 is driven and, thus the associated bit is set in the IRR.

▶ The 8259A receives this and reacts by sending an INT signal to the processor.

▶ The CPU receives the INT signal and replies with a first $\overline{\text{INTA}}$ cycle, if the IE flag is set.

▶ With the receipt of the first $\overline{\text{INTA}}$ cycle from the CPU, the most significant priority bit in the IRR register is reset, and the corresponding bit in the ISR register is set.

▶ The processor produces a second $\overline{\text{INTA}}$ cycle, instructing the 8259A to release an 8-bit indicator through the data bus. The CPU fetches this indicator as the number of the interrupt handler to be called.

▶ At the end of the second $\overline{\text{INTA}}$ impulse in AEOI mode, the ISR bit is automatically reset. Otherwise, the CPU must transfer an EOI command to the 8259A to clear the ISR bit manually.

The interrupt mask register (IMR) is available, in order to selectively suppress certain interrupt requests. To complete the picture, I would like to mention that the 8259A can be *cascaded*, such that it can handle more than eight interrupt requests. For this, at least two PICs are necessary, which create two levels. The first level is created by a master PIC, the second by one of up to eight slave PICs.

14.1.2 Pins and signals

Firstly, I would like to introduce you to the control and data signals of the APIC 82489DX. It comes in a 132-pin PQFP. The pin layout is shown in Figure 14.1.

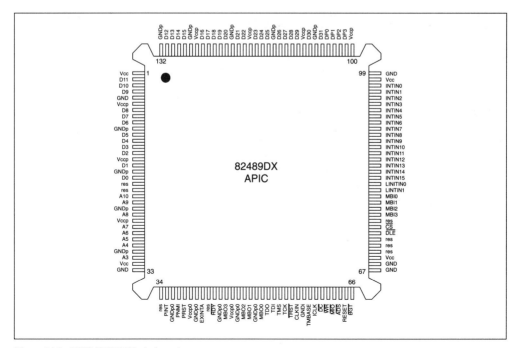

Figure 14.1: APIC 82489DX pin layout.

Without wanting to waste too much space, I will only explain the signals in group form. Each pin is an element of one of the following groups: system, timer, interrupt, register access, processor pin, ICC bus and power supply.

System group: RESET, EXINTA, CLKIN, $\overline{\text{TRST}}$, TCK, TDI, TDO, TMS (I, 0, I, I, I, I, O, I)

Reset, external interrupt, CLK input, test reset, test CLK, test data input, test data output, test mode select
An active reset signal resets the 82489A. EXINTA is activated if an external PIC (that is, an 8259A) reacts to an interrupt. CLKIN defines the clock for most bus signals. $\overline{\text{TRST}}$, TCK, TDI, TDO and TMS implement the boundary scan interface to the on-chip TAP controller.

Timer group: TMBASE (I)

Time base
The signal delivers the reference frequency for the internal timer of the 82489DX. Alternatively, CLKIN can serve as the reference frequency. Furthermore, both can be divided by 2, 4, 8 or 16, so that a total of 10 different reference frequencies are available to the timer: CLKIN, TMBASE, CLKIN/2, CLKIN/4, CLKIN/8, CLKIN/16, TMBASE/2, TMBASE/4, TMBASE/8 and TMBASE/16 are available.

Interrupt group: INTIN15–INTIN0, LINTIN1, LINTIN0 (I, I)

Interrupt input, local interrupt input
The INTINx pins are supplied with external interrupt request signals, which should issue an interrupt at the local, or other, processor. In comparison, and without exception, interrupt requests are transmitted to the local processors.

Register access group: ADS, M/IO, D/C, W/R, BGT, CS, A10–A3, DLE, D31–D0, DP3–DP0, RDY (I, I, I, I, I, I, I, I/O, I, I/O, I/O, O)

Address strobe, memory I/O, data/command, write/read, bus grant, chip select, address, data latch enable, data, data parity, ready
An active ADS signal determines the start of a bus cycle, the type of which is defined by the three bus control signals $M/\overline{\text{IO}}$, $D/\overline{\text{C}}$ and $W/\overline{\text{R}}$. As a result of the possibility of implementing the 82489DX register I/O or memory mapped, $M/\overline{\text{IO}}$ is merely used for the decoding of an INTA cycle ($M/\overline{\text{IO}} = D/\overline{\text{C}} = W/\overline{\text{R}} = 0$). The optional signal $\overline{\text{BGT}}$, specifies the addressing phase of a bus cycle. An active $\overline{\text{CS}}$ signal indicates that another logic component (for example, the Pentium) wishes to access the 82489DX register. The register address is transferred via A10–A3. An active $\overline{\text{DLE}}$ signal specifies the data phase of a bus cycle. The 82489DX registers are read and written via the data bus D31–D0, to which bytes the parity bits DP3–DP0 are assigned. The $\overline{\text{RDY}}$ signal indicates, in a known way, the completion of a bus cycle.

Processor interface group: PINT, PRST, PNMI (O, O, O)

Processor interrupt output, processor reset output, non-maskable interrupt
An active PINT signal indicates that at least one hardware interrupt is pending. PINT is connected to the INTR input of the Pentium. With the activation of the 82489DX RESET input or a reset message via the ICC bus, the 82489DX transmits a signal at the PRST output, also in order to reset the Pentium. In a similar manner, the PNMI is activated if the 82489DX receives an NMI message.

ICC bus group: ICLK, MBI3–MBI0, MBO3–MBO0 (I, I, O)

ICC bus CLK, ICC bus in, ICC bus out
The clock signal for the ICC bus is supplied to ICLK. Incoming ICC messages are fed to the ICC bus input pins MB13–MB10. The 82489DX outputs such messages via pins MBO3–MBO0.

Supply group: Vcc, Vccp, Vccpo, GND, GNDp, GNDpo, GNDi

The pins are supplied with the supply voltage (+5 V) and ground potential (0 V), respectively.

All other pins are reserved.

14.1.3 Structure and function of the APIC 82489DX

During development of the APIC architecture, the aim was to have flexible management and distribution of interrupt requests to the CPUs in a multiprocessor system. To this end, each 82489DX integrates a *local interrupt unit* and an *I/O interrupt unit*. Figure 14.2 shows the internal structure of the APIC. In addition to both of the previously mentioned interrupt units, a 32-bit timer, a JTAG test logic, and a bus and system control unit are also available.

The local interrupt unit is connected via the PRST, PINIT and PNMI pins to the applicable Pentium. It can accept two local interrupts via LINTIN0 and LINTIN1, which are always passed to the local processor. In comparison, the interrupt requests to the I/O interrupt unit, which arrive via all 16 interrupt pins INTIN15 to INTIN0, are redirected to the local interrupt unit of another APIC with the help of a redirection table and the ICC bus and, thus, to an external processor. Each of the INTINx pins is assigned to a 64-bit redirection entry. It contains all of the necessary information, on the one hand regarding the recognition of an interrupt at the assigned pin (for example, edge or level triggering), and on the other regarding its additional handling. Also included is, for example, what priority the interrupt has, which vector is assigned, the transfer mode (fixed target, dynamic target, NMI, ExtINT and so on) and the transfer target. Thus, the priority sequence of all 16 interrupt pins is entirely optional. Even an NMI can be managed via the APIC. All that is necessary is to set the transfer mode to NMI. Then the target APIC activates its PNMI output, in order to release an NMI from the attached processor. A similar table register is contained in the local interrupt unit, which receives the necessary inputs for both local interrupts LINTINx and the timer interrupt.

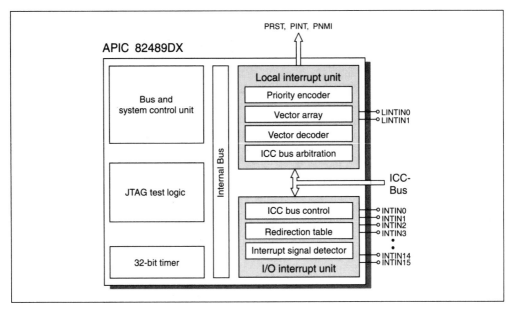

Figure 14.2: Internal structure of the APIC 82489DX.

The whole idea behind interrupt redirecting is that a processor is not interrupted when executing a higher priority task. Instead, the interrupt is redirected to a processor with a task of lower priority, where it becomes an interrupt. The priority of the currently active task in each processor is determined for the local processor by an input in the task priority register of the 82489DX. This task is typically undertaken by the operating system – that is, during a task switch and, in addition to other proceedings, the task priority register is also loaded with an appropriate value. In this way, the task priority can be altered dynamically. The system 82489DX APICs elect to operate with static or dynamic interrupt assignments. With a static assignment, the processor, which is determined from the start, is interrupted in order to handle the interrupt request. With dynamic assignments, all installed APICs search via the ICC bus for the processor, which executes the task with the lowest priority.

So-called *focus processors* are also included in the 82489DX architecture. If the processor has served a particular interrupt, and if the same interrupt appears again, then it is allotted once again to the same processor (the focus processor of the interrupt). There is the hope that the on-chip and L2 caches of the focus processor will retain a vast amount of information and code, which can be used for re-performing the interrupt. In the most favourable case, the complete handler code is situated in cache, and does not have to be downloaded from the slower main memory.

The ICC bus consists of four lines for arbitration and message signals, as well as a clock line, which is typically clocked with 10 MHz from ICLK. In addition to the system bus, the ICC bus creates a complete self-standing, small interrupt system bus for the communication between the APICs themselves, without placing a load on the system bus. The redirecting of the interrupt is executed with the aid of so-called *messages*. You will find out more about these in the next section.

Other possible interrupt sources, in addition to requests via the pins LINTINx and INTINx, are the 82489DX timer as well as the local processor itself. Normally, the 32-bit timer is supplied from the clock signal TMBASE and can be programmed such that it releases an interrupt after a reduction to 0. In this way, for example, the time slices for multitasking operating systems can be implemented. A system processor can also release interrupts to the other processors in the system via the local 82489DX for synchronization, communication or other purposes.

Of the possible 256 theoretical interrupt vectors 0 to 255 of the 82489DX, the first 16 should not be used, because, among other things, they have been reserved for exceptions by Intel. Thus, the APIC supports 240 vectors with the numbers 16 to 255. It operates alternately edge or level triggered.

In a well-known manner, the JTAG test logic implements a boundary scan test. Therefore, like the Pentium or even the L2 cache system, the APIC 82489DX can be included in such a test. I would like to point out, though, that the 82489DX can also work with an 8259A. For this, the ExINTA signal is used. A high level indicates that the external 8259A has responded to the INTA cycle. The 82489DX is then transparent.

14.1.4 Multi-APIC systems and the ICC bus

It is normal in a multi-Pentium system for each Pentium to be allocated its own APIC. Thus, the local interrupt unit of each 82589DX is connected to the local Pentium, and the I/O interrupt unit to many I/O devices. The APICs communicate via the ICC bus. This set-up is shown in Figure 14.3.

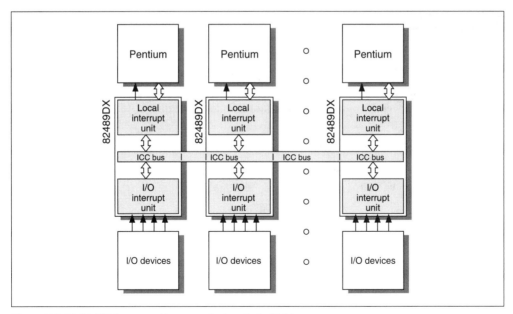

Figure 14.3: Multi-APIC system with communication via the ICC bus.

You should note that despite each Pentium having to be allocated a local interrupt unit, it is sufficient for all I/O devices to be served by one APIC. The external interrupts are transferred via the ICC bus to the desired target Pentium.

Two procedures are available for the choice of the target processor of an interrupt request: fixed mode and lowest priority mode. In *fixed mode*, all requests that fulfil the target requirements are supplied to the APICs. The target requirements are determined in the so-called *physical mode* by an 8-bit identification, and in *logical mode* by a 32-bit target field. In the *lowest priority mode*, all APICs together search for the 82489DX, whose local processor is executing the task with the lowest priority. During the interrupt allocation, all APICs communicate via the ICC bus, whereby another identification ID is allotted to each APIC.

In order to transfer a message, the ICC bus must first execute an arbitration. During the course of this, the APIC with the lowest priority is determined. This lasts four bus cycles. Subsequently, the message is transferred in an additional 15 (short message) or 24 (long message) ICC bus cycles. It includes the target mode, control bits, vector, target and a checksum. The local interrupt unit of the target APIC has now received all of the necessary information and can interrupt its local processor, in order to serve the interrupt.

An *inter-processor interrupt* is issued if a local CPU writes to the interrupt command register in the local unit of the allocated 82489DX. This command register records the same information as a redirection input. Directly after the write, the local interrupt unit outputs an interrupt message to the ICC bus, which is taken on by the target APIC. The local unit then issues an interrupt to the local processor.

14.2 The L2 Pentium cache subsystem 82496/82491 and the MESI cache consistency protocol

Intel had a special cache controller developed for the Pentium – the 82496 – which, together with the cache SRAM modules, can create an L2 cache. In the following sections I would like to discuss this cache system developed for the Pentium in more detail.

14.2.1 The structure of the L2 cache subsystem

Figure 14.4 shows the structure of the L2 cache, which is created from a 82496 cache controller and several 82491 cache SRAM modules.

The cache controller and the SRAM modules are located between the Pentium, the memory bus and the memory controller, which controls the DRAMs of the main memory. The necessary address, data and control signals are transferred between the components over a total of six channels. The interfaces between these components are optimized for the chip set consisting of the Pentium CPU, 82496 cache controller, 82491 cache SRAM and the memory system. As usual, the 82496 checks all memory accesses from the CPU – here, the Pentium. In addition, it either makes the data available from the 82491 SRAM modules, or controls the memory bus and the memory controller, in order to read the data from the main memory if a cache miss occurs. The 82496 is also responsible for the implementation and execution of the MESI protocol, so as to attain cache consistency over several such L2 caches.

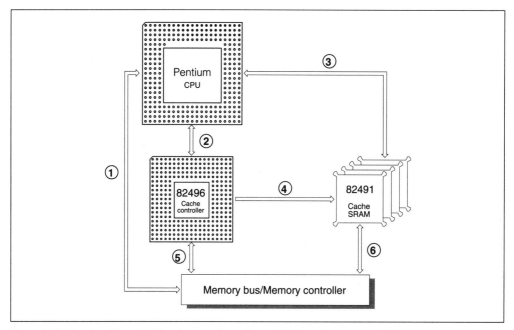

Figure 14.4: L2 cache with an 82496 cache controller and several 82491 cache SRAM modules.

14.2.2 Pin schematic and functionality of 82496 and 82491

Next, I would like to introduce you to the pin diagrams of the 82496 and the 82491 SRAM modules, as shown in Figures 14.5 and 14.6.

The 82496 in the Pentium is an improved version of the i486 82495DX cache controller. It can be configured as an L2 cache with 256 kbytes or 512 kbytes memory capacity. The 82496 operates with two-way set-associative cache architecture; all tags and management bits (read-only, MESI, MRU) are contained in the 82496.

The 82496 cache controller supports cache line sizes of 32, 64, and 128 bytes and also implements the MESI protocol for consistency with the Pentium on-chip caches and other caches in the system. 4k of the 8k tags are available, depending on the size of the cache and the cache lines. In contrast to the Pentium on-chip caches, the 82496 also supports write allocation.

The cache SRAM 82491 modules implement the data memory for the L2 cache subsystem with the 82496 cache controller. They each have a memory capacity of 32 kbyte or 256 kbit and an internal logic; thus, they are more than just pure SRAM chips. They includes, for example, a test function corresponding to the boundary scan test. The 82491 SRAM modules can be configured in a number of ways; there is more about this in Section 14.2.4. During main memory accesses by the Pentium, the 82491 chips act as gateways between the Pentium and the DRAMs; all data transfers flow through them, and not directly through a data bus.

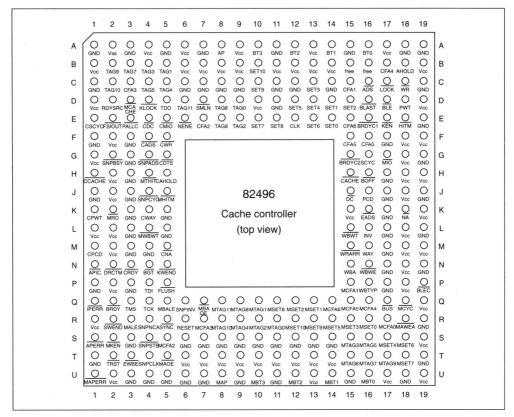

Figure 14.5: 82496 cache controller pin layout.

For this, the cache SRAM modules have four memory buffers, each of which can hold a complete cache line of 128 bytes maximum (therefore, the maximum size of the cache line): two memory cycle buffers for normal memory accesses, a write-back buffer for write-back cycles and a snoop buffer for inquiry cycles. Note that the maximum width applies to all installed SRAM modules; in other words, 128 bytes are achieved with 16 82491 chips because, only by the expansion of the L2 cache to 512 kbytes, is a cache line size of 128 bytes possible. A buffer in an 82491 chip is, therefore, eight bytes in size. The two memory cycle buffers are used alternatively, depending on which is available.

At this stage, on grounds of space, and to prevent repetitions in the next section, I do not wish to list individually the vast quantity of 82496 and 82491 pins. They are described in Section 14.2.3, depending on their affiliation to the six different signal channels.

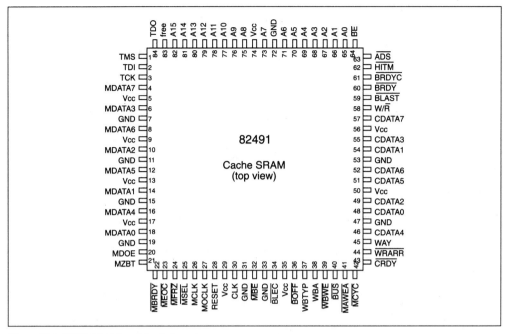

Figure 14.6: 82491 SRAM module pin layout.

14.2.3 Signal channels between the components

As you can see from Figure 14.4, there is a total of six signal channels available between the individual system components.

Signal channel 1

This signal channel transfers the signals between the Pentium, the memory bus and the memory controller. All signals have already been discussed in connection with the Pentium pin schematic in Chapter 10. Therefore, I would just like to summarize in Table 14.1, without further explanation.

Signal(s)	I/O	Pin	Signal(s)	I/O	Pin
APCHK	O	W3	INTR	I	N18
BP3, BP2	O	B2, B3	IU, IV	O	J2, B1
PM1/BP1–PM0/BP0	O	C3, D2	NMI	I	N19
BRDY	I	L4	PCHK	O	R3
BREQ	O	V2	PEN	I	M18
BUSCHK	I	T3	PRDY	O	U3
CLK	I	K18	RESET	I	L18
FERR	O	H3	R/S	I	R18
FLUSH	I	U2	SMI	I	P18

Signal(s)	I/O	Pin	Signal(s)	I/O	Pin
$\overline{\text{HIT}}$	O	W2	$\overline{\text{SMIACT}}$	O	T5
HOLD, HLDA	I, O	V5, Q3	TCK	I	T4
IBT	O	T19	TDI	I	T21
$\overline{\text{IERR}}$	O	C2	TDO	O	S21
$\overline{\text{IGNNE}}$	I	S20	TMS	I	P19
INIT	I	T20	$\overline{\text{TRST}}$	I	S18

Table 14.1: Pentium/memory bus signals

Signal channel 2

This signal channel transfers the signals between the Pentium and the 82496 cache controller. All Pentium signals, which I have already discussed in connection with the pin schematic in Chapter 10, are summarized in Table 14.2, without further explanation.

Signal(s)	I/O	Pin	Signal(s)	I/O	Pin
A31–A3	I/O	T9–T17, U8–U21, V6, V19–V21, W5, W19	$\overline{\text{EWBE}}$	I	A3
			$\overline{\text{HITM}}$	O	M4
$\overline{\text{ADS}}$	O	P4	INV	I	A1
AHOLD	I	L2	$\overline{\text{KEN}}$	I	J3
AP	I/O	P3	$\overline{\text{LOCK}}$	O	V3
$\overline{\text{BOFF}}$	I	K4	$\overline{\text{M/IO}}$	O	A2
$\overline{\text{BRDY}}$	I	L4	$\overline{\text{NA}}$	I	D13
BT3–BT0	O	T7, T8, W20, W21	PCD, PWT	O, O	W4, S3
$\overline{\text{CACHE}}$	O	J4	SCYC	O	R4
$\overline{\text{D/C}}$	O	V4	$\overline{\text{W/R}}$	O	N3
$\overline{\text{EADS}}$	I	M3	WB/$\overline{\text{WT}}$	I	M2

Table 14.2: Pentium/cache controller signals

$\overline{\text{ADSC}}$ (O)

Pentium pin N4

This address strobe pin of the Pentium is identical to the $\overline{\text{ADS}}$ pin P4, except that it is also connected to the $\overline{\text{ADS}}$ input C16 of the 82496. The $\overline{\text{ADS}}$ output of the Pentium is, however, connected to the cache SRAM modules or the bus controller.

$\overline{\text{BRDYC1}}$ (O)

82496 pin E16

The burst ready cache 1 pin of the 82496 is connected with the BRDYC input of the Pentium. In this way, the cache controller indicates to the CPU that it has received data from it or transmitted data to it.

CFA6–CFA0, SET10–SET0, TAG11–TAG0

82496 pins B2–B5, B10, B17, C2–C5, C10, C13, C15, D6, D8, D9, D12–D15, E7–E11, E13–E15, F15, F16

These 29 pins are connected to the Pentium address pins A31–A3. The exact connection is dependent on the system configuration. This is explained further below.

Signal channel 3

Signal channel 3 serves to exchange signals between the Pentium and the 82491 cache SRAM modules. Table 14.3 shows the Pentium signals discussed previously.

Signal(s)	I/O	Pin
ADS	O	P4
HITM	O	M4

Table 14.3: Pentium/cache SRAM signals.

A15–A1

82491 pins 66–71, 73, 75–82

The cache SRAM pins A15–A1 are always connected to the address pins A17–A3 of the Pentium. The cache SRAM pin A0 is always connected to ground (GND).

CDATA7–CDATA0

82491 pins 46, 48, 49, 51, 52, 54, 55, 57

The eight cache data pins are connected to the data bus pins D63–D0, the byte enable pins BE7–BE0 or the data parity pins DP3–DP0 of the Pentium. The exact connection is dependent on the system configuration.

Signal channel 4

This signal channel transfers the signals between the 82496 cache controller and the 82491 cache SRAM modules.

BLAST (O, I)

82496 pin D16, 82491 pin 59

The BLAST output of the 82496 is connected to the BLAST input of the 82491. When BLAST is activated, the cache controller indicates to the SRAM modules that the current BRDY or BRDYC specifies the last cycle (BLAST = burst last) within one burst transfer. Subsequently, the burst cycle is ended.

$\overline{\text{BLEC}}$ (O, I)

82496 pin P19, 82491 pin 34

The $\overline{\text{BLEC}}$ output ($\overline{\text{BEx}}$ latch enable) of the 82496, is always connected to the $\overline{\text{BLEC}}$ input of a 82491. When BLEC is activated, the Pentium byte enable signals $\overline{\text{BEx}}$ are latched in the SRAM modules.

$\overline{\text{BOFF}}$ (O, I)

82496 pin H16, 82491 pin 36

The 82496 can interrupt a Pentium bus cycle and also the 82491 SRAM modules by the activation of the back-off signal. The 82491 modules erase all signals and data that are connected with the interrupted bus cycle.

$\overline{\text{BRDYC2}}$, $\overline{\text{BRDYC}}$ (O, I)

82496 pin G15, 82491 pin 61

The $\overline{\text{BRDYC2}}$ output (burst ready cache 2) of the 82496 is always connected to the $\overline{\text{BRYDC}}$ input of the 82491. Through the activation of BRDYC2, the 82496 cache controller indicates to the 82491 that it has transferred data to or received data from the CPU.

$\overline{\text{BUS}}$ (O, I)

82496 pin Q17, 82491 pin 40

The $\overline{\text{BUS}}$ output of the 82496 is connected to the $\overline{\text{BUS}}$ input of the 82491. The $\overline{\text{BUS}}$ signal determines whether the read data, for a read access of the Pentium, comes from the cache SRAM 82491 ($\overline{\text{BUS}}$ is inactive; that is, high level) or from memory bus ($\overline{\text{BUS}}$ is active; that is, at low level). Depending on the $\overline{\text{BUS}}$, the 82491 switches an internal multiplexer, in order to serve the read access accordingly.

$\overline{\text{MAWEA}}$ (O, I)

82496 pin R18, 82491 pin 41

The $\overline{\text{MAWEA}}$ output (memory bus array write enable or allocation) of the 82496 is connected to the $\overline{\text{MAWEA}}$ input of the 82491. During a read procedure, an active $\overline{\text{MAWEA}}$ signal with a low level from the 82496 instructs the 82491 to also write the data, read from the main memory, into the 82491 – that is, execute a line fill. If $\overline{\text{MAWEA}}$ is active during a write operation, the 82491 cache SRAMs will subsequently execute a write allocate.

$\overline{\text{MCYC}}$ (O, I)

82496 pin Q18, 82491 pin 42

The $\overline{\text{MCYC}}$ output (memory bus cycle) of the 82496 is connected to the $\overline{\text{MCYC}}$ input of the 82491. An active 82496 MCYC signal at a low level indicates to the 82491 that the current cycle is using the memory buffer – that is, placing the current address in a memory address buffer.

WAY (O, I)

82496 pin M16, 82491 pin 45
The WAY output of the 82496 is connected to the WAY input of the 82491. The WAY signal from the 82496 indicates the way that the current cache access cycle is addressing. A low level WAY signal represents way 0, whereas a high level WAY signal represents way 1.

WBA, $\overline{\text{SEC2}}$ (O, I)

82496 pin N15, 82491 pin 38
The WBA/$\overline{\text{SEC2}}$ output of the 82496 is connected to the WBA/$\overline{\text{SEC2}}$ input of the 82491. WBA (write-back buffer address) and $\overline{\text{SEC2}}$ (lines per sector) share this pin. If the 82496 SEC2 pin transmits a low – that is, active – signal to the 82491, it shows that each tag represents two cache SRAM lines in the 82491, otherwise only one cache SRAM line.

For a cache configuration with two cache lines per sector, the WBA signal indicates which of these two cache lines will be written back. A low level WBA signal selects line 1, a high level signal selects line 2. During a write-back, WBA is always at a low level for a cache configuration with only one cache line per sector.

WBTYP, LR0 (O, I)

82496 pin P16, 82491 pin 37
The WBTYP/LR0 output of the 82496 is connected to the WBTYP/LR0 input of the 82491. WBTYP (write-back cycle type) and LR0 (line ratio) share this pin.

The WBTYP signal indicates which type of write-back cycle will be executed. A high level WBTYP signal represents a snoop write-back cycle; a low level WBTYP represents a replacement write-back cycle. This is used in deciding which write-back buffer will be used for the writing back of 82491.

LR0, together with LR1 ($\overline{\text{WBWE}}$), indicates which line size ratio of the memory controller will be used. LR1 and LR0 are generated by a reset of the 82491 cache SRAM module.

The following line size ratios are valid: 1(LR1=0, LR0=0), 2 (LR1=0, LR0=1) and 4 (LR1=1, LR0=0).

$\overline{\text{WBWE}}$, LR1 (O, I)

82496 pin N16, 82491 pin 39
The $\overline{\text{WBWE}}$/LR1 output of the 82496 is connected to the $\overline{\text{WBWE}}$/LR1 input of the 82491. $\overline{\text{WBWE}}$ (write-back buffer write enable) and LR1 (line ratio) share this pin.

An active 82496 WBWE signal at low level indicates to the 82491 that the next cycle represents a write-back cycle. LR1, together with LR0 (WBTYP), indicates which line size ratios of the memory controller will be used (see above).

$\overline{\text{WRARR}}$ (O, I)

82496 pin M15, 82491 pin 44

The $\overline{\text{WRARR}}$ output of the 82496 is connected to the $\overline{\text{WRARR}}$ input of the 82491. This signal controls the writing of data in the 82491 cache SRAMs, the so-called cache array (write to cache array).

Signal channel 5

This signal channel transfers the signals between the 82496 cache controller and the memory bus for controlling the main memory. Additionally, the test pins are available for the boundary scan tests.

$\overline{\text{APERR}}$ (O)

82496 pin S1

An active address parity error signal indicates that the 82496 has recorded an address parity error on the CPU bus.

$\overline{\text{APIC}}$ (O)

82496 pin N1

An active (advanced programmable interrupt controller address decoding) signal indicates that the current output address is an APIC address, therefore, fee00000h to fee003ffh.

$\overline{\text{BGT}}$, CLDRV (I)

82496 pin N4

The $\overline{\text{BGT}}$ (bus guaranteed transfer) and CLDRV (cache low drive configuration) signals share this pin. The memory controller indicates to the 82496 through the activation of $\overline{\text{BGT}}$ that it has taken over control of the memory cycle; the 82496 is now available for other activities. During the course of a reset, CLDRV indicates whether one or two buffers will be used for the cache SRAM control signals (for example, $\overline{\text{BLAST}}$, $\overline{\text{BLEC}}$ and so on).

BLE (O)

82496 pin D17

The 82496 activates its byte latch enable output in order to read the control signals PCD, PWT, $\overline{\text{BE7}}$–$\overline{\text{BE0}}$, $\overline{\text{CACHE}}$ and SCYC from the Pentium into an external latch, where they are latched. The $\overline{\text{BLE}}$ signal is only necessary for SRAM modules other than the 82491. The 82469/82491 automatically fetches these control signals and latches them.

$\overline{\text{BRDY}}$ (I)

82496 pin Q2
The memory controller indicates by the activation of BRDY (burst ready) that it has transmitted valid data to or received valid data from the 82496.

$\overline{\text{CADS}}$ (O)

82496 pin F4
The 82496 indicates to the main memory by the activation of CADS (cache address strobe) that a main memory access is currently taking place.

CAHOLD (O)

82496 pin H5
The cache AHOLD signal simply represents the level of the Pentium AHOLD signal – in other words, it indicates whether the 82496 is executing a Pentium inquiry cycle or an invalidation.

$\overline{\text{CCACHE}}$ (O)

82496 pin H1
The cache CACHE signal represents, in an unchanged form, the level of the Pentium $\overline{\text{CACHE}}$ signal. With this, the memory controller can determine how many $\overline{\text{BRDY}}$ signals it must return; that is, whether a single access with a maximum of eight bytes will be executed, or a burst cycle with 64 bytes.

CD/$\overline{\text{C}}$, CM/$\overline{\text{IO}}$, CW/$\overline{\text{R}}$ (O, O, O)

82496 pins E4, E5, F5
The signals cache data/control (1=data cycle, 0=command/special cycle), cache memory/IO (1=memory cycle, 0=I/O cycle), cache write/read (1=write cycle, 0=read cycle) determine the current bus cycle type. If CD/$\overline{\text{C}}$ and CM/$\overline{\text{IO}}$ are at a high level and, therefore, a data access of the memory is executed, the bus cycle comes from the 82496. I/O accesses are only performed by the Pentium.

The possible signal combinations have the following significance:

▶ (0xx) no 82496 cycle (82496 only reads data; no command fetching)
▶ (x0x) no 82496 cycle (I/O cycle from the Pentium)
▶ (110) reading of data from memory
▶ (111) writing of data to memory

$\overline{\text{CDTS}}$ (O)

82496 pin G5
An active $\overline{\text{CDTS}}$ signal (cache data strobe) indicates that the CPU or memory bus is available with the next clock CLK.

CFG2–CFG0 (O)

82496 pins N5, R2, M5
During the course of a reset, the 82496 checks this configuration pin and thus determines the cache configuration with respect to the cache/Pentium line size ratio, the tag size and the cache lines per sector. Note that in each case, CFG0 and $\overline{\text{CNA}}$, CFG1 and $\overline{\text{SWEND}}$ as well as CFG2 and $\overline{\text{KWEND}}$, share one pin.

CLK (I)

82496 pin E12
This pin is supplied with the same clock signal as the Pentium and the 82491.

$\overline{\text{CNA}}$, CFG0 (I)

82496 pin M5
Through a low level signal at this cache next address pin, the memory controller instructs the 82496 to release the next address. Thus, an address pipelining can be carried out. $\overline{\text{CNA}}$ and CFG0 share the pin.

CPCD, CPWT (O, O)

82496 pins M1, K1
The cache PCD signal CPCD and the cache PWT signal CPWT are the latched versions of the Pentium page cache disable signal and the page write-through signal, respectively.

$\overline{\text{CRDY}}$, $\overline{\text{SLFTST}}$ (I)

82496 pin N3
An active $\overline{\text{CRDY}}$ signal (cache memory bus ready) from the memory controller indicates that the current memory cycle is completed. In the course of a reset, the 82496 checks the $\overline{\text{SLFTST}}$ (self-test) pin in order to determine whether it should execute an internal self-test ($\overline{\text{SLFTST}}$ at low level). $\overline{\text{CRDY}}$ and $\overline{\text{SLFTST}}$ share the pin.

CWAY (O)

82496 pin K4
As opposed to the memory controller, the cache way signal specifies which path of the cache the read data will be transferred across, and from which path the write data comes.

$\overline{\text{DRCTM}}$ (I)

82496 pin N2
An active $\overline{\text{DRCTM}}$ signal (direct to M state) informs the 82496 to place a newly loaded cache line directly into the M state. For example, direct cache-cache transfers can be executed without the involvement of the main memory.

$\overline{\text{FLUSH}}$ (I)

82496 pin P5
If the cache flush pin is supplied with a low level $\overline{\text{FLUSH}}$ signal, then the 82496 writes back all changed cache lines to the main memory and invalidates the cache. Furthermore, the 82496 executes an inquiry of the Pentium on-chip cache, writes back all changed cache lines of the data cache, and invalidates both Pentium caches. The $\overline{\text{FLUSH}}$ signal is as good as connected to the Pentium.

$\overline{\text{FSIOUT}}$ (O)

92496 pin E2
The $\overline{\text{FSIOUT}}$ signal indicates the start (with a drop to a low level) and the finish (a climb to a high level) of a flush, synchronization or initialization process.

$\overline{\text{HIGHZ}}$ (I)

82496 pin Q5
A high level high impedance pin $\overline{\text{HIGHZ}}$ signal causes the outputs of the 82496 to adopt a tristate condition and so be separated from the bus.

$\overline{\text{IPERR}}$ (O)

82496 pin Q1
An active 82496 $\overline{\text{IPERR}}$ signal (internal parity error) indicates that a parity error has occurred in a tag RAM or an address path.

$\overline{\text{KLOCK}}$ (O)

82496 pin D4
With the activation of $\overline{\text{KLOCK}}$ (cache controller LOCK), the 82496 can execute a locked access of the main memory.

$\overline{\text{KWEND}}$, CFG2 (I)

82496 pin N5
With the activation of $\overline{\text{KWEND}}$ (cacheability window end), the cacheability window that was opened by $\overline{\text{CADS}}$ is ended. The 82496 then scans the $\overline{\text{MKEN}}$ and $\overline{\text{MRO}}$ signals. $\overline{\text{KWEND}}$ and CFG2 share the same pin.

MALE $(\overline{\text{WWOR}})$, $\overline{\text{MAOE}}$, MBALE $(\overline{\text{HIGHZ}})$, $\overline{\text{MBAOE}}$ (I, I, I, I)

82496 pins R3, T5, Q5, Q7
The 82496 internal address latch is controlled by the following four signals: memory address latch enable, memory address output enable, memory sub-line address latch enable and

memory sub-line address output enable. MALE and $\overline{\text{WWOR}}$, as well as MBALE and $\overline{\text{HIGHZ}}$, share a pin.

MAP (O, I)

82496 pin U8

MAP produces a parity bit for an even memory bus address during a write access of memory ($\overline{\text{MAOE}}$=0); MAP is fed with a parity bit for an even address during a read access ($\overline{\text{MAOE}}$=1).

$\overline{\text{MAPERR}}$ (I, O)

82496 pin U1

The signal at the $\overline{\text{MAPERR}}$ pin (memory address bus parity error) indicates whether an address parity error is present on the memory bus ($\overline{\text{MAPERR}}$=0).

MBT3–MBT0 (O)

82496 pins U10, U12, U14, U16

The memory branch trace address bits MBT3–MBT0 reproduce the values of the branch trace address bits BT3–BT0 from the Pentium. MBT2–MBT0 specify the bits A2–A0 of the linear branch address in a branch trace message cycle; BT3 defines the standard operand size (BT3=1: standard operand size 32 bits; BT=0: 16 bits).

$\overline{\text{MCACHE}}$ (O)

82496 pin D3

An active 82496 $\overline{\text{MCACHE}}$ signal indicates that the data of the current cycle can be transferred into the L2 cache. This will, in fact, only happen if the $\overline{\text{MKEN}}$ signal is activated from the memory controller.

MCFA6–MCFA0, MSET10–MSET0, MTAG11–MTAG0 (I, O)

82496 pins P15, Q8–Q16, R7–R17, S5, S15–S18, T15–T18

These 30 pins form the memory address bus between the 82496 cache controller and the memory bus.

$\overline{\text{MHITM}}$ (O)

82496 pin J5

The memory snoop hit signal produces the result of an inquiry cycle. By referencing a changed line in cache, the 82496 sets the $\overline{\text{MHITM}}$ signal to a low level. The pin produces a high level signal for a hit or a miss of an unchanged line.

$\overline{\text{MKEN}}$ (I)

82496 pin K2

The 82496 determines at the end of the cacheability window ($\overline{\text{KWEND}}$ at low level), via $\overline{\text{MKEN}}$ (memory cache enable) whether the current cycle is 'cacheable' and, therefore, whether the addressed address area of the cache can be transferred. If this is the case, and if the 82496 has issued a cacheable cycle (thus, $\overline{\text{MCACHE}}$ is active), then a cache line fill will be executed. As $\overline{\text{MKEN}}$ comes from the memory bus system, using $\overline{\text{MKEN}}$, certain address areas can be protected by the hardware prior to cacheing through the L2 cache 82496/82491. $\overline{\text{MKEN}}$ has a similar significance for the 82496 as $\overline{\text{KEN}}$ has for the Pentium.

$\overline{\text{MRO}}$ (I)

82496 pin S2

With the aid of an active $\overline{\text{MRO}}$ signal (memory read only), the cache line, which has just been read, can be marked as read only ($\overline{\text{MRO}}$=0). It is identified in the L2 cache as being shared with a set read-only bit.

$\overline{\text{MTHIT}}$ (O)

82496 pin H4

The 82496 activates this $\overline{\text{MTHIT}}$ signal (memory snoop hit to valid state) if an inquiry cycle has hit a cache line in the M, E or S state, the inquiry address is, therefore, available.

MWB/$\overline{\text{WT}}$ (I)

82496 pin L4

The L2 cache 82496/82491 operates normally using a write-back strategy. A write-through strategy can also be set for the cache lines individually. For this, the line need only be saved in the S state. The 82496 does exactly that, when the MBW/$\overline{\text{WT}}$ (write-back/write-through) pin is set to a low level for a cache line fill.

$\overline{\text{NENE}}$ (O)

82496 pin E6

If the current access falls in the same 2-kbyte page as the previous access, the 82496 activates the $\overline{\text{NENE}}$ signal (next near). This supports the memory controller during access of the DRAM main memory in the page or static column mode.

$\overline{\text{PALLC}}$ (O)

82496 pin E3

With the activation of $\overline{\text{PALLC}}$ (potential allocate), the 82496 indicates, in view of the memory controller, that it wishes to execute a write allocate after the current write access. The main memory has to respond with a $\overline{\text{MKEN}}$, so that the write allocate does in fact occur.

RDYSRC (O)

82496 pin D2
The 82496, with the aid of RDYSRC (ready source), determines the source of the $\overline{\text{BRDY}}$ signal for the Pentium. A high RDYSRC signal indicates that the memory controller should produce the $\overline{\text{BRDY}}$ signal, and in comparison, a low RDYSRC signal indicates that the 82496 itself will make the $\overline{\text{BRDY}}$ signal available.

RESET (I)

82496 pin R6
A high level signal at this pin causes a reset of the 82496 cache controller.

$\overline{\text{SMLN}}$ (O)

82496 pin D7
An active high level $\overline{\text{SMLN}}$ signal (same line) indicates that the address of the current cycle is in the same cache line as the previous cycle.

$\overline{\text{SNPADS}}$ (O)

82496 pin G4
The 82496 indicates by the activation of $\overline{\text{SNPADS}}$ (cache snoop address strobe) that all address, data and control signals are valid for a write-back cycle. Thus, $\overline{\text{SNPADS}}$ is functionally identical to $\overline{\text{CADS}}$; in contrast to this, $\overline{\text{SNPADS}}$ is only activated for snoop write-back cycles and not for normal accesses.

$\overline{\text{SNPBSY}}$ (O)

82496 pin G2
AN active $\overline{\text{SNPADS}}$ signal (snoop busy) indicates that the current inquiry cycle will be delayed, because the elements necessary for this are currently in use by another process.

SNPCLK, SNPMD (I)

82496 pin G2
The SNPCLK signal shares a pin with the snooping mode signal SNPMD. During the course of a reset, SNPMD determines whether the 82496 uses a synchronized snooping mode (SNPMD=0), a strobed mode (SNPMD=1) or a clocked mode. In the latter case, the clock signal of the memory controller has to be fed to the SNPCLK (snooping clock) pin, which then determines the frequency of inquiry cycles.

$\overline{\text{SNPCYC}}$ (O)

82496 pin J4
An active $\overline{\text{SNPCYC}}$ signal (snoop cycle) indicates that an inquiry cycle is currently taking place.

SNPINV (I)

82496 pin Q6
By feeding a high level signal to the 82496 SNPINV input (snoop invalidate), the cache line in the inquiry address is invalidated.

$\overline{\text{SNPSTB}}$, SNPNCA (I, I)

82496 pins S4 and R4
When an external bus controller executes an access, $\overline{\text{SNPSTB}}$ (snoop strobe) is activated in order to release an inquiry cycle in the 82496. If the result of this snoop is a hit, then the corresponding cache line is marked as being shared. SNPNCA (snoop non-cache access) is activated in order to prevent the situation where, for example, the external bus controller does not transfer this line to its own cache. Therefore, the state of the affected cache line will not be changed.

$\overline{\text{SWEND}}$, CFG1 (I)

82496 pin R2
The snoop window opened by $\overline{\text{CADS}}$ is ended through the activation of $\overline{\text{SWEND}}$ (snoop window end). The 82496 then checks the signals $\overline{\text{DRCTM}}$ and $\overline{\text{MWB/WT}}$. $\overline{\text{SWEND}}$ and CFG1 share this pin.

$\overline{\text{SYNC}}$, MALDRV (I)

82496 pin R5
When $\overline{\text{SYNC}}$ (synchronize) is activated, the 82496 writes all of the modified cache lines back to the main memory, but does not invalidate the internal tags. All lines marked as shared and exclusive remain unchanged, but the modified lines will be marked as exclusive. This is possible because they have been written-back to the main memory. $\overline{\text{SYNC}}$ and MALDRV share this pin. During the course of an initialization, the 82496 scans the MALDRV input (memory address low drive) in order to determine whether the address driver should be activated for one or two buffers.

TCK, TDI, TDO, TMS, $\overline{\text{TRST}}$ (I, I, O, I, I)

82496 pins Q4, P4, D5, Q3, T2
The five pins represent the pin to the boundary scan test of the 82496 cache controller.

$\overline{\text{WWOR}}$ (I)

82496 pin R3
An active signal at the $\overline{\text{WWOR}}$ input (weak write ordering) during the course of a reset directs the 82496 to implement a weak write ordering. The ordering, in which write accesses operate on the memory bus, is no longer required to be synchronized, as is the case with an access from the CPU. In this way, it is possible, using a suitable rearrangement of the write accesses, to increase system performance.

Signal channel 6

The purpose of signal channel 6 is to exchange signals between the 82491 cache SRAM, the memory bus and the main memory controller. In addition, there are four test pins available for the boundary scan test, and, as opposed to the 82496, in this case the TRST reset pin is missing.

$\overline{\text{BRDY}}$ (I)

82491 pin 60
The memory controller indicates, by the activation of $\overline{\text{BRDY}}$ (burst ready), that it has transmitted valid data to or received valid data from the 82491.

CLK (I)

82491 pin 30
This pin is supplied with the same clock signal as the Pentium and the 82496.

$\overline{\text{CRDY}}$ (I)

82491 pin 43
An active $\overline{\text{CRDY}}$ signal (cache ready) from the memory controller indicates that the current memory cycle is completed.

$\overline{\text{MBE}}$, $\overline{\text{PAR}}$ (O, I)

82491 pin 32
$\overline{\text{MBE}}$ represents the locked version of the corresponding Pentium $\overline{\text{BE7}}$–$\overline{\text{BE0}}$ signals. During the course of a reset, $\overline{\text{PAR}}$ is used as an input for a configuration signal, which signifies whether the 82491 cache RAM module is serving as a parity memory ($\overline{\text{PAR}}$=0).

$\overline{\text{MBRDY}}$, MISTB (I, I)

82491 pin 22
When the L2 cache 82496/82491 is operating with a clocked memory bus, $\overline{\text{MBRDY}}$ (memory burst ready) indicates that the current data transfer is complete and that the burst address counter can be incremented in order to transfer the next section. $\overline{\text{MBRDY}}$ and MISTB share this pin. MISTB is used in the strobed memory bus mode to insert data into the 82491.

MCLK, MSTBM (I, I)

82491 pin 26
When the L2 cache 82496/82491 is operating with a clocked memory bus, the clock signal MCLK (memory bus clock) is supplied for the memory bus. Then all accesses of the main memory are synchronized to MCLK. MCLK and MSTBM share this pin. MSTBM (memory strobed mode) is used as a configuration pin. During the course of a reset, the level of the MSTBM signal is checked. If the MSTBM is fixed at a low, or a high level, then the 82491 will

operate with a strobed memory bus. However, if the 82491 receives a clock signal at the MSTBM input, then it will use a clocked memory bus.

MDATA7–MDATA0 (I, O)

82491 pins 4, 6, 8, 10, 12, 14, 16, 18
These eight pins represent the memory data bus between the 82491 and the main memory. Data is transferred via these pins to and from the 82491 and the main memory. MDATA7–MDATA0 (memory data) are controlled directly by the $\overline{\text{MDOE}}$ signal.

$\overline{\text{MDOE}}$ (I)

82491 pin 20
An active low level signal at the $\overline{\text{MDOE}}$ (memory data output enable) pin directs the 82491 to release data to its memory data bus MDATA7–MDATA0.

$\overline{\text{MEOC}}$ (I)

82491 pin 23
An active low level signal at the $\overline{\text{MEOC}}$ (memory end of cycle) pin ends the current 82491 memory bus cycle. The internal memory buffers are prepared for a new cycle.

$\overline{\text{MFRZ}}$, MDLDRV (I, I)

82491 pin 24
If the $\overline{\text{MFRZ}}$ (memory data freeze) pin is supplied with a low level signal, then the written data from the 82491 contained in the current write cycle is frozen. A subsequent write allocate replenishes the affected cache line in the 82491 with the amount of 'frozen' data – that is, this data is not overwritten. Therefore, it is unnecessary to connect the write access of the main memory; instead, the write data is held in the 82491 and only the unsaved data is reloaded from the main memory. The effect is like that of a cache write hit in a write-back cache – that is, the modified, valid cache line is only contained in the cache and not the main memory. $\overline{\text{MFRZ}}$ and MDLDRV share this pin. During the course of an initialization, the 82491 checks the MDLDRV (memory data low drive) input, in order to determine whether the address driver should be activated for one or two buffers.

$\overline{\text{MOCLK}}$, MOSTB (I, I)

82491 pin 27
If, when using a clocked memory bus, the MOCLK (memory data output clock) pin is supplied with a high level signal, then the memory data bus will be clocked by MCLK. MOCLK and MOSTB share this pin. With a strobed memory bus, in comparison, the MOSTB pin is supplied with a scan control signal.

$\overline{\text{MSEL}}$, MTR4/$\overline{8}$ (I, I)

82491 pin 25

If the $\overline{\text{MSEL}}$ (memory buffer chip select) pin is supplied with a low level signal, then the 82491 will be activated. $\overline{\text{MSEL}}$ and MTR4/$\overline{8}$ share this pin. During the course of an initialization, the 82491 checks the MTR4/$\overline{8}$ input (memory 4/8 transfers) in order to determine how many transfers are necessary to fill, or write-back, a cache line; a high level signifies four transfers for a cache line; a low level signifies eight. The quantity is dependent upon the configurable cache line size of the L2 cache system 82496/82491 and the width of the memory bus.

$\overline{\text{MZBT}}$, MX4/$\overline{8}$ (I, I)

82491 pin 21

If the $\overline{\text{MZBT}}$ (memory zero base transfer) pin is supplied with a low level signal, then the 82491 always starts a burst transfer for a cache line fill or a write-back with the base address 00h. A Pentium base address that deviates from this will be ignored. The address sequence is always xx00h, xx08h, xx10h and so on for a 64-bit memory bus, and xx00h, xx10h, xx20h and so on for a 128-bit memory bus. $\overline{\text{MZBT}}$ and MX4/$\overline{8}$ share this pin. During the course of an initialization, the 82491 checks the MX4/$\overline{8}$ (memory 4/8 I/O bus width) pin in order to determine how many of its data bus pins MDATA7–MDATA0 it should use. The 82491 only uses the four pins MDATA3–MDATA0 for a high level; for a low level, all eight pins MDATA7–MDATA0 are used.

RESET (I)

82491 pin 28

A high level signal at this pin causes a reset of the 82491 cache SRAM module.

TCK, TDI, TDO, TMS (I, I, O, I)

82491 pins 3, 2, 84, 1

These four pins represent the interface to the boundary scan test of the 82491 cache SRAM.

14.2.4 Configuration and operating modes

The configuration of the L2 cache system is set during the course of a reset. The following 82496 and 82491 configuration inputs are used for this purpose: CFG2–CFG0, CLDRV, $\overline{\text{FLUSH}}$, $\overline{\text{HIGHZ}}$, MALDRV, MDLDRV, MSTBM, MTR4/$\overline{8}$, MX4/$\overline{8}$, PAR, SLFTST, SNPMD and WWOR. You can see which initialization signals are fed to the individual components of the Pentium/L2 cache sub-system in Figure 14.7. The settings cannot be changed after successful configuration. For that, a reset is necessary. Aspects that can be set include:

▶ 256 kbytes or 512 kbytes cache size
▶ 64-bit or 128-bit memory bus
▶ one or two cache lines per sector
▶ a 1:1, 1:2 or 1:4 size ratio for cache lines of the Pentium and 82496
▶ four or eight bus transfers for one cache line fill or write-back

▶ 4k or 8k tags
▶ snoop mode
▶ memory bus mode
▶ strong/weak write ordering

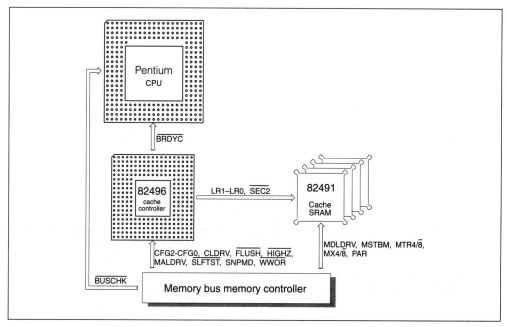

Figure 14.7: Initialization signals for the various components of a Pentium/82496–82491 system.

The possible physical configurations of the L2 cache 82496/82491 are given in Table 14.4. Therefore, the L2 cache chips are very flexible. The setting of the listed cache parameters is achieved by the configuration signal CFG2–CFG0.

Configuration	1	2	3	4	5	6
Cache size (kbytes)	256	256	512	512	512	512
Number of 82491 modules	8	8	16	16	16	16
Memory bus width (bits)	64	64	64	64	128	128
Cycles for line fills or write-backs	4	8	4	8	4	8
Size ratio for Pentium/82496 line	1	2	2	2	2	4
Number of tags	8k	4k	8k	8k	8k	4k
Cache lines per sector	1	1	1	1	1	1
CFG2, CFG1, CFG0	0, 0, 1	1, 1, 1	0, 0, 0	0, 1, 1	0, 1, 1	1, 1, 0

Table 14.4: Physical configurations of L2 cache 82496/82491.

A cache size of 256 kbytes or 512 kbytes is possible for the L2 cache subsystem consisting of the 82496 cache controller and the 82491 cache SRAM modules. Eight or sixteen 82491 elements are necessary, respectively. In addition, two further 82491 modules can be included, in order to store parity information. These two parity modules must then be configured specially (see below).

The 82496/82491 system includes a memory bus between the SRAM modules and the main memory; the bus can have a width of 64 bits or 128 bits. A 128-bit memory bus can only be used with sixteen 82491 modules – thus, only with the full L2 cache extension of 512 kbytes. The size of a cache line in the L2 cache can also be set, possible values being 32 bytes, 64 bytes and 128 bytes. Setting is achieved by the relationship of the (flexible) cache line size for the L2 cache to the (fixed) cache line size of the Pentium with 32 bytes. This relationship, together with the bus width, determines the necessary number of bus cycles (four or eight) that are necessary in order to execute a cache line fill or write-back. Setting of the 82491 module is undertaken by a corresponding configuration signal and its MTR4/$\overline{8}$ pin. For example, a 64-byte cache line for a 128-bit memory bus, which is double the size of that of the Pentium, is filled or written-back within eight bus cycles.

The 82496 also supports *cache sectoring*. Generally, with cache sectoring, several cache lines are combined into one cache sector. Sectors with only one or two cache lines are included in the case of the 82496. The first instance is synonymous with an unsectored cache. A tag is attached to each sector, and not to each individual cache line. However, each line retains its own MESI bits. The cache itself can be enlarged by cache sectoring, without an increase in the number of tags. Thereby, unfortunately, cacheing becomes less effective, and there is a negligible reduction in the possibility of a hit. Note that during cache sectoring with two cache lines per sector, only one line will be filled or written-back with each cache line fill or write-back. Therefore, two cache line fills or write-backs must be executed in order to serve the complete sector. The number of queries and back invalidation cycles (which are necessary for the maintenance of cache consistency) are set automatically by the 82496.

The size of the tag RAM and the number of tag inputs are determined by the cache line size and the bus width. The 82496 can accept 4k (4096) or 8k (8192) tags. As you already know from Chapter 9, the tag entries serve for the determination of cache hits. Together with the SRAM modules, the 82496 implements a two-way set-associative L2 cache. This means that 2k or 4k sets are included in each of the two ways, depending on the size of the cache. That is why the 4k and 8k tags are necessary. Each way has 15 tag bits, 4 bits for the status of the cache line and a write protection bit. Furthermore, if a cache miss occurs, an LRU bit is allocated to a way 0 set and the corresponding way 1 set, which the 82496 uses for replacing a cache line. The CPU address bits are, in differing forms, represented by the configurable pins CFA6–CFA0, the address pin TAG11–TAG0 and the set address pins SET10–SET0, depending on the set quantity and the size of cache line. The various assignments are given in Table 14.5.

Depending on the configuration, the address signals that are fed to the pins CFA6–CFA0, are used internally by the 82496 as set addresses, tag addresses, the address of a line within one sector or as a sub-line address. The 82496 uses the Pentium address signals A31–A3 to determine whether there is a hit or a miss. Simultaneously, the cache SRAM is addressed via the Pentium address signals A17–A3. With a cache size of 256 kbyte, the Pentium address signals A16–A3 are fed to the 82491 address pins A15–A2, and the 82491 address pins A1 and A0 are at

GND. In the case of a cache size of 512 kbytes, the Pentium address signals A17–A3 are fed to 82491 address pins A15–A1 and only 82491 address pin A0 is at GND.

Configuration (see Table 14.4)	CFA6	CFA5	CFA4	CFA3	CFA2	CFA1–CFA0	TAG11–TAG0	SET10–SET0
1	A5	GND	A31	A30	A29	A4–A3	A28–A17	A16–A6
2	A5	GND	A31	A30	A29	A4–A3	A28–A17	A16–A6
3	A6	A5	GND	A31	A30	A4–A3	A29–A18	A17–A7
4	A6	A5	GND	A31	A30	A4–A3	A29–A18	A17–A7
5	A6	A5	GND	A31	A30	A4–A3	A29–A18	A17–A7
6	A6	A5	GND	A31	A30	A4–A3	A29–A18	A17–A7

Table 14.5: Assignment of address signals A31–A3 from Pentium and 82496 pins.

For a hit, the 82491 SRAM array transfers the data to the Pentium. For a miss, the 82496 outputs the address to the main memory, via the MCFA6–MCFA0, MSET10–MSET0 and MTAG11–MTAG0 pins, in order to execute a cache line fill. The address bus between the 82496 cache controller and the main memory is controlled by the four control signals MALE, MBALE, $\overline{\text{MAOE}}$ and $\overline{\text{MBAOE}}$. Depending on the width of the memory data bus and the number of 82491 modules, the 82491 SRAM module must be configured to the main memory with respect to the particular data bus widths. The 82491 elements operate four or eight MDATA lines, depending on the signal level that will be fed to the MX4/$\overline{8}$ pins during a reset. The width of the data bus CDATA7–CDATA0 will also be set according to the Pentium, in order to fulfil the differing configuration possibility requirements. The possible combinations and their necessary configuration signal levels are given in Table 14.6.

Configuration (see Table 14.4)	Cache size (kbytes)	Cache line size ratio	MX4/8	MTR4/8	Memory bus width (bits)	CDATA pins	MDATA pins	Bus cycles	82491 modules
1	256	1	0	1	64	8	8	4	8
2	256	2	0	0	64	8	8	8	8
3	512	1	1	1	64	4	4	4	16
4	512	2	1	0	64	4	4	8	16
5	512	2	0	1	128	4	8	4	16
6	512	4	0	0	128	4	8	8	16

Table 14.6: Data bus width and configuration signals .

If, during a reset, a low level signal is fed to the 82491 $\overline{\text{PAR}}$ pin, then the SRAM module will be configured as a parity memory. In this configuration, the pins CDATA3–CDATA0 are used to store four parity bits, and CDATA7–CDATA4 are used as activation pins allocated to the four CDATA3–CDATA0 pins. Using CDATA7–CDATA4, individual parity bits can be written or read. Two 82491 SRAM modules, irrespective of the size of cache (256 kbytes or 512 kbytes) and the memory bus width (64 bits or 128 bits), are always necessary for the operation of the complete 8-bit data bus between the Pentium and the 82491. In addition to the physical settings for cache size, memory bus width and so on, the 82496 can also be configured for the following three different snoop modes:

▶ Synchronous snoop mode: here, all relevant snooping data is read and stored synchronously to the CPU clock signal CLK. The snoop itself then takes place with the next CLK; the result is given with the subsequent clock signal. Snoops operate at their quickest in sychronized mode.

▶ Asynchronous clocked mode: here, all relevant snooping data is read and stored synchronously to an external snoop clock signal SNPCLK. Normally, SNPCLK has a reduced frequency to that of the CPU clock signal (otherwise a synchronous snoop mode could be performed). The 82496 synchronizes all external activities with CLK.

▶ Strobed snoop mode: all snoop information is read and stored with the descending edge of $\overline{\text{SNPSTB}}$ (snoop strobe). The 82496 then synchronizes all external activities with CLK.

Even the 82491 cache SRAM modules can execute two different memory bus modes; the memory bus mode determines the type and manner of the data exchange between the 82491 and the data bus to the memory:

▶ Clocked mode: all data is transferred or read synchronously to an external memory clock signal MCLK. Thus, MCLK is independent of CLK. In order to achieve maximum transfer efficiency, MCLK should be synchronized to the period, or at least to the half-period, of CLK.

▶ Strobed mode: in this mode the 82491 outputs data synchronized to a strobe signal and reads data synchronized to a (if possible, another) strobe signal.

Note that the memory bus mode is totally independent of the snoop mode; every combination is possible (a strobed memory bus mode, for example, does not necessarily lead to a strobed snoop mode).

As the final configuration possibility for the 82496/82491 cache system, there is still the setting of the strong or weak write ordering. In a system with strong write ordering – the standard setting for a system with Pentium and 82496/82491 L2 cache – all write accesses are switched through the bus in the same sequence as when they arrive from the CPU. In a system with weak write ordering, which, for this purpose, has a write buffer and, normally, a cache subsystem, the write cycle order can deviate from the order dictated by the processor. Systems with weak write ordering are more flexible and have somewhat higher performance, though the software requirement in a multiprocessor is greater, because the CPU must always be prevented from reading data that has not been updated on the grounds of a weak write order. If, during the course of a reset, the 82496 $\overline{\text{WWOR}}$ (weak write ordering) pin is fed with a low level signal, then the cache controller operates with a weak write order. Then it always specifies an active $\overline{\text{EWBE}}$ signal (external write buffer empty) to the Pentium, to indicate that the next write cycle can be executed, even if the external write buffer is not yet empty.

Finally, a few observations with regard to improved performance in connection with an L2 cache. The obtainable performance is dependent on many parameters. The number of write accesses is clearly reduced by the write-back strategy. This goes to show that the performance of the whole system is less dependent on the Pentium cache strategy as on the L2 cache strategy.

An L2 cache configured as write-back delivers a performance increase of 30% in comparison to an L2 cache with a write-through strategy. If the L1 cache is also configured as write-back, a further increase of only 5% can be expected. The reason is obvious: in most cases, no wait cycles are necessary for a Pentium write access of the L2 cache; on the other hand, this appears different for a write access of the 82496 66 MHz L2 cache controller of a 70 ns DRAM main memory. Thus, the L2 cache should always be configured as a write-back cache. Tests show, in typical application programs, that cache association plays a large role: direct mapped caches (corresponding to one-way caches) are approximately 15% slower than two-way set-associative caches. Surprisingly, the size of the cache plays a much smaller role than would be expected: the transition from a 128-kbyte cache to a 256-kbyte cache produces a 4–5% increase; a further increase to 512 kbytes, a meagre 2–2½%. The greatest significance for improved performance is as a result of the two Pentium on-chip caches, when compared to the i486. If you deactivate these caches, the performance is reduced by more than two-thirds. This result implies that, in a single processor system based on the Pentium, a moderate L2 cache brings with it an obvious, but not miraculous, performance improvement. In comparison, money is better spent on a good graphics adaptor and a faster hard disk controller, than on expensive SRAM modules to extend the L2 cache to a full 512 kbytes.

14.2.5 Cache consistency with an L2 cache

The system consisting of the Pentium and a 82496/82491 L2 cache delivers cache consistency through so-called *inclusion*. What is meant by this is that all addresses in the Pentium on-chip cache are also available in the L2 cache (of course, this does not apply in reverse, because the L2 cache is larger). Note that this does not necessarily imply that the data of these address is the same – for example, the CPU caches can have more up-to-date values than the L2. Figure 14.8 shows the inclusion schematic.

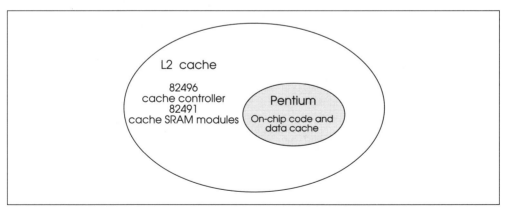

Figure 14.8: Cache consistency by inclusion.
All addresses in the Pentium on-chip caches are also present in the L2 cache.

The transfer of data between the CPU cache and the main memory takes place over the L2 cache, so that the MESI protocol (see Chapter 9) is also fully valid via the three-stepped CPU cache, L2 cache and the main memory. To this end, the MESI state of an L2 cache line always runs one step in front of the MESI state of the corresponding L1 cache line in the Pentium (in accordance with Table 9.1 and the MESI transfer diagram in Figure 9.4).

The inclusion of the on-chip caches is realized by inquiry and back invalidation cycles, as well as by a *write once policy*.

The 82496/82491 L2 cache establishes, during an inquiry cycle of the L2 cache on the Pentium, whether a certain cache line in the Pentium is available, and in that case, whether the line in the data cache is changed – that is, whether it is in the M state. The Pentium indicates a hit by the activation of the $\overline{\text{HIT}}$ signal. In addition, the Pentium produces a $\overline{\text{HITM}}$ signal (hit modified) if the searched line in the data cache has been changed. In this case the Pentium writes back the modified cache to the L2 cache, thus executing a write-back cycle to the L2 cache, in order to update the affected line where it is. Furthermore, during a back invalidation cycle, the snoop access invalidates the affected cache line; thus, the 82496 sends an active INV signal to the Pentium.

The 82496 inquiry and back invalidation cycles to the Pentium are released by the bus activities of the other Pentium/L2 cache units in the multiprocessor system. Each access by the bus master of the shared memory bus and, with this, the main memory is controlled by the memory controller of the respective Pentium/L2 cache unit (see also Figure 14.4). In this way, it is guaranteed that the cache consistency is not only secured through a Pentium/L2 cache unit, but also in the complete system. Each access of a unit practically produces a snoop in all other units. Only by this is it possible to request data from other caches, invalidate data in other caches by a write access of a bus master, and share data between several caches. 82496 inquiry and back invalidation cycles of the Pentium are executed in the following cases:

▶ An external snoop, which is issued by the bus activity of another bus master, has hit an M line in the 82496.
▶ A cache flush, from an external FLUSH signal, refers to a modified line.
▶ A synchronization of the 82496 takes place with the help of the SYNC signal, which writes back all modified cache inputs in the main memory.
▶ A line is replaced in the L2 cache; thus, a cache line fill is executed. If the same line is also available in the on-chip cache of the Pentium, then it must be replaced or at least invalidated.

The write once policy has the task of ensuring that the 82496 is always aware of the modified lines in the on-chip data cache of the Pentium. To that end, it uses the WB/$\overline{\text{WT}}$ signal to inform the Pentium of the cache strategy of the current cycle. Only then will the 82496 allow the Pentium to transfer a cache line in the exclusive state, if the same cache line in the 82496/82491 subsystem is also available in the modified state. The affected cache line must be transferred with the TBD cycle in the 82496 – that is, from the exclusive to the modified state – or it must already be in the modified state. As a result of the inclusion principle, each exclusive line in the Pentium cache is available as a modified line in the L2 cache. This causes the 82496 to execute an inquiry cycle to the Pentium for each write-back cycle, irrespective of the cause of this cycle, in order to, first, write-back the possibly modified line (Pentium on-chip caches use a write-back strategy as standard) to the L2 cache, and then to the main memory. Thus, the requirement for cache consistency is guaranteed, not only for an individual Pentium/L2 cache/main memory configuration, but also for a multiprocessor system with several such units.

14.3 Memory bus systems, powerful memory organizations and operating modes

In this section I would like to present both types of memory that can be considered for cache memory or main memory. These are dynamic and static random access memory, abbreviated as DRAM and SRAM, respectively. The background behind these abbreviations, which identify the modern and efficient working principles of these most highly integrated elements (there are approximately 10 million components on the 4-Mbit DRAM chip, and 40 million components on the 16-Mbit DRAM) are constantly being discussed. Firstly, though, to the most extensively used chip, the dynamic RAM.

14.3.1 DRAM basics

The name dynamic RAM or DRAM comes about as a result of the working principle of this memory chip: it maintains the saved information at the ready, in the form of electrical charges in a capacitor. All technically possible capacitors have, unfortunately, the annoying characteristic that they discharge slowly. After a certain amount of time the memory chip 'forgets', as it were, the saved information. In order to prevent this, from time to time the information has to be refreshed – that is, the capacitor is recharged – according to the information stored. In a DRAM, the information can therefore only remain saved through a dynamic operation, namely that of the periodical recharging of the capacitors.

Structure and function

Several functional groups, of course, are necessary for saving data, selecting information and the internal management of the DRAM. A block diagram of a dynamic RAM is given in Figure 14.9.

The main component of the memory chip is the *memory cell array*. Normally, a bit is stored in an individually addressable unit memory cell which, along with the others, is arranged in the form of a matrix of rows and columns. Thus, a 4-Mbit chip has 4 194 304 cells which are, for example, arranged in a matrix of 2048 rows and 2048 columns. The cells can be clearly identified by specifying a row and a column number.

The address buffer accepts the address, which is output by the memory controller, corresponding to the CPU address. To this end, the address is then split into two component parts – that is, a row and a column address. These are read, one after the other, into the address buffer. This is also know as multiplexing. The reason behind this separation is obvious: 22 address bits (11 for the row and 11 for the column) are necessary in order to address a cell in the 4-Mbit chip with 2048 rows and 2048 columns. If all address bits were to be transferred at the same time, then 22 address pins would also be necessary – the chip package would be very large. Furthermore, a larger address buffer would need to be integrated. All assemblies that create a link to the outside world, such as the address buffer or the data buffer, have to be strong in order to produce enough current for the control of external components. Unfortunately, strong components are large and so are detrimental to the level of chip integration.

Therefore, it is advantageous to supply the memory address in two sections. Normally, the address buffer reads in the row address followed by the column address. This address multiplexing is controlled with the help of the control signals $\overline{RAS}$ and $\overline{CAS}$. If the memory controller transfers a row address, it activates the $\overline{RAS}$ signal – that is, it lowers $\overline{RAS}$ to a low level. $\overline{RAS}$ is the abbreviation for row address strobe, and indicates to the DRAM chip that the address supplied is a row address. As a result of this, the DRAM controller activates the address buffer, reads the address in and forwards it to the row decoder, which decodes the address. If, at a later time, the memory controller feeds the column address to the address buffer, it activates the column address strobe signal $\overline{CAS}$. The DRAM controller now recognizes that the currently supplied address represents a column address. Once again, it activates the address buffer, which accepts the column address and passes it on to the column decoder. The length of the $\overline{RAS}$ and $\overline{CAS}$ signals, as well as their delay – the so-called *RAS/CAS delay* – must satisfy the requirements of the DRAM chip.

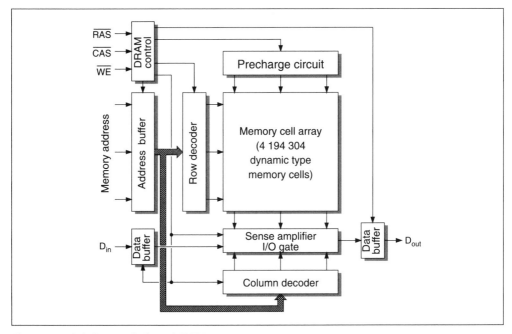

Figure 14.9: Block diagram of a dynamic RAM.
The dynamic memory cells are arranged in a matrix, the so-called memory cell array. The address buffer accepts the row and later the column address and transfers them to the row and column decoders, respectively. The two decoders drive internal lines and gates so that, after a short time, the data of the addressed memory cell is supplied to the data buffer for output, or the applied write data is written into the addressed memory cell.

The addressed cell outputs the stored data, which is amplified by a sense amplifier and fed to a data output buffer via an I/O gate. Subsequently, the buffer outputs the data as read data D_{out} to the memory element data pins.

If data has to be written, the memory controller activates the $\overline{WE}$ signal (write enable) and supplies the data to be written (D_{in}) to the data input buffer. The information is amplified by an

I/O gate and a sense amplifier and is transferred to the addressed cell, where it is stored. The precharge circuit is used for supporting the sense amplifier.

Memory control of a DRAM main memory is quite extensive, having three main tasks: separation of the CPU address into a row and a column address, correct activation of the $\overline{\text{RAS}}$, $\overline{\text{CAS}}$ and $\overline{\text{WE}}$ signals, and the transmission and receipt of read or write data. Modern memory concepts, such as interleaving and page mode, have to request flexible wait cycles and prepare the memory chips for this operating mode. From the description, you can tell that the direct address and data signal from the CPU is not suitable for a DRAM chip. Thus, external memory controllers are an important part of the computer's memory bus system.

Various organization forms of DRAM chips

The 4-Mbit chips are quite simply too large for many applications, especially if the width of the data bus is eight or more bits. For example, a fast graphics adaptor has an internal 32-bit data bus, but with a 4-Mbit chip having one data pin, 32 chips are necessary to serve the data bus. Even at today's standards, this leads to an exaggerated memory capacity of 16 Mbytes for the graphics adaptor. The solution to the problem lies in a somewhat different internal organization of the DRAM memory chips used.

The 4-Mbit chip with only one data pin has a so-called 4M word * 1-bit organization. This means that the memory chip has 4M (thus, 4 194 304) words with one bit each, therefore, having exactly one data pin. It can store or release exactly one bit per access. Another regularly used organizational form for a 4-Mbit chip is the 1M word * 4-bit organization. In this case, the DRAM chip has 1M words, each having a width of four bits, and in this case, the memory capacity is also 4 Mbits. Internally, the chip has four data input and data output buffers; furthermore, with these chips, the memory cell array is separated into at least four sub-arrays which are each assigned to one data pin. Therefore, the data can only ever be input or output, word for word, and, in this case, in sections of four bits each. In this way, 1-Mbyte single in-line memory modules (SIMMs) are, for example, produced with two 1M*4bit DRAMs for the data and 1M*1bit DRAM for the parity bits.

The first number always gives the quantity of words, the second number, the quantity of bits per word. Compared to the 4M*1 chip, the 1M*4 chip has four data pins, because during a memory access, in principle, one word of the memory chip is output (do not confuse this word with a word in the integer sense – that is, 16 bits). Especially with SRAM chips, substantially wider organizations are standard, for example, 128k*8. With four such chips you can realize a large L2 cache with a capacity of 512 kbytes and a width of 32 bits.

14.3.2 DRAM: Fast operating modes

In addition to the normal operating modes described above, when the row and column address is supplied for each access, there are also different column modes to reduce the access time. The best known of these is the page mode, which is currently supported by all modern DRAM chips. I would now like to explain briefly what is so special about this and the less well known static column, nibble and serial modes. Figure 14.10 shows the relationship of the most important memory signals, if the chip executes a read in one of these high speed modes. Examine Figure 14.10(a) and compare this with the course the signal takes in normal mode.

Page mode

Above, you should have learned that when using the activated $\overline{RAS}$ signal for access of a uniform cell, the row address is transferred, and subsequently the column address with an active $\overline{CAS}$ signal. Furthermore, internally, all memory cells of the addressed row are always read onto the corresponding bit line pairs. If the following memory access concerns a memory cell in the same row but in a different column, then the row address remains the same and only the column address is changed therefore, it is not necessary for the row address to be input and decoded again. This would only delay the access. Thus, the memory controller only changes the column address in page mode; the row address remains unaltered. Therefore, a page is exactly equivalent to a row in the memory cell array. The course of the page mode signal is given in Figure 14.10(b).

As usual, to initiate the read procedure in page mode, the memory controller first activates the $\overline{RAS}$ signal and transfers the row address. If the address is transferred to the row decoder, where it is decoded and the corresponding word line selected, then the memory controller activates the CAS signal and transfers the column address to the requested memory cell. The column decoder decodes this address and transfers the corresponding value from the addressed bit line pair to the data output buffer. Then, in normal mode, the external memory controller would deactivate the $\overline{RAS}$ and $\overline{CAS}$ signals, and the access would be ended.

When, in page mode, the memory controller accesses a memory cell of the DRAM in the same row – that is, the same page – then it does not deactivate $\overline{RAS}$ after the initial access; instead it remains active at a low level. Only the $\overline{CAS}$ signal is briefly deactivated and then after a short time, reactivated in order to inform the DRAM controller that the previously decoded row address is still valid, and that only a different column address will be supplied. Therefore, all access transistors of the selected row, which are connected with the activated word line, remain open. All data read from the bit line pairs is maintained in a stable condition by the sense amplifier. The column decoder decodes the new column address and opens the corresponding transfer gate. In page mode, therefore, the RAS precharge time, and also the transfer and decoding of the row address, do not apply to the second and all subsequent accesses to memory cells in the same row; only the column address is transferred and decoded. Thus, in page mode, when compared to normal mode, the access time is reduced by about 50% and the cycle time is reduced by as much as 70%. This is only applicable to the second and subsequent accesses. On grounds of stability, the time during which the $\overline{RAS}$ signal is active must remain short. Typically, approximately 200 accesses can be executed to a page before the memory controller has to deactivate the $\overline{RAS}$ signal for one cycle.

Operation in page mode is not just restricted to the reading of data; on the contrary, data can be written in page mode and read and write procedures can be mixed within a page, without the DRAM having to leave page mode. For a 4-Mbit chip with a memory cell array of 1024 rows for every 4096 columns, a page will still cover 1024 memory cells. If the main memory has a width of 32 bits, thus 32 4-Mbit chips are available, and a main memory page is 4 kbytes in size. The page mode can be used very effectively to reduce the access and cycle times of the memory components, because the instruction codes and most of the data tends towards blocking, and the processor rarely accesses data that is more than 4 kbytes away from the previous value. If, on the other hand, the CPU addresses a cell in another row – that is, another page – the DRAM has to leave the present page mode and the $\overline{RAS}$ precharge time, once more, comes into effect for the necessary page change. This is, of course, also valid if the $\overline{RAS}$ signal is deactivated by the memory controller after the maximum active time.

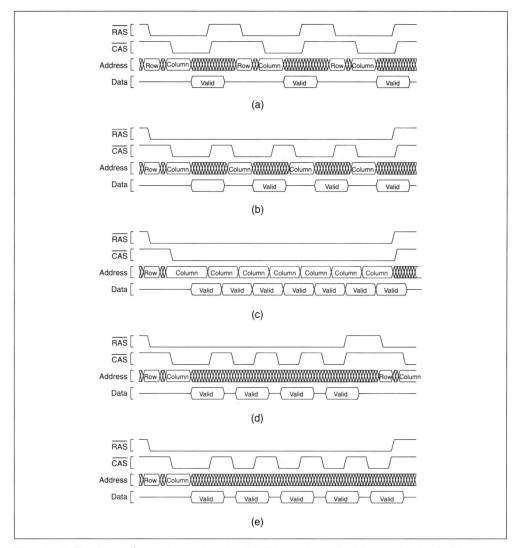

Figure 14.10: Signal course for a read access in various DRAM operation modes: (a) conventional mode, (b) page mode, (c) static column mode, (d) nibble mode and (e) serial mode.

Static column mode

Static column mode is closely linked with page mode (see Figure 14.10(c) for the course of the signal). In this case, not even the $\overline{CAS}$ signal is switched if the memory controller is supplied with a new column address. Instead, only the column address is changed, and $\overline{CAS}$ remains unaltered at a low level. After a brief response time, the internal DRAM controller itself recognizes that the column address supplied has changed. In comparison to page mode, this saves an additional part of the $\overline{CAS}$ switching and response times. Thus, static column mode is somewhat faster than page mode. Also, in this case, $\overline{RAS}$ and $\overline{CAS}$ are not allowed to be at a low level for a lengthy period of time – that is, remain active. Within the chip, only the gates that correspond to the new column address are opened to the output buffer. All memory cells within a row are randomly accessible in static column mode, as they are in page mode.

Nibble mode

Nibble mode is a simple serial mode: four data bits are successively clocked out of an addressed row (a nibble is equivalent to four bits or half a byte) by toggling $\overline{CAS}$, which is repeated four times. The first data bit is determined by the column address supplied, the other three directly follow this address. In nibble mode, the DRAM chip internally has a 4-bit intermediate buffer, which receives the four successive data bits at one time and, one after the other, writes them to the output buffer clocked by the $\overline{CAS}$ signal. This all happens very quickly, because all four addressed data bits (one explicit and three implicit) have already been transferred to the intermediate buffer. The three later data bits only have to be delayed, and not read. When compared to page mode or static column mode, nibble mode has only found a minor use for its application.

Serial mode

Serial mode can be regarded as an extended version of nibble mode. Here, too, data bits are successively clocked out of an addressed row by toggling $\overline{CAS}$. The difference, when compared to nibble mode, is that the number of $\overline{CAS}$ toggles and, thus, the data bits, is not reduced to four. Instead, in principle, the chip can output a complete row of data in series. In this case, the internal organization of the chip plays a part because, for example, a 4-Mbit chip row can have 1024, 2048 or 4096 columns. The supplied row and column addresses only identify the start of the access, when toggling $\overline{CAS}$; the DRAM chip increases the column address count independently. Serial mode is especially advantageous for the reading of video memory or the filling of a cache line, because the read accesses of the CRT controller or the cache controller are naturally serial over long distances.

14.3.3 DRAM: Advanced refresh modes

In DRAM, the data is stored in minute capacitors in the form of electrical charges. The simple one-transistor/one-capacitor memory cell permits a very high degree of DRAM chip integration. Unfortunately, there is no such thing as a perfect capacitor, not even in a DRAM chip. With time, it discharges itself over the access transistor or its dielectric. Thus, the stored charges and, therefore, the data is lost. The capacitors must therefore be recharged on a periodic basis. As I mentioned above, automatic refreshing of the memory cells in the addressed row takes place when reading or writing. Depending on the type, normal DRAM has to be refreshed every 1 to 16 ms. For this purpose, three essential but different forms of refresh are used: RAS-only refresh, CAS-before-RAS refresh and hidden refresh. You can see the signal courses of these forms of refresh in Figure 14.11.

RAS-only refresh

The simplest form of refreshing a memory cell is accomplished by the execution of a dummy read cycle, whereby the $\overline{RAS}$ signal is activated and the DRAM is supplied with a row address, the so-called refresh address, and the $\overline{CAS}$ signal remains inactive. A column address is not necessary. Internally, the DRAM then reads a row from the bit line pairs and amplifies the data that was read. However, as a result of the inactive $\overline{CAS}$ signal, the data is not transferred to the I/O line pair and, therefore, is not transferred to the data output buffer either. In order to refresh the complete memory, an external logic, or the CPU itself, will have to supply the DRAM with all of the row addresses. This form of refreshing is known as RAS-only refresh (only the $\overline{RAS}$ signal is activated). The disadvantage is that an external logic, or a program at least, is necessary in order to carry out the refreshing. For example, channel 0 of the DMA chip in the PC is periodically activated by counter 1 of the timer chips 8253/8254 and issues a dummy transfer.

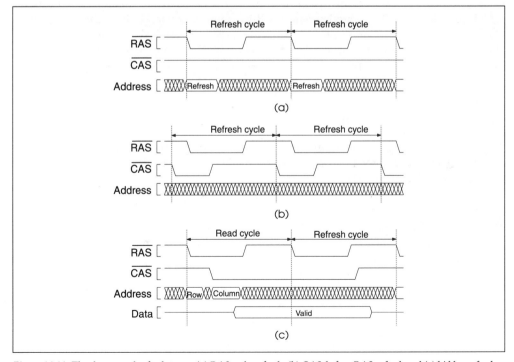

Figure 14.11: The three usual refresh types: (a) RAS-only refresh, (b) CAS-before-RAS refresh and (c) hidden refresh.

CAS-before-RAS refresh

Most modern DRAM chips also have access to one or more internal refresh modes. The most important is the so-called CAS-before-RAS refresh. To this end, an individual refresh logic with an address counter is implemented on the DRAM chip. With CAS-before-RAS refresh, the external memory controller maintains the $\overline{CAS}$ signal at a low level for a predetermined period of time before $\overline{RAS}$ drops – hence, the name 'CAS-before-RAS'. Here, the on-chip refreshing (that is, the internal refresh logic) is activated and the refresh logic executes an automatic, internal refresh. What is special about this is that the refresh address is produced internally by the address counter in the refresh logic, and does not need to be supplied externally. After each CAS-before-RAS cycle, the internal address counter is increased such that it indicates the new address to be refreshed. Refreshing is simply triggered by the memory controller; refreshing itself is performed independently by the DRAM chip.

Hidden refresh

Hidden refresh is a further, elegant time-saving possibility. Here, the refresh cycle is, as it were, 'hidden' behind a normal read access – hence, the name 'hidden'. On completion of a memory access, when using hidden refresh, the $\overline{CAS}$ signal is continually maintained at a low level and only the $\overline{RAS}$ signal is switched over. The data that was read during the read cycle will continue to be output by the DRAM chip, even during the refresh cycle. As the duration of the refresh cycle is normally shorter than the read cycle, this form of refresh saves some time. As with the CAS-before-RAS refresh, the hidden refresh DRAM address counter itself produces the refresh address. The row and column addresses given in Figure 14.11 are applicable for the read cycle. If the $\overline{CAS}$ signal is maintained at a low level for long enough, several refresh cycles can be executed one after another. For this, it is necessary to toggle the $\overline{RAS}$ signal regularly between a low and a high level.

14.3.4 Advanced memory organization

The next possibility of getting around delays caused by the $\overline{RAS}$ precharge, which would also exist for a page change or without page and static column mode, is the interleaving of different memory areas. The DRAM memory is separated into several sections, called *banks*, which are interleaved in a predetermined relationship. I would like to explain this for a Pentium two-way interleaved memory (the Pentium burst mode is ideally suited to such a memory). As a result of the Pentium 64-bit data bus, the memory is also organized with a width of 64 bits. During two-way interleaving, the memory is split into two banks, each of which is 64 bits wide. All data with even quad word addresses (such as 0000h, 0010h, 0020h, ...) can be found in the 0 bank; all data with odd quad word addresses (such as 0008h, 0018h, 0028h, ...) can be found in the 1 bank. Both banks are addressed alternatively during a sequential or burst access of the Pentium to the memory. This means that the RAS precharge time of a bank, overlaps the access time of another bank, or put another way, bank 0 is precharged, while the CPU accesses bank 1 and vice versa. Figure 14.12 shows a representation of the control and data signals.

The rate can be doubled, because the access time, and not the cycle time, is all that is relevant for the access rate of the CPU (the number of successive memory accesses per second) – the cycle time is typically double the duration of the access time. The effective access time for several successive memory accesses is halved, as it appears to the CPU. The same procedure without interleaving is shown in the lower part of Figure 14.12; the difference is easy to see.

Three-way and four-way interleaving follow the same principle, but in these cases the memory is separated into three and four banks, respectively, and instead of the $\overline{RAS}$ and $\overline{CAS}$ time shifts being halved, they are a third and a quarter of the normal cycle time. The memory must then be separated into three or four banks, respectively.

If the DRAM main memory is constructed with page mode chips, you can combine the advantages of interleaving with page mode. Today, most memories are configured as paged/interleaved memories. When interleaving with page mode, successive pages are located in different banks; in this way, a page change is executed more quickly.

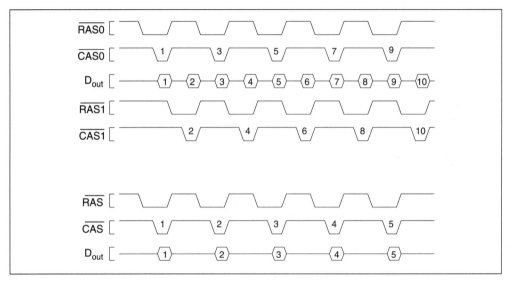

Figure 14.12: Two-way interleaving.
By means of interleaving (top) the RAS precharge time is avoided when the two memory banks are accessed alternately. Thus, only the access time, not the cycle time, of the chip is decisive. Without interleaving (below), on the other hand, the nearly twice as long cycle time is decisive for successive accesses. Repeated accesses can perform at only half the speed.

In a two-way interleaved memory, the column address $\overline{CAS1}$ signal for bank 1 is, when compared to the $\overline{CAS0}$ signal for bank 0, phase delayed by 180°. Bank 0 accepts column addresses, decodes them and outputs data, whereas the scan signal $\overline{CAS1}$ for bank 1 is inactive in order to change the column address, and vice versa. Thus, when compared to a simple interleaving or page mode, the access rate is increased. With normal interleaving, the DRAMs are interleaved as double words or quad words, depending on the width of the memory, whereas with page/interleaving, this is achieved on a page basis. If a $\overline{RAS}$ precharge cycle is necessary for a page change, the access will, with a 50% probability, take place in the other bank; thus, for page changes, interleaving is conveyed in the same manner as normal memory operation. Tests using typical application programs show that, on average, a two-way interleaving produces a performance increase of just under 10%; further interleaving to a four-way, however, will only produce an additional increase of just below 4%. A two-way interleaving organization of the

DRAM therefore represents the best compromise (especially if an L2 cache is available) between performance, on one hand, and a simple and cheap DRAM controller on the other.

The innovative concepts described above, such as page or static column mode and interleaving, do not always lead to success. After all, they have a simple statistical foundation. As I have already mentioned, it is necessary for memory accesses to occur on the same page, so that the benefits of page mode can be reaped. As in normal mode, a page change leads to a RAS precharge time and, therefore, to a delay. In the same manner, it is necessary for interleaving to be advantageous, that, with the Pentium 64-bit data bus, the accesses alternatively take place between odd and even quad word addresses. However, if the Pentium grasps an odd or even quad word address twice, one after the other, then in this case, the RAS precharging makes itself known as being disadvantageous. Luckily, code and data tend to form blocks; furthermore, prefetching runs sequentially so that in most cases (but not always) page mode and interleaving notably increase the access rate of the memory. Typically, for page/interleaving, the hit rate is in the region of 80%. Intelligent memory controllers are a prerequisite. For page mode, they must know whether the access takes place in the same page, or, with interleaving, whether the other bank should be addressed. If this is not achieved, the memory controller has to implement flexible wait states until the DRAMs react, by either making the data available, or being ready to accept data. Of course, for the Pentium main memory, only fast DRAMs with page or static column mode and a two-way interleaved organization come into question. Therefore, in the most advantageous of cases, DRAMs can attain an access time of approximately 30 ns; this represents one wait cycle during a memory access.

14.3.5 SRAM

In this section, I would like discuss the fastest of the memory components currently available, the SRAM. With SRAM, the information is not stored as a charge in a capacitor. Instead, it is retained as the state of a special circuit. Normally, a flip-flop is used, which has two stable states that can be switched over by a strong external signal – which is what is implied by the name 'flip-flop'. The structure of the SRAM cell is substantially more complicated than that of a DRAM memory cell. The integration of a SRAM memory cell is only possible with the assistance of extremely complicated technological processes, therefore SRAM components are expensive and usually have reduced memory capacity when compared to DRAM chips. SRAMs are used on this basis, in the first instance, for small and fast cache memories, whereas DRAM chips are used for the larger and slower main memories. Very good SRAM chips in ECL or BiCMOS technology attain an access time of 10 ns, CMOS SRAMs between 15 and 25 ns.

The flip-flop is identified as being a bistable multivibrator, because it can be switched by external signals between two stable internal states. The existence of a pair of stable states leads to a form of hysteresis in the characteristics of the flip-flop; the larger the hysteresis, the greater the state stability and the greater the extent required to switch the flip-flop between both states. This occurs through a strong electrical signal when writing data.

SRAM chips do not carry out multiplexing of row and column addresses. Instead, row and column addresses are supplied simultaneously. Thus, a SRAM chip requires substantially more address pins; its package is much larger than that of a DRAM. The SRAM then splits the address internally into a row and column address.

In contrast to the DRAM, no lengthy RAS/CAS recovery times are necessary; under normal circumstances, the specified access time is always equal to the SRAM cycle time. Advanced DRAM memory concepts such as page mode, static column mode or interleaving offer no real advantage as a result of the absence of address multiplexing and RAS recovery time. Thus, SRAM chips are always operated in 'normal mode', whereby row and column addresses are always supplied.

As a result of the simultaneous supply of row and column addresses, the memory controller for SRAM chips is substantially simpler than that for DRAMs. The internal control of memory cells is easier, because no complex modes such as page or static column mode need to be executed. Refreshing is also unnecessary as a result of the static design; the state of the memory flip-flops remains constant as long as the SRAM chip is supplied with a voltage. These characteristics simplify the SRAM chip periphery when compared to that of the DRAM chips, somewhat equalizing the substantially complicated memory cell structure. In spite of this, the density of integration of DRAM chips is approximately four times greater than that of SRAM chips using the same technology.

15 Bus systems

In this chapter I would like to introduce the latest bus systems, as used by the Pentium. As a result of its compatibility with the whole 80x86 family, its field of application lies, naturally, in the area of the PC – or, when considering a 166 MIPS processor, should we be speaking of a personal *workstation*? The enormous performance of calculations requires a very effective bus system; only EISA, microchannel or the new local bus systems come into question. Still, I will mention the ISA bus briefly, because it is expected that some manufacturers will combine local bus slots with ISA bus slots, in order to, on one hand, achieve compatibility in the area of I/O adaptor boards and, on the other, to use the enormous transfer capacity of a highly clocked local bus.

15.1 ISA and Pentium

To begin with, IBM introduced the so-called AT bus with the AT, but it was never clearly defined; all standards in this area were, therefore, rather weak. Seven years after the introduction of the AT, the computer industry finally agreed to a (fairly) defined standard for the AT bus, the result being the ISA bus, which is almost fully orientated to the AT bus of the original IBM AT. ISA is the abbreviation for *Industry Standard Architecture* – thus, ISA should define the bus standard for manufacturers of AT compatible PCs.

Among other things, this standard specifies that the bus slots should operate with a maximum of 8.33 MHz (the fundamental difference of the local bus is simply the higher bus frequencies of up to 50 MHz). The slot clock frequency is created by parts of the CPU clock. In comparison, the main memory on the mother board runs at the full processor frequency, even if this is 100 MHz. At best, the memory controller instructs the CPU to insert corresponding wait cycles if the RAM component is too slow. If a 100-MHz Pentium wishes to access an area of memory, which can only be reached via the ISA 16-bit slots, it has to insert a large number of wait states. A bus cycle that is being read requires, for example, two bus clock cycles; but in this instance, one bus clock cycle is 12 times longer than a CPU clock cycle, so 24 CPU clock cycles are necessary – and all this for a bus width of just 16 bits. The maximum transfer rate of the ISA bus is a mere 8.33 Mbytes/s, compared to a Pentium burst transfer rate of more than 500 Mbytes/s – a factor of 60! As it is, this impressively goes to show that the ISA bus, on its own, is totally unsuitable for a Pentium system. If, in the ISA slots, only serial and parallel ports or other adaptors with a minimal transfer rate (this also includes even 10 Mbits/s Ethernet adaptors) are used, and if the critical components, such as graphical adaptors and hard disk controllers, for example, are addressed via the local bus, then the ISA bus can be tolerated as a standard expansion bus for low end Pentium systems.

The bus frequency is attained by dividing the CPU clock – thus, the bus essentially works synchronously with the CPU. This is totally different, for example, when working with microchannel, which has its own clock generator for the bus, such that the microchannel works asynchronously to the CPU. The ISA bus also carries out asynchronous cycles, for example, if a DMA chip, which is run at 5 MHz (a tall order, even for an i386 or i486 system), initiates a bus cycle. The fixed clocking of the ISA bus leads to the constant input of wait cycles from the bus controller, especially when related to components operating asynchronously, even if an adaptor is too slow by only a few nanoseconds. Thus, EISA permits the extending of such cycles, in order to avoid unnecessary wait states. A bus is rather more than just a contact strip on the mother board, which for an AT, encompasses a mere 98 contacts. In addition to the shape of the bus slots and the signal levels, the ISA standard also defines time characteristics for the address, data and control signals. In the following paragraphs I would like to outline briefly the architecture of an ISA or AT system and the ISA part of a local bus system (see Section 15.4).

The processor is the central component in the latest systems, including the i386, the i486 and the Pentium; in the original AT you will find the 80286. The physical address space accessible via the ISA bus is a mere 16 Mbytes due to the 24-bit address bus of the 80286. The ISA standard (like EISA) makes provision for five different address buses:

▶ Local address bus: this includes the 24 to 32 address signals from the CPU (only 24 in the 80286; 32 in all others). An external address buffer and address latches separate the local bus from the system bus.

▶ System address bus: this is, essentially, the ISA address bus and includes the latched address bits A0–A19 of the local address bus – the system address bus is, therefore, merely a 20-bit address bus (a hangover from the stone age PC, which began with the 8086/88 and its 20-bit address bus). With the ISA system, the system address bus is implemented as A0–A19, together with the L-address bus, in the bus slots.

▶ Memory address bus: this address bus is only implemented on the mother board. The row and column addresses are transferred, one after the other, to the DRAM chips (see Section 14.3.1); it is therefore multiplexed. Its width is dependent upon the installed memory controller.

▶ X-address bus: this serves the purpose of addressing the I/O units and the ROM BIOS on the mother board like, for example, the register of the interrupt controller. However, I/O ports and the ROM BIOS on expansion adaptors are addressed via the system address bus.

▶ L-address bus: this address bus consists of the seven most significant (L = large) and unlatched address bits A17–A23 of the local address bus. Together with the system address bus, it is implemented in ISA slots. Thus, the address bits A17–A19 are available twice.

Furthermore, four different data buses are provided for ISA:

▶ Local data bus: this includes the 16 or 32 data signals from the processor (only 16 in the 80286; 32 in all others).

▶ System data bus: this represents the latched version of the local bus and is 16 bits wide. The system data bus ends at the ISA slots.

▶ Memory data bus: this data bus is only available on the mother board; it creates the connection between main memory and the system data bus. Normally, the memory data bus has the same width as the processor data bus, in order to achieve a maximum rate of data transfers between the CPU and the main memory.

▶ X-data bus: this addresses I/O units and the ROM BIOS on the mother board. However, I/O ports and additional BIOSs on expansion adaptors are supplied from the system data bus.

The ISA bus only supports the CPU and the DMA chips on the mother board, unrestricted, as a bus master. No pure bus master on external plug-in boards in the bus slots can operate and control the ISA bus. This is not acceptable for a powerful computer with a multitasking operating system or multiprocessor system. An important goal with the introduction of EISA and multiprocessor systems was, therefore, the support of an external bus master; for example, to accelerate data transfers in a LAN. With the ISA bus, transfer of the bus control is only achieved via a DMA channel and not through a master request.

Several support chips are provided by the ISA standard for support of the CPU and peripheral devices. Two programmable interrupt controllers (PIC) 8259A are available, a master PIC and a slave PIC. Thus, 15 IRQ levels are available in an ISA PC. Meanwhile, the PIC 8259A is more than 15 years old; in addition to this, it is part of the 8-MHz ISA bus. You cannot expect real performance miracles. On this basis, the 82489DX advanced programmable interrupt controller was developed for the Pentium, which can also be used in conjunction with the i486. The priority of the interrupt channels in an ISA system is predetermined. Interrupts with high priority mask all interrupts with a lower priority.

In an ISA system, in addition to the CPU, two DMA chips 8237A are available as the second data transfer channel between memory and the I/O address space. They are cascaded so that a total of seven DMA channels are available. The first four channels serve 8-bit peripheral units (back to the dark ages again); the three channels 5 to 7 are set aside for 16-bit peripheral devices.

To complete the picture (and even though these components no longer belong to the ISA bus) I would like to mention that one more CMOS RAM is available, which stores the system configuration and makes the BIOS available when booting. EISA and microchannel extend this concept further: here, also, you can determine the DMA and IRQ channels used by plug-in boards, using a more friendly program, by an input in an expanded CMOS RAM. Together with the CMOS RAM, a real time clock is integrated, which, even when the PC is switched off, constantly updates the date and time.

All support chips are addressed via ports in the address space; ISA systems usually use an I/O mapped input/output.

In ISA systems with an i386 or i486 processor, the internal data and address buses of the mother board are usually a full 32 bits wide. However, as in the original AT, the bus slots only end in 24 address lines and 16 data lines. Shifting to 32-bit values for the 32-bit data bus is achieved using a special swapper and buffer. The whole thing becomes rather crass if a Pentium is installed. It has a 64-bit data bus, whereas an ISA bus has one of only 16 bits. In addition to the apparently poor relationship between the data transfer rate of the Pentium bus in burst mode (about 500 Mbytes/s compared to 8 Mbytes/s), this is a further reason why the ISA bus has justification for being, at the most, an additional expansion channel to a local bus.

15.2 EISA and Pentium

The term EISA, an abbreviation for *Extended ISA*, already indicates the evolutionary concept of 32-bit expansion for the AT bus. During the development of EISA, the maxim was the total problem-free inclusion of ISA components into the EISA system. The pure EISA adaptors inform the EISA system, via control signals ($\overline{EX32}$ and $\overline{EX16}$), that it concerns EISA components with extended functions, which are provided for EISA. Internally, though, EISA machines differ greatly, in many ways, from their ISA predecessors. Only 16- or 32-bit EISA components use the advantages of the EISA bus system, for example the burst cycles or 32-bit DMA. The EISA bus manages a data transfer rate of up to 33 Mbytes/s compared to 8.33 Mbytes/s for the ISA bus. This is still a lot lower than the Pentium's transfer rate of more than 500 Mbytes/s. Now, with the 33 Mbytes/s (and even 66 or 133 Mbytes/s with enhanced master burst) it is no longer the bus that acts as a brake; more so, the hard disk and other peripheral devices reveal themselves to be the cause of the bottleneck.

Technically speaking, the EISA is more complicated than microchannel, because EISA not only has to execute EISA cycles, but, on the grounds of compatibility, it also has to execute ISA cycles. This affects, for example, DMA, where the EISA system must decide whether an 8237A compatible DMA cycle with its known disadvantages should be executed, or a full valued 32-bit DMA cycle. The hardware must be able to do both and is, therefore, very complicated. In this respect, microchannel has had it easier – it simply threw the unsuitable concept of the PC/XT/AT overboard, and started again from scratch. The same applies for the local bus. Nevertheless, EISA should be given consideration as an efficient bus system, mainly for compatibility, because an excessive number of adaptor cards are available for almost every conceivable application.

15.2.1 The EISA bus architecture

Figure 15.1 shows a schematic diagram of the EISA architecture. The clock generator supplies the Pentium as well as the EISA bus, after the frequency has been reduced in the frequency divider. EISA is, therefore, a synchronous bus system, because the CPU and the EISA bus are supplied with the same clock signal and, therefore, work synchronously. Like ISA, the maximum frequency for the EISA bus lies at 8.33 MHz. This frequency determines the access of the CPU to all external units in the EISA channel. The Pentium is allowed to continue to access the main memory at maximum clock frequency, in so far as it is not braked by wait cycles. The EISA bus buffer serves the purpose of controlled data transfers between the local bus and the EISA bus.

The heart of the EISA bus is the EISA bus controller. It distinguishes EISA from ISA bus cycles, generates all of the necessary ISA and EISA bus signals, controls normal and burst cycles, and manages the complete control of the bus in the EISA PC. Together with the data swapper, it divides 32-bit quantities into parts, putting them into 8- or 16-bit portions for 8- and 16-bit peripheral units, or rejoins such portions to form a 32-bit quantity. This is necessary, for example, if you insert a 16-bit ISA adaptor in an EISA slot.

EISA plug-in boards with their own bus master contain a bus master interface, which makes it possible for the local CPU (the bus master) to control the EISA bus independently. EISA is, therefore, a large step towards a multiprocessor environment – a necessity for the Pentium, conceived from the start as an element in a multiprocessor system.

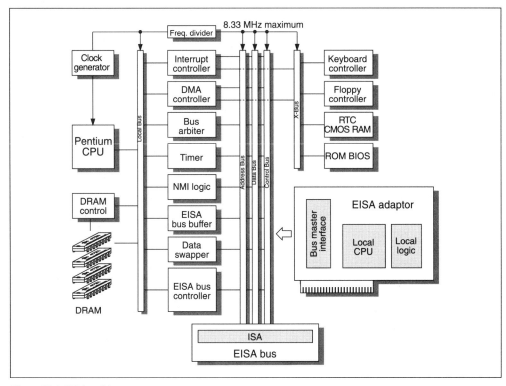

Figure 15.1: EISA architecture.

The EISA bus can execute various bus cycles:

▶ standard bus cycle
▶ burst cycle
▶ bus cycle with BCLK stretching
▶ enhanced master burst cycles EMB-66 and EMB-133

The standard bus cycle is a normal Pentium single transfer cycle, as far as the performing of the applicable address, data and control signals are concerned. As the EISA bus runs at a maximum bus clock BCLK of 8.33 MHz, a large number of CPU wait cycles are necessary, even for a slow clocked i386 CPU. The standard cycle requires two BCLK cycles for the transfer of a 32-bit value. The EISA burst cycle corresponds to the burst mode of the i486, except that the bus clock BCLK instead of the CPU clock PCLK is used. Note that the Pentium burst mode deviates from that of the i486. The Pentium only outputs the memory address for the first data transfer of a burst cycle; for all subsequent transfers, the subsystem has to create its own addresses in accordance with Table 12.1. This difference between the Pentium burst mode and the EISA bus has no real relevance. The Pentium only executes a burst mode for a cache line fill or write-back. A cache line fill or write-back merely affects the main memory, which is connected to the memory bus on the mother board, and operates at the full external 66 MHz of the Pentium. In contrast, the EISA bus is not affected by such fast data transfers. The only plausible possibility would be a cache line fill or write-back that has the video RAM and a graphic adaptor as a transfer source and destination, respectively. Normally, these address areas are identified as being non-cacheable because, ultimately, all changes to the video RAM should also be shown on the monitor. Thus, the EISA burst mode solely uses the DMA chips, which can execute a burst transfer in EISA DMA mode C, in the same way as in the i486.

In addition to the burst cycle, the bus cycle with BCLK stretching is also new. The EISA bus controller can extend a half cycle of BCLK, in order to serve slower units optimally, and subsequently to re-establish the synchronization of the CPU frequency. Thus, the number of wait cycles for slower peripheral units is reduced and the system throughput is improved. With the aid of BCLK stretching, the EISA bus can insert half wait cycles, because the increase is only a half cycle of BCLK.

The advance of VLB and PCI is also reflected by the EISA specification. The EISA interest group has recently defined a new *enhanced master burst cycle*, which should increase the transfer rate up to 66 Mbytes/s (EMB-66) or even 133 Mbytes/s (EMB-133). To achieve this, a data transfer is no longer only triggered by the ascending BCLK edge: both the ascending and the descending BCLK edges can issue a data transfer. Thus, the transfer rate is doubled, while the bus frequency remains unchanged at a maximum of 8.33 MHz for compatibility reasons. Together with a data bus width of 32 bits, this leads to a transfer rate of 66 Mbytes/s. To reach the mentioned 133 Mbytes/s, the 32-bit address part of the EISA bus is additionally used for the data transfer, since this part is unused during the data transfer phase in burst mode. Therefore, the data bus width increases to 64 bits.

15.2.2 EISA bus arbitration

When compared to the ISA bus, an important advance is the flexible bus arbitration. This means that even an external microprocessor on an EISA plug-in board has full control over the bus and, thus, can access the system's main memory, the hard disk and all other system components, without the need for assistance from the Pentium. This is necessary for an efficient multiprocessor operation if, for example, a LAN controller wishes to access the main memory and the hard disk, in order to handle a LAN query. Such external EISA bus masters can request bus control from the Pentium to the mother board, via a special EISA control signal (MREQ, master request). The host CPU – the Pentium – thus represents the standard bus master.

For allocation of the EISA bus to different bus masters, the EISA uses an arbitration model with three levels: DMA/refresh (highest level), CPU/master, and other master (lowest level). Several masters may be available on each level; then, within the affected level, the bus is allocated in a rotational sequence. The memory refresh has the highest priority, because a blocking of the refresh by another master would lead to loss of data from the main memory. If the refresh control requests the bus, via an arbitration, it always receives the refresh after a short response time; all other requesting bus masters must wait until the requested refresh cycle has ended.

EISA bus masters do not have to look after refresh of the main memory on the mother board; this is achieved by its own refresh logic. In contrast, in an ISA system using primitive arbitration, the pseudo-ISA bus master has to take control of an ISA adaptor and also memory refreshing, via a DMA channel, if it has control of the bus.

15.2.3 EISA DMA system

The EISA DMA system is also greatly improved when compared to the ISA standard. Now, for each DMA transfer, not only is the full 32-bit address space available (with ISA, only 64-kbyte or 128-kbyte blocks are allowed), but EISA also implements three modern DMA operating modes with improved data throughput: the DMA types A, B and C. The mode, known from the ISA standard, is identified by the EISA as being a compatible mode. In compatible mode, as with the ISA bus, addresses are produced for the same clock cycles with identical clock length, as is the case with the 8237A.

The new EISA operating type A for the DMA reduces the memory phase of the DMA transfer; the I/O phase remains the same. A DMA cycle is executed in six BCLK cycles, and the maximum data throughput increases to (an appalling) 5.56 Mbytes/s. Modern ISA units can be operated without problems in an EISA system in DMA mode A. With DMA type B, the I/O cycle is also shorter, so that only four BCLK cycles are necessary for a DMA transfer. The data throughput runs at a maximum of 8.33 Mbytes/s. The burst type C is exclusively for EISA units that support EISA burst cycles. Here, one DMA transfer is executed in a single BCLK cycle. Using the DMA burst type C, with full use of the 32-bit width of the EISA data bus, DMA transfer rates of up to 33 Mbytes/s can be achieved – the maximum value for the EISA bus. With EISA, the transfer of data that has been read from, or data to be written to, the hard disk via DMA once again becomes interesting.

Control of the EISA DMA channels is no longer achieved following a predetermined stepped priority as with AT; instead, it is distributed over three levels, within which the channels are given out according to a rotational pattern. This should prevent a peripheral unit with a high DMA priority from blocking the other units that have a low priority, with numerous DMA requests. In addition, compared to the AT, this contrived DMA hierarchy serves to support multitasking operating systems, in which several tasks fight over the DMA channels. The microchannel follows a similar strategy. EISA is provided with a total of seven DMA channels, which can serve 8-, 16- or 32-bit devices.

15.2.4 The EISA interrupt system

Like the ISA, the EISA is provided with 15 interrupt levels, which are managed by the EISA interrupt controller. Here also, on grounds of compatibility with ISA, IRQ2 is occupied by cascading. The EISA interrupt controller conducts itself in exactly the same way as both of the cascaded PICs 8259A in the AT. Something new is that the occupied interrupt channels of the EISA boards can also work with level triggering in place of edge triggering. The level of an IRQ line above a certain value then releases an interrupt request, and not the increase itself. Thus, it is possible for several sources to share an IRQ. ISA, however, exclusively uses edge triggering for the release of an interrupt. Because the interrupt subsystem of a computer represents a pure hardware component, the new 82489DX can also be used in place of the really old 8259A. The ROM BIOS, as hardware-like software, only has to undertake approved intialization and serve the 82489DX accordingly.

15.2.5 EISA adaptors and automatic configuration

You will search in vain for the DIP switches on EISA adaptors; sometimes the configuration of ISA boards leads to a lottery with an uncertain outcome. EISA eradicates the configuration problem much more simply and efficiently: each EISA adaptor is accompanied by a disk with the configuration data (CFG = configuration file). The CFG stores the required system elements of the EISA PC, such as, for example, the occupied IRQ and DMA channels. The information is used by the configuration utility, which is supplied with every EISA PC, for correctly configuring the PC and adaptors.

The configuration information is saved in the extended CMOS RAM. With EISA, the CMOS RAM is extended by 4 kbytes. Typical information is which I/O ports of the adaptor should be used, which IRQ and DMA channels of the adaptor are occupied, and so on. This EISA system information can be called through various functions of the INT 15h. Other peripheral units on the mother board are addressed via the X-bus. With EISA, the CFG data mentioned was part of the total concept right from the start – the companies involved in EISA have agreed to a standard for the data format.

15.2.6 EISA slots

EISA has a total of 90 new contacts, provided for the expansion of the ISA bus from 16 to 32 bits, of which currently only 16 are used as data lines, 23 as address lines and 16 as control and status lines. In addition to the 98 ISA contacts already available, the 90 new contacts would lead to a gigantic EISA contact strip on the mother board, which would be larger than the board itself. With microchannel, this problem can be overcome in that the contacts are simply smaller and placed closer together. Thus, microchannel is already incompatible.

In order to be able to integrate ISA elements in an EISA system, the geometry of the EISA slots must be harmonized with the existing ISA boards. For this purpose, EISA is provided with a second level of contacts in the EISA contact strip, which, when compared to former ISA contacts, are so transposed that they can only be reached by an EISA board. ISA boards cannot short circuit the contacts, because an ISA board cannot penetrate deep enough into the EISA slot. Coding bridges in the slots prevent false insertion of an EISA board, or the too deep insertion of an ISA board into the slot, whereby the contact would be short circuited. Considering its enormous number of contacts, the EISA slot is very compact and, in addition, it is 100 % compatible with ISA plug-in boards, which have only one level of contacts.

15.3 Microchannel and Pentium

With the introduction of microchannel, and with respect not only to the architecture but also to the geometrical structure of the bus slots, IBM crossed over into completely new areas. Microchannel no longer represents the completely open architecture that the manufacturer and user are accustomed to with PC/XT/AT. Associated with the large functional extent of microchannel, it can be referred to as being the radical transformation on the path to a proper 32-bit system. Right from the start, microchannel was stigmatized as being incompatible with existing AT architecture. This argument lost its meaning entirely with the introduction of the even less compatible local bus systems. This architecture became firmly established, not least as a result of the hitherto unaccustomed price offensive (this, of course, was not entirely voluntary) placed upon IBM. The considerable linearity and consequent orientation in the direction of powerful computers (for example, using the 64-bit streaming data procedures) allows for greater efficiency, making microchannel an interesting alternative to EISA and the local bus systems.

Identical problems usually lead to similar solutions – it is no great surprise that, apart from a totally incompatible bus slot, microchannel is not much different to EISA. Subsequently, at operating system level and, of course, at user level, compatibility with AT should exist. Programs that do not explicitly access the register of the computer hardware run without problem on a PS/2 machine and without you noticing any difference.

15.3.1 The MCA bus architecture

Figure 15.2 shows a schematic block diagram for the microchannel architecture (MCA). A big difference, when compared to EISA, is the separate system clock generator, which supplies all components of the microchannel with a frequency of 10 MHz maximum. Only the memory bus between the CPU and memory runs faster, in order to execute the CPU data access of the main memory at maximum speed (with a Pentium, up to 66 MHz). Thus, the microchannel is an asynchronous bus system; the CPU is supplied by its own CPU clock.

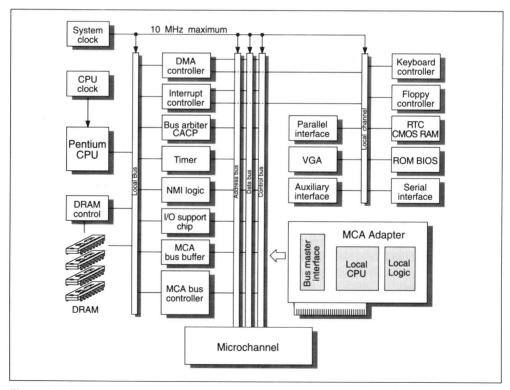

Figure 15.2: Microchannel architecture.

Initially, three different bus cycles were provided when microchannel was introduced:

▶ standard bus cycle
▶ synchronous extended bus cycle
▶ asynchronous extended bus cycle

The standard bus cycle is equivalent to a standard CPU bus cycle of 10 MHz without wait cycles. Wait cycles are inserted for extended bus cycles via a control signal (CHRDY) from the addressed unit. If CHRDY is actively synchronized with the data bus cycle of the MCA bus cycle, this is said to be a synchronous extended bus cycle; otherwise, asynchronous. Note that with this, CHRDY affects the 10 MHz bus clock and not the CPU clock, which can be much greater with a Pentium of 100 MHz. The Pentium always inserts several CPU wait cycles for an access to the microchannel; these are, however, controlled by the bus controller via the processor $\overline{\text{READY}}$ signal. Without wait cycles, an MCA bus cycle lasts two bus clock cycles for every 100 ns. Initially, microchannel was constructed with a maximum data transfer rate of 20 Mbytes/s (in special burst mode, the EISA attained 33 Mbytes/s). Using certain MCA control signals ($\overline{\text{MMC}}$ and $\overline{\text{MMCR}}$), the transfer rate for so-called matched memory cycles can be increased to 21.4 Mbytes/s. This is worth mentioning in order to complete the picture (only the model 80 operated at 16 MHz).

An important jump to higher transfer rates, which are adequate for fast clocked processors with a 32- or even 64-bit data bus, is represented by the *streaming data procedures* (SDPs) concept. Currently three SDPs have been conceived:

▶ 32-bit SDP
▶ 64-bit SDP
▶ extended 64-bit SDP

IBM not only uses the microchannel in its PS/2 series, but also in the substantially more powerful workstations, based on the RISC System/6000. These demand a vastly higher data throughput over that of a PC based on the i386, the high-end chip at the time when the microchannel came into the market.

With its signal flow, the 32-bit SDP is identical to the i486 burst mode. Note, however, that the Pentium implements a different burst mode to that of the i486. On the same grounds as above, the differences are negligible for an access of components in the microchannel. In order to request a 32-bit SDP, the bus master deactivates a control signal of the microchannel, namely $\overline{\text{BLAST}}$ (burst last). The addressed unit responds with a BRDY (burst ready), in order to show that it can execute a 32-bit burst mode. Now, for a 32-bit SDP, 4 bytes are transferred with every MCA bus clock. With this, the data transfer rate temporarily increases to 40 Mbytes/s. This is somewhat more than the burst mode of the EISA bus at 33 Mbytes/s.

A further increase can be achieved with the aid of the 64-bit SDP. In this case, the address is only transferred during the first bus cycle; the addressed unit accepts it and stores it (this corresponds to the Pentium burst mode). Subsequently, the data is transferred over both the 32-bit data bus and the 32-bit address bus – that is, with a total width of 64 bits or 8 bytes. The addressed unit has an address counter, which, in 64-bit SDP, counts up the addresses independently and so only requires the start address from the CPU. 64-bit SDPs achieve a transfer rate of 80 Mbytes/s. The extended 64-bit SDP is even more powerful. Here, the bus cycle is reduced from 100 to 50 ns; the bus frequency is thus doubled to 20 MHz. The actual transfer operates like that of the normal 64-bit SDP, but at 20 MHz. This gives rise to a transfer rate of 160 Mbytes/s, close to five times the transfer rate for the EISA. Note that this refers to the transfer rate in microchannel and not the transfer rate between the Pentium and memory. Microchannel typically serves hard disks and network adaptors. Thus, the 160 Mbytes/s should be adequate for the next couple of years. The disadvantage of the 64-bit SDPs is that additional control signals are necessary, which indicate whether such a transfer should be executed. Up until now, they have not been implemented in the PS/2 series. This will probably be changed soon for high-end machines, such as powerful Pentium-based servers, for example, especially in response to the local bus systems.

15.3.2 The MCA bus arbitration

Similarly to EISA, MCA also supports an external bus master on adaptor boards; with the inclusion of the CPU, a maximum of 16 different bus masters can be integrated. For this purpose, IBM has provided an element, the so-called *central arbitration control point (CACP)*, which undertakes the bus arbitration and transfer of control to a bus master. For MCA, bus masters can be the CPU of the mother board, the refresh logic, the DMA controller and the external bus master of adaptor boards. Memory refresh is assigned priority 2. This means that if a refresh has to be executed, the arbitration logic of the refresh always transfers control via the bus. Memory refreshing takes place on the mother board and controls the arbitration logic via an internal signal (refresh request). The lowest priority is assigned to the CPU. Thus, the mother board CPU always has control over the system bus, if no other bus master requests control of the bus.

Using a control signal, namely $\overline{\text{PREEMPT}}$, all other bus masters can request control of the bus. The bus arbitration gives control to one of the requesting bus masters, corresponding to a strategy based on equal treatment. Each bus master adaptor has a local bus arbiter, which drives $\overline{\text{PREEMPT}}$ and the arbitration control signals of the adaptor board. If a bus master does not return control within 7.8 µs, the CACP interprets this as being an error. It then separates the bus master from the bus, transfers control to the CPU and releases an NMI.

15.3.3 The MCA DMA subsystem

In view of their functions, the microchannel support chips do not differ significantly from their EISA counterparts. However, they are completely harmonized with the new bus system. Thus, in a 32-bit microchannel, the DMA controller always carries out a 32-bit DMA transfer for the complete address space – no 8237A-compatible DMA transfers are executed. Moreover all eight DMA channels can be active simultaneously. MCA is really well directed to multitasking operating systems.

15.3.4 The MCA interrupt subsystem

In addition to the bus system and the DMA controller, the interrupt controller is also harmonized with the new architecture. All interrupt channels work exclusively with level triggering, whereas with EISA the interrupts can be level or edge triggered in order to insert

ISA adaptors into EISA slots, like, for example, serial interfaces, which work exclusively with edge triggering. Several sources can share an interrupt line IRQx as a result of pure level triggering. Furthermore, level triggering is less susceptible to disruption than edge triggering, because an erroneous impulse only releases a brief increase in current, whereas for level triggering, a much greater level is necessary. There are 255 possible different hardware interrupts for the microchannel; in the AT, only 15 are authorized. On grounds of compatibility, the occupation of the IRQ lines and the assigning of hardware interrupts and associated interrupt vectors is agreed for the AT and EISA.

15.3.5 MCA adaptors and automatic configuration

Here, when compared with the old AT concept, an important advantage is that an adaptor board can be identified automatically by the system. Like their EISA counterparts, microchannel adaptors are no longer configured via a jumper; instead, they are configured through dialogue with the supplied system software. Since IBM was responsible for developing microchannel, it allocates a reference number for every adaptor from any manufacturer, which can be read and evaluated by the system. Even third-party manufacturers receive such reference numbers for their MCA products; this is managed centrally by IBM. As with EISA, the configuration information is deposited in an extended CMOS RAM. The individual MCA slots, and therefore also the implemented MCA adaptors, can be addressed individually. With this, MCA slots are directed as being active or suspended. This is advantageous if a plug-in board is defective, or at least suspect. It is deactivated without problem, until the repair technician arrives, there being no need for you to take the PC apart to remove the board. Consequently, for example, you can operate two adaptors alternately, which would normally interfere with each other, without having to constantly fiddle with the PC.

15.3.6 The MCA slot

After deciding to throw the AT concept overboard, IBM was of course free to redesign the layout of the bus slots. 8-, 16- and 32-bit slots are required, with the 8-bit slot already implementing all of the important control lines. The kernel of the MCA slot is the 8-bit section with its 90 contacts. Unlike EISA, the MCA slot only has contacts on a single layer, but they are much narrower and every fourth contact of a row is ground or at the power supply level. The ground and supply contacts on both sides are shifted by two positions so that, effectively, every second contact pair has a ground or supply terminal. By the defined potential of these contacts, the noise resistance is significantly better than on an AT.

Besides the 8-bit section there are various extensions: the 16-bit section for 16-bit MCA adaptors, the 32-bit section for 32-bit MCA adaptors, the video extension for additional graphics adaptors, and the matched memory extension for memories with a higher access rate. The 16-bit PS/2 models do not have any 32-bit extensions, of course. Because of the narrow contacts, the MCA slot is nevertheless quite compact, although it holds up to 202 contacts.

15.4 Peripheral component interconnect PCI bus

At 8 MHz and 10 MHz, respectively, the maximum clock frequencies of the EISA bus and microchannel are much too slow for fast image build-up within graphically orientated operating systems or system expansions, such as OS/2 or Windows, for example. Even a small dialogue window with 512*384 points, which in high resolution mode only covers a quarter of the screen surface, consists of 192k pixels. Therefore, in TrueColor mode (with 24-bit colour depth), the 192k pixels first have to be saved, and then rewritten, which is equivalent to 1152 kbytes of picture data. Even with complete utilization of the bus band widths, it takes so long, that the process is actually visible to the human eye.

One possibility for overcoming these problems – especially if you consider the rather high processor clock frequencies when compared to the bus clocks – is the driving of the bus between the graphic subsystem and the CPU at the same frequency as the processor. This is exactly what local bus attempts to do. The first of the local buses on a mother board was, in the main, a fast interface for the video memory, so that the CPU could transfer data faster than in a commercial system with a standard extended bus. Of course, this concept was then applied to other devices that require a high rate of data transfer. An example would be fast hard disks with integrated cache memory. Here, though, other problems occur: host adaptors or controllers of hard disks are usually supplied as plug-in boards, which are inserted into a bus slot. A standard is required so that compatibility of products between the various manufacturers is maintained. Currently, two standards have developed: the PCI (peripheral component inter-connect) bus from Intel, and the VL bus (VESA local bus) from the VESA committee.

Today, PCI represents a high-end solution for powerful PCs and workstations. As an introduction, I would like to list a few characteristics of this Intel-initiated bus system.

▶ Coupling of the processor and expansion bus by means of a bridge
▶ 32-bit standard bus width with a maximum transfer rate of 133 Mbytes/s
▶ Expansion to 64 bits with a maximum transfer rate of 266 Mbytes/s
▶ Support for multiprocessor systems
▶ Burst transfers with arbitrary length
▶ Support for 5 V and 3.3 V power supplies
▶ Write posting and read prefetching
▶ Multimaster capabilities
▶ Operating frequencies from 0 MHz to a maximum of 33 MHz
▶ Multiplexing of address and data bus, reducing the number of pins
▶ Support for ISA/EISA/MCA
▶ Configuration through software and registers
▶ Processor-independent specification

15.4.1 PCI bus structure

An essential characteristic of the PCI concept is the strict decoupling of the processor main memory subsystems and the standard expansion bus. You can see the structure of the PCI bus in Figure 15.3.

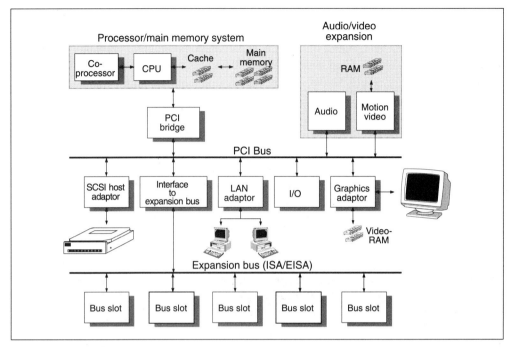

Figure 15.3: The PCI bus.

The *PCI bridge* represents the connection between the subsystems of the processor main memory and the PCI bus. Bridges are invisible interfaces between two bus systems (and also networks). All of the PCI units (also known as *PCI agents*) are connected to the PCI bus, for example, a SCSI host adaptor, a LAN adaptor, an I/O unit or a graphics adaptor (see Figure 15.3). Unlike the VL bus, these units should, as far as possible, be integrated onto the mother board. However, they are mostly constructed as adaptors. In total, a maximum of three slots are provided for PCI units; for example, two slots can be used for an audio and motion video unit. Motion video concerns moving pictures, which require a staggering number of complicated calculations. For this reason, the corresponding PCI unit is often very large, making integration impossible. The audio/video extensions should make the PCI bus most suitable for future multimedia applications. The interface to the expansion bus is a third type of PCI unit. This means that the standard expansion bus – whether ISA, EISA, microchannel or another bus system – can be considered here as a PCI unit. In this way, in principle, every bus system can be integrated, enabling the PCI bus to be connected at a later date. In total, it is possible to connect the PCI bus with up to 10 PCI units.

The PCI bus and its bus cycles use a multiplexing scheme in which the lines are alternately used as address and data lines. This saves on the number of lines required, but two to three clock cycles are now required for a single transfer, because the address is transferred in the first cycle, write data in the second, and read data in the third. For this reason, the maximum data transfer rate is only 66 Mbytes/s (write access) and 44 Mbytes/s (read access) with a 32-bit bus width. In addition, the PCI bus includes a very powerful burst mode, in which the address is only transferred once. Then, the sender and receiver increase the amount of data transferred for the address with each clock cycle because the address is always implicitly known. With burst mode, any number of transfer cycles can be performed. The maximum data transfer rate in burst mode increases to 133 Mbytes/s with a 32-bit data bus and 266 Mbytes/s with a 64-bit data bus. Whether the addressed PCI units can keep up with this is, of course, another matter.

An essential characteristic of the PCI bridge is – and herein clearly lies the main difference from all other bus systems – that it independently forms burst accesses. This means that the PCI bridge independently joins together incoming single transfer read and write operations to form burst accesses, if the addresses of the individual accesses follow one another sequentially. This is also the case, for example, with a 32-bit bus, if the CPU communicates with the double-word addresses DW0–DW1–DW3–DW4–DW5 one after the other. Note that DW2 is not called up. The PCI solves this problem elegantly, in that the bridge produces the burst DW0–DW1–DW2–DW3–DW4–DW5 and simply deactivates all $\overline{BEx}$ signals for DW2, to indicate that no data will be transferred.

15.4.2 Bus cycles

The PCI bridge is considerably more intelligent than an ISA/EISA or MCA bus controller. It switches CPU accesses through to the addressed PCI unit, or 'filters' such accesses in order to address the unit optimally (through the PCI bridge).

The PCI bridge can, in this way, almost function as a fast buffer between the initiator and the target, thus synchronizing the two PCI units. Only in this way is it possible for the bridge to convert CPU single accesses into a PCI burst. With the help of $\overline{IRDY}$ and $\overline{TRDY}$ signals, the PCI bridge can also perform write posting and read prefetching. During *write posting*, the CPU first writes the data at a much higher speed (faster than the PCI bus can currently pass it on) to a buffer. The posting buffer then transfers the data to the addressed PCI unit. During *read prefetching*, the PCI bridge reads data from the target faster than necessary and stores it in a prefetch buffer; it passes the data on to the CPU later.

15.4.3 Bus arbitration

PCI bus arbitration is performed separately for each access – in other words, a busmaster cannot hold up the PCI bus between two accesses. This may occur with EISA and MCA. For this reason, a PCI burst, which in the sense of bus arbitration represents a single access, can extend over any number of transfer cycles. However, this single arbitration does not impair the transfer bandwidth of the PCI bus because the arbitration is 'hidden' behind the active bus – a *hidden arbitration* takes place. This means that the arbitration is already being performed if the active bus access is still running. In this way, no PCI bus cycles are required for the arbitration.

PCI includes two control signals for arbitration: $\overline{REQ}$ and $\overline{GNT}$. Each busmaster has its own request and grant signal, which are intercepted and used by a central arbitration logic. However, the PCI specification does not lay down a model for the arbitration; this is a task for the system designer. Usually, a model corresponding to the CACP from microchannel or the bus arbiters from EISA is used.

15.4.4 DMA

Unlike ISA/EISA and microchannel, no direct memory access (DMA) is implemented. The 'normal' DREQx and DACKx signals known from the PC are missing. At first, this may appear to be a backward step because, above all in EISA and MCA PCs, the transfer of large quantities of data from peripheral devices to the main memory and vice versa can be performed very quickly via a DMA (even though PC manufacturers very rarely use this channel). The busmaster concept (not only in PCI, but also in EISA and microchannel) actually makes DMAs superfluous.

15.4.5 Interrupts

Only optional interrupts are included in the PCI specification: they should be level-triggered and active-low. One interrupt line, namely $\overline{\text{INTA}}$, is assigned to each PCI unit. Only so-called multifunctional units can also use the other three interrupt lines $\overline{\text{INTB}}$, $\overline{\text{INTC}}$ and $\overline{\text{INTD}}$. The PCI interrupts are formed in the CPU PCI bridge like the interrupt requests IRQx of the AT architecture. This usually occurs in a flexible way with help from the setup in the computer BIOS.

15.4.6 Configuration address area

A configuration area of 256 bytes is provided for every PCI unit (and every separate function in a multifunction unit), thus, 64 *registers* for each 32 bits. They define the functions and the behaviour of each PCI unit in the PCI system. In addition to instruction registers, a status register is also provided. It indicates the status of the applicable unit for a PCI operation.

15.4.7 PCI slots

PCI not only frees itself from ISA – like microchannel a few years previously – but with its slot geometry and contact layout, it is completely independent from all existing bus systems. Only the dimensions of the slots recall microchannel to mind. PCI is laid out for an address and data bus width of 32 bits without compromise – you are wasting your time looking for 8-bit and 16-bit segments. Instead, an expansion increase to 64 bits is planned.

In total, a maximum of three PCI slots can be available. However, as each slot can be filled by a PCI adaptor containing a number of functional units and, in addition, PCI units can also be included on the mother board, the number of possible PCI devices is not restricted to three. With a PCI clock speed of 33 MHz and the high current driving capabilities that adaptors request compared to on-board units, more than three external adaptors would overload the PCI components or would become too error-prone.

The 64-bit section is separated from the 32-bit part by a coding bridge. It is optional and stores the most significant double word of a quad word value or a quad word address. Note that the control and status pins $\overline{\text{REQ64}}$ and $\overline{\text{ACK64}}$ for the activation of the 64-bit extension are included in the 32-bit part. Because the contacts are close together, the 64-bit PCI slot is very compact despite its total of 188 contacts. The address/data multiplexing reduces the number of contacts, even with the 64-bit slot, to less than that in a microchannel slot (maximum of 202 pins).

15.5 VESA local bus

The VESA local bus (VLB) has been designed as much more of a local bus than its later appearing competitor, PCI. It is directly connected to the local CPU bus of an i386, i486 or Pentium (from specification 2.0 onwards). In this way, it uses bus cycles that are largely the same as those of the 80x86 processors. Note, however, that the cycles even within the 80x86 family can vary; for example, the i386 does not include a burst cycle. To begin with, I would like to introduce a few of the distinguishing features of this bus system.

▶ No decoupling of processor and expansion bus
▶ Other bus systems can be connected through their own bridge
▶ VLB runs with the bus frequency of the processor: maximum 66 MHz on-board or 40 MHz (specification 1.0) and 50 MHz (specification 2.0) in a slot
▶ 32-bit standard bus width with a maximum 133 Mbytes/s (specification 1.0) and 160 Mbytes/s (specification 2.0) transfer rate
▶ Expansion to 64 bits with a maximum 266 Mbytes/s transfer rate (specification 2.0)
▶ Burst transfers of up to four cycles maximum
▶ Multimaster capabilities
▶ Only single host CPU
▶ Separate address and data lines for simultaneous transfers of address and data bytes
▶ Combined VLB/ISA slots
▶ Processor-dependent specification for the 80x86 family
▶ Supporting of dynamic changes of the clock frequency
▶ Simpler and therefore cheaper solution than PCI, but in end effect somewhat less powerful
▶ Maximum of three VL busmasters in addition to the VL bus controller of each VLB subsystem
▶ Support for write-back caches

15.5.1 VLB bus structure

The concept layout of the VL bus system is shown in Figure 15.4. As in the PCI bus, the VL bus is situated between the processor and memory system, and the standard expansion bus. From the figure, you can clearly see that the VL bus is not so strictly decoupled from the processor system on one side and the standard expansion bus on the other, as in PCI. The VL bus can include up to three VL bus units, which can be inserted in the corresponding VL slots on the mother board. The VLB subsystem is controlled by a VL bus controller. It generates all necessary address, data and control signals for the local bus, or acts on them accordingly.

Like the microchannel slots, the VL slots have a 116-pole mounting (four of which, however, are used for the coding bridge). The main difference is that each VLB slot lies 5 mm behind the slot of a standard expansion bus. In this way, a VL bus adaptor can not only use the signals and contacts of the VL bus, but, with the corresponding geometry, can also use the standard slot if necessary. As in the PCI bus, the standard bus width is 32 bits, but it can be halved to 16 bits.

With the new specification 2.0, an expansion of the VL bus to 64 bits is planned. For this, a further 37 signals are necessary, but they must be transferred through the existing contacts (multiplexing). A VLB unit can request a 64-bit cycle using the $\overline{LBS64}$ signal.

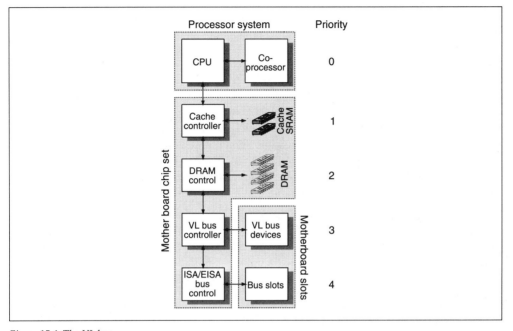

Figure 15.4: The VL bus.

The VL bus runs at the external clock frequency of the CPU. Thus, i386SX/DX, i486SX/DX, i486DX2, i486DX4 and Pentium processors supply the VL bus with differing frequencies. The VL bus is laid out in such a way that it can be operated at a maximum of 66 MHz. However, this is only possible if no local bus slots are included and the VL units are integrated directly onto the mother board. Damping, signal reflections and the capacity of the VL bus slot impede such high frequency. For this reason, using expansion slots, the VL bus runs at a maximum of 50 MHz – even this is six times that of EISA. In too highly clocked CPUs, a frequency divider reduces the supplied clock speed.

The integrated bus buffer of the VL bus makes it possible to perform write accesses to VL units at 33 MHz without wait cycles; like the PCI bus, the VLB also carries out write posting. During read accesses, these buffers do not give any advantage, therefore read accesses are always accomplished with a wait state. The VL bus specification also makes provision for a burst mode like that of the i486 and so implements the necessary control signals.

The theoretical data transfer rate with a data bus width of 32 bits at 50 MHz (the maximum for VL slots) during a write is 160 Mbytes/s. For the first transfer of a read operation, an additional wait cycle is necessary. The burst thus runs 3–1–1–1 and the data transfer rate falls to 133 Mbytes/s. An expansion to 64 bits gives almost twice the rate, namely 266 Mbytes/s for a write burst and 222 Mbytes/s for a read burst. The multiplexing of the most significant data double word prevents a true doubling of the bus bandwidth.

Logically, the three possible VL units are subdivided into a so-called *local bus master* (*LBM*) and a *local bus target* (*LBT*). An LBM can – as in an EISA or MCA busmaster – independently take control of the VL bus and initiate a data transfer. An LBT, on the other hand, is not capable of doing this and only controls the VL bus during the data transfer. It cannot produce any bus signals itself. In addition to the VL bus controller, three other VL busmasters are provided. Naturally, more VLB subsystems can be integrated onto a single mother board. The number of slots and external busmasters increases accordingly.

15.5.2 Bus cycles

The VL bus cycles for single transfers and INTA sequences follow exactly the same rules and phases as for an i386, i486 or Pentium CPU. The VL bus uses a burst cycle corresponding to the i486 read burst. This was also the only possible burst for VLB boards according to specification 1.0. The VLB read transfer burst is best performed (no wait cycles) as a 3–1–1–1 burst. In specification 2.0, VESA has also specified a burst write transfer. It is carried out in exactly the same way as a burst read transfer except, of course, that it is in the other direction.

In specification 2.0, an optional expansion of the VL data bus to 64 bits is also included, without the need to enlarge the VLB slot or to increase the quantity of contacts. Much more, the expansion is achieved by multiplexing the additional data and control signal pins required with already existing pins. The 64-bit transfer should, above all, aid burst cycles.

15.5.3 Bus arbitration

The VL bus supports up to three LBMS. The arbitration protocol is very simple: the control of the VL bus is handed over in accordance with a set priority. Two arbitration signals $\overline{\text{LREQ}<x>}$ and $\overline{\text{LGNT}<x>}$ are used for this purpose. One $\overline{\text{LREQ}}/\overline{\text{LGNT}}$ pair is included in every VLB slot <x>. An LBM with a high priority can snatch control of the bus from an LBM with a lower priority, but not the other way around. If an LBM wishes to take control of the bus, it activates its $\overline{\text{LREQ}}$ signal. If no LBM with a higher priority currently has control, then the VLB controller reacts with a $\overline{\text{LGNT}}$ and so hands over control of the bus. In order to make the bus available again, the currently active LBM deactivates its $\overline{\text{LREQ}}$ signal and the bus control confirms this, in that it also increases the $\overline{\text{LGNT}}$ signal to a high level.

15.5.4 DMA

As in the PCI, no DMA is provided. The main difference to the PCI is the fact that a VLB adaptor usually uses an ISA or EISA slot as well, and therefore, also uses the (E)ISA control signals (incidentally, in the case of VLB, this also justifies the title 'local bus'). VLB adaptors generally include the signals DREQx and DACKx. Thus, a DMA access in the style of an AT or EISA PC is still possible. However, it is then carried out by the (E)ISA bus and *not* by the VL bus, with all limitations regarding the data transfer rate and so on. If a VLB unit uses only the VL bus in order to perform a data transfer, then it must represent a VL busmaster that can fully control the VL bus. This strategy normally permits a far greater data transfer rate than the classic DMA technique, because the VL busmaster can use the wide (32 bits or even 64 bits) and fast (up to 50 MHz in the slots) VL bus in burst mode. The necessary bus arbitration is performed by means of a VL bus controller, as in the PCI. Thus, in the VL bus also, the concept of the DMA is replaced by the more flexible, and more powerful, external bus master principle.

15.5.5 Interrupts

Only a single interrupt pin is included in the VLB specification, namely IRQ9. It is level-triggered, active at a high level and is directly connected to IRQ9 of the (E)ISA bus. If the VL bus is integrated into a microchannel system, then the VLB IRQ9 is connected to the MCA $\overline{\text{IRQ9}}$ through an inverter. Normally, the VLB adaptor also uses the existing ISA, EISA or MCA slot, so that sufficient interrupt lines are available.

15.5.6 VLB slots

As I have already mentioned, the VL slots have a 116-pole standard microchannel mounting. Each lies behind a standard expansion bus slot, so that a VL bus adaptor can also use the signals and contacts of the standard slots (and this usually enables them to have access to the hardware interrupts). In the new specification 2.0, with its expansion of the VL bus to 64 bits, the 37 new signals necessary are multiplexed with the address signals through the existing contacts.

Part 5
Competing concepts

In Part 5, I would like to finish by discussing RISC implementations and other concepts that are just as efficient. Chapter 16 details the different RISC implementations and explains where they are typically used. Chapter 17 discusses concepts that are sometimes still undergoing research, but which are already producing amazing results with very little hardware complexity – how many people are aware, for example, that luggage at many airports is examined by a neural net?

16 Alternative RISC implementations

This chapter details the different RISC implementations that are in competition with the Pentium. Without the need to include x86 compatibility, unlike the Pentium, here we must deal with essentially 'purer' RISCs.

16.1 DEC's Alpha

The Alpha, and the AXP computer series based on it, has been produced by DEC as the successor to the VAX. The Alpha architecture should form DEC's basic framework for the next 25 years. During this time period, the plan is to increase Alpha's system performance by a factor of 1000, compared to that of today. The first chip in the Alpha processor series, the 21064 (21 represents the 21st Century, 64 the 64-bit architecture) was presented to the public at the end of 1992. It is clocked at an incredible 200 MHz and can execute a maximum of two instructions per clock cycle, resulting in a command execution performance of at least 400 MIPS (for comparison, the Pentium can attain 166 MIPS). The 21064 is constructed from 0.75 μm CMOS technology; its successors will be built with 0.5 μm structure size. In this way, and with other improvements, DEC wishes to achieve a clock speed of 400 MHz.

The Alpha includes superscalar architecture and, right from inception, a superpipelined concept; the integer and floating-point pipelines have 7 and 10 stages, respectively. Memory accesses are executed strictly in accordance with the load/store principle – that is, ALU instructions can only contain register operands and not memory operands. The Alpha is a 100% 64-bit chip all registers are 64-bits wide. It communicates with its surroundings through a 128-bit data bus and a 34-bit address bus; during a reset, the data bus can also be configured to 64-bit width. Internally, the 21064 uses virtual 64-bit addresses. This results in a fantastic 16-Ebyte (16-exabyte) or 16 000 000 000 000 000 000-byte virtual address area. This would enable every water molecule in a drop of water to be addressed. Externally, it can address 16 Gbytes with its 34-bit address bus. In Figure 16.1, you can see a photograph of the Alpha 21064 and its components.

In addition, I would like to mention that in the meantime, the value-for-money Alpha variant 21066, clocked at 166 MHz, is available for PCs and workstations. It consumes between 5 and 9 W and has been developed for both desktops and portable computers. On the processor chip, the 21066 integrates a PCI controller and a memory controller for driving DRAMs. Together with the 64-Mbit DRAMs available in 1995 or 1996, the main board of an AXP system with a 16-Mbyte main memory will consist of only a 166 MHz 21066 and four 64-Mbit chips. This could almost be installed in the casing of a fashionable wrist watch.

Figure 16.1: The Alpha 21064. Source: Digital Equipment GmbH (Germany).
The photograph shows the Alpha die, which is about 14 mm∗17 mm in size with structures of 0.75μm.

The 21068 is also planned for use in embedded controllers. In addition, DEC has stated that future 21064 processors will not only perform simple parity checks, but will also perform ECC correction for individual bit faults in 128-bit data units with the help of a 7-bit ECC. This will increase the data security in an AXP system quite considerably.

16.1.1 Internal structure of the Alpha 21064

Figure 16.2 shows the internal structure of the Alpha 21064. The connection to its surroundings is represented by the bus interface, which uses a 128-bit data bus, a 34-bit address bus and a control bus. The external bus clock cycle can be adjusted between 18.75 MHz and 75 MHz. The full internal 200 MHz is unnecessary because neither peripheral chips as fast as SRAMs, nor system controllers can achieve a cycle time of 5 ns (5 ns is substantially shorter than the typical life of excited atomic and molecular states that cause light to be emitted). An L2 cache, or so-called B cache (backup cache), can be connected directly to the Alpha without the need for an additional buffer. The B cache can be between 128 kbytes and 8 Mbytes. Two L1 caches are integrated on the Alpha chip itself, namely the instruction or I cache and the data or D cache. They are both 8 kbytes in size and operate with a cache line size of 32 bytes – that is, a cache line fill is completed within two clock cycles. The data cache uses a write-through strategy; all data is immediately written through to the main memory (or B cache). In the I cache, eight branch bits are available for every cache line, which are used by the branch prediction unit for branch predictions; more on that later.

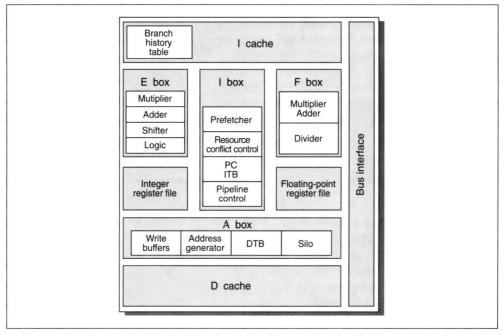

Figure 16.2: Internal structure of the Alpha 21064.

The Alpha 21064 itself is contained within a pin grid array (PGA) housing that contains 431 pins for 291 signals and 140 for supply voltages (Vcc and GND). The Alpha operates with a voltage of only 3.3 V, at maximum 200 MHz performance. However, it uses 30 W of power so the cooling problems are considerable. For this reason, the third metal layer of the chip is used to transfer heat to the housing, on which a truly monstrous heat sink is installed. Finally, the 21064 contains approximately 1.7 million transistors. Despite the expansion to 64-bits, this is only half as many as in the Pentium – a further indication that Intel must use more than 50% of the work-load and transistors for compatibility with the i386/i486 and also for the extensive test functions.

The actual performing of instructions takes place in three functionally independent units: the control unit (I box), the integer execution unit (E box) and the floating-point execution unit (F box). An additional addressing unit (A box) is available for the formation of addresses. The

E box and F box execution units also include two register files consisting of 32 integer registers of 64 bits and 32 floating-point registers of 64-bits. The 32 integer registers are mnemonically identified as R0 to R31, whereby R31 is similar to the global register 0 of Sparc processors, in that it always returns a value of 0 when read. A write operation using R31 as the target register always results in the losing of the write value. You could say that R31 has the value 0 hardwired into it. In this way, the Alpha can always have the most frequently used initialization value 0 in integer format, readily available for a program. In a similar way, the 32 floating-point registers are identified as F0 to F31 in mnemonic code. F31, like R31, always returns the value 0 when read; a write operation using F31 as the target address also results in the loss of the value to be written. In this way, the Alpha can very quickly make available the value 0 in floating point format.

The control unit (I box) contains a program counter, which, in the usual way, indicates the address of the next instruction to be executed. This can be changed by a branch instruction, for example. A prefetcher is installed immediately in front of the program counter. It fetches instructions from the I cache in advance. Two instruction translation buffers (ITBs) are also integrated and are used for converting virtual addresses into physical addresses. The first ITB stores the corresponding entry for a maximum of eight 8-kbyte pages; the second, four entries for the large 4-Mbyte pages. For the implementation of the superscalar principle, the I box always reads two instructions in parallel and checks them with respect to dual issue in the three independent functional units for integer, floating-point and load/store operations in the E box, F box and A box, respectively. In this way, a maximum of two instructions can be started and completed in one clock cycle (thus giving the theoretical 400 MIPS at 200 MHz). Through the strict load/store architecture of the Alpha, a higher parallel execution rate of memory accesses and ALU or FPU operations is possible. The following instruction pairs lead to a dual issue:

▶ Integer operation and floating-point operation

▶ Floating-point operation and floating-point branch

▶ Integer operation and integer branch

▶ Load/store operation and any other integer or floating-point operation

Thus, the Alpha also operates with instruction pairing similar to that in the Pentium. It is, however, on a much larger scale because here the limitations only affect the instruction groups and not the individual instructions (after all, all Alpha instructions are 'simple', because hardwired, complex instructions are externally linked through the privileged architecture library (PAL) code).

If the instructions of a pair can be executed in parallel, then the I box passes them on to the applicable operations boxes, the E box, F box and A box. The instructions then either pass through the seven stages of the integer pipeline (E box and A box), or through the ten stages of the floating-point pipeline (F box). If, due to the pairing rules, only one instruction can be issued, then the I box holds back the next sequential instruction and sends the first instruction through the applicable pipeline. Of significance is the fact that the single instruction that was held back is then passed on separately to the applicable pipeline. The I box does not read in the next instruction in order to possibly execute it as a pair with the instruction that was held back.

A branch prediction logic is also implemented in the I box which, as in the Pentium, should predict the result of a conditional jump. For this purpose, the I cache makes a note of all branch results for the stored instructions in a 2-kbyte table for the branch history bits.

In addition to the usual hardwired instructions of the Alpha, the control unit I box also recognizes PAL code instructions. They are used for the external implementation of complex functions that until now have been the responsibility of microcode in CISCs or CRISCs. The AXP series from DEC based on the Alpha uses PAL code, for example, for the handling of interrupts and misses to the ITB. This PAL code ensures that the Alpha is very flexible; in some respects, it can be adjusted to the requirements of most operating systems at the hardware level (in this way especially, 80x86 machine codes can be emulated); you will find more on this subject in Section 16.1.4.

The integer execution unit (E box) executes all integer operations, for example, additions, multiplications, divisions and also integer branches and so on. Immediately assigned to the E box is the integer register file; the registers are accessible through four read and two write ports.

The floating-point execution unit (F box) is, in principle, very similar to the structure of the E box. It executes all floating-point operations in DEC's own specific format and also in IEEE format. DEC's own format is supported, mainly because, although the Alpha AXP architecture will replace the VAX, the porting of existing VAX programs should be supported by the AXP series. The previously described   floating-point register file with its 32 64-bit registers is connected directly to the F box.

The addressing unit (A box) is the last of the three functional execution units. Together with the data translation buffer (DTB), it generates the physical and virtual addresses for the load/store instructions, in order to access the bus interface for a memory access. The four 32-bit write buffers increase the throughput of the bus interface by acting as temporary buffers and, in some cases, by rearranging the sequence of read and write accesses. As an example, cache line fills have the highest priority. The write buffers store the corresponding data so that, in the meantime, other write operations can take place. If the Alpha issues a further write access while data is still in the write buffers, then the A box logic checks whether the applicable address is temporarily stored in the write buffers. If this is the case, the later write access updates the entry in the write buffer; in other words, no further write buffer is required for the new write operation – the A box carries out an internal write operation.

Storage areas in the A box store read accesses that have led to a miss in the D cache and thus require an external bus cycle. They are then executed when the previous cache or main memory access has been completed. The storage areas are necessary because a miss can only be discovered when the subsequent instructions have already been loaded into the pipelines and are located in different execution stages.

The Alpha also has the ability to count specific hardware incidents, such as the execution of specific instructions or the occurrence of external hardware interrupts, in a similar way to the Pentium, with its performance monitoring. If the corresponding counter overflows, the Alpha will issue an interrupt.

During the system start-up – that is, when the Alpha is switched on – unlike the 80x86 processors, for example, the 21064 does not jump to a fixed address. Instead, it first transfers the content of a serial ROM (SROM) into the I cache, then it loads the instruction at address 0 in the I cache into the prefetcher as the first instruction to be executed. In this way, it initiates the boot sequence for the system start.

16.1.2 The Alpha's pipelines

I have already mentioned above that the Alpha contains a seven-stage integer and load/store pipeline. You can see the individual stages of the integer pipeline in Figure 16.3.

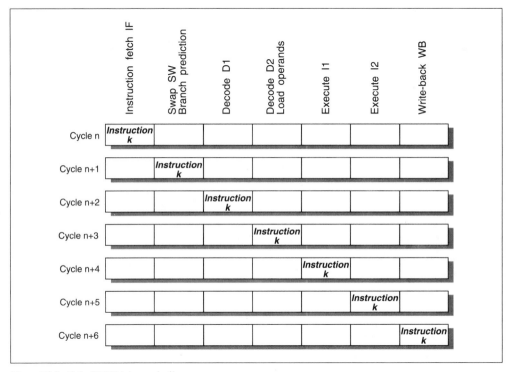

Figure 16.3: Alpha 21064 integer pipelines.

The first two stages IF and SW fetch two instructions and check whether simultaneous execution is possible. If necessary, the two instructions in the SW stage are exchanged in order to achieve a dual issue. At the same time, the SW stage executes a branch prediction if the loaded instruction represents a branch. The two decoding stages D1 and D2 decode the instruction or instructions and load the operands into the applicable register. Until this stage, the integer and floating-point pipelines are identical; they share the first four stages as in the Pentium. The execution of the integer instruction then follows in the integer execution stages I1 and I2 so that finally, in the seventh and last stage, the result can be written back to the destination register. The first four stages IF, SW, D1 and D2 are executed by the I box. Only then, is the E box or A box addressed. A bypass immediately sends the result at the output of stages I1, I2 or WB to the input of stage I1, so that this part of the complete result is available earlier for the subsequent instruction.

In place of the stages I1, I2 and WB, the memory reference pipeline contains the stage AC, in which the effective data address is calculated, the stage TB for DTB look-ups, and finally the stage HM, which determines a cache hit or miss and, if necessary, writes to the register file. The first four stages of the memory reference pipeline are identical to those of the integer pipeline shown in Figure 16.3.

Note that an integer or load/store instruction at 200 MHz only remains in each of the pipeline stages for 5 ns. During this time, light – and also the electrical signal in the chip – will only have moved 15 cm; that is less than 10 times the width of the Alpha chip. Each stage, however, contains a number of electronic components which form many circuit stages. You can quite easily see that a clock cycle of 200 MHz is at the absolute limit of current CMOS technology.

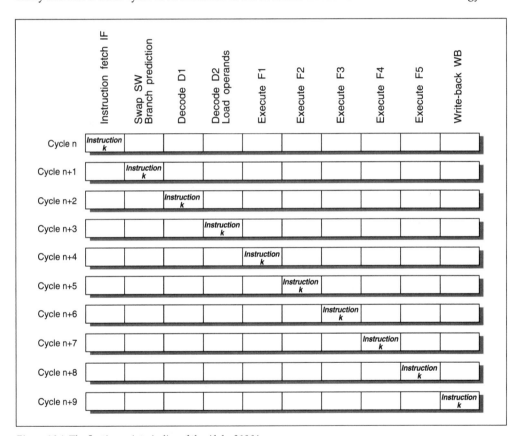

Figure 16.4: The floating-point pipeline of the Alpha 21064.

Figure 16.4 shows the structure of the floating-point pipeline of the Alpha 21064. The first four stages IF, SW, D1 and D2 are identical to those of the integer pipeline. The floating-point instruction is executed in the five execution stages F1 to F5. They are located in the F box. The tenth and last stage, WB, writes the result to the destination register. A bypass is also included in the floating-point pipeline, which makes the result of the previous stage available by bypassing the destination register.

As I stated above, the I box includes a branch prediction logic which, as far as possible, prevents pipeline stalls caused by the delayed availability of branch results. For this purpose, the I cache notes all branch results for the stored instructions in a 2-kbyte table for the branch history bits. When a branch instruction is executed for the first time, the I cache obviously has no experience to use for the prediction. In this case, the branch prediction logic predicts a branch taken, as standard, providing the displacement field in the opcode (see Section 16.1.3) contains a negative value. This indicates that the branch instruction is part of a loop that will normally be repeated many times (otherwise a loop is not necessary) and, thus, that there is a great possibility that the first branch at the end of the loop will point back to the start of the loop. If, on the other hand, the displacement field in the opcode has a positive value, then it indicates a branch in accordance with a CASE instruction in C. Here, the branch prediction logic predicts a not taken branch as standard – that is, the program execution is continued with the instruction immediately following the branch instruction.

The Alpha, like the Pentium, does not make use of branch delay slots. However, the reasons for this are different. While branch delay slots are not possible in the Pentium because both old code and code not optimized for the slots must be executed, the reason in the case of the Alpha is the number of pipeline stages. Branch delay slots are only effective if they can be filled with instructions that actually precede the branch. The number of these slots is equal to the number of clock cycles that are required between the sending out of the branch instruction to the pipeline and the writing of the branch result in the instruction fetch stage. This number can be reduced by one because of the register bypass. Generally, however, the number of branch delay slots produced is in the region of half the number of pipeline stages implemented. In the Alpha, this would be between four and five delay slots. This number is so large that it would be unlikely that all delay slots could be filled with productive instructions. This is especially so if the popular CASE instruction were to be converted into a series of successive conditional branches. Then, the only possibility would be to insert the corresponding number of unproductive NOPs. Thus, for the superpipelined architecture of the Alpha, a branch prediction is considerably more effective.

The branch prediction stack is a second mechanism for supporting branch predictions. The Alpha implements procedure calls through a simple jump instruction – that is, there is no difference between subprogram calls and normal jumps. Through a special bit in the opcode field, the program can instruct the Alpha to store the return address also in the branch prediction stack. For a return jump, the Alpha can then use this return address stored in the prediction stack, to determine the most likely return jump address. The conditional MOV instruction of the Alpha also supports the quickest possible execution of branches: if a specific condition is true, then the content of a register is shifted to another register. In the Pentium, this would be implemented as the result of a conditional branch with an additional (unconditional) MOV instruction. Since such conditional load operations occur frequently, the conditional MOV instruction of the Alpha is very efficient.

16.1.3 The Alpha's instruction structure

As a true RISC processor, the Alpha uses horizontal instruction encoding with a uniform instruction length of 32 bits. In total, four different types of instructions are provided, which are shown in Figure 16.5.

The PAL code format is the first instruction format shown in Figure 16.5. PAL code instructions activate procedures and system functions stored in a library. You will find more on this subject in Section 16.1.4. The branch instruction format contains a 21-bit displacement. It is shifted two bits to the left, thus the value of the displacement is multiplied by four. This is possible because the Alpha's instructions are of 32-bit uniform length, and so always begin at the boundaries 0000h, 0004h, 0008h and so on. For internal usage, the Alpha expands the 23-bit displacement produced thus to a full 64 bits with sign formation. This 64-bit offset is added to the updated program counter value, in order to determine the destination address for the branch. Conditional branches examine the value in the R_a register, to check whether or not the branch should be executed.

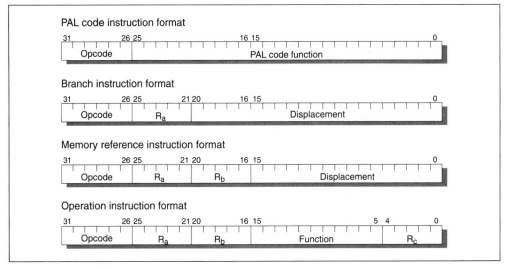

Figure 16.5: The structure of the 32-bit Alpha instruction codes.

The memory instruction format concerns the load and store instructions of the Alpha. Firstly, the 16-bit displacement is expanded to 64 bits with sign formation. This 64-bit value is then added to the register value R_b, to generate a virtual 64-bit memory address. The 32- or 64-bit data at the position determined thus is loaded into the register R_a or, from there, written to memory.

The last basic instruction format remaining, is the operation instruction format. All operations within the Alpha, that do not belong to one of the groups mentioned above (such as addition, logical AND and so on) are code with this format. Normally, the two registers R_a and R_b are used as source registers, and the register R_a is used as the destination register. The 11-bit function field identifies the operations more exactly. There are also integer instructions that use bits 12 to 15 of the function field for other purposes, or join them together with the R_b field to give an 8-bit value.

16.1.4 The PAL code

The true RISC architecture of the Alpha prohibits complex functions that need to be implemented with microcode. In addition, the Alpha should replace the VAX but, despite this, should not have a true DEC-specific architecture. The AXP desktops, especially, are clearly targeted at the PC and workstation market, under the Windows NT operating system. For this, very great flexibility is required, above all, if many operating systems need to be supported in parallel. In Alpha's case, the solution lies with PAL code. The PAL code would be better described as a macroscopic microcode, because it can directly address the larger part of the Alpha's operating components, such as the A box for load/store operations or the translation buffers. For this, it can use the already available Alpha instructions and it is held ready in an external memory. The PAL code should, for example, support targeted operating system functions of UNIX, Open VMS and Windows NT, and also implement complex functions similar to REP MOVS of the 80x86 processors. In this way, in principle, it is possible to emulate the instruction set of the Pentium, in order to integrate a relatively slow (as compared to the usual Alpha performance), but completely compatible, DOS box under Windows NT.

Thus, the PAL code has to be arranged for each individual operating system and its fundamental hardware. Because of the placing of the PAL code in a writable external memory, it can be very flexibly supplemented, updated or exchanged with a version for a different operating system. Even though the PAL code only uses the already available hardwired Alpha functions, it operates with a higher privilege level than normal program code.

The PAL code takes over complete control of the whole Alpha system; however, it has no, or very little, influence on normal program code, such as the generation and execution of load/store operations. Since PAL code is also used mainly for the handling of interrupts and exceptions, it also controls the generation and handling of these interruptions, which are essentially an element of the hardware, or of hardware-like software.

Five instructions and their corresponding opcodes are reserved for the PAL code (PALRES0 to PALRES4). They can only be called from within the vicinity of the PAL code. If the Alpha is not currently working with the PAL code, then the call of such an opcode leads to an exception. PALRESx is used for reading and writing internal registers, or for the return from an interrupt or exception.

The Alpha calls PAL code under clearly defined conditions. Firstly, the Alpha empties its pipelines and prepares the condition of the processor for performing PAL code – for example, the current program counter value is saved to an internal register. Finally, the Alpha executes the PAL code, as CISC processors would execute the internally stored microcode. There are four hardware conditions that activate the PAL code:

▶ A reset sets the Alpha into the PAL code mode and executes a reset PAL code to initialize the processor. In this way, the processor start condition can be adjusted to the requirements of the hardware and system software without problems.
▶ When a hardware error or exception occurs, PAL code is called up for its handling.
▶ External interrupts are also handled by PAL code.
▶ Misses in the translation buffer activate the PAL code, which reloads the buffer as it is adjusted to the hardware and system software.

PAL code can also be directly activated by the CALLPAL function. The parameters transferred with CALLPAL specify the PAL code function to be executed. For each PAL code set, DEC has specified two instructions that must always be implemented, HALT and IMB.

The HALT instruction, similar to the HLT instruction of the Pentium, stops the Alpha. The I stream memory barrier (IMB) instruction is executed if an instruction or hardware component in the instruction flow has changed, for example, if an opcode has been overwritten by another (self-modifying code).

16.2 The PowerPC from Motorola

A few years ago, a stir was caused in the computer industry when it was announced that IBM, Apple and Motorola had formed an alliance in order to break the market-dominating position of Microsoft and Intel in the field of PCs. The role of Apple was essentially to provide its generally well-liked operating system, and Motorola was to deliver a high performance processor – the result was the PowerPC line. The first examples for evaluation were delivered in 1993; mass production started in 1994. The name PowerPC (Performance Optimized With Enhanced RISC) suggests that elements of the IBM power architecture, which were implemented in the RISC System/6000, have been used in order to construct a PC. The PowerPC 601 (also known as the Motorola PC or MPC 601, for short) is currently available. This is discussed in more detail in the following section. Figure 16.6 is a photograph of this new high-performance chip.

Figure 16.6: The MPC 601. Source: Motorola GmbH (Germany), Geschäftsbereich Halbleiter.

16.2.1 Internal structure of the MPC 601

You can see the internal structure of the MPC 601 in Figure 16.7. It contains an instruction unit with a prefetch queue for eight instructions, from which the distribution logic reads a maximum of three instructions at a time, and passes them on to the integer unit (IU), the branch prediction unit (BPU) and the floating-point unit (FPU). Both the IU and the FPU have an associated register file containing 32 registers of 32 bits (IU) and 64 bits (FPU). Both arithmetic units contain an adder, multiplier and divider, in order to execute mathematical calculations very quickly. The floating-point unit implements simple floating-point instructions such as FADD, FMUL and so on, but not, however, complete floating-point functions (such as FTAN), as is the case in the Pentium. Such values must be implemented through function libraries at a machine code level. Similarly to the i860, the MPC 601 supports typical Taylor series through the FMUL–FADD function.

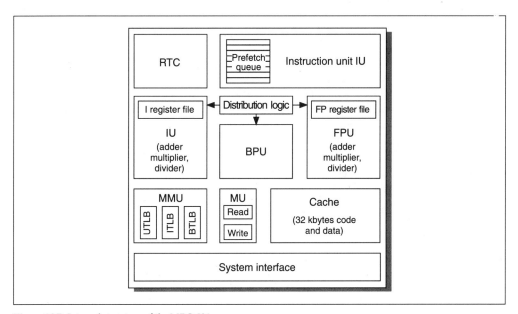

Figure 16.7: Internal structure of the MPC 601.

In order to load the prefetch queue with sufficient speed (as a superscalar, the MPC 601 can execute up to three instructions in parallel) and thus to accelerate data accesses, a single 32-kbyte cache is available. It stores both code and data, and supports cache consistency by using the MESI protocol. The on-chip cache is organized as an eight-way set-associative cache, with a cache line size of 64 bytes, which is divided into two sectors, each of 32 bytes. Normally, the cache uses a write-back strategy; on a page or block basis, however, a write-through strategy can also be selected. Cache lines are exchanged according to an LRU strategy, and not randomly. The data in the cache is addressed with physical, not virtual, addresses – in other words, the virtual addresses must first be converted to physical addresses in the memory management unit (MMU). As this occurs at a very early stage of the three pipelines, it does not produce a delay for the cache access.

The logical 52-bit address space of the MPC 601 contains 4 Pbytes (Petabyte; 4 Pbytes=4096 Tbytes, or approximately 4 million Gbytes), the physical address space 4 Gbytes (completely sufficient for PC applications). The system interface has a 32-bit address bus available and a 64-bit data bus. The address space of the MPC 601 is divided into 16 segments, each of 256 Mbytes. Obviously, the PowerPC also supports demand paging (with page sizes of 4 kbytes) and block addressing for blocks with 128 kbytes, 256 kbytes and so on, up to 8 Mbytes. Three different translation lookaside buffers – UTLB, ITLB and BTLB – are implemented in the MMU. The two-way set-associative UTLB (unified TLB) stores 256 entries for normal data and code accesses, the fully associative ITLB (instruction TLB) stores four entries for instruction addresses, and the fully associative BTLB (block TLB) stores four entries for block accesses. The entries in the three TLBs can overlap, for example, if a code access (with the help of the ITLB), and a data access (with the help of the UTLB) refer to the same page. The MMU also implements access protection with the two supervisor and user levels.

All instructions are executed in the MPC 601 with the help of the three pipelines, which can operate in parallel. They are the integer, floating-point and branch prediction pipelines. They are described in more detail in the following section.

The memory access unit (MU) contains a read buffer, which can buffer a maximum of two read accesses, and a write buffer, which can store up to three pending write accesses. The write buffer entries can each buffer up to 32 bytes – that is, a complete cache line sector. In particular, they are used for the writing back of cache lines during a cache flush or write-back. Write and read accesses can be rearranged by the MU so that maximum performance is achieved, thus the PowerPC operates using weak write ordering. The MU supports single transfers and burst cycles of four individual accesses. This is sufficient to fill or to write-back a sector of a cache line (four cycles with a 64-bit data bus). Like all Motorola processors, the MPC 601 uses the big endian format as standard – that is, the most significant bytes of multiple byte entities have the low address. By setting a control bit, the processor changes from using this standard method to using the little endian format known from Intel processors.

As a last element, the MPC 601 also contains a real time clock (RTC). With its help, the processor has a time frame resolution in the region of nanoseconds. The RTC will probably not be integrated into subsequent PowerPC processors.

16.2.2 The pipelines of the MPC 601

As I have already mentioned, the MPC 601 contains three pipelines, which can operate in parallel. The simplest is the single-stage BPU pipeline, which decodes and executes branch instructions completely within one single clock cycle and in one stage. The integer pipeline contains the usual three decoding (D) execution (EX) and write-back (WB) stages. The floating-point pipeline is five stages long: buffer BF, decoding D, execution E1, execution E2 and write-back WB. Every floating-point instruction must first wait one clock cycle in a buffer, before being transported to the first 'true' FPU pipeline stage. As is generally the case with the new generation of high performance RISC CPUs, the PowerPC also implements a number of bypasses in order to prevent, as far as possible, or at least to shorten, pipeline stalls due to register and data dependencies. The three pipelines are shown in Figure 16.8.

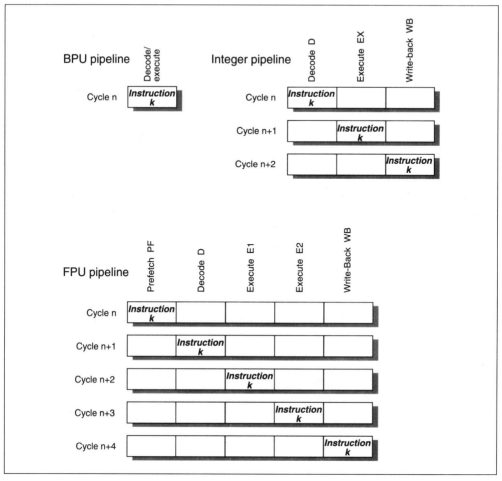

Figure 16.8: The three MPC 601 pipelines.

The prefetch queue in the instruction unit (IU), and the distribution logic operate very closely together with the three pipelines. The prefetch queue can store up to eight machine instructions. They can be written from the on-chip cache into the queue all at once, or in a number of smaller quantities. The lower four entries are then distributed to the three pipelines by the distribution logic. This does not occur – and here the MPC 601 differs from other RISCs – strictly in the sequence in which they occur in the instruction flow. More accurately stated, the lowest floating-point instruction in the four lowest queue entries is transferred to the FPU pipeline, where a BPU or integer instruction could be located at a lower position. The same applies to BPU instructions. The lowest BPU instruction is transferred to the BPU pipeline, even if integer and FPU instructions are waiting at a lower level. Integer instructions are then only passed on to the integer pipeline when they are located at the very bottom of the prefetch queue. For every instruction transferred, all of the instructions located above it in the queue shift one position downwards. In addition, the prefetch queue is continually refilled from the on-chip cache. Naturally, instructions can only be transferred to the pipelines if the pipelines are free, thus the first stage is empty. Since the pipelines can be halted if certain conditions arise (pipeline stalls), the consequence is a seemingly disorganized releasing of instructions, which at times are unavailable for execution. It is presumed that the prefetch queue is completely full with eight instructions, which are transferred to make space available for other instructions.

The example in Figure 16.9 clearly shows to what extent the instructions can be rearranged. The workload of the MPC 601 increases considerably if it is necessary to identify and handle inter-related or interdependent instructions that are not issued strictly sequentially. Note that the Pentium, on the other hand, strictly executes instructions sequentially in its two pipelines. For example, the instruction in the v pipeline cannot overtake the sequentially previous instruction in the u pipeline, even if there is no interdependency between them. The more intermixed the instructions are (that is, integer, floating-point and branch instructions statistically do not occur together), the better the pipelines of the MPC 601 are balanced. Unlike the Pentium, each pipeline can only execute one type of instruction. Thus, two successive integer instructions always require two clock cycles. This is somewhat different in the Pentium, for example. If both integer instructions are simple (for example, MOV-INC), then they can be executed in parallel, in a single clock cycle; this saves one clock cycle. On the other hand, the rules for instruction pairing in the Pentium are much stricter.

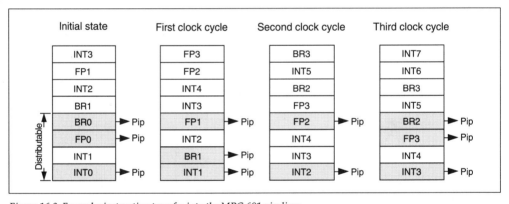

Figure 16.9: Example: instruction transfer into the MPC 601 pipelines.
The prefetch queue is shown with eight entries by way of an example for integer instructions INTx, floating-point instructions FPx and branch instructions BRx. Only instructions located in the lower half of the queue can be distributed to the pipelines. Instructions that are transferred to a pipeline upon the indicated clock cycle are marked. The sequential instruction flow is:
INT0–INT1–FP0–BR0–BR1–INT2–FP1–INT3–INT4–FP2–FP3–BR2–INT5–BR3–INT6–INT7
However, the instructions are transferred into the pipelines and executed in the following order:
(INT0+FP0+BR0) – (INT1+BR1+FP1) – (INT2+FP2) – (INT3+FP3+BR2) and so on.

While the MPC 601 can always, for example, execute an integer and branch instruction in parallel (here, I would like to leave out all mention of data dependencies), this is only possible in the Pentium if the pairing rules have been fulfilled. The reason for this is mainly the reduced and plain instruction set of the MPC 601, in accordance with RISC principles. Extensive microcode instructions are not included.

16.2.3 The branch prediction

In the MPC 601, as with all processors that implement instruction pipelining, branch instructions can have a fatal effect on performance. The integrated BPU should prevent this. It decodes and executes branch instructions in a pipeline with only a single stage. The procedure for unconditional jumps and conditional jumps where the jump condition is already known is considerably different to that of conditional jumps where the jump condition must first be calculated by a different pipeline, while the branch instruction is already being loaded into the BPU pipeline. Conditional jumps make full use of the condition register, but not of the registers in the integer or FPU register file.

In the case of unconditional branches and conditional branches with a known jump condition, the BPU does not need to give a correct prediction – the jump target is already clearly known. Then, the BPU pipeline simply calculates the destination address, and exchanges the jump instruction with the instruction at the jump target address. Finally, the instruction unit continues by reading into the prefetch queue the instruction sequentially following the jump target instruction. In this way, the PowerPC carries out a branch folding (the exchanging of branch instructions with the jump target instruction, as described). Such branches with known jump targets can only disrupt the flow of instructions in the pipelines if the instruction at the jump target is not located in the on-chip cache, and must be loaded from the slower main memory. Thus, a maximum delay is indirectly produced by a delayed load.

Naturally, this is completely different in the case of conditional branches, in which the jump condition is calculated immediately prior to the branch instruction. This occurs quite frequently, typically because the branch condition is calculated first, then the branch is executed immediately afterwards. Thus, the calculation takes place in the integer or FPU pipeline if the BPU should predict the branch. For this, a prediction of the jump target is required – that is, whether the branch will be executed (taken branch) or not (not taken branch). The somewhat disorganized sending out of instructions in the MPC 601 (see Figure 16.9) supports the BPU by making early predictions possible. A branch instruction can be transferred to the BPU pipeline, at the earliest, when it reaches the fourth lowest position in the prefetch queue. It is possible that up to three (integer) instructions are located below it. In the best possible case, the branch can thus be executed two clock cycles before the time when it is actually required. Also, in the worst case, there is still enough time to fetch the new instruction at the jump target from the on-chip cache or the slower main memory, and to insert it into the prefetch queue.

The branch prediction strategy of the BPU in the PowerPC is very simple. It is accomplished purely on the static basis of the jump target. 'Backwards' branches – branches to lower instruction pointer values – are generally assessed as taken branches. They are interpreted by the MPC 601 as loop instructions, which should initiate the multiple execution of loops. For this reason, the probability that the jump back will be executed is greater than the likelihood that the program will leave the loop. After a maximum of two loop completions (thus, a jump back), a dynamic prediction algorithm would also have decided that the jump back should be executed, due to the previous ('historical') execution of the branch instruction. Thus, the easier to implement static branch prediction is no less efficient for frequently occurring branches than is the dynamic algorithm using historical information, as implemented in the Pentium and the Alpha. In addition, the dynamic algorithm must also employ a standard strategy for when it reaches a specific branch for the first time – it does not yet have values based on previous experience. On the other hand, when executing a CASE instruction in C with multiple conditional branches, for example, static prediction often falls behind dynamic prediction. Conditional branches, which are executed with the help of a prediction, differ somewhat in their effects to those that are handled using branch folding. As long as a prediction is active – that is, as long as the prediction has not yet been finally confirmed, through the actual calculation of the jump condition – the instructions following the jump instruction cannot write any register values; the instructions are held up before they reach the register write stage WB. In addition, no further branch instructions can be transferred to the BPU pipeline; they are only decoded, not executed. Thus, two simultaneously active predictions are not possible. However, all instructions that follow an unconditional branch, or a conditional branch whose jump condition is already known, can overwrite their destination register, and, in addition, other branch instructions can be transferred to the BPU pipeline.

16.2.4 Power PC instruction structure

The instructions of the PowerPC are a uniform 32 bits long and have 4-byte addresses. Bits 0 to 5 always indicate the primary opcode, which is supplemented by a secondary opcode located in bits 21 to 30. Figure 16.10 shows the basic structure of the PowerPC's instructions (note the big-endian format).

The integer instructions and the instructions for conditional branches contain a primary 6-bit opcode, a secondary 10-bit or 9-bit opcode, and also a maximum of two control fields Ctr. Depending on the instruction, a destination register dest, and up to two source registers scr1 and src2 are possible. The five bits of the register positions are sufficient to address one of the 32 registers in the integer register file. An immediate operand can be available in place of src2, Ctr and the secondary opcode.

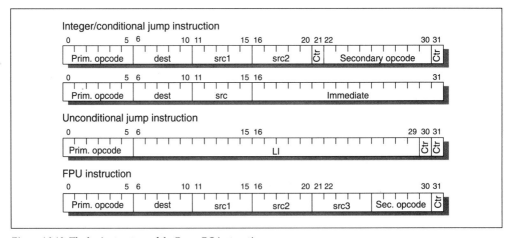

Figure 16.10: The basic structure of the PowerPC instructions.

Unconditional branches only include a primary 6-bit opcode, two control bits Ctr, and a 24-bit offset LI which gives the absolute or relative offset of the jump target in two's complement representation. Floating-point instructions can contain up to three source operands (for example, the instruction FMADD dest, src1, src3, src2 for the dest=[src1*src3]+src2 operation). If only src1 and src2 are used, then src3 and the 5-bit field of the secondary opcode produce a 10-bit secondary opcode. The encoding scheme of the PowerPC shown in Figure 16.10 indicates that the MPC 601 does not operate destructively – that is, source and destination registers are generally different.

16.3 MIPS

One of the main special features of MIPS, as compared to the Alpha from DEC or the i860 or i960 from Intel, is that both the architecture and the full implementation of the MIPS CPUs have essentially been developed by one university (Stanford). For this reason, the new concepts stand foremost, followed by profitable marketing. The result has been the two MIPS and MIPS-X RISC CPUs. As commercial companies, DEC and Intel are naturally profit orientated. Primarily, they have a different target for their own development than a university would have. However, Stanford University's slight fear of commercial dealings has quickly led to the formation of a company – MIPS Computer Systems – which has concerned itself with the further development and profitable marketing resulting from previous research. This has been a very great success. The results are essentially the two CMOS processor chip sets R2000 and R3000, and the high performance ECL processor chip set R6000. MIPS Computer Systems has developed the concepts and architecture (and has also patented them), but does not carry out its own manufacturing – instead, it gives manufacturing licences to the individual integrated circuit manufacturers. These are currently Siemens, NEC, Integrated Device Technology and LSI Logic. The manufacturer holding the licence is only obligated to produce binary compatible versions of the MIPS chips. The chips must also be completely pin-compatible. Currently, MIPS RISC CPUs are mainly inserted into high performance workstations such as the DS 3100 from DEC, Graphic Workstations from Silicon Graphics or the Cyber 910-600 from Control Data. In the following description, I would like to concentrate on the widespread MIPS R3000 processor. The R2000 and the high end implementation R6000 are addressed only briefly.

16.3.1 R3000 architecture

Figure 16.11 shows the internal layout of the R3000 RISC processor. Unlike SPARC architecture, the R3000 contains only a simple register file consisting of 32 general-purpose registers, each of which is 32 bits in size. Thus, the R3000 does not implement register window technology for the fast call of subroutines. However, by means of assigning registers across procedure boundaries, a corresponding compiler strategy ensures that the whole register file need not be saved or reproduced with every CALL or RETURN, respectively. Naturally, this requires a higher optimization workload for the (more complex) compiler, but negates the disadvantage of not having a register window. The advantage of a much quicker task switch, due to the lower number of registers that must be saved, makes the R3000 well suited to real-time applications and multitasking operating systems. Multiple register files provided for fast task switches, however, require a considerably higher hardware workload. Thus, the R3000 has enough room remaining on the chip for the integration of a memory management unit (MMU) and a cache controller, in addition to the RISC kernel. The R3000 CPU kernel considers the MMU as the first coprocessor (with the number 0) and not as a directly connected part of the RISC CPU.

Naturally, in addition to the usual ALU units such as the adder, a faster multiplier and divider are also available.

The five-stage MIPS pipeline is the central, and most important, part for processor performance. It executes every R3000 instruction in a single clock cycle, or – better stated – it delivers an instruction result for every clock cycle. Figure 16.12 shows the individual stages of this pipeline.

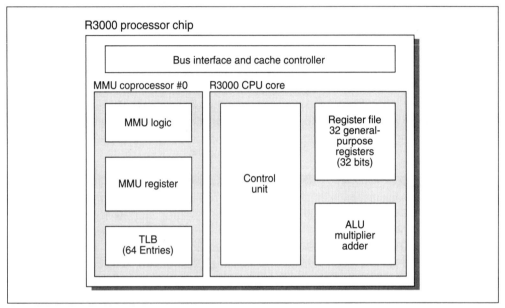

Figure 16.11: The internal structure of the R3000 RISC processor.
The R3000 processor chip integrates a R3000 CPU core, an MMU, which is implemented as coprocessor 0, and a cache controller for driving external SRAM chips.

The instruction fetch stage directs the reading in of the instruction, and also accesses the translation lookaside buffer of the MMU in order to determine the physical address of the instruction. The instruction cache is also prepared for a read access.

The operand or register read stage then executes the access to the instruction cache and reads in the instruction. The instruction is decoded at the same time; this occurs very quickly because of the extremely simple instruction format. Depending on the result of the decoding, the operand is also collected from the corresponding register. The execution or ALU stage then carries out the decoded instruction.

If an access to the data cache or the main memory is necessary during the execution of a load or store instruction, this operation is accomplished during the memory access stage. The last write-back stage (register write stage) stores the result of the instruction in the given destination register (if specified by such an instruction).

This five-stage R3000 pipeline is not free from the danger of stalls. They are resolved either by hardware measures or by a request to the compiler not to allow the possibility of stalls. Here are the individual pipeline conflicts and their solutions:

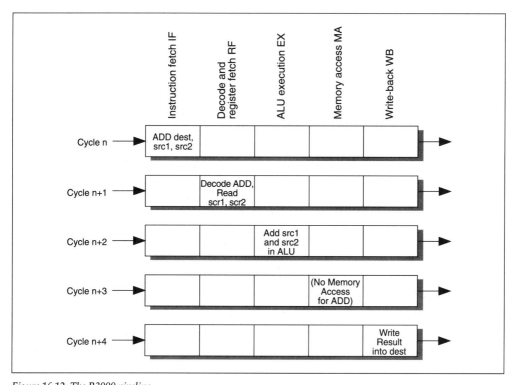

Figure 16.12: The R3000 pipeline.
The R3000 pipeline comprises five stages. The three-address instruction ADD dest, src1, src2 is shown as an example which does not require any memory access. Thus, stage four does not carry out any operation.

▶ An instruction contains a register operand, the value of which is currently being calculated. Thus, the register operand must be read in the operand fetch stage before its value has been written by the register write stage. Thus, in this case, the instruction would be incorrectly executed using the old register value if precautions were not taken. In order to prevent such faults, the R3000 writes the new register value into a buffer, which immediately serves the ALU and the destination register. Thus, the R3000 executes bypassing internally. In this way, the pipeline stages are not dependent on one another with respect to multiple stages (naturally, every pipeline stage depends on the previous stage for receiving the instructions and operands to be executed). This should make the term MIPS clear: MIPS is an acronym for Microprocessor without Interlocked Pipeline Stages.

▶ A register that is loaded by a load instruction cannot be used as an operand in the next clock cycle. The MIPS concept categorically prevents such cases; it simply leaves it to the compiler to produce appropriate code (delayed load).

▶ Most jumps and branches involve an addition operation, in order to determine the jump off-set and the current instruction pointer value of the target address. In this way, the target address is first available one clock cycle later. The R3000 requires that the applicable compiler correctly uses the delayed branch concept and rearranges the code suitably to prevent pipeline conflicts.

▶ Complicated floating-point instructions require more than one clock cycle for execution. In this (seldom occurring) case, the R3000 must hold back the pipeline until the result is available from the coprocessor. This conflict does not, however, directly concern the R3000 and so the term MIPS is still justified.

▶ Load and store instructions are similar. If the required value is already located in the cache (as is the case in more than 90% of all accesses), then it can be read within a single clock cycle. Thus, such accesses do not lead to a pipeline stall. This is entirely different if the value is stored in the main memory and the memory cannot keep up with the CPU. With the relatively low clock frequency of the R3000 – currently up to 33 MHz – most modern DRAMs in page or static column mode are often fast enough. Otherwise, nothing more can be done other than holding up the pipeline until the value is available, or the compiler must insert sufficient NOPs.

16.3.2 R3000 MMU and R3000 address space

The MMU is implemented in the R3000 as a coprocessor. It executes paging in a similar way to the post-80286 x86 processors. For this, the MMU divides the 4-Gbyte address space of the R3000 into pages, each of 4 kbytes. Thus, the R3000 operates internally with virtual 32-bit addresses, which are converted into a physical 32-bit address by the MMU in the same way as in the PU of the i386. The translation lookaside buffer (TLB) is of importance for the performance of the R3000 during address translation, which, in the form of a cache, holds ready 64 'translation entries'.

In this way, the translation of a virtual into a physical address is possible in less than a single clock cycle if a TLB hit occurs. If a TLB miss occurs, on the other hand, the corresponding page directory entry must be read from memory. The TLB operates in a similar way to the TLB of the i386. The only difference is that in addition to the 20 most significant physical address bits and the four general entry management bits (N = non-cacheable, D = dirty, V = valid and G = global), every entry is assigned a 6-bit task mark. This gives the number of the task, to which the applicable TLB entry applies. This is useful for task switches, because then it is not necessary to invalidate the complete TLB (in the i386, all TLB entries apply to the currently active task; thus, the complete TLB must be invalidated for a task switch). As all RISC processors have been planned for high-end machines working under a multitasking operating system, developers have made allowance for task identification. If a TLB miss occurs, the TLB entry is exchanged according to a predefined strategy, as is also the case with normal caches.

An essential difference of the R3000 TLB, as compared to the i386 TLB for example, is that the choosing of the TLB entry to be exchanged and the exchange strategy are implemented by software. In the case of a TLB miss, the R3000 only issues an exception and leaves it to the exception handler to update the appropriate TLB. In comparison, the i386 in such cases reads the page table entry and automatically updates the applicable TLB entry according to a predefined strategy.

The R3000 MMU, like the PU of the i386, implements a two-stage data protection model with kernel or supervisor, and application or user levels. However, there is no segmentation by segment registers – the R3000 contains 32 general-purpose registers with equal rights – and so there is also no segment protection mechanism, as in the i386. Unlike the i386, the R3000 does not implement the protection mechanism at a physical page level, but instead at the level of four preset and very large memory areas (here also known as segments) of the virtual address space. The virtual 4-Gbyte address space of the R3000 is thus split into four segments (see Figure 16.13).

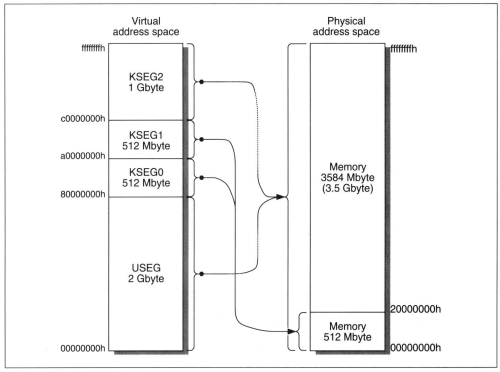

Figure 16.13: The four segments of the R3000 address space.
The virtual address space of 4 Gbytes is divided into the three kernel segments KSEG0, KSEG1 and KSEG2 as well as a user segment USEG. The virtual address space is mapped by the R3000 MMU onto an equal-sized physical address space.

Of these, the three segments KSEG0 to KSEG2 concern the kernel level, and the USEG segment, the application level. The 512-Mbyte KSEG0 kernel segment starts at the virtual address 8000 0000h. It can only be addressed by a supervisor and can be transferred to the cache. KSEG0 usually contains the code and data of the operating system kernel, and thus corresponds to the privilege level 0 of the i386. The segment KSEG1 also encompasses 512 Mbytes. It starts immediately after KSEG1 at the virtual address a000 0000h and can only be addressed by a supervisor. KSEG1 usually contains I/O registers (in the absence of I/O instructions, the R3000 executes a memory mapped I/O), boot ROM and similar elements. For this reason, it is not cacheable. The last kernel segment KSEG2 begins after KSEG1 at the virtual address c000 000h and encompasses 1 Gbyte. This segment, also, can only be addressed by a supervisor. Like KSEG0, KSEG2 is cacheable. The single user segment USEG occupies the lowest 2 Gbytes of the virtual address area and is cacheable. The two segments KSEG0 and KSEG1 of the virtual address area are formed at the first 512 Mbytes of the physical address area; the kernel segment

KSEG2 and the user segment USEG, at the above 3584 Mbytes. The R3000 can physically address bytes, words and double words in memory.

16.3.3 R3000 instruction structure

Considerably more so than with most other RISC processors, there is much closer cooperation between the R3000 (and the RISC MIPS in general) hardware and software development teams. According to the development requirements, the hardware should be as simple as possible and therefore fast, because all complicated harmonization and optimization tasks are handled by the compiler. In this way, the actual compiler is at the forefront, and the MIPS processor is a type of subsystem for the use of the compiler. Instructions have only been included in the instruction set of the R3000 that increase the complete performance of the system by a minimum of 1%. The result is a horizontal instruction set with a total of 58 machine instructions in the four groups load/store, ALU, jump and coprocessor. They are coded by three basic instruction formats (see Figure 16.14).

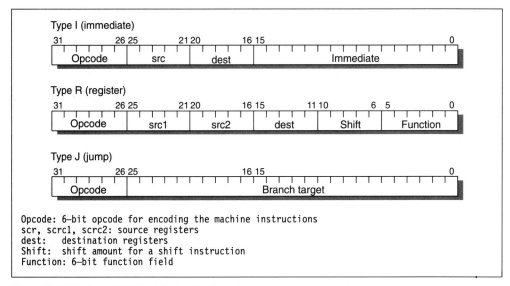

Figure 16.14: The three R3000 basic instruction formats.
The R3000 instructions uniformly comprise 32 bits and show a horizontal encoding.

MIPS identifies the basic instruction formats as I type (with immediate operands), R type (with register operands) and J type (Jumps; that is, jumps and branches). The individual instruction groups are as follows:

▶ Load/store: all instructions in this group are I instructions. The memory address is formed from the source register and an immediate 16-bit offset. Thus, the R3000 implements only a single type of address. During the initialization of the R3000, the CPU can be set to either the little-endian or big-endian format. Loads are implemented as delayed loads and must be organized by the compiler accordingly. Stores are supported by the corresponding temporary registers. In this way, loads and stores can be executed in only one single clock cycle.

▶ ALU: the instructions in this group are of either I or R type. Thus, only three address instructions occur, namely two source registers (R type), a source register and an immediate operand (I type), or a destination register. The two special registers LO and HI are implicitly used only with multiplication and division instructions. They are both 32 bits in size, and store the 64-bit multiplication result in the case of a multiplication, or, in the case of a division (encompassing a maximum of 32 bits), they store the result of the division (HI) or the remainder (LO). If the destination register is not the same as the source register, the ALU instructions are executed non-destructively, in accordance with the requirements of RISC.

▶ Jump: conditional jumps (branches) are in I format, unconditional jumps are in I or R format. For a conditional jump where the source register makes use of the I format, the immediate 16-bit operand of the I format is shifted two positions to the left, and the resulting value is added to the current value of the instruction pointer; the destination register entry of the I format is ignored. The result gives the absolute jump address. Thus, conditional jumps are always relative. The shifting of two positions is possible, because all instructions contain 32 bits and are always aligned with a double word address. The immediate operand is handled as a signed integer, and so both forwards and backwards jumps are possible. In this way, the maximum jump area encompasses $\pm 2^{(15+2)}$ bytes = ± 128 kbytes.

For unconditional jumps, the immediate operand and the two registers of the I format are joined together to form a signed 26-bit jump offset, which is added to the instruction pointer value. The jump area in I format is thus $\pm 2^{25}$ bytes = ± 32 Mbytes. The R format can also be used, whereby the source register entry indicates the register defined by the absolute jump address. In this way, a jump within the complete 4-Gbyte address space is possible. All jumps and branches are implemented as delayed branches and must be organized by the compiler accordingly. Thus, jumps and branches can also be executed in a single clock cycle.

Unlike most CISC processors – and also the i386/i486 and Pentium – the R3000 does not contain a flag register. Instead, the R3000 stores the conditional codes delivered by comparison instructions such as AND, in one of the 32 general-purpose registers. Thus, it is not necessary to make immediate use of the comparison result.

▶ Coprocessor: the R3000 automatically knows whether or not the coprocessor necessary for such an instruction is available. In the latter case, it generates a trap so that a suitable software routine can emulate the functions of the missing coprocessor. This is also possible in the i386. Up to four coprocessors can be connected to an R3000. Coprocessor 0 is formed by the on-chip MMU, thus, an additional three external coprocessors can be inserted. Usually, a mathematical coprocessor R3010 is used as coprocessor 1. Coprocessor interfaces 2 and 3 are freely available for other processors (for example, communications coprocessors).

16.3.4 The R3000 interrupt system

The interrupt system of the R3000 differs quite considerably from that of the x86 processor family. The R3000 only includes three exception vectors, which are reached by a jump as the result of an exception and an interrupt: reset at the virtual address bfc00000h, TLB miss at 80000000h and general exception at 80000080h. Thus, after a reset, the R3000 restarts operation with the instruction at the address bfc00000h in the kernel segment KSEG1. The two other exception handlers are part of the kernel segment KSEG0. The exception for a TLB miss is necessary because the R3000 leaves the TLB exchanging strategy and its execution to a software routine.

The R3000 contains six interrupt pins for issuing hardware interrupts, each of which can generate one interrupt request. Such hardware interrupts do not immediately lead to the call of the corresponding handler through an interrupt vector, which, like the i386 or the Pentium, is transferred by an interrupt controller. Instead, they only lead to a general exception independently of the source. Thus, the software must determine the cause of the exception or interrupt. This is achieved with the help of a special cause register, which is shown in Figure 16.15. In the i386 or Pentium, on the other hand, the interrupt controller transfers the number of the interrupt vector, depending on the source of the interrupt, during the INTA sequence.

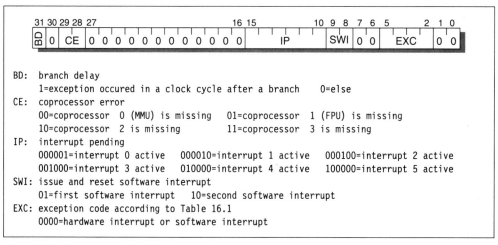

BD: branch delay
      1=exception occured in a clock cycle after a branch   0=else
CE: coprocessor error
      00=coprocessor 0 (MMU) is missing   01=coprocessor 1 (FPU) is missing
      10=coprocessor 2 is missing   11=coprocessor 3 is missing
IP: interrupt pending
      000001=interrupt 0 active   000010=interrupt 1 active   000100=interrupt 2 active
      001000=interrupt 3 active   010000=interrupt 4 active   100000=interrupt 5 active
SWI: issue and reset software interrupt
      01=first software interrupt   10=second software interrupt
EXC: exception code according to Table 16.1
      0000=hardware interrupt or software interrupt

Figure 16.15: The structure of the R3000 cause register.

If the entry in the field EXC equals zero, either an external hardware interrupt or an internal software interrupt has occurred. The codes of the other exception causes are listed in Table 16.1.

The handler must determine the source of the exception, by examining the cause register entries, and handle it accordingly. This procedure gives a considerable speed advantage, despite the apparently more complex strategy, especially if the processor has a fast clock speed. The INTA sequence for the i386 is determined by a very slow (typically 5–8 MHz) interrupt controller 8259A. The 33 MHz version of the R3000 can complete many instructions while the 8259A is still busy transferring the interrupt vector. Thus, controllers on the R3000 basis have a very low interrupt latency.

Code	Source
0	Hardware or software interrupt
1	TLB change
2	TLB miss (data or code fetch)
3	TLB miss (data write)
4	Address fault (data or code fetch)
5	Address fault (data write)
6	Bus error (code fetch)
7	Bus error (data read or write)
8	System call by R3000 instruction SYSCALL
9	Breakpoint through R3000 instruction BREAK
10	Reserved opcode
11	Coprocessor not present
12	ALU overflow
13–15	Reserved

Table 16.1: Exception codes

16.3.5 R3000 caches

The clock frequency of the R3000 is a very high 33 MHz. Further advantages due to the integration of components can be expected to produce even higher clock rates in the future. In addition, between 20 and 30% of a program's content is typically load and save instructions which, together with a slow memory subsystem, can have a very detrimental effect on the performance. Thus, a quicker cache memory is essential for the R3000. For this purpose, the R3000 implements a cache controller for separate code and data caches on its chip. The actual cache memory is realized by external SRAM components. The code and data caches can each be between 4 kbytes and 256 kbytes in size. If a cache miss occurs, the data is loaded in a burst mode. For this reason, the R3000 implements instruction streaming; that is, the R3000 control unit starts with the execution of an instruction as soon as the code is loaded into the cache after a cache miss. In parallel to this instruction execution, the remaining data of the burst mode is also transferred to the cache. Therefore, the R3000 need not wait for the end of the burst mode and, thus, the complete filling of a cache line.

The R3000 uses a write-through strategy, so that the write data for every write access is written through to the main memory, independently of whether a cache hit or miss has occurred. In order not to brake the write operation unnecessarily, a write buffer has been inserted between the cache and the main memory. Thus, the R3000 need not wait for the completion of the write operation, which, at 33 MHz, could lead to a number of wait states. MIPS has developed a special FIFO write buffer for the R3000 – the R3020. It is one byte wide and four levels deep; four such chips are necessary for the R3000, in order to cover the R3000 data bus width of 32 bits. Without a write buffer, the execution time of the store instruction would be set by the access time of the slow main memory, and so a cache would have no effect. Also, 'normal' i386 systems with a cache mostly implement such a write buffer. This can lead to the fact that the number of wait cycles for a write access to the main memory being less than that required for a read operation. The reason for this is that during a write operation, the write buffer immediately takes the data from the CPU and stores it temporarily, then leisurely passes it on to the main memory, whereas during a read operation the CPU must wait for the memory.

16.3.6 The R3010 coprocessor

Regarding mathematics, the R3000 only implements integer instructions. Floating-point formats and transcendental functions, such as sines or logarithms, are not supported. Workstations, however, are frequently used in areas that require such mathematical functions. For this reason, a mathematical coprocessor has been developed for the R3000 – the R3010. As in the i387, or the on-chip coprocessor of the i486 and Pentium, it conforms strictly to the IEEE standard 754-1985 for the representation and handling of floating-point numbers. The R3010 is managed by the R3000 as coprocessor 1 (0 is already occupied by the MMU).

Internally, the R3010 contains 16 floating-point registers, each with a width of 64 bits. For the quick execution of floating-point instructions, the R3010 also contains a hardwired floating-point adder, multiplier and divider. In this way, very complex floating-point instructions can also be completed very quickly. In addition, the R3010 implements a six-stage floating-point pipeline (the R3000 pipeline has five stages). However, it does not execute register bypassing and so, therefore, must be halted if pipeline conflicts occur. Unlike, for example, the i386/i387 combination, a coprocessor opcode occurring in the instruction flow need not be explicitly transferred to the R3010, which would slow the execution speed. Instead, the R3010 begins with the instruction execution, as soon as the instruction code is read during the instruction fetch stage of the R3000. In this way, the R3010 behaves as if it were a floating-point unit integrated on the R3000 chip, similarly to the i486DX.

16.3.7 The R2000

The performance of the MIPS processor architecture is reduced in the R2000 and its associated coprocessor R2010 and write buffer 2020. The R2000 is the predecessor to the R3000. A special feature of the R3000 and R2000 is their pin compatibility – they have the same housing and the same pin layout. Obviously, the R2000 and R3000 are also object code compatible – programs for the R2000 can run on the R3000 and vice versa, without the need to recompile. Like the R3000, the R2000 integrates a memory management unit and a cache controller in addition to the CPU kernel. However, neither burst mode for the filling and writing back of cache lines, nor instruction streaming, is supported. The cache controller is constructed for controlling an external data and instruction cache, each of a maximum 64-kbyte memory capacity. Together with the lower clock frequency of 8–16.7 MHz, the R2000 clearly falls behind the R3000 with respect to performance. The 16 MHz variant of the R2000 achieves an instruction throughput of 12 MIPS, as compared to 28 MIPS for the 33 MHz R3000 (for comparison, the high-end MIPS R6000 version achieves 65 MIPS at 80 MHz, the Pentium 166 MIPS at 100 MHz).

16.3.8 The R6000 in ECL technology

The 32-bit high-end implementation of MIPS RISC concepts is currently represented by the R6000 and its coprocessor R6010. It is clocked at a maximum of 80 MHz and is constructed using only emitter coupled logic (ECL) technology. This is a bipolar technology; it does not operate using MOSFETs, but instead uses bipolar transistors. In this way, the chip is considerably quicker; it does, however, have a much higher power consumption and is not so compactly integrated (BiCMOS in the Pentium is not a compromise between speed, heat production and compactness without reason). An ECL chip typically requires two to three times the energy and is only half as tightly integrated as a comparable CMOS chip. For this reason, it can cope with the doubled clock frequency without problems.

The basic circuit (see Figure 16.16) in ECL technology consists of a differential amplifier, whereby the two transistors Tr_1 and Tr_2 are bipolar. They are not operated in the saturated state, even though the circuit is digital (in digital circuits constructed using CMOS technology, on the other hand, the transistors operate in a saturated state). In this way, a switching time of well under 1 ns is achieved for the logic gates. Using MOS technology, only circuits based on GaAs achieve shorter switching times.

Through the use of bipolar transistors, where current flows continuously even in the closed condition, the power loss is considerably higher. A further disadvantage of ECL circuits is that the dynamic range of the output voltage is very small (typically 0.8 V), thus the difference between the logic levels for 0 and 1 is much less. For this reason, ECL circuits require additional impedance converters and voltage shifting stages in order to produce suitable input voltages for subsequent ECL circuit stages. Together with already lower structure density of bipolar circuits due to the more complicated layer structure, this means that the density of integration is considerably reduced.

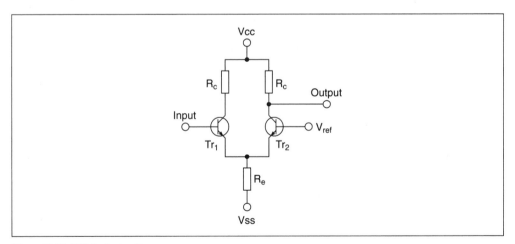

Figure 16.16: ECL basic circuit.
The emitters of the two transistors are connected (thus the name emitter coupled logic) and are connected to GND (Vss) via the emitter resistor R_e. The collectors of the transistors are connected to Vcc via separate collector resistors R_c. The second transistor Tr_2 receives a reference voltage, the first transistor Tr_1 the input voltage. The output voltage is produced at the collector of the second transistor.

The R6000 processor chip set consists of the R6000 CPU, the coprocessor R6010 with associated external multiplier/divider, and the system bus controller 6020 with integrated write buffer – thus, four ECL chips in total. The pipeline, register file and MMU structure are, in principle, the same as in the R2000/R3000; the R6000, for example, also contains a pipeline with five stages.

Many other characteristics of the R6000 differ from the R2000/R3000. The address bus has been expanded from 32 bits to 36 bits, so the R6000 is object-compatible, but no longer pin-compatible with the R2000/R3000. Thus, the physical address area has increased to 64 Gbytes. The virtual memory per task, in comparison, remains as before at 4 Gbytes because of the unchanged 32-bit registers. However, these 32-bit addresses are expanded by an 8-bit task identification to 40 bits, so that the complete virtual address area encompasses 1 Tbyte.

A further essential difference to the R2000/R3000 is that the cache in the on-chip cache controller is already implemented as a two-stage cache. An external L2 cache controller was necessary for this in the R2000/R3000. The two separated primary caches for code and data are realized with very fast 8 ns ECL SRAMs. The secondary (L2) cache, however, stores both code and data and is formed from somewhat slower BiCMOS SRAMs. The primary cache is direct-mapped and uses a write-through strategy via write buffers to the L2 cache. The secondary L2 cache, on the other hand, is organized as a two-way set-associative cache and usually operates using a write-back strategy in order to avoid, as much as possible, lengthy write accesses to the main memory.

As I have already explained, the R6010 coprocessor uses an external ECL multiplier/divider (usually the B3110), which can also calculate cubic roots independently. This has become necessary, because of the low integration compactness on the R6010 chip – there was simply no room remaining for this complex circuit. The B3110 is only connected to the R6010 and not to the R6000.

The fourth chip of the R6000 chip set – the R6020 – represents the complete system bus controller and not just a write buffer, as was the case in the R2020/R3020. It also executes other tasks, for example, burst mode transfers with a band width of up to 320 Mbytes/s at a clock speed of 80 Mhz.

16.3.9 The 64-bit MIPS R4000

The latest MIPS chip is the R4000. It represents a full-value 64-bit processor, but for reasons of compatibility, it can also be programmed for 32-bit operation. The R4000 integrates a 64-bit CPU, a 64-bit FPU, an integer register stack with 32 64-bit registers, an FP register stack with 32 64-bit registers and separate code and data caches on one chip. The caches can store between 8 and 32 kbytes of data. The L1 code cache is direct-mapped and operates with 16-byte or 32-byte cache lines. The L1 data cache is also direct-mapped and implements a write-back strategy; a 16-byte or 32-byte cache line size can be selected. The on-chip caches use a protocol similar to MESI in order to ensure cache consistency with other caches. A cache controller for an L2 cache is already available on the R4000 chip. This also functions as direct-mapped with a write-back strategy but, however, 16-byte, 32-byte, 64-byte or 128-byte cache lines can be selected.

The R4000 uses virtual 64-bit addresses, which it forms in the physical address area of its 36-bit address bus. This produces a physical address area of 64 Gbytes. In 32-bit mode, the virtual address area encompasses 2^{31} bytes = 2 Gbytes; in 64-bit mode 2^{41} = 1 Tbyte. The TLB contains 32 entries; pages in the R4000 can be selected as 4 kbytes, 16 kbytes, 64 kbytes, 256 kbytes, 1 Mbyte, 4 Mbytes or 16 Mbytes in size. The external data bus is 128 bits wide. The instruction set has been expanded by 58 instructions, which mainly support multiprocessor and multitasking operating systems.

Compared to the R3000, the pipeline of the R4000 has been extensively reworked. The R4000 pipeline, shown in Figure 16.17, contains eight stages.

The first two prefetch stages IF and IS of the R4000 pipeline, read in an instruction where the operation of the TLB is necessary in order to determine the correct physical address. The register fetch stage RF decodes the instruction and fetches the required operands from the register file. The ALU executes the instruction in the execution stage EX. The two data fetch stages DF and DS fetch the data from the data cache or write it to the TLB. In the seventh tag check stage TC, the tag executes a tag check for load/store instructions, in order to determine whether a hit or a miss has occurred. The last WB stage finally updates the register with the new value.

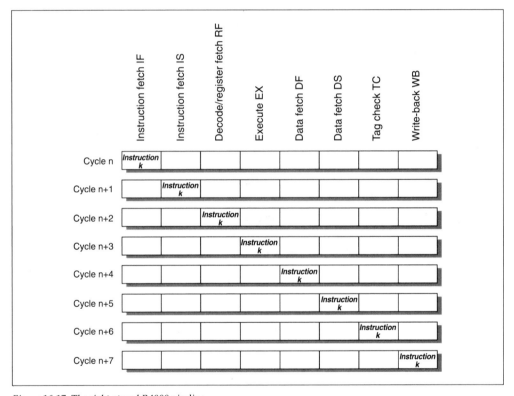

Figure 16.17: The eight-staged R4000 pipeline.

The R4000 normally operates with an external clock speed of 50 MHz, but doubles this internally for the pipeline – that is, the R4000 pipeline runs at 100 MHz. Stated differently, two instructions are started per (50 MHz) clock cycle, even though no superscalar architecture is implemented. The greatest difference compared to its predecessors – and in conflict with the term MIPS – is the fact that the R4000 pipeline can also contain interlocks, which can stall the complete pipeline or at least hold back an instruction (and thus, all subsequent instructions). Until now, the most important requirement of the MIPS concept was not to allow interlocks, even if the compiler had to insert the corresponding quantity of NOPs. With the extension of the pipeline to eight stages, the same problem arises regarding the use of delay and branch slots as in the Alpha. In addition, the use of L1 and L2 caches makes it almost impossible to predict when a value will be available after a load. Thus, the new MIPS R4000 has left the previously used track, whereby such complex problems were handled exclusively by software, and now supports such situations through its hardware. Branches, for example, lead to a branch delay of three pipeline cycles (100 MHz), and load operations to a load delay of two pipeline cycles.

16.4 SPARC

SPARC (Scalable Processor Architecture) was developed by Sun Microsystems based on the Berkeley RISC concept. Therefore, SPARC follows a somewhat different concept, mainly for the realization of the pipeline, to that of the MIPS processors. SPARC is not, however, a slave-like implementation of Berkeley RISCs; it does contain significant improvements for the organization of the registers. As a result of a very open licensing concept (similar to that of the MIPS), there are a number of manufacturers of SPARC chips (It should be noted that SPARC, unlike MIPS, was developed by a company and not a university). Currently, these include Bipolar Integrated Technology, Cypress Semiconductors, Fujitsu, LSI-Logic and Philips. SPARC CPUs are available with clock frequencies from 16 to 80 MHz (ECL), and MIPS values of between 10 and 65 MIPS. All SPARCS from the different manufacturers are binary compatible; however, they can sometimes differ greatly in their performance.

16.4.1 SPARC architecture and register organization

The SPARCs, like all RISC processors, implement a simple instruction set which, in this case, is executed in a pipeline with four stages (for comparison, MIPS generally operate with a pipeline containing five stages). Through the three address models of the instructions, SPARCs operate non-destructively – that is, the source operands remain available for further execution after an instruction has executed. A considerable difference compared to MIPS, for example, is the modular architecture of a SPARC system (see Figure 16.18).

A SPARC system consists of an integer CPU at a minimum (and of course, a main memory). In addition, a floating-point unit (FPU), a further coprocessor (for example, for communication tasks), a cache and a memory management unit (MMU) may be available. These elements are optional; the CPU and the two coprocessors each contain their own register set. SPARC does not integrate the coprocessors; instead, it only defines the interface to their connections. This applies to the mathematical coprocessor, for example, so that improvements to its internal layout do not mean that the SPARC CPU has to be redesigned. It is also interesting that the MMU is not integrated. Thus, SPARCs operate purely with virtual addresses; if an external MMU is available, the processor sends a virtual address and not a physical address to its terminals. The cache is also added on to the processor as a separate subsystem. Thus, SPARC processors have a very simple structure, but must be supported by external support chips. Only in this way, for example, was it possible to implement the first SPARC processor as a simple gate array and still achieve a 40 MHz clock frequency. The modular structure is also important for ensuring the scalability of the SPARC architecture – not without reason is the acronym for scalable processor architecture used. Such a layout makes SPARCs suitable for multiprocessor operation. A considerable strength of the SPARC workstation is the ease with which it can be integrated into a network – also a form of scaling.

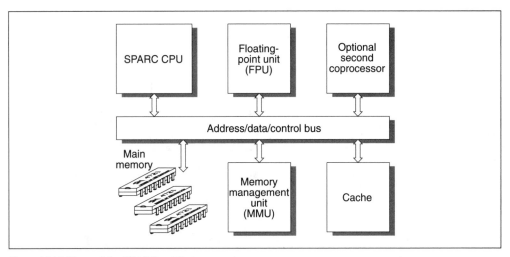

Figure 16.18: The modular SPARC architecture.
A SPARC system is structured in a modular manner. Only the SPARC CPU and the main memory are required; FPU, coprocessor, MMU and cache are optional but increase the system performance. SPARC only defines the interface between the devices. Thus, manufacturers have extensive freedom to choose the best and most powerful way of implementing the support devices.

The pipeline of the SPARC CPU, shown in Figure 16.19, executes an instruction in only four stages.

The instruction fetch stage reads in the instruction. The decoding stage decodes the instruction that has been read and, if necessary, addresses the source operand register. The decoding is executed very quickly as a result of the simple instruction format. The execution stage that follows then executes the decoded instruction with the operand fetched. The last write-back stage (register write stage) stores the instruction result in the given destination register (if one is specified by the instruction). Pipeline stalls are processed through register bypassing and scoreboarding. An optimizing compiler, however, can largely avoid such stalls.

An essential characteristic of the SPARC architecture is the number of registers (40 to 520, sometimes more), which are joined together in multiple register windows, which partly overlap. Thus, SPARC implements a multiple register file. In this way, very fast subroutine calls are possible. At any given time, exactly one register window with 32 registers is always visible using this register window strategy. The 32 registers of this register window are divided into eight IN registers, eight local registers, eight OUT registers and eight global registers. During a subroutine call (or the return from it), the register window pointer that sets the beginning of the register window within the much larger SPARC register file is simply changed. In this way, the register window can be shifted simply and quickly; the number of memory accesses for the saving and replacing of parameters and variables falls dramatically. The eight OUT registers of the procedure at a higher level overlap with the eight IN registers of the procedure at a lower level. Thus, together with the eight static global registers, a register window of 32 general-purpose registers is always visible. This is shown in Figure 16.20.

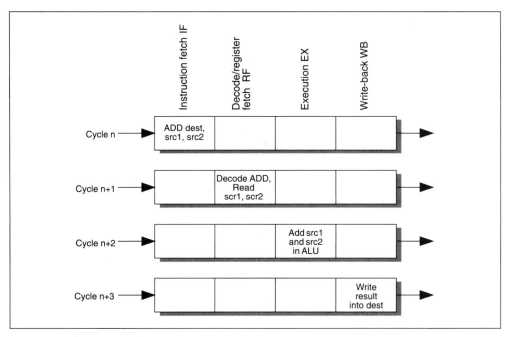

Figure 16.19: The SPARC pipeline.
The pipeline of the SPARC CPU comprises four stages. The three-address instruction ADD dest, src1, src2 is shown as an example that does not require any memory access.

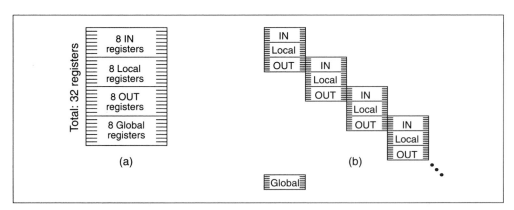

Figure 16.20: The register windows of the SPARC architecture.
(a) The register window visible at a certain time is divided into eight IN, eight OUT, eight local and eight global registers.
(b) Upon a subroutine call (or a return from one) the register window pointer is simply altered so that the register window is shifted. Together with the eight static global registers, one register window with 32 general-purpose registers is always visible. The eight OUT registers of the higher level procedure overlap with the eight IN registers of the lower level procedure. Thus a fast subroutine call is possible.

The OUT registers store the input parameters for the called subroutine. As they are physically identical to the eight IN registers of the subroutine, the parameter transfer is accomplished without delays. The global register 0 always contains the value 0 – it cannot be changed, even by an over-write. In this way, the most frequently used constant can be made available for programs in a very simple way, without the need for immediate operands.

For the realization of the SPARC minimum configuration with two register windows, a minimum of 40 registers are necessary: eight IN, eight local and eight OUT registers for the first level; eight IN (identical to the eight OUT registers of the first level), eight local and eight OUT registers for the second level. The eight global registers are separate and are managed statically. The software for high-end versions with 520 registers – corresponding to 32 register windows plus eight global registers – and the simple version described with only two register windows, is completely identical. Thus, the register structure is completely transparent. From the compiler's side, no provisions are necessary in order to serve SPARC processors with differing numbers of registers.

An essential change in the definition of SPARC, as compared to the basic Berkeley RISC concept, is the decoupling of instructions that set (SAVE) and reset (RESTORE) the pointer – the so-called *current window pointer* – to the register window used from that for the call of the sub-routines themselves. In this way, the compiler is much more flexible for the reorganization of registers, even across procedure boundaries – for example, if the called subroutine does not activate any more subroutines, and thus the management of its variables in a separate register window is not strictly necessary. *Register window overflows* resulting from too deep a nesting level can be effectively prevented. The SAVE instruction switches the register window one level further. If, however, the complete multiple register file of the SPARC processor is used up – and thus the SAVE instruction cannot be executed – then a register window overflow occurs and the processor generates the corresponding exception. As the multiple register file contains a ring structure, the exception handler must only store the oldest register window externally – that is, the register window that belongs to the highest procedure level – in order to make sufficient room for the execution of the SAVE instruction.

A RESTORE instruction, on the other hand, switches the register window one level back, so that the register window of the above procedure level is again addressable. A RESTORE instruction is typically executed immediately before or after a RETURN instruction. If, during the previous subroutine call and the accompanying SAVE instruction, a register window overflow has occurred, and the processor has stored a register window externally in memory, then the RESTORE instruction in the corresponding level causes a register window underflow. The processor again produces an exception, and the applicable handler loads the register window from memory back into the multiple register file of the processor. It is clear that such register window overflows and underflows occur less frequently the more registers the SPARC processor contains.

Task switches represent a general problem – not just for SPARC and other RISC processors, but also for CISC CPUs – because, during their operation, the updated register values of the current task must be saved, and the new register values of the newly activated task must be loaded from memory. The more registers there are to save and restore, the longer the whole operation takes. Multitasking systems or controllers with a heavy workload spend a large proportion of their time executing such storing and retrieving operations when task switches occur continuously. If all 520 registers of the multiple register file must be saved and restored, a task switch can take a very long time. For this reason, during a task switch, the operating system for SPARC processors stores only those registers in memory that actually contain valid data (and also only restores those applicable). Thus, having a large number of registers does not always bring only advantages. The developer must find a compromise between using a large number of registers suitable for the fast call of subroutines without register window overflows and underflows, and using fewer registers to increase the speed of task switches. Alternatively, a large multiple register file can also be divided into many smaller multiple register files, each assigned to a task. In this way, not only register window overflows due to extensive subroutine calls are negated – in addition, task switches (in most cases) do not then require lengthy saving and restoring phases.

The SPARC CPU contains many control and status registers in addition to the registers described – including the current window pointer. They are used, for example, for managing the coprocessors. The condition code register is important for instruction execution. It stores the condition code for the single SPARC comparison instruction, SUBCC (subtract and set condition codes). The destination register for this instruction is usually the global register 0 (which cannot be overwritten). The instruction stores a condition code in the condition code register, which can then be used by a branch instruction.

SPARC processors include a very extensive interrupt structure, with 128 exceptions or software interrupts, and 128 hardware interrupts. Thus, they are well suited to controller applications.

16.4.2 The SPARC address space

Through the load and store instructions, SPARC CPUs address a 4-Gbyte address space. Individual bytes, words or double words can be addressed. The SPARC CPU also produces the addresses for all load and store operations through the FPU or an optional coprocessor, whereby the FPU and coprocessor immediately receive data from or send data to memory. Thus, no memory access takes place through the CPU, as is the case in the i386/i387, where the coprocessor performance is significantly influenced. The memory addresses must be aligned at 32-bit boundaries, otherwise an alignment exception is generated. Unlike the i386, Pentium and MIPS processors, SPARC uses the big-endian format exclusively; thus, the most significant bytes are stored at the least significant addresses and vice versa.

SPARC implements a simple access protection, in that an 8-bit address space identifier (ASI) is provided for many load and memory instructions, which is combined with the 32-bit memory address. Four of the possible address areas are preset by the SPARC architecture: supervisor code, supervisor data, application code and application data. The other address areas can be used by the hardware and the accompanying hardware-like system software, for example, in order to address system elements not visible to the user. Note that each address area can contain a full 4 Gbytes; thus, the complete address area is very large.

16.4.3 The SPARC instruction structure

The SPARC instruction set contains 55 CPU instructions, 14 floating-point instructions and two coprocessor instructions, all of which contain 32 bits and are uniformly coded, in order to increase the speed of the decoding operation in the second pipeline stage. Figure 16.21 shows the three basic instruction formats.

The first format codes a CALL instruction, which contains a 30-bit displacement as the target address. Because the target address always points to a 32-bit double word, the 30-bit displacement is, in fact, a 32-bit byte address, so that a call to any position in the 4-Gbyte address area can result. The second format serves initially for the coding of a SETHI (set high) instruction and also for branch instructions. For this, the CC field defines the jump condition, which must be identical to the value in the condition register of the SPARC CPU. All other instructions are code in format 3; they implement a three-address structure, whereby the source register can also be replaced by an immediate operand. In the case of a load or store instruction, the eight ASI bits operate as an address space identifier, which defines the address area used for the memory access. For floating-point instructions, the FP Op-bits extend the opcode by a further eight bits (31/30 and 24–18).

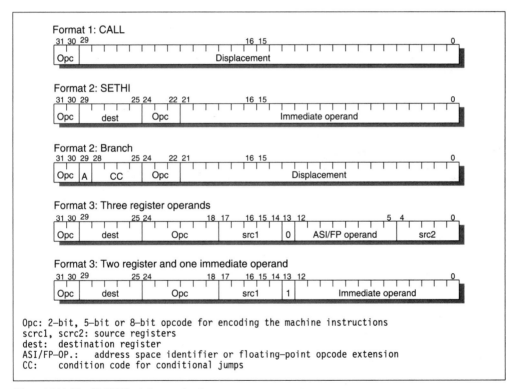

Figure 16.21: The SPARC basic instruction formats.
The SPARC instructions are uniformly 32 bits in size and show a horizontal encoding. The opcode can be distributed over a maximum of three fields.

With a normal arithmetic instruction coded in format 3, only immediate 13-bit operands can be loaded into a 32-bit register. The 19 most significant bits are not accessible. The 32-bit registers can only be loaded in a single instruction using LOAD, which leads to an unwanted memory access. On the other hand, only small values are normally loaded into registers, such as 0, ±1, or occasionally 100 for loops, perhaps. Values in the region of ±2G, which fill the complete 32-bit capacity, occur only very seldom. For this reason, in most cases it is sufficient to use an immediate 13-bit operand in order to load a constant into a register (13 bits correspond to a range of ±4096). In the few cases where a larger fixed value must be loaded into a 32-bit register, it is accomplished using SETHI. The SETHI instruction writes the 22 most significant bits of a register with a specific value. The 13 least significant bits can be loaded by an immediate operand, so that with two instructions, the complete 32-bit register is written; an overlapping of the values from SETHI and the immediate operand occurs in bits 12–14. The direct loading of a 32-bit value from memory into a 32-bit register would not be any quicker, because a LOAD generally leads to a pipeline delay of one clock cycle.

It is interesting to note that SPARC does not contain an instruction for the complete multiplication of integers (and so does not include a multiplier unit on the chip). Instead, the multiply stage set CC (MULSCC) instruction is implemented, which, in a more or less lengthy and roundabout way, delivers the 64-bit product of two 32-bit numbers. MULSCC uses a method corresponding to Figure 6.1. The least significant bit of the multiplicator register decides whether the multiplicand of the already determined part result is added. Finally, MULSCC shifts the resulting value one bit to the left. In this way, after a maximum of k + 4 clock cycles, a k * 32 multiplication is completed, without the need for a multiplier unit. Through instruction pipelining, SPARCs can still execute the multiplication very quickly. Highly complex mathematical tasks are executed by the floating-point coprocessor, which implements a very fast hardware multiplier unit.

16.4.4 Floating-point and other coprocessors

In accordance with the SPARC specification, the floating-point coprocessor or floating-point unit (FPU), like the SPARC CPU, contains a register file with 32 general-purpose registers, each of 32 bits. These 32-bit registers can be used individually, or joined together in pairs of registers (64-bit), or in groups of four registers (128-bit). The groups must be aligned at pair or quad boundaries. In this way, the FPU can store a maximum of 32 floating-point numbers with a low accuracy, 16 with double the accuracy, or eight with a higher accuracy. Like the MIPS coprocessors or x87 series, SPARC FPUs also implement the IEEE standard 754-1985. If the floating-point coprocessor is not available in the system, the SPARC CPU generates an exception, so that the FPU functions can be emulated by a mathematical software library.

The need for parallel operation was foremost during the development of the FPU. For this reason, the SPARC FPU can execute floating-point additions and floating-point multiplications in parallel. In addition, these operations are also completed in parallel to the program execution in the CPU. Load and store instructions are also accomplished in the FPU, in parallel to instruction execution. As I have already explained, SPARC only defines the interface between the CPU and the FPU, and not the architecture of the FPU itself. A SPARC FPU usually executes the floating-point instructions in a pipeline, which operates using scoreboarding in order to master pipeline conflicts.

In addition to the floating-point coprocessor, SPARC includes a further coprocessor that can be integrated into the system. This may, for example, be a communications coprocessor. For these optional coprocessors also, only the interface to the SPARC CPU is defined – the exact implementation is the responsibility of the manufacturer. According to the requirements of the SPARC specification for such coprocessors, an individual register set is available, and so these coprocessors also execute instructions in parallel to the CPU and FPU. This emphasizes that SPARC is most suitable for the parallel processing of instructions in high performance networked workstations.

16.5 i860

The i860 is Intel's first 64-bit microprocessor with more than a million transistors. It integrates not only an integer and a floating-point unit, but also a 3D unit in order to support the representation of three-dimensional (3D) graphics on a monitor. The i860 can operate its three internal pipelines in parallel. Clock frequencies of 33 to 50 MHz deliver a maximum theoretical performance of 150 MIPS or 80 Mflops for single precision floating-point numbers. These figures lie within the range of supercomputers. Separate code and data caches supply the execution unit and access the memory through a 64-bit wide data bus.

16.5.1 i860 architecture

The i860 contains a total of nine functional units. They are the RISC core unit, the floating-point unit, the floating-point adder, the floating-point multiplier, the graphics unit, the memory management unit (MMU), the bus and cache controllers, the code cache and the data cache. Figure 16.22 is a block diagram of the i860.

The central part is the RISC core unit, which controls the complete i860. In addition to the execution of normal integer and control flow instructions, the core unit also reads the floating-point instructions and distributes them to the floating-point unit and the two floating-point pipelines. The RISC core unit further implements a register file of 32 general-purpose registers r0 to r31, each of which encompasses 32 bits. They can, however, also be addressed as 16 64-bit registers. For this, the register pairs must be aligned with pair limits (r0, r2 and so on). Further local or global registers are not available, thus the i860 does not implement multiple register files or register windows. The r0 register always returns the value 0 when read; write operations are, thus, implicitly ignored. In this way, the 32-bit constant 00000000h is always available.

The floating-point unit contains its own set of 32 general-purpose registers f0 to f31 with a width of 32 bits. They can, however, also be addressed as sixteen 64-bit registers or as eight 128-bit registers. For this, the register pairs or register quads must be aligned with pair (f0, f2 and so on) or quad (f0, f4 and so on) limits, respectively. All floating-point instructions exclusively refer to floating-point registers. The floating-point registers f0 and f1 always return the value 0 when read. Thus, write operations are implicitly ignored, as with the r0 register. In this way, the 64-bit constant 0000000000000000h is always available. In addition to floating-point instructions, many graphics instructions also use the floating-point registers.

The floating-point adder and the floating-point multiplier can operate in parallel, for example to execute a multiply accumulate instruction in the form A * B + C. Thus, in pipeline mode, the i860 can execute two floating-point instructions in a single clock cycle. If you add to this the simultaneous execution of an instruction in the RISC core unit, then three instructions in a single clock cycle are possible. The problem then is that the external data bus can no longer load the instructions from the main memory with enough speed. For this reason, an essential task during the development of the i860 was to find a good balance between the execution speed of the internal calculation units and the band width of the external data bus.

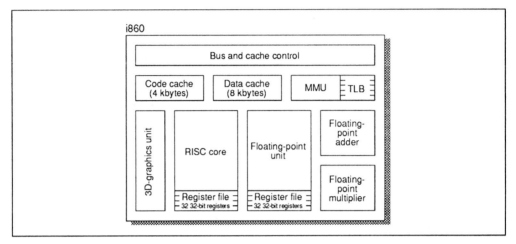

Figure 16.22: The internal structure of the i860.
The i860 integrates a RISC core, a floating-point unit, a floating-point adder, a floating-point multiplier, a 3D-graphics unit, a memory management unit (MMU), a bus and a cache controller, as well as code and data caches.

The 3D graphics unit mainly supports graphical transformations and a 3D rendering for the elimination of hidden surfaces and edges. It uses special pixel formats, which are regarded as bit chains, and special graphics instructions. The graphics unit makes an approximation of graphical objects by means of polygons. By using the full internal 64-bit architecture of the i860, this task is executed very quickly, without the need for an external clipping processor.

The MMU integrates a paging unit (PU), the function of which is essentially the same as that in the i486 and Pentium. The protection of data and codes from each other is implemented through a two-level user/supervisor model. The protected mode of the x86 architecture is not applied. Virtual addresses are converted into physical addresses by a translation lookaside buffer (TLB).

The instruction cache is organized as a two-way set-associative cache with 32-byte cache lines, and contains 4 kbytes; thus, 128 cache lines are available in total. The instruction cache is connected to the bus controller through an internal 64-bit instruction bus, and to the RISC core and the floating-point unit through two 32-bit buses – thus, together, a 64-bit bus. Therefore, at 50 MHz, it has an internal instruction transfer rate of 400 Mbytes/s, because only one clock cycle is necessary for a 64-bit transfer. The data cache is also organized as a two-way set-associative cache with 32-byte cache lines, but has a memory capacity of 8 kbytes; thus, 256 cache lines are available in total. The data cache is connected to the bus controller through an internal 128-bit data bus, and to the RISC core and the floating-point unit through two 64-bit data buses – thus, together, a 128-bit data bus. Here, the internal data transfer rate is 800 Mbytes/s at 50 MHz. The data cache generally uses a write-back concept, in order to keep external memory accesses to a minimum. Both caches operate using virtual addresses, in order to save an address conversion cycle in the PU and to increase the speed of accesses to the instructions and data in the caches.

The bus and cache controllers execute all accesses to data and code. They operate with pipelined addressing and support up to three pending bus cycles. Write buffers accelerate the memory access further. The i860 bus, however, does not know burst mode, for example, to quickly refill or to store a cache line. Furthermore, the i860 does not implement a separate I/O address area, as known from the x86 family and the Pentium. All access to external control or status registers must therefore be executed as memory mapped.

16.5.2 Control, status and special registers

In addition to the total of 64 general-purpose registers, the i860 contains numerous other control and special registers. The first group includes the processor status register (PSR), the expanded processor status register (EPSR) the data breakpoint (DB) register, the directory base register (DIRBASE), the fault instruction register (FIR) and the floating-point status register (FSR). The structure of the PSR and the EPSR is shown in Figure 16.23.

The PSR contains various information about the current processor and task condition. The two *pixel size* and *pixel mask* fields are used by graphics instructions. They define the number of bits for each pixel, and also the mask for the pixel updating instruction. The *shift count* entry stores the number of shifts in the last shift right instruction. The *KNF* bit sets whether or not the next floating point instruction should be ignored. This is typically the case after a floating-point trap (an exception), if the floating-point instruction that released the trap should not be executed again. After a trap, the *DIM* bit indicates whether the i860 was operating in dual instruction mode when the trap occurred. After the return from the trap handler, the i860 restarts normal operation in dual instruction mode if this bit is set. The *DS* bit is set after a trap, if the trap occurred with an instruction that precedes the entry into, or the exit from, dual instruction mode. The *FT*, *DAT*, *IAT*, *IN* and *IT* bits indicate the cause of a trap. By interrogating these bits, the trap handler can determine the source of the trap and handle it accordingly. For example, an external interrupt releases an interrupt trap. The two 1-bit *PU* and *PIM* fields save the current value of the U and IM status bits if a trap occurs. A trap can change U and IM. The *U* bit is set if the i860 is operating in user mode, thus the active task has low access privileges. U is reset in supervisor mode. A set *IM* bit allows external interrupts, and therefore corresponds to the IE flag in the i386 and Pentium. The *LCC* sets the condition for the repeating of loops. It is set and interrogated by the BLA (branch and add) instruction. *CC* indicates the condition code, for example, of a comparison operation. The two *BW* and *BR* bits permit data access traps if a write to, or read from, a specific breakpoint occurs.

The EPSR contains further information concerning the current task and also control instructions for the i860. *OF* is set if an overflow occurs in the RISC core. The *BE* bit is a control flag and sets the byte sequence. The i860, like all Intel processors, normally uses the little-endian format and so BE is reset. If data accesses should be executed in the big-endian format, you must set the BE bit. Code accesses, and also accesses to page directories and page tables, can only be executed in the little-endian format independently of the BE value. The *PBM* bit sets whether the value of the CD bit (PBM=0) or the value of the WT bit (PBM=1) in the page table entry for the current access is sent out from the PTB pin of the i860. The *DCS* bit indicates the size of the on-chip data cache; DCS can only be read. The *INT* bit indicates the current level at the INT pin of the i860. The *WP* bit sets whether write accesses to page level entries should lead to a trap in user mode only, or also in supervisor mode. A set *IL* bit indicates that the trap has occurred in a locked cycle. The two other processor type and model number fields describe the i860 and the current version, respectively.

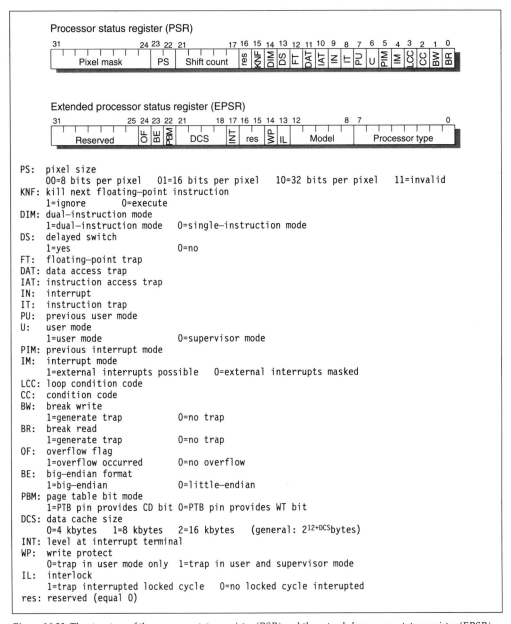

PS: pixel size
      00=8 bits per pixel   01=16 bits per pixel   10=32 bits per pixel   11=invalid
KNF: kill next floating-point instruction
      1=ignore   0=execute
DIM: dual-instruction mode
      1=dual-instruction mode   0=single-instruction mode
DS: delayed switch
      1=yes   0=no
FT: floating-point trap
DAT: data access trap
IAT: instruction access trap
IN: interrupt
IT: instruction trap
PU: previous user mode
U: user mode
      1=user mode   0=supervisor mode
PIM: previous interrupt mode
IM: interrupt mode
      1=external interrupts possible   0=external interrupts masked
LCC: loop condition code
CC: condition code
BW: break write
      1=generate trap   0=no trap
BR: break read
      1=generate trap   0=no trap
OF: overflow flag
      1=overflow occurred   0=no overflow
BE: big-endian format
      1=big-endian   0=little-endian
PBM: page table bit mode
      1=PTB pin provides CD bit 0=PTB pin provides WT bit
DCS: data cache size
      0=4 kbytes   1=8 kbytes   2=16 kbytes   (general: 2^{12+DCS}bytes)
INT: level at interrupt terminal
WP: write protect
      0=trap in user mode only 1=trap in user and supervisor mode
IL: interlock
      1=trap interrupted locked cycle   0=no locked cycle interupted
res: reserved (equal 0)

Figure 16.23: The structure of the processor status register (PSR) and the extended processor status register (EPSR).

The 32-bit data breakpoint register *DB* stores the address of a breakpoint in a similar way to the debug register of the i386 or Pentium. In this way, only read or write data accesses can be intercepted in the i860. If a data access occurs that overlaps with the stored address, and the BR or BW bit in the PSR is set, the i860 generates a trap. A debugger can intercept the trap and handle it accordingly. In the case of a trap, the FIR stores the address of the active instruction at the point in time when the trap occurred. The directory base register DIRBASE (see Figure 16.24) is used for controlling the MMU and, especially, the PU located within it. The *directory table base* supplies the 20 most significant page table physical address bits of the first order. Together with the *RB* bits, the *RC* bits control the cache replacement strategy for the code and data cache, as well as the TLB (which also represents a cache). For a cache miss, a value of 00b determines the standard replacement algorithm, with which all blocks (ways) in all caches can be replaced. With 01b, only those blocks that were set by RB are replaced in the three caches by a cache miss. Code and data caches always ignore the most significant RB bit. Using a value of 10, the block defined by RB is replaced in the data cache; the code cache and TLB use random replacement. In the case of a value of 11, block replacement is deactivated in the data cache; the code cache and TLB use random replacement. In the case of a code cache miss, a set *CS8* bit instructs the i860 to reload the code being searched for with 8-bit bus cycles. In this way, during the boot phase, 8-bit ROM chips can, for example, be used for the loading of the operating system. If the *ITI* bit is set during the writing of DBR, then the i860 invalidates all code cache and TLB entries. The *BL* bit activates or deactivates the i860 $\overline{\text{LOCK}}$ output, in order to execute locked bus cycles. With the *DP*, the i860 bus cycle can be matched to the configuration of the memory subsystem. In this way, in page mode or static column DRAMs, short access times are achieved within a page or column. Subsequently, the *ATE* bit enables or disables the PU, in order to execute a conversion of virtual addresses into physical addresses. Paging of the i860 operates in the same manner as that in the i386/i486 or Pentium. For example, the page tables and page table entries match those in the i486.

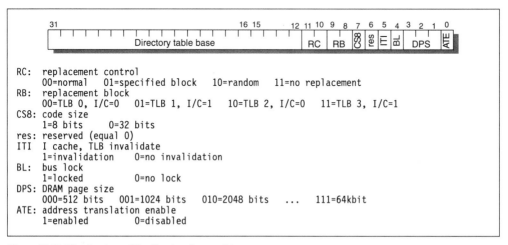

Figure 16.24: The structure of the directory base register.

The final available control and status register is the floating-point status register (FSR). It contains various status information about the current state of the floating-point unit and its pipelines, and supplies control instructions for them. The *ARP, MRP, IRP* and *LRP* bits serve to reinstate the state of the pipeline after a trap or a task switch and specify the accuracy of the result of the last stage. They are set by the i860 hardware and cannot be altered. The *result register* entry specifies the destination registers f0 to f31 of the instruction, for which a trap has occurred.

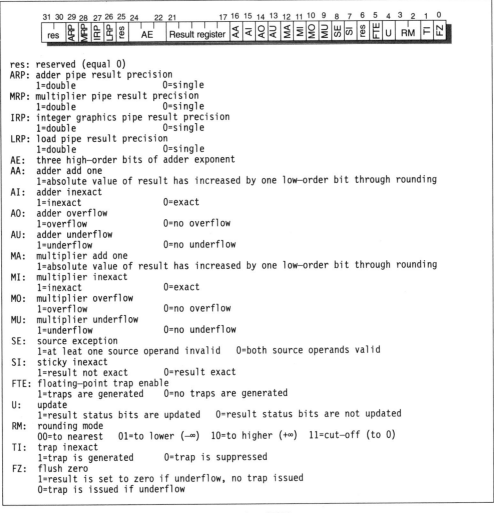

res: reserved (equal 0)
ARP: adder pipe result precision
     1=double   0=single
MRP: multiplier pipe result precision
     1=double   0=single
IRP: integer graphics pipe result precision
     1=double   0=single
LRP: load pipe result precision
     1=double   0=single
AE: three high-order bits of adder exponent
AA: adder add one
     1=absolute value of result has increased by one low-order bit through rounding
AI: adder inexact
     1=inexact   0=exact
AO: adder overflow
     1=overflow   0=no overflow
AU: adder underflow
     1=underflow   0=no underflow
MA: multiplier add one
     1=absolute value of result has increased by one low-order bit through rounding
MI: multiplier inexact
     1=inexact   0=exact
MO: multiplier overflow
     1=overflow   0=no overflow
MU: multiplier underflow
     1=underflow   0=no underflow
SE: source exception
     1=at leat one source operand invalid   0=both source operands valid
SI: sticky inexact
     1=result not exact   0=result exact
FTE: floating-point trap enable
     1=traps are generated   0=no traps are generated
U: update
     1=result status bits are updated   0=result status bits are not updated
RM: rounding mode
     00=to nearest   01=to lower (-∞) 10=to higher (+∞) 11=cut-off (to 0)
TI: trap inexact
     1=trap is generated   0=trap is suppressed
FZ: flush zero
     1=result is set to zero if underflow, no trap issued
     0=trap is issued if underflow

Figure 16.25: The structure of the floating-point status register (FSR).

The *AA, AI, AO* and *AU* result status bits indicate the result of the last adding stage; *AE* stores the three most significant exponent bits of the addition result. In a similar manner, the *MA, MI, MO* and *MU* result status bits specify the result of the last multiplication stage. The *SE* bit is set if one of the source operands is invalid – that is, de-normalized, infinite or a NAN. The *SI* bit indicates that the result of the last stage from the adder or multiplier is not exact. An *FTE* bit permits floating-point traps. If the update bit *U* is set when writing to the FSR, then the AE, AA,

AI, AO, AU, MA, MI, MO, and MU result status bits are overwritten in the corresponding locations by the new values and transferred to the first stage of the adder or multiplier pipelines.

The two *RM* bits determine the rounding process. A set *TI* bit leads to a trap if an instruction result is not exact. If the *FZ* bit is set, then the result is set to zero for an error without generating a trap.

The three floating-point special registers KR, Kl and T are used by the dual operation instructions of the floating-point unit (for example, ADD and multiply), which simultaneously involve an addition and a multiplication function. Such instructions would actually require six operands (two source operands and one destination operand, for both the adder and the multiplier). In order to prevent this, the three special registers store the results intermediately, implicitly supplying them as source operands to the next function. MERGE is only used by the graphics unit and its associated graphic instructions. It is used for the implementation of the Z-buffer algorithm and for shading the surfaces of three-dimensional bodies.

16.5.3 The i860 pipelines

The i860 can execute integer instructions in the RISC core with 32- or even 64-bit operands. Load and store instructions can include 8-, 16-, 32-, 64- or 128-bit operands. For the execution of integer instructions, the RISC core has a four-stage pipeline containing instruction fetch, decode, execute and write-back stages. The pipeline is able to execute one instruction per clock cycle, if no pipeline conflicts occur. This is handled by scoreboarding and register bypassing, so that, according to Intel, the average CPI value of the RISC core is approximately 1.1. The RISC core is also responsible for the distribution of instructions to the floating-point unit, should such an instruction occur. In single instruction mode, the unit reads a 32-bit instruction from the code cache and supplies it to the corresponding pipeline. In comparison, in dual instruction mode, the unit simultaneously fetches 32-bit instructions from the code cache and supplies one of them to the integer pipeline and the other to the floating-point unit.

In accordance with the IEEE standard 754-1985, floating-point instructions are executed in the floating-point unit using the single precision 32-bit format and the double precision 64-bit format. All instructions are 32 bits long. The basic format is represented in Figure 16.25. The floating-point unit in question implements four pipelines: a multiplication pipeline, an addition pipeline, a graphics pipeline and a load pipeline.

The addition pipeline incorporates the following three stages: mantissa comparison/pre-normalization scanning, rounding bit prediction/pre- or de-normalization, and mantissa addition/rounding. Pre-normalization is necessary, because for the addition of two floating-point numbers the exponents of both sums must be equal, and so for the smaller sums, the mantissa must be displaced to the right (thus, to smaller mantissa values) until the exponents of both sums are identical. The addition pipeline can add single precision 32-bit or double precision 64-bit floating-point numbers, and delivers the correspondingly single or double precision result. The multiplication pipeline has three stages. The first stage consists of a hard-wired multiplication tree. For single precision the tree is run through once; for double precision, twice. With double precision, the tree creates both the first and the second pipeline stages, so that, in fact, for double precision the pipeline has four stages. The following second stage executes the necessary addition of the least significant sub-product bits, the forming of the carry, and certain predictions about the width of the product – that is, the most significant product bits. The last stage then executes the subsequent addition, also for most significant bits, so that the result is ready.

The graphics pipeline simply consists of a single stage; the load pipeline of three stages, for both single and double precision. Graphics instructions work with fields of pixels having 8, 16 or 32 bits. The i860 always works with 64-bit groups, independently of the pixel quantity – that is, eight, four or two pixels at once. The 3D graphics unit supports the visualization of computer results, especially through an instruction for selective pixel saving, in order to erase hidden surfaces and corners, and an instruction for pixel insertion, in order to support coloured shading of 3D bodies. Transformations, which are necessary for the projection of a 3D object on the monitor from a two-dimensional projection, or the rotation of a body in space, can be executed quickly by the floating-point unit. Together with five special graphics instructions for a Z buffer algorithm, the specialized 3D graphics unit executes 3D rendering and clipping very quickly.

The difference to the Pentium is that the parallel execution of several instructions in the pipelines of the RISC core and the floating-point units is not transparent – that is, the program code must explicitly advise parallel operation. An optimizing compiler (or assembler programmer) can match the instructions optimally with one another and achieve a maximum arithmetic efficiency for the i860.

Note that the i860, for example, has no hardware divider, as compared to the R3010. The machine code instructions FRCP (floating point reciprocal) and FRSQR (floating point reciprocal square root) are therefore implemented as microcode. Also apparent is the fact that the i860 does not implement a single transcendental function, such as SIN or LOG for example. In comparison, these are already implemented in the x87 family of processors, even as early as the 8087 model. As a RISC processor, the i860 should not implement any complex functions in microcode, but instead, in the first instance, it should make simple but extremely fast instructions available. Transcendental function values can be calculated very quickly, especially by the dual operation instructions PFAM (add and multiply) in the pipelined mode of the floating-point unit, using an external software routine. Thus, the i860 leaves all x87 coprocessors far behind. In view of the missing floating-point functions compared to the Pentium, this is one of the reasons why the i860, as a 64-bit processor, is only integrated with about one million transistors, a third of the number used in the Pentium, even though it has a larger data cache and an additional graphics unit. The circuitry on the Pentium for implementing the functions mentioned takes considerable space.

16.5.4 The i860 instruction execution modes

The RISC core unit always executes the instructions in the pipeline described – thus, it always works in pipelined mode if no pipeline obstructions are active. These are handled with scoreboarding and are reduced by register bypassing.

Scalar and pipelined mode

Things look a little different in the floating-point unit: it knows the so-called scalar and pipelined modes. In scalar mode an instruction passes completely through the floating-point pipeline before the i860 loads the next instruction into the first stage. Thus, addition requires three clock cycles, and, depending on its precision, multiplication requires three or four clock cycles. The scalar mode is used in the case of data dependency, if the following instruction requires the result of the previous instruction. The dual operation instructions solve these problems somewhat differently; more about this later.

In comparison, in pipelined mode, the next floating-point instruction is loaded into the first pipeline stage as soon as the previous instruction has left. Therefore, addition results – for a swung-in pipeline – are available in every clock cycle. Double precise multiplication has to pass through the multiplication tree of the first pipeline stage twice, so a multiplication instruction can only be loaded into the first stage of the pipeline every second clock cycle. Therefore, depending on the precision, multiplication requires one or two clock cycles.

The machine code instructions must be explicitly assigned to the scalar or pipelined mode. The mode is coded in a bit of the instruction. Nearly all floating-point instructions have a variant for scalar or pipelined execution (for example, FMUL for floating-point multiply and PFMUL for pipelined floating-point multiply). The type of execution, therefore, is not controlled by the hardware of the i860 with scoreboarding, but instead exclusively by the software, and thus by the machine code instructions produced by the compiler. The i860 automatically switches the floating-point unit over between the scalar and pipelined modes, if it receives a corresponding value of the mode bit in the machine code instruction.

Dual operation instructions

Under certain circumstances, the addition and multiplication pipelines can work in parallel. Such a parallel operation must be explicitly instructed by the program using the dual operation instructions PFAM (add and multiply), PFSM (subtract and multiply), PFMAM (multiply and add) and PFMSM (multiply and subtract). As you can see from the mnemonics, these instructions always release an instruction for the adder and the multiplier. Both instructions, joined together to form one single instruction, actually require six operands – namely, two source and one destination operand each – the instruction format dest, src1, scr2 only authorizes two. This problem is solved with the assistance of the special registers Kl, KR and T. The dual operation instructions are used particularly for solving linear equations and are suitable for fast transformations, and also for the determination of values for transcendental functions such as LOG, for example, using a Taylor series, in which many expressions occur in the form of A * B + C or (A + B). Typically, dual operation instructions appear in blocks, so the three special registers Kl, KR and T temporarily store results and operands and supply the next dual operation instruction as an operand. Figure 16.26 shows the corresponding signal path in the floating-point unit. For a dual operation instruction, the KR and Kl registers can store the value of src1 and supply it to the multiplier for the following dual operation instruction, in place of src1. The T register (transfer register) stores the product from the multiplier and supplies it to the adder for the subsequent dual operation instruction, in place of src1. The following cases apply to a 4-bit field DPC (data path control) in the opcode, available for the coding of source and destination operands:

▶   mop1 of the multiplier is KR, Kl or src1
▶   mop2 of the multiplier is src2 or the output from the adder

▶ aop1 of the adder is src1, the T register or the output of the adder
▶ aop2 of the adder is src2, the output of the multiplier or the output of the adder

In this way, interlocked algorithms with many additions and multiplications that are dependent on each other can be executed very quickly. An example is the calculation of extensive scalar products, as they appear in the matrix calculation:

$$(a_1, a_2, a_3, a_4, \ldots a_n) * (b_1, b_2, b_3, b_4, \ldots b_n)^T = a_1 * b_1 + a_2 * b_2 + \ldots a_n * b_n$$

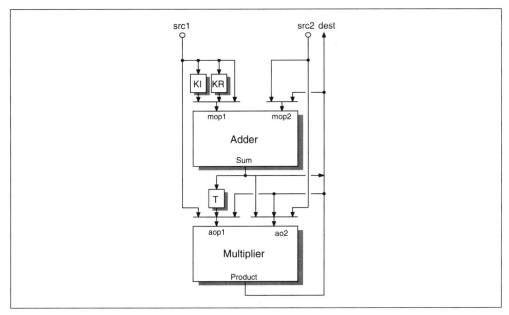

Figure 16.26: The signal path in the floating-point unit for dual-operation instructions.
Beside the three ordinary operands src1, src2 and dest for dual operation instructions, the registers KI, KR and T can also be specified.

Using the dual operation instructions of the i860, the products $a_i * b_i$ can be calculated in the multiplier pipeline and, simultaneously, the product can be totalled in the adder.

Of course, instructions that contain two additions or multiplications cannot be implemented as dual operation instructions. There is only one such pipeline available for each. Under these circumstance, pipelined mode is all that is available.

Single and dual instruction mode

The RISC core pipeline can work independently from the both of the floating-point pipelines, because it only executes integer and instruction flow instructions. Floating-point instructions are only executed in the floating-point unit. Thus, in principle, there is a possibility of operating the RISC core pipeline in parallel with the floating-point unit. The i860 then executes the core and floating-point instructions in parallel. This type of operation is also not transparent to the software – that is, both units are not automatically operated in parallel even if this is theoretically possible. More so is the case whereby the instruction code has to explicitly indicate this.

Core and floating-point instructions will, then, always be executed in parallel, if the D bit (dual mode) is set in the machine code instruction. The instruction flow then no longer consists of individual core and floating-point instructions, each of 32 bits; instead it is made up from 8-byte limit aligned 64-bit instruction pairs, in which the floating-point instruction code the 32 least significant bits and the core instruction code occupies the 32 most significant bits. Therefore, in dual instruction mode, core and floating-point instructions must always appear in pairs. The RISC core unit is then always able to read 64 bits from the instruction cache, separate the two instructions, and supply them to the core and floating-point units, respectively. In dual instruction mode at 50 MHz (in theory), the i860 can execute 100 MIPS. If the floating-point unit is working with dual operation instructions, it can achieve as much as 150 MIPS. This requires intelligent code optimization and an extremely efficient bus system, generally speaking, so that many instructions can be reloaded, parallel to instruction execution. To close, I would like to specify the basic code formats for core and floating-point instructions, as shown in Figure 16.27.

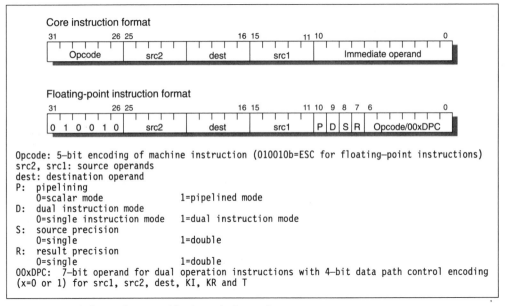

Figure 16.27: Code formats for core and floating-point instructions.

16.6 At a glance: RISC chips for embedded controllers

An important area of use for RISC processors was initially the area of the market that requires powerful, graphically orientated workstations – such as CAD applications. However, between the area of the PC (IBM compatible, Apple) at the lower performance end, and mainframes at the high performance end, RISC CPUs were not able to establish themselves in the beginning. The reason for this, in the area of the PC, is the lack of compatibility with existing hardware platforms and the initial high price for these high performance chips. In comparison, the first RISCs were lacking in performance for use with mainframes. Meanwhile, all this is changing at rather fast tempo, as, along with the Pentium, RISC elements are finding new openings in the area of the PC, while mainframes are noticeably being replaced by high performance PC and workstation networks with distributed, local calculating power. A very important area of application for RISCs is offered by embedded controllers, which you insert, for example, in every laser printer or communication device, such as a fax. Such isolated solutions are, on one hand, free from compatibility requirements, but on the other they must offer a high arithmetic efficiency – an ideal area of application for RISC processors. Analysis of the market currently shows that approximately 70% of RISC CPUs are being used as controllers and 30% are being used with (notably more complex) computer systems. Therefore, in the following text I would like to briefly discuss two RISC CPUs that are often found in such embedded controllers, the Am29000 and the i960.

16.6.1 Am29000

The Am29000 is a 32-bit RISC processor that was purposely conceived for use in embedded controllers. On one hand, embedded controllers should be able to react as quickly as possible; on the other, the control tasks are usually homogeneous and only require, for example, a modest memory or I/O method when compared to a word processing program. The Am29000 should be able to get by without a cache, without a reduction in the calculation efficiency. A cache and the associated hardware would only make the embedded controller more expensive. The Am29000 is available up to 33 MHz and requires approximately 1.2 clock cycles per instruction (CPI).

Internally, the Am29000 implements a data bus with an associated data address bus, and an instruction bus with an associated instruction address bus. The data and instruction paths are totally separate; the Am29000 realizes Harvard architecture. In order to prevent the interface to the outside from leading nowhere, both of the address buses are directed to the outside in common. Thus, externally, the Am29000 only has one address bus, but, as before, a separated data and instruction bus. The bus can execute single, pipelined or burst accesses. In burst mode, a maximum of 256 units of data can be transferred in groups of 32 bits. The burst mode of the Am29000 is more extensive than that of the Pentium. Because the Am29000 has no on-chip cache, the burst mode is important for fast, repeated memory accesses during a task switch (saving of many internal registers), or simply for the reloading of instructions. As the Am29000 executes one instruction in one clock cycle, an instruction must be loaded in every clock cycle. This is only applicable in burst mode.

Because of the burst mode, cheap page mode or static column DRAMs can be installed instead of a cache or faster SRAMs, without an increase in the memory access time. Usually, only the first access requires several wait states; all remaining cycles in the same burst mode do without wait states. If an external cache is provided (for example, if the memory or the bus is slow), then normally, on the grounds of the Harvard architecture, the code and the data cache are implemented separately. Figure 16.28 shows a block diagram of the Am29000.

The central component is the four-stage Am29000 pipeline with instruction fetch stage, decoding stage, execution stage and register write stage (write-back stage). It executes nearly every instruction in a clock cycle, in a swung-in state. With the Am29000, pipeline conflicts are, in the first instance, solved by the hardware. A load forwarding is executed for memory accesses in order to prevent interlocks. However, if a value is not ready in time, the pipeline must be halted. This is where the starting point for the Am29000 optimizing compilers also lies. Some pipeline stalls can be prevented through the restructuring of the code. Bypassing is carried out in order to prevent register dependencies; with this, under certain conditions, ALU results are supplied directly to the ALU input for subsequent instructions, and are simultaneously written to the destination register. A special feature of the IP instruction counter in the Am29000 is the integrated IP shadow register. It stores the jump back address during subroutine calls and interrupts.

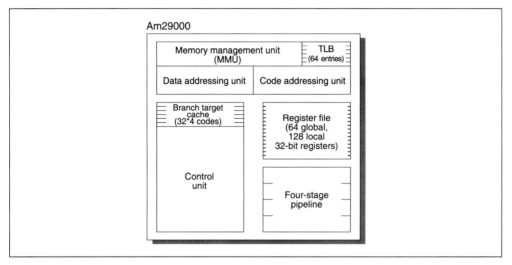

Figure 16.28: The internal structure of the Am29000.
The Am29000 integrates a memory management unit (MMU) with a translation lookaside buffer (TLB), which holds 64 entries. The data and code paths are separate, according to the Harvard architecture. For fast branch execution a branch target cache is implemented, which holds the first four instructions of 32 target addresses. The Am29000 has a multiple register file with a total of 64 global and 128 local registers. All instructions are executed in a four-stage pipeline.

The Am29000 has an extensive register file with a total of 192 general-purpose registers. These are divided into 64 global registers with absolute addressing, and 128 local registers with relative addressing. Like the SPARCs, the Am29000 uses a register window scheme in order to allocate a procedure to a set of local registers (the global registers are always visible). However, unlike SPARC, the number of registers per subroutine or subroutine level is not set to 32, but instead is dynamically adjusted to suit the requirements. Thus, with every SAVE or RESTORE, the register pointer is not switched forwards or backwards by a predetermined value, but instead by a value dependent on the number of registers required by the subroutines. In this way, the 128 local registers are used notably more economically, and larger procedure subdivisions are possible, without having to increase the multiple register files. Like SPARC processors, the Am29000 also uses overlapping register windows, in order to be able to transfer parameters quickly to the called subroutine. Thus, the variable register windows are subdivided into IN, local and OUT registers, but this is not fixed with the Am29000 (compare, for example, the eight IN, eight local and eight OUT registers of the SPARC), but can be adjusted by the compiler to meet the requirements.

During a task switch, all registers containing valid values are transferred to memory, and the registers for the newly activated tasks are loaded. For this purpose, the Am29000 uses the burst mode in order to execute this register swapping as quickly as possible.

Furthermore, an MMU is integrated onto the Am29000 chip, which executes the translation of virtual addresses into physical addresses. The MMU and ALU operation can thus be executed in parallel. In comparison, an external MMU would require a sequential execution of address calculations in the pipeline and the address translation in the external MMU. The MMU has a TLB with 64 entries for the translation of a virtual address into a physical address. Compared to the TLBs, which are usually executed as direct-mapped cache on the grounds of speed, the Am29000 TLB is organized as two-way set-associative. As with the MIPS processors, no hardware replacement algorithm is implemented. The Am29000 generates an exception for a TLB miss, so that, depending on user requirements, the operating system can carry out the replacement. The Am29000 therefore has suitable instructions for the access of the TLB. In accordance with the Harvard architecture, the addressing unit is included twice, in order to achieve complete separation of the code and data accesses.

Branches do not just represent a big problem for the Am29000: in addition to the frequently unavoidable pipeline stalls, which occur without a delayed branch, the AM29000 still has the problem that the instructions at the target address – that is, for executed branches – first have to be read from memory into the instruction fetching stage. This, more or less, takes time depending on the speed and availability, or misses of an external cache. Therefore, the Am29000 implements a so-called branch target cache (BTC) as a middle course between a fast on-chip cache and a somewhat slower main memory. It consists of 512 bytes and stores the first 32-bit instructions of 32 branch targets. If a branch is executed to an address, which is saved in the branch target cache, the result is a BTC hit, and the Am29000 reads the first four instructions from the branch target cache. The addressing unit of the Am29000 simultaneously addresses the main memory in order to read the subsequent instructions. In this way, memory is allowed to request up to two wait states, without a delay occurring as the result of a memory that is too slow (a further two cycles are lost as a result of the output of the address and the transfer of the first code). Pipeline stoppages, due to a delayed transfer of the target address to the instruction fetching stage, via the execution stage – note the bypassing – cannot, of course, be prevented. This can only be prevented using a delayed branch, which is, therefore, the task of the optimizing compiler. In this way, the Am29000 can also execute branch instructions in only one clock cycle. AMD specifies 60% as a typical BTC hit quota, and as much as 90% for short program loops without further branches.

As a RISC processor, the Am29000 also exclusively works with three-address instructions such as ADD dest, src1, src2, which, as operands, can only contain registers of the register files. Only the two LOAD and STORE instructions access memory (unlike the Pentium, instructions such as ADD eax, mem32 do not exist). As I have already mentioned, the Am29000 does not have an on-chip floating-point unit (FPU). floating-point instructions have already been implemented, but, of course, without an FPU they cannot be executed and, therefore, they generate an exception. They are intercepted by the operating system and then a suitable software routine can emulate the coprocessor function. Another possibility for executing floating-point instructions quickly is offered by the mathematical coprocessor Am29027 – AMD calls this the *Arithmetic Accelerator Unit (AAU)* – for fixed-point and floating-point functions.

It can be directly coupled to the Am29000. In a defined cycle, the Am29000 transfers the operands and the opcode to the Am29027 for the required operation. This happens simultaneously via the 32-bit data bus and the 32-bit address bus, so that at any one time, 64 bits can be transferred. As soon as the Am29027 has received the opcode, it executes the instruction and transfers the result to the Am29000. At this time, the Am29027 can operate in two modes: flow-through mode and pipelined mode. In flow-through mode, the Am29027 receives the operands and the opcode, executes the operation and makes the result available. Thus, for a following instruction, the Am29000 has to re-transfer the operands. This is disadvantageous, especially for iterative mathematical calculations, which contain many so-called multiply/accumulate instructions in the form of A * B + C. Therefore, in pipelined mode, the Am29027 stores the results – for example, the value of A * B – in internal registers, so that for the following instructions, the Am29000 only has to transfer a few (for addition) operands, or (only C) none at all. Because the Am29027 executes arithmetical instructions very quickly, and transfer of operands does not represent a large overhead, the pipelined mode reduces the execution time to half or even less.

There are also a vast number of Am29000 models, which I do not wish to withhold from you. They are given in Table 16.2.

Model	On-chip FPU	On-chip MMU	On-chip cache	Clock rate (MHz)
Am29000	No	Yes	BTC:32*4 codes	16–33
Am29005	No	No	No	16
Am29030	No	Yes	8-kbyte (code)	25–33
Am29035	No	Yes	4-kbyte (code)	16
Am29050	Yes	Yes	BTC:128*2 or 64*4 codes	20–40

Table 16.2: The Am29000 family.

16.6.2 The i960CA

Intel has also developed a special line of RISC processors for embedded controllers: the 80960 CPUs. The newest representative is the i960CA. At 33 MHz, it offers calculation performance of at least 66 MIPS. MIPS that are twice the size of the MHz value are on the way to being super-scalar technology. In reality, the i960CA implements three independent pipelines, which are able to operate in parallel, so that the 66 MIPS can be attained. Furthermore, as a controller CPU, the i960CA integrates an interrupt controller, a DMA controller, a programmable bus controller, a 1-kbyte instruction cache and a 1.5-kbyte data SRAM on the same chip. Only very few components are necessary; the controller is compact and cheap.

Figure 16.29 shows the internal structure of the RISC superscalar i960CA. The central component is the *instruction scheduler (IS)*. The IS decodes the instructions from the prefetcher, controls the various processor elements and reads and writes the registers of the register files. The important point is that several processor elements can be active simultaneously from the IS, and in this way the superscalar architecture is realized.

The i960CA has three independent pipelines: a register operation pipeline, a memory operation pipeline and a control flow pipeline. Each of these pipelines executes corresponding instructions. The memory operations pipeline is necessary because, unlike most RISC CPUs, the i960CA can also execute instructions with memory references and implement very complicated possibilities for addressing. As a result of the three independent pipelines, a maximum of three instructions can be initiated, as long as they belong to one of these three classes of instruction. Thus, the scheduler must decode three instructions within a clock cycle, which are subsequently distributed to the three pipelines for execution, according to their class. Via an internal 128-bit bus, the prefetcher transfers a total of four instructions to the instruction scheduler each clock cycle.

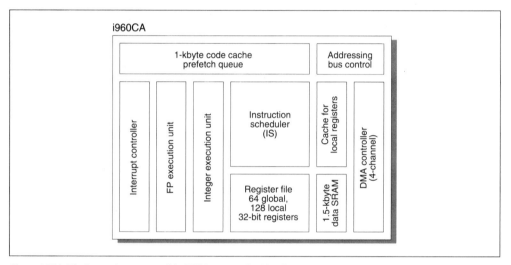

Figure 16.29: The internal structure of the RISC superscalar i960CA.

In most cases, the instructions are taken from the prefetch queue or a microcode ROM. This affects the sequential execution of instructions with prefetching. With branches, it is possible that the prefetcher has not yet read the necessary instruction. This is then directly transferred from the instruction cache to the IS. In the case of a cache miss, the bus controller must carry out a memory read cycle, so that a more or less extensive delay occurs.

Another observation regarding the microcode ROM: instructions that have been micro-encoded actually contradict the RISC concept, which requires hardwired instructions. In fact, very simple instructions such as CALL or RETURN, for example, can lead to very complicated code as a result of the necessary backup and restoring procedures for register contents, if only the elementary RISC instructions are available. Thus, the designers of the i960CA were of the opinion that it is better to implement such instructions as a type of macro. This means that in the microcode ROM of the i960CA for the CALL instruction, for example, microcodes are not available as a direct program statement to the control unit of the i960CA. Instead, there is a sequence of i960CA instructions, which have the same effect as the CISC instruction CALL with all register backup procedures. There are no micro-instructions to be found in the microcode ROM of the i960CA; instead, there are standard i960CA instructions, which are joined together as macros in order to emulate, for example, the CALL instruction of an i386 as already mentioned (only very few lines of the microcode address the memory unit directly). In this way, the programmer is relieved and the programmer code more compact, without a 'real' execution of micro-encoded machine code instructions being necessary. In addition to the CALL and RETURN instructions, DMA instructions and initialization sequences, especially, are stored in the microcode ROM.

Most instructions are executed in a three staged pipeline: instruction fetch stage/decoding stage, distribution and execution stage/write-back stage. Instructions with operands are fetched between the distribution and execution stage. Like the other pipeline stages, this is governed by the control from the instruction scheduler. In this way, it practically establishes a further pipeline stage.

The instruction fetch stage/decoding stage fetches the instruction and decodes it. The instruction can be an inseparable machine code instruction (like, for example, ADD) or a macro instruction (like, for example CALL), which is stored in the microcode ROM as a series of inseparable machine code instructions. In the first case, the instruction is passed on for execution, whereas the macro instruction is broken down and executed in its elementary instructions according to the microcode. The distribution stage completes the decoding and transfers the decoded instruction to one of the three pipelines. The execution stage/write-back stage controls the necessary processor elements, in order to determine the instruction result and, subsequently, the writing of the result in the destination register.

The three pipelines only work fully in parallel if respective triple groups consisting of a register instruction, a memory instruction and a control instruction are loaded. This is, of course, not generally the case. However, with the three pipelines, a theoretical maximum performance of 99 MIPS at 33 MHz could be possible; the practical value for optimized code with many quickly executed loops is a maximum of approximately 66 MIPS.

As always with instruction pipelining, problems affect the conditional branches. Through decoding, the instruction scheduler recognizes whether the current instruction is a conditional branch. If, during the decoding, the conditions of the branch are not yet set (for example, because the previous instruction determines this), then, on the grounds of a prediction as in the Pentium, the i960CA executes the branch. If this prediction is later found to be false, the i960CA empties all of the subsequent instructions from the pipeline and fetches the correct instructions. However, if the prediction is correct, then the instruction flow is not interrupted. The IS recognizes branch instructions very early – it always decodes three instructions at a time, even if at least two of them belong to the same class and therefore cannot be executed in parallel – and is thus in a position to calculate the jump addresses before the actual instruction execution. This is known as *branch look ahead*. A branch instruction is executed within zero clock cycles – that is, immediately – if it can be executed in parallel with other instructions and either the branch code conditions were known in advance or the branch prediction was correct. Otherwise, two clock cycles are necessary for this (that of both parallel executed instructions currently being compensated for in the other pipelines). Of course, optimizing compilers can also implement a delayed branch or other optimizing strategy, in order to prevent pipeline conflicts.

Register dependencies are greatly increased due to the three parallel pipelines. Register dependencies may not only occur within a single pipeline, but also between the pipelines themselves. Such situations are handled by scoreboarding from the i960CA hardware side. Through clever code transformation, the optimizing compiler can, as far as possible, prevent register dependencies.

The i960CA register file consists of 16 global and 16 local 32-bit registers. The i960CA implements a register cache, which normally encompasses five sets, consisting of groups of 16 local registers each. They are placed in the data SRAM of the i960CA, which is not accessible in another form. In addition, a further 10 sets of local registers can be reserved in the data SRAM, to handle deeply nested subroutines. The available memory space becomes correspondingly smaller for other applications in the on-chip data SRAM. Note that the register sets in the SRAM only serve the storage of the actual register values. Physically, the local registers remain the same – only 16 of them are implemented. For a subroutine call, the i960CA independently assigns a new set of local registers in the data SRAM and backs up the current values of the local registers in the (virtual) registers in the data SRAM. With a return, the procedure is reversed – the i960CA produces the old values in the local registers via register values stored in the SRAM. This occurs via the 128-bit wide internal data bus, so only four clock cycles are necessary for the saving and restoring of the register values.

As with the well-know register window technology, the register sets in the data SRAM are managed via a window pointer, which determines the current set. The difference between this and SPARC processors or the Am29000 is that, due to the physical identity of the local registers from calling and called procedures, no overlapping between the registers of the calling and called procedures occurs. Therefore, all parameters must be transferred via the constantly visible global registers. This i960CA implementation of the register window simply saves the memory accesses for the saving and restoring of registers, but the subroutine parameters must be explicitly transferred. For this reason, the i960CA implements a special call instruction for subroutines, that do not call any other procedures (these are known as *leaf routines*). They do not require any local register sets, thus the associated call instruction *branch and link* also does not save the local registers in the SRAM. The subroutines called use exactly the same register set as the calling procedure.

The physical 4-Gbyte address area of the i960CA is subdivided into 16 areas, each of 256 Mbytes, which are individually configurable. For this, the i960CA implements a special area table with 16 entries, each of 32 bits. Each entry defines the configuration of the associated 256-Mbyte memory area and of the i960CA bus when accessing it, as shown in Figure 16.30.

The *BO* bit determines whether the little-endian or the big-endian format should be used. Furthermore, the data bus width can be set to 8, 16 or a full 32 bits. In this way, without further bus logic, very different components can be addressed (for example, small 8-bit EPROMs with start-up routines and large 32-bit main memory). The number of waitstates for different bus cycles can also be set. This is necessary so that the i960CA can dynamically insert wait cycles if the subsystem does not supply a ready signal. Subsequently, the three bits *PE*, *RE* and *BE* define whether the i960CA executes an address pipelining or a burst mode, and whether the addressed subsystem supplies a ready signal. At a clock frequency of 33 MHz, together with pipelined addressing, the burst mode still provides a maximum data transfer rate of 132 Mbytes/s.

As the i960CA – and also the previous series of the 80960 – was primarily conceived for embedded controllers, the interrupt subsystem plays an important role in this case. The i960CA has an on-chip interrupt controller for the management of hardware interrupt requests. It can handle up to 248 interrupt sources. In addition to hardware interrupts, software interrupts can also be generated using the SYSCTL instruction; the effects are the same.

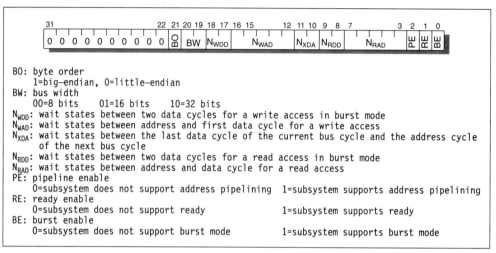

BO: byte order
    1=big–endian, 0=little–endian
BW: bus width
    00=8 bits   01=16 bits   10=32 bits
N_{WDD}: wait states between two data cycles for a write access in burst mode
N_{WAD}: wait states between address and first data cycle for a write access
N_{XDA}: wait states between the last data cycle of the current bus cycle and the address cycle
    of the next bus cycle
N_{RDD}: wait states between two data cycles for a read access in burst mode
N_{RAD}: wait states between address and data cycle for a read access
PE: pipeline enable
    0=subsystem does not support address pipelining 1=subsystem supports address pipelining
RE: ready enable
    0=subsystem does not support ready   1=subsystem supports ready
BE: burst enable
    0=subsystem does not support burst mode   1=subsystem supports burst mode

Figure 16.30: The structure of an area entry.

Each of the interrupts is allocated an 8-bit index, which is used as an index in a vector table, similar to that of the i386 and the Pentium. Each vector consists of 32 bits and gives the entry point of the service routine. Each interrupt is allocated a priority level from 1 to 31, which are coded by the five most significant bits of the vector: 1 indicates the lowest, and 31 the highest priority. At any given point in time, the interrupt with the highest priority is served. With an active interrupt, additional interrupts are only recognized if they have a higher priority. Otherwise, they are marked as pending in a reserved area of the interrupt vector table and handled later. The reserved areas in the interrupt vector table occupy the first 32 bytes, so that interrupts with an index of between 0 and 7 cannot appear. Thus, the i960CA only recognizes 248 interrupts with indexes between 8 and 255. With an interrupt, the i960CA stores its condition automatically and branches to the interrupt handler, through a CALL. Simultaneously, the local registers are stored in the SRAM and a special interrupt stack in memory is used.

The on-chip interrupt controller of the i960CA can be operated in three different programmable modes. It serves external hardware interrupt requests at the eight interrupt interfaces XINT0 to XINT7 of the i960CA, as well as hardware interrupt requests through the on-chip DMA controller. In *dedicated mode*, the eight interrupt pins XINT0 to XINT7 are each allocated an external interrupt source; therefore, eight different external interrupt requests can occur. In addition, the four channels of the on-chip DMA controller are connected with four further entries of a lower priority. Each of the interfaces must be allocated a vector index, which serves as an index into the interrupt vector table. This assignment is partly fixed and partly freely programmable. As a result of the fixed connection, the four least significant index bits are preset to the value of 0010. In comparison, the four most significant can be freely programmed. In this way, the interrupt source, which is connected to the input of the XINT0 of the on-chip interrupt controller, need not always be assigned to the most significant bit. The further processing of a hardware interrupt is similar to that of the 8259A. Next, a recognized interrupt is transferred into the interrupt pending register and then an interrupt is released to the CPU kernel of the i960CA. Interrupts can be targeted and individually masked by entries in the interrupt mask register. Using dedicated mode, up to four different external and four internal (DMA) hardware interrupts can be managed. Naturally, this number can be increased by additional external hardware such as, for example, a multiplexer.

The expanded mode is set up to serve up to 248 different interrupt sources. The important difference is that in expanded mode, the eight bits are used to manage the inputs XINT0 to XINT7 for the coding of 248 different interrupts (interrupts 0 to 7 are not implemented). XINT0 is equivalent to the least significant bit and XINT7 is equivalent to the most significant bit of the 8-bit interrupt number. However, in dedicated mode, each of the pins XINT0 to XINT7 were individually allocated a single interrupt source. Therefore, in most cases in expanded mode, additional external hardware is necessary, which, following a fixed priority, transforms the individual interrupt lines of the device into a type of 'interrupt address' and supplies it to the XINT0 to XINT7 interfaces of the i960CA.

In mixed mode, the five XINT0 to XINT4 interfaces are merely operated in expanded mode and the three XINT5 to XINT7 interfaces in dedicated mode. Thus, in this mode $2^5 + 3 = 35$ external hardware interrupts can be managed. Mixed mode permits a very flexible interrupt structure.

The on-chip interrupt controller of the i960CA can work as both edge and level triggered. Furthermore, a fast mode for the quick recognition of interrupt requests within two clock cycles (at the expense of reliability) and a debounced mode for the very reliable recognition of such requests within six clock cycles (at the expense of speed) are implemented. Especially with flank triggered channels, the debounced mode should prevent an interference signal from deceiving an interrupt in the interrupt line. The i960CA attains an interrupt latency of less than 1 μs. It is, therefore, well suited for complex controller functions.

A DMA controller with four independent channels is an additional functional unit found on the i960CA chip. The DMA controller operates totally unconnected from the instruction scheduler and can, therefore, execute all data transfers parallel to instruction execution. It implements three different types of application. From a software instruction in *block mode*, the DMA controller transfers a complete data block, typically from one memory position to another memory position. Here, the DMA control signals do not play a role. In comparison, the *demand mode* handles data transfers between an I/O unit and the main memory. In this mode, the transfer is released by one of the DMA request signals DREQ0 to DREQ3; the controller confirms the request with a corresponding signal DACK0 to DACK3. After reading, in block mode as well as in demand mode, the data to be transferred is stored temporarily in the i960CA, then transferred to the destination unit in a write cycle. This, of course, costs time, but does make an external buffer unnecessary. In comparison, in fly-by mode, there is no temporary storage in the i960CA; the data is read from the system data bus by control signals of the DMA controller. Directly thereafter, the controller instructs the target, using suitable control signals, simply to get rid of the data from the system data bus. This mode is equivalent to the compressed mode of the 8237A. In fly-by mode, the i960CA attains the highest data transfer rate of up to 59 Mbytes/s at a clock frequency of 33 MHz. In comparison, in each of the block and demand modes, a complete bus cycle per two clock cycles is necessary for reading and writing the 32-bit data; in this case, the maximum transfer rate is 33 Mbytes/s at 33 MHz.

The i960CA indicates the end of a DMA transfer with signals at the EOP0 to EOP3 (end of process) terminals – in this case, also known as TC0 to TC3 (terminal count) – or it receives a corresponding completion signal from the transferring unit at these pins. A priority is attached to each of the DMA channels. The i960CA can be programmed for fixed and rotational priorities. In the first case, channel 0 has the highest priority and channel 3 the lowest. A low priority channel is only then served if no DMA request of a higher priority is available. With rotational priority this is changed through cyclically using the schematic 0→1→2→3→0, whereby the lowest priority is assigned to the channel just served, and the highest priority is assigned to the channel following the schematic.

A more effective mechanism for the transfer of several unconnected blocks in a single DMA transfer is created by concatenated lists. An internal descriptor pointer register of the DMA controller in the i960CA points to a descriptor, which defines the source address, the target address, the number of bytes to be transferred and – for concatenation – the next descriptors of the concatenated lists. The end of a concatenated list is given by a so-called NULL descriptor. Using this mechanism, several separate DMA transfers can be joined to form a single transfer. This only works for memory to memory transfers. DMA transfers are started with the loading of a descriptor in the descriptor pointer register. The DMA controller transfers the given number of bytes from the specified source address to the required target address. Finally, the controller loads the fixed descriptor for the next data block or ends the DMA transfer, if it comes across a NULL descriptor. The descriptors of the concatenated lists can still be altered, if the DMA transfer has already started.

16.7 Relentlessly parallel: The transputer

In 1985, when INMOS brought the first of the transputers onto the market with its IMS T414 (for example, the Acorn Archimedes is based on that chip), it created a sensation, especially because of its uncompromising structure for multiprocessor systems. The term 'transputer' is an abbreviation of 'transfer computer'. Here, it should be stated that a number of transputers can be connected together to form a multiprocessor system, in exactly the same way as a number of transistors (from transfer resistor) can be connected together to increase the total current driving capability. Like the Pentium, transputers implement 32-bit architecture.

Before the details of the transputer architecture are explained, I would like to introduce the important characteristics of a transputer. As you can see, many components were integrated on a transputer chip very early, while the competition was still working with discrete components:

▶ CPU kernel with 10 (T414) to 200 MIPS (T9000)
▶ FPU with up to 25 MFLOPs
▶ faster on-chip SRAM with 2–4 kbytes
▶ on-chip memory controller for external DRAM or SRAM memories
▶ two or four serial links (communication interfaces) with up to 80 Mbytes/s of bidirectional transfer capacity
▶ RISC pipeline for simple instructions
▶ CISC microprogramming for complex instructions

Transputers not only use RISC concepts, but also CISC concepts, in order to achieve maximum performance. They have a very special instruction coding, which I would like to explain in more detail in 16.7.2.

16.7.1 The general architecture of transputers and transputer systems

In addition to the standard components, like the CPU kernel and the bus interface, every transputer has, as an important component, two or more bidirectional, serial communications interfaces, the so-called *links*. These serve exclusively for the communication of transputers between themselves, and not for the usual memory access; the bus interface is responsible for that. Links directly access (read or write) the memory areas of other transputers as if there was no involvement of the transputer CPU kernels. Therefore, the links can also be identified as being a bidirectional, serial interface controller. Their function and means of operation are very similar to those of the DMA chips. When compared to the 'classic' solution of using the CPUs themselves for interprocessor communication, links have the big advantage that the communication process hardly burdens the CPU kernels. As a result of this second data channel in a multitransputer system, the otherwise normal bottleneck of the interprocessor communication is spread. Right from the start, this shows the uncompromising structure of the transputer for multiprocessor systems (links are worthless in a in one-transputer system – they cannot communicate with any other transputer). Figure 16.31 shows the general structure of a transputer.

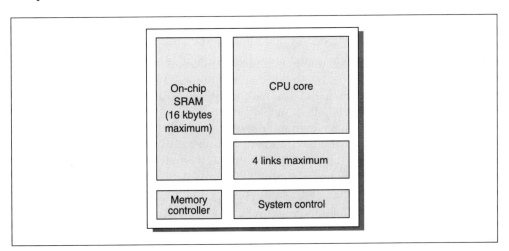

Figure 16.31: The general structure of a transputer.

In a multitransputer system, each transputer is allocated its own private memory. Only through the links can the other transputers in the system also use this private memory – that is, the links determine memory couplings, which are necessary for interprocess communication. It is important that these memory accesses are controlled via various transputers away from the transputer hardware and are, therefore, very fast. An important characteristic of the on-chip SRAM of the transputer, which differentiates the transputer in another way from standard

CPUs, is its organization and management. Normally, on-chip memories are formed as caches, which temporarily store any portions of data from within the complete physical processor address area. This is not so with the transputer. Here, the on-chip memories merely form the start of the physical address area. Externally, the physical address area is continued through additional DRAM or SRAM memory chips. Due to the 32-bit address bus, the physical address area is restricted to a maximum of 4 Gbytes. With the T800, the 4-kbyte on-chip cache SRAM is found between the addresses 00000000h and 00000fffh: finishing with the address 00001000h, a maximum 4-Gbyte-4-kbyte sized external memory. I would also like to mention that the transputer always manages the memory with physical addresses, and, unlike most other CPUs, virtual addressing does not take place.

Transputers have an overall reduced set of registers. In comparison with, for example, SPARCs, which can serve as many as 2048 registers, in the CPU kernel of a transputer there are usually only six 32-bit registers available for virtual data processing (see Figure 16.32). Nevertheless due to the fast on-chip SRAM memory, no essential access latencies appear, even when a memory operand is referred to instead of a register.

Of the six transputer registers, the three A to C registers form the so-called *evaluation stack*, which contains the source and destination registers A to C for the majority of ALU operations. In this way, for many ALU instructions, the explicit indication of an operand register is unnecessary; for example, the transputer instruction ADD automatically adds the register values A and B and places the result in A. You can already see from this example that transputers, like the 80x86 family, for example, implement a destructive manner of operation; they are, therefore, not pure RISCs. Because of the many instructions with implicit register addressing, the instruction codes are extremely compact; more about this in Section 16.7.2.

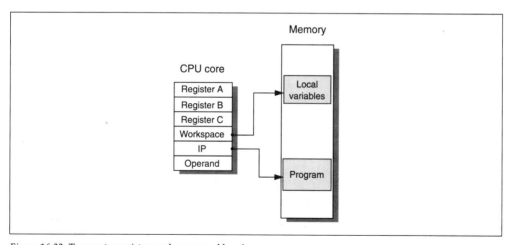

Figure 16.32: Transputer registers and memory addressing.

The *workspace pointer* supplies the address of local variables in the memory (either to the on-chip SRAM or to the external memory). These represent a type of expansion of the transputer register sets. They are memory operands, as known from other CPUs, and can be directly addressed in instructions. Pure RISCs only refer to memory operands indirectly via a LOAD or STORE and a subsequent and previous register access, respectively. The workspace is also used as a stack for procedure calls and link messages. The *instruction pointer (IP)* indicates the address of the next instruction in a known way; thus, transputers also operate using sequential instruction execution. Finally, the *operand register* serves the creation of operands using a very specific transputer mechanism, which is explained in more detail in Section 16.7.2. Because of the reduced number of registers and the workspace pointer, task switches are executable very quickly. Only six registers have to be saved and the workspace pointer for the new task loaded.

A task scheduler is also integrated in the system controller. It is micro-encoded and controls the multitasking of different tasks. Its function is much more extensive than the simple saving and reading of the TSS with the Pentium. The scheduler has a front and a back pointer, which respectively determine the beginning and the end of a task wait queue. The wait queues hold information at the ready about the active tasks of the workspaces. Transputers implement a priority model for the tasks. This means that every task is assigned to one of two priority stages. The higher prioritized tasks do not undergo time slicing; they are first disrupted, if they have to wait for an event (input/output or timer pulse). In comparison, lower prioritized tasks are disrupted at the end of a set time. The transputer contains its own task wait queue for each of the two priority stages. In this case, the chaining of the tasks is achieved by a pointer in the working memory; with the Pentium, this is done via the task gates and the associated TSS (which are also a form of pointer). Transputers with integrated FPU, such as the T800 or the T9000, for example, have an additional 64-bit FPU register as well as the six CPU kernel registers. The transputer architecture provides a further four registers for the support of multi-tasking operating systems.

16.7.2 Transputer instruction structure and instruction encoding

The basic structure of the transputer instructions is extremely simple; they are each only a single byte long and have a uniform format. The basic structure is represented in Figure 16.33.

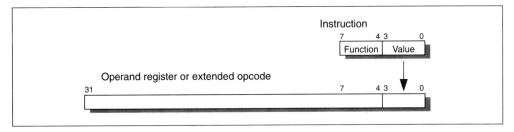

Figure 16.33: The structure of a transputer opcode.

The 1-byte opcode is subdivided into a most significant function nibble and a least significant value nibble. Therefore, to begin with, 16 different instructions, each with different operand values, can be coded – not really very many. The 16 instructions that can be directly coded are identified as *direct instructions*, of which 13 are used as actual executable opcodes. Together with the three other 1-byte instructions, they are given in Table 16.3.

Because of the 4-bit wait field with a single 1-byte instruction, for example, constants between 0 and 15 can be loaded or stored in one cycle. In addition, the first 16 variables relative to the workspace pointer are accessible. Operand values between 0 and 15 are, of course, not sufficient for all applications. For larger values, the transputer uses the operand registers and both prefix instructions in a very special way. Here, with the assistance of both prefix instructions, larger operands can be put together from 4-bit portions. The schematic is given in Figure 16.34. Normally, an instruction loads the four value bits into the four least significant bits of the operand register; all of the most significant bits are simultaneously initialized to zero. After the execution of the instruction, the operand register is reset to zero.

Instruction	Code	Description
Jump	00h	Unconditional jump
Load local pointer	01h	Evaluate local address
Load non-local	03h	Load variable via pointer in A
Load constant	04h	Load constant value
Load non-local pointer	05h	Evaluate non-local address
Load local	07h	Load local variable via workspace pointer
Add constant	08h	Add constant value
Call	09h	Procedure call
Jump conditional	0ah	Conditional jump
Adjust workspace	0bh	Load workspace pointer register
Equals constant	0ch	Compare value in A with constant
Store local	0dh	Store local variable via workspace pointer
Store non-local	0eh	Store variable via pointer in A
Prefix	02h	Prefix for operand extension
Negative prefix	06h	Pegative prefix for operand extension
Operate	0fh	Prefix for composed instruction

Table 16.3: 1-Byte transputer instructions.

In comparison, the prefix instructions work totally differently. Exactly like all other instructions, the *prefix* instruction loads its four value bits in the four least significant bits of the operand register. Subsequently, the operand register is shifted by four bits to the left (quasi-multiplied by 16), so that the four least significant bits of the operand register are, once again, free and equal to zero. As usual, the next instruction loads its value bits in these operand register bits. Thus, from this one prefix instruction, an 8-bit operand is formed. Of course, several prefix instructions can follow one another; for example, in order to fill the complete 32-bit operand register and to execute an instruction, seven prefix instructions and one 1-byte instruction are necessary. In this way, each prefix instruction writes the already loaded operand values four bits to the left. In contrast to the other instructions following a prefix instruction the operand register is not reset (the prefix function would otherwise be worthless). The *negative prefix* instruction works in a similar manner to the prefix instruction – that is, it too loads its four value bits in the four least significant bits of the operand register. Prior to the final shift to the left, the complete register (including bits already loaded with prefix or negative prefix) is inverted. You can see the working manner of the prefix instructions in Figure 16.34.

With the help of the prefix and negative prefix instructions, operands can be built up to any length. This is especially advantageous for high level language compilers, because the operand size produced is independent of the word length (usually the register width) of the underlying transputer.

After the direct and the two prefix instructions, only the opcode 0fh remains; it is used for the *operate* instruction. Through one of the prefixes and a very similar mechanism, operate opens the door to an almost arbitrary large number of indirect instructions. If the value 0fh for operate appears in the function field of the 1-bit instruction code, then the transputer interprets the value field as an extension of the opcode and no longer as an operand value. Above all, with this, 16 additional 1-byte instructions can be encoded, but no operand values are possible. Therefore, such indirect 1-byte instructions mostly address the A to C registers of the evaluation stack implicitly. An example would be the ADD instruction. ADD executes the following operation:

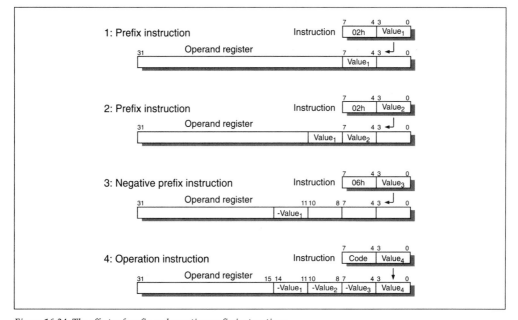

Figure 16.34: *The effects of prefix and negative prefix instructions.*
In the example shown, first two prefix instructions load value1 and value2, then the negative prefix instruction loads value3 and inverts the 12 bits input up to now. The actual instruction completes the 16-bit operand with value4. Afterwards the instruction is executed.

A ← B + A

B ← C

Thus, the A to C registers are implicitly addressed: A and B are added and the result is placed in A; additionally, the content of C is transferred to B; C is subsequently undefined. Here, in the opcode, an explicit operand value is not necessary.

Put more exactly, the operate instruction interprets the associated operands as opcode expansion. In this way, it is possible to use the prefix mechanism for the expansion of the opcode. For example, a prefix instruction results in 4-bit opcode expansion and the subsequent operate instruction results in a 12-bit opcode. This scheme can be continued at will, so that a very large instruction set is possible. INMOS states that approximately 80% of all transputer instructions can be coded with only one byte and, therefore, are direct instructions or 1-byte indirect instructions. They are also mostly executed within one clock cycle. Thus, the opcode structure of the transputer shows a very distinct strategy: the more instructions are regularly used, the shorter their coding time and, therefore, their execution time as a result of the reduced decoding phase. In contrast, infrequently used instructions are coded with more bytes – actually by two and more (prefix) instructions.

Because of the instruction structure of the transputer, the assembler programming is very complicated (who would take pleasure in programming a 16-bit operand or an indirect function with an exact number of prefix instructions by hand?), but the codes produced by a compiler are very compact, as a result of the 8-bit basic structure of the instructions, and can be decoded quickly. Transputers are – because multiprocessor systems are targeted – accomplished with programming in high level language. The compiler developer then only has to get to grips with the complicated assembler programming. In the first instance, the programming language occam and the operating system Helios led the way for transputer based systems.

16.7.3 The links and intertransputer communication

Not only in a multitasking system, but also in a multiprocessor system, do different processes and tasks have to communicate with each other in order to exchange data. This affects, for example, the transfer of function values, which are calculated from a process, to another process, or the transfer of control information, in order to synchronize the transputer of a system. For this purpose, instructions (mainly input message and output message) are implemented in the transputer, which make possible communication between processors even over transputer boundaries.

The communication itself takes place via so-called *channels*, which represent a connection between the processors. In this way, it is totally transparent for the software, whether it is dealing with a process that will be executed in the same transputer or whether another transputer will be used. In the first case, a data word in RAM (the on-chip SRAM or the external memory) is used. In comparison, communication with an external transputer takes place via the links. The decision whether, for the input/output instruction, a local communication via a RAM data word or an external transputer via a link is necessary, is decided independently by the microcode of the instruction during the runtime of the program. Therefore, the compiler does not have to take any precautions, in order to initialize a link for a communication. In both cases, the process that requests the communication stores the address of the communication channel, a pointer to the message block that should be written or read, and the length of this block, on the stack. Subsequently, the input message or output message instruction is released and the hardware determines, independently, whether an internal channel via the shared memory is adequate. If this is the case, then the transputer executes a block shift corresponding to the move block instruction of the transputer.

If, on the other hand, an external channel via a link is necessary, in order to execute the input message or output message instruction, then the microcode activates the corresponding link. The communication with the link of the target transputer is achieved by a handshake procedure: Initially, the transmitter outputs a data packet, which consists of two start bits 11b, the actual data bits and a stop bit 0b (see Figure 16.35). If the link of the target transputer has received the data packet, and if it is ready to accept a further packet, it returns a 2-bit acknowledge message 10b. In order to attain as even a data flow via the links as possible and, thereby, to maximize the transfer rate, the link of the target transputer can return the acknowledge message while, at the same time, a data packet is being transferred. Thus, the T9000 reaches a communication rate of up to 80 Mbytes/s. This is already equivalent to the maximum bus band width of a 40 MHz i386. You should remember that, in addition to the standard CPU bus, the links represent a second data channel.

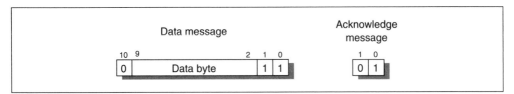

Figure 16.35: The format of the data and acknowledge messages.

Later transputers also implement a so-called *virtual channel*, so that, via a single link, several processes can communicate simultaneously. The links and these virtual channels are especially responsible for the relatively problem-free connection of transputers for establishing a multi-processor system. However, this requires a specialized operating system based on a transputer and communication via links, and a compiler that supports interprocess communication via channels. In the case of the transputer, these are Helios and occam respectively.

16.7.4 An example: The T9000

In this section, I would like to introduce the latest representative of the transputer – The T9000 – in more detail. It was conceived as the successor to the T800 series and implements RISC concepts, such as instruction pipelining with superscalar architecture. The internal structure of the T9000 is shown in Figure 16.36.

The T9000 has a 32-bit ALU and a 64-bit FPU. The 32-bit integer kernel can process byte, word and double word operands (32 bits); the FPU, 32-bit and 64-bit operands. Like all transputers, the CPU works with a linear addressing of the 4-Gbyte large physical address area. There is also a *protected mode* (just like that of the 80x86) implemented with the T9000. In this mode, all memory accesses are checked and translated by an MMU before they are placed on the bus and actually access the memory. The reason for the implementation of the protected mode is that, in future, transputers will be operated with operating systems other than Helios, and programmed with programming languages other than occam. These have a simple memory protection, already implemented at software level, but C and Fortran, for example, do not. This should be delivered at hardware level by protected mode.

Another major shortcoming of the transputer has been solved in the T9000. All of its predecessors could only handle errors and exceptions globally – there were no handler sets allocated to each process for the handling of such errors. However, with every task switch, a new interrupt table is activated in the TSS via the IDT (interrupt descriptor table) entry. Only now has this become possible with the T9000. For every process, the T9000 can intercept and handle errors and exceptions, although their global handling is also possible as an option. Like all other transputers, the T9000 is clocked by an external 5 MHz signal; internally, though, it operates at 10 times that, namely 50 MHz. With all transputers, the external frequency and the internal processor clock are not coupled. The transputer itself produces the processor clock from an internal PLL synthesizer; the external clock only serves as a trigger. In this way, the clock design of a transputer system is very simple. All transputers are supplied with the same frequency, but can be operated internally with a very different speed. Transputers, also, do not necessarily have to be supplied from the same oscillator with 5 MHz. Thus, phase shifts caused by signal propagation times no longer play a role, because the transputer communication mutually runs via the links, serially and totally unconnected from the internal processor clock.

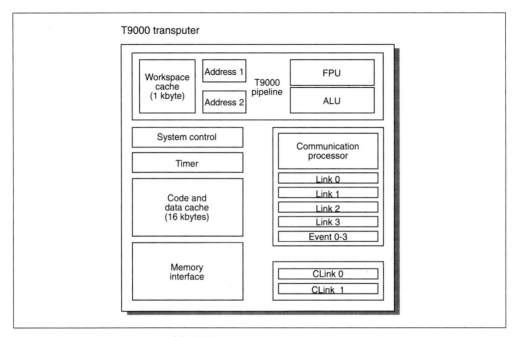

Figure 16.36: The internal structure of the T9000.

Structure of the T9000 CPU

A small workspace cache is directly integrated in the CPU kernel. It stores the 32 first words (with 32 bits each) of the procedure stack and of the workspace. In this way, local variables can be read extremely quickly – as quickly, in fact, as if 32 32-bit registers were available. The workspace cache is also equivalent to a register stack of 32 general-purpose registers, like that implemented in a similar manner for many RISC CPUs. The cache reaches an access rate of up to 150 Mwords/s. For a word width of 32 bits this is equivalent to an internal transfer rate of 600 Mbytes/s.

The T9000 also has an evaluation stack with the three registers A, B and C (see Figure 16.32). Also available in a known form are a workspace pointer, an instruction counter IP and an operand register. If an interrupt occurs, the evaluation stack is simply duplicated in the workspace cache, so that interrupt latency times of less than 1 μs occur. Task switchs also run very quickly, due to the reduced number of registers, which have to be saved in memory (usually the on-chip cache). Ultimately, the FPU also contains an evaluation stack with the three FPU registers similar to registers A to C.

The central component of the CPU kernel is the superscalar pipeline. It can complete up to four instructions in one clock cycle. For an internal processor clock of 50 MHz, this corresponds to a considerable instruction rate of 200 MIPS. You should note though, that this includes the simple prefix instructions, which are used for the structure of 16- or 32-bit operands. In comparison, most other RISC CPUs implement instructions, which can load such operands in a single instruction into the ALU, where they are executed. You will learn more about the pipelines and their special instruction execution strategy below. For completeness, I would like to mention that the FPU typically executes a floating-point instruction within two clock cycles, and thus attains 25 MFLOP.

Additional T9000 elements

In addition to the small 1-kbyte workspace cache, a 16-kbyte cache for data and code is also found on the T9000 chip. The cache is subdivided into four banks, each of 4 kbytes, which are addressed via address bits 4 and 5 of the 32-bit memory address. The four least significant address bits 0 to 3 select a byte from the respective cache line consisting of 16 bytes. In this way, each bank contains 256 cache lines for each 16 bytes. The cache controller logic of the T9000 always ensures that at least one cache line is free. For a cache miss, this cache line is filled by a cache line fill, and the addressed data, which has led to the cache miss, is transferred to the CPU kernel. Finally, by chance, the controller logic invalidates one of the other 255 cache lines in the associated bank, and the content is written back when the cache line changes – that is, becomes 'dirty'. This strategy, of always making at least one empty cache available, is known as *early write-back*.

Another special feature is the possibility of configuring the 16-kbyte on-chip cache as a standard memory, which occupies the start of the physical address area (as is the case in the on-chip SRAM of the previous transputers T4xx and T8xx), or as 'true' cache, which temporarily stores any size of address area in the complete address space. A division between the types of use is also possible. Alternatively, you get a fast 16-kbyte SRAM memory between the addresses 00000000h and 00003fff, an 8-kbyte SRAM between 00000000h and 00001fff as well as an 8-kbyte cache for the whole address space or a 16-kbyte cache, which covers the whole physical address space.

The memory interface incorporates a complete memory controller for the control of DRAM chips. A maximum of 16 1M * 4bit DRAMs can be attached, without additional buffers and amplifiers, which results in a memory of 8-Mbyte capacity. The memory interface automatically outputs the $\overline{RAS}$ and $\overline{CAS}$ signals, and splits the memory address into a row address and a column address. The 8-Mbyte limit only occurs because of the limited ability of the driver in the on-chip circuitry, and not on grounds of principle. The memory can be increased to a maximum size of 4 Gbytes, with external buffers for the address and data signals, without the need for an additional memory controller. The interface can also be configured for the connection with SRAMs, which do not execute address multiplexing, or ROMs. The use of page mode DRAMs is also possible.

For communication with other transputers, the T9000 chip has a complete communications sub-system with communication processor, four 100-Mbit/s links for duplex data exchange, two control links for the input and output of control data, as well as four event channels, which can be used for interrupts or other synchronization tasks, for example.

In addition to the two data links, there are also two control links CLink0 and CLink1 on the T9000. CLink0 outputs status information and receives instructions from other transputers or a control processor. In comparison, CLink1 creates a cascading to the control links of other trans-puters. In this way, in addition to the standard data bus and the data links, there is a third channel implemented, namely a control network. The main component of the control links is its *routeing hardware*, by which the transputer only extracts the control information that is specified for it from the entering flow of data. Without delay, all other information is further transferred to the next transputer. This is very similar to a local network, in which the individual work-stations also (apparently) have direct access to any other workstation. The control links CLinkx are used for communication among the *transputers* – that is,, the hardware – in comparison to the data links Linkx, which are used for communication purposes between the *processes* – that is, the software. After power-on, the system can also use the CLinks for booting the transputer and its memory. Another possibility is to use the classic method via a ROM BIOS.

The four event channels can be configured as input or output. An input event channel is typically used for interrupt requests, an output channel for the control of external units such as the registers of a drive controller. The interrupt management principle differs greatly for a transputer when compared to standard processors. Interrupts are seen as a special form of communication. From the model of the synchronized communication of processors, as implemented by transputers, a communication can only be executed if both communication participants – transmitter and receiver – are ready. The faster process must, therefore, wait for the slower process. Transfer to interrupts and their associated event channels means that the interrupt handler is always the faster process, and so has to wait for communication with the slower process – that is, the interrupt itself (even better, the event). The willingness to communicate (that is, the activation of the interrupt signal) automatically activates the associated process (thus, the handler) and thereby releases the interrupt operation. In their conception, interrupt handlers themselves do not differ from other processes, which wait for the willingness of the partner processes to be communicated with.

Finally, the T9000 has two internal timers, which increase the counter value by one every $1\,\mu s$ (timer 0) or 64 μs (timer 1). The transputer uses the timer for internal control of multitasking via a hardware scheduler. Programs can also access the timer and read the counter value.

The T9000 pipeline

The T9000 is a superscalar processor and, therefore, it implements a pipeline that can work on several instructions in parallel. It does this using a special mechanism called *instruction grouping*, in order to execute as many as eight instructions. With every clock cycle, the processor can only read a 32-bit double word, which contains four instructions, because of the simple 1-byte structure of the instruction. In this way, at 50 MHz, the T9000 attains a continuous instruction rate of (in theory) 200 MIPS. If an instruction requires more than one clock cycle, then a larger group is joined together, which can incorporate a maximum of eight instructions (that is, eight instruction bytes), and which are subsequently loaded into the T9000 pipeline. The pipeline itself has five stages (see Figure 16.37).

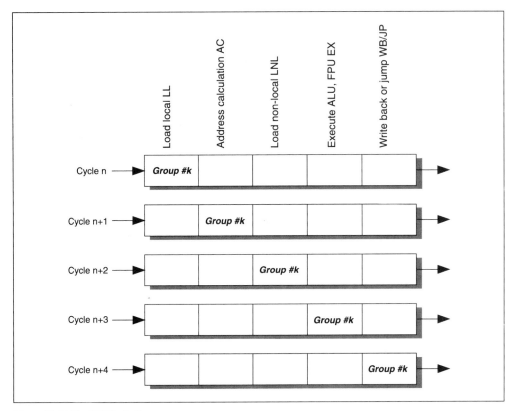

Figure 16.37: The T9000 pipeline.

The first stage *LL* (load local) fetches a maximum of two local variables from the current workspace. The second pipeline stage *AC* executes an address calculation for up to two non-local or indexed variables; that is, variables that are addressed via one of the A to C registers or a combination of two such registers, respectively. The third stage, *LNL* (load non-local), subsequently loads the non-local variables into the pipeline. The execution stage *EX*, forms the pipeline stage and executes the instructed ALU or FPU instruction. Finally, the fifth and last stage, *WB/JP* writes back the instruction results in the corresponding registers, or executes a jump. An important component of the pipeline is the *grouper*, which independently puts together instruction groups from the instruction flow. In this way, the pipeline architecture of the T9000 can be used optimally, without the necessary optimization from a compiler (although, of course, with respect to the special T9000 architecture, code optimization is never inappropriate and will extract every last percentage from the T9000). The largest portion of the executable instructions of a program are found in register stores and loads. This is highlighted because of the smaller register set for the transputer. On the other hand, such processes are executed easily in parallel, because only a small number of registers, but a large number of internal data buses, are available.

With the T9000, instead of principally sending two, or, in accordance with the pairing rule, a maximum of two, instructions to the pipeline, the grouper puts together an instruction group and loads this as a unit into the pipeline. Then, within the pipelines, each of which have two parallel stages, the group is executed in the usual pipelined way. In this way, only two pipelines are actually available, but because the grouper puts the instructions together such that in each group, a maximum of two instructions are found that use the same pipeline stage, a group can contain more than two instructions, which are completed within one clock cycle in accordance with the pipelining principle. Using an example, I would like to explain what appear, in the first instance, to be abstract characteristics.

Example: a[k+4] = b[1+8] +c[m+23]

The example instruction in a high level language adds the two elements of fields b and c, and places the result in a field element of a. The compiler produces, for example, the following codes:

Instruction	Stage	Process	
LDL 1	1a	load local variable 1	
LDL b	1b	load basis address from field b	Group 1
WSUB	2a	calculate address from b[1]	
LDNL 8	2b,3a	load element b[1+8]	
LDL m	1a	load local variable m	
LDL c	1b	load basis address from field c	
WSUB	2a	calculate address from c[m]	Group 2
LDNL 23	2b,3a	load element c[m+23]	
ADD	4a	add b[1+8] and c[m+23]	
LDL k	1a	load local variable k	
LDL a	1b	load basis address from field a	Group 3
WSUB	2a	calculate address from a[k]	
STNL 4	2b,5a	store element a[k+4]	

As you can see from the instructions listed and the pipeline stages used, each pipeline stage is covered, at the most, twice. As a result of the T9000 superscalar structure, these requests are executed in parallel. Therefore, the T9000 can execute the example instruction given in only three clock cycles, because only one clock cycle is needed per group. The large number of machine code instructions necessary for the evaluation of the expression a[k+4] = b[1+8] + c[m+23] comes from the fact that the transputer only implements relatively simple addressing methods. The Pentium effects the expression with fewer instructions as follows:

```
MOV ebx, 1            ; load 1 after ebx (1)

MOV ecx, m            ; load m after ecx (2)

MOV eax, b[ebx+8]     ; load field element b[1+8] after eax (3)

ADD eax, c[ecx+23]    ; add b[1+8] and c[m+23], result to eax (4)

MOV ebx, k            ; load k after ebx (5)

MOV a[ebx+4], eax     ; store eax=b[1+8]+c[m+23] in a[k+4] (6)
```

The instructions (1) and (2), as well as (4) and (5), can be paired because they are simple and do not have register dependencies. For optimal operation, the Pentium requires four clock cycles for the execution of a high level language instruction, one more than the T9000.

The T9000 links and virtual channels

The four data links are sufficient in order to connect five transputers with each other. In this way, via its four links, each transputer is connected with the other four transputers. With the insertion of a C104 message router, the number of channels can be further increased, but the possibility of maintaining the established direct connections between all transputers is lost. This is adequate for small systems but, for massively parallel operating multiprocessor systems based on the transputer that contain more than 64 transputers, this is not enough even though two channels are allocated to every link, namely a channel and a return channel for duplex transfers. To increase the number of communication channels further, more links could be integrated. The purely hardware level solution encounters a limit to the number of possible connecting lines, and an integration limit for the manufacture of the transputer chip.

A possible solution is given by the *virtual channels*, which have been implemented with the T9000. Therefore, a virtual channel processor (VCP) has been implemented on the transputer chip, which controls the links and creates the virtual links. The VCP operates in parallel to the transputer CPU – that is, the program operation is not slowed by it (processes on transputers are automatically shut down if they are waiting for a message from another process; for this, a waiting process is again restarted). Furthermore, the VCP separates every message, depending on the extent of the data, into a more or less large number of packets. Each packet is given a so-called header, which defines the target process for the data transfer. The VCP in the target transputer then reassembles the original message from the packets and passes it on to the target process. The procedure is, therefore, very similar to a packet switched data network. The virtual channels are distinguished by several advantages:

▶ the number of channels available is almost unlimited
▶ a physical link can be used by almost any number of virtual channels
▶ virtual channels can be separated into several physical links
▶ the data packets of a virtual channel can be transferred via different links and, therefore, do not have to wait for a free transfer channel
▶ the data packets of different virtual channels can be linked together; thus more virtual channels can transfer parallel data, as there are physical links

The transfer of the packet itself is achieved very similarly to existing data transfers. After the receipt of a data group, the receiver passes an acknowledgement back to the transmitter. The transfer protocol at packet and token level is shown in Figure 16.38.

In order to transfer a message between two processors via a virtual channel, the transmitter, more or less, outputs many packets. Without a header and packet or end of message token, a packet can transport a maximum of 32 data bytes. A short message encompasses, at the most, 32 data bytes and can be transferred with one packet; an end of message is transferred as an end token. In comparison, the number of the data bytes for a long message is not restricted. All packets, including the last one, are completed with an end of packet token. Like a short message, the last one encompasses 32 data bytes and is completed with an end of token message. After the receipt of every packet, the recipient returns an acknowledge packet, which also has a header, in order to identify the sending process. The data field is not available (or has zero length, if you want to look at it that way).

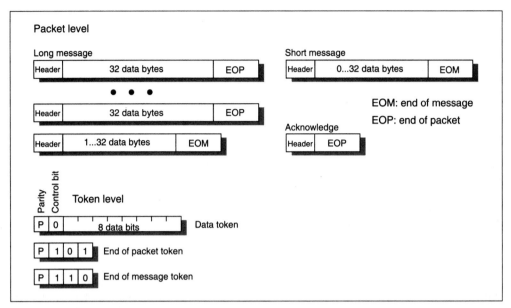

Figure 16.38: The link protocol on a packet and token level.

A parity bit is allocated to every token at token level, irrespective of whether it is data, an end of packet or an end of token. The control bit differentiates between data tokens and control tokens. Finally, a data token contains eight data bits, the control token only two. Both the header and the data field of a packet are assembled by a data token.

Support chips for the T9000

Two important support chips are also available for the T9000. Firstly, the packet switch C104 links 32 inputs with a choice of 32 outputs, using a so-called crossbar switch. The C104 represents a very small distribution centre with a very short switching time of less than 1 μs. As you have already learned above, the T9000 protocol for the control and data signals via the control and data links has changed somewhat, when compared to previous transputers. It is available to the system protocol converter C100, which converts the control signals and data signals of the links between the T8xx (and previous) and the T9000.

16.7.5 The transputer family

In the meantime, the transputer family encompasses a large quantity of chips with varying performance, from the simple 16-bit transputer T212, to the high performance transputer T9000 with up to 200 MIPs. The family members and their important characteristics are given in Table 16.4.

INMOS has made it known that future transputers will integrate more than four links on one chip for powerful parallel operating systems, in order to widen somewhat the communication bottleneck between the individual transputer elements of such a system.

Transputer	Register (bits)	Clock (MHz)	Links	RAM (kbytes)	Further elements
T212	16	20	4	2	Memory controller
M212	16	20	2	2	Memory controller, disk controller
T222	16	20	4	4	Memory controller
T400	32	30	2	2	Memory controller
T414	32	20	4	2	Memory controller
T425	32	30	4	4	Memory controller
T800	32	30	4	4	Memory controller, FPU
T801	32	30	4	4	Memory controller, FPU
T9000	32	50	4	16	Memory controller, FPU

Table 16.4: The transputer family.

With a further increase in the density of integration, it can be expected that, in future, transputers will have even larger on-chip memories, so that a powerful parallel operating computer based on a transputer will possibly only consist of many transputers and almost no memory chips.

17 Outlook: Other innovative concepts

In this chapter I would like to highlight a few concepts that are currently undergoing research, although in some cases they have already been introduced practically. They are especially suited to applications related to human thought processes or to the adaptation of problems that require independent conclusions in the realm of biological systems. This is, in the first instance, fuzzy logic with its 'routine' philosophy and the neural network, with a technical likeness to – in any case, until today – simple nerve systems.

17.1 Fuzzy logic

Fuzzy logic is a term cloaked in secrecy, which appears to be synonymous with information processing for the dawning third millennium. It is based on the theory of so-called fuzzy sets – or fuzzy numbers – and thus represents our 'fuzzy' thinking and conversation, which is only intelligible if we also take into account the context in which it takes place. This means that, in reality, the maths remains strictly logical, whereas the handled objects, and mappings to alter the objects (every addition of paired numbers is a mapping of two numbers onto a third) are, in the classical sense, fuzzy. The theoretical foundation of fuzzy sets was developed int the late 1960s and early 1970s by Zadeh, but initially had no application. Only since the explosive expansion in the 1980s of information technology, and the fact that processing capacity reaches limits, even for very powerful computers, especially during tasks that are a typical part of everyday life and that should support people, has there been a requirement to search for totally different and innovative concepts. For example, a complex production line with fuzzy logic allows itself to be easily controlled and is, therefore, cheaper than one using standard logic based on powerful microprocessors. A fuzzy logic system with a simple 8-bit microprocessor shows itself to be much more efficient for these control tasks than a system based on classical logic and using a fast clocked 32-bit chip. Therefore, in the following sections, I would like to introduce the basics of fuzzy logic. Readers who wish to delve more deeply into this new and interesting subject are advised to consult a more specialized text.

In classical logic and, therefore, also classical data processing, all characteristics are either clearly available or not available; 'partially available' does not exist. Put another way, an object can be allocated the number 1, if it has a particular characteristic, and 0 if the characteristic is not available.

Example: A car is green (1) or not green (0).

Using this functional characteristic you can create a defined set; for example, the set GrC for all green cars is, put mathematically, GrC = {Cars | Colour = green}. This is known as an analytical representation of the set, because the affiliation ('is an element of') is abstractly expressed by a characteristic. Another (and for finite sets, regularly used) possibility is the counting up of all elements, thus, all green cars – a rather time and space consuming operation. The elements of a set can – and with this we are already approaching a possible mathematical formulation of fuzzy logic – therefore also be identified, in that each object is assigned an *affiliation function* X, which indicates whether the object belongs to the set ($X=1$), or does not belong to the set ($X=0$). The values 0 and 1 are, of course, randomly selected, but lean towards stochastics, in which an event safely occurs if the probability is equal to 1 (or 100%), and does not occur if the probability is equal to 0.

If you consider the example above once again, then you will quickly realize that the simple differentiation of green or not green in borderline cases will certainly lead to differences of opinion between several people. Ultimately, colour sensitivity is not completely the same (as seen through the eyes of people who are red/green colour blind). If, of two people, one is of the opinion that the car is still green, while the other is of the view that the car is blue (which could be the case for a dark turquoise car), from the viewpoint of democracy it would be appropriate to allocate a value of 1/2 to the affiliation function X; thus, the fuzzy value is 1/2. In comparison, in classical logic, a decision has to be made as to whether the car is exactly green, or exactly not green. The circumstances surrounding the affiliation function is shown in Figure 17.1.

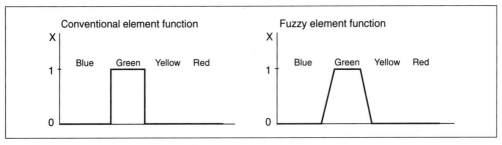

Figure 17.1: A classical and a fuzzy element function.

In the figure you can see the classical affiliation function, which forms a defined square function. All cars on the right of it are yellow (or red and so on), all cars on the left of it are blue; transitional colours such as yellow-green or blue-green do not occur. In comparison, the trapezoidal fuzzy affiliation function reflects human sensitivity much better, in that it permits transitional areas, the reduced intensity of green being identified by a functional value of less than 1. Of course, in place of the trapezoidal function, other fuzzy functions are also possible; for example, a triangular (if the characteristic is pretty well defined such as the air temperature is 28 °C; you would also calculate on having 27.9 °C and 28.1 °C) or a flat Gauss distribution without defined corners. Which affiliation function is best suited, depends on the system being modelled and each respective characteristic. Currently, there are still no general obligatory rules for the use of specific functions and the modelling of systems. Besides the concept of fuzzy logic, the application itself also appears to be fuzzy.

The three most important operations that can be carried out with sets are union, intersection and complement (within a larger set). Union and intersection are both dual operations, because two initial sets are necessary, which are mapped onto a target set . In comparison, the formation of a complement (within a specified large set) is a monovalent function, because it only requires one initial set. In order to continue with the description, in addition to the set of all green cars, the set of all blue cars is taken into consideration. The union set would then be the set of all green and blue cars, whereas the intersection set would contain all cars that are simultaneously green and blue. These set formations for both classical set logic and fuzzy logic are shown in

Figure 17.2. To complete the picture, the complement mapping is also given – that is, the set of cars that are not green.

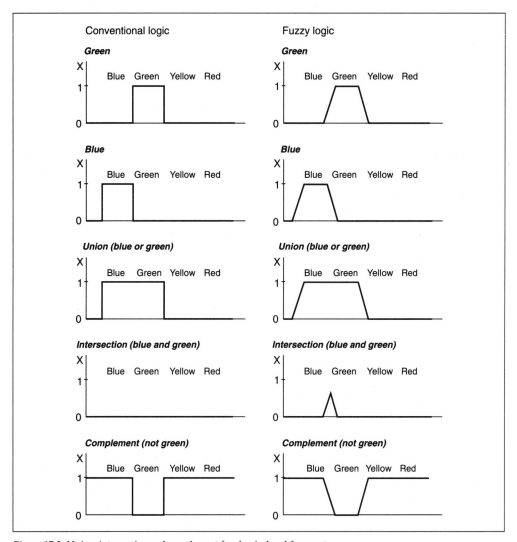

Figure 17.2: Union, intersection and complement for classical and fuzzy sets.

It is quite apparent, as an important difference between the two columns, that the fuzzy section is not empty. However, in the classical sense, a car cannot, of course, be green and blue simultaneously (and we are not talking about a green interior with a blue roof). In comparison, the fuzzy section set reflects the difference of opinion as to whether a particular blue/green car is actually green or blue. In reality, fuzzy controllers – controller systems based on fuzzy logic – turn out to be more efficient, especially in the limit and transfer areas of two characteristics, when compared to classical control machines because the 'not empty' section set of two actually contradictory sets prevents the controller from following only one control path.

Other elements are important to the basics of fuzzy theory, in addition to sets and the three set functions already mentioned. For example, put colloquially, important things are often described by the attribute 'very', less important things by 'little'. There is definitely a difference, if we consider green cars or very green cars. This means that, for Figure 17.2, for the characteristic green, the affiliation function would be much smaller and the transfer area narrower, and would, in an extreme case, adopt the form of a defined peak. The section between very green and very blue is, also according to fuzzy logic, then empty. The attributes 'very' or 'little' (and of course others) are identified in this case as being *modifiers*, because they modify the affiliation function.

Although rather rapidly – at least within the tight boundaries of this chapter – you now have the basics of fuzzy logic (an exact mathematical handling is, of course, more detailed), but the true implementation of the controller system is still in the distance. To date, there are no exact instructions on how to configure such systems. Instinct, intuition and 'pi-times-thumb' measurements, as well as the distinct trial and error strategy, replace the otherwise usual exactness. The majority of controller systems based on fuzzy logic always have the same basic structure. To begin with, the system and input data (for the cars, for example, the signal of a spectrograph) have to be 'fuzzied'. For this, parameterizing of the system and the fuzzy function used are necessary. (In the case of the car, it would be a good idea to define the colours based on the wavelength of light emitted by the cars in question.) With the assistance of the conventional standard base of today, the characteristics, so parameterized and fuzzified, are connected with each other in an inference member, so that the output value of the inference member identifies a characteristic that can be used for control (for example, the conveyor belt runs rather quickly). This unclear characteristic is transformed into a control signal inside the defuzzifier (for example, in order to supply the conveyer belt motor with the correct power, so that instead of running too fast, the belt runs at the correct speed). For the standard base, depending on the processes to be controlled, a more or less extensive knowledge acquisition has to be operated, which is also necessary in the case of artificial intelligence for classical systems. How extensive and how fine the knowledge base has to be is quite simple: if the controller is functioning, then the knowledge is adequate; otherwise the standard base has to be extended. The strength of the fuzzy logic for control functions lies in the fact that it can also bridge gaps in the standard base, where a normal processor would get tied up and crash the whole system.

With the assistance of standard computers, fuzzy controllers, based on fuzzy logic, can be modelled, in which the undefined affiliation functions and their connections (see Figure 17.2) must be replaced by, as it were, continual graduations (which are obtained from a number of smaller/larger comparison operations). Meanwhile, with the help of normal processors, in addition to this fuzzy emulation, there are also proper fuzzy chips, which already have the important fuzzy characteristics and combinations built in. Even an emulation on an 8-bit microprocessor such as the 8080 or Z80, for example, is often much more effective for control tasks, or cheaper than the corresponding standard classical controllers. Of course, not all systems are suited for control using the assistance of fuzzy logic. The greater the distinction is in the definition of the characteristic to be controlled, the more the advantage shifts towards known logic. For example, fuzzy logic would be out of place in attempting to calculate the absolute exact number pi. The fundamental characteristic of pi is that only one absolute exact number exists. Rough estimations between 3.1 and 3.2 are adequate if you want to evaluate the volume of water in a round bowl, but certainly not when you need to evaluate high precision scientific experiments.

Currently, known applications of fuzzy logic are the shutter control of photographic cameras (for example, the synchronization between f-stop and exposure time for still and moving objects in conditions with a lot of light and very little light), the prevention of shaky pictures in video cameras, and the control of the Sendai underground railway in Japan. A disadvantage of the fuzzy system is that the system has to be modelled and a suitable standard base set up. If this is not adequate, then somebody will have to expand the standard base. Of course, it would be desirable for the fuzzy system itself to recognize its 'missing knowledge' and independently expand its standard base accordingly – in other words, the machine should learn and not the man. I will address such self-learning systems – neural nets – in Section 17.2.

17.2 Neural nets

Until today, commonly used computers have been excellently suited to strictly determinable calculations. During the Second World War, there was a need to execute calculations related to determining the trajectory of shells, and in the development of the atomic bomb – the main driving force behind the development of electronic calculators. The foundations are provided by accurate basic equations in physics. There is no better example than that of the difference between the requirements placed on a biological nerve system and that of a computer for the calculation of mathematical expressions on one hand, and the idea of programming a robot such that it can execute a handstand on the edge of a balcony on the tenth floor. An Olympic gymnast can do it with ease; the robot would have to be scrapped after the first attempt (of course, recognition that there are also differences within the biological system can be related to the fact that the author himself would not attempt such a feat). It should be accepted that, in reverse, even a relatively simple computer can calculate the multiplication of a pair of 80-bit floating-point numbers a lot faster than an Olympic gymnast.

The two most influential recognition capabilities are pattern and language recognition. It is easy to identify an object from an angle another than that from which it has already been observed (for example, the observation of a person from an oblique forward angle, even though, until now, the person has only been seen from directly in front), or the object can be allocated to· a class (such as table), although the objects within this class can look very different. More difficult is the recognition of language. If you write a short colloquial expression down on paper, in order to analyses it later in greater detail, you will soon realize how imprecise human speech really is. It only becomes clear what each of the conversationalists is saying if the context is known. The general thought process capability and the ability to replace missing parts of an object from thought is almost impossible to simulate with standard computers using common algorithms.

Biological nerve systems usually consist of an enormous amount of nerve cells, the neurons, which, using synapse signals, accept other neurons via an extensively branched *dendrite* tree, reworking and changing them in a specific manner, and supplying the synapses to other neurons via their axons. Typically, a neuron has a thousand synapses on the dendrite tree (a form of parallel input interface) and an axon, which is itself branched and, thus, can control many synapses. It has come to light that, for the functioning of the brain, control among the nerve cells is important, whereby each of the synapses has an allocated and individual amplification factor. The controlling model of the neurons appears to be controlled partially by transmission mechanisms. For example, the first layers of the brain should recognize movement from information received from the eye; with all humans (and also animals) this is a very characteristic control structure. On the other hand, mental notes and learning process are very important; this affects the coupling strength of the neurons among one another via their synapses. Learning processes alter the weight of the individual synapses for a neuron.

It is, more or less, plain to see that the thought function of the brain or even the control function for the mechanism is realized by certain memory patterns in the complete system – that is, it does not store information locally. This also explains why biological nerve systems are very resistant to the loss of individual components. However, in a standard computer, if only one transistor of the many millions in the memory or CPU is defective, then eventually the whole system will crash (looked at biologically, the computer 'dies'). If our brains were as intolerant to failure, then our first hangover (which costs approximately one thousand out of an estimated 10 billion brain cells) would also have been our last. Until now, neither the exact structure nor the detailed function of the brain has been known (at this point, philosophy poses the question of whether the brain is capable of understanding itself).

Neural nets should simulate the capabilities that are typical of a biological system in order to make them (in a greatly reduced form) available to machines. Necessary at the outset is a model of the biological nerve system, which can be used to map the brain onto an electronic structure (or software). All that is differentiated are the diverse net topologies. With a layered net, the neurons are brought together with tasks of the same level. In general, this produces one input layer, k intermediate layers and an output layer. What is special about this is that the k intermediate layers are only addressed after a filtering of the input signal, and are not directly influenced by the input signals; they execute encoding of the input sample. In comparison, in nets without layers, all neurons are connected with one another. As the biological prototypes go to show, the development is currently going more in the direction of layered nets. In Figure 17.3, you can see the general structure of a layered net with three levels.

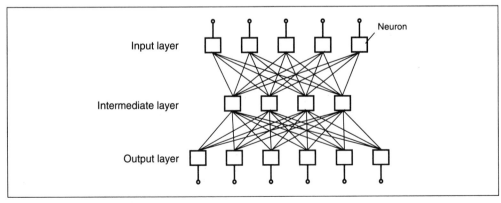

Figure 17.3: Multi-layered net with three layers.

Even the direction of the activation spread is differentiated by the neural net – that is, the direction in which the output signals of a neuron are given. For so-called feed forward nets, the signals are always transferred to the next layer, even possibly to the same neuron. With feed-back nets, the signals can also be directed to the same neuron, the same neuron layer or a preceding layer, in order to execute re-coupling, which is necessary for the learning process, for example.

You can see a typical black box structure of a neuron in Figure 17.4 with N synapses through which the input signals e_i are fed to the neuron, and M axons (corresponding to an axon with M branches), which provide the output signals a_j after the internal processing in the neuron.

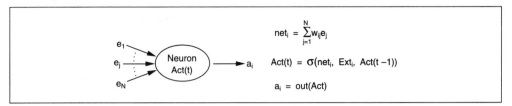

Figure 17.4: The black box structure of a neuron.

Each of the net neurons in the mathematical model is allocated three quantities: the propagation function *net*, the activation function σ and the output function *out*. The propagation function net_i identifies the net input on the basis of all neurons allied with the inputs e_j of the neurons. The factors w_{ij} form a matrix with the weight factors of the individual synapses i for the axon a_i of the neuron i. In addition to net_i, external inputs Ext_i (for layered nets, this usually only applies to the input layer) and the former activation condition Akt_i (t–1) can contribute to the current activation condition. Normally a function is selected for the activation function σ, which initially increases slowly from 0, then increases greatly in a relatively tight transfer area, and subsequently ends asymptotically in 1. For example, the fermi function (from quantum statistics) is suitable. The output signal a_i is a function of the current activation condition. A biological neuron then fires differing amounts of impulses per time unit. The stronger the activation, the more impulses that are supplied via the axon. However, the strength of the individual impulses remains the same.

The neural net can calculate the degree of activation of the individual neurons and, thus, their output signals either in layers, or via a swing process. In the first case, all neurons of a layer initially determine synchronously the total input net and subsequently the output functions. The output value is then transferred to the next layer as an input, which, for its part, starts to determine the degree of activation. These layer for layer, synchronized calculations can be repeated several times (which is essential for feed-back), until the output is stable. With a swing process, a randomly selected neuron commences with the calculation and provides the result to all those who, for their part, will start the activation investigation. In this way, the signal avalanches out, leading to a swing process of the whole net through feed-backs. If the total output value of the net is stable – that is, if it does not change (much) from stage to stage any more – then the activation calculation is ceased. A problem that can occur with both procedures is that the neuronal net finds a local minimum or a local stable condition, which does not correspond with the required end condition. Therefore, some nets also implement a statistical mechanism, which is suitable for leaving such local conditions, in order to find the global minimum or the global stable condition.

Neural nets operate in two different modes – a recall and training mode. In recall mode, the information stored in the net is output by a specific search pattern. The neurons then calculate their activation condition, and after a few stages the result is available in a stable condition. This happens relatively quickly. From the input of learning patterns during the training mode, the weight of the link, and, with this, the final link structure is set. This process takes somewhat longer. Normally, the degree of coupling and weighting w_{ij} is increased, if both neuron i as well as neuron j are active. The weight w_{ij} has to be matched until a given search learn pattern re-produces a specific output pattern. Therefore, the strength of a neural net lies in the fact that a later search pattern does not have to agree exactly with a previously trained learn pattern in order to produce an almost identical output pattern. Thus, neural nets are highly adaptable. For example, without much problem, you can reproduce a missing section of picture, if the rest of the picture is available as a search pattern. We ourselves know that the missing part should not be too extensive, if the picture is to remain recognizable. To a large degree, neural nets operate redundantly and are error tolerant, because a neuron contributes very little to the complete net and, thus, to the stored information. Subsequently, a missing section of a picture is equivalent to nothing other than an error during data storage. Other redundant memory media are, for example, holographic memories. Here too, the stored information can be reconstructed error-free, if a relatively large part of the information has been destroyed. The strength of contrast simply drops – that is, the possibility of confusion increases.

Neurons can be realized by both hardware and software. Current hardware implementations are operational amplifiers with a variable degree of amplification, which, for example, is defined by the loading condition of a capacitor. Neural nets can also be simulated by a computer program. Due to the discrete structure of the binary logic used you only receive quasi-continuous net conditions.

Neural nets are currently still heavily involved in the research and development phases. There are already some definite applications, though; for example, an explosives detector at airports, which can reliably detect explosives with the aid of a neural net and a neutron source. Because of the high nitrogen content of explosives, the neutrons display a characteristic pattern, after passage through the suitcase, and the possibly present explosive material, independently of its structure. In order to train the net, suitcases with and without explosives are passed through the detector hundreds of times during a training phase, at the same time teaching the net that the applicable object it is dealing with is explosives.

Appendices

A ASCII codes

The following table lists ASCII codes 0 to 127, as well as the extended ASCII codes 128 to 255. The values 0 to 31 are assigned control codes; they are listed separately. Each code is given in decimal (dec) and hexadecimal (hex) form, together with the assigned character (char).

Ctrl	dec	hex	char	code	Description
^@	0	00		NUL	Null character
^A	1	01	▼	SOH	Start of header
^B	2	02	–	STX	Start of text
^C	3	03	♥	ETX	End of text
^D	4	04	♦	EOT	End of transmission
^E	5	05	♣	ENQ	Enquiry
^F	6	06	♠	ACK	Acknowledge
^G	7	07	.	BEL	Bell
^H	8	08	.	BS	Backspace
^I	9	09		HT	Horizontal tabulation
^J	10	0A		LF	Line feed
^K	11	0B		VT	Vertical tabulation
^L	12	0C		FF	Form feed
^M	13	0D		CR	Carriage return
^N	14	0E		SO	Shift out
^O	15	0F		SI	Shift in
^P	16	10	►	DLE	Data link escape
^Q	17	11	◄	DC1	Device control 1
^R	18	12	↕	DC2	Device control 2
^S	19	13	‼	DC3	Device control 3
^T	20	14	¶	DC4	Device control 4
^U	21	15	§	NAK	Negative acknowledgement
^V	22	16	▬	SYN	Synchronous idle
^W	23	17	↨	ETB	End of transmission block
^X	24	18	↑	CAN	Cancel
^Y	25	19	↓	EM	End of medium
^Z	26	1A	→	SUB	Substitute
^[	27	1B	.	ESC	Escape
^\	28	1C	∟	FS	File separator
^]	29	1D	↔	GS	Group separator
^^	30	1E	▲	RS	Record separator
^_	31	1F		US	Unit separator

dec	hex	char
32	20	
33	21	!
34	22	"
35	23	#
36	24	$
37	25	%
38	26	&
39	27	'
40	28	(
41	29	)
42	2A	*
43	2B	+
44	2C	,
45	2D	–
46	2E	.
47	2F	/
48	30	0
49	31	1
50	32	2
51	33	3
52	34	4
53	35	5
54	36	6
55	37	7
56	38	8
57	39	9
58	3A	:
59	3B	;
60	3C	<
61	3D	=
62	3E	>
63	3F	?

dec	hex	char
64	40	@
65	41	A
66	42	B
67	43	C
68	44	D
69	45	E
70	46	F
71	47	G
72	48	H
73	49	I
74	4A	J
75	4B	K
76	4C	L
77	4D	M
78	4E	N
79	4F	O
80	50	P
81	51	Q
82	52	R
83	53	S
84	54	T
85	55	U
86	56	V
87	57	W
88	58	X
89	59	Y
90	5A	Z
91	5B	[
92	5C	\
93	5D	]
94	5E	^
95	5F	_

dec	hex	char
96	60	'
97	61	a
98	62	b
99	63	c
100	64	d
101	65	e
102	66	f
103	67	g
104	68	h
105	69	i
106	6A	j
107	6B	k
108	6C	l
109	6D	m
110	6E	n
111	6F	o
112	70	p
113	71	q
114	72	r
115	73	s
116	74	t
117	75	u
118	76	v
119	77	w
120	78	x
121	79	y
122	7A	z
123	7B	{
124	7C	|
125	7D	}
126	7E	~
127	7F	⌂

dec	hex	char
128	80	Ç
129	81	ü
130	82	é
131	83	â
132	84	ä
133	85	à
134	86	å
135	87	ç
136	88	ê
137	89	ë
138	8A	è
139	8B	ï
140	8C	î
141	8D	ì
142	8E	Ä
143	8F	Å
144	90	É
145	91	æ
146	92	Æ
147	93	ô
148	94	ö
149	95	ò
150	96	û
151	97	ù
152	98	ÿ
153	99	Ö
154	9A	Ü
155	9B	¢
156	9C	£
157	9D	¥
158	9E	Pt
159	9F	ƒ

dec	hex	char
160	A0	á
161	A1	í
162	A2	ó
163	A3	ú
164	A4	ñ
165	A5	Ñ
166	A6	ª
167	A7	º
168	A8	¿
169	A9	⌐
170	AA	¬
171	AB	½
172	AC	¼
173	AD	¡
174	AE	«
175	AF	»
176	B0	░
177	B1	▒
178	B2	▓
179	B3	│
180	B4	┤
181	B5	╡
182	B6	╢
183	B7	╖
184	B8	╕
185	B9	╣
186	BA	║
187	BB	╗
188	BC	╝
189	BD	╜
190	BE	╛
191	BF	┐

dec	hex	char
192	C0	└
193	C1	┴
194	C2	┬
195	C3	├
196	C4	─
197	C5	┼
198	C6	╞
199	C7	╟
200	C8	╚
201	C9	╔
202	CA	╩
203	CB	╦
204	CC	╠
205	CD	═
206	CE	╬
207	CF	╧
208	D0	╨
209	D1	╤
210	D2	╥
211	D3	╙
212	D4	╘
213	D5	╒
214	D6	╓
215	D7	╫
216	D8	╪
217	D9	┘
218	DA	┌
219	DB	█
220	DC	▄
221	DD	▌
222	DE	▐
223	DF	▀

dec	hex	char
224	E0	α
225	E1	ß
226	E2	Γ
227	E3	π
228	E4	Σ
229	E5	σ
230	E6	µ
231	E7	τ
232	E8	Φ
233	E9	θ
234	EA	Ω
235	EB	δ
236	EC	∞
237	ED	φ
238	EE	∈
239	EF	∩
240	F0	≡
241	F1	±
242	F2	≥
243	F3	≤
244	F4	⌠
245	F5	⌡
246	F6	÷
247	F7	≈
248	F8	°
249	F9	•
250	FA	·
251	FB	√
252	FC	^{n}
253	FD	^{2}
254	FE	■
255	FF	

B Pentium instruction set

In the following you will find all Pentium machine instructions, and an indication of the 80x86 processor in which the corresponding instruction has been implemented. The machine instructions for the integer core and the floating-point unit are listed separately in Section B.1 and B.2, repectively.

B.1 Integer core instructions

AAA	*ASCII Adjust After Addition (8086/88)* Adjusts the result of a BCD addition.
AAD	*ASCII Adjust Before Division (8086/88)* Converts non-packed BCD to binary number.
AAM	*ASCII Adjust After Multiply (8086/88)* Converts 8-bit binary number to non-packed BCD.
AAS	*ASCII Adjust After Subtraction (8086/88)* Converts the result of a subtraction to BCD.
ADC	*Add with Carry (8086/88)* Adds source operand, destination operand and carry flag.
ADD	*Add (8086/88)* Adds source and destination operands.
AND	*Logical AND (8086/88)* Bit by bit logical AND of two operands.
ARPL	*Adjust Requested Privilege Level (80286)* The instruction replaces the requested privilege level RPL in a segment selector by a less privileged value.
BOUND	*Check Array Bounds (80186)* Checks a value as to whether it is within the preset boundaries of an array.
BSF *BSR*	*Bit Scan Forward/Bit Scan Reverse (i386)* Scans the operand in forward or reverse direction to look for the first bit set (=1).
BSWAP	*Byte Swap (i486)* Swaps to bytes.

BT BTC BTR BTS	*Bit Test (i386)* Copies the value of a certain bit into the carry flag.
CALL	*Call Procedure (8086/88)* Calls a procedure.
CBW	*Convert Byte to Word (8086/88)* Converts signed byte to signed word.
CDQ	*Convert Double to Quad (i386)* Converts signed double word into signed quad word.
CLC	*Clear Carry Flag (8086/88)* Sets carry flag to zero.
CLD	*Clear Direction Flag (8086/88)* Clears direction flag for string instructions.
CLI	*Clear Interrupt Flag (8086/88)* Blocks out maskable interrupts.
CLTS	*Clear Task Switched Flag (80286)* Clears the task-switched flag in the machine status word MSW.
CMC	*Complement Carry Flag (8086/88)* Complements the carry flag.
CMP	*Compare (8086/88)* Compares two operands.
CMPS CMPSB CMPSW	*Compare String (8086/88)* Compares two strings.
CMPSD	*Compare String (i386)* Compares two strings.
CMPXCHG	*Compare and Exchange (i486)* Compares and exchanges source and destination operands, dependent on the comparison result.
CMPXCHG8B	*Compare and Exchange 8 Bytes (Pentium)* Compares the 8-byte value in EDX:EAX with the destination operand. If they match then ECX:EBX is stored into the destination operand, else the destination operand is transferred into EDX:EAX.
CPUID	*CPU Identify (Pentium)* The instruction returns an identification in the EAX register.
CWD	*Convert Word to Double (8086/88)* Converts signed word to signed double word.

CWDE	*Convert Word to Extended Double (i386)*
	Converts a signed word to a signed double word.
DAA	*Decimal Adjust After Addition (8086/88)*
	Converts result of addition to packed BCD.
DAS	*Decimal Adjust after Subtraction (8086/88)*
	Converts result of subtraction to packed BCD.
DEC	*Decrement (8086/88)*
	Subtracts 1 from destination operand.
DIV	*Unsigned Divide (8086/88)*
	Divides destination operand by source operand.
ENTER	*Make Stack Frame (80186)*
	Generates a stack frame for a local variable of a procedure.
ESC	*Escape (8086/88)*
	Supplies instruction and optional operand for coprocessor.
HLT	*Halt (8086/88)*
	Halts the processor.
IDIV	*Signed Divide (8086/88)*
	Divides signed destination operand by signed source operand.
IMUL	*Signed Multiply (8086/88)*
	Multiplies signed destination operand with signed source operand.
IN	*Input from Port (8086/88)*
	Transfers byte, word or double word (i386 and above) from port to accumulator.
INC	*Increment (8086/88)*
	Adds 1 to destination operand.
INS INSB INSW	*Input from Port to String (80186)* Transfers a string from a port into a string.
INSD	*Input from Port to String (i386)*
	Transfers a string from a port to a string.
INT	*Interrupt (8086/88)*
	Issues a software interrupt.
INTO	*Interrupt on Overflow (8086/88)*
	Issues interrupt 4 if overflow flag is set.
INVD	*Invalidate Cache (i486)*
	Invalidates the entries in the on-chip cache.

INVLPG	*Invalidate TLB Entry (i486)* Invalidates the entries in the translation lookaside buffer of the paging unit.
IRET	*Interrupt Return (8086/88)* Returns control from interrupt handler to interrupted program.
IRETD	*Interrupt Return (i386)* Returns control from an interrupt handler to the interrupted program.
JB/JNAE JAE/JNB JBE/JNA JA/JNBE JE/JZ JNE/JNZ JL/JNGE JGE/JNL JLE/JNG JG/JNLE JS JNS JC JNC JO JNO JP/JPE JNP/JPO	*Jump Conditionally (8086/88)* Executes a jump, dependent on a certain condition.
JCXZ JECXZ	*Jump if CX is Zero (8086/88)* Jumps if value of CX is equal to zero.
JMP	*Jump Unconditionally (8086/88)* Jumps always.
LAHF	*Load Flags into AH Register (8086/88)* Transfers flag bits 0 to 7 into register AH.
LAR	*Load Access Rights (80286)* Loads the access rights of a selector into a certain register.
LDS LES	*Load Far Pointer (8086/88)* Reads and stores the far pointer of source memory operand in a segment/register pair.
LEA	*Load Effective Address (8086/88)* Calculates the effective address (offset) of the source memory operand.

LEAVE	*High Level Procedure Exit (80186)* Opposite to ENTER.
LFS LGS LSS	*Load Far Pointer (i386)* Reads and stores the far pointer of the source memory operand in a segment/register pair.
LGDT LIDT LLDT	*Load Descriptor Table (80286)* Loads the value of an operand into a descriptor table register.
LMSW	*Load Machine Status Word (80286)* Loads the value of a memory operand into the machine status word.
LOCK	*Lock the Bus (8086/88)* Locks out other processors from the bus.
LODS LODSB LODSW	*Load String Operand (8086/88)* Loads a string from memory into accumulator.
LODSD	*Load String Operand (i386)* Loads a string from the memory into the accumulator.
LOOP	*Loop (8086/88)* Returns repeatedly to a certain label and executes one or more loops.
LOOPE/LOOPZ LOOPNE/LOOPNZ	*Loop if (8086/88)* Executes a loop conditionally.
LSL	*Load Segment Limit (80286)* Loads the segment limit of a selector into a register.
LTR	*Load Task Register (80286)* Loads the value of an operand into the current task register.
MOV	*Move Data (8086/88)* Copies the value of the source into the destination operand.
MOVS MOVSB MOVSW	*Move String Data (8086/88)* Copies a string from one memory area into another memory area.
MOVSD	*Move String Data (i386)* Copies a string from one memory area to another.
MOVSX	*Move with Sign Extend (i386)* Copies an operand and extends its sign to 16/32 bits.
MOVZX	*Move with Zero Extend (i386)* Copies an operand and extends its value with zeros.

MUL	*Unsigned Multiply (8086/88)* Multiplies two unsigned operands.
NEG	*Two's Complement Negation (8086/88)* Replaces the operand by its two's complement.
NOP	*No Operation (8086/88)* Does not execute any process.
NOT	*One's Complement Negation (8086/88)* Replaces each operand bit by its complementary value.
OR	*Inclusive OR (8086/88)* Bit by bit logical OR of two operands.
OUT	*Output to Port (8086/88)* Transfers a byte, word or double word from the accumulator to a port.
OUTS *OUTSB* *OUTSW*	*Output String to Port (80186)* Transfers a string to a port.
OUTSD	*Output String to Port (i386)* Transfers a string to a port.
POP	*Pop (8086/88)* Pops the last value off the stack and transfers it to the operand.
POPA *POPAD*	*Pop All (80186)* Transfers the last eight values from the stack into the general purpose registers.
POPF	*Pop Flags (8086/88)* Transfers the last value on the stack into the flag register.
POPFD	*Pop Flags (i386)* Transfers the last value on the stack into the flag register.
PUSH	*Push (8086/88)* Transfers the operand onto the stack.
PUSHA *PUSHAD*	*Push All (80186)* Transfers the general purpose registers onto the stack.
PUSHF	*Push Flags (8086/88)* Transfers the flag register onto the stack.
PUSHFD	*Push Flags (i386)* Transfers the flag register onto the stack.

RCL	*Rotate (8086/88)*
RCR	Rotates the bits of the operand.
ROL	
ROR	
RDMSR	*Read Model-Specific Register (Pentium)*
	The instruction reads a model-specific register (for example, test
	register and so on) and transfers its value into EDX:EAX.
REP	*Repeat String (8086/88)*
	Repeats the string instruction CX times.
REPE	*Repeat String Conditionally (8086/88)*
REPNE	Repeats the string instruction until the condition is true.
REPZ	
REPNZ	
RET	*Return from Procedure (8086/88)*
RETN	Returns from a procedure to the calling program.
RETF	
RSM	*Resume from System Management Mode (Pentium)*
	Resumes program execution after an SMI and leaves system
	management mode for this purpose.
SAHF	*Store AH into Flags (8086/88)*
	Transfers AH into the bits 0 to 7 of the flag register.
SAL	*Shift (8086/88)*
SAR	Shifts the operand bits.
SHL	
SHR	
SBB	*Subtract with Borrow (8086/88)*
	Subtracts the source from the destination operand and additionally
	subtracts the carry flag.
SCAS	*Scan String Flags (8086/88)*
SCASB	Scans a string for a certain value.
SCASW	
SCASD	*Scan String Flags (i386)*
	Scans a string for a certain value.

SETB/SETNAE	Set Conditionally (i386)
SETAE/SETNB	Sets the byte of the operand conditionally
SETBE/SETNA	
SETA/SETNBE	
SETE/SETZ	
SETNE/SETNZ	
SETL/SETNGE	
SETGE/SETNL	
SETLE/SETNG	
SETG/SETNLE	
SETS	
SETNS	
SETC	
SETNC	
SETO	
SETNO	
SETP/SETPE	
SETNP/SETPO	
SGDT	Store Descriptor Table (80286)
SIDT	Stores a descriptor table register in a certain operand.
SLDT	
SHLD	Double Precision Shift (i386)
SHRD	Shifts the bits of an operand into another operand.
SMSW	Store Machine Status Word (80286)
	Stores the machine status word in a memory operand.
STC	Set Carry Flag (8086/88)
	Sets carry flag to 1.
STD	Set Direction Flag (8086/88)
	Sets direction flag to 1.
STI	Set Interrupt Flag (8086/88)
	Sets interrupt flag to 1.
STOS	Store String Data (8086/88)
STOSB	Writes the accumulator value into a string.
STOSW	
STOSD	Store String Data (i386)
	Stores the value of the accumulator in a string.
STR	Store Task Register (80286)
	Stores the current task register in an operand.

SUB	*Subtract (8086/88)* Subtracts two operands.
TEST	*Logical Compare (8086/88)* Tests certain bits of an operand.
VERR *VERW*	*Verify Read or Write (80286)* Verifies that a certain segment selector is valid and can be read or written.
WAIT	*Wait (8086/88)* Halts the CPU until a corresponding signal from the coprocessor is received.
WBINV	*Write-Back and Invalidate Data Cache (i486)* Writes the contents of the on-chip data cache back into main memory and invalidates the cache entries.
WRMSR	*Write Model-Specific Register (Pentium)* The instruction writes a model-specific register (for example, rest register and so on) with the value in in EDX:EAX.
XADD	*Exchange and Add (i486)* Exchanges and adds source register and destination register or memory operand and destination register and writes the result into the destination register.
XCHG	*Exchange (8086/88)* Exchanges the value of two operands.
XLAT *XLATB*	*Translate (8086/88)* Translates a value from one encoding system into another encoding system by replacing the table index in Al into the table at DS:(E)BX by the corresponding entry.
XOR	*Exclusive OR (8086/88)* Bit by bit exclusive OR of two operands.

B.2 FPU instructions

Many 80x87 instructions have a format with or without WAIT. Instructions without WAIT are characterized by a N after the initial F (for floating; that is, ESC instruction).

F2XM1	*2 to X minus 1 (8087)* Calculates $y=2^{x-1}$ with $0 \leq x \leq 0.5$. x is taken from TOP and the result y is stored in TOP again afterwards.
FABS	*Absolute (8087)* Converts the value in TOP to its absolute value.

FADD FADDP FIADD	*Add/Add and Pop (8087)* Adds source and destination operand.
FCHS	*Change Sign (8087)* Changes the sign of TOP.
FCLEX FNCLEX	*Clear Exceptions (8087)* Clears the exception flags, busy flag and bit 7 in the status word.
FCOM FCOMP FCOMPP FICOM FICOMP	*Compare (8087)* Compares source with TOP.
FCOS	*Cosine (80287XL/i387)* Calculates the cosine of TOP.
FDECSTP	*Decrement Stack Pointer (8087)* Decrements the pointer to the register (TOP) on top of the register stack.
FDISI FNDISI	*Disable Interrupt (8087)* Masks off all interrupts; only valid on the 8087, all other coprocessors ignore FDISI/FNDISI.
FDIV FDIVP FIDIV	*Divide (8087)* Divides the destination by the source operand and stores the result in the destination operand.
FDIVR FDIVRP FIDIVR	*Divide Reversed (8087)* Divides the source by the destination operand and stores the result in the destination operand.
FENI FNENI	*Enable Interrupts (8087)* Clears the IE flag in the control word and thus enables the interrupts; only valid on the 8087, all other 80x87 processors ignore FENI/FNENI.
FFREE FREE	*Free (8087)* Changes the tag entry of a register to empty without changing the register value.
FIADD FISUB FISUBR FIMUL FIDIV FIDIVR	*Integer Add/Subtract/Multiply/Divide (8087)* Carries out addition, subtraction, multiplication and division using integers.

FICOM FICOMP	*Compare Integer (8087)* Compares two integers.
FINCSTP	*Increment Stack Pointer (8087)* Increments the pointer referring to the register (TOP) on top of the register stack.
FINIT FNINIT	*Initialize Coprocessor (8087)* Initializes the coprocessor and resets all registers and flags.
FLD FILD FBLD	*Load (8087)* Converts the operand to the temporary real format and pushes it onto the register stack.
FLD1 FLDZ FLDPI FLDL2E FLDL2T FLDLG2 FLDLN2	*Load Constant (8087)* Loads +1, +0, π, $\log_2(e)$, $\log_2(10)$, $\log_{10}(2)$ and $\log_e(2)$, respectively, onto the register stack.
FLDCW	*Load Control Word (8087)* Loads the control word from memory into the control register of the coprocessor.
FLDENV	*Load Environment State (8087)* Loads the environment state from memory into the coprocessor. The environment state comprises control word, status word, tag word, instruction pointer and operand (data) pointer.
FMUL FMULP FIMUL	*Multiply (8087)* Multiplies the source with the destination operand and stores the result in the destination operand.
FNOP	*No Operation (8087)* Does not carry out any process.
FPATAN	*Partial Arctangent (8087)* Calculates $z = \arctan(y/x)$. y is taken from register TOP, x from register TOP+1, x is popped off the stack and the result is stored in the new TOP (y).
FPREM	*Partial Remainder (8087)* Calculates the partial remainder of TOP when divided by TOP+1, the result is stored in TOP.
FPREM1	*Partial Remainder/IEEE (80287XL/i387)* Calculates the remainder of TOP when divided by TOP+1 according to the IEEE standard, the result is stored in TOP.

FPTAN	*Partial Tangent (8087)*
	Calculates y/x = tan(z); z is taken from register TOP; y is pushed into register TOP and x into register TOP −1.
FRNDINT	*Round to Integer (8087)*
	Rounds broken TOP to an integer.
FRSTOR	*Restore Saved State (8087)*
	Restores the coprocessor state from the data stored memory.
FSAVE	*Save Coprocessor State (8087)*
FNSAVE	Saves the current coprocessor state as a data array in memory.
FSCALE	*Scale (8087)*
	Scales with powers of 2 by calculating $y = y * 2^x$. y is taken from TOP +1, y from register TOP. The result is stored in TOP.
FSETPM	*Set Protected Mode (80287)*
	Switches the 80287 into protected mode. The 80387 ignores this instruction because it handles addresses in the same way in real and protected mode.
FSIN	*Sine (80287XL/i387)*
	Calculates the sine of TOP.
FSINCOS	*Sine and Cosine (80287XL/i387)*
	Calculates the sine and cosine of TOP. The sine is stored in TOP and the cosine is pushed onto the register stack; that is, into TOP−1.
FSQRT	*Square Root (8087)*
	Calculates the square root of TOP.
FST	*Store Real/Store Real and Pop/Store Integer/Store Integer and*
FSTP	*Pop/Store BCD and Pop (8087)*
FIST	Writes the value in TOP in memory or a register.
FISTP	
FBSTP	
FSTCW	*Store Control Word (8087)*
FNSTCW	Writes the control word into a memory operand.
FSTENV	*Store Environment State (8087)*
FNSTENV	Stores the coprocessor environment state in memory. The environment state comprises control word, status word, tag word, instruction and operand (data) pointer.
FSTSW	*Store Status Word (8087)*
FNSTSW	Writes the status word into a memory operand.

FSTSW AX	*Store Status Word into AX (i486)* Stores the floating-point unit's status word in the accumulator of the CPU core.
FSUB *FSUBP* *FISUB*	*Subtract (8087)* Subtracts the source from the destination operand and stores the difference in the destination operand.
FSUBR *FSUBPR* *FISURB*	*Subtract Reversed (8087)* Subtracts the destination from the source operand and stores the difference in the destination operand.
FTST	*Test for Zero (8087)* Compares TOP with +0.
FUCOM *FUCOMP* *FUCOMPP*	*Unordered Compare (8087)* Compares the source operand with TOP.
FWAIT	*Wait (8087)* Halts the CPU operation until the coprocessor has completed the current process.
FXAM	*Examine (8087)* Examines the contents of TOP and stores the result in condition code C3–C0 of the status word.
FXCH	*Exchange Registers (8087)* Exchanges the contents of the destination register and TOP.
FXTRACT	*Extract Exponent and Mantissa (8087)* Stores the exponential part of TOP in TOP and pushes the mantissa into TOP -1.
FYL2X	*Y log2(X) (8087)* Calculates $z = y \log_2(x)$. x is taken from the register TOP and y from the register TOP+1, after a pop the result is stored in the new TOP.
FYL2XP1	*Y log2(X+1) (8087)* Calculates $z = y \log_2(x+1)$. x is taken from the register TOP and y from the register TOP+1, after a pop the result is stored in the new TOP.

B.3 Instruction pairing

The following list summarizes which machine instructions can be paired internally by the Pentium and to what extent this is possible. U + V means that the instruction can be executed in both pipelines u and v, U alone means that the instruction can be paired with a (U + V) or V instruction, if it is in the u pipeline and the other can be executed in the v pipeline. Finally, V means that the instruction can be paired with a (U + V) or U instruction, if it is in the v pipeline and the other can be executed in the u pipeline. Please note that the list does not claim completeness. It has been evaluated from the pairing rules according to Section 8.4.1. Instructions that are not undoubtly pairable in one or the other way are not indicated.

Instruction	Pairing
ADD	U+V
AND	U+V
CALL (immediate only)	V
CMP	U+V
DEC	U+V
INC	U+V
Jcc	V
JMP (immediate only)	V
LEA	U+V
MOV (general-purpose register and memory operands only)	U+V
NOP	U+V
OR	U+V
POP (register only)	U+V
PUSH (register only)	U+V
RCL (only one bit or immediate)	U
RCR (only one bit or immediate)	U
ROL (only one bit or immediate)	U
ROR (only one bit or immediate)	U
SAR (only one bit or immediate)	U
SHL (only one bit or immediate)	U
SHR (only one bit or immediate)	U
SUB	U+V
TEST (register–register, memory–register and immediate–EAX only)	U+V
XOR	U+V

Table B.1: Pairing ordered according to instructions.

Pairing	Instruction
U+V	ADD
	AND
	CMP
	DEC

Pairing	Instruction
U+V	INC
	LEA
	MOV (general-purpose register and memory operands only)
	NOP
	OR
	POP (register only)
	PUSH (register only)
	SUB
	TEST (register–register, memory–register and immediate–EAX only)
	XOR
U	RCL (only one bit or immediate)
	RCR (only one bit or immediate)
	ROL (only one bit or immediate)
	ROR (only one bit or immediate)
	SAR (only one bit or immediate)
	SHL (only one bit or immediate)
	SHR (only one bit or immediate)
V	CALL (immediate only)
	Jcc
	JMP (immediate only)

Table B.2: Pairing ordered according to pairing types

Beside many integer instructions, certain FPU instructions can also be paired in a restricted manner with the FXCHG instruction. FXCHG is always carried out in the v pipeline, the paired instruction in the u pipeline and the following stages of the floating-point pipeline. Please note that this list, also, does not claim completeness. It has been evaluated from the pairing rules according to Section 8.5.3. Instructions that are not undoubtly pairable in one or the other way are not indicated.

FABS
FADD/FADDP
FCHS
FCOM/FCOMP/FCOMPP
FDIV/FDIVP/FDIVR/FDIVRP
FLD (single/double, precision memory operand)
FLD ST(i)
FMUL/FMULP
FSUB/FSUBP/FSUBR/FSUBRP
FTST
FUCOM/FUCOMP/FUCOMPP

Table B.3: Floating-point instructions that can be paired with FXCHG.

All other instructions can not be paired and are, therefore, executed solely and individually in the u pipeline.

C Pentium pin cross references

The following table lists all Pentium pins and signals together with their coordinates. It also shows the signal transfer direction (I: <—; O: —>, I/O: <—>) as well as the active level (↑: high; ↓: low).

Pin signal	Coord.	Direc.	Active level	Pin signal	Coord.	Direc.	Active level	Pin signal	Coord.	Direc.	Active level
A3	T17	<—>	↑	$\overline{BE5}$	S4	—>	↓	D24	B10	<—>	↑
A4	W19	<—>	↑	$\overline{BE6}$	U7	—>	↓	D25	C8	<—>	↑
A5	U18	<—>	↑	$\overline{BE7}$	W1	—>	↓	D26	C11	<—>	↑
A6	U17	<—>	↑	$\overline{BOFF}$	K4	<—	↓	D27	D9	<—>	↑
A7	T16	<—>	↑	BP2	B2	—>	↑	D28	D11	<—>	↑
A8	U16	<—>	↑	BP3	B3	—>	↑	D29	C9	<—>	↑
A9	T15	<—>	↑	$\overline{BRDY}$	L4	<—	↓	D30	D12	<—>	↑
A10	U15	<—>	↑	BREQ	V2	—>	↑	D31	C10	<—>	↑
A11	T14	<—>	↑	BT0	T8	—>	↑	D32	D10	<—>	↑
A12	U14	<—>	↑	BT1	W21	—>	↑	D33	C17	<—>	↑
A13	T13	<—>	↑	BT2	T7	—>	↑	D34	C19	<—>	↑
A14	U13	<—>	↑	BT3	W20	—>	↑	D35	D17	<—>	↑
A15	T12	<—>	↑	$\overline{BUSCHK}$	T3	<—	↓	D36	C18	<—>	↑
A16	U12	<—>	↑	$\overline{CACHE}$	J4	—>	↓	D37	D16	<—>	↑
A17	T11	<—>	↑	CLK	K18	<—	↑	D38	D19	<—>	↑
A18	U11	<—>	↑	D0	D3	<—>	↑	D39	D15	<—>	↑
A19	T10	<—>	↑	D1	E3	<—>	↑	D40	D14	<—>	↑
A20	U10	<—>	↑	D2	E4	<—>	↑	D41	B19	<—>	↑
A21	U21	<—>	↑	D3	F3	<—>	↑	D42	D20	<—>	↑
A22	U9	<—>	↑	D4	C4	<—>	↑	D43	A20	<—>	↑
A23	U20	<—>	↑	D5	G3	<—>	↑	D44	D21	<—>	↑
A24	U8	<—>	↑	D6	B4	<—>	↑	D45	A21	<—>	↑
A25	U19	<—>	↑	D7	G4	<—>	↑	D46	E18	<—>	↑
A26	T9	<—>	↑	D8	F4	<—>	↑	D47	B20	<—>	↑
A27	V21	<—>	↑	D9	C12	<—>	↑	D48	B21	<—>	↑
A28	V6	<—>	↑	D10	C13	<—>	↑	D49	F19	<—>	↑
A29	V20	<—>	↑	D11	E5	<—>	↑	D50	C20	<—>	↑
A30	W5	<—>	↑	D12	C14	<—>	↑	D51	F18	<—>	↑
A31	V19	<—>	↑	D13	D4	<—>	↑	D52	C21	<—>	↑
$\overline{A20M}$	U5	<—	↓	D14	D13	<—>	↑	D53	G18	<—>	↑
$\overline{ADS}$	P4	—>	↓	D15	D5	<—>	↑	D54	E20	<—>	↑
AHOLD	L2	<—	↑	D16	D6	<—>	↑	D55	G19	<—>	↑
AP	P3	<—>	↑	D17	B9	<—>	↑	D56	H21	<—>	↑
$\overline{APCHK}$	W3	—>	↓	D18	C6	<—>	↑	D57	F20	<—>	↑
$\overline{BE0}$	U4	—>	↓	D19	C15	<—>	↑	D58	J18	<—>	↑
$\overline{BE1}$	Q4	—>	↓	D20	D7	<—>	↑	D59	H19	<—>	↑
$\overline{BE2}$	U6	—>	↓	D21	C16	<—>	↑	D60	L19	<—>	↑
$\overline{BE3}$	V1	—>	↓	D22	C7	<—>	↑	D61	K19	<—>	↑
$\overline{BE4}$	T6	—>	↓	D23	A10	<—>	↑	D62	J19	<—>	↑

Pin signal	Coord.	Direc.	Active level	Pin signal	Coord.	Direc.	Active level	Pin signal	Coord.	Direc.	Active level
D63	H18	—>	↑	HLDA	Q3	—>	↑	$\overline{PEN}$	M18	<—	↓
$\overline{D/E}$	V4	<—>	↑	HOLD	V5	<—	↑	PMO/BPO	D2	—>	↑
DPO	H4	<—>	↑	IBT	T19	—>	↑	PM1/BP1	C3	—>	↑
DP1	C5	<—>	↑	$\overline{IERR}$	C2	—>	↓	PRDY	U3	—>	↑
DP2	A9	<—>	↑	$\overline{IGNNE}$	S20	<—	↓	PWT	S3	—>	↑
DP3	D8	<—>	↑	INIT	T20	<—	↑	RESET	L18	<—	↑
DP4	D18	<—>	↑	INTR	N18	<—	↑	$\overline{R/S}$	R18	<—	↑
DP5	A19	<—>	↑	INV	A1	<—	↑	SCYC	R4	—>	↑
DP6	E19	<—>	↑	IU	J2	—>	↑	$\overline{SMI}$	P18	<—	↓
DP7	E21	<—>	↑	IV	B1	—>	↑	$\overline{SMIACT}$	T5	—>	↓
$\overline{EADS}$	M3	<—	↓	$\overline{KEN}$	J3	<—	↓	TCK	T4	<—	↑
$\overline{EWBE}$	A3	<—	↓	$\overline{LOCK}$	V3	—>	↓	TDI	T21	<—	↑
$\overline{FERR}$	H3	—>	↓	$\overline{M/IO}$	A2	—>	↑	TDO	S21	—>	↑
$\overline{FLUSH}$	U2	<—	↓	$\overline{NA}$	K3	<—	↓	TMS	P19	<—	↑
$\overline{FRCMC}$	M19	<—	↓	NMI	N19	<—	↑	$\overline{TRST}$	S18	<—	↓
$\overline{HIT}$	W2	—>	↓	PCD	W4	—>	↑	WB/$\overline{WT}$	M2	<—	↑
$\overline{HITM}$	M4	—>	↓	$\overline{PCHK}$	R3	—>	↓	W/R	N3	—>	↑

Coord.	Pin signal	Direc.	Active level	Coord.	Pin signal	Direc.	Active level	Coord.	Pin signal	Direc.	Active level
A1	INV	<—	↑	C5	DP1	<—>	↑	D6	D16	<—>	↑
A2	$\overline{M/IO}$	—>	↑	C6	D18	<—>	↑	D7	D20	<—>	↑
A3	EWBE	<—	↓	C7	D22	<—>	↑	D8	DP3	<—>	↑
A9	DP2	<—>	↑	C8	D25	<—>	↑	D9	D27	<—>	↑
A10	D23	<—>	↑	C9	D29	<—>	↑	D10	D32	<—>	↑
A19	DP5	<—>	↑	C10	D31	<—>	↑	D11	D28	<—>	↑
A20	D43	<—>	↑	C11	D26	<—>	↑	D12	D30	<—>	↑
A21	D45	<—>	↑	C12	D9	<—>	↑	D13	D14	<—>	↑
B1	IV	—>	↑	C13	D10	<—>	↑	D14	D40	<—>	↑
B2	BP2	—>	↑	C14	D12	<—>	↑	D15	D39	<—>	↑
B3	BP3	—>	↑	C15	D19	<—>	↑	D16	D37	<—>	↑
B4	D6	<—>	↑	C16	D21	<—>	↑	D17	D35	<—>	↑
B9	D17	<—>	↑	C17	D33	<—>	↑	D18	DP4	<—>	↑
B10	D24	<—>	↑	C18	D36	<—>	↑	D19	D38	<—>	↑
B19	D41	<—>	↑	C19	D34	<—>	↑	D20	D42	<—>	↑
B20	D47	<—>	↑	C20	D50	<—>	↑	D21	D44	<—>	↑
B21	D48	<—>	↑	C21	D52	<—>	↑	E3	D1	<—>	↑
C2	$\overline{IERR}$	—>	↓	D2	PMO/	—>	↑	E4	D2	<—>	↑
C3	PM1/	—>	↑	D3	DO	<—>	↑	E5	D11	<—>	↑
	BP1			D4	D13	<—>	↑	E18	D46	<—>	↑
C4	D4	<—>	↑	D5	D15	<—>	↑	E19	DP6	<—>	↑

Coord.	Pin signal	Direc.	Active level	Coord.	Pin signal	Direc.	Active level	Coord.	Pin signal	Direc.	Active level
E20	D54	<—>	↑	N19	NMI	<—	↑	U5	$\overline{A20M}$	<—	↓
E21	DP7	<—>	↑	P3	AP	<—>	↑	U6	$\overline{BE2}$	—>	↓
F3	D3	<—>	↑	P4	$\overline{ADS}$	—>	↓	U7	BE6	—>	↓
F4	D8	<—>	↑	P18	$\overline{SHI}$	<—	↓	U8	A24	<—>	↑
F18	D51	<—>	↑	P19	TMS	<—	↑	U9	A22	<—>	↑
F19	D49	<—>	↑	Q3	HLDA	—>	↑	U10	A20	<—>	↑
F20	D57	<—>	↑	Q4	$\overline{BE1}$	—>	↓	U11	A18	<—>	↑
G3	D5	<—>	↑	R3	$\overline{PCHK}$	—>	↓	U12	A16	<—>	↑
G4	D7	<—>	↑	R4	SCYC	—>	↑	U13	A14	<—>	↑
G18	D53	<—>	↑	R18	R/S	<—	↑	U14	A12	<—>	↑
G19	D55	<—>	↑	S3	PWT	—>	↑	U15	A10	<—>	↑
H3	FERR	—>	↓	S4	BE5	—>	↓	U16	A8	<—>	↑
H4	DPO	<—>	↑	S18	$\overline{TRST}$	<—	↓	U17	A6	<—>	↑
H18	D63	<—>	↑	S20	$\overline{IGNNE}$	<—	↓	U18	A5	<—>	↑
H19	D59	<—>	↑	S21	TDO	—>	↑	U19	A25	<—>	↑
H21	D56	<—>	↑	T3	$\overline{BUSCHK}$	<—	↓	U20	A23	<—>	↑
J2	IU	—>	↑	T4	TCK	<—	↑	U21	A21	<—>	↑
J3	$\overline{KEN}$	<—	↓	T5	$\overline{SMIACT}$	—>	↑	V1	BE3	—>	↓
J4	$\overline{CACHE}$	—>	↓	T6	$\overline{BE4}$	—>	↓	V2	BREQ	—>	↑
J18	D58	<—>	↑	T7	BT2	—>	↓	V3	$\overline{LOCK}$	—>	↓
J19	D62	<—>	↑	T8	BT0	—>	↑	V4	D/E	—>	↑
K3	NA	<—	↓	T9	A26	<—>	↑	V5	HOLD	<—	↑
K4	$\overline{BOFF}$	<—	↓	T10	A19	<—>	↑	V6	A28	<—>	↑
K18	CLK	<—	↑	T11	A17	<—>	↑	V19	A31	<—>	↑
K19	D61	<—>	↑	T12	A15	<—>	↑	V20	A29	<—>	↑
L2	AHOLD	<—	↑	T13	A13	<—>	↑	V21	A27	<—>	↑
L4	$\overline{BRDY}$	<—	↓	T14	A11	<—>	↑	W1	$\overline{BE7}$	—>	↓
L18	RESET	<—	↑	T15	A9	<—>	↑	W2	$\overline{HIT}$	—>	↓
L19	D60	<—>	↑	T16	A7	<—>	↑	W3	$\overline{APCHK}$	—>	↓
M2	WB/$\overline{WT}$	<—	↑	T17	A3	<—>	↑	W4	PCD	—>	↑
M3	EADS	<—	↓	T19	IBT	—>	↑	W5	A30	<—>	↑
M4	$\overline{HITH}$	—>	↓	T20	INIT	<—	↑	W19	A4	<—>	↑
M18	PEN	<—	↓	T21	TDI	<—	↑	W20	BT3	—>	↑
M19	$\overline{FRCMC}$	<—	↓	U2	$\overline{FLUSH}$	<—	↓	W21	BT1	—>	↑
N3	W/R	—>	↑	U3	PRDY	—>	↑				
N18	INTR	<—	↑	U4	$\overline{BEO}$	—>	↓				

Glossary

1"

Abbreviation for 1 inch, equal to 2.54 cm.

1-Cycle Machine Instruction

A machine instruction that can be executed within one single clock cycle or, with a full instruction pipeline, that can be completed in each clock cycle. In the latter case the execution takes more time, but with every clock a result is available because with each clock cycle one instruction is completed.

68000 family

A Motorola CISC processor family, used mainly in Apple computers. They are the counterparts to the Intel 80x86 family.

8086

A 16-bit processor with 16-bit registers, 16-bit data bus and 20-bit address bus. It is employed in the XT and is the ancestor of the 80x86 family. The 8086 operates in real mode only, the address space comprises 1 Mbyte.

8088

A 16-bit processor with 16-bit registers, 16-bit data bus and 20-bit address bus. It is used in the PC and apart from the smaller data bus width is identical to the 8086.

80186/88

These processors are the successors of the 8086/88. In addition to improved and extended instructions, an interrupt controller, a DMA chip and a timer chip are integrated on the 80186/88.

80286

The second generation of the 80x86 family. The 80286 represents a 16-bit processor with 16-bit registers, 16-bit data bus and 24-bit address bus. With the 80286 the protected mode was introduced, which enables an address space of up to 16 Mbytes.

80287/80287XL

The mathematical coprocessor for the 80286. The 80287XL is improved compared to the normal 80287 and comprises all i387 functions.

80386/80386SX

Another name for i386/i386SX (see i386/i386SX).

80387/80387SX

Another name for i387/i387SX (see i387/i387SX).

80486/80486SX

Another name for i486/i486SX (see i486/i486SX).

80486DX2

Another name for i486DX2 (see i486DX2).

80487SX

Another name for i487 (see i487).

8087

The mathematical coprocessor for the 8086/88.

80x86 family

The family of the downward compatible 80x86 chips. At present the family comprises the 8086/88, 80186/88, 80286, i386/i386SX, i486/i486SX and Pentium. Up to the i386 they are all CISC processors with an extensive and micro-encoded instruction set. The i486 already implements some RISC elements, such as instruction pipelining, for example. The Pentium uses modern RISC concepts to a higher extent.

8237A

An 8-bit DMA controller with four independently programmable DMA channels. In the PC/XT one such chip is present, in the AT two chips are cascaded so that seven DMA channels are available.

82489DX

The Advanced Programmable Interrupt Controller (APIC) for supporting the Pentium and multiprocessor systems. It can operate at up to 50 MHz and is the successor of the 8259A.

82491

A 256-kbit SRAM module for an L2 cache with the 82496 cache controller.

82496

A cache controller for an L2 cache with 82491 SRAM modules. Its external interface is optimized in view of a cooperation with the Pentium.

8259A

A programmable interrupt controller (PIC) with eight different interrupt lines. In the PC/XT one such chip is used, in the AT two 8259A are cascaded so that 15 different interrupt levels are available.

8514/A

An IBM graphics adaptor with in-built graphics processor.

Abort

An exception that leads to an abortion of the task because the reason cannot be recovered. An abort typically occurs if the calling of a exception handler leads to another exception.

Access Time

The value for the time period between the output of an access request and the return of data.

Accumulator

A CPU register that is optimized in view of executing instructions. In former processors the accumulator was the only register which could be used as the instruction destination – that is, for storing the result.

ACK

Abbreviation for acknowledge.

Active-high

A signal is called active-high if a high potential level has the effect or shows the status that is indicated by the signal's name. For example, the 8086's signal READY is active-high because a high potential level indicates that the addressed unit is ready. On the other hand a low-level states that the unit is not yet ready.

Active-low

A signal is called active-low if a low potential level has the effect or shows the status that is indicated by the signal's name. For example, the 8086's signal $\overline{RD}$ is active-low because a low potential level indicates that data is read. On the other hand a high-level states that data is written. Active-low signals are usually characterized by an overbar ($\overline{RD}$), a preceding slanted line (/RD), a succeeding star (RD*) or, in fewer cases, by a succeeding tilde (RD~).

Adaptor Card

Also called extension card or plug-in card. A board with electronical circuitry that is inserted into a bus slot and enhances the capabilities of the PC. Typical representatives are interface adaptor cards, graphics adaptor cards and controller cards.

ADC

Abbreviation for analogue to digital converter. An ADC converts an analogue signal into a predetermined number of bits that represent the value of the analogue signal.

Address

A quantity that describes the location of an object. Specifically an address is a word or a number that characterizes a storage location or a port.

Address Bus

A plurality of generally parallel lines that transmit an address.

Address Space

The number of objects that a CPU or another chip can address.

Alpha

A very powerful 64-bit RISC processor from DEC. At present, it can be clocked up to 200 MHz and has two pipelines with seven (integer and addressing) and ten (FPU) stages. Moreover, 8-kbyte code and data caches are integrated on the chip. The Alpha should form the basis of all DEC systems from desktops up to mainframes for the next 25 years.

ALU

Abbreviation for arithmetical and logical unit. The ALU is the part of a CPU that executes the arithmetical and logical operations.

Am29000

A RISC processor from AMD for embedded controllers. It has an on-chip memory management unit and a branch target cache. The Am29000 was the first member of a whole family, which currently consists of Am29000, Am29005, Am29030, Am29035 and Am29050.

AMD

Abbreviation for Advanced Micro Devices. A US firm that produces microelectronic components such as processors, ASICs, RAM chips and so on. AMD became known because of its Intel-compatible 80x86 and 80x87 processors, and could win a considerable market share with its 386 clones.

Analogue

Without intermediate steps, continuous. An analogue signal, for example, can have continuous values without intermediate steps.

ANSI

Abbreviation for American National Standards Institute. An authority in the US that sets technical standards. ANSI is comparable with the German DIN.

Arbitration

The transfer of control over a unit from the present holder of the control rights to another unit. This is done by arbitration signals and an arbitration strategy.

Architecture

The overall concept for the design and structure of computer or a computer system.

ASCII code

Abbreviation for American Standard Code for Information Interchange. A 7-bit code that encodes 32 control characters for data transfer and 96 alphanumerical characters.

ASCIIZ string

A string that is terminated by the ASCII character \0 – that is, a null.

ASIC

Abbreviation for application-specific integrated circuit. An integrated circuit that is focused to a specific application. ASICs are often manufactured by means of gate arrays.

Assembler

A program that translates mnemonic code and symbolic addresses into machine code. Assemblers are the programming possibility closest to the machine that still accepts symbolic addresses and quantities.

Associative Memory

See CAM.

Asynchronous

Not corresponding to a phase or clock signal or without clock signal.

AT

1. Abbreviation for Advanced Technology.
2. The successor of the PC/XT with 80286 CPU and 16-bit bus slots.

AT bus

The AT bus system with various support chips (DMA, PIC, PIT and so on) and a 16-bit bus slot. The AT bus is strictly defined by ISA.

ATA

Abbreviation for AT atachment. A standard mainly for connecting hard disk drives to an AT bus; synonymous with IDE.

AUX

Abbreviation for auxiliary. With DOS synonymous with COM1, otherwise generally an additional signal or an additional line.

Average Access Time

The average value for the time period between the output of an access request and the return of data.

Axon

The (biological) nerve fibre or (technically or logically) signal line via which a neuron provides an output signal.

BASIC

Abbreviation for beginners all-purpose symbolic instruction code. A very simple structured programming language with easy to remember instruction names like 'PRINT'. Very often BASIC is implemented in the form of an interpreter, but nowadays there exist several powerful BASIC compilers that have some structural elements of C or Pascal.

BCD

Abbreviation for binary coded decimal. BCD encodes a decimal digit as a binary value of one byte. Example: BCD = 04h corresponds to decimal 4. BCD wastes a lot of storage because one byte is able to encode 256 different values but BCD uses only ten (0 to 9) of them.

Berkeley RISC Architecture

A RISC architecture developed at the University of Berkeley, characterized by register scoreboarding and an extensive register file. The first prototypes of this architecture were the RISC I and RISC II processors. Commercial implementations include Sun's SPARC processors.

Beyond RISC Architecture

Proposals for future RISC processors combining the advantages of RISCs and CISCs and which intend to apply superscalar and superpipelined concepts, for example.

Biased Exponent Representation

A representation of floating-point numbers in the form value = ±mantissa * base$^{exponent+bias}$, where exponent + bias is interpreted as an unsigned integer. To get the actual exponent you must therefore subtract the bias from the exponent value (exponent + bias) – in other words, *exponent = exponent value - bias* holds.

Bidirectional

In the case of a bidirectional transmission data can be exchanged in either direction between the communication participants. Thus, the two participants can serve both as transmitter and receiver.

Big Blue

Nickname for IBM, because IBM is a big business group and the company's logo is blue.

Big-Endian Format

In the big-endian format the high bytes of a multiple-byte quantity are stored at lower addresses and the low bytes are stored at higher addresses. Motorola's 68000 family uses the big-endian format.

BIOS

Abbreviation for basic input/output system. The BIOS comprises the system programs for the basic input and output operations and represents the software interface to the PC hardware. Typical BIOS functions are accesses to the floppy disk and hard disk drives, interfaces and graphics adaptors.

BIST

Abbreviation for built-in self-test. A test function of microchips, implemented by hardware or microcode. The BIST is typically carried out at power-on or directed through the RUNBIST command of the boundary scan test. It checks more or less all chip components and writes a check code into a register.

Bit

Abbreviation for binary digit. A digit, number or value that can show only two different conditions. These are normally named 0 and 1 or 0 and L. Very often, the bit is also called the smallest information unit.

Bit Line

The line in the column direction of a memory cell array in a RAM or ROM to which the stored value of a selected memory cell is transferred. The bit line is usually connected to the source terminal of the selection transistor.

Boundary Scan Test

A test function according to the IEEE standard 1149.1 which, by means of test cells and a test path, enables the serial input and output of test data and results. The boundary scan test implements a certain test command set to perform various checks of connections and chips.

Branch Delay Slot

A possible instruction location immediately after a branch instruction, which is always executed independently of the branch result (taken/not taken branch). By means of this, branch problems can be handled in that the compiler rearranges the instruction so that these branch delay slots contain useful instructions. Also called Delay Slot.

Branch Folding

The replacement of a branch instruction by the branch target instruction.

Branch Look Ahead

The calculation of a jump address in advance of the actual execution of the branch instruction. Thus, the target address is available at once.

Branch Prediction

A Pentium innovation for predicting branches and therefore for accelerating program execution. The branch prediction logic comprises a control unit and the branch trace buffer (BTB). The BTB is a cache which holds, as the tag, the address of the instruction preceding the branch instruction. Furthermore it contains the target address of jump as the cache data entry as well as some history bits. They provide statistical information about the frequency of each branch. The dynamic branch prediction algorithm attempts to predict the branches according to the instructions that the Pentium has executed in the past. If such a prediction is later verified as correct, then all instructions that have been loaded into the pipeline after the jump instruction are correct. The pipeline operation is continued without interruption. Thus, jumps and calls are executed within one clock cycle and in parallel to other instructions – if the prediction was correct. The branch prediction serves for compatibility because the powerful concept of delayed branches cannot be applied in the Pentium: existing 80x86 code has not been optimized in this respect.

Branch Prediction Buffer

See Branch Trace Buffer.

Branch Target Cache

A small cache on a CPU chip that holds the first few instructions at the branch target address. Thus, the branch target addresses form the tag and the code bytes the assigned cache data entry. By means of this the CPU can read the new instructions at the target address immediately after the branch has been taken. It need not wait for a lasting main memory access. Therefore, branch target caches have a similar job as on-chip code caches, but hold only a few code bytes. Data accesses are not accelerated, of course. Also called Branch Target Buffer.

Branch Trace Buffer

A small buffer or cache that holds the target addresses of jump instructions dependent on their occurrence in the past. The tag comprises the address of the instruction that precedes the branch instruction. The assigned cache data entry can be the address of the instruction sequentially following the branch instruction (that is, no branching is executed), or the branch target address (that is, branching is carried out). Which of the two possibilities is selected depends on whether the branch is more likely to have been executed or not executed during the past loops. Also called Branch Prediction Buffer.

Breakpoint

A means for supporting debuggers. If program execution reaches a breakpoint, the debugger suspends execution and displays a message. The user can restart program execution afterwards by an explicit command. Breakpoints can be activated by code and data accesses. They are supported at the hardware level, beginning with the i386, by the debug registers.

BTB

1. See Branch Target Buffer.
2. See Branch Trace Buffer.

Built-In Self-Test

See BIST.

Burst Mode

A special high speed mode for the transmission of larger data blocks in the form of an uninterrupted burst of smaller data units. For example, a cache line of 16 bytes can be transferred as a burst of four data units of 4 bytes each.

Bus

A plurality of generally parallel signal lines that transmit control, data and address signals.

Bus Master

A device or chip that can control a bus autonomously. Examples are the CPU and DMA chip.

Bus Slot

A dual contact strip in a PC into which adaptor cards can be inserted. The bus slot comprises the contacts for all necessary control, data and address signals.

Byte

A group of eight bits.

C

A very flexible programming language, which is very close to the machine but nevertheless comprises all elements of a high-level language. Characteristic of C is that there are almost no reserved names and commands; instead, all extensive commands that are known from other languages are implemented in the form of function libraries.

Cache

A very fast intermediate memory between a fast CPU and a slower memory subsystem.

Cache Consistency

The property in a multi-cache system that in an access by any CPU to a cache, that cache always returns the correct value. This means that in the course of updating a cache entry in an arbitrary cache all other caches are informed about that modification. The MESI protocol supports cache consistency.

Cache Flush

Writing the cache contents into main memory or to another data medium. Cache flushes are necessary only for those cache systems that do not support a write-through strategy.

Cache Hit

A cache hit occurs if a CPU in a computer system containing a cache outputs an address to read data, and if the data addressed thus is already in the cache SRAM and does not need to be read from the slow main memory. If this is not true and the addressed data is in main memory only, and not in the SRAM, this is called a cache miss.

Cache Miss

See Cache Hit.

Call Gate

A data structure of protected mode, which is defined by a descriptor. It serves to provide protected access to code of another privilege level.

CAM

Abbreviation for contents addressable memory; often called associative memory. CAM concernes a memory or memory chip in which the information is not addressed by means of an address but via a part of the information itself – thus, part of the memory contents. By means of this the CAM associates further data with this partial information, so that eventually various pieces of information are addressed. The information can become ambiguous. CAMs are used mainly for cache systems.

$\overline{\text{CAS}}$

Abbreviation for column address strobe. A control signal for a DRAM memory chip, which instructs the chip to accept the provided address as the column address and to interpret the address accordingly.

CAS-before-RAS Refresh

In the CAS-before-RAS refresh the external memory controller holds the $\overline{\text{CAS}}$ signal on a low level for a predetermined time, before $\overline{\text{RAS}}$ falls also – hence the name CAS-before-RAS refresh. Upon this happening, the internal refresh logic is enabled and carries out an internal refresh. The refresh address is generated internally by an address counter which is part of the refresh logic. Thus, the refresh is only triggered by the memory controller. The actual refresh is done by the DRAM chip itself.

Chip

A fingernail-sized silicon plate with up to several million circuits and electronic elements.

Chipset

A group of integrated circuits that serve for a certain job, for example to build an AT. A chipset integrates the function of many discrete elements, such as, for example, CPU, PIC, PIT, DMA and so on, on a small number of chips.

CISC

Abbreviation for complex instruction set computer. Microprocessors that comprise a very extensive instruction set of 100 to 400 machine instructions. Characteristic of CISC is the micro-encoding of the machine instructions.

CMOS

Abbreviation for complementary metal oxide semiconductor. CMOS is a technology for semiconductor elements with very low power consumption. Generally this is achieved by connecting one NMOS and one PMOS element.

COBOL

Abbreviation for common business oriented language. COBOL is a programming language designed specifically for banking and business applications.

Code Rearrangement

A strategy of optimizing the compiler that accelerates program execution by altering the 'natural' instruction flow. Such code rearrangements are mainly used mainly for MIPS RISC processors to fill branch delay slots with useful instructions instead of NOPs or to handle stalls caused by delayed loads.

COLIBRI

Abbreviation for Coprocessor for LISP Based on RISC. A specialized RISC processor for well-directed support of the programming language LISP. LISP is used in the field of artificial intelligence.

Compiler

A program that translates the commands written in a high-level language like, for example, C or Pascal into a series of machine instructions for the computer.

Control Bus

A plurality of lines that which transmit control information or control signals, generally in parallel.

Controller

1. An electronic device that controls and supervises the function of a peripheral; examples are floppy disk controller, hard disk controller, LAN controller and so on.
2. An electronic device that executes a certain function; for example a DMA controller.

Coprocessor

Also called processor extension. A microchip specially designed for a certain CPU to enhance or support the functions of that CPU. Examples are numerical coprocessors, which enhance the capabilities of the CPU by calculating numerical expressions with floating-point numbers.

Copy-Back

See write-back.

CP/M

Abbreviation for control program for microcomputers. A simple operating system for 8-bit processors such as, for example, the 8080/85 or Z80. CP/M was the predecessor of DOS. Therefore DOS still shows some CP/M concepts (the FCBs, for example).

CPU

Abbreviation for central processing unit. The CPU is the heart of a computer, and is also often called the (central) processor. Examples are the Intel 80x86 family and the Motorola 68000.

CRISC

Abbreviation for Complexity Reduced Instruction Set Computer. A contraction for characterizing computers or processors that, beside pure RISC concepts, also implement CISC elements such as, for example, a partially micro-encoded FPU.

CU

Abbreviation for control unit. The CU is part of a processor or CPU and controls the ALU and the registers, as well as other components.

DAC

Abbreviation for digital analogue converter. A DAC converts a digital signal made up of a certain number of bits into an analogue signal representing the value of those bits.

Data Bus

A plurality of lines that transfer data, generally in parallel.

Data Dependency

See Register Dependency.

Delayed Branch

If a jump or branch occurs – that is, a branch instruction leads to a new instruction address – the new instruction pointer value is not known until the command is completed in a later stage of the instruction pipeline. This is called delayed jump or delayed branch, because the jump or branch is carried out with some delay. While the jump or branch instruction is passing through the pipeline, several new instructions, which sequentially follow the branch instruction, are loaded into the pipeline and partially executed. One possibility for handling the branch problem is for the compiler to insert one or more NOPs immediately after the jump instruction. These NOPs actually have no consequences. Alternatively the compiler may rearrange the instructions in such a manner that these branch delay slots contain useful instructions.

Delayed Jump

See Delayed Branch.

Delayed Load

When an instruction contains a memory operand, the CPU must fetch that operand from cache or main memory. However, even an access to the fast on-chip cache usually requires one clock cycle. Transferring the instruction from the operand fetch to the execution stage of an instruction pipeline needs to be delayed accordingly. Alternatively the processor can execute NOPs. Both strategies slow down program execution and are called delayed load.

Delay Slot

See Branch Delay Slot.

Dendrite Tree

A widespread structure via which a neuron collects signals by means of the synapses formed thereon, and transfers them to the neuron itself.

Descriptor

An 8-byte data block that describes a segment or gate in protected mode.

Die

The 'bare' and therefore unprotected, processor or memory chip before it is bonded and packed.

Digital

With intermediate steps, discontinuous, divided in discrete steps. A digital signal, for example, can only reach certain values on a scale but no intermediate values.

DIP

Abbreviation for dual inline package. A package with contacts on the two opposite lateral sides.

DIP Switch

A small switch block in a DIP package, comprising several small switches. Jokingly, often called mouse piano.

DMA

Abbreviation for direct memory access. Besides the CPU, DMA forms a second data channel between peripherals and main memory, through which a peripheral can access directly the main memory directly without the help of the CPU and read or write data. In the PC DMA is implemented by the DMA controller 8237A.

Doping

The controlled deposition of impurities into a semiconductor substrate to affect its electrical properties in a certain way.

Double Word

A 4-byte quantity, therefore 32 bits.

Drain

One conduction terminal of a field effect transistor.

DRAM

Abbreviation for dynamic RAM. DRAM is a direct accessible memory (RAM) where the information is usually stored in the form of charges in a capacitors. Because all capacitors are gradually discharged by leak currents the storage capacitor and therefore the whole DRAM must be refreshed periodically, hence the name dynamic.

Driver

A software or hardware unit for driving a software or hardware component. The driver usually has a clearly defined interface so that, for example, a program has the possibility of accessing the device without needing to know the device's structure and functioning in detail.

Dual-Port RAM

A RAM chip comprising two independent access ports to the memory cells in the RAM chip. By means of this, two devices can access the information in RAM without disturbing each other. Dual-port memories are used mainly for the video RAM of graphics adaptors, where CPU and adaptor logic access the display memory concurrently. Another application is the use as communication memory in a multiprocessor system so that two or more processors can exchange data through this memory.

DWord

Abbreviation for double word. See Double Word.

Dynamic Branch Prediction

See Branch Prediction.

Early Write-Back

Writing back a cache line in advance of a cache miss which will cause a cache line fill. Using an early write-back strategy, at least one cache line is always free in the cache and can be filled immediately without the need to save its content in main memory.

EBCDIC Code

Abbreviation for extended binary coded decimal interchange code. An 8-bit character code corresponding to the ASCII code, used mainly in IBM mainframes.

ECL

Abbreviation for emitter coupled logic. A certain family of logic circuits. A family of integrated logic circuits that uses bipolar transistors. Thus, the chip operates faster but has a significantly higher power consumption and less integration density. The basic ECL circuit is a differential amplifier.

EEPROM

Abbreviation for electrically erasable PROM. A programmable read-only memory that can be erased by a high level voltage pulse. EEPROMs are implemented mainly with FAMOSTs.

Effective Address

The complete offset of an address which can be composed of a base register, scaled index and a displacement.

EISA

Abbreviation for extended industry standard architecture (ISA). EISA defines a 32-bit extension for the ISA or AT bus to integrate the 32-bit processors i386/i486. EISA is downward compatible with the XT and AT bus. Therefore XT and ISA adaptors can be used without any problems (theoretically).

EISA Master

A bus master able to carry out EISA bus cycles.

EISA Slave

A device able to serve EISA bus cycles.

Element Function

A function in the field of fuzzy logic for indicating the extent to which an object belongs to a certain set. Usually the element function X has a range of values between 0 (is not element at all) and 1 (is completely an element). In classical logic only the two discrete function values 0 and 1 are possible because an object either belongs to the set ($X = 1$) or not ($X = 0$). The range of values between 0 and 1 is arbitrarily chossen, but follows the stochastics: an event occurs with certainty (the object belongs 100% to the set) if its probability is equal to 1, and it does not occur (the object does not belong 100% to the set) if its probability is equal to 0.

Embedded Controller

Small microcomputers that serve for controlling electronic and electro-mechanical equipment, such as, for example, laser printers, drives or air conditioning devices. Characteristically, they have no external input means such as keyboards. Embedded controllers fulfil their role by means of the firmware stored in a ROM without any external intervention. Further typical properties are the powerful interrupt system, a rather small memory in most cases, and the lack of mass storages. For embedded controllers, RISC CPUs are especially well suited (for example, Am29000 or i960).

ENIAC

Abbreviation for Electronic Numerical Integrator and Calculator. One of the first fully electronic digital computers, which ran with vacuum tubes. It was developed in the US between 1943 and 1946.

EPROM

Abbreviation for erasable PROM. A programmable read-only memory that can be erased by irradiation with ultraviolet light. EPROMs are mainly implemented with FAMOST technology.

ESC Instruction

All opcodes for the numerical coprocessor 80x87 start with the bit sequence 11011 corresponding to 27. This is the ASCII code for the character ESC, therefore they are called ESC instructions.

EU

Abbreviation for execution unit. The part of a CPU that actually executes the instructions under the control of the control unit (CU).

Exception

If an internal processor error occurs the CPU issues an interrupt which is called an exception. The source of an exception can be, for example, a segment that is not present in memory, an unloaded page, a division by zero, a set breakpoint or a protection error.

Extended ASCII Code

An 8-bit code whose codes from 0 to 127 meet the standard ASCII code. The codes 128 to 255 are allocated to block graphics and other characters.

FAMOST

Abbreviation for floating gate avalanche injection MOS transistor. A FAMOST has a floating gate that can be loaded with electrons by a high level voltage pulse, which leads to an avalanche breakthrough. By means of this the characteristic of the FAMOST is changed. FAMOSTs are used mainly for EPROMs, EEPROMs and flash memories.

Fault

An exception that is recognized by the processor in advance of executing the faulty instruction. Thus the return address for the exception handler points to the instruction that caused the exception. Therefore, after the return the processor automatically attempts to re-execute the faulty instruction. A typical fault is an exception because of a swapped page. The exception handler reads the missing page and after the return the instruction accesses the now available data again without causing an exception.

FDC

Abbreviation for floppy disk controller.

Feed-back Net

A topology for neural nets where the neuron signals of one neuron layer can be fed to the same neuron, or the same or a preceding neuron layer. In that way feedbacks can be achieved, which are important, for example, for a training effect. Compare to feed-forward net.

Feed-forward Net

A topology for neural nets where the neuron signals of one neuron layer are always fed to the following neuron or neuron layer. Compare to feed-back net.

FET

Abbreviation for field effect transistor. In a FET the control of the conductivity is carried out by means of an electrical field between gate and source.

Flip-Flop

Also called bistable multivibrator. An electronical circuit with two stably defined states, which can be switched by a strong write pulse. Flip-flops are used as latches or SRAM memory cells.

Floating-Point Numbers

A representation of numbers in the scientific notation value $= \pm$mantissa $*$ base$^{\pm exponent}$. By altering the exponent the decimal point in the mantissa can be shifted without changing the value. Normally a representation with biased exponent is used.

Floating-Point Unit

See FPU.

FPU

Abbreviation for floating-point unit. A circuitry in a processor for executing floating-point instructions. The FPU is often implemented as a mathematical coprocessor.

Fuzzy Logic

A logic based on fuzzy sets. In the field of fuzzy logic the sharp distinction between, for example, larger and smaller/equal disappears. Instead, the transition area between two such strictly distinguishable properties is smeared out. This is shown in a graphical representation by replacing a square-shaped function with its sharply defined border by a more 'fuzzy' trapezoidal function. Thus, two quantities are no longer either larger or smaller/equal, but much larger, somewhat larger, nearly equal, somewhat smaller and much smaller. Fuzzy logic is more adopted to the human sensation of the transition between properties than that was the case with classical logic. Fuzzy logic is very successful mainly in the field of machine control or image recognition. At present, many applications are still in the development or research phase, but less complicated applications have already come onto the market.

G

Symbol for giga; that is, one billion of a quantity as, for example, in $1\,GW=1\,000\,000\,000$ W. Note that 1 Gbyte usually means 2^{30} bytes$=1\,073\,741\,800$ bytes.

Gallium Arsenide

Chemical symbol GaAs. A semiconductor material for extremely fast operating circuits.

Gate

The control terminal of a field effect transistor (FET). By changing the gate voltage the conductivity of the transistor can be varied.

Gate Array

A microchip with a plurality of logic gates. To carry out a certain function the connection of the gates is determined by a mask not before the last manufacturing step. By means of this the gate array can be adapted very easily to various jobs because the function concerned affects only a single manufacturing step. Today gate arrays are used mainly for ASICs or highly integrated controller chips in the PC.

Gbyte

2^{30} bytes = 1 073 741 800 bytes; *not* 1 000 000 000 bytes.

GDT

Abbreviation for global descriptor table. A table of 8-byte entries (the descriptors), which describe segments and gates in protected mode.

GDTR

Abbreviation for global descriptor table register. A memory management register from the 80286, which holds the base address and the limit of the GDT in memory.

Global Descriptor Table

See GDT.

Gradual Underflow

A floating-point number which is different from zero but can no longer be represented in normalized form.

Graphics Processor

A specialized microprocessor that processes graphics commands. By means of this the processor can draw, for example, lines and geometric objects using only the coordinates of a few characterizing points without any intervention of the CPU. With a graphics processor the CPU is relieved from ordinary graphics tasks.

Handler

A routine or task that is called as the result of an exception or interrupt. It should 'handle' the cause of the exception or interrupt.

Harvard Architecture

This architecture implements separate data and address buses, at least, internally in a processor. Externally, these two buses can be partially or completely combined.

HD

1. Abbreviation for hard disk.
2. Abbreviation for high density.

HDC

Abbreviation for hard disk controller.

Helios

Helios is an operating system for transputers, which supports the communication facilities of the transputers via their links and implements point-to-point connections among processes via these links.

HEX

Abbreviation for hexadecimal number.

Hidden Refresh

Here, the refresh cycle is 'hidden' behind a normal read access. After a memory access the $\overline{CAS}$ is further kept at a low level and only the $\overline{RAS}$ signal is toggled. The data read in the normal read cycle is provided by the DRAM chip while the refresh cycle is in progress. An address counter inside the DRAM generates the refresh address internally.

Horizontal Machine Code Format

The weak encoded form of machine instructions. With a horizontal machine code format the encoding fields in the various instructions are equal in size. In addition every instruction comprises the same number of bytes. For example, each machine instruction is four bytes (32 bits) long. Thus, for example, the encoding position of the registers used in the machine instruction is fixed.

Hz

Symbol for Hertz. 1 Hz = 1 period/s.

i386/i386SX

The third generation of the 80x86 family. The i386 represents a 32-bit processor with 32-bit registers, 32-bit data bus and 32-bit address bus. With the i386 the virtual 8086 mode was introduced. The physical address space comprises 4 Gbytes. The SX modification i386SX is internally identical to the i386 but has only a 16-bit data bus and a 24-bit address bus.

i387/i387SX

The mathematical coprocessor for the i386 and i386SX, respectively.

i486/i486SX

The fourth and up to now last generation of the 80x86 family. The i486 represents a 32-bit processor with 32-bit registers, 32-bit data bus and 32-bit address bus. It also comprises an improved i387 coprocessor, a cache controller and an 8-kbyte cache SRAM. The i486SX lacks only the coprocessor.

i486DX2

An i486 with internally doubled processor frequency; that is, the internal processor clock is twice the external clock supplied by the clock generator. The bus interface and therefore the bus cycles, on the other hand, run with the external clock only.

i487SX

The upgrade for an i486SX. The i487SX not only supplies the coprocessor but is a complete i486 CPU with on-chip cache and so on. If the i487SX is installed it disables the i486SX CPU and takes over its jobs, too.

i960

A RISC processor from Intel for embedded controllers. It has two pipelines; that is, is a super-scalar.

IC

Abbreviation for integrated circuit. A circuit consisting of several electronic elements, which is provided on a single carrier (substrate). DRAMs and microprocessors belong to the highest integrated ICs.

IDT

Abbreviation for interrupt descriptor table. A table of 8-byte entries (the descriptors), which describe gates for handling interrupts in protected mode.

IDTR

Abbreviation for interrupt descriptor table register. A memory management register from the 80286, which holds the base address and limit of the IDT in memory.

IEEE

Abbreviation for Institute of Electrical and Electronics Engineers; sometimes called IE^3 (I-triple-E). An engineers' organization in the US which defines standards.

IIL

Abbreviation for integrated injection logic; also called I^{2}L. A family of logic elements.

Inquiry Cycle

Also called snoop cycle. A bus cycle to a processor with an on-chip cache or to a cache controller to investigate whether a certain address is present in the applicable cache.

Instruction Pipelining

Generally, instructions show rather similar execution steps; for example, every instruction has to be fetched, decoded and executed, and the results need to be written back into the destination register. With instruction pipelining the execution of every instruction is separated into more elementary tasks. Each task is carried out by a different stage of an instruction pipeline (ideally in one single clock cycle) so that, at a given time, several instructions are present in the pipeline at different stages in different execution states.

Intel

An important US firm, which manufactures microelectronic components such as memory chips and processors. The most important processor family is the 80x86. Intel is regarded as the inventor of the microprocessor.

Interleaving

A modern memory organization concept for DRAMs to avoid delays caused by the $\overline{\text{RAS}}$ precharge time. For this purpose, the memory is divided into several banks where, for example, in a 64-bit memory all data with even quad word address (that is, 0000h, 0010h, 0020h, …) is located in bank 0 and all data with odd quad word address (that is, 0008h, 0018h, 0028h, …) in bank 1. Thus, in successive memory reads or writes the banks are accessed alternately. This means that the $\overline{\text{RAS}}$ precharge time of one bank overlapps the access time of the other. The effective access time for several succeeding memory reads and writes, as they appear to the CPU, is thus reduced. Today, most DRAM storages are configured as paged/interleaved memories. If interleaving is used together with page mode then successive pages are located in different banks, which accelerates page changes.

Interlock

If a stage in a pipeline needs the result or the system element of another stage that is not yet available this is called an interlock. Interlocks arise, for example, if in the course of calculating a composite expression the evaluation of the partial expressions is still in progress. The requesting pipeline stage then has to wait until the other pipeline stage has completed its calculations.

Interrupt (Software, Hardware)

A software interrupt is issued by an explicit interrupt instruction INT; a hardware interrupt, however, is transmitted via an IRQ line to the processor. In both cases the processor saves flags, instruction pointer and code segment on the stack and calls a certain procedure, the interrupt handler.

Interrupt Descriptor Table

See IDT.

Interrupt Gate

A gate descriptor for calling an interrupt handler. Unlike a trap gate the interrupt gate clears the interrupt flag and therefore disables external interrupt requests.

Interrupt Handler

See interrupt.

I/O

Abbreviation for input/output.

I/O Mapped I/O

With I/O mapped I/O the registers of peripherals are accessed via the I/O address space; that is, ports.

I/O Permission Bitmap

A data structure in a TSS that serves for an individual protection of I/O addresses. Each I/O address in the 64k I/O address space is assigned exactly one bit of the map.

IRQ

Abbreviation for interrupt request. A line or signal which is activated by a peripheral to issue a hardware interrupt to the CPU.

ISA

Abbreviation for industry standard architecture. A defined standard that has replaced the vague AT bus specification. ISA defines the bus structure, the architecture of CPU and support chips and the clock frequency of the ISA bus.

ISA Master

A bus master that is able to carry out ISA bus cycles.

ISA Slave

A device that is able to serve ISA bus cycles.

IU

Abbreviation for instruction unit. The part of the CPU that drives the execution unit.

k

Symbol for kilo; that is, one thousand of a quantity as, for example, 1 kW = 1 000 W. Note that kbyte generally means 2^{10} bytes = 1 024 bytes.

kbit

2^{10} bits = 1 024 bits.

kbyte

2^{10} bytes = 1 024 bytes.

kHz

1 000 Hz = 1 000 periods/s.

L1 Cache

The first level nearest to the CPU in a hierarchically structured cache subsystem. The L1 cache is usually much smaller than a possibly present L2 cache and integrated on the same chip as the CPU itself. The L1 cache can typically be accessed within one processor clock cycle.

L2 cache

Also called second-level cache. The second level of a hierarchically structured cache subsystem, nearer to the main memory. Between the CPU and main memory, the L1 cache and then the L2 cache are located. The L2 cache is typically 10 to 50 times larger than the L1 cache. It is formed by several SRAM chips and an L2 cache controller.

LAN

Abbreviation for local area network. LAN characterizes data networks that are restricted in space. Typical distances are less than 500 m. For LANs Ethernet and Token Ring are mainly used.

Latch

A circuit usually composed of two parallel connected inverters which holds (latches) once-written external data even if the external data has been deactivated again. The data writing is controlled by a clock or strobe signal.

LDT

Abbreviation for local descriptor table. A table of 8-byte entries (the descriptors), which describe segments in protected mode. These segments are local for the task concerned.

LDTR

Abbreviation for local descriptor table register. A memory management register from the 80286, which holds a selector, which in turn indicates the descriptor for the local descriptor table in the global descriptor table.

Leaf Routines

Subroutines that are called by other procedures, but do not themselves call further subroutines. Thus, leaf routines always form the lowest procedure nesting level.

Linear Address

An address in a linear address space. On the 80x86 processors the linear address is evaluated from the segment number and the offset. This is accomplished in real mode by multiplying the segment number by a factor of 16 and adding the offset afterwards. In protected mode another data structure is referred to, namely the segment descriptor, which holds the linear base address of the segment. With paging enabled, the linear address is further translated into a physical address.

Little-Endian Format

In the little-endian format the high bytes of a multiple byte quantity are stored at higher addresses and the low bytes are stored at lower addresses. Intel's 80x86 family uses the little-endian format. When writing multiple byte entities in the usual way with the highest order bit left and the lowest order bit right, the arrangement in memory seems to be reversed.

Load Forwarding

Here, in a read access to memory, the memory operand is not transferred to the destination register first and then from the register to the instruction pipeline. Instead the control unit applies the operand immediately after the read access to the ALU and saves it in a temporary register. Then the data is stored in the destination register referenced by the read instruction.

Load/Store Architecture

Here, only the two instructions load and store can access the memory. All other instructions (such as, for example, ADD or MOV) reference only internal processor registers (instructions like ADD reg, mem, for example, are therefore not possible). RISC CPUs, in particular, implement a load/store architecture to reduce the number of memory accesses and the variety of addressing schemes.

Local Bus

A new bus system for the PC which operates with 32 bits and, unlike EISA, at up to 50 MHz. Unfortunately the local bus is not as universally applicable as the ISA, EISA or MCA bus, but is currently used only for the integration of fast graphics adaptors and hard disk controllers. Two new standards exist for the local bus: Intel's PCI and the VESA VL bus.

Local Descriptor Table

See LDT.

Local Network

See LAN.

Logical Address

See Virtual Address.

LSB

Abbreviation for least-significant bit or least-significant byte.

LSI

Abbreviation for large-scale integration. This means the integration of 10 000 to 100 000 elements on a single chip.

μ

Symbol for micro; that is, one millionth of a quantity, for example 1 μm = 0.000 001 m

μm

Symbol for micrometre; that is, one millionth of a metre or 0.000 001 m.

μP

Abbreviation for microprocessor.

M

Symbol for mega; that is, one million of an unit as, for example, 1 MW = 1 000 000 W. Note that Mbyte usually means 2^{20} bytes = 1 048 576 bytes.

m

Symbol for milli; that is, one thousandth of a quantity, for example. 1 mm = 0.001 m

Machine Instruction

An instruction for a microprocessor that is decoded and interpreted by the processor without further modification or translation by software or hardware. Machine instructions consist of a more or less long sequence of bits, which specify the operation type, the addressing scheme, the affected registers and so on. The machine instruction is the lowest level of processor instructions accessible by a programmer. Assembler and high-level language instructions are translated into machine instructions by the assembler and compiler, respectively.

Main Memory

That memory of a computer that stores the program and the data that is necessary for program execution or that is processed by the program. Generally, the main memory is implemented with DRAM.

Mantissa

The number by which the power in scientific notation is multiplied to give the value of the expression. Example: $1.83 * 10^4$; 1.83 is the mantissa, 10 the base and 4 the exponent of the number 18 300 in scientific notation.

Matrix

A generally two-dimensional arrangement of objects such as, for example, numbers or memory cells. An individual object within the matrix is determined by specifying its line and column.

Mbit

2^{20} bits = 1 048 576 bits.

Mbyte

2^{20} bytes = 1 048 576 bytes.

Mega

See M.

Memory Bank

A group of memory chips that are accessed in common.

Memory Chip Organization

The internal organization of memory chips. Usually it is indicated as *m words * n bits*. The first number always indicates the number of storage words and the second the number of bits per word. Thus a 4M*1-chip has 4M words with a width of one bit each; that is, a storage capacity of 4 Mbits. Only one data terminal is formed. On the other hand, the 1M*4 chip has four data pins but still a storage capacity of 4 Mbits. Note that the words are always addressed and output.

Memory Mapped I/O

With memory mapped I/O all registers of the peripherals are located in the normal address space and thus are accessed via the normal memory instructions such as, for example, MOV.

MESI Protocol

A protocol for managing cache entries on a cache line base. This protocol is used mainly for multi-cache systems. The protocol assigns each cache line one of the states modified, exclusive, shared or invalid. Transitions between the individual states are issued by read or write accesses to the cache lines.

MHz

1 000 000Hz = 1 000 000 periods/s.

Micro

See μ.

Microchannel

A modern IBM bus system for the PS/2 PCs. The microchannel is designed for an 8-bit to 32-bit data and address bus and the support of multitasking operating systems on the hardware level. Unlike EISA the microchannel is completely incompatible with the PC/XT and ISA bus.

Microchip

A highly integrated circuit on a single substrate plate – the chip. More particularly microchip refers to ICs with extensive logic such as, for example, microprocessors or DRAMs.

Micro-encoding

The encoding of machine instructions of a processor by a sequence of more elementary instructions to the instruction and execution unit in a CPU. The microcode is stored in the processor's microcode ROM and is not accessible to the programmer, but is burnt-in in the course of manufacturing.

Microprocessor

A microchip with high intelligence for the execution of instructions. Therefore a microprocessor is programmable and the program is usually stored in a ROM or main memory.

MIPS

1. Abbreviation for million instructions per second. MIPS indicates the number of instructions executed by a processor within one second and serves sometimes as a (not very powerful) measure of the performance of the CPU.
2. Abbreviation for microprocessor without interlocked pipeline stages. A RISC architecture where no interlocks occur between the pipeline stages. Well-known MIPS implementations are the Siemens processors R3000/4000 and IBM's R6000.

MIPS/MIPS-X

See Stanford RISC Architecture.

MMU

Abbreviation for memory management unit. The MMU is either part of a processor or integrated on a separate chip. It carries out the address transformations for segmentation and paging.

Mnemonics

Easy to remember abbreviations that characterize the machine instructions of a processor and that are translated by an assembler according to the addressing scheme, the operands and so on into machine instructions. Example: MOV.

Monitor

1. A device for computers to display text and graphics.
2. A supervision program for a hardware or software unit. Example: virtual 8086 monitor; a system program to supervise the i386 and succeeding processors and one or more tasks in virtual 8086 mode.

MOS

Abbreviation for metal oxide semiconductor. A technology for manufacturing electronic components or integrated circuits that comprise a layer structure of the indicated form.

MOSFET

Abbreviation for metal oxide semiconductor FET (field effect transistor). A field effect transistor that comprises a control gate (metal), a substrate (semiconductor) and an isolating film (oxide) that separates the gate and substrate.

Motherboard

Also called mainboard. The board in a PC comprising the central components such as CPU, main memory, DMA controller, PIC, PIT and so on, as well as the bus slots.

Motorola

An important US manufacturer of microelectronic components such as, for example, memory chips and processors. The most important processor family of Motorola is the 68000. At present Motorola is very involved in the telecommunications field.

MSB

Abbreviation for most-significant bit or most-significant byte.

MSI

Abbreviation for medium scale integration. The integration of 100 to 10 000 elements on a single chip.

MSW

Abbreviation for machine status word. An 80286 control and status register for protected mode.

Multilayer Net

A topology for neural nets, in which neurons with equal function are connected in so-called neuron layers. Generally this leads to one input layer, k intermediate layers and one output layer. The k intermediate layers are only accessed after 'filtering' the input signals and not, therefore, affected by the input signals directly. The intermediate layers perform a re-coding of the input pattern.

Multiple Register File

In processors with a multiple register file a complete logical register file, is available for each procedure nesting level that is managed by a register file pointer. Upon a CALL the register file pointer is simply switched (increased) by one file and, thus, points to a register file not used at that time. The called subroutine is allocated this register file. Therefore additional write-backs of register values into memory upon a CALL are obsolete. If the program returns from the subroutine (by a RETURN) then the CPU simply switches back the register file pointer by one nesting level. Now the program 'sees' the old register values again.

Multiplexer

A device that transfers the data of several input channels to a smaller number of output channels in a strictly defined way. For example, the 20-bit memory address of the 80286 is divided into two successive 10-bit packets, namely the row and the column address, by the DRAM controller; here the number of input channels is equal to 20 but the number of output channels is only equal to 10. The DRAM controller therefore represents a multiplexer and the multiplexing manner described is called time-division multiplexing.

Multitasking

The concurrent execution of several tasks in a computer. Users have the impression that the tasks are executed in parallel; actually the computer only switches very quickly between the tasks.

Multitasking Operating System

An operating system that is able to manage several tasks in a computer system simultaneously, to activate them for a short time period and interrupt them later again. Examples are OS/2, UNIX or mainframe operating systems such as VMS or BS2000.

n

Symbol for nano; that is, one billionth of a quantity, for example, 1 nm = 0.000 000 001 m.

NAN

Abbreviation for not a number. A floating-point number that is different from zero but does not meet the IEEE definitions for the representation of floating-point numbers in a computer.

Nano

See n.

Nanometre

One billionth of a metre; that is, 0.000 000 001 m.

Nanosecond

One billionth of a second; that is, 0.000 000 001 s.

Neuron

The biological or technical cell of a neural net, which first collects signals via the dendrite tree and the synapses, processes them internally and outputs them via the axon afterwards. Also called nerve cell.

Neural Net

A form of data processing that attempts to imitate the connection and thought process of biological nerve systems. Characteristic of this is that the processing is carried out in an analogue or semi-analogue way. As is the case for real nerve systems, forward processing takes place – that is, many inputs are summarized for one output. Many of these outputs in turn are used as the inputs for the next stage, which, in turn, generates only one output. For the training phase of a neural net (also a feature of biological nerve systems) the final result is fed back to the input (for example, by the back-propagation algorithm). Neural nets can be formed by hardware; the neurons are then composed mainly of analogue amplifiers, the dendrites and the axon by electrical input wires and one output line, respectively. Also, simulation of neural nets on a computer – that is, by ordinary software – is possible. A predetermined combination between input parameters takes over the role of the neurons and the return value of the 'neuron procedure' is more or less the axon of the software nerve cell in question.

Nibble

A group of four bits, half a byte.

Nibble Mode

A certain operation mode of DRAM memory chips, where after supplying and decoding a row and a column address the $\overline{CAS}$ signal is toggled as a clock signal for data output. Thus, a maximum of four bits (one nibble) within one row can be addressed very quickly in a serial manner. The provided row and column address defines the start of the data output. With each of a maximum of three following $\overline{CAS}$ toggles an internal address counter is incremented and the next value is output. Unlike the serial mode, only four bits can be output here; in serial mode, however, a maximum of one complete row (1024 or more) can be output.

nm

Abbreviation for nanometre; that is, one billionth of a metre or 0.000 000 001 m.

NMI

Abbreviation for non-maskable interrupt. A hardware interrupt request to a CPU that cannot be masked internally in the processor by a bit but must be served immediately.

NMOS

Abbreviation for n-channel MOS. A technology for manufacturing MOS transistors in which the channel conductivity is based on negatively charged electrons.

Non-Destructive Operation

With non-destructive operation the operands are available in an unchanged manner after the instruction has been completed. The result is stored in another register. Thus, the destination operand is different from the source operand(s). RISC processors usually implement three-address instructions for this purpose.

Normalized Representation

In normalized floating-point number representation it is assumed that the leading digit is always equal to 1. Because by this the leading digit is thus always known implicitly, it is neglected and the exponent is adjusted accordingly, so that the value of the number remains equal. By means of this the precision is increased by one digit without enlarging the number format.

Not Taken Branch

See Branch Prediction.

ns

Abbreviation for nanosecond; that is, one billionth of a second or 0.000 000 001 s.

NVR

Abbreviation for non-volatile RAM. A memory that does not lose its memory contents even after the power is switched off.

occam

A high-level language for programming transputers. occam is adopted to the communication capabilities of transputers via their links and supports point-to-point connections among processes via these links.

Offset

The address within a segment; that is, the number of bytes from the beginning of the segment.

On-Chip Cache

See L1 Cache.

Operating System

Hardware-near software that controls and supervises the operation of a computer, establishes an interface between application programs and the hardware and file system, and manages the various tasks.

Organization

See Memory Chip Organization.

Overdrive

An upgrade for processors, which improves the performance by using another processor generation (for example, Pentium Overdrive for the i486DX) and, especially, by internally increasing the clock rate (for example i486DX/2 instead of i486DX). See also Upgrade.

Overflow

The condition that occurs when the result of an arithmetic operation is too large for the reserved memory location. For example, the multiplication of two integers may cause an overflow if the destination register can only accept an integer but the result is longer than 16 bits.

P5

The short form or development name for the Pentium

Packed BCD

Binary coded decimal numbers where each nibble of a byte encodes a decimal digit, for example: 72h = decimal 72. Packed BCD saves storage area compared to ordinary BCD.

Page

A section of an address space that is handled as a unit.

Page Directory

The first-order page table in a system with paging which holds the addresses of the second-order page table. The page directory is always in memory and, unlike the second-order page tables, not swapped onto disk.

Page Mode

A certain operating mode of modern DRAM memory chips in which after supplying and decoding a row address, only the column address is changed further. Similar to the static column mode, data within one row can be addressed randomly. Upon application of a new column address the column address strobe signal $\overline{CAS}$ needs to be disabled for a short time and then activated again. This instructs the DRAM chip to fetch and decode the new address. In static column mode, on the other hand the $\overline{CAS}$ signal need not be toggled in advance of providing a new column address. The duration of the page mode is limited, typically to 100 memory cycles. If the required data is located outside the page then a lasting page change is necessary.

Page Table

A table that holds the addresses of the corresponding pages in a system where paging is effective. The first-order page table is called the page directory. Unlike the first-order page table, the second-order page tables can be swapped like ordinary pages.

Paging

1. Generally: the division of an address space into smaller units – the pages.
2. Demand paging: the swapping of pages in main memory onto an external mass storage if the data stored therein is currently not needed by the program. If the CPU wants to access the swapped data the whole page is transfered into memory again and another currently unused page is swapped. In this way, a much larger virtual address space than the actually present physical one can be generated.

PAL code

Abbreviation for Privileged Architecture Library Code. A feature of the Alpha processor for externally implementing complex functions that have been handled by microcode up to now. Wirh PAL code, operating system-related or hardware-specific peculiarities of a system can be implemented and taken into account.

Parity

A simple method of detecting errors in data recording or transmission. For that purpose a data quantity is allocated a parity bit whose value is computed from the data bits. With even parity the number of 1s of all data and parity bits is even, thus the modulo-2 sum of all bits is equal to 0. With odd parity, however, the number of 1s is odd, thus the modulo-2 sum of all bits is equal to 1. Furthermore, the parities mark and space exist.

Performance Monitoring

An innovative functionality of the Pentium to evaluate various parameters such as, for example, the cache hit rate that are decisive for the overall performance of the Pentium.

Peripheral

A device or unit located outside the system CPU/main memory.

PGA

Abbreviation for pin grid array. A package where the terminals are provided in the form of pins at the package's bottom.

Physical Address

That address that appears at the address terminals of a processor. With paging enabled, it is generated from the linear address. Otherwise physical and linear address match.

Physical Address Space

The number of physically addressable bytes. It is determined by the number of address lines of a processor or the amount of installed memory.

PIC

Abbreviation for programmable interrupt controller. A chip for the management of several hardware interrupts and the ordered transfer of the requests to a CPU, which usually has only one input for such an interrupt request. Thus the PIC serves as a multiplexer for hardware interrupts. In the PC you will find the 8259A.

PIO

Abbreviation for programmed I/O. With PIO data are exchanged between main memory and a peripheral not by means of DMA but with IN and OUT instructions via the CPU.

Pipeline Stage

A unit or stage within a pipeline, which executes a certain partial task. A pipeline for a memory access may include the four pipeline stages address calculation, address supply, reading the value and storing the value in a register. An instruction pipeline comprises, for example, the stages instruction fetch, instruction decode, execution and register write-back.

Pipelining

The execution of a function of the next cycle beginning before the function of the current cycle is completed. For example the 80286 provides the address for the next read cycle in advance of receiving the data of the current cycle. This is called address pipelining or pipelined addressing. Similarly, a processor can start the execution of parts of a complex instruction in an early pipeline stage before the preceding instruction has been completed in the last pipeline stage.

PLA

Abbreviation for programmable logic array. A highly integrated chip with logic gates, which is employed as an ASIC and whose logic can be freely programmed during manufacturing or by the user. A PLA usually comprises a field of AND gates and a field of OR gates. By combining AND and OR any logical combination can be realized. This is similar to the fact that all natural numbers can be generated with 0 and 1.

PLCC

Abbreviation for plastics leaded chip carrier. A package where the contacts are formed on all four sides.

PMOS

Abbreviation for p-channel MOS. A technology for manufacturing MOS transistors in which the channel conductivity is based on positively charged holes.

Port

An address in the 80x86 I/O address space. Registers in peripherals usually are accessed via ports.

POST

Abbreviation for power-on self-test. A program in ROM that detects and checks all installed components during power-on.

PQFP

Abbreviation for plastics quad flatpack package. A package where the contacts are formed on all four sides.

Prefetch Queue

A small intermediate memory in a CPU where the prefetcher stores the following instructions before the processor has executed the current instruction. The prefetch queue serves for relief of the bus system and for predecoding the instructions in CISC processors.

Probe Mode

An innovative function of the Pentium for supporting external debugging hardware. In probe mode the Pentium drives the debug port to externally monitor the execution of a program inside the Pentium.

Procedure Window Method

Here every subroutine or procedure is allocated its own window into a register file. Upon a procedure call the register window pointer is simply switched one position so that all register accesses now take place relative to the register windows of the active procedure. By overlapping the parameter passing and result return areas of the individual nesting levels very fast parameter passing and result returning is possible because these are physically identical. The common parameter passing via an external stack is obsolete.

Process Computer

A small computer, usually without monitor and keyboard, for controlling machines such as, for example, automobile engines, robots or chemical reactors.

Processor

An intelligent microchip, which is highly programmable. Often used synonymously for CPU.

PROM

Abbreviation for programmable ROM. A read-only memory where the stored data can be programmed in the last manufacturing step or in the field by the user.

Protected Mode

An advanced operating mode, from the 80286 on, in which the access of a task to code and data segments and the I/O address space is automatically checked by processor hardware. The address generation in protected mode is completely incompatible to that in real mode. Thus real mode applications like DOS cannot be executed in protected mode.

PS/2

An IBM PC series with microchannel; conceived as a successor to the AT.

R2000

See R3000.

R3000

A common 32-bit implementation of the Stanford MIPS concept, which has a simple register file composed of 32 general-purpose registers with 32 bits each. All complex problems such as pipeline stalls (which must not occur according the definition of MIPS as microprocessor without interlocked pipeline stages) are handled by the compiler – that is, by software. Thus, the internal structure of the R3000 is quite simple. The R3000 has a five-stage pipeline and integrates an MMU and a cache controller on its chip. Floating-point instructions are executed by the R3010 coprocessor. Further members of the MIPS family are the R2000 (maximum clock rate 20 MHz compared to 40 MHz with the R3000, no instruction streaming and so on), the fast-clocked ECL derivate R6000 (up to 80 MHz) and the new 64-bit MIPSer R4000.

R4000

See R3000.

R6000

See R3000.

RAM

Abbreviation for random access memory. In a RAM, data can be directly and randomly read or written (that is, with any choice of the address).

$\overline{\text{RAS}}$

Abbreviation for row address strobe. A control signal for a DRAM chip, which instructs the chip to accept the supplied address as a row address and to interpret it accordingly.

RAS-only Refresh

A refresh method for DRAMs, by performing a dummy read cycle in which the $\overline{RAS}$ signal is activated and the DRAM is supplied with a row address (the refresh address). However, the $\overline{CAS}$ signal remains disabled; a column address is not required. Internally the DRAM reads one row onto the bit line pairs and amplifies the read-out data, but they are not transferred to the I/O line pair and thus to the data output buffer because the $\overline{CAS}$ signal is disabled. To refresh the whole memory an external logic or the CPU itself must apply all row addresses successively.

Real Mode

An 80x86 operating mode in which the segment value is just multiplied by 16 and the offset is added to generate the physical memory address. In real mode no access checks are carried out for the code and data segments and the I/O address space. All 80x86 CPUs up to the i486 support real mode for compatibility reasons.

Register

1. Internal memories of a CPU, the contents of which can be loaded or modified by instructions or by the CPU itself.
2. Components or intermediate memories of peripherals whose values result in a certain action in the device (control register) or indicate the status of the device (status register). The registers are accessed either via ports – that is, the I/O address space (I/O mapped I/O) – or via the ordinary address space (memory mapped I/O).

Register Bypassing

A method for reducing pipeline stalls. Normally the last stage of an instruction pipeline writes the result of the preceding execution stage back into the destination register. If a succeeding instruction needs this result as a source operand then, with bypassing, the result is directly, or by the write-back stage, applied to the operand fetch stage. This accelerates program execution because the operand is available to the succeeding instruction either two or one clock cycles earlier, respectively. Therefore no or at least a less severe, pipeline stall results.

Register Dependency

Also called data dependency. A state in which a later instruction uses source operands that are the destination of a former instruction. If the former instruction is not yet completed – that is, it is still in a later pipeline stage – then the register cannot be used at the moment. A pipeline stall or interlock occurs.

Register File

RISC CPUs often have a large number of general-purpose registers (32 to 2048). Their functionality and addressing is, unlike the 80x86 general-purpose registers, completely identical. The totality of these symmetrical general-purpose registers is called the register file of the RISC CPU.

Register Window

A usually linear sector of a register file, which has a certain size (for example, always 32 registers). The beginning of a register window is defined by a register window pointer (typically simply the number of the window's first register), the window size is either fixed (for example, 32 registers in principle) or variable. Then it is determined by a second pointer, which defines the end of the window, or a size indicator for the number of registers in that window.

REQ

Abbreviation for request.

RISC

Abbreviation for reduced instruction set computer (or also reusable information storage computer). Microprocessors that have a significantly reduced instruction set compared to a CISC (typically less than 100 machine instructions). Characteristic of RISC is that the machine instructions are no longer micro-encoded, but may be executed immediately without decoding. Well-known RISC processors are MIPS (microprocessor without interlocked pipeline stages) and SPARC.

RISC I/RISC II

See Berkeley RISC Architecture.

ROM

Abbreviation for read-only memory. ROM characterizes a memory chip from which data can be read that has been written in advance but cannot be written in the field. The stored data is determined once and cannot be modified afterwards, or only with some special equipment. The data stored in a ROM remains even if the power is switched off.

ROM BIOS

The PC BIOS routines in the ROM on the mother board.

Safe Instruction Recognition

See SIR.

Scoreboarding

A method for handling pipeline stalls. Scoreboarding is implemented by the RISC processors according to the Berkeley concept. Every register is assigned one bit. If the register is the desti-nation of an instruction – that is, that instruction must have run through the write-back stage of the pipeline before the register content can be used by another instruction – then the CPU sets the scoreboarding bit of the register as soon as the instruction has been loaded into the pipeline. Thus the register is blocked. Upon leaving the write-back stage the bit is cleared again. If a succeeding instruction in an earlier pipeline stage attempts to use the blocked register, for example, a source operand, then the instruction is suspended until the preceding instruction has left the write-back stage and cleared the scoreboarding bit. Therefore, the situation of an instruction using a register content that is not up to date, and thus carrying out erroneous calculations, is avoided.

Second-Level Cache

See L2 Cache.

Segment

A section in memory that is described by a segment register or a segment descriptor. Within the segment the objects are addressed by an offset.

Selector

An index into a descriptor table to select the segment or gate described by the descriptor.

Self-Test

See BIST.

Serialization (of Instruction Execution)

Here, all instructions that are currently in a more or less advanced state in the instruction pipeline are completed before another instruction is loaded into the first pipeline stage. On the Pentium certain instructions issue such a serialization.

Serial Mode

A certain high-speed mode of DRAM chips in which after supplying and decoding a row and a column address only the $\overline{CAS}$ signal is toggled as a clock signal for data output. Unlike page and static column mode, the data within one row can be addressed very quickly in a serial manner. The passed row and column address defines the begin of the output. Upon each $\overline{CAS}$ toggle an internal address counter is incremented and the next value is output.

Server

A central computer in a network, which manages the common data and supplies it to the workstations in the net. Usually it controls the access of the individual netnodes to peripherals such as printers and modems.

Set

Every tag and the assigned cache line are elements of a set. The set address determines the intended set, within all possible sets. Thus, a set is composed of a cache directory entry and the corresponding cache data entry for each way.

Silicon

Chemical symbol Si. A semiconductor, which has attained an outstanding importance in microelectronics. By introducing impurity atoms (doping) such as arsenic or phosphorus the electrical properties of silicon can be varied in a very wide range. Silicon is the main constituent of quartz – that is, ordinary sand – and is therefore available in unrestricted amounts.

Simple Instructions

A class of Pentium instructions that can be paired for simultaneous execution in the u pipeline and v pipeline. The simple instructions are completely hardwired, therefore no intervention of microcode is required. Thus, they can usually be executed within one clock cycle. To the group of simple instructions belong MOV, ALU, INC, DEC, PUSH, POP, LEA, JMP/Jcc near, CALL and NOP. ALU is synonymous for any arithmetical or logical instruction.

Single-Layer Net

A topology for neural nets in which all neurons are connected to all other neurons. Compare with multilayer net.

SIR

Abbreviation for safe instruction recognition. A process in one of the first stages of a floating-point pipeline, which determines whether the instruction to be executed gives rise to an exception (for example, underflow, overflow and so on) if the passed operands are used. For example, the multiplication of two floating-point numbers in temporary real format cannot lead to an overflow exception if the exponents of both operands are smaller than 1fffh. Then the instruction is regarded as safe. Inn the case of an instruction, the next floating-point instruction may be loaded into the pipeline before the current instruction has been completed, otherwise a possibly occurring exception could not be handled and the task would be aborted.

Slip

The suspension of an instruction in a pipeline where the preceding instructions in later pipeline stages are, however, executed further. Only the suspended, and thus all succeeding, instruction is not continued at the moment. Compare with stall.

Snoop Cycle

See Inquiry Cycle.

SOAR

Abbreviation for smalltalk on a RISC. A specialized RISC processor for well-directed support for the programming language Smalltalk.

Source

One conduction terminal of a field effect transistor.

SPARC

A RISC architecture which includes, as a specific feature, a plurality of registers (up to 2048 or more) and a ring-like organized register set. A task or a routine is allocated only a register window of 32 registers. SPARC processors can carry out a task switch rapidly fast because only the register window has to be moved and no storing of the task environment in memory is necessary (at least as long as the register set is not exhausted).

SPUR

Abbreviation for symbolic processing using RISC. A specialized RISC processor for well-directed support of the programming language Smalltalk.

SRAM

Abbreviation for static RAM. SRAM is a random access memory (RAM) where the information is usually stored as the state of a flip-flop. Because the circuit state of the flip-flop is not changed without a write pulse, a SRAM need not be refreshed, as is the case with a DRAM. This is the reason for the name static.

SSI

Abbreviation for small scale integration. This means the integration of less than 100 elements on a single chip.

Stall

The stoppage of the complete pipeline so that none of the instructions presently in various pipeline stages is executed further. Compare with slip.

Stanford RISC Architecture

A RISC architecture developed at the University of Stanford. Characteristic of this architecture is the transfer of all complex tasks into the compiler. Beside other things the compiler is responsible for ensuring that no interlocks are generated, because the Stanford architecture does not implement register scoreboarding. The first prototypes of this architecture were the MIPS and MIPS-X processors. Commercial implementations are the MIPS processors R2000 to R6000.

Static Column Mode

A certain high-speed mode of DRAM chips in which after supplying and decoding a row address only the column address is changed. Similarly to page mode, the data within one row can be addressed randomly and very quickly. Unlike page mode, however, in static column mode the $\overline{CAS}$ signal need not be toggled in advance of applying a new column address. The static column chip detects a column change automatically and decodes the new address even without column address strobe signal $\overline{CAS}$.

String

A group of successive characters terminated by \0 (ASCIIZ) or whose length is stored in a string descriptor.

Strobe

A signal that instructs a device, such as a DRAM, or a latch to read another signal, like an address.

Structure Size

The size of the elementary components of a microchip in its smallest extension, therefore usually the width of these components. Source, drain and gate of MOSFETs, bit lines and so on.

belong to the elementary components. The most highly integrated chips have structure sizes of less than 1 μm.

Substrate

The carrier of the microchip circuitry. The transistors and connections are formed on the substrate. In most cases silicon, which is doped to adjust the electrical properties as intended, is used as the substrate material.

Superpipelined Architecture

An architecture in which each machine instruction is split into a large number of elementary steps, which the processor executes in a separate pipeline stage for each. Unlike the well-known pipeline architectures that typically have four or five pipeline stages, the superpipelined architectures implement 10 or even more stages. Because of the less extensive nature of the tasks of every stage, they can be passed through more quickly; that is, the clock rate can be increased. At present superpipelined architectures are under development, because with an increased number of stages the likelihood of interlocks is enhanced.

Superscalar architecture

A RISC processor architecture that is able to issue more than one instruction in separate pipelines; for example, a comparison in an ALU pipeline and a floating-point instruction in a floating-point pipeline. Therefore, some instructions require less than one clock cycle on average if programming is carried out accordingly. The Pentium and i860 from Intel and Motorola's MC88110 apply superscalar principles.

Synapse

The coupling element with the axons of other neurons on the dendrite tree of a neuron via which output signals from other neurons are collected.

Synchronous

Corresponding in phase or clock signal or with the use of a clock signal.

System Management Mode

A specific operating mode of, for example, the Pentium. The system management mode (SMM) serves mainly for implementing a stand-by state in which the processor requires less power, for example by switching off or at least reducing the processor clock. The SMM is usually issued by an external signal to a dedicated terminal and leads to an interrupt which reorders addressing of the usual memory or addresses a certain SMM memory. Typically either all important register contents are saved in a non-volatile memory or the processor is constructed in such a way that it keeps all register values even after switching off the clock. Fast-clocked CMOS CPUs then gain a 99.99% reduction in power consumption.

T

Symbol for tera; that is, one trillion of a quantity as, for example, 1 THz = 1 000 000 000 000 Hz. Note that Tbyte generally means 2^{40} bytes and not 10^{12} bytes.

Tag

The tag forms the most important part of a cache directory entry. By means of the tag the cache controller determines whether a cache hit or a cache miss occurs. The tag holds the tag address; that is, certain address bits of the assigned cache line.

Taken Branch

See Branch Prediction.

Task

Also called process or job. A task is a called program loaded into memory, which is managed by the operating system. The operating system activates the individual tasks periodically and interrupts them. Each task has its own environment. The distinction between task and program is only significant with multitasking operating systems.

Task State Segment

A data structure in protected mode that describes one task.

Task Switch

The switching from one active task to another task that is currently interrupted. For this purpose the active task is interrupted, all important parameters are saved in the TSS, and the new and up to now inactive task is activated by the operating system.

Tbyte

2^{40} bytes; not 1 000 000 000 000 bytes.

TIGA

Abbreviation for Texas Instruments Graphics Adaptor. A graphics adaptor with its own graphics processor.

TR

Abbreviation for task register. A memory management register from the 80286 containing a selector, which in turn indicates the descriptor for the active TSS in the global descriptor table.

Transputer

A family of RISC processors from INMOS characterized, for example, by an instruction set with very compact encoding. A significant property of the transputers is that the processor chip integrates one to four interfaces – the so-called links. They serve for data exchange with other transputers. Transputers were directed to multiprocessor systems right from the start.

Trap

An exception that is recognized by the processor after executing the instruction that leads to the exception condition. Thus, the return address for the exception handler points to the instruction immediately following the instruction that caused the exception. A typical trap is the debug breakpoint exception. The exception handler activates the debugger, for example, to display the current register contents. After a return for restarting program execution the processor continues the interrupted task with the next instruction.

Trap Gate

A gate descriptor for calling an interrupt handler. Unlike the interrupt gate the trap gate does not clear the interrupt flag.

Triggering

The starting or stoping of a process by an external signal.

TSOP

Abbreviation for thin small outline package. A very flat package with contacts on two sides. TSOP packages are used mainly for flash memories.

TSS

See Task State Segment.

TTL

Abbreviation for transistor-transistor logic. A family of logic elements.

Two's Complement

A representation of negative numbers where the negative number is generated by complementing all bits of the corresponding positive number and adding the value 1 afterwards.

ULSI

Abbreviation for ultra-large-scale integration. This means the integration of more than 1 000 000 elements on a single chip.

Underflow

The condition that occurs when the result of an arithmetic operation is too small for the reserved memory location. That is possible if, for example, the divisor in the division of two single-precision real numbers is so big that the result cannot be represented as a single-precision real number any longer, but is nevertheless different from null. If the result is representable by a single-precision real number but not in normalized form this is called a gradual underflow.

Upgrade

Unlike the coprocessor, the upgrade not only supplies an enhancement for floating-point operations but also takes over the previous CPU jobs. Therefore an upgrade is a complete and usually much more powerful CPU. In the case of the i486SX, which lacks the coprocessor, the corresponding upgrade (the i487SX) supplies a coprocessor beside a faster CPU.

u Pipeline

One of the two Pentium integer pipelines. The u pipeline can execute all integer instructions and forms more or less the 'main pipeline'. Also called u pipe.

Vertical Machine Code Format

The highly encoded format of machine instructions. A vertical machine code format often has encoding fields of variable size or instructions that comprise various numbers of bytes. Thus, for example, the encoding position of the registers used in the machine code is not fixed, or the registers are binary encoded and do not show a one-to-one assignment with an individual bit per register.

VGA

Abbreviation for video graphics array or video graphics adaptor. VGA was introduced by IBM with the PS/2 series as a successor to EGA. Unlike the other graphics adaptors VGA supplies an analogue signal. Therefore 256 different colours from a palette of 262 144 ($=2^{18}$) colours may be displayed simultaneously.

Video Memory

See Video RAM.

Video RAM

Also called video memory or display memory. In text mode the screen words and in graphics mode the pixel values are stored in video RAM. With most of the graphics adaptors the video RAM is divided into several pages. The graphics control chip then reads the video RAM continuously to display the written information as text or graphics on the monitor.

Virtual 8086 Mode

An advanced operating mode from the i386 in which the access of a task to code and data segments and the I/O address space is automatically checked by the processor hardware, but the address generation with segment and offset is done in the same manner as in real mode. In this way, real-mode applications can be executed in a protected environment. With paging, several virtual 8086 tasks are possible in parallel.

Virtual Address

The address that is used in the logical addressing of the memory. On the 80x86 processors the logical address is composed of a segment number and an offset.

VLSI

Abbreviation for very-large-scale integration. This means the integration of 100 000 to 1 000 000 elements on a single chip.

v Pipeline

One of the two Pentium integer pipelines. The v pipeline can only execute so-called simple instructions and is only used for the second instruction of an instruction pair (if instruction pairing is possible). Also called v pipe.

VRAM

Abbreviation for video RAM. Dual-port RAM chips used specifically for the video RAM of graphics adaptors.

Way

The term *way* indicates the associativity of a cache. For a given set address the tag addresses of all ways are simultaneously compared to the tag part of the address provided by the CPU to determine a cache hit or miss. Thus, a data group that corresponds to a cache line can be stored at a different locations, the number of which matches the number of implemented ways.

$\overline{\text{WE}}$

Abbreviation for write enable. A control signal for a RAM chip, which indicates that the access is a write cycle and the RAM chip should store the supplied data at the specified address.

Word

Two bytes; that is, 16 bits.

Word Line

The line in row direction within a memory cell array of a RAM or ROM that turns on the access transistors of one memory row or page. The word line is usually connected to the gate of the access transistors.

Wraparound

If the address exceeds the maximum possible value a wraparound occurs because the highest order address bit cannot be put into the address register or onto the address bus. This applies to the 8086 if the segment register and the offset register both hold the same value, ffffh. The result is the 20-bit address 0ffefh. The leading 1 is, as the 21st address bit, neglected and the address jumps from a value at the top of memory to a value very near to the bottom of memory.

Write Allocation

If a cache miss for a write access occurs in a system with cache and main memory – that is, the address to be written is not located in the cache – them the cache carries out a cache line fill to read the corresponding data. Usually a cache line fill is executed only in case of a read miss.

Write-Back

Also called copy-back. Write-back refers to a cache strategy in which, when writing data, the data is written into the cache but not into main memory. The data writing into main memory is carried out only upon an explicit request (cache flush) or if a cache line must be replaced.

Write-Through

Write-through characterizes a cache strategy in which the data is always written into main memory when data is written by the CPU. Therefore, the write-through is carried out through the cache system. In addition the data may be written into the cache SRAM, but this is not necessary.

X-Bus

The part of the PC/XT/AT system bus that accesses the I/O ports on the mother board, for example the registers of the PIC, PIT or the keyboard controller.

Index